HOUGHTON LIBRARY BIBLIOGRAPHICAL CONTRIBUTIONS

DIE PRESSE
an ihre Erlöser!

Dankbar dargebracht
von U. Klopf sen. und A. Eurich's Buchdruckerei in Wien
am 17. März 1848.

Ein Wort! denn frei ist's Jedermann,
    Und jubeln darf und fröhlich singen,
Wer jubeln will und singen kann
    Und noch ein Blatt zum Kranze bringen!

Die freie Presse dankt es Euch,
    Dass Ihr die Fesseln ihr gelöset
Und in dem grossen Oesterreich
    Kein Wort mehr in der Brust verweset.

Vor Allem ruft sie Jenen „**Hoch!**"
    Die erst das stolze Wort gesprochen,
Das lange zaghaft sich verkroch,
    Als ob es Schweres hätt' verbrochen.

Sie ruft und Alles stimmet ein:
    „Es sollen die **Studenten** leben!
Die mit den **Bürgern** im Verein
    Die gold'ne Freiheit uns gegeben.

Sie rufet: Hoch dem **Vaterland!**
    „Und **hoch** dem väterlichen **Kaiser!**"
Der lang gefesselt und verkannt,
    Jetzt dasteht frei — ein grosser Kaiser!

**The Press to its Liberators! Poem by a printing firm in Vienna celebrating
the abolition of censorship.**

(3.17.48)

1848

AUSTRIAN REVOLUTIONARY BROADSIDES AND PAMPHLETS:

A Catalogue of the Collection

in the

Houghton Library

Harvard University

Compiled by
James E. Walsh

G. K. HALL & CO., 70 LINCOLN STREET, BOSTON, MASS.

Library of Congress Cataloging in Publication Data

Harvard University. Library. Houghton Library.
   1848 Austrian revolutionary broadsides and pamphlets.

   Bibliography: p.
   1. Austrian--History--Revolution, 1848--Pamphlets--
--Bibliography--Catalogs. 2. Broadsides--Bibliography--
Catalogs. 3. Harvard University. Library. Houghton
Library. I. Walsh, James Edward,
1918-   II. Title.
Z2124.V6H32   1976 (DB83)   016.9436'13'04
ISBN 0-8161-7870-4   76-14853

This publication is printed on permanent/durable acid free paper
MANUFACTURED IN THE UNITED STATES OF AMERICA

Contents

Foreword

The catalogue here offered to the public is of a kind of
material not usually thought worthy of detailed listing in the
files of the library or archive that possesses it: ephemera.
But the historian who wants to write a more than superficial history of a period of great social stress and political turmoil will
neglect the ephemeral productions of that period at his peril; for
it is from these small *cris de coeur*, these individual airings of
grievances, these poetic effusions of a perhaps unlettered muse,
that he can gain the kind of insight into the spirit of the times
that is denied him by more formal records.[1] The larger the
library, the more it needs a complete record of its holdings,
down to the last pamphlet and broadside. As a matter of preservation, also, a full listing of material is desirable. If a
single entry in a catalogue is made to cover a large number of
items ("Collection of..."), anyone who wants to examine that material must usually be given the entire lot and allowed to sort
through it piece by piece for the items that will serve his pur-
pose. He may find ten but will have handled a hundred. A catalogue of the kind here presented will enable him to be precise in
his requests for material, and it will also, we hope, serve those
at a distance from the library in which the material is preserved.

The revolutions that convulsed Europe in 1848, coming as they
did after the long period of nearly unbroken peace that followed
the Congress of Vienna, undammed pent-up frustrations and dissatis-
factions with the absolutist regimes that had made that peace
possible--imposed it, one might even say. Among the first fruits
of the revolutionary movement was the abolition of press censorship, a hated instrument always employed by repressive rulers.
The new and unaccustomed freedom of expression thus suddenly available was quickly seized on by people of all ranks and classes,

---

1. For an example of the effective use of such material by a historian, see R. J. Rath, *The Viennese revolution of 1848* (Austin, Tex.
[1957]).

including such figures as Richard Wagner and Franz Grillparzer,[2] with the result that 1848 is probably one of the best-documented years in modern history. "Die Aufhebung der Censur erlaubt uns jetzt unsere Wünsche auszusprechen, drucken zu lassen, und in Tausenden von Blättern zu verbreiten," wrote an anonymous pamphleteer in the first days following the lifting of censorship.[3] "Da nun Pressfreiheit ist, so hat ein Staatsbürger so gut als der andere das Recht, seine Ansicht auszusprechen," declared another.[4] The universal rush into print was criticized by some, however: "Das 'Zu viel' ist schon von der Sündfluth her immer ein Uebel. Ich glaube dieses 'Zu viel' ist auch jetzt bei unsern Flugschriften eingetreten."[5] Others satirized it: "Wundert Euch nicht, meine guten Leser! dass ein Mops auch schon anfängt, als Schriftsteller aufzutreten.... Ueberhaupt habe ich schon die Bemerkung gemacht, dass schon Viele von dem Thierreiche jetzt schreiben; fast alle Tage tritt ein anderer Esel als öffentlicher Schriftsteller auf."[6]

As might be expected, the physical form of much of what was published in the rapid course of day-to-day revolutionary events was ephemeral--broadsides, wall placards, leaflet poems, pamphlet essays, and the like--and it is exceptional for ephemeral material of such a nature to be preserved. When, therefore, I was in Vienna in the spring of 1967 and in the course of a call on Michael Krieg was shown a remarkable collection of just such material dealing with the Viennese revolution of 1848, it was not difficult to make the decision that it should be acquired for the Harvard College Library.

The collection that Herr Krieg showed me was arranged chronologically, with every dated broadside or pamphlet filed in a folder for the particular day; undated pieces were filed by *Schlagwort* in folders under the letters of the alphabet. These folders were then filed in two series of large portfolio boxes, one under month, the other alphabetically. The collection did not contain boxes for the months of November and December 1848, but there may never have been any, for the revolution was effectively ended by

---

2. See Wagner's *Gruss aus Sachsen an die Wiener* (6.1.48); Grillparzer's *Feldmarschall Radetzky* (6.8.48).

3. See *Volksblatt ohne Censur* (3.32.48).

4. M. Schickh, *Mitbürger!* (4.20.48).

5. I. F. Castelli, *Gutgemeinte Wünsche* (3.32.48).

6. *Neues Gekritzel über die alten Spitzel* (3.32.48).

the capitulation of the revolutionary forces to the army under
Windischgrätz on October 31st. Nor was there any material for the
letters T-Z. However, the consent of the Nationalbibliothek in
Vienna had to be obtained in order for the collection to be sent
out of Austria,[7] and in his negotiations Herr Krieg arranged for
the acquisition of 420 duplicates from the Nationalbibliothek's
own collection of similar material in exchange for allowing photo-
graphic reproductions to be made of any pieces in his collection
not already owned by the library. Of these there were between
five and six hundred. It will be seen what proportion of the
whole these figures represent when it is stated that the Harvard
collection here catalogued contains in the neighborhood of 2600
items. The lacunae in Herr Krieg's collection could thus be to
some extent filled in by Nationalbibliothek duplicates, though it
is possible that the collection remains less complete for the
months of November and December and for the letters T-Z than it
would be had we received it in the fullness in which it was formed
by the original collector. Who that collector was we do not know.
Herr Krieg informed us that the portfolio boxes in which the collection was kept had been in his father's stock for many years and
that his father had bought it from another dealer, who had acquired it from the estate of a government official, who had
probably inherited it. Beyond that we cannot go, but it seems
likely that the collection was formed during or shortly after the
revolution itself while it was still possible to lay hands on so
perishable a mass of material. Some of the broadsides appear to
have come from a printer's archive, for they bear such contemporary
manuscript notations as "125 Stück 9. Mai 1848." Others are dated
in a hand that may be that of the collector.

I have retained a chronological arrangement of the material
in this catalogue, since in that way the user will be able to
follow the day-to-day progress of the revolution. The date of a
particular piece is indicated by the third line of the shelf-mark:
3.17.48 = March 17, 1848; 10.3.48 = October 3, 1848. I was able
to fit many of the undated pieces into their proper sequence, some
precisely, others nearly, by reference to the event or subject
with which they deal; some I could date only approximately by
month, and in these cases the third line of the shelf-mark uses
the next number after the last day of the month, e.g., 3.32.48,
4.31.48, etc.; and some I had to relegate to a catch-all section
at the end of the year (12.32.48), since I was unable to assign
them with certainty to any month. Specialists may be able to do

---

7. Herr Krieg originally offered to sell the collection to the
Nationalbibliothek, but they declined to buy it.

so. I would be glad to be informed of any corrections they can make. The gist of most of the pieces is clear from their titles or headings or from the opening words of their text, but where it is not, I have added an explanatory note.

Many of the documents in this collection have been printed in standard histories of the Viennese revolution, particularly the Reschauer-Smets *Das Jahr 1848*, and when this was the case I have referred to such sources in a note on the individual entries. A selection of them from the collection in the Wiener Stadtbibliothek has also been reproduced in facsimile in Kurt Mellach's *1848: Protokolle einer Revolution* (Vienna [1968]), but that volume was not available in time for me to make much use of it in cataloguing the Harvard collection.

James E. Walsh
Keeper of Printed Books

The Houghton Library
Cambridge, Massachusetts
29 October 1975

List of Works Referred To

Helfert, Joseph Alexander, Freiherr von: "Die confessionale Frage
   in Oesterreich 1848." In: *Oesterreichisches Jahrbuch*,
   6.Jahrg., 1882, pp. [86]-182; 7.Jahrg., 1883, pp. [61]-196;
   8.Jahrg., 1883, pp. [113]-220.

_____. *Geschichte der österreichischen Revolution im Zusammen-
   hange mit der mitteleuropäischen Bewegung der Jahre 1848-1849.*
   Freiburg im Breisgau u. Wien, 1907-09. 2 vols.

_____. *Der Wiener Parnass im Jahre 1848.* Wien, 1882.

Lyser, Johann Peter: *Die Wiener-Ereignisse vom 6. Oktober bis 12.
   November 1848.* Wien, 1849.

Reschauer, Heinrich, & Smets, Moritz: *Das Jahr 1848. Geschichte
   der Wiener Revolution.* Wien, 1872. 2 vols.

Unterreiter, Friedrich: *Die Revolution in Wien.* Wien, 1848-49.
   8 pts.

*pGB8
V6755R
2.25.48

Ausserordentliche Depesche aus Frankreich.
Grosse Revolution in Paris und Proclamirung des
Louis Napoleon zum Kaiser von Frankreich.
[Wien]Zu haben in der Kölnerhofgasse Nr.740.
Gedruckt bei Leop.Sommer(vorm.Strauss).[1848]

broadside. 41x26cm.

---

*pGB8
V6755R
3.1.48

Kalchegger von Kalchberg, Joseph, freiherr,
1801-1882.
Auszug aus einem Schreiben des k. k. Rathes
und erzherzoglichen Cameral=Directors zu
Teschen, Herrn v. Kalchberg, vom 1. März 1848
an die Bürgermeister der k. k. Haupt= und
Residenzstadt Wien.
[Wien,1848]

broadside. 40.5x25cm.
Describing conditions of pestilence & famine.

---

*GB8
V6755R
3.11.48

Dercsényi, János Lajos, báró, 1802-1863.
Erklärung des Herrn Hofrathes Baron Dercsényi,
vom 11. März 1848 zur Petition der Wiener Bürger
an die Nieder=Oesterreichischen Stände um
Pressfreiheit, Constitution &c.
[Wien,1848]

broadside. 30x23cm.
Dated: Wien, am 11. März 1848.
The petition is printed in Reschauer-Smets
I.143.

---

*pGB8
V6755R
3.13.48

Austria. Sovereigns, etc., 1835-1848
(Ferdinand I)
Kundmachung. Um die Rhue in dieser seit gestern
bewegten Residenzstadt zu sichern, haben Seine
Majestät der Kaiser auch die Bewaffnung der
Studierenden, mit Ausschluss aller Ausländer und
unter zweckmässiger Reglung anzuordnen geruht.
[Wien,1848]

broadside. 57.5x46cm.
Dated: Wien am 13. März 1848.

---

*pGB8
V6755R
3.13.48

Austria, Lower. Regierungs-Präsident.
Kundmachung. Eine bedauerliche Störung der
niederösterr. ständ. Versammlung ist heute
eingetreten ...
[Wien,1848]

broadside. 44.5x56.5cm.
Dated & signed: Wien den 13. März 1848. Johann
Talatzko Freiherr von Gestieticz, k. k.
Nieder=Oester. Regierungs-Präsident.
Reschauer-Smets I.270.

---

*pGB8
V6755R
3.13.48

Austria, Lower. Regierungs-Präsident.
Kundmachung. Eine bedauerliche Störung der
niederösterreichischen ständischen Versammlung
ist heute eingetreten ...
[Wien,1848]

broadside. 38x23cm.
Dated & signed: Wien den 13. März 1848. Johann
Talatzko Freiherr von Gestieticz, k. k.
Nieder=Oester. Regierungs=Präsident.
Reschauer-Smets I.270.

---

*pGB8
V6755R
3.14.48

Austria. Armee.
Von Sr. k. k. apostolischen Majestät mit
vollständiger Vollmacht ausgerüstet, Ruhe und
Ordnung in der in Belagerungsstand erklärten
Residenz herzustellen ...
[Wien,1848]

broadside. 45x57cm.
Dated & signed: Wien am 14. März 1848. Alfred
Fürst zu Windischgrätz, k. k. Feldmarschall=
Lieutenant.
Reschauer-Smets I.388.

---

*pGB8
V6755R
3.14.48

Austria. Sovereigns, etc., 1835-1848
(Ferdinand I)
In Erwägung der gegenwärtigen politischen
Verhältnisse haben Wir beschlossen, die Stände
Unserer deutschen und slavischen Reiche ... zu
versammeln ...
[Wien,1848]

broadside. 45x57cm.
Dated & signed: Wien am 14. März 1848.
Ferdinand m. p.
Reschauer-Smets I.390.

---

*pGB8
V6755R
3.14.48

Austria, Lower. Regierungs-Präsident.
Bekanntmachung. Die gegenwärtigen Ereignisse
berühren das Wohl des Staates eben so wie der
Stadt Wien ...
[Wien,1848]

broadside. 44.5x57cm.
Dated & signed: Wien am 14. März 1848. Johann
Talatzko Freiherr von Gestieticz, k. k. Nieder=
Oester. Regierungs=Präsident.
Reschauer-Smets I.344.

---

*pGB8
V6755R
3.14.48

Austria, Lower. Regierungs-Präsident.
Kundmachung. Seine Majestät der Kaiser haben
die Bewegung des gestrigen Tages durch Gewährung
einiger Ihm vorgebrachten Bitten ...
[Wien,1848]

broadside. 45x57cm.
Dated & signed: Wien am 14. März 1848. Johann
Talatzko Freiherr von Gestieticz, k. k.
Nieder=Oester. Regierungs=Präsident.
Reschauer-Smets I.366.

*pGB8
V6755R
3.14.48

Austria, Lower. Regierungs-Präsident.
Seine k. k. apostolische Majestät haben die
Aufhebung der Censur und die alsbaldige
Veröffentlichung eines Pressgesetzes
allergnädigst zu beschliessen geruht.
[Wien,1848]

broadside. 45x57cm.
Dated & signed: Wien am 14. März 1848. Johann
Talatzko Freiherr von Gestieticz, k. k. Nieder=
Oester. Regierungs=Präsident.
Reschauer-Smets I.379.

---

*pGB8
V6755R
3.14.48

Austria, Lower. Regierungs-Präsident.
Se. Majestät haben die Errichtung einer
Nationalgarde zur Aufrechthaltung der
gesetzmässigen Ruhe und Ordnung der Residenz und
zum Schutze der Personen und des Eigenthumes ...
[Wien,1848]

broadside. 45x57cm.
Dated & signed: Wien am 14. März 1848. Johann
Talatzko Freih. von Gestieticz, k. k. Nieder=
Oester. Regierungs=Präsident.
Reschauer-Smets I.379.
Also announcing the appointment of Graf
Hoyos as commander of the Nationalgarde.

---

*GB8
V6755R
3.14.48

Bürger von Wien! Das Volk hat gestern lang
unterdrückte Wünsche laut werden lassen,
und Ihr wisst Alle, wie darauf geantwortet
wurde! ...
[Wien,1848]

folder([4]p.) 22x15cm.
Caption title; another issue has imprint on p.
[4].
Reschauer-Smets I.385; ascribed by Unterreiter
(I.79) to Eduard von Bauernfeld.

---

*GB8
V6755R
3.14.48

Bürger von Wien! Das Volk hat gestern lang
unterdrückte Wünsche laut werden lassen, und Ihr
wisst Alle, wie darauf geantwortet wurde! ...
Gedruckt bei Jos.Stöckholzer v.Hirschfeld in
Wien.[1848]

folder([4]p.) 22.5x15cm.
Caption title; imprint on p.[4]; another issue
is without imprint.
Reschauer-Smets I.385; ascribed by Unterreiter
(I.79) to Eduard von Bauernfeld.

---

*GB8
V6755R
3.14.48

Frankl, Ludwig August, 1810-1894.
Die Universität.
[Wien]Erstes censurfreies Blatt aus der
Josef Stöckholzer von Hirschfeld'schen
Buchdruckerei.[1848]

broadside. 22x15cm.
Helfert (Wiener Parnass) 310.
"Während des Wachstehens geschrieben von Ludw.
Aug. Frankl."

---

*GB8
V6755R
3.14.48

Frankl, Ludwig August, 1810-1894.
Die Universität.
[Wien]Erstes censurfreies Blatt aus der Josef
Stöckholzer von Hirschfeld'schen Buchdruckerei.
Gedruckt bei Rud.Ronrer's sel.Wittwe.[1848]

broadside. 26x21cm.
Helfert (Wiener Parnass) 310.
"Während des Wachstehens geschrieben von
Ludw. Aug. Frankl."

---

*GB8
V6755R
3.14.48

Frankl, Ludwig August, 1810-1894.
... Die Universität.
[Wien]Wurde von der dankbaren Studentenschaft
in der Buchdruckerei von U.Klopf sen.und A.Eurich
zum zweiten Male censurfrei abgedruckt.[1848]

broadside. 21x13cm.
Helfert (Wiener Parnass) 310.
At head of title: Dank dem Herrn Dr. Ludw.
Aug. Frankl.
"Während des Wachstehens geschrieben von
Ludw. Aug. Frankl."

---

*GB8
V6755R
3.14.48

Liebe Freunde und Mitbürger! Grosses ist
gewonnen, die feste Grundlage nämlich, auf
welcher sich das Glück der Völker und der
Einzelnen allmählich aber sicher aufbauen lässt
...
[Wien,1848]

broadside. 29x23cm.
Reschauer-Smets (I.356) print this document
with the date: Wien, am 14.März 1848.
Signed: A. Auersperg (Anastasius Grün). Ferd.
Colloredo=Mannsfeld [& 3 others].

---

*GB8
V6755R
3.14.48

[Maithstein, Ignaz Wildner von, 1802-1854]
Wackere Mitbürger des grossen herrlichen
Oesterreichs!
[Wien,1848]

[2]p. 25.5x21.5cm.
Caption title.
Dated & signed at end: Wien, den 14. März 1848,
im Augenblicke nach der Verkündigung der
Censurfreiheit. Dr. Wildner-Maithstein.
Reschauer-Smets I.386.

---

*GB8
V6755R
3.14.48

[Maithstein, Ignaz Wildner von, 1802-1854]
Wackere Mitbürger des grossen herrlichen
Oesterreichs!
Druck bei Hirschfeld in Wien.[1848]

folder([4]p.) 23x15.5cm.
Caption title; imprint on p.[4].
Dated & signed at end: Wien, den 14. März
1848, im Augenblicke nach der Verkündigung der
Censurfreiheit Dr. Wildner-Maithstein.
Reschauer-Smets I.386.
In this edition, the last line on p.[1]
ends: ein System, das

*GB8
V6755R
3.14.48

[Maithstein, Ignaz Wildner von, 1802-1854]
Wackere Mitbürger des grossen herrlichen
Oesterreichs!
[Wien,1848]

folder([4]p.) 19x12cm.
Caption title.
Dated & signed at end: Wien, den 14. März 1848,
im Augenblicke nach der Verkündigung der
Censurfreiheit. Dr. Wildner-Maithstein.
Reschauer-Smets I.386.
In this edition, the last line on p.[1] ends:
in ganz Italien ( ) und

---

*GB8
V6755R
3.15.48

Aufruf eines Nationalgardisten an seine
geehrten Herren Cameraden.
[Wien]A.Dorfmeister's Buchdruckerei.[1848]

[2]p. 25x15cm.
Caption title; imprint on p.[2].
Dated & signed at end: Wien, den 15. März
1848. h.S*****.

---

*GB8
V6755R
3.14.48

Mayr, Josef.
Ein Wort der Verehrung dem Herrn Professor
Hye.
[Wien]Druck von U.Klopf sen.und A.Eurich,
Wollzeile 782.[1848]

broadside. 21x13.5cm.
Helfert (Wiener Parnass) 307.
Dated & signed: Wien den 14. März 1848. Josef
Mayr, Jurist im I. Jahre.

---

*pGB8
V6755R
3.15.48

Austria. Armee.
Von Sr. k. k. apostolischen Majestät mit
vollständiger Vollmacht ausgerüstet, Ruhe und
Ordnung in der Residenz herzustellen ...
[Wien,1848]

broadside. 45x57cm.
Reschauer-Smets I.390.
Dated & signed: Wien am 15. März 1848. Alfred
Fürst zu Windischgrätz, k. k. Feldmarschall=
Lieutenant.
A revision of ( ) his similar proclamation
of the previous day.

---

*GB8
V6755R
3.14.48

Meyerhofer, A
Der Bauer bei der Mariahilfer=Linie am Morgen
des 14. März 1848. Ein Gedicht in Wiener Mundart
von A. Meyerhofer.
Wien,gedruckt und zu haben bei Leopold Grund,
am Stephansplatze im Zwettelhof.[1848]

broadside. 26.5x21cm.
Helfert (Wiener Parnass) 308.

---

*pGB8
V6755R
3.15.48

Austria. Sovereigns, etc., 1835-1848
(Ferdinand I)
Wir Ferdinand der Erste, von Gottes Gnaden
Kaiser von Oesterreich ... haben nunmehr solche
Verfügungen getroffen, die Wir als zur Erfüllung
der Wünsche Unserer treuen Völker erforderlich
erkannten. Die Pressfreiheit ist durch Unsere
Erklärung der Aufhebung der Censur in derselben
Weise gewährt, wie in allen Staaten, wo sie
besteht ...
[Wien,1848]
(See next card)

---

*GB8
V6755R
3.15.48

Aufruf an unsere Brüder auf dem Lande am 15.
März 1848.
[Wien]Gedruckt bei Ant.Benko.[1848]

folder([4]p.) 21.5x14cm.
Caption title; imprint on p.[4].
Also published with title: Aufruf an unsere
Brüder für Stadt und Land ...

---

*pGB8
V6755R
3.15.48

Austria. Sovereigns, etc., 1835-1848
(Ferdinand I)   Wir Ferdinand der Erste ...
[1848]   (Card 2)

folder([2]p.) 45x28.5cm.
Reschauer-Smets I.418.
"Gegeben in Unserer kaiserlichen Haupt= und
Residenzstadt Wien, den fünfzehnten März, im
eintausend achthundert acht und vierzigsten ..."
Ferdinand's proclamation of freedom of the
press, the establishment of the Nationalgarde,
and the calling of the estates for the drafting
of a constitu-) tion.

---

*GB8
V6755R
3.15.48

Aufruf an unsere Brüder für Stadt und Land
am 15. März 1848.
[Wien]Gedruckt bei Ant.Benko.[1848]

folder([4]p.) 21x14cm.
Caption title; imprint on p.[4].
Also published with title: Aufruf an unsere
Brüder auf dem Lande ...

---

*pGB8
V6755R
3.15.48

Austria, Lower. Landstände.
Kundmachung. Die Nieder=Oesterreichischen
Stände haben heute den Beschluss gefasst, einen
provisorischen Ausschuss zu bilden, welcher
daasjenige vorzukehren hat, was in diesem
wichtigen Momente zur Besorgung der ihnen
zukommenden Geschäfte erforderlich ist ...
[Wien,1848]
broadside. 45x57cm.
Reschauer-Smets I.429.
Dated & signed: Wien den 15. März 1848. Die
Nieder=Oester- ( ) reichischen Stände.

*GB8
V6755R
3.15.48

Authentische Nachricht von dem am 14. März
1848 erfolgten Hinscheiden und dem
Leichenbegängnisse der Frau Bonadonna Censur,
gebornen Mitternacht.
[Wien,1848]

[2]p. 19.5x12.5cm.
Caption title.
Reschauer-Smets I.382.

*GB8
V6755R
3.15.48

[Bermann, Joseph, b.1810]
Neues Volkslied am 15. März 1848. Von Benno
Phisemar [pseud.]. Für die Serenade des
Männergesang=Vereins bestimmt.
Gedruckt bey Ant.Benko.Wien,bey Joseph
Bermann,am Graben zur goldenen Krone.[1848]

broadside. 28.5x22cm.
Helfert (Wiener Parnass) 344.

*GB8
V6755R
3.15.48

[Bermann, Joseph, b.1810]
Neues Volkslied. Ferdinand der erste
constitutionelle Kaiser.
K.k.Hofbuchdruckerei des L.Sommer,vormals
Strauss.Wien,bei Jos.Bermann,Kunsthändler am
Graben.[1848]

broadside. 29.5x22.5cm.
Helfert (Wiener Parnass) 344.
Dated: 15. März 1848.
Other editions are signed with the pseudonym
"Benno Phisemar", an anagram of Bermann's
name.

*GB8
V6755R
3.15.48

[Bermann, Joseph, b.1810]
Neues Volkslied. Ferdinand der erste
constitutionelle Kaiser.
[Wien,1848]

broadside. 19x12cm.
Helfert (Wiener Parnass) 344.
In this edition the 3d line of the title
measures 79mm. in length; other editions are
signed with the pseudonym "Benno Phisemar",
an anagram of Bermann's name.

*GB8
V6755R
3.15.48

[Bermann, Joseph, b.1810]
Neues Volkslied. Ferdinand der erste
constitutionelle Kaiser.
[Wien,1848]

broadside. 21x13cm.
Helfert (Wiener Parnass) 344.
In this edition the 3d line of the title measures 91mm. in length; other editions are signed
with the pseudonym "Benno Phisemar", an anagram
of Bermann's name.

*GB8
V6755R
3.15.48

[Bermann, Joseph, b.1810]
Neues Volkslied von Benno Phisemar [pseud.].
(Für die Serenade des Männergesang=Vereins
bestimmt.) Ferdinand der erste constitutionelle
Kaiser.
K.k.Hofbuchdruckerei des L.Sommer, vormals
Strauss.Wien,bei Jos.Bermann,Kunsthändler am
Graben.[1848]

broadside. 29.5x23cm.
Helfert (Wiener Parnass) 344.
Dated: 15. März 1848.

*GB8
V6755R
3.15.48

Bowitsch, Ludwig, 1818-1881.
Den braven Studenten. Von Ludwig Bowitsch.
[Wien,1848]

broadside. 22.5x14.5cm.
Helfert (Wiener Parnass) 322.
Dated: Wien, am 15. März 1848.

*GB8
V6755R
3.15.48

Cerri, Cajetan, 1826-1899.
Ein Auferstehungslied. Bei der ersten
Verkündigung der Pressfreiheit.
K.k.Hof=Buchdruckerei des L.Sommer (vormals
Strauss) in Wien.[1848]

broadside. 30x22cm.
Helfert (Wiener Parnass) 323.
"Zweites censurfreies Blatt."
"Wien, während des Wachestehens erfasst."

*GB8
V6755R
3.15.48

[Cornet, Enrico, b.1823]
Salmo politico.
Libreria di Tendler & comp. in Vienna.[1848]

folder([2]p.) 27.5x19.5cm.
Helfert (Wiener Parnass) 342.
Caption title; imprint on p.[2].
Dated & signed: Vienna, li 15 marzo 1848.
Enrico Cornet.

*GB8
V6755R
3.15.48

Dem Palatin Ungarns Stephan. Am Tage seiner
Ankunft in Wien, den 15. März 1848. (Im Namen
der in Wien anwesenden Ungarn.)
Druck von Bl.Höfel in Wien.[1848]

[2]p. 25x18.5cm.
Helfert (Wiener Parnass) 318.
Caption title; imprint on p.[2].

Eckardt, Ludwig, 1827-1871.
*GB8   Neue Volkshimne der Wiener=Studenten. Von L.
V6755R   Eckardt, Nazionalgardist. (Geschrieben in der
3.15.48   Nacht des 15. März, des "idus martis" für
die Finsterlinge.)
[Wien,1848]

[2]p. 21x14.5cm.
Helfert (Wiener Parnass) 324.
Caption title.

Eckardt, Ludwig, 1827-1871.
*GB8   Neue Volks-Himne der Wiener Studenten. Von
V6755R   Ludwig Eckardt, Nazionalgardist. (Geschrieben in
3.15.48   der Nacht des 15. März, des "idus martis" für
die Finsterlinge.)
[Wien,1848]

[2]p. 18.5x12cm.
Helfert (Wiener Parnass) 324.
Caption title.

     Das erste censurfreie Wort eines
*GB8   österreichischen Soldaten. Nach Verkündung der
V6755R   Constitution an alle seine lieben Mitbürger!
3.15.48   [Wien,1848]

broadside. 22.5x13.5cm.
Helfert (Wiener Parnass) 317.

     Ferdinand und die Engel. Vision am 15. März
*GC8   1848. Dritte Auflage.
V6755R   Wien 1848.Fr.Beck's Universitäts=Buchhandlung.
Z848fc

15,[1]p. 21cm.,in case 22.5cm.
Helfert (Wiener Parnass) 316.
Printer's imprint on p.[16]: Druck von U.
Klopf sen. und A. Eurich in Wien.
Ascribed to Eduard von Lackenbacher.
Poems on various figures of the revolution of
1848, with contemporary ms. identifications in
the margins.
Unbound, stitched as issued; in cloth
case.

Frankl, Johann Adam.
*GB8   Böhmen mein Vaterland. Lied, gedichtet um
V6755R   Mitternacht den 15. März 1848, auf dem
3.15.48   Wachtposten in Wien bei der Kaiser Ferdinand-
Nordbahn, von Dr. J. Ad. Frankl vom Marienbad.
Druck von Josef Stöckholzer von Hirschfeld in
Wien.[1848]

folder(2ℓ.) 27x22cm.
Helfert (Wiener Parnass) 313.

Gentilli, Giuseppe, d.1862.
*GB8   Dì 15. marzo 1848, primo della constituzione
V6755R   austriaca.
3.15.48   [Wien,1848]

broadside. 21x13cm.
Helfert (Wiener Parnass) 352.

Gerhard, Friedrich, fl.1848.
*GB8   Die Presse frei! Wien, 15. März 1848. Von
V6755R   Friedrich Gerhard, aus Danzig. Erstes
3.15.48   censurfreies Gedicht.
[Wien,1848]

folder([4]p.) 20x14cm.
Helfert (Wiener Parnass) 327.
Printer's imprint on p.[2]: Zu haben in der
Buchdruckerei von Ul. Klopf sen. und Alex.
Eurich, Wollzeile Nr. 782.

Graz. Bürgerschaft.
*GB8   Petition der Bürgerschaft der Hauptstadt
V6755R   Gratz an Se. Majestät.
3.15.48   [Graz,1848]

[2]p. 27x22cm.
Helfert (Geschichte) I.290.
Caption title; dated on p.[2]: Gratz am 15.
März 1848.
"Diese Petition wurde heute Nachmittags den
15. März von der versammelten Bürgerschaft
Sr. Excellenz dem Herrn Landesgouverneur
überreicht, und   ) von demselben alsogleich an
Se. k. k.   ) Majestät befördert."

Gussmann, Rudolf.
*GB8   Jm Doppelfrühling des Jahres 1848. Gedicht von
V6755R   Rudolf Gussmann.
3.15.48   [Wien,1848]

broadside. 22.5x15cm.
Helfert (Wiener Parnass) 329.
Another edition has imprint at foot.

Gussmann, Rudolf.
*GB8   Jm Doppelfrühling des Jahres 1848. Gedicht
V6755R   von Rudolf Gussmann.
3.15.48   K.k.Hof=Buchdruckerei des L.Sommer (vormals
Strauss) in Wien[1848]

broadside. 19x12cm.
Helfert (Wiener Parnass) 329.
Another edition is without imprint at foot.

*GB8
V6755R
3.15.48

Gustus, George.
    Allen hochherzigen Verfechtern der
öffentlichen Wohlfahrt, am Mittwoch, den 15. März
1848, gewidmet von George Gustus. Der Erlös
den Armen der Leopoldstadt zugedacht.
    Gedruckt bei Hirschfeld in Wien.[1848]

    folder([4]p.) 23x15cm.
    Helfert (Wiener Parnass) 331.

*GB8
V6755R
3.15.48

[Haas, Johann Baptist]
    Prolog: "Nacht".
    [Wien,1848]

    [2]p. 22.5x15cm.
    Helfert (Wiener Parnass) 332; Helfert combines
this poem with his no.333, another poem with
title "Hellstrahlender Tag" dated 15 March 1848;
perhaps the poem present here represents only the
1st leaf of a 2-leaf folder.
    Caption title.

*GB8
V6755R
3.15.48

Härdtl, Joseph, freiherr von.
    Das alte Volkslied: neu angestimmt am 15.
März 1848.
    [Wien,1848]

    broadside. 22x14.5cm.
    Helfert (Wiener Parnass) 334.
    In this edition, the 2 lines of the heading
are approximately the same length.

*GB8
V6755R
3.15.48

Härdtl, Joseph, freiherr von.
    Das alte Volkslied: neu angestimmt am 15. März
1848.
    [Wien,1848]

    broadside. 22x12.5cm.
    Helfert (Wiener Parnass) 334.
    In this edition, the 2d line of the title is
longer than the 1st.

*GB8
V6755R
3.15.48

[Hermann von Hermannsthal, Franz, 1799-1875]
    An den Kaiser Ferdinand I. von Oesterreich.
    [Wien,1848]

    [2]p. 21x13.5cm.
    Helfert (Wiener Parnass) 335.
    Dated & signed: Wien den 15. März 1848.
Hermannsthal.
    In this edition, the last stanza on p.[1] is
in 4 lines.

*GB8
V6755R
3.15.48

[Hermann von Hermannsthal, Franz, 1799-1875]
    An den Kaiser Ferdinand I. von Oesterreich.
    [Wien,1848]

    [2]p. 22x13.5cm.
    Helfert (Wiener Parnass) 335.
    Dated & signed: Wien, den 15. März 1848.
Hermannsthal.
    In this edition, the last stanza on p.[1]
is in 5 lines.

*GB8
V6755R
3.15.48

Hradetzky, Joseph, fl.1848.
    Kaiser Ferdinand's Traum! vom 14. auf den 15.
März 1848. von Jos. Hradetzky, als Sänger genannt
Kraus.
    [Wien,1848]

    folder([4]p.) 21.5x14cm.
    Helfert (Wiener Parnass) 312.
    Printer's imprint on p.[4]: Gedruckt bei
Carl Ueberreuter.

*GB8
V6755R
3.15.48

Jasper, Friedrich Moritz, 1805-1849.
    Den Studenten Wiens. Von einem der dankbaren
Bürger.
    Wien,zu haben bei Jasper,Hügel und Manz,
Herrngasse Nr.251.[1848]

    broadside. 22.5x15cm.
    Helfert (Wiener Parnass) 337.
    Dated & signed: Wien, den 15. März 1848. M. F.
Jasper.

*GB8
V6755R
3.15.48

Lenzi di Torcegno, Michele Antonio.
    Per il giorno faustissimo della costituzione,
concessa all'Austria dall'augustisimo
imperatore Ferdinando I[mo], seguita addi 15 marzo
l'anno 1848. Terzine. Composte da Mich. Antonio
Lenzi di Torcegno ...
    Coi tipi di Giuseppe de Hirschfeld in Vienna.
[1848]

    folder([4]p.) 21.5x13.5cm.
    Helfert (Wiener Parnass) 345.

*GB8
V6755R
3.15.48

Litolff, Henry, 1818-1891.
    Zur Feier der 4 Tage im März 1848! 12. 13. 14.
15. der heldenmüthigen Studirenden-Legion an der
Wiener Hochschule brüderlich geweiht von Henry
Litolff und Siegfried Kapper. Dritte Auflage.
    Wien,am 15.März 1848,dem ersten Tage der
Constitution.

    folder([4]p.) 22.5x15.5cm.
    Helfert (Wiener Parnass) 311.
    Printer's imprint on p.[4]: K. k. Hof=Buch-
druckerei des L.   Sommer (vormals Strauss)
in Wien.
                (See next card)

*GB8
V6755R
3.15.48

Litolff, Henry, 1818-1891.   Zur Feier ...
1848.   (Card 2)

The poem by Kapper has title "Chorgesang
der Wiener Studenten-Legion"; includes the
music by Litolff.

---

*GB8
V6755R
3.15.48

[Nesper, Eugen, 1816-1887]
Oesterreichs hochsinnigem Kaiser an
Oesterreichs wichtigstem Tage, dem 15. März
1848. Von Dr. Falkner [pseud.].
[Wien,1848]

broadside. 23x14.5cm.
Helfert (Wiener Parnass) 326.
In ms. at top: 45 Stk. 18ten März 1848.

---

*pGB8
V6755R
3.15.48

Manifest der Schriftsteller Wiens.
Druck von U.Klopf sen.und Alex.Eurich in Wien,
Wollzeile Nr.782.[1848]

broadside. 47.5x30.5cm.
Reschauer-Smets I.379.
Acclaiming Ferdinand's proclamation of freedom
of the press; signed by I. F. Castelli, Eduard
von Bauernfeld, L. A. Frankl, & 26 others.

---

*GB8
V6755R
3.15.48

Palme, Alois, 1793-1864.
Palmenzweig, den hochverehrten Wiener
akademischen Jünglingen gewidmet von A. Palme,
Bürger von Wien. Am 15. März 1848.
[Wien,1848]

folder(2ℓ.) 21.5x15cm.
Helfert (Wiener Parnass) 341.
Title in 9 lines; another edition has a
printer's imprint.

---

*pGB8
V6755R
3.15.48

Metternichs Reisepass.
[Wien,1848]

broadside. 39x25cm.
Unterreiter II.108ff.
Dated: 15. März 1848.
Another edition has imprint at foot.
Printed on the verso of this broadside is
another work, Der gefangene Liguorianer, which
appeared on 3 May 1848.

---

*GB8
V6755R
3.15.48

Palme, Alois, 1793-1864.
Palmenzweig, den hochverehrten Wiener
akademischen Jünglingen, gewidmet von A. Palme,
Bürger von Wien. Am 15. März 1848.
[Wien,1848]

folder([4]p.) 23x15cm.
Helfert (Wiener Parnass) 341.
Title in 10 lines; printer's imprint on p.[4]:
Druck bei Hirschfeld in Wien.

---

*pGB8
V6755R
3.15.48

Metternich's Reisepass.
[Wien]Gedruckt und zu haben bei U.Klopf sen.
und Alexander Eurich.[1848]

broadside. 39x25cm.
Unterreiter II.108ff.
Dated: 15. März 1848.
Another edition is without imprint.

---

*GB8
V6755R
3.15.48

[Payer, Karl]
Die grosse Stunde der Freiheit.
[Wien]Gedruckt bei Leopold Grund.[1848]

folder([4]p.) 21x13cm.
Helfert (Wiener Parnass) 343.
Caption title; imprint on p.[4].
Dated & signed: Wien den 15. März 1848. Karl
Payer.

---

*GB8
V6755R
3.15.48

[Much, Adolf, b.1818]
Am 15. März 1848. Abends.
[Wien,1848]

[2]p. 19.5x12.5cm.
Helfert (Wiener Parnass) 340.
Caption title; signed on p.[2]: Adolf Much,
Raths=Auskultant und National=Gardist.

---

*GB8
V6755R
3.15.48

Programm. Die 3 Märztage 1848. Charac-
teristiches Tongemälde.
[Wien,1848]

broadside. 15x12cm.
Includes Joseph Bermann's "Volks-Hymne"
(Helfert, Wiener Parnass, 344).

---

*GB8
V6755R
3.15.48

Schulz, Joseph, fl.1848.
Dem durchlauchtigsten Herrn Erzherzog Stephan,
Reichspalatinus von Ungarn, ehrfurchtsvollst
dargebracht von Joseph Schulz.
[Wien]Mechitharisten=Buchdruckerei.[1848]

folder([4]p.) 22.5x14cm.
Helfert (Wiener Parnass) 319.
Caption title; imprint on p.[4].

---

*GB8
V6755R
3.15.48

Vienna. Magistrat.
Dank=Adresse überreicht von den Unterfertigten.
Hoch lebe unser konstitutioneller Kaiser!
Hoch! Hoch! Hoch!
[Wien,1848]

[2]p. 29x22.5cm.
Unterreiter I.90.
Signed: Der Magistrat und Bürgerausschuss der
Stadt Wien.
On the verso is printed Ferdinand's proclama-
tion of freedom of the press, the establishment
(See next card)

---

*GB8
V6755R
3.15.48

Steiger, L   E
Am 15. März 1848.
[Wien,1848]

broadside. 21x14cm.
Helfert (Wiener Parnass) 348.

---

*GB8
V6755R
3.15.48

Vienna. Magistrat.   Dank=Adresse ... [1848]
(Card 2)

of the Nationalgarde, and the calling of
the estates for the drafting of a constitution.
Also published with title: Hoch lebe unser
konstitutioneller Kaiser!

---

*GB8
V6755R
3.15.48

Titl, Anton Emil, 1809-1882.
Marsch=Lied der östreichischen Nationalgarde.
Gedichtet auf dem Marsche für Freiheit und
Sicherheit den 15. März 1848 von August
Silberstein. Musik von A. Emil Titl.
[Wien,1848]

folder([4]p.) 22.5x15cm.
Helfert (Wiener Parnass) 347.
Printer's imprint on p.[4]: K.k. Hof=Buch-
druckerei des L. Sommer in Wien.
Includes the music.

---

*pGB8
V6755R
3.15.48

Vienna. Magistrat.
Hoch lebe unser konstitutioneller Kaiser!
Hoch! Hoch! Hoch!
[Wien,1848]

broadside. 39.5x24.5cm.
Unterreiter I.90.
Signed: Der Magistrat und Bürgerausschuss der
Stadt Wien.
Also published with title: Dank=Adresse
überreicht von den Unterfertigten.

---

*GB8
V6755R
3.15.48

... Le tre giornate di Vienna.
[Wien,1848]

folder([3]p.) 24.5x17cm.
Caption title; at head: Costituzione.
Libertà della stampa.
Dated at end: Vienna 14 marzo 1848.

---

*pGB8
V6755R
3.15.48

Vienna. Nationalgarde.
Vorläufige Anordnung für die Organisirung der
Nationalgarde.
[Wien,1848]

broadside. 45x57cm.
Reschauer-Smets I.402.
Dated & signed: Wien am 15. März 1848. Ernst
Graf Hoyos, Ober=Commandant der Nationalgarde.

---

*pGB8
V6755R
3.15.48

Vienna. Magistrat.
Aufforderung. Sämmtliche Herren Handels=
und Geschäftsleute, so wie die Herren Gewölbs=
Inhaber werden ersucht, zur grösseren Beruhigung
des Publikums alsogleich Ihre Schreibstuben,
Geschäfts= und Verkaufslokalitäten dem
öffentlichen Verkehre zu öffnen ...
[Wien,1848]

broadside. 37.5x23cm.
Reschauer-Smets I.406.
Signed & dated: Vom Magistrate der k. k. Haupt-
und Residenzstadt   Wien am 15. März 1848.

---

*pGB8
V6755R
3.15.48

Wien. Se. k. k. Majestät haben folgendes
allerhöchste Cabinetsschreiben an den Obersten
Kanzler allergnädigst zu erlassen geruhet ...
[Wien,1848]

broadside. 38x29.5cm.
A news-sheet, incorporating 2 of the Emperor's
and one of Talatzko's proclamations dated 14
March 1848; commentary begins: Ein bedeutungs-
voller Tag, einer der bedeutungsvollsten in der
österreichischen Geschichte, liegt hinter uns ...
In this edition, the last line begins: hatten.

*pGB8
V6755R
3.15.48

Wien. Seine k. k. Majestät haben folgendes
allerhöchste Cabinetsschreiben an den Obersten
Kanzler allergnädigst zu erlassen geruhet ...
[Wien,1848]

broadside. 38x28cm.
A news-sheet, incorporating 2 of the Emperor's
and one of Talatzko's proclamations dated 14
March 1848; commentary begins: Ein bedeutungs-
voller Tag, einer der bedeutungsvollsten in der
österreichischen Geschichte liegt hinter uns ...
. In this edition, the last line begins: für das

---

*GB8
V6755R
3.16.48

Brühl, Carl Bernhard, 1820-1899.
Ein Lebehoch den Studenten Wiens. Dargebracht
von Med. Dr. Brühl, Nationalgardist.
[Wien,1848]

[2]p. 22x14cm.
Helfert (Wiener Parnass) 359.
Caption title; dated on p.[2]: Am 16. März
1848.

---

*pGB8
V6755R
3.16.48

Austria. Sovereigns, etc., 1835-1848
(Ferdinand I)
... Wir Ferdinand der Erste, von Gottes Gnaden
Kaiser von Oesterreich ... haben nunmehr solche
Verfügungen getroffen, die Wir als zur Erfüllung
der Wünsche Unserer treuen Völker erforderlich
erkannten. Die Pressfreiheit ist durch Meine
Erklärung der Aufhebung der Censur in derselben
Weise gewährt, wie in allen Staaten, wo sie
besteht ...
[Wien,1848]

(See next card)

---

*GB8
V6755R
3.16.48

[Callot, Eduard, freiherr von]
An die wackern Oesterreicher!
Druck von Bl.Höfel in Wien.[1848]

[2]p. 25x19.5cm.
Helfert (Wiener Parnass) 360.
Caption title; imprint on p.[2].
Dated & signed on p.[2]: Wien, am 16. März
1848. Eduard Freiherr von Callot ...

---

*pGB8
V6755R
3.16.48

Austria. Sovereigns, etc., 1835-1848
(Ferdinand I)   ... Wir Ferdinand der
Erste ... [1848]   (Card 2)

[2]p. 42.5x26.5cm.
At head of title: Nachstehende Proklamation
wurde gestern Abends 6 Uhr ausgegeben:
"Gegeben in Unserer kaiserlichen Haupt= und
Residenzstadt Wien, den fünfzehnten März, im
eintausend achthundert acht und vierzigsten ..."
Ferdinand's proclamation of freedom of the
press, the establishment of the Nationalgarde,
and the calling   of the estates for the
drafting of a   constitution.

---

*GB8
V6755R
3.16.48

Etienne, Michael, 1827-1879.
Der Universität und den Bürgern. Dargebracht
von Miguel Etienne.
[Wien,1848]

folder([4]p.) 21x13.5cm.
Helfert (Wiener Parnass) 362.
Printer's imprint on p.[2]: Zu haben in der
Buchdruckerei von Ul. Klopf sen. und Alex.
Eurich, Wollzeile Nr. 782.
Dated at end: Wien am 16. März 1848.

---

*pGB8
V6755R
3.16.48

Austria, Lower. Regierungs-Präsident.
Es wird zur Kenntniss gebracht, dass der
Wiener Bürgermeister v. Czapka sich aus der
Haupt= und Residenzstadt entfernet ...
[Wien,1848]

broadside. 45x57cm.
Reschauer-Smets II.10; Unterreiter I.93.
Dated & signed: Wien am 16. März 1848. Johann
Talatzko Freiherr von Gestieticz, k. k. Nieder=
Oester. Regierungs=Präsident.

---

*GB8
V6755R
3.16.48

[Eyb, Otto, freiherr von]
Worte eines neugebornen Kindes an seine
Brüder.
[Wien,1848]

folder([4]p.) 19.5x12cm.
Caption title; dated & signed at end: Wien,
den 16. März 1848. Otto Freiherr von Eyb.

---

*GB8
V6755R
3.16.48

[Bernklau, Jacob]
An die Gefallenen.
[Wien]A.Dorfmeister's Druck und Verlag (Stadt,
Kühfussgasse Nr.575).[1848]

[2]p. 23x15cm.
Helfert (Wiener Parnass) 358.
Dated & signed on p.[2]: Wien, am 16. März
1848. Bernklau.
Caption title; imprint on p.[2].

---

*GB8
V6755R
3.16.48

[Kolbenheyer, Moritz, 1810-1884]
1648 / 1848.
[Wien,1848]

folder([4]p.) 22x15cm.
Helfert (Wiener Parnass) 365.
Title within woodcut wreath; printer's imprint
on p.[4]: Gedruckt bei J. v. Hirschfeld in Wien.
Dated & signed at end: Am 16ten März. Moritz
Kolbenheyer, evang. Prediger in Oedenburg.

*GB8
V6755R
3.16.48

[Leidesdorf, Eduard]
Aufruf an die Nationalgarde!
[Wien,1848]

[2]p. 21x13cm.
Caption title; signed & dated on p.[2]:
Eduard Leidesdorf, Nationalgardist ... Wien, am
16. März 1848.

*pGB8
V6755R
3.16.48

Vienna. Magistrat.
Aufforderung. Das anhaltende Zusammenströmen
der Menschen auf den öffentlichen Plätzen und
Strassen, und das bestimmungslose Herumziehen in
denselben stört nicht allein die öffentliche
Ordnung und Ruhe, sondern entzieht auch der
Industrie und dem Handel die nothwendigen
Arbeitskräfte ...
[Wien,1848]

broadside. 36.5x22cm.
Unterreiter I.94.
Signed & dated: (Vom Magistrate und prov.
Bürgerausschusse (der Stadt Wien am 16.
März 1848.

*GB8
V6755R
3.16.48

[Motloch, Moriz Albert, 1825-1851]
Eljen.
[Wien,1848]

broadside. 22x14.5cm.
Helfert (Wiener Parnass) 357.
Signed: Moriz Albert [pseud.].

*pGB8
V6755R
3.16.48

Vienna. Nationalgarde.
Bekanntmachung. Erstens. Die Einschreibung
für die Nationalgarde geschieht für die Stadt
auf dem Rathhause ...
[Wien,1848]

broadside. 38.5x23cm.
Dated & signed: Wien am 16. März 1848. Vom
Ober-Commando der Nationalgarde.

*GB8
V6755R
3.16.48

[Rosenfeld, Albert, fl.1848]
Der Empfang des Kaisers Ferdinand. Als sich die
Pforten der ehrwürdigen Burg wieder öffneten.
[Wien]Druck von U.Klopf sen.und Alex.Eurich,
Wollzeile Nr.782.[1848]

[2]p. 20.5x13cm.
Helfert (Wiener Parnass) 368.
Caption title; imprint on p.[2].
Signed & dated at end: Albert Rosenfeld,
Nationalgardist. Wien, 16. März 1848.

*pGB8
V6755R
3.16.48

Vienna. Nationalgarde.
Tagsbefehl für die Nationalgarde am 16. März
1848.
[Wien,1848]

folder([3]p.) 44.5x28.5cm.
Signed on p.[3]: Hoyos, k. k. Feldmarschall=
Lieutenant und Ober=Commandant der Bürger= und
Nationalgarde.

*GB8
V6755R
3.16.48

[Strampfer, Heinrich]
An Oesterreich's Völker.
Druck und Eigenthum von Josef Stöckholzer
v.Hirschfeld in Wien.1848.

folder([4]p.) 27.5x22cm.
Helfert (Wiener Parnass) 370.
Dated & signed at end: Am 16. März 1848.
Heinrich Strampfer.

*pGB8
V6755R
3.16.48

Vienna. Nationalgarde.
Vorläufige Anordnung über den Dienst der
Nationalgarde.
[Wien,1848]

broadside. 38x23cm.
Dated & signed: Wien am 16. März 1848. Vom
Ober-Commando der Nationalgarde.

*GB8
V6755R
3.16.48

[Swiedack, Karl, 1815-1888]
Prolog. Gedichtet von Carl Elmar [pseud.]. Bei
Gelegenheit der Wiedereröffnung des Theaters
an der Wien, nach den drei denkwürdigen Tagen
des 13., 14. und 15. März des Jahres 1848.
Gesprochen von Herrn Lussberger.
[Wien,1848]

[2]p. 22x15cm.
Helfert (Wiener Parnass) 361.
Caption title.
Printed on yellow paper.

*pGB8
V6755R
3.16.48

Vienna. Nationalgarde.
Weitere Anordnung über die Organisirung der
Nationalgarde.
[Wien,1848]

broadside. 38x23cm.
Dated & signed: Wien am 16. März 1848. Vom
Ober-Commando der Nationalgarde.

Wia's halt is, wann mas in da Geschwindigkeit
aussaaredt, weil am s'Herz übergeht.
*GB8 [Wien]Druck von Bl.Höfel,Mariahilfer
V6755R Hauptstrasse Nr.407.[1848]
3.16.48
[2]p. 19.5x12.5cm.
Caption title; imprint on p.[2].
Dated & signed: Wien, am 16. März 1848. A
Oestreicha.

○

[Zerboni di Sposetti, Julius, 1805-1884]
An meine Brüder im freien Vaterlande
*GB8 Oesterreich!
V6755R [Wien]Bei Fr.Tendler & Comp.,Buchhändler am
3.16.48 Graben Nr.618.[1848]
[2]p. 29x22cm.
Helfert (Wiener Parnass) 372.
Caption title; imprint on p.[2].
Dated & signed at end: Am 16. März 1848.
Julius von Zerboni di Sposetti.

○

Auf den Tod des Technikers Carl Heinrich
Spitzer. Von einer jungen Dame.
*GB8 [Wien]Druck vou [!] U.Klopf sen.und A.Eurich,
V6755R Wollzeile Nr.782.[1848]
3.17.48
broadside. 19.5x13cm.
Helfert (Wiener Parnass) 420.

○

Austria. Armee.
Befehl Sr. Durchlaucht des k. k.
*pGB8 Feldmarschall=Lieutenants, k. k. Civil= und
V6755R Militär=Gouverneurs, Fürsten Alfred zu
3.17.48 Windischgrätz, an den Commandirenden der
National=Garde, Grafen von Hoyos: "Nachdem die
Bürgergarde den Dienst zur Aufrechthaltung der
Ruhe und Ordnung zugleich mit der Nationalgarde
versieht ...
[Wien,1848]
broadside. 44.5x28.5cm.
Dated: Wien am   17. März 1848.
Appointing   ○   Hoyos commander of the
Bürgergarde.

○

Breuer, Hermann, fl.1848.
Am Grabe der gefallenen Brüder. Von Hermann
*GB8 Breuer.
V6755R [Wien]Gedruckt bei M.Lell,vormals Anna St.
3.17.48 von Hirschfeld.[1848]
[2]p. 22x14.5cm.
Helfert (Wiener Parnass) 391.
Caption title; imprint on p.[2].

○

Brix, Alexander, d.1869.
Jubellied seinen Brüdern, den Wiener
*GB8 Studenten, am Tage der Befreiung unseres
V6755R Vaterlandes aus übervollem Herzen zugejauchzt
3.17.48 von Alexander Brix, Mediziner.
[Wien]Druck von U.Klopf sen.und A.Eurich,
Stadt,Wollzeile Nr.782.[1848]
broadside. 21x13cm.
Helfert (Wiener Parnass) 377.

○

Brix, Alexander, d.1869.
Jubellied seinen Brüdern, den Wiener Studenten,
*GB8 am Tage der Befreiung unseres Vaterlandes aus
V6755R übervollem Herzen zugejauchzt von Alexander
3.17.48 Brix, Mediziner.
[Wien]Zweiter Abdruck.Druck von U.Klopf sen.
und A.Eurich,Stadt,Wollzeile Nr.782.[1848]
broadside. 21x13cm.
Helfert (Wiener Parnass) 377.

○

Busch, Isidor.
Der Gefallenen Ehrendenkmal.
*GB8 [Wien,1848]
V6755R
3.17.48 broadside. 22x14cm.
Helfert (Wiener Parnass) 392.
Dated: Wien den 17. März 1848.

○

Castelli, Ignaz Franz, 1781-1862.
Lied für die Nationalgarde.
*GB8 [Wien,1848]
V6755R
3.17.48 broadside. 21x13cm.
Helfert (Wiener Parnass) 378.

○

[Castelli, Ignaz Franz, 1781-1862]
Lied für die Nationalgarde.
*GB8 [Wien,1848]
V6755R
3.17.48 [2]p. 18x13cm.
Helfert (Wiener Parnass) 378.
Caption title; signed at end: J. F. Castelli.

○

*GB8
V6755R
3.17.48

Drei wichtige Actenstücke! i.Kossuth's Rede
bei seiner Ankunft mit den ungarischen
Deputirten in Pressburg den 17. März. ii.Brief
Sr. k. k. Hoheit des Erzherzogs Reichspalatin
an Grafen Ludwig Bathyány, Premier-Minister.
iii.Abschiedsworte der ungarischen Reichstagsjugend an die Wiener Universitätsjugend.
[Wien]K.k.Hof-Buchdruckerei des L.Sommer,
vormals Strauss.[1848]
    folder([4]p.) 22.5x14.5cm.
    Caption title; imprint on p.[4].
    The 3d document is signed: Friedrich Szarvady,
im Auftrage der   sämmtlichen Reichstagsjugend.

*GB8
V6755R
3.17.48

Geyer, Fr
    Worte der Theilnahme beim Begräbniss der
Gefallenen vom 13. März 1848.
[Wien,1848]
    broadside. 18.5x11cm.
    Helfert (Wiener Parnass) 396.

*GB8
V6755R
3.17.48

Ellinger, Joseph von, 1814-1877.
    Nur Ruhe!
[Wien,1848]
    broadside. 19x12cm.
    Dated & signed: Wien den 17. März 1848.
Advokat Ellinger.
    In this edition the first line of text ends:
unseres

*GB8
V6755R
3.17.48

Gulitz, A
    Die Leichenfeier der Gefallenen.
[Wien,1848]
    broadside. 22.5x14.5cm.
    Helfert (Wiener Parnass) 397.
    Dated: Am 17. März 1848.

*GB8
V6755R
3.17.48

Ellinger, Joseph von, 1814-1877.
    Nur Ruhe!
[Wien,1848]
    broadside. 22.5x14cm.
    Dated & signed: Wien den 17. März 1848.
Advokat Ellinger.
    In this edition the first line of text ends:
unseres gelieb=

*GB8
V6755R
3.17.48

[Irmscher, Carl Gottlieb]
    Lied eines Schustergesellen. An die edlen
Vorkämpfer für die gute Sache und an die
hochherzigen Gefallenen für's Vaterland am 13.
und 14. März 1848.
[Wien]Druck von U.Klopf sen.und A.Eurich,
Wollzeile 782.[1848]
    [2]p. 20x13.5cm.
    Helfert (Wiener Parnass) 399.
    Caption title; imprint on p.[2].
    Signed at end: Carl Gottlieb Irmscher,
ehemaliger   Schustergeselle aus
Chemnitz in   Sachsen (dermalen
Bedienter).

*GB8
V6755R
3.17.48

Engländer, Hermann.
    Grabgeleite für die Gefallenen bei der
erhaltenen Constitution.
[Wien]A.Dorfmeister's Druck und Verlag,Stadt,
Kühfussgasse Nr.575.[1848]
    broadside. 20x12cm.
    Helfert (Wiener Parnass) 394.

*GB8
V6755R
3.17.48

[Kauffmann, G   ]
    Am Grabe der Gefallenen vom 13. und 14. März
1848.
[Wien]Mechitharisten-Buchdruckerei.[1848]
    [2]p. 29x22.5cm.
    Caption title; imprint on p.[2].
    Signed: G. Kauffmann, Mitglied der
Nationalgarde.

*GB8
V6755R
3.17.48

Gärtner, Wilhelm, 1811-1875.
    An Oesterreichs Völker. Der Wiener
Universität! Von ihrem Verehrer Wilhelm
Gärtner, Priester an der Universitätskirche.
[Wien,1848]
    folder([4]p.) 22.5x15.5cm.
    Helfert (Wiener Parnass) 380.
    Printer's imprint on p.[4]: Druck und Verlag
von Jos. Stöckholzer v. Hirschfeld.
    Dated at end: Wien, am 17. März 1848.

*GB8
V6755R
3.17.48

[Kirschner, Karl, d.1878]
    Am Grabe der gefallenen Brüder.
[Wien]Druck von U.Klopf sen.und Alex.Eurich,
Wollzeile 782.[1848]
    broadside. 21.5x12.5cm.
    Helfert (Wiener Parnass) 393.
    Signed: Carl Dolde [pseud.].

Klopf und Eurich, firm, printers, Vienna.
*GB8   Die Presse an ihre Erlöser! Dankbar
V6755R dargebracht von U. Klopf sen. und A.Eurich's
3.17.48 Buchdruckerei in Wien am 17. März 1848.
[Wien,1848]

broadside. 21x12.5cm.
Helfert (Wiener Parnass) 376.
Printed within ornamental border.

Mannheimer, Isak Noah, 1793-1865.
*GB8   Rede am Grabe der Gefallenen. Gesprochen von
V6755R J. N. Mannheimer. Freitag den 17. März 1848.
3.17.48 [Wien]Gedruckt bei Franz Edl.v.Schmid.[1848]

folder([4]p.) 22.5x15cm.
Reschauer-Smets II.16.

Kloss, Joseph Ferdinand, 1807-1883.
*GB8   Am Grabe der Opfer für die Freiheit, gefallen
V6755R am 13. u. 14. März 1848. Von Carl Haffner.
3.17.48 Musik nach Graun's Melodie für 4 Singstimmen
eingerichtet von J. F. Kloss, National=
Gardisten ...
Wien,Mechitharisten=Buchdruckerei.[1848]

folder(2ℓ.) 22.5x14cm.
Helfert (Wiener Parnass) 398.
Includes the music.
Also published   with title: Hymne für
Oesterreichs Volk.

[Moeschl, F   A   J   ]
*GB8   Den Manen der am Montag, den 13. März 1848,
V6755R für das Vaterland gefallenen Helden.
3.17.48 [Wien]Druck und Eigenthum von Hirschfeld.
[1848]

folder([4]p.) 22.5x13cm.
Helfert (Wiener Parnass) 403.
Signed at end: F. A. J. Moeschl.

König, Ferdinand, fl.1848.
*GB8   Am Grabe der am 13. März 1848 gefallenen
V6755R Bürger.
3.17.48 [Wien]A.Dorfmeister's Druck und Verlag,Stadt,
Kühfussgasse Nr.575.[1848]

broadside. 20x12cm.
Helfert (Wiener Parnass) 400.

Montecuccoli, Albert Raimund Zeno, graf,
*GB8   1802-1852.
V6755R Rede des Landmarschalles an die akademische
3.17.48 Jugend.
[Wien,1848]

broadside. 28x22cm.
Cf. Helfert (Geschichte) I.281.
Another issue has date added following title:
Den 17. März 1848.

Kreichel, Andreas, 1828-1889.
*GB8   Am Begräbnisstage unserer gefallenen
V6755R Mitbrüder. Von And. Kreichel, Mediziner.
3.17.48 [Wien,1848]

broadside. 21x13.5cm.
Helfert (Wiener Parnass) 401.

Montecuccoli, Albert Raimund Zeno, graf,
*GB8   1802-1852.
V6755R Rede des Landmarschalles an die akademische
3.17.48 Jugend. Den 17. März 1848.
[Wien,1848]

broadside. 28.5x22cm.
Cf. Helfert (Geschichte) I.281.
Another issue does not have the date following
the title.

Kulka, Adolf, 1823-1898.
*GB8   Denkstein für die am 13. März Gefallenen.
V6755R Meinen Herren Collegen den hochherzigen
3.17.48 Studenten Wiens liebevoll gewidmet von A. E.
Kulka.
[Wien,1848]

folder([4]p.) 21x13.5cm.
Helfert (Wiener Parnass) 402.
Printer's imprint on p.[2]: Druck von Ul.
Klopf sen. und Alex. Eurich, Wollzeile Nr. 782.

Neumann, Josef, 1815-1878.
*GB8   Rede, gehalten am Grabe der am 13. März 1848
V6755R in Wien gefallenen Patrioten, von Prof. Dr. Jos.
3.17.48 Neumann.
[Wien,1848]

folder([3]p.) 21.5x13.5cm.
Reschauer-Smets II.18.
Caption title.

Neutitscheiner, Anton.
*GB8   Wiener Märzen-Veigerl'n. Von Anton
V6755R   Neutitscheiner.
3.17.48   [Wien,1848]

           folder([4]p.) 25x16.5cm.
           Helfert (Wiener Parnass) 382.
           Caption title; dated at end: Wien, am 17.
           März 1848.

Petri, Hugo Jacques.
*GB8   An die Gefallenen am 13. und 14. März 1848.
V6755R   Von Hugo Jacques Petri.
3.17.48   [Wien,1848]

           folder([4]p.) 21x13.5cm.
           Helfert (Wiener Parnass) 404.

Petrichevich Horváth, Lázár, 1807-1851.
*GB8   An die verehrlichen Nationalgarden Wiens.
V6755R   [Budapest,1848]
3.17.48
           broadside. 30x23.5cm.
           Dated: Buda-Pest, den 17. März 1848.
           Urging subscriptions and dissemination of his
           journal "Ungarns Morgenröthe".

           Programm der am Freitag, den 17. März
*GB8   1848, stattfindenden Feierlichkeiten.
V6755R   [Wien,1848]
3.17.48
           broadside. 22.5x15cm.
           Programme for ceremonies of the Nationalgarde
           held on the evening of March 17, following the
           state funeral of the victims of the March 13
           revolution in the afternoon.

Rosenfeld, Albert, fl.1848.
*GB8   Zwischen beiden Welten. Geschrieben auf dem
V6755R   Schmelzer Friedhofe den 17. März 1848 von
3.17.48   Albert Rosenfeld, Nationalgardist.
           [Wien]Druck von U.Klopf sen.und A.Eurich,
           Wollzeile 782.[1848]

           broadside. 20x13cm.
           Helfert (Wiener Parnass) 405.

Saphir, Moritz Gottlieb, 1795-1858.
*pGB8   Die Studenten beim Leichenbegängnisse der
V6755R   Tapfern. Den Studirenden Wiens gewidmet von
3.17.48   M. G. Saphir.
           [Wien]Gedruckt bei Leopold Grund.[1848]

           broadside. 33x26cm.
           Helfert (Wiener Parnass) 406.

[Scheda, Julius]
           Bei dem Grabe der am 13. März 1848 Gefallenen
*GB8   von ihren trauernden Mitbrüdern.
V6755R   [Wien]A.Dorfmeister's Druck und Verlag(Stadt,
3.17.48   Kühfussgasse Nr.575).[1848]

           [2]p. 22.5x14.5cm.
           Helfert (Wiener Parnass) 407.
           Caption title; imprint on p.[2].
           Signed at end: Julius Scheda, Jurist im 3.
           Jahre. Gedichtet auf der Wache in der Villa
           Metternich.

[Scherb, ———]
           Gedanken während des Begräbnisses der in der
*GB8   Wiener-Merzrevolution Gefallenen.
V6755R   [Wien]Druck von U.Klopf sen.und Alex.Eurich,
3.17.48   Wollzeile 782.[1848]

           [2]p. 21x13cm.
           Helfert (Wiener Parnass) 409.
           Caption title; imprint on p.[2].
           Signed at end: Scherb.

Schick, Leopold.
*GB8   Am Grabe der für das Vaterland und die
V6755R   Freiheit Gefallenen. Von Leopold Schick.
3.17.48   [Wien]Gedruckt bei Carl Gerold.[1848]

           [2]p. 28.5x22cm.
           Caption title; imprint on p.[2].
           Dated: Wien, am 17. März 1848.

[Schindler, Franz Vincenz, b.1821?]
           Gedanken an den Särgen der Gefallenen (am 17.
*GB8   März 1848).
V6755R   [Wien]K.k.Hof-Buchdruckerei des L.Sommer
3.17.48   (vormals Strauss),Dorotheergasse Nr.1108.[1848]
           folder([4]p.) 19x12.5cm.
           Caption title; imprint on p.[4].
           Signed: Franz Vinc. Schindler, Nationalgardist.

*GB8
V6755R
3.17.48

Seligmann, Romeo, 1808-1892.
    Rede am Grabe der am Montag, den 13. März 1848,
im Kampf für Oesterreichs freie Verfassung,
Gefallenen, verfasst von Dr. Romeo-Seligmann,
gesprochen im Namen der Wiener Bürgerschaft von
J. G. Scherzer, Bürger=Officier.
[Wien,1848]
    broadside. 1 illus. 22x13.5cm.
    "Gratis."

*GB8
V6755R
3.17.48

Uhl, Friedrich, 1825-1906.
    Für die Bürger, die am Montag den 13. März
1848 in Wien gefallen.
[Wien,1848]
    broadside. 21x14cm.
    Helfert (Wiener Parnass) 413.
    Printed within mourning border 5mm. wide;
another edition has imprint.

*GB8
V6755R
3.17.48

Stern, Max Emanuel, 1811-1873.
    Es werde Licht! Von M. E. Stern.
[Wien]Druck von U.Klopf sen.und Alex.Eurich,
Wollzeile 782.[1848]
    [2]p. 21x12.5cm.
    Helfert (Wiener Parnass) 385.
    Caption title; imprint on p.[2].

*GB8
V6755R
3.17.48

Uhl, Friedrich, 1825-1906.
    Für die Bürger, die am Montag, den 13. März
1848, in Wien gefallen.
Josef v.Hirschfeld'sche Officin in Wien.[1848]
    broadside. 22.5x15cm.
    Helfert (Wiener Parnass) 413.
    Printed within mourning border 2mm. wide;
another edition is without imprint.

*GB8
V6755R
3.17.48

Szántó, Simon, 1819-1873.
    Gedanken-Freiheit! Aufruf an Wiens hochherzige
Bürger von Simon Szántó.
[Wien]Zu haben in der Buchdruckerei von Ul.
Klopf sen.und Alex.Eurich,Wollzeile Nr.782.
[1848]
    folder([4]p.) 21x13cm.
    Helfert (Wiener Parnass) 386.
    Caption title; imprint on p.[4].

*pGB8
V6755R
3.17.48

Vienna. Magistrat.
    ... Kundmachung. In Folge der von den nied.
österr. Herren Ständen erlassenen Kundmachung vom
15. d. M. wurde bey dem Magistrate und dem
provisorischen Bürgerausschusse die Wahl jener
12 Mitglieder aus dem Bürgerstande vorgenommen ...
[Wien,1848]
    broadside. 42x26.5cm.
    Signed & dated: Von dem Magistrate und prov.
Bürgerausschusse der Stadt Wien am 17. März 1848.
    At head: ad Nr.   520. P.

*GB8
V6755R
3.17.48

[Szarvady, Frigyes, 1822-1882]
    Abschiedsworte der ungarischen Reichstags-
jugend an die Wiener Universitätsjugend.
[Wien,1848]
    [2]p. 21.5x13.5cm.
    Reschauer-Smets II.14.
    Caption title; dated & signed on p.[2]: Wien
am 17. März 1848. Friedrich Szarvady, im
Auftrage der sämmtlichen Reichstagsjugend.

*pGB8
V6755R
3.17.48

Vienna. Magistrat.
    Kundmachung. Nachdem die Bewohner Wiens ihre
Freude über die ihnen allerhöchst zugestandenen
Rechte bereits einige Tage durch allgemeinen
Jubel und Beleuchtung an den Tag gelegt haben
...
[Wien,1848]
    broadside. 29x45cm.
    Signed & dated: Vom Magistrate und prov.
Bürger-Ausschusse der Stadt. Wien am 17. März
1848.
    Urging the   restoration of order.

*GB8
V6755R
3.17.48

Tauber, Josef Samuel, 1822-1879.
    Alle Brüder! Am Grabe der gefallenen
Freiheits=Helden.
[Wien,1848]
    broadside. 21x13.5cm.
    Helfert (Wiener Parnass) 411.

*pGB8
V6755R
3.17.48

Vienna. Nationalgarde.
    Tagsbefehl für die Nationalgarde. Am 17.
März 1848.
[Wien,1848]
    broadside. 38x23cm.
    Signed: Hoyos.

*GB8
V6755R
3.17.48
[Wolf-Leitenberger, Johanna, 1818-1893]
Oesterreich's Frühling.
[Wien,1848]

broadside. 22x13.5cm.
Helfert (Wiener Parnass) 388.
Dated & signed: Wien, am 17. März Abends.
Maria Litahorsky [pseud.]

*pGB8
V6755R
3.18.48
Austria, Lower. Landständischer Ausschuss.
Der N. Oest. ständische Ausschuss an seine
Mitbürger! Durch öffentlichen Anschlag vom 15.
d. M. wurde bekannt gegeben, dass von den N. Oest.
Ständen zur Besorgung der ihnen zukommenden und
für diesen Augenblick wichtigsten Geschäfte ein
provisorischer Ausschuss von 24 Mitgliedern
niedergesetzt worden ist ...
[Wien,1848]

broadside. 45x57cm.
Dated: Wien, den 18. März 1848.

*GB8
V6755R
3.17.48
[Zerboni di Sposetti, Julius, 1805-1884]
Oesterreich hoch!
[Wien]Bei Fr.Tendler & Comp.,Buchhändler am
Graben Nr.618.[1848]

[2]p. 29x22cm.
Helfert (Wiener Parnass) 387.
Caption title; imprint on p.[2].
Dated & signed at end: Am 17. März 1848.
Julius von Zerboni di Sposetti.

*GB8
V6755R
3.18.48
Brief eines Soldaten aus Mailand, von der
Begebenheit der grossen Revolution.
[Wien]Gedruckt bei Josef Ludwig.[1848]
[2]p. 26x20cm.
Caption title; imprint on p.[2].

*GB8
V6755R
3.18.48
An die Bürger Wiens!
[Wien,1848]
folder([4]p.) 22.5x14cm.
Caption title; dated & signed on p.[4]:
Wien, am 18. März 1848. Ein Mitkämpfer vor,
und an den Tagen der Schlacht.

*GB8
V6755R
3.18.48
Dem Manne uns'rer Verehrung, Professor Hye.
[Wien,1848]
folder([4]p.) 22.5x14.5cm.
Helfert (Wiener Parnass) 422.
Title within ornamental wreath; signed on p.
[4]: Heinrich D....... Nationalgardist im
Juristen=Corps.

*GB8
V6755R
3.18.48
An Oesterreichs Jugend.
[Wien]Druck von J.St.v.Hirschfeld.[1848]
[2]p. 22.5x15cm.
Helfert (Wiener Parnass) 426.
Caption title; imprint on p.[2].
Signed: E. v. M.

*GB8
V6755R
3.18.48
[Landau, Herrmann Josef, 1815-1889]
An den todtgeglaubten Dichter und Mitkämpfer
Ludwig Eckardt. (Als ich ihn zum ersten Male
wieder sah.)
[Wien,1848]
folder([4]p.) 22.5x14.5cm.
Helfert (Wiener Parnass) 434.
Signed at end: Herrmann Landau.

*pGB8
V6755R
3.18.48
Austria. Armee.
Kundmachung. Ordnung und Ruhe kehrt nunmehr,
Dank sei es der von dem oft bewährten guten
Geiste geleiteten thätigen Mitwirkung aller
Bürger=Classen dieser Residenz, in dieselbe
zurück ...
[Wien,1848]
broadside. 45x57cm.
Dated & signed: Wien am 18. März 1848. Alfred
Fürst zu Windischgrätz, k. k. Feldmarschall=
Lieutenant.

*GB8
V6755R
3.18.48
[Löbenstein, Alois]
Glaubensfreiheit.
[Wien]Zu haben in der Wollzeile Nr.782.[1848]
folder([3]p.) 21x13cm.
Caption title; imprint on p.[3].
Signed & dated at end: Löbenstein Alois,
Candidat des ev. Predigeramtes. Wien, 18. März
1848.

*GB8
V6755R
3.18.48

[Metzerich, Wilhelm von, 1818-1867]
Noch eines Wieners Lied. Dem Mitgliede der
National-Garde, Joseph Englisch, gewidmet.
[Wien]Gedruckt bei Carl Gerold.[1848]

[2]p. 22.5x14.5cm.
Helfert (Wiener Parnass) 423.
Caption title; imprint on p.[2].
Dated & signed at end: Am 18. März 1848. Wilh.
v. Metzerich.

*pGB8
V6755R
3.18.48

Vienna. Magistrat.
Kundmachung. Se. k. k. Majestät haben laut
Hofkanzlei=Präsidialdekretes vom 17. d. M. Z.
620 das hohe Hofkanzlei=Präsidium zu ermächtigen
geruht ...
[Wien,1848]

broadside. 36.5x22.5cm.
Signed & dated: Vom Magistrate und prov.
Bürger=Ausschusse der Stadt Wien am 18. März
1848.
In this edition the last line of text begins:
gleiche rühmliche   Haltung

*GB8
V6755R
3.18.48

Der oberöstreichische Baur am 18. März 1848.
Wien 1848.Gedruckt bei Carl Gerold.

[2]p. 22.5x14.5cm.
Helfert (Wiener Parnass) 432.
Caption title; imprint on p.[2].

*pGB8
V6755R
3.18.48

Vienna. Magistrat.
Kundmachung. Se. k. k. Majestät haben laut
Hofkanzlei=Präsidialdekretes vom 17. d. M. Z.
620 das hohe Hofkanzlei=Präsidium zu ermächtigen
geruht ...
[Wien,1848]

broadside. 37x22cm.
Signed & dated: Vom Magistrate und prov.
Bürger=Ausschusse der Stadt Wien am 18. März
1848.
In this edition the last line of text begins:
Haltung bewähren

*GB8
V6755R
3.18.48

Palme, Alois, 1793-1864.
Der Kaiser hat geweint!
[Wien]K.k.Hof=Buchdruckerei des L.Sommer
(vormals Strauss).[1848]

broadside. 21x13cm.
Helfert (Wiener Parnass) 429.
Dated: Wien, im März 1848.

*pGB8
V6755R
3.18.48

Vienna. Nationalgarde.
Tagsbefehl für die Nationalgarde. Am 18.
März 1848.
[Wien,1848]

[2]p. 44.5x28.5cm.
Signed: Hoyos, k. k. Feldmarschall=Lieutenant.

*GB8
V6755R
3.18.48

Rotter, Richard.
An Kaiser, Volk und Studenten. Von Richard
Rotter.
[Wien,1848]

broadside. 22x13cm.
Helfert (Wiener Parnass) 430.
Dated: Am 18. März 1848.
Another issue has imprint.

*pGB8
V6755R
3.18.48

Vienna. Universität.
Nachricht. Nachdem die Verhältnisse, welche
bisher den edlen Eifer und die rastlose
Thätigkeit sämmtlicher Studierenden in
Anspruch genommen haben ...
[Wien,1848]

broadside. 38.5x23cm.
Dated & signed: Wien den 18. März 1848. Von
der Universität.
Announcing the resumption of classes on 20
March.

*GB8
V6755R
3.18.48

Rotter, Richard.
An Kaiser, Volk und Studenten. Von Richard
Rotter.
[Wien]Verlag von Singer u.Göring,Buchhändler
im Fürsterzbischöfl.Palais,Wollzeile Nr.869.
[1848]

broadside. 21x13.5cm.
Helfert (Wiener Parnass) 430.
Dated: Am 18. März 1848.
Another issue is without imprint.

*GB8
V6755R
3.18.48

Vogl, Johann Nepomuk, 1802-1866.
Nationalgardistenlied.
[Wien,1848]

broadside. 19x12cm.
Helfert (Wiener Parnass) 431.

*GB8
V6755R
3.19.48

... Aufgefangener Brief des Fürsten Metternich an den Minister Guizot in London.
[Wien,1848]

folder([4]p.) 26.5x21cm.
At head of title: (Preis: 3 kr. CM.)
Printer's imprint on p.[4]: Gedruckt bei M. Lell, Leopoldstadt Weintraubengasse Nr.505.
Fictitious.
Dated in contemporary ms.: 19. März 848.

---

*pGB8
V6755R
3.19.48

Faster, Peter, b.1801.
Mitbürger, Landsleute, Brüder! Eueren Stimmen gehorsam, lassen wir das Haus und Alles, was uns theuer, in Euerer Mitte zurück, um Euere Wünsche an den erhabenen Thron unseres Königs zu bringen ...
[Prag,1848]

broadside. 36x22cm.
Dated & signed: Prag, den 19. März 1848. Im Namen der Deputirten: Peter Faster. Prawoslaw Aloys Trojan.
Printed in red; Czech & German in double columns; Czech text begins: Spolumeštané, krajané, bratři!

---

*pGB8
V6755R
3.19.48

Austria. Sovereigns, etc., 1835-1848
(Ferdinand I)
Wir Ferdinand der Erste, von Gottes Gnaden Kaiser von Oesterreich ... In Anbetracht der dringenden Nothwendigkeit, die öffentlichen Geschäfte in einen geregelten Gang zurückzuführen ...
[Wien,1848]

broadside. 44.5x28.5cm.
"Gegeben in Unserer kaiserlichen Haupt= und Residenzstadt Wien, den neunzehnten März, im eintausend achthundert acht und vierzigsten ..."

---

*GB8
V6755R
3.19.48

Der Grossvezier auf Reisen.
[Wien,1848]

[2]p. 22.5x15cm.
Helfert (Wiener Parnass) 479.
On the resignation & flight of Metternich.

---

*GB8
V6755R
3.19.48

[Bidschof, Franz Xavier]
Der Bauer Hansjürgel und die Pressfreiheit.
[Wien]Gedruckt bei Josef Ludwig,Josefstadt Florianigasse Nr.52.[1848]

folder([4]p.) 19x12cm.
Helfert (Wiener Parnass) 452.
Caption title; imprint on p.[4].
Signed at end: Franz X. Bidschof.

---

*GB8
V6755R
3.19.48

[Hassaurek, Friedrich, 1832-1885]
Trauergesang am Grabe meines geliebten Kollegen Karl Konitschek. (Verwundet den 13. und gestorben den 17. März 1848.)
[Wien,1848]

[2]p. 21x13cm.
Helfert (Wiener Parnass) 438.
Caption title; signed on p.[2]: Friedrich Hassaureck.

---

*GB8
V6755R
3.19.48

[Bidschof, Franz Xavier]
Der betrogene Satan.
[Wien]Gedruckt bei Josef Ludwig,Josefstadt Florianigasse Nr.52.[1848]

folder([4]p.) 19x12cm.
Helfert (Wiener Parnass) 488.
Caption title; imprint on p.[4].
Signed at end: Franz X. Bidschof.
On the resignation & flight of Metternich.

---

*GB8
V6755R
3.19.48

Heinisch, Constantin.
Wo mag denn der Metternich hingekommen sein! oder: Wenn er in Russland wäre - - Ein Wort im Fluge von Constantin Heinisch, Nationalgardist der akademischen Legion ...
[Wien,1848]

folder([4]p.) 22x14.5cm.
Helfert (Wiener Parnass) 482.
Imprint on p.[4]: Gedruckt bei M. Lell, Leopoldstadt, Weintraubengasse Nr.505.

---

*GB8
V6755R
3.19.48

[Buchheim, Carl Adolf, 1828-1900]
Das waren die braven Studenten!
[Wien]Zu haben bei U.Klopf sen.und Alex. Eurich,Stadt,Wollzeile Nr.782,im ersten Stock. [1848]

[2]p. 21x13cm.
Helfert (Wiener Parnass) 437.
Caption title; imprint on p.[2].
Signed: Adolf Buchheim, absolvirter Philosoph.

---

*GB8
V6755R
3.19.48

[Hermann von Hermannsthal, Franz, 1799-1875]
Die Nationalgarde.
[Wien]Ausgegeben von Tendler & Comp.[1848]

[2]p. 22.5cm.
Helfert (Wiener Parnass) 439.
Caption title; imprint on p.[2].
Dated & signed at end: Wien, am 19. März 1848. Hermannsthal.

*GB8
V6755R
3.19.48

Janitschka, Johann, b.1797.
Oesterreich in den letzten Dezennien bis zum
13. März 1848.
[Wien]A.Dorfmeister's Druck und Verlag.[1848]

broadside. 27x22cm.
Helfert (Wiener Parnass) 459.
Printed within ornamental border on pink
paper.

---

*GB8
V6755R
3.19.48

[Loritz, Adolf]
Offenes Sendschreiben an meine Mitkämpfer.
[Wien]Gedruckt bei Carl Gerold.[1848]

[2]p. 22x14.5cm.
Caption title; imprint on p.[2].
Dated & signed at end: Geschrieben den 19.
März 1848. Adolf Loritz.

---

*GB8
V6755R
3.19.48

König, Ferdinand, fl.1848.
An Wien's Bürger!
[Wien]A.Dorfmeister's Druck und Verlag (Stadt,
Kühfussgasse Nr.575).[1848]

[2]p. 22.5x14.5cm.
Helfert (Wiener Parnass) 491.
Caption title; imprint on p.[2].

---

*GB8
V6755R
3.19.48

Ludwig, Johann, fl.1848.
Die vier Elemente.
[Wien]Druck von U.Klopf sen.und A.Eurich.
[1848]

broadside. 20x13cm.
Helfert (Wiener Parnass) 490.
On the resignation & flight of Metternich.

---

*GB8
V6755R
3.19.48

Das Lied vom Bürgermeister.
[Wien,1848]

folder([4]p.) 20x13.5cm.
Helfert (Wiener Parnass) 486.
Printer's imprint on p.[4]: Druck von U.
Klopf sen. und A. Eurich, Wollzeile Nr.782.
On the resignation & flight of Metternich.

---

*GB8
V6755R
3.19.48

Markl, Franz.
Zur Erinnerung an den 13., 14. und 15. März
1848. Der Nationalgarde gewidmet.
[Wien]Druck von U.Klopf sen.und A.Eurich,
Wollzeile 782.[1848]

broadside. 20x13cm.
Helfert (Wiener Parnass) 448.

---

*pGB8
V6755R
3.19.48

Linz, Austria. Bürgerschaft.
Adresse. An die Bürger der k. k. Haupt- und
Residenzstadt Wien.
[Wien]Druck von U.Klopf senior und Alexander
Eurich,Wollzeile 782.[1848]

broadside. 44.5x28cm.
Signed & dated: Die Bürger der Stadt Linz am
19. März 1848.

---

*GB8
V6755R
3.19.48

[Medis, J   Alexander]
Die neue Geschichte von einem alten grossen
Herrn.
[Wien]Verlag von J.Wenedikt.Gedruckt bei F.E.v.
Schmid.[1848]

[2]p. 22x14.5cm.
Helfert (Wiener Parnass) 480.
Caption title; imprint on p.[2].
Signed at end: Alexander Medis.
On the resignation & flight of Metternich.

---

*pGB8
V6755R
3.19.48

Linz, Austria. Bürgerschaft.
Adresse an Sr. kais. kön. Majestät Kaiser
Ferdinand I.
[Wien]Druck von U.Klopf senior und Alexander
Eurich,Wollzeile 782.[1848]

broadside. 45x29cm.
Signed & dated: Die treuen Bürger der Stadt
Linz des constitutionellen Kaiserreiches
Oesterreich am 19. März 1848.

---

*GB8
V6755R
3.19.48

Meisl, Karl, 1775-1853.
Der Kalife und seine Vezier. Zeitgemässes
Gedicht von Carl Meisl.
[Wien,1848]

folder([4]p.) 23x14.5cm.
Helfert (Wiener Parnass) 481.
Printer's imprint on p.[4]: Gedruckt bei M.
Lell, vormals Anna St. von Hirschfeld.
On the resignation & flight of Metternich.

*GB8
V6755R
3.19.48

Meisl, Karl, 1775-1853.
    Wien's Jubelruf am Tage des feyerlichen Te
Deums, abgehalten in der Metropolitankirche zu St.
Stephan. Verfasst von Carl Meisl.
    Wien.Gedruckt und zu haben bei Leopold Grund,
am Stephansplatz im Zwettelhof.[1848]

    folder([4]p.) 26.5x21cm.
    Helfert (Wiener Parnass) 441.

*GB8
V6755R
3.19.48

Rick, Carl, 1815-1881.
    Das Lied vom braven Kanonier. Worte von Carl
Rick. In Musik gesetzt für eine Singstimme mit
Begleitung des Pianoforte von A. M. Storch ...
Dem braven Kanonier Joh. Pollet. Gewidmet vom
Dichter und Compositeur.
    [Wien]Gedruckt bei J.B.Wallishausser.[1848]

    [2]p. 21.5x13.5cm.
    Helfert (Wiener Parnass) 477.
    Caption title; imprint on p.[2].
    Without the music.

*GB8
V6755R
3.19.48

Minzloff, Leopold.
    An den Jubel-Abenden Wiens den 15ten, 16ten,
17ten März 1848. Der St. Stephansthurm (in
seiner Kuppel illuminirt). Von Leopold Minzloff,
aus Königsberg in Preussen.
    [Wien]Gedruckt bei Carl Gerold.[1848]

    [2]p. 25.5x19.5cm.
    Helfert (Wiener Parnass) 457.
    Caption title; imprint on p.[2].

*GB8
V6755R
3.19.48

Sloboda se z vatre stvori u Beču 13. 14. 15.
ožujka 1848.
    [Wien?]Tiskom Jermenah.[1848]
    folder(2ℓ.) 26.5x17cm.
    Helfert (Wiener Parnass) 473.
    Signed: Jedan Petrinjac.
    The 1st leaf contains the text in the Latin
alphabet, the 2d in the Cyrillic.

*GB8
V6755R
3.19.48

Der neue Frühling.
    [Wien,1848]

    broadside. 28x21cm.
    Helfert (Wiener Parnass) 435.
    Dated & signed: Wien, den 19. März 1848. E. B.

*GB8
V6755R
3.19.48

Urschler, Joseph.
    Die Wiener-Insurrekzion im Jahre 1848 an den
glorreichen Tagen des 13., 14. und 15. März.
Wien's grossherzigen Bewohnern zur Erinnerung
vom Nazionalgardisten Jos. Urschler.
    [Wien]Gedruckt bei Ant.Benko.[1848]

    [2]p. 25.5x21cm.
    Helfert (Wiener Parnass) 444.
    Caption title; imprint on p.[2].

*GB8
V6755R
3.19.48

[Petri, Hugo Jacques]
    Des Teufels Kleeblatt.
    [Wien,1848]

    folder([3]p.) 21.5x13cm.
    Helfert (Wiener Parnass) 489.
    Caption title; signed on p.[3]: Hugo Jacques
Petri.
    On the resignation & flight of Metternich.

*GB8
V6755R
3.19.48

Der verantwortliche Ministerrath.
    [Wien,1848]

    folder([4]p.) 21.5x13.5cm.
    Printer's imprint on p.[4]: Druck und
Eigenthum von Hirschfeld in Wien.
    Dated at end: Wien, am 19. März 1848.

*GB8
V6755R
3.19.48

[Redlich, J   ]
    Das Militär. Ein Wort der Versöhnung.
    [Wien]Gedruckt bei M.Lell,vormals Anna St.von
Hirschfeld.[1848]

    [2]p. 19x12.5cm.
    Helfert (Wiener Parnass) 442.
    Caption title; imprint on p.[2].
    Dated & signed at end: Wien den 19. März 1848.
J. Redlich.

*pGB8
V6755R
3.19.48

Vienna. Magistrat.
    Kundmachung. Die zur Unterbringung von
Verhafteten disponiblen Lokalitäten wurden bei
der gegenwärtigen Bewegung von den vorzüglich
aus den Ortschaften vor den Linien eingebrachten
Individuen dermassen überfüllt ...
    [Wien,1848]

    broadside. 36.5x22cm.
    Signed & dated: Vom Magistrate und prov.
Bürger=Ausschusse der Stadt Wien, am 19. März
1848.

*GB8
V6755R
3.19.48

Von den Jugendgenossen Carl Heinrich
Spitzer's, des Erstgefallenen. An die ruhm= und
sieggekrönten studierenden Jünglinge in Wien.
[Wien,1848]

[2]p. 20x12.5cm.
Caption title; dated & signed on p.[2]:
Bisenz in Mähren, Sonntag den 19. März 1848.
Die Bisenzer Jugend.

---

*pGB8
V6755R
3.20.48

Austria, Lower. Regierungs-Präsident.
Kundmachung. Die Staats=Verwaltung hat
beschlossen, zu Gunsten der ärmeren Classe der
Bevölkerung bei der Einhebung der Verzehrungssteuer in Wien folgende wesentliche Er-
leichterungen eintreten zu lassen ...
[Wien,1848]

broadside. 45x28cm.
Dated & signed: Wien am 20. März 1848. Johann
Talatzko Freiherr v. Gesticticz, k. k. Nieder=
Oester. Regierungs=Präsident.

---

*GB8
V6755R
3.19.48

Weinberger, Eduard.
Des Kaisers Monument.
[Wien]Druck von U.Klopf sen.und Alex.Eurich,
Wollzeile 782.[1848]

broadside. 20x13cm.
Helfert (Wiener Parnass) 464.

---

*GB8
V6755R
3.20.48

Castelli, Ignaz Franz, 1781-1862.
Was ih jetzt sein möcht. Populäres Lied in
Wiener Mundart, von J. F. Castelli.
[Wien,1848]

broadside. 21.5x13cm.
Helfert (Wiener Parnass) 493.

---

*GB8
V6755R
3.20.48

Alt, Leopold.
An die deutschen Brüder. Von Leopold Alt.
[Wien]Gedruckt bei Joh.N.Fridrich,Josephstadt
Nr.58.[1848]

[2]p. 24x19cm.
Helfert (Wiener Parnass) 501.
Caption title; imprint on p.[2].
Dated at end: Geschrieben am 20. März 1848.

---

*GB8
V6755R
3.20.48

Castelli, Ignaz Franz, 1781-1862.
Was ih jetzt sein möcht? Populäres Lied in
Wiener Mundart von J. F. Castelli.
[Wien,1848]

[2]p. 22x13cm.
Helfert (Wiener Parnass) 493.
Caption title.

---

*pGB8
V6755R
3.20.48

Austria. Sovereigns, etc., 1835-1848
(Ferdinand I)
Wir Ferdinand der Erste, von Gottes Gnaden
Kaiser von Oesterreich ... Um Unseren getreuen
Unterthanen einen weiteren Beweis Unseres
Vertrauens zu geben, und ihnen zu zeigen, wie
sehr Wir geneigt sind, selbst gegen Verirrte
Gnade zu üben ...
[Wien,1848]

folder([2]p.) 44.5x28.5cm.
Reschauer-Smets II.23.   (See next card)

---

*GB8
V6755R
3.20.48

[Denarowski, Karol]
Młodzież wszechnicy Wiedeńskiéj.
[Wien? 1848]

[2]p. 21x13cm.
Helfert (Wiener Parnass) 354.
Caption title; dated & signed on p.[2]:
Napisał na czatach nocnych z 15. na 16. Lutego.
przy z burzonej fabryce w Kettenhofie koło
Wiednia Karol Denarowski.
In contemporary ms. at head: 200 Stk 20 März
1848.

---

*pGB8
V6755R
3.20.48

Austria. Sovereigns, etc., 1835-1848
(Ferdinand I)   Wir Ferdinand der Erste ...
[1848]   (Card 2)

"Gegeben in Unserer kaiserlichen Haupt= und
Residenzstadt Wien, den zwanzigsten März, im
eintausend achthundert acht und vierzigsten ..."
Proclamation of amnesty.

---

*pGB8
V6755R
3.20.48

Denksteine zur Erinnerung. Umständliche
Erzählung der Ereignisse der drei Tage am 13.,
14. und 15. März 1848 in Wien, nebst allen
erlassenen Knndmachungen [!] und Verordnungen,
welche sofort gesammelt erscheinen.
[Wien,1848]
folder(4p.) 36.5x22.5cm.
Caption title.
Includes proclamations dated 14-18 March.
At end: (Fortesetzung folgt.)
No more pub-   lished?

*pGB8
V6755R
3.20.48

Die drei Tage in Wien, oder: Die Entfernung
des alten Uebels, den 13., 14. und 15. März
1848.
   [Wien]Gedruckt und zu haben bei Leopold Grund,
am Stephansplatze im neugebauten Zwettelhofe.
[1848]
   [2]p. 41x25cm.
   Caption title; imprint on p.[2].
   In this issue, the lst line of the title
measures 172mm. in length & its capitals are
13mm. high.

*GB8
V6755R
3.20.48

Kulka, Adolf, 1823-1898.
   Der befreite Gefangene. Bei Gelegenheit der von
Sr. Majestät erlassenen Amnestie für alle
politische Gefangene. Von A. E. Kulka.
   [Wien,1848]
   folder([4]p.) 23x15cm.
   Helfert (Wiener Parnass) 496.
   Printer's imprint on p.[2]: A. Dorfmeister's
Buchdruckerei.

*pGB8
V6755R
3.20.48

Die drei Tage in Wien, oder: Die Entfernung
des alten Uebels, den 13., 14. und 15. März
1848.
   [Wien]Gedruckt und zu haben bei Leopold Grund,
am Stephansplatze im neugebauten Zwettelhofe.
[1848]
   [2]p. 41x25.5cm.
   Caption title; imprint on p.[2].
   In this issue, the lst line of the title
measures 111mm. in length & its capitals are
8mm. high.

*GB8
V6755R
3.20.48

   Der Morgengruss eines Wieners an Oesterreichs
wieder gefundene Brüder, die Magyaren, Slaven
und Lombardo-Veneter.
   [Wien,1848]
   broadside. 22.5x15cm.
   Signed: C. S. Mitglied des jur. pol. Lese-
Vereines.

*GB8
V6755R
3.20.48

Fürchterliche Ereignisse. Revolution von
Berlin und Sturz des Ministeriums.
   [Wien]Gedruckt und zu haben bei Leopold Grund,
am Stephansplatze im neugebauten Zwettelhofe.
[1848]
   folder(4p.) 27x21.5cm.
   Caption title; imprint on p.4.
   Dated: Berlin am 20. März 1848.
   "Aus der Berliner Zeitungshalle und Vossischen
Zeitung."

*GB8
V6755R
3.20.48

   Offener und herzlicher Dank der getreuen
Oestreicher an ihren geliebten Kaiser.
   [Wien]Ausgegeben von Tendler et Comp.[1848]
   broadside. 28.5x22cm.

*GB8
V6755R
3.20.48

[Heller, Camill, 1823-1917]
   Bedeutung der Begebenheiten am 13. 14. und 15.
März 1848.
   [Wien,1848]
   folder([4]p.) 21.5x13cm.
   Caption title; signed at end: Camill Heller.

*GB8
V6755R
3.20.48

[Petri, Hugo Jacques]
   Ein Abschieds-Wort an einen Minister.
   [Wien]Druck und Eigenthum von Hirschfeld.
[1848]
   folder([4]p.) 22x14cm.
   Signed at end: Hugo Jacques Petri.
   On Metternich.

*GB8
V6755R
3.20.48

Kossuth, Lajos, 1802-1894.
   Freiheits-Rede des dermaligen ungarischen
Ministers Kossuth Layos, siegreichen Vorkämpfers
für Volksrechte. Deutsch vorgetragen von dem
Juristen Putz aus Tyrol, am 13. März 1848,
am Brunnen, im Hofe des Ständehauses. Zur
Erinnerung an die, durch diese Rede
hervorgerufene, beispiellos folgenreiche
Begeisterung. Aufgenommen und herausgegeben von
J. B. Mauss.
   [Wien,1848]
   folder(4p.)   25.5x20cm.
   Woodcut illus.   on t.-p.

*GB8
V6755R
3.20.48

Rick, Carl, 1815-1881.
   Neues Osterlied. Zu singen wie: "Der Heiland
ist erstanden."
   [Wien]Gedruckt bei Anton Benko.[1848]
   broadside. 22.5x14cm.
   Helfert (Wiener Parnass) 497.
   Without the music.

*GB8
V6755R
3.20.48

Saphir, Moritz Gottlieb, 1795-1858.
Ausrückungslied der Nationalgarde. Gedichtet
von M. G. Saphir, Musik von Heinrich Proch,
Nationalgardist.
[Wien]Druck von U.Klopf sen.& A.Eurich.[1848]

broadside. 26x19.5cm.
Helfert (Wiener Parnass) 500.
Without the music.

*pGB8
V6755R
3.20.48

Vienna. Nationalgarde.
Tagsbefehl für die Nationalgarde. Am 20.
März 1848.
[Wien,1848]

folder([3]p.) 45x28cm.
Signed: Hoyos, k. k. Feldmarschall=Lieutenant.
Note at end: Der gestrige Nationalgarde=
Befehl wurde nicht durch den Druck veröffentlicht.

*GB8
V6755R
3.20.48

Stern, Moriz.
Oesterreichs Heil. Von Moriz Stern.
[Wien]Gedruckt bei F.E.v.Schmid.[1848]

[2]p. 22.5x14cm.
Helfert (Wiener Parnass) 498.
Caption title; imprint on p.[2].
Dated at end: Wien, 20. den März 1848.

*pGB8
V6755R
3.20.48

Vienna. Universität. Rektor.
Kundmachung. Der Ober=Commandant der
Nationalgarde, Feldmarschall=Lieutenant, hat
mit Befehl vom 20. März 1848 die Universität in
Kenntniss gesetzt, dass er nach eingeholter
höherer Genehmigung befugt sei, allsogleich zur
Organisation einer permanenten akademischen
Legion als integrirender Theil der Nationalgarde
nach den hier unten folgenden Grundlinien zu
schreiten ...
[Wien,1848]   (See next card)

*pGB8
V6755R
3.20.48

Eine Versammlung in Wien wohnhafter
Engländer hat folgende Adresse beschlossen:
Oesterreichische Brüder! ...
[Wien]Gedruckt bei Carl Gerold.[1848]

broadside. 46.5x31cm.
Dated & signed: Wien, den 20. März 1848. John
Wheatley, commander Royal navy Präsident. J. H.
Hedley, Sekretär.

*pGB8
V6755R
3.20.48

Vienna. Universität. Rektor.   Kundmachung ...
[1848]   (Card 2)

broadside. 44.5x57.5cm.
Reschauer-Smets II.24.
Dated & signed: Wien den 20. März 1848.
Jemull m. p. d. Z. Rektor der Wiener=
Universität.

*pGB8
V6755R
3.20.48

Vienna. Magistrat.
Kundmachung. Zur Ergänzung und Verstärkung des
provis. Bürger=Ausschusses, aus dessen Mitte laut
hierortiger Kundmachung vom 17. d. M. mehrere
Mitglieder den Verhandlungen bei den n. ö.
Herren Ständen beigezogen werden ...
[Wien,1848]

broadside. 37x22.5cm.
Unterreiter I.109.
Signed & dated: Vom Magistrate und prov.
Bürger=Ausschusse der Stadt Wien am 20. März
1848.

*GB8
V6755R
3.21.48

[Arnstein, Ignaz, baron]
Ein Wiener an die künftige constitutionelle
Polizei.
[Wien]Druck von U.Klopf sen.und Alex.Eurich,
Wollzeile 782.[1848]

folder(4p.) 20x13cm.
Caption title; imprint on p.4.
Dated & signed at end: Wien den 21. März 1848.
Ignaz Baron Arnstein.

*GB8
V6755R
3.20.48

Vienna. Nationalgarde.
Soldaten des österreichischen Kaiserstaates!
Lasst die grossen folgereichen Begebenheiten der
letzten Tage keine Kluft bilden zwischen Euch
und dem Volke ...
[Wien]Gedruckt bei Ant.Benko.[1848]

folder([2]p.) pl. 27.5x19cm.
Caption title; imprint on p.[2]; signed at
end: Von einer grossen Anzahl Mitglieder der
Nationalgarde.
The plate is a lithograph with caption: Bürger
und Soldat   biethen sich die Hand
zur Versöhnung.

*pGB8
V6755R
3.21.48

Austria. Vereinte Kameral-Gefällen-Verwaltung.
Uebersicht der Mengen verzehrungs-
steuerpflichtiger Gegenstände, welche nach den
Bestimmungen des ersten Absatzes der Kundmachung
vom 20. März 1848 steuerfrei über die Linien
Wiens eingeführt werden können.
[Wien,1848]

[2]p. 45x28cm.
Signed & dated: Von der k. k. vereinten
Cameral-Gefällen-Verwaltung für Oesterreich ob
und unter der Enns. Wien am 21. März 1848.

*pGB8
V6755R
3.21.48

Austria, Lower. Appellations- und
  Criminalobergericht.
  Kundmachung. Von dem k. k. Nieder=Oester.
  Appellations= und Criminal=Obergerichte wird zur
  Beseitigung umlaufender Gerüchte bekannt
  gemacht ...
  [Wien,1848]

  broadside. 45x57cm.
  Dated & signed: Wien am 21. März 1848.
  Hermann Freiherr v. Hess, Präsident.

*GB8
V6755R
3.21.48

Hammer-Purgstall, Joseph, freiherr von,
  1774-1856, tr.
  Weiss auf Schwarz. Zum Newrus, d. i. zur
  Frühlingsfeier der freien Presse, von Hammer=
  Purgstall.
  [Wien]In der Tag= und Nachtgleiche des Jahres
  1848,erstes censurfreies Blatt mit orientalischer
  Schrift aus der k.k.Hof=Buchdruckerei des L.
  Sommer(vormals Strauss).

  broadside. 29.5x23cm.
  Two Arabian distichs, translated by Hammer-
  Purgstall.

*GB8
V6755R
3.21.48

Die Bekleidung der Nationalgarde, einfach, gut
  und malerisch, wie sie sein soll. Eine freie
  Musterzeichnung. Mit einer Lithographie von G.
  Reiffenstein.
  Wien,den 21.März 1848.

  folder(2l.) plate. 20.5x13 & 30.5x23.5cm.
  Printer's imprint on p.[3]: K. k. Hof=Buch-
  druckerei des L. Sommer (vormals Strauss).

*GB8
V6755R
3.21.48

[Kirchberger, Josef]
  Pressfreiheits=Regulirung.
  [Wien,1848]

  folder([4]p.) 22.5x14.5cm.
  Printer's imprint on p.[4]: Druck und Eigenthum
  von Hirschfeld in Wien.
  Dated & signed at end: Wien am 21. März 1848.
  Jos. Kirchberger.
  Title within ornamental wreath border.

*GB8
V6755R
3.21.48

[Buchheim, Carl Adolf, 1828-1900]
  Judenpech.
  [Wien]Druck von U.Klopf sen.und Alex.Eurich,
  Wollzeile 782.[1848]

  [2]p. 20x13cm.
  Caption title; imprint on p.[2]; signed &
  dated: Adolph Buchheim. Wien den 21. März 1848.
  First edition, including the account of the
  student A. Brix's intercession for the Jews in
  the paragraph beginning "Die Juden sind
  misstrauisch, sind kleinmüthig"; according to
                             (See next card)

*GB8
V6755R
3.21.48

Knöpfelmacher, Bernhard.
  Guter Rath. Von Bernhard Knöpfelmacher.
  Mediziner.
  [Wien]Druck von U.Kopf[!] sen.und A.Eurich.
  [1848]

  [2]p. 19.5x12.5cm.
  Helfert (Wiener Parnass) 506.
  Caption title; imprint on p.[2].
  Dated at end: Wien den 21. März 1848.

*GB8
V6755R
3.21.48

[Buchheim, Carl Adolf, 1828-1900]   Judenpech
  ... [1848]   (Card 2)
  Helfert ("Die confessionelle Frage in
  Oesterreich 1848", in Oesterreichisches
  Jahrbuch, 1882, p.138), this passage was omitted
  in later editions.

*pGB8
V6755R
3.21.48

Opava, Czechoslovak republic. Bürgerschaft.
  Adresse der Troppauer Bürgerschaft an die
  Studirenden der Wiener Universität.
  [Wien,1848]

  broadside. 40x25.5cm.
  Dated: Troppau am 21. März 1848.

*GB8
V6755R
3.21.48

Gugler, Josef, fl.1848.
  An die hochherzigen Wienerinnen, welche
  während der drei Märztage sich durch ihr edles
  Benehmen gegen die studirende Jugend besonders
  auszeichneten.
  [Wien]Druck von U.Klopf sen.und A.Eurich,
  Wollzeile Nr.782.[1848]

  broadside. 20x13cm.
  Helfert (Wiener Parnass) 507.
  Dated: Wien, am 1. Frühlingstage 1848.

*GB8
V6755R
3.21.48

Rauscher, H
  Alles was wahr und recht ist! Für und gegen
  die Juden. Von H. Rauscher, Jurist.
  [Wien]Gedruckt bei M.Lell,Leopoldstadt,
  Weintraubengasse Nr.505.[1848]

  folder([4]p.) 24.5x14.5cm.
  Caption title; imprint on p.[4].
  Dated in contemporary ms.: 21. März 848.

*pGB8
V6755R
3.21.48

... Wien, 20. März, 6 Uhr Abends. So eben
erscheint folgende Kuudmachung [!]. Die
Staatsverwaltung hat beschlossen ...
[Wien,1848]

[2]p. 34x26cm.
Caption title; at head: Ausserordentliche
Beilage zum "Oesterreichischen Beobachter" vom
21. März Nr. 81.
A news sheet, incorporating Talatzko's
proclamation of 20 March & that of the
Niederösterreichischer Landständischer
Ausschuss of 18   March.

---

*GB8
V6755R
3.22.48

[Irmscher, Carl Gottlieb]
Epistel an meine theuern Glaubensgenossen
Augsb. und Helvet. Confession, am Morgen des
freien und befreiten Vaterlandes ...
[Wien,1848]

folder(4p.) 26.5x21cm.
Helfert (Wiener Parnass) 519.
Printer's imprint on p.[2]: Druck von U.
Klopf sen. und A. Eurich, Wollzeile 782.
Dated & signed at end: Wien, am 22. März 4848
[i.e.1848]. Carl Gottlieb Irmscher, ehemaliger
Schuhmachergesell   aus Chemnitz in Sachsen
(dermalen   Bedienter).

---

*pGB8
V6755R
3.22.48

Austria. Armee.
Kundmachung. Die Aufgeregtheit im öffentlichen
Leben und Treiben hat sich bei uns gelegt, und
somit haben auch die ausserordentlichen
militärischen Massregeln ihr Ende gefunden ...
[Wien,1848]

broadside. 45x57cm.
Reschauer-Smets II.25.
Dated & signed: Wien am 22. März 1848. Alfred
Fürst zu Windischgrätz, k. k. Feldmarschall=
Lieutenant.

---

*GB8
V6755R
3.22.48

Kaiser, Friedrich, 1814-1874.
Prolog bei dem Feier-Concerte dessen
Erträgniss für die Errichtung eines Monumentes
für die am 13. März 1848 Gefallenen
bestimmt war. Gedichtet und gesprochen von
Friedrich Kaiser.
Wien 1848.Bei Tendler & Comp.

folder([4]p.) 22x14.5cm.
Helfert (Wiener Parnass) 521.
Printer's imprint on p.[4]: Gedruckt bei Ferd.
Ullrich.

---

*GB8
V6755R
3.22.48

Czerny, Joseph Paul.
Neues Volkslied. (Geschrieben nach erhaltener
Einreihungs=Karte in die National=Garde; am 22.
März 1848.) Von Joseph Paul Czerny.
[Wien,1848]

broadside. 20x13cm.
Helfert (Wiener Parnass) 523.

---

*GB8
V6755R
3.22.48

Kretschmar, Hermann.
Echo von Lande!
[Wien]Zu haben bei U.Klopf sen.und Alex.
Eurich,Stadt,Wollzeile Nr.782,im ersten Stock.
[1848]

broadside. 21x13cm.
Helfert (Wiener Parnass) 526.
Dated: Dürnkrut am 22. März 1848.

---

*pGB8
V6755R
3.22.48

Endlicher, Stephan, 1804-1849.
An das akademische Mediziner=Corps.
[Wien,1848]

broadside. 45x57cm.
Dated & signed: Wien, den 22. März 1848.
Professor Endlicher m. p.

---

*GB8
V6755R
3.22.48

März, Julius.
Warum? Eine Frage an das neunzehnte Jahr-
hundert. Von Julius März.
[Wien]Gedruckt bei M.Lell,Leopoldstadt,
Weintraubengasse Nr.505.[1848]

folder(2ℓ.) 24x15cm.
Helfert (Wiener Parnass) 1170.
Dated in contemporary ms.: 22. März 848.

---

*pGB8
V6755R
3.22.48

Rye von Glunek, Anton, freiherr, 1807-1894.
An sämmtliche Theilnehmer des bisherigen
akademischen Juristen-Corps.
[Wien,1848]

broadside. 45x57cm.
Dated & signed: Wien den 22. März 1848.
Professor Rye m. p., als abtretender
provisorischer Ober=Commandant des bisherigen
akademischen Juristen=Corps.

---

*pGB8
V6755R
3.22.48

[Naske, Adolf Carl, 1814-1864]
Pia desideria der subalternen Staatsbeamten.
Veröffentlicht von Einem aus ihrer Mitte.
[Wien]Zu haben bei dem Buchhändler Jakob Bader,
Stroblgasse.Gedruckt bei Anton Benko.[1848]

folder([4]p.) 38x25cm.
Caption title; imprint on p.[4].
Dated & signed at end: Wien, am 22. März 1848.
Adolf Carl Naske.

[Neumann, Josef, 1815-1878]
*GB8 An meine Mitbürger, betreffend den verkündeten
V6755R provisorischen Ausschuss.
3.22.48 [Wien,1848]

folder(4p.) 22.5x15cm.
Dated & signed at end: Wien am 22. März 1848.
Prf. Dr. Jos. Neumann.
Caption title.

[Bosio von Klarenbrunn, Casimir]
*pGB8 Wie ist der Wiener Magistrat neu einzurichten?
V6755R [Wien,1848]
3.23.48

[2]p. 35.5x22.5cm.
Caption title; dated & signed at end: Wien den
23. März 1848. Dr. Casimir Bosio v. Klarenbrunn.

Prechtler, Otto, 1813-1881.
*GB8 Drei Tage! Gedicht von Otto Prechtler. Nach
V6755R einer Melodie von Fr. Rücken.
3.22.48 [Wien,1848]

broadside. 21x13cm.
Helfert (Wiener Parnass) 520.
Helfert records this poem under 22 March, but
this copy has contemporary ms. date: 19. März
848.
Without the music.

König, Moriz.
*GB8 Oesterreichs Ziel und Waffe. Den Männern
V6755R des 13. März 1848 gewidmet von Moriz König.
3.23.48 [Wien]Mechitaristen=Buchdruckerei.[1848]

folder([3]p.) 21.5x13.5cm.
Helfert (Wiener Parnass) 534.
Caption title; imprint on p.[3].
'Aus F. Glöggl's "Allgem. musikalischen
Anzeiger" Nr. 12.'

Sauter, Ferdinand, 1804-1854.
*GB8 Geheime Polizei.
V6755R [Wien]Gedruckt bei Franz Edlen von Schmid,--zu
3.22.48 haben bei J.Wenedikt.[1848]

broadside. 22.5x14.5cm.
Helfert (Wiener Parnass) 524.
Includes at foot a prose parody of the Lord's
prayer beginning: Vater Metternich, der Du bist
in Wien ...

[Markbreiter, Moritz]
*GB8 Kaiser Ferdinand's Gnadenwort, oder: Befreiung
V6755R der Italiener und Pohlen.
3.23.48 Wien,gedruckt und zu haben bei Leopold Grund,
am Stephansplatze im Zwettelhofe.[1848]

[2]p. 26x21cm.
Helfert (Wiener Parnass) 533.
Caption title; imprint on p.[2].
Signed at end: Moriz Markbreiter.

Scheibe, Theodor, 1820-1881.
*pGB8 Der heutige Siegescourier. Die Belagerung von
V6755R Mailand und die neue Republik.
3.22.48 [Wien]Gedruckt bei M.Lell.[1848]

broadside. 47x30.5cm.

Neumann, J G
*pGB8 Aufruf an die Schriftsteller und gebildeten
V6755R Bewohner Wiens.
3.23.48 [Wien]Gedruckt bei Carl Gerold.[1848]

broadside. 44.5x29cm.
Dated & signed: Wien, am 23. März 1848. J. G.
Neumann, National=Garde.
Calling for the unity of the Nationalgarde
rather than the establishment of individual
corps.

Vienna. Nationalgarde.
*pGB8 ... Tagsbefehl für die Nationalgarde. Am 22.
V6755R März 1848.
3.22.48 [Wien,1848]

[2]p. 45x28cm.
Numbered at head: 5.
Signed: Hoyos, k. k. Feldmarschall=Lieutenant
und Ober=Commandant der Bürger= und Nationalgarde.
Note at end: Der gestrige Tagsbefehl wurde
nicht durch den Druck veröffentlicht.

Vienna. Nationalgarde.
*pGB8 ... Tagsbefehl für die Nationalgarde. Am 23.
V6755R März 1848.
3.23.48 [Wien,1848]

broadside. 45x28.5cm.
Numbered at head: 6.
Signed: Hoyos, k. k. F. M. L.

*pGB8
V6755R
3.24.48

Austria. Ministerium des Innern.
Seine Majestät der Kaiser haben über die
weiter folgenden Bitten der Bürger und Einwohner
der Hauptstadt Prag nachstehendes Allerhöchstes
Cabinetschreiben an den Minister des Inneren zu
erlassen geruhet.
[Wien,1848]

6p. 45x29cm.
Dated & signed at end: Wien am 24. März 1848.
Der Minister des Inneren: Freih. v. Pillersdorff
m. p.

(See next card)

---

*pGB8
V6755R
3.24.48

Hessler, Ferdinand, 1803-1865.
An das Corps des polytechnischen Institutes.
[Wien,1848]

broadside. 44.5x57cm.
Dated & signed: Wien, den 24. März 1848.
Professor Hessler m. p. als abtretender
provisorischer Ober=Commandant des Polytechniker=
Corps.

---

*pGB8
V6755R
3.24.48

Austria. Ministerium des Innern.   Seine
Majestät ... [1848]   (Card 2)

Includes the text of the main points of the
Prague petition.
Czech & German in parallel columns.

---

*pGB8
V6755R
3.24.48

Vienna. Nationalgarde.
... Tagsbefehl für die Nationalgarde. Am 24.
März 1848.
[Wien,1848]

broadside. 44.5x28cm.
Numbered at head: 7.
Signed: Hoyos, k. k. F. M. L.

---

*GB8
V6755R
3.24.48

Bedeutung und Geist der National Garde. (Aus
der Wiener=Zeitung vom 24. März 1848.)
[Wien,1848]

folder([4]p.) 22.5x14cm.
Printer's imprint on p.[4]: Gedruckt bei den
Edlen von Ghelen'schen Erben.

---

*GB8
V6755R
3.25.48

Antwort der deutschen Nation an den König von
Preussen.
[Wien,1848]

folder([4]p.) 20.5x13.5cm.
Reprinted from Wiener Zeitung, No.85, March 25,
1848.

---

*GB8
V6755R
3.24.48

[Brühl, Carl Bernhard, 1820-1899]
Einige Worte zur Verständigung über Lehr=
und Lernfreiheit an die Studirenden und Doktoren
der verschiedenen Fakultäten zunächst, sodann
an jeden für den zeitgemässen Fortschritt
allgemeiner Bildung begeisterten Bürger.
[Wien]Gedruckt bei Karl Ueberreuter.[1848]

folder([4]p.) 26.5x22.5cm.
Caption title; imprint on p.[4].
Dated & signed at end: Wien am 24. März 1848.
Dr. Brühl, Mitglied der Wiener med. Fakultät ...

---

*GB8
V6755R
3.25.48

[Arthur, pseud.]
Ausserordentliche merkwürdige Begebenheit. Der
Pulverthurm in Venedig oder sechzehn Heldensöhne
der Steyermark. Bericht nach einer wahren
Begebenheit der letzten Tage unserer Zeit.
[Wien]Gedruckt bei Jos.Ludwig,Josefstadt,
Florianigasse Nr.52.[1848]

[2]p. 26x21cm.
Caption title; imprint on p.[2]; signed:
Arthur.

---

*GB8
V6755R
3.24.48

[Häufler, Joseph von]
Oesterreichs Parole.
Fr.Beck's Universitäts=Buchhandlung in Wien.
[1848]

[2]p. 28x19cm.
Helfert (Wiener Parnass) 833.
Caption title; imprint on p.[2].
In contemporary ms. at head: 1000 [Stücke?]
24 März 1848.

---

*GB8
V6755R
3.25.48

[Becher, Alfred Julius, 1803-1848]
Der deutsche Kaiser.
[Wien]Gedruckt bei Ferdinand Ullrich.[1848]

[2]p. 26x20cm.
Caption title; imprint on p.[2].
Dated & signed at end: Wien, den 25. März 1848.
Dr. A. J. Becher.

*pGB8
V6755R
3.25.48

Vienna. Nationalgarde.
... Tagsbefehl für die Nationalgarde. Am 25.
März 1848.
[Wien,1848]

broadside. 45x28cm.
Numbered at head: 8.
Signed: Hoyos, k. k. Feldmarschall=Lieutenant
und Ober=Commandant der Bürger= und Nationalgarde.

*pGB8
V6755R
3.26.48

Vienna. Nationalgarde.
... Kundmachung vom 26. März.
[Wien,1848]

[2]p. 45x29cm.
Numbered at head: 9.
Signed: Hoyos, k. k. Feldmarschall=Lieutenant
und Ober=Commandant der Bürger= und National-
garde.
On questions of discipline.

*pGB8
V6755R
3.26.48

Austria. Ministerium des Innern.
Ueber ein Einschreiten der Wiener
privilegirten Seidenzeug=Fabrikanten wird
von Seite des Ministeriums erklärt ...
[Wien,1848]

broadside. 45x57cm.
Dated & signed: Wien den 26. März 1848. Der
Minister des Inneren: Freiherr v. Pillersdorff.

*pGB8
V6755R
3.26.48

Vienna. Nationalgarde.
... Tagsbefehl für die Nationalgarde. Am 26.
März 1848.
[Wien,1848]

broadside. 45x28cm.
Numbered at head: 10.
Signed: Hoyos, Feldmarschall=Lieutenant und
Ober=Commandant der Bürger= und Nationalgarde.

*GB8
V6755R
3.26.48

[Deutsch, Simon, b.ca.1822]
Offener Brief an die Juden.
[Wien,1848]

folder(4p.) 20x13cm.
Caption title; dated & signed at end: Wien,
den 26. März 1848. Simon Deutsch.
Another issue has imprint on p.4.

*pGB8
V6755R
3.27.48

Austria. Ministerium des Innern.
An Seine des Herrn Gouverneurs vom Küstenlande,
Altgrafen von Salm, Excellenz.
[Wien,1848]

broadside. 38.5x23cm.
Dated & signed: Wien am 27. März 1848. Der
Minister des Inneren: Freiherr von Pillersdorff,
m. p.

*GB8
V6755R
3.26.48

[Deutsch, Simon, b.ca.1822]
Offener Brief an die Juden.
[Wien]Druck von U.Klopf sen.und A.Eurich,
Wollzeile Nr.782.[1848]

folder(4p.) 22x15.5cm.
Caption title; imprint on p.4.
Dated & signed at end: Wien, den 26. März 1848.
Simon Deutsch.
Another issue is without imprint on p.4.

*GB8
V6755R
3.27.48

[Buschman, Gotthard, freiherr von, 1810-1888]
Die Standarte der Pressfreiheit, von Eginhard
[pseud.].
[Wien,1848]

[2]p. 23.5x15cm.
Helfert (Wiener Parnass) 554.
Caption title; dated at end: Wien, im März
1848.

*GB8
V6755R
3.26.48

Der Schutzengel von Oesterreich: Kaiser
Ferdinand der Gütige!
Gedruckt bei U.Klopf sen.und A.Eurich in Wien.
[1848]

folder([4]p.) 20x13cm.
Dated & signed at end: Wien, den 26. März 1848.
A. B., Student.

*GB8
V6755R
3.27.48

Castelli, Ignaz Franz, 1781-1862.
Offener Brief an die Arbeiter in Wien. Von J.
F. Castelli.
[Wien]Verlag und Eigenthum von Tendler et Comp.
Gedruckt bei F.Ullrich.[1848]

[2]p. 26x20cm.
Caption title; imprint on p.[2].
Dated: Wien den 27. März 1848.

*pGB8
V6755R
3.27.48

Salzburg, Austria. Universität. Studentencorps.
An die Studenten Wiens.
[Wien,1848]

broadside. 40.5x25.5cm.
Dated & signed: Salzburg, den 27. März 1848.
Im Namen und Auftrage des Studentencorps: Die
Senioren.

---

*GB8
V6755R
3.28.48

[Schmitz, Severin von]
Die Vertrauten.
[Wien,1848]

folder([3]p.) 21.5x13cm.
Caption title; dated & signed on p.[3]:
Wien am 28. März. Severin v. Schmitz.

---

*pGB8
V6755R
3.28.48

Austria. Sovereigns, etc., 1835-1848
(Ferdinand I)
Wir Ferdinand der Erste, von Gottes Gnaden
Kaiser von Oesterreich ... Mit Unserer
Entschliessung vom 15. December 1846 haben Wir
die geeignete Bestimmung getroffen, um
freiwillige Uebereinkommen zur Ablösung der
Roboten nach Thunlichkeit zu erleichtern ...
[Wien,1848]
[2]p. 35x30cm.
"Gegeben in Unserer kaiserlichen Haupt= und
(See next card)

---

*pGB8
V6755R
3.29.48

Kopřiva, J   N
Auf! nach Italien!!! Das Abendblatt der
Wiener Zeitung vom 28. d. M. bringt folgenden
Aufruf zur Vertheidigung des lomb. venet.
Königreiches von C. E. Schindler. Wien, am
27. März.
[Wien]Mechitharisten=Buchdruckerei.[1848]

broadside. 46.5x29.5cm.
Signed: J. N. Kopřiva, National=Gardist,
Mariahilf Nr.135.
Helfert (Geschichte) I.404.

---

*pGB8
V6755R
3.28.48

Austria. Sovereigns, etc., 1835-1848
(Ferdinand I)   Wir Ferdinand der Erste ...
[1848]   (Card 2)
Residenzstadt Wien, den acht und zwanzigsten
März, im eintausend achthundert acht und
vierzigsten ..."
Caption title.
Helfert (Geschichte) I.406.

---

*pGB8
V6755R
3.29.48

Vienna. Magistrat.
Kundmachung. Nach der bestehenden Marktordnung
ist den Markt=Viktualienhändlern, das ist
solchen Händlern, welche die Viktualien auf den
Märkten zu dem Ende ankaufen ...
[Wien,1848]

broadside. 37.5x22.5cm.
Signed & dated: Von dem Magistrate und dem
prov. Bürger=Ausschusse der Stadt Wien, am 29.
März 1848.

---

*GB8
V6755R
3.28.48

[Francesconi, Carlo]
Die Revolution in Venedig, und Mailand's
Bombardement. Geschildert von einem Augenzeugen.
Gedruckt bei Hirschfeld in Wien.[1848]

folder([4]p.) 26.5x22cm.
Caption title; imprint on p.[4]; signed at end:
Carlo Francesconi.

---

*pGB8
V6755R
3.30.48

Bernard, Franz Alois.
Zeitgemässe Aeusserungen über den gewesenen
Bürgermeister Herrn J. Czapka Ritter v.
Winstetten. Von Franz Alois Bernard ...
[Wien,1848]

[2]p. 33.5x26cm.
Caption title.

---

*GB8
V6755R
3.28.48

[Frieser, J   ]
Noch ein Aufruf an Oesterreichs Völker.
[Wien,1848]

[2]p. 21x13cm.
Caption title; signed at end: J. Frieser.
Calling for financial support for the campaign
in Italy.

---

*GB8
V6755R
3.30.48

Hesser, Anton.
Sänger voran!
[Wien]Gedruckt bei Joh.N.Fridrich.[1848]

broadside. 19.5x12cm.
Not in Helfert (Wiener Parnass).
Dated in contemporary ms.: 30. März 848.

*GB8
V6755R
3.30.48

[Könyvi, A   ]
    Protestanten, aufgeschaut!
[Wien]Kommission bei Leo & Schmidt.--Gedruckt
bei Ferdinand Ullrich.[1848]

    [2]p. 26x21cm.
    Caption title; imprint on p.[2].
    Dated & signed at end: Wien 30. März 1848.
    A. Könyvi.

(

*pGB8
V6755R
3.30.48

Sommaruga, Franz, freiherr von, 1780-1860.
    Rede des Ministers des öffentlichen
Unterrichtes Dr. Franz Freiherrn von Sommaruga,
gehalten in der Aula der Wiener Universität.
am 30. März 1848.
[Wien,1848]

    folder([3]p.) 44.5x28.5cm.
    Caption title.

(

*GB8
V6755R
3.30.48

    Offene und ehrliche Bitte der getreuen
Oestreicher an ihren geliebten Kaiser.
    [Wien,1848]
    [2]p. 26x21cm.
    Caption title.
    Another issue has imprint on p.[2]:
Geschrieben am 30. März 1848.--Ausgegeben durch
Tendler et Comp.

(

*pGB8
V6755R
3.30.48

Vienna. Akademie der bildenden künste.
    In Uebereinstimmung mit der, unter Genehmigung
des hohen Ministeriums des Innern unterm 26.
dieses Monats erflossenen Bekanntmachung, die
Erörterung der Wünsche der Studierenden an der
Wiener Universität betreffend, nimmt das
Präsidium und der Rath der kaiserl. Akademie
der vereinigten bildenden künste keinen Anstand
...
    [Wien,1848]

    broadside. 45x57cm.
((See next card)

*GB8
V6755R
3.30.48

    Offene und ehrliche Bitte der getreuen
Oestreicher an ihren geliebten Kaiser.
    [Wien]Geschrieben am 30.März 1848.--
Ausgegeben durch Tendler et Comp.

    [2]p. 26.5x20.5cm.
    Caption title; imprint on p.[2].

(

*pGB8
V6755R
3.30.48

Vienna. Akademie der bildenden künste.   In
    Uebereinstimmung mit der ... [1848]
                    (Card 2)
    Dated & signed: Wien den 30. März 1848. Von
dem Präsidium und dem Rathe der kaiserl.
Akademie der vereinigten bildenden Künste.
Ludwig von Remy, als Präses=Stellvertreter.

(

*GB8
V6755R
3.30.48

Rigler, Andreas.
    Ein Recept für ein krankes Vaterland. Von
Andreas Rigler ...
    Wien,1848.Gedruckt bei Karl Ueberreuter.

    folder([4]p.) 30x23.5cm.
    Dated in contemporary ms.: 30. März 848.

(

*pGB8
V6755R
3.30.48

Vienna. Magistrat.
    ... Von dem Magistrate der k. k. Haupt= und
Residenzstadt Wien. Der Magistrat hat die von
der Gesellenschaft der bürg. Schneider
überreichten 2 Vorstellungen um Einführung
einiger neuer Einrichtungen in Berathung gezogen
und findet hierüber Folgendes zu verfügen ...
    [Wien,1848]

    [2]p. 36.5x22cm.
    Caption title; at head: G.Z.17289.
    Dated & signed: Wien am 30. März 1848.
Bergmüller Vice-   (bürgermeister.

*GB8
V6755R
3.30.48

Schmidt, W   0
    Politische Meinung eines Bürger Wiens über
die lombardisch=venetianischen Republikaner in
den oesterreichischen Agregat=Staaten. Am 30.
März 1848.
    [Wien]Gedruckt bei Franz Edlen von Schmid.
[1848]

    broadside. 29x23cm.

(

*pGB8
V6755R
3.31.48

Austria. Ministerium des Innern.
    Kundmachung. Auf die zur Kenntniss des
Ministeriums des Inneren gelangte Anzeige von
mehrfachen, zwischen den Arbeitern und Innungs=
Vorstehern bestehenden Misshelligkeiten und den
auf Abstellung von Missbräuchen gerichteten
Wünschen der Arbeiter ist die Verfügung bereits
getroffen worden ...
    [Wien,1848]

    broadside. 45x57cm.
    Dated & signed: Wien den 31. März 1848. Der
Minister des   (Inneren.

*pGB8
V6755R
3.31.48

Austria. Ministerium des Innern.
Verordnung. Im Nachhange zu der Allerhöchsten
Kundmachung vom 14. März und zum Patente vom 15.
März 1848 wegen Aufhebung der Censur und
alsbaldiger Veröffentlichung eines Gesetzes
gegen den Missbrauch der Presse haben Seine k. k.
Majestät ... nachstehende provisorische
Vorschrift zu genehmigen geruhet ...
[Wien,1848]

8p. 44.5x29cm.

(See next card)

---

*GB8
V6755R
3.31.48

Gewappnetes Sonett.
[Wien]Bei Kaulfuss W^{we},Prandel & Comp.[1848]

broadside. 22.5x15cm.
Helfert (Wiener Parnass) 579.
Signed: S. v. M.

---

*pGB8
V6755R
3.31.48

Austria. Ministerium des Innern.   Verordnung
... [1848]   (Card 2)

Helfert (Geschichte) 407.
Dated & signed: Wien den 31. März 1848. Der
Minister des Inneren: Franz Freiherr von
Pillersdorff.

---

*pGB8
V6755R
3.31.48

Malisz, Carl.
Begrüssungsrede bei der Ankunft der
Deputation aus den österreichisch-polnischen
Ländern durch Dr. Carl Malisz, Mitglied dieser
Deputation, am Wiener Kaiser Ferdinand's
Nordbahnhof am 31. März 1848 gehalten.
[Wien]Gedruckt bei Edl.v.Schmidbauer und
Holzwarth.[1848]

broadside. 38x26cm.

---

*GB8
V6755R
3.31.48

Castelli, Ignaz Franz, 1781-1862.
Gehst denn nit dani von Wagen? Ein
wienerisches Sprichwort mit Variationen. Von J.
F. Castelli.
[Wien]Gedruckt und zu haben bei Leop.Grund,am
Stephansplatze im Zwettelhofe.[1848]

[2]p. 27x21.5cm.
Helfert (Wiener Parnass) 577.
Caption title; imprint on p.[2].

---

*GB8
V6755R
3.31.48

[Naske, Adolph Carl, 1814-1864]
Das Todtenlied für die Polizei=Spione.
Zeitgemässe Reflexion über die alte und die neue
Polizei.
[Wien]Zu haben bei dem Buchhändler Jakob Bader,
Stadt,Strobelgasse.Gedruckt bei Anton Benko.
[1848]

folder(4p.) 24.5x19cm.
Caption title; imprint on p.4.
Dated & signed at end: Wien am 31. März 1848.
Adolph Carl Naske.

---

*GB8
V6755R
3.31.48

[Dorn, Gustav]
Der Naschmarkt=König und der Untergang seines
Reiches. Eine Darstellung der Ursachen und
Wirkungen des am 28., 29. und 30. März d. J.
auf dem Naschmarkte stattgehabten Aufstandes.
[Wien]Zu haben bei dem Buchhändler Jakob Bader,
Stadt,Strobelgasse.Gedruckt bei Anton Benko.
[1848]

folder(4p.) 25x19cm.
Caption title; imprint on p.4.
Dated & signed at end: Wien am 31. März 1848.
Gustav Dorn.

---

*GB8
V6755R
3.31.48

Schleichert, J   M
Die Bürgerschlacht an der Spree, oder: Ein
königliches Missverständniss. Historisches Drama
in 3 Aufzügen, v. J. M. Schleichert, Nationalgardist im Juristenkorps.
[Wien,1848]

folder([4]p.) 1 illus. 27x21.5cm.
Helfert (Wiener Parnass) 578.
Caption title; dated at end: Wien am 31. März
1848.
Another edition has title: Der Kartätschen= u.
Granaten=König und)   seine lieben Berliner.
Satire on the   )   King of Prussia.

---

*GB8
V6755R
3.31.48

Frankl, Johann Adam.
Zwei Worte.
[Wien,1848]

broadside. 21x13cm.
Helfert (Wiener Parnass) 580.

---

*GB8
V6755R
3.31.48

Schleichert, J   M
Der Kartätschen= u. Granaten=König und seine
lieben Berliner. Historisches Heruntersetzen in
3 Aufzügen, v. J. M. Schleichert. Nationalgardist
im Juristenkorps.
[Wien,1848]

folder([4]p.) 27x21.5cm.
Helfert (Wiener Parnass) 578.
Caption title; dated at end: Wien am 31. März
1848.
Another edition has title: Die Bürgerschlacht
an der Spree,   oder: Ein königliches
Missverständniss.
Satire on the King of Prussia.

*GB8
V6755R
3.32.48

[Achilles, J C]
Eine Meinung über Uniformirung [!] und
Bewaffnung der Nationalgarde.
[Wien,1848]

[2]p. 22.5x14.5cm.
Caption title; signed on p.[2]: J. C. Achilles,
Gardekorporal.

*pGB8
V6755R
3.32.48

An die Studenten! Böswillige, das Licht des
Fortschrittes scheuende Menschen werfen die
Saat des Misstrauens und des Hasses zwischen
Bürger, Nationalgarde und Studenten ...
[Wien]Druck von U.Klopf sen.und Alex.
Eurich.[1848]

broadside. 39.5x26cm.

*pGB8
V6755R
3.32.48

Albert, F
Jüdischer Betrug. Der Leser, der diese
Zeilen gekauft, in der süssen Hoffnung, eine
Schmähschrift mehr gegen die Juden in Händen zu
haben, hat sein Geld umsonst ausgeben ...
[Wien,1848].

broadside. 43x27cm.

*GB8
V6755R
3.32.48

Anekdoten aus den Befreiungstagen.
[Wien,1848]

2 pts. 21x13cm.
Pt. 1 is a broadside; pt. 2 has [2]p.
Each pt. has note: Beiträge werden mit Dank
angenommen in Ul. Klopf sen. und Alex. Eurich's
Buchdruckerei. Wollzeile 782.

*GB8
V6755R
3.32.48

Alt, Leopold.
An Oesterreichs Söhne und Töchter. Von Leopold
Alt, National-Gardisten.
Wien.Druck und Verlag von Joh.Nep.Fridrich,
Josephstadt Nr.58.[1848]

folder([4]p.) 26x20.5cm.

*GB8
V6755R
3.32.48

Anrede an die Studirenden der Wiener
Universität.
[Wien]Ged.bei Rud.Rohrer's sel.Witwe.[1848]

broadside. 30.5x24cm.

*pGB8
V6755R
3.32.48

An die brave Garnison der Haupt= und
Residenzstadt Wien und sämmtliche tapfere
Krieger des constitutionellen österreichischen
Kaiserstaates.
[Wien,1848]

broadside. 42.5x27cm.
Signed: Eine grosse Anzahl Mitglieder der
National=Garde.

*GB8
V6755R
3.32.48

Appel, Karl, fl.1848.
Loblied der Damen Wiens.
[Wien,1848]

broadside. 21x12.5cm.
Helfert (Wiener Parnass) 618.

*GB8
V6755R
3.32.48

An die Bürger und Studenten! Der 13te, 14te
und 15. März sind vorüber! ...
[Wien]Gedruckt bei Carl Gerold.[1848]

[2]p. 22x14cm.
Caption title; imprint on p.[2]; signed at
end: H— — Sohn eines Bürgers, früher Student,
jetzt Soldat.

*GB8
V6755R
3.32.48

Arndt, Ernst Moritz, 1769-1860.
Des deutschen Vaterland.
Gedruckt bei U.Klopf sen.und Alexander Eurich
in Wien.[1848]

broadside. 25x20cm.
Helfert (Wiener Parnass) 628.
Printed in 2 columns.

*GB8
V6755R
3.32.48

[Arndt, Ernst Moritz, 1769-1860]
Des deutschen Vaterland.
[Wien,1848]

[2]p. 21x13.5cm.
Helfert (Wiener Parnass) 628.
Caption title; signed at end: E. M. Arndt.

---

*GB8
V6755R
3.32.48

Aufruf an Oesterreich's biedere Bürger.
[Wien]Druck und Eigenthum von Josef Stöckholzer
v.Hirschfeld.[1848]

folder([4]p.) 20.5x13.5cm.

---

*pGB8
V6755R
3.32.48

Arnold, Johann, fl.1848.
An die unchristlichen Hetzer! Mit tiefer
Betrübniss muss es das Herz jedes fühlenden
unpartheiischen Menschen erfüllen, die Bekenner
des mosaischen Glaubens gerade in dem Zeitpunkte
auf die schmählichste, kränkendste und zugleich
gemeinste Weise verfolgt zu sehen ...
[Wien]Druck von Josef St.v.Hirschfeld.[1848]

broadside. 40x25.5cm.
A plea for tolerance.

---

*GB8
V6755R
3.32.48

Aufruf an Oesterreichs studirende Jugend.
Druck und Eigenthum von Hirschfeld in Wien.
[1848]

broadside. 22.5x14cm.

---

*GB8
V6755R
3.32.48

[Arthur, pseud.]
Hoch Oesterreich! ... Ich frage dich? Gedanken
eines Naturdichters!
[Wien]Gedruckt bei Josef Ludwig,in der
Josefstadt Florianigasse Nr.52.[1848]

folder([4]p.) 22x15cm.
Helfert (Wiener Parnass) 606.
Signed at end: Arthur.

---

*GB8
V6755R
3.32.48

Aufforderung an alle Patrioten des
österreichischen Kaiserstaates.
[Wien]Druck und Eigenthum von Josef Stöckholzer
v.Hirschfeld.[1848]

folder([4]p.) 22x13.5cm.
Woodcut (angel with trumpet & wreath) at head
of title.
Signed at end: Die Studenten.

---

*pGB8
V6755R
3.32.48

[Arthur, pseud.]
Ist eine Prise gefällig? oder Es kratze sich
wem es juckt.
[Wien]Gedruckt bei Josef Ludwig,Josefstadt
Florianigasse Nr.52.[1848]

[2]p. 38x24.5cm.
Caption title; imprint on p.[2]; signed:
Arthur.

---

*pGB8
V6755R
3.32.48

Aufruf an alle wohlgesinnten Österreicher,
unsere Lebensfrage betreffend.
[Wien,1848]

broadside. 60x47cm.
Signed: Von einem Nationalgardisten ...
Asking for contributions for the army in Italy.

---

*pGB8
V6755R
3.32.48

[Arthur, pseud.]
Schauerliche Begebenheit, Selbst=Mord des so
allgemein berühmten und beliebten Herrn Jeremias
Lumpatius Vagabundus.
[Wien]Gedruckt bei Josef Ludwig,Josefstadt
Florianigasse Nr.52.[1848]

[2]p. 42x25cm.
Caption title; imprint on p.[2]; signed:
Arthur.
Satire on Metternich.

---

*GB8
V6755R
3.32.48

Aufruf an alle wohlgesinnten Oesterreicher,
unsere Lebensfrage betreffend.
[Wien]Druck von A.Pichler's Wittwe.[1848]

[2]p. 22x14cm.
Caption title; imprint on p.[2]; signed at
end: Von einem Nationalgardisten ...
Asking for contributions for the army in Italy.

*GB8
V6755R
3.32.48

Aufruf zur Wiedervereinigung derzeit
getrennter Gemüther, von Baron G. L. M.,
Oberlieutenant der Nationalgarde aus der
Leopoldstadt.
[Wien]Druck und Eigenthum von Josef
Stöckholzer v.Hirschfeld.[1848]

folder([4]p.) 22x13.5cm.

---

*GB8
V6755R
3.32.48

Bidschof, Franz Xavier.
Der Artillerist und der Polizeimann.
Zweigespräch zwischen die Wäschermädchen Toni
und Leni. Von F. X. Bidschof.
[Wien]Gedruckt bei Josef Ludwig,Josefstadt
Florianigasse Nr.52.[1848]

folder([4]p.) 25x19cm.
In the Viennese dialect.

---

*pGB8
V6755R
3.32.48

[Bardach, D   ascribed author]
Die Juden=Herrschaft.
[Wien]Gedruckt bei M.Lell.[1848]

broadside. 38x23cm.
Signed: B———ch.

---

*pGB8
V6755R
3.32.48

Bidschof, Franz Xavier.
Die grosse Litanei.
[Wien]Gedruckt bei Joseph Ludwig Josephstadt
Florianigasse Nr.52.[1848]

broadside. 38x24cm.

---

*GB8
V6755R
3.32.48

Bartsch, J   G
Was ist Censur, Pressfreiheit und
Constitution? Was haben wir damit gewonnen?
Eine gemeinfassliche Darstellung, für Jedermann
verständlich verfasst von J. G. Bartsch.
[Wien]Gedruckt bei Edl.v.Schmidbauer und
Holzwarth.[1848]

[2]p. 25.5x18cm.
Caption title; imprint on p.[2].

---

*pGB8
V6755R
3.32.48

Bidschof, Franz Xavier.
Der grosse neue Katechismus der Freiheit im
deutschen Kaiserreich, von Franz X. Bidschof.
[Wien]Gedruckt bei Josef Ludwig,Josefstadt
Florianigasse Nr.52.[1848]

broadside. 37x22.5cm.

---

*GB8
V6755R
3.32.48

Berger, Johann Nepomuk, 1816-1870.
Die zehn Gebote des constitutionellen
Staatsbürgers. Von Dr. J. N. Berger.
[Wien,1848]

folder([4]p.) 25x16.5cm.
Printer's imprint on p.[4]: Bei Fr. Tendler
& Comp., Buchhändler am Graben Nr. 618.

---

*pGB8
V6755R
3.32.48

Bidschof, Franz Xavier.
Speise-Zettel in dem neu eröffneten Gasthofe
zur Constitution, von F. X. Bidschof.
[Wien]Gedruckt bei Josef Ludwig,Josefstadt
Florianigasse Nr.52.[1848]

[2]p. 40x27cm.
Caption title; imprint on p.[2].

---

*GB8
V6755R
3.32.48

[Bernklau, Jacob]
Drei Worte. (Der Nationalgarde gewidmet.)
[Wien]A.Dorfmeister's Druck und Verlag
(Stadt,Kühfussgasse Nr.575).[1848]

[2]p. 22.5x14.5cm.
Helfert (Wiener Parnass) 644.
Caption title; imprint on p.[2].
Signed at end: J. Bernklau.

---

*GB8
V6755R
3.32.48

Bidschof, Franz Xavier.
Die Wiener Bürger Deputation auf der k. k.
Hof Stiegen, oder die Entstehung der National=
Garde durch den Bürger Herrn Albert Hardt,
nach sichern Quellen in Ergebenheit allen
Nationalgarden in den k. k. constitutionellen
Staaten gewidmet von Franz X. Bidschof ...
[Wien]Gedruckt bei Josef Ludwig.[1848]

folder([4]p.) 29.5x22.5cm.

*GB8
V6755R
3.32.48

Bodanzky, Arnold.
Rede, verfasst von Arnold Bodanzky.
[Wien,1848]

broadside. 22.5x15cm.

---

*GB8
V6755R
3.32.48

Brix, Alexander, d.1869.
Oestreich frei! Von Alex. Brix. Mediziner.
Zum Besten seiner armen Kollegen in Wien.
[Wien]Druck von U.Klopf sen.und Alex.Eurich,
Wollzeile 782.[1848]

broadside. 20.5x12.5cm.
Helfert (Wiener Parnass) 616.

---

*GB8
V6755R
3.32.48

Botgorschek, Ferdinand.
Te Deum laudamus, für die Jetztzeit
übertragen und der Universität zu Wien
gewidmet von Ferdinand Botgorschek.
[Wien,1848]

folder([4]p.) 18x10.5cm.
Helfert (Wiener Parnass) 648.
Caption title.

---

*GB8
V6755R
3.32.48

[Brixner, Josef]
Halts eng zam, von einen National=Gardisten
für seini Kameraden der Vorstadt Neubau ...
Gedruckt bei J.Stöckholzer v.Hirschfeld in
Wien.[1848]

folder([4]p.) 22.5x14.5cm.
Helfert (Wiener Parnass) 615.
Signed at end: Josef Brixner, Wiener=Bürger
und National Gardist.

---

*pGB8
V6755R
3.32.48

Breinreich, Ludwig.
Freundliches Schreiben an die Unterthanen
der Herrschaft Feldsberg. Von ihrem Justiziär,
Ludwig Breinreich. Zu ihrer Aufklärung über
die jüngst erlangte Constitution und Pressfreiheit.
[Wien?,1848]

[2]p. 43x27cm.
Caption title.

---

*GB8
V6755R
3.32.48

[Buchheim, Carl Adolf, 1828-1900]
Kundmachung.
[Wien,1848]

[2]p. 20x12cm.
Helfert (Wiener Parnass) 655.
Caption title; at end: Gegeben während der
merkwürdigen Märzereignisse im Jahre 1848 im
Namen des Magistrates der Capitale Justitia von
Adolph Buchheim.

---

*pGB8
V6755R
3.32.48

[Brenner, Johann Nepomuk]
Oesterreichs Morgenröthe. Wodurch ist
Oesterreichs Morgenröthe angebrochen? Durch
die unsterblichen, unsers glorreichen Kaisers
Alles beglückenden Worte Nationalgarde,
Pressfreiheit, Constitution und Amnestie.
[Wien]Gedruckt bei M.Lell.[1848]

[2]p. 44x27cm.
Caption title; imprint on p.[2]; signed at end:
Joh. Nep. Brenner.
Includes a poem "Das freie Oesterreich an
seinen hochher-   zigen Kaiser"; not in
Helfert (Wiener   Parnass).

---

*pGB8
V6755R
3.32.48

Castelli, Ignaz Franz, 1781-1862.
Gutgemeinte Winsche von J. F. Castelli.
[Wien]Gedruckt und zu haben bei Leop.Grund,
am Stephansplatze im neugebauten Zwettelhofe.
[1848]

[2]p. 37x22.5cm.
Caption title; imprint on p.[2].

---

*GB8
V6755R
3.32.48

Breuer, Hermann, fl.1848.
Freiwilliges Corps. Von Herrmann Breuer.
[Wien]Gedruckt bei Josef Ludwig.[1848]

[2]p. 22x13.5cm.
Caption title; imprint on p.[2].
Not in Helfert (Wiener Parnass).
The first letters of the poem form an acrostic
of the title.

---

*pGB8
V6755R
3.32.48

Castelli, Ignaz Franz, 1781-1862.
Was ist denn jetzt g'schehn in Wien? Eine
Mittheilung für meine lieben österreichischen
Landsleute ausser Wien. Von J. F. Castelli.
[Wien]Gedruckt und zu haben bei Leopold Grund,
am Stephansplatze im neugebauten Zwettelhofe.
[1848]

[2]p. 42x26cm.
Caption title; imprint on p.[2].

*GB8
V6755R
3.32.48

Constitutionelle Bockssprünge, oder: der politische Lumpensammler.
[Wien,1848]

folder([4]p.) 22x14cm.
Imprint on p.[4]: Druck von A. Pichler's Witwe.

---

*GB8
V6755R
3.32.48

I. [i.e. Erstes] Dreschen. Für grobe Beamte und Geschäftsleute. Grosse Viecharbeit für Drescher oder Weltzopfreissen in Wien ...
[Wien,1848]

folder([4]p.) 26x20.5cm.
Imprint on p.[4]: Gedruckt bei Josef Ludwig, Josefstadt Florianigasse Nr.52.
Illustration on t.-p.

---

*GB8
V6755R
3.32.48

Egenhöfer, Johann.
Ruf eines National-Gardisten der vierten Compagnie im Bezirke Wimmerviertel an seine Kameraden im Monat März 1848. Von Johann Egenhöfer, Bürger in Wien ...
Wien 1848.Mechitharisten-Buchdruckerei.

folder([4]p.) 22x15cm.
Helfert (Wiener Parnass) 668.

---

*pGB8
V6755R
3.32.48

Eure Majestät! In einem Augenblick, wo der Jubelruf allerhöchstihrer getreuen Unterthanen von einem Ende der Monarchie zum andern widerhallt, sind Eurer Majestät nicht katholische und israelitische Unterthanen, die Einzigen, die bis jetzt nicht ohne Wehmuth an der allgemeinen Begeisterung Theil nehmen können ...
[Wien,1848]

broadside. 40x24.5cm.
A petition for equality of religious beliefs; no names have been signed.

---

*GB8
V6755R
3.32.48

Ehrlich, Wilhelm, fl.1848.
Oesterreich's constitutionelle Zukunft. Ein Aufruf an die Bürger Wiens von Wilhelm Ehrlich ...
[Wien,1848]

folder([4]p.) 23.5x19cm.

---

*pGB8
V6755R
3.32.48

Ferdinand der Gütige, Kaiser von Oesterreich. Der 1. Staatsbürger!
[Wien]Gedruckt bei Franz Edlen von Schmid.
[1848]

broadside. illus.(port.) 42x26cm.

---

*pGB8
V6755R
3.32.48

Einladung zur Bildung eines Frauenvereines, dessen schöner Zweck sein soll, für die Nationalgarde deutsche Fahnen zu schaffen und zwar so, dass jeder vi. Compagnie eine solche Fahne als Anerkennung der hohen Bestimmung dieses Jnstitutes zu Theile werden soll.
[Wien,1848]
broadside. 46.5x30cm.
"Zur Besprechung hierüber ladet jeden Tag bis 10 Uhr Morgens ein zu St. Ulrich, Pelikangasse Nr. 26, die Hauseigenthümerin."

---

*GB8
V6755R
3.32.48

Feyertag, Johann.
An Seine Durchlaucht dem Herrn Fürsten Vinzenz Auersperg, Commandant der Nationalgarde des Bezirkes Josefstadt.
[Wien,1848]

broadside. 28.5x22cm.
In verse; not in Helfert (Wiener Parnass).

---

*GB8
V6755R
3.32.48

Die ersten Keimlinge der freien Presse. 1848. Bisher censurwidrige, nun laut und frei ausgesprochene fromme Wünsche.
[Wien]Druck und Eigenthum von Josef Stöckholzer von Hirschfeld.[1848]

folder([4]p.) 22x15cm.

---

*GB8
V6755R
3.32.48

Fischer, Johann, fl.1848.
Freiheits-Jubel für das Jahr 1848.
Druck und Eigenthum von Hirschfeld in Wien.
[1848]

broadside. 22.5x14.5cm.
Helfert (Wiener Parnass) 593.

*pGB8
V6755R
3.32.48
Forderungen der Nation, welche in einer durch das provisorische Nationalcomitée einberufenen und in der Hauptstadt Agram im National=Gebäude am 25/13 März abgehaltenen Nationalversammlung der drei vereinigten Königreiche Dalmatien, Kroatien und Slawonien einstimmig beschlossen und mittelst einer grossartigen Nationaldeputation an den allerhöchsten Thron zur Bestätigung entsendet worden sind. (Aus dem ilirischen übersetzt).
[Wien,1848]
[2]p.   45x29.5cm.
Caption title.

*GB8
V6755R
3.32.48
Grosse Hunde=Versammlung auf der Simmeringer=Haide.
Wien,1848.Gedruckt bei J.N.Friedrich,Josephstadt Langegasse Nr.58.

folder([4]p.)   23.5x19cm.

*GB8
V6755R
3.32.48
Das freie Wort, oder: Die constitutionelle Monarchie.
[Wien,1848]
folder([4]p.)   26x21.5cm.
Imprint on p.[4]: Gedruckt bei Ant. Benko.

*GB8
V6755R
3.32.48
Die grosse Revolution von Italien, das schreckliche Blutvergiessen in Mailand und die Ermordung des Kommandanten Martinowich in Venedig.
Wien.1848.Druck von J.N.Fridrich,Josephstadt Nr.58.

folder([4]p.)   26x21cm.
Signed at end: Sch——e [i.e. Theodor Scheibe?].

*GB8
V6755R
3.32.48
Freunde, Brüder! Eilet, Euch den Reihen der National=Garde anzuschliessen, sie ist der festeste Grundstein der Constitution ...
[Wien,1848]

broadside. 21x12.5cm.
At end: Beherziget diess Wort eines National-Gardisten.

*GB8
V6755R
3.32.48
Grundfest, Emanuel.
Traum und Wirklichkeit, von Emanuel Grundfest. [Wien]Druck von U.Klopf senior und Alexander Eurich,Wollzeile 782.[1848]

broadside. 26x20cm.
Dated: Wien im März 1848.

*GB8
V6755R
3.32.48
Frühauf, Carl Raimund, 1818?-1858.
Die Kaiser Josephsstatue in der Mitternacht vor dem 13. März 1848.
[Wien,1848]

broadside. 22.5x14.5cm.
Helfert (Wiener Parnass) 700.

*GB8
V6755R
3.32.48
[Gürtler, J   ]
Oesterreich's Freiheit und Worte!
[Wien,1848]
[2]p.   20.5x13cm.
Helfert (Wiener Parnass) 599.
Caption title; signed at end: J. Gürtler.

*GB8
V6755R
3.32.48
[Goldner, Ignaz]
Aufruf.
[Wien]Gedruckt und zu haben bei Leop.Grund, am Stephansplatze im Zwettelhofe.[1848]

[2]p.   21x12.5cm.
Helfert (Wiener Parnass) 692.
Caption title; imprint on p.[2].
Signed at end: Ignaz Goldner.

*GB8
V6755R
3.32.48
Haas, Philipp, fl.1848.
Ich wache für meinen Kaiser! Von Philipp Haas, National=Gardist.
Druck und Eigenthum von Hirschfeld in Wien. [1848]

broadside. 22.5x14cm.
Helfert (Wiener Parnass) 647.

[Hammer, ————]
    Die Bureaukratie in Galizien.
*pGB8   [Wien]Gedruckt bei Edl.v.Schmidbauer und
V6755R   Holzwarth.[1848]
3.32.48
        [2]p. 42x26cm.
        Caption title; imprint on p.[2]; signed at
end: Dr. Hammer.

Heinisch, Constantin.
    Der Kaiser--frei! Ein Lied aus offener Brust
*GB8   von Constantin Heinisch, Nationalgardist der
V6755R   academischen Legion.
3.32.48 [Wien]Druck von U.Klopf sen.und A.Eurich,
        Wollzeile 782.[1848]

        [2]p. 20.5x12.5cm.
        Helfert (Wiener Parnass) 684.
        Caption title; imprint on p.[2].

Hammerschmidt, J   B
    Die Emancipation der Juden betreffend.
*GB8   [Wien?]Gedruckt bei Franz Gastl.[1848]
V6755R
3.32.48 broadside. 24x19cm.
        Signed: Dr. Hammerschmid.
        Attacking a pamphlet by Hubert Müller entitled
"Ein ruhiges Wort gegen die Juden-Emancipation!"

Heinrich, Christian.
    ... Die Juden Böhmens in den letzten Tagen.
*pGB8   Ein Wort eines Christen an seine Brüder.
V6755R   Gedruckt bei C.W.Medan in Prag.[1848]
3.32.48
        broadside. 40x25cm.
        At head of title: Beilage zur Prager=Zeitung
Nr.68.

Hammerschmidt, J   B
    Die Emanzipation der Juden betreffend. Von Dr.
*GB8   Hammerschmidt.
V6755R   [Wien]Gedruckt und zu haben bei Leopold Grund
3.32.48 am Hundsthurm Nr.1.—Verlag:Stadt Zwettelhof.
        [1848]

        [2]p. 27x22cm.
        Caption title; imprint on p.[2].
        Attacking a pamphlet by Hubert Müller entitled
"Ein ruhiges Wort gegen die Juden-Emancipation!"

Heldenmüthige Vertheidigung des Castells in
Como, vom 19. bis 27. März 1848, durch das
*pGB8   österreichische Militär.
V6755R   [Wien]Gedruckt bei Edl.v.Schmidbauer und
3.32.48 Holzwarth.[1848]

        [2]p. 42.5x26.5cm.
        Caption title; imprint on p.[2].
        Signed at end: N. M.

Haschl und Mauschel. Nix ze handeln?
    [Wien,1848]
*GB8
V6755R   folder([4]p.) 27x21.5cm.
3.32.48 Two woodcut illus. on t.-p.
        Another issue has title: Nix zu handeln?
        For the emancipation of the Jews.

Hennig, Josef Heinrich.
    Ein Wort an die braven Wiener Bürger und
*pGB8   Nationalgarde, aber auch ein ernstes,
V6755R   belehrendes und treuherziges Wort an die
3.32.48 biedern Landleute und auswärtigen Mitbürger,
        denen die Ereignisse in Wien theils von
        bösgesinnten Missiggängern, theils von elenden
        Prahlern und Grosssprechern ganz falsch
        mitgetheilt werden. Von Jos. Heinrich Hennig,
        Nationalgarde.
        [Wien]Gedruckt und zu haben bei Leopold Grund,
am Stephansplatze,   im Zwettelhofe.[1848]
                        (See next card)

[Heider, Gustav, 1819-1897]
    Freundschaftliche Worte an die Künstler-Jugend!
*GB8   [Wien,1848]
V6755R
3.32.48 [2]p. 29x22cm.
        Caption title; signed at end: G. Heider.

Hennig, Josef Heinrich.   Ein Wort ... [1848]
                        (Card 2)
*pGB8
V6755R   [2]p. 42x26.5cm.
3.32.48 Caption title; imprint on p.[2].

*GB8
V6755R
3.32.48

Hirschfeld, J   H
    Freiheitslied. Den freiheitsmuthigen
Studenten aus liebevollem Herzen gewidmet von
Ihrem Collegen Drnd. J. H. Hirschfeld.
    [Wien]Gedruckt bei Franz Edlen v. Schmid.[1848]

    folder([4]p.) 23.5x15cm.
    Helfert (Wiener Parnass) 652b.
    Revised & enlarged edition of a poem first
published with title: Freiheits=Marsch für
die Studenten.

*GB8
V6755R
3.32.48

[Holzinger, Johann]
    Die Freiheit.
    [Wien,1848]

    [2]p. 20.5x13cm.
    Helfert (Wiener Parnass) 587.
    Caption title; signed at end: Johann Holzinger.

*GB8
V6755R
3.32.48

Hirschfeld, J   H
    Freiheits=Marsch für die Studenten.
    Druck und Eigenthum von Hirschfeld in Wien.
[1848]

    broadside. 22.5x13.5cm.
    Helfert (Wiener Parnass) 652a.
    A revised & enlarged edition has title:
Freiheitslied.

*GB8
V6755R
3.32.48

Holzinger, Johann.
    Die Gleichheit.
    [Wien,1848]

    broadside. 21.5x12.5cm.
    Helfert (Wiener Parnass) 588.

*GB8
V6755R
3.32.48

[Hirschfeld, J   H   ]
    Hoch lebe der Kaiser! Dankeshymne zur Feier
Oesterreichs glorreicher Märztage. In Musik
gesetzt vom Professor S. Sulzer.
    [Wien]Tendler & Comp.[1848]

    folder([4]p.) 21x13.5cm.
    Helfert (Wiener Parnass) 669.
    Signed at end: J. H. Hirschfeld.
    Without the music.

*GB8
V6755R
3.32.48

    Der Invalide und sein Guckkasten.
    Wien,1848.Druck von U.Klopf sen.und A.Eurich,
Wollzeile 782.[1848]

    folder([4]p.) 21.5x13.5cm.

*pGB8
V6755R
3.32.48

    Der Hofnarr und die Constitution. Ein
anmuthiges Geschichtlein, welches sich
irgendwo in der Welt zugetragen haben soll.
    Wien,gedruckt und zu haben bei Leop.Grund,
Stephansplatz,Zwettelhof.[1848]

    [2]p. 40.5x25cm.
    Caption title; imprint on p.[2].

*GB8
V6755R
3.32.48

Janisch, Anton.
    Wie das Monument Kaiser Joseph II. lebendig
wurde, und was es zu seinen lieben
Oesterreichern sprach. Ein Traum von Anton
Janisch.
    Wien,1848.Gedruckt in der Josephstadt,
Langegasse Nr.58.

    folder([4]p.) 23.5x19cm.

*GB8
V6755R
3.32.48

Holger, Philipp Aloys, ritter von, 1799-1866.
    Religionsgleichheit. Was heisst Gleichstellung
der Religion und in welchem Sinne kann sie von
der Regierung gefordert werden. Von Professor von
Holger.
    [Wien]Gedruckt und zu haben bei Leopold Grund
am Stephansplatze im Zwettelhofe.[1848]

    folder(4p.) 21x13cm.
    Caption title; imprint on p.4.

*GB8
V6755R
3.32.48

Janowitz, Moritz.
    An die freien Männer der christlichen
Bekenntnisse.
    [Wien]Gedruckt bei J.B.Wallishausser.[1848]

    broadside. 25x19cm.
    Signed: Moritz Janowitz, Hörer der Rechte, im
Namen seiner Glaubensgenossen.
    A plea for the equality of the Jews.

*GB8
V6755R
3.32.48

[Jilly, Gustav]
Was früher unmöglich geschienen.
[Wien]Gedruckt bei Josef Ludwig.[1848]

[2]p. 20.5x13cm.
Caption title; imprint on p.[2]; signed at end:
Gustav Jilly.

(

*GB8
V6755R
3.32.48

[Kneissler, Hippolyt, 1831-1883]
Das edle, treue Oesterreich!!
[Wien]Gedruckt bei Carl Gerold.[1848]

[2]p. 22.5x14.5cm.
Not recorded by Helfert (Wiener Parnass).
Caption title; imprint on p.[2].
Dated & signed at end: Wien, 1848. Im Monat
März. Hippolyt Kneissler, Poet am akademischen
Gymnasium.

(

*pGB8
V6755R
3.32.48

Die Juden wie sie waren, sind—und bleiben
werden. Eine getreue Charakter=Schilderung,
Winke und Warnungen für das Volk.
[Wien]Gedruckt bei Joh.N.Fridrich.[1848]

[2]p. 43x27cm.
Caption title; imprint on p.[2].
Ms. ascription (not contemporary) at head: Von
Johann Quirin Endlich?

(

*GB8
V6755R
3.32.48

[Koehler, Alexander von, attributed author]
Die Bedingung zur Emancipation der Juden.
Mit Bezug auf die neuesten Ereignisse. Von E. K.
...
Wien,1848.Bei Jasper,Hügel und Manz,
Herrngasse Nr.251,im Fürst Lichtensteinischen
Palais.

13p. 18.5x11.5cm.

(

*GB8
V6755R
3.32.48

Kadisch, L   J
Feuer!
[Wien,1848]

broadside. 22.5x14.5cm.
In verse; not in Helfert (Wiener Parnass).

(

*GB8
V6755R
3.32.48

Körner, A   A
Neues Volkslied (nach der Melodie: Gott
erhalte) dessen Ertrag den, bei gegenwärtigen
grossen Ereignissen Verwundeten zugewendet wird.
[Wien,1848]

broadside. 19x11.5cm.
Helfert (Wiener Parnass) 685.
Without the music.

(

*GB8
V6755R
3.32.48

Kargl, Franz.
Wer hat die arbeitende Classe zu ihrer jetzigen
Entwürdigung geführt? Nebst einigen Worten über
die Juden=Emancipation. Von Franz Kargl, Bürger
und Nationalgardist.
[Wien,1848]

folder([4]p.) 23x15.5cm.
Caption title.

(

*pGB8
V6755R
3.32.48

Kundmachung. Wer für völlige Gleichstellung
aller Confessionen ist, wird eingeladen, eine
an Seine kaiserliche Majestät gerichtete
allunterthänigste Adresse zu unterzeichnen,
welche in allen Buch= und Kunsthandlungen und
Kaffeehäusern Wiens aufliegt ...
[Wien]Gedruckt bei F.E.v.Schmid.[1848]

broadside. 34x25.5cm.
Includes the text of the petition, which
begins: Eure Majestät! In einem Augenblicke, wo
der Jubelruf ...   (

*GB8
V6755R
3.32.48

Keine Juden in der Nationalgarde???! Ein
Wort an Alle, die's trifft!
[Wien,1848]

broadside. 25.5x20cm.
Signed: Rudolf G.......

(

*GB8
V6755R
3.32.48

[Leidesdorf, Eduard]
Kartätschen.
[Wien,1848]

[2]p. 21x13.5cm.
Caption title; signed at end: J.[i.e.E.] Ldf.

(

1848 Austrian Revolutionary Broadsides and Pamphlets

*pGB8
V6755R
3.32.48

Leitermayer, August.
Aufruf. Die Freiheit ist errungen; überall
fühlt man ihren beseligenden Einfluss, ihren
wohlthätigen Strahl ...
[Wien,1848]

broadside. 44x29cm.
Suggesting the organization of choral
societies.

---

*GB8
V6755R
3.32.48

[Mauss, J   B   ]
Metternichs Geist in Petersburg, oder: Was
wollen jetzt die Russen. Die Unterjochung
Europas im Sinne des Testaments von Peter dem
Grossen, Kaiser von Russland.
[Wien,1848]

folder([4]p.) 25.5x19.5cm.
At end: Zusammengestellt von J. B. Mauss.
Imprint on p.[4]: Wien, gedruckt bei Leopold
Grund, Hundsthurm Nr.1. Verlag: Stadt,
Stephansplatz im Zwettelhofe.
"Das Testament   Peters des Grossen,
Kaisers von Russ-   land": p.[2-3].

---

*GB8
V6755R
3.32.48

Machanek, Ignaz, b.1825.
Deutsches Freiheitslied. Von J. Machanek.
Druck v.U.Klopf sen.u.A.Eurich in Wien.[1848]

broadside. 26.5x21cm.
Helfert (Wiener Parnass) 594.

---

*GB8
V6755R
3.32.48

[Mauthner, Bernard]
Angstruf eines Israeliten ...
[Wien,1848]

folder([4]p.) 23x14.5cm.
Signed at end: Bernard Mauthner, National
Gardist.

---

*GB8
V6755R
3.32.48

Manger, Franz.
An die Wiener. Von Franz Manger.
[Wien]Gedruckt bei Ferd.Ullrich.[1848]

[2]p. 21x13cm.
Helfert (Wiener Parnass) 609.
Caption title; imprint on p.[2].
In Viennese dialect.

---

*GB8
V6755R
3.32.48

[Mayer, Joseph, fl.1848]
Auch die Frauen wollen, was wir Männer haben.
Humoristische Gelegenheitsskizze.
[Wien]K.k.Hofbuchdruckerei des L.Sommer
(vormals Strauss).[1848]

[2]p. 26x21.5cm.
Caption title; imprint on p.[2]; signed at
end: Joseph Mayer.

---

*GB8
V6755R
3.32.48

[Mantelmann, pseud.]
Die Geschichte von der grossen italienischen
Aufwieglerin Prinzessin Beliocojoso, genannt
die blutdürstige Mörderin der Oesterreicher.
Wien,1848.Gedruckt in der Josephstadt,
Langegasse Nr.58.[1848]

folder([4]p.) 26.5x21cm.
Signed at end: Mantelmann.

---

*GB8
V6755R
3.32.48

Medis, J   Alexander.
Ein Licht vom Westen. Gedicht von J. Alexander
Medis, Nationalgardisten.
[Wien,1848]

[2]p. 22.5x14cm.
Helfert (Wiener Parnass) 583.
Caption title.

---

*GB8
V6755R
3.32.48

Materna, Wenzl.
Die entwölkte Sonne. Von Wenzl Materna,
Techniker und Nationalgardist.
[Wien]Druck von U.Klopf sen.und A.Eurich,
Stadt,Wollzeile Nr.782.[1848]

broadside. 20x12cm.
Helfert (Wiener Parnass) 617.

---

*pGB8
V6755R
3.32.48

Meisl, Karl, 1775-1853.
Politischer Katechismus eines neugebornen
Oesterreichers. Von Carl Meisl.
[Wien]Gedruckt und zu haben bei Leopold Grund,
am Stephansplatze im neugebauten Zwettelhofe.
[1848]

[2]p. 38x25cm.
Caption title; imprint on p.[2].

*GB8
V6755R
3.32.48

Meisl, Karl, 1775-1853.
Politisches Evangelium für die neue Zeit
Oesterreichs, von Carl Meisl.
Wien,gedruckt und zu haben bei Leopold Grund,
am Stephansplatz im Zwettelhof.[1848]

[2]p. 25x19.5cm.
Caption title; imprint on p.[2].

---

*GB8
V6755R
3.32.48

[Moretti, ——]
Aufruf an edelgesinnte österreichische Bürger.
Druck und Eigenthum von J.v.Hirschfeld in
Wien.[1848]

folder([4]p.) 22x13.5cm.
Signed at end: Dr. Moretti.

---

*GB8
V6755R
3.32.48

Meisl, Karl, 1775-1853.
Was ist gestern Neues in Wien geschehen?
Morgengespräch eines wienerischen Balbiers
mit seiner politischen Kundschaft. Von Carl
Meisl.
[Wien]Gedruckt bei Leop.Grund,am Hundsthurm Nr.
1.Verlag:Stadt,Zwettelhof.[1848]

[2]p. 25x19.5cm.
Caption title; imprint on p.[2].

---

*GB8
V6755R
3.32.48

[Müller, C F]
Danklied eines freien Volkes an die Gottheit
als wahres, inniggefühltes Te Deum laudamus.
[Wien]A.Dorfmeister's Druck und Verlag,Stadt,
Kühfussgasse Nr.575.[1848]

[2]p. 22.5x14.5cm.
Helfert (Wiener Parnass) 677.
Caption title; imprint on p.[2].
Signed at end: C. F. Müller.

---

*pGB8
V6755R
3.32.48

Merket auf! Was wir wollen.
Gedruckt bei U.Klopf sen.und Alexander Eurich
in Wien.[1848]

broadside. 40x24.5cm.
Signed: M. O.

---

*pGB8
V6755R
3.32.48

[Miller, Hubert, fl.1848, ascribed author]
Nur keine Juden=Emancipation! Von einem Freunde
der guten Sache.
[Wien]Zu haben bei dem Buchhändler Jacob
Bader,Stroblgasse.Gedruckt bei Ant.Benko.[1848]
[2]p. 38.5x24.5cm.
Caption title; imprint on p.[2].
In this edition, the last line of text on p.
[2] begins: sie einstehen und handeln!
Also published with title: Ein ruhiges Wort
gegen die Juden-Emancipation.
Sometimes wrongly attributed to J. B.
Weis.

---

*GB8
V6755R
3.32.48

Metternich's und seiner Gattin Melanie
Zichy's Ränke in London und Russland's
gegenwärtige Politik. Beleuchtet von einem
Patrioten.
[Wien,1848]

folder([4]p.) 24.5x19.5cm.
Imprint on p.[4]: A. Dorfmeister's Officin.
Signed at end: Ein Patriot.

---

*pGB8
V6755R
3.32.48

[Miller, Hubert, fl.1848, ascribed author]
Nur keine Juden=Emancipation! Von einem
Freunde der guten Sache.
[Wien]Zu haben bei dem Buchhändler Jacob
Bader,Stroblgasse.Gedruckt bei Ant.Benko.[1848]
[2]p. 38x24cm.
Caption title; imprint on p.[2].
In this edition, the last line of text on p.
[2] begins: machen,——dann wollen wir gern ...
Also published with title: Ein ruhiges Wort
gegen die Juden-Emancipation.
Sometimes wrongly attributed to J. B.
Weis.

---

*GB8
V6755R
3.32.48

Mitbürger und Freunde! In der Einigkeit und
Ordnung haben wir Recht und Freiheit gefunden!
...
Bei Hirschfeld in Wien.[1848]

broadside. 22.5x15.5cm.

---

*pGB8
V6755R
3.32.48

[Miller, Hubert, fl.1848, ascribed author]
Ein ruhiges Wort gegen die Juden=Emancipation!
Von einem Freunde der guten Sache.
[Wien?,1848]

[2]p. 42x26.5cm.
Caption title.
Also published with title: Nur keine Juden-
Emancipation!

*pGB8
V6755R
3.32.48

[Miller, Hubert, fl.1848, ascribed author]
Ein ruhiges Wort gegen die Juden=Emancipation.
Von einem Freunde der guten Sache.
[Wien]Zu haben bei dem Buchhändler Jacob
Bader,Stroblgasse.Gedruckt bei Ant.Benko.[1848]
[2]p. 38x24.5cm.
Caption title; imprint on p.[2].
In this edition, the last line of text on
p.[2] begins: machen,——dann wollen wir gern ...
Also published with title: Nur keine Juden-
Emancipation!

*GB8
V6755R
3.32.48

... Neues Gekritzel über die alten Spitzel.
Von einem ehrlichen Mops.
[Wien,1848]
folder([4]p.) 27x21.5cm.
At head of title: Mit dem Bildniss des
Verfassers. [woodcut of a dog]

*pGB8
V6755R
3.32.48

[Miller, Hubert, fl.1848, ascribed author]
Ein ruhiges Wort gegen die Juden=Emancipation!
Von einem Freunde der guten Sache.
[Wien]Zu haben bei dem Buchhändler Jacob Bader,
Stroblgasse.Gedruckt bei Ant.Benko.[1848]
[2]p. 38x24.5cm.
Caption title; imprint on p.[2].
In this edition, the last line of text on p.
[2] begins: sie einstehen und handeln!
Also published with title: Nur keine Juden-
Emancipation!

*GB8
V6755R
3.32.48

[Neuwall, Leopold, ritter von]
Neue Volks=Hymne.
[Wien]Gedruckt bei Carl Gerold.[1848]
[2]p. 22.5x14.5cm.
Helfert (Wiener Parnass) 679.
Caption title; imprint on p.[2].
Signed at end: Leopold Ritter von Neuwall,
Doktor der Rechte.

*GB8
V6755R
3.32.48

[Begins:] Nacht war's--/ Schwere Wetterwolken/
Schwankten drohend durch das Dunkel--/ ...
[Wien]F.Beck's Universitäts=Buchhandlung,
Bischofgasse Nr.638.[1848]
broadside. 28x19cm.
Helfert (Wiener Parnass) 585.

*GB8
V6755R
3.32.48

Nichts für ungut!
[Wien,1848]
folder([4]p.) 22x14cm.
Title within oval wreath border.

*GB8
V6755R
3.32.48

Neidl, Julius.
Freiheitsblitze. Früher censurwidrige doch
nun öffentlich ausgesprochene Gedanken, Wünsche
und Betrachtungen. Von Julius Neidl.
[Wien,1848]
folder([4]p.) 23.5x15cm.
Imprint on p.[4]: Druck von A. Pichler's
Witwe.

*GB8
V6755R
3.32.48

Nix zu handeln?
[Wien,1848]
folder([4]p.) 27x21.5cm.
One woodcut illus. on t.-p.
Another issue has title: Haschl und Mauschel.
Nix ze handeln?
For the emancipation of the Jews.

*GB8
V6755R
3.32.48

Neuer Volks=Vaterunser!
[Wien]Druck von U.Klopf sen.und A.Eurich,
Wollzeile 782.[1848]
broadside. 26.5x21cm.

*GB8
V6755R
3.32.48

Nordmann, Johannes, 1820-1887.
Trutznachtigall. Eine Reihe von Liedern. Von
Johannes Nordmann. Erstes[-drittes] Lied ...
[Wien,1848]
3 pts. 22.5x15cm.
Helfert (Wiener Parnass) 661, 650, & 619.
Contents: Erstes Lied: Die freie Presse.--
Zweites Lied: Den Studenten.--Drittes Lied: Von
den Frauen.
Each pt. has printer's imprint on p.[2] (of
a [4]p. folder): Wien, gedruckt bei Franz
Edl. v. Schmid.

*GB8
V6755R
3.32.48

Notna, K., pseud.
Der Wanderbursch. Ein Wanderbursche von einer Weltreise kommend, ruht im freien und treuen Wien einige Tage aus.
[Wien, 1848]

broadside. 1 illus. 24x15cm.

---

*GB8
V6755R
3.32.48

Patrioten der österreichischen Monarchie!
Bei Hirschfeld in Wien.[1848]

broadside. 22x15cm.
Signed: Die Studenten.

---

*pGB8
V6755R
3.32.48

Ein Oesterreicher an seine Landsleute.
[Wien]Druck von U.Klopf sen.und Alex.Eurich, Wollzeile 782.[1848]

broadside. 40.5x26cm.
This large broadside edition has publisher's address in imprint.

---

*pGB8
V6755R
3.32.48

Pauer, Julius.
Was die Juden denn eigentlich wollen?
[Wien]Gedruckt bei den Edlen v.Ghelen'schen Erben.[1848]

broadside. 38x24cm.
A plea for the emancipation of the Jews.

---

*GB8
V6755R
3.32.48

Ein Oesterreicher an seine Landsleute.
[Wien]Druck von U.Klopf sen.und Alex.Eurich.
[1848]

broadside. 21.5x13.5cm.
This small broadside edition is without publishers' address in imprint.

---

*GB8
V6755R
3.32.48

Pauly, Wilhelm, ritter von.
Dichtkunst und Pressfreiheit. Von Wilhelm Ritter von Pauly.
[Wien]A.Dorfmeister's Druck und Verlag(Stadt, Kühfussgasse Nr.575).[1848]

[2]p. 22.5x14.5cm.
Helfert (Wiener Parnass) 665.
Caption title; imprint on p.[2].

---

*GB8
V6755R
3.32.48

Oesterreichische Volkshymne. Neuer verfassungsmässiger Text nach der volksthümlich gewordenen Haydn'schen Tonweise: Gott erhalte &c.
Wien 1848.Verlag von J.G.Heubner am Bauernmarkt Nr.590.Druck von Ferd.Ullrich.

[2]p. 19x12cm.
Helfert (Wiener Parnass) 682.
Caption title; imprint on p.[2].
Without the music.

---

*GB8
V6755R
3.32.48

[Petri, Hugo Jacques]
An Oesterreich's Volk!
Verlag von Hirschfeld in Wien.[1848]

folder([4]p.) 22x13.5cm.
Signed at end: Hugo Jaques Petri.

---

*GB8
V6755R
3.32.48

Offener Brief an die Bürger der k. k. Hauptstadt Olmütz.
[Wien]Gedruckt bei Carl Gerold.[1848]

[2]p. 28.5x22cm.
Caption title; imprint on p.[2]; signed at end: B. Sz. Bürger und Kaufmann.

---

*pGB8
V6755R
3.32.48

Politisch=constitutionell=monarchisches Glaubensbekenntniss. Zweite Auflage.
[Wien]Gedruckt bei U.Klopf sen.und Alexander Eurich,Wollzeil Nr.782.[1848]

broadside. 40x25cm.
Signed: P. K. ch.

Prague. Citizens.
Petition der Bewohner Prags an Seine kais.
kön. Majestät.
[Wien,1848]

[2]p. 47x30cm.
Text in Czech on verso headed: Žádost
obyvatelů Pražkých k Jeho c. k. Milosti.

*pGB8
V6755R
3.32.48

[Richter, Franz Johann]
Die Adler Oesterreichs.
[Wien]Mechitharisten-Buchdruckerei.[1848]

[2]p. 22.5x15cm.
Helfert (Wiener Parnass) 696.
Caption title; imprint on p.[2]; signed at end:
Dr. Franz Joh. Richter, Quiescent.

*GB8
V6755R
3.32.48

[Pratobevera-Wiesborn, Adolf, freiherr von,
b.1806]
Offenes Sendschreiben an die Herren
Studierenden Wiens.
Wien 1848.Gedruckt bei Carl Gerold.
folder((4]p.) 22x14cm.
Caption title; imprint on p.[4]; signed at end:
Pratobevera, Dr. d. R., Appellations=Rath und
Nationalgarde im Namen vieler Gleichgesinnten.

*GB8
V6755R
3.32.48

Richter, Karl, fl.1848.
Ein Wort im Interrese der Juden. An alle
Menschenfreunde in und ausser Wien. Von Karl
Richter.
[Wien]Gedruckt bei Ulrich Klopf sen.und Alex.
Eurich.[1848]

folder((4]p.) 20x13cm.
Caption title; imprint on p.[4].

*GB8
V6755R
3.32.48

Purschke, Carl.
Antwort auf das am 22. März 1848 dem Tagblatte
für constitutionelles Volksleben und Belehrung
"Die Constitution," eingerückte Schreiben an
den Herrn Prälaten des Stiftes Klosterneuburg;
von Fr. Römersdorfer, Bürger daselbst. Von C.
Purschke, Justiziär und Commissär.
[Wien,1848]

[2]p. 42.5x26.5cm.
Caption title.

*pGB8
V6755R
3.32.48

Rosental, Klemens.
Ich war dabei! Nach der Melodie: "Zu Warschau
schwuren Tausend auf den Knien."
[Wien,1848]

[2]p. 22.5x14cm.
Helfert (Wiener Parnass) 613.
Caption title.

*GB8
V6755R
3.32.48

[Redlich, J   ascribed author]
Der Juden=Galgen.
[Wien]Druck von M.Lell.[1848]

broadside. 38x23cm.
Signed: J. R.

*pGB8
V6755R
3.32.48

[Sauter, Ferdinand, 1804-1854, ascribed author]
Freiheitsblüthen.
[Wien]Druck von U.Klopf sen.und A.Eurich,
Wollzeile 782.[1848]

folder([4]p.) 20x13cm.
Helfert (Wiener Parnass) 596 (ascribed to
Sauter in index).
Caption title; imprint on p.[4]; signed at end:
S.
Two poems, "Des Landmanns Ahnen" & "Lied".

*GB8
V6755R
3.32.48

Reno, ———.
Tags=Fragen. In zwanglosen Heften.
Herausgegeben von Dr. Reno.
Wien.Gedruckt bei Carl Gerold.1848.

folder([4]p.) 38x25.5cm.
Caption title, p.[3]: Die Frage über
Gleichstellung der Israeliten aus einem anderen
als dem in diesem Augenblicke gewöhnlichen
Gesichtspunkte betrachtet.
No more published?

*pGB8
V6755R
3.32.48

Schleichert, J   M
Nur jetzt keine Judenfreiheiten!
[Wien,1848]

broadside. 43x27cm.

*pGB8
V6755R
3.32.48

*GB8
V6755R
3.32.48

[Schleichert, J   M   ]
    Sedlnitzky's Geist als Nachtwächter, Nacht-
wandler, Kaffeehausgast, Zeitungsausträger und
Marktschreierweib.
    [Wien,1848]
    folder([4]p.) 27x21.5cm.
    Signed at end: J. M. Schleichert, National=
Gardist im Juristenkorps.

*GB8
V6755R
3.32.48

Schwarz, Roth, Gold.
    [Wien,1848]
    folder([4]p.) 22x14.5cm.
    Helfert (Wiener Parnass) 626.
    Imprint on p.[4]: Gedruckt bei den Edlen von
Ghelen'schen Erben.
    Signed at end: Teutschland, Lenzmonat 1848.

*GB8
V6755R
3.32.48

Schmidtler, Friedrich Mathäus.
    Freiheitslied, von Friedr. Math. Schmidtler.
    [Wien,1848]
    broadside. 19.5x12.5cm.
    Not in Helfert (Wiener Parnass).

*GB8
V6755R
3.32.48

Selinger, Engelbert Maximilian, 1802-ca.1854.
    Österreich über Alles, wenn es nur will!
Von Dr. Engelbert Selinger.
    [Wien]Gedruckt und zu haben bei L.Grund,
Hundsthurm,Schlossgebäude Nr.1.Verlag am
Stephansplatze im Zwettelhofe.[1848]
    [2]p. 27x21.5cm.
    Caption title; imprint on p.[2].

*GB8
V6755R
3.32.48

[Schumacher, Andreas, 1803-1868]
    Ein Wort im Fluge!
    [Wien]Gedruckt bei Edl.v.Schmidbauer und
Holzwarth,Bürgerspital Nr.1100.[1848]
    8p. 18x12.5cm.
    Caption title; imprint on p.8; signed at end:
Andr. Schumacher.

*GB8
V6755R
3.32.48

[Seyfried, Franz]
    An die Nationalgarde Oesterreichs.
    [Wien,1848]
    folder([3]p.) 20.5x13cm.
    Caption title; signed at end: Franz Seyfried,
k. k. Beamter und Oberlieutenant der Nationalgarde.

*GB8
V6755R
3.32.48

Schwartz, Eugen, fl.1848.
    Beschreibung von dem Wappen der
österreichischen National-Garde.
    [Wien,1848]
    broadside. 27x21.5cm.
    "Das Bild ist in gross Folio-Format
lithographirt und gemalt, zu haben bei Schenett,
Vergolder, Wieden nächst der Paulaner=Kirche."

*pGB8
V6755R
3.32.48

[Simić von Hohenblum, Joseph]
    Grundbedingungen des Gedeihens der Constitu-
tion in den österreichischen Staaten.
    [Wien]Gedruckt bei den Edlen v.Ghelen'schen
Erben.[1848]
    [2]p. 38.5x26.5cm.
    Caption title; imprint on p.[2]; signed at end:
J. S. Hohenblum.

*pGB8
V6755R
3.32.48

Schwarz, Roth, Gold.
    [Wien]Gedruckt bei den Edlen von Ghelen'schen
Erben.[1848]
    broadside. 37.5x25.5cm.
    Signed: Teutschland, Lenzmonat 1848.
    Helfert (Wiener Parnass) 626.

*GB8
V6755R
3.32.48

[Stegmayer, Carl]
    Constitutionelles Volkslied. Melodie: Gott
erhalte u.s.w.
    M.Haas in Wels.[1848]
    [2]p. 18.5x11cm.
    Caption title; imprint on p.[2]; signed at
end: Carl Stegmayer.
    Without the music.
    "Der Ertrag dieses Liedes ist zum Beitrage für
das Monument der am 13. März 1848 in Wien
Gefallenen bestimmt."

*pGB8
V6755R
3.32.48

Suchomel, ——.
    Die österreicher Bauern, hoffen das Beste!
[Wien]Druck von U.Klopf senior und Alexander
Eurich,Wollzeile Nr.782.[1848]

    broadside. 53x42cm.

---

*GB8
V6755R
3.32.48

Das viele Unediche.
[Wien]Gedruckt bei Josef Ludwig.[1848]

[2]p. 26.5x21cm.
Caption title; imprint on p.[2].

---

*GB8
V6755R
3.32.48

[Tuvora, Franz, d.1866]
    Gedanken über die völlige Gleichstellung der
Confessionen in Oesterreich. Verfasst über den
öffentlichen Aufruf zur Unterschrift einer in
dieser Angelegenheit für Se. Majestät den
Kaiser bestimmten Adresse. Von einem Katholiken.
Wien.Druck und Verlag von Joh.Nep.Fridrich,
Josephstadt Nr.58.[1848]

    folder([4]p.) 28.5x22cm.
    The petition referred to begins: Eure Majestät!
In einem Augenblick, wo der Jubelruf ...
    Another edition is not anonymous.

---

*pGB8
V6755R
3.32.48

Vienna. Comité für die Errichtung eines
        Gemeinde-Ausschusses.
    Comité-Bericht über die Bildung eines Gemeinde=
Ausschusses für die Stadt Wien zum Gebrauche für
die darüber zu pflegende Berathung.
[Wien,1848]

[2]p. 57.5x38cm.
Caption title.

---

*GB8
V6755R
3.32.48

Tuvora, Franz, d.1866.
    Gedanken über die völlige Gleichstellung aller
Confessionen in Oesterreich. Verfasst über den
öffentlichen Aufruf zur Unterschrift einer in
dieser Angelegenheit für Se. Majestät den
Kaiser bestimmten Adresse. Von Franz Tuvora.
Wien.Druck von U.Klopf sen.und Alex.Eurich,
Wollzeile 782.[1848]

    folder([4]p.) 26x20.5cm.
    The petition referred to begins: Eure Majestät!
In einem Augenblick, wo der Jubelruf ...
    Another edition is anonymous.

---

*pGB8
V6755R
3.32.48

Vienna. Nationalgarde.
    Auszug der Commando-Wörter. Aus dem Exercier=
Reglement der kais. kön. Infanterie, für die
kais. kön. National-Garde der kais. kön. Haupt=
und Residenzstadt Wien.
[Wien]Mechitharisten=Buchdruckerei.[1848]

[2]p. 39x24cm.
Caption title; imprint on p.[2].

---

*GB8
V6755R
3.32.48

[Ullmeyer, Anton]
    Das magistratisch politische Raubnest oder die
Wiener magistratische Beamten Bureaukratie.
[Wien,1848]
    folder([3]p.) 1 illus. 27x21.5cm.
    Caption title; signed at end: Anton Ullmeyer,
Leopoldstadt, grosse Stadtgutgasse No.376.
    Engraved throughout; another edition is in
letterpress.

---

*pGB8
V6755R
3.32.48

Vienna. Universität. Ausschuss der Studierenden.
    Arbeiter! Ihr Männer wisst, dass es die
Studenten mit Euch immer gut gemeint haben ...
[Wien,1848]

    broadside. 44.5x57.5cm.
    Signed: Für die Studenten: Dr. Goldmark. Dr.
Fischhof. Dr. Giskra. Unger.

---

*GB8
V6755R
3.32.48

[Ullmeyer, Anton]
    Das magistratisch=politische Raubnest, oder:
die Wiener magistratische Beamten=Bureaukratie.
[Wien,1848]
    folder([3]p.) 1 illus. 26.5x21.5cm.
    Caption title; signed at end: Anton Ullmeyer,
Leopoldstadt, grosse Stadtgutgasse Nr.376.
    Letterpress edition; another edition is
engraved.

---

*GB8
V6755R
3.32.48

Volksblatt.
[Wien]Gedruckt bei Carl Gerold.[1848]

[2]p. 26x19.5cm.
Caption title; imprint on p.[2]; signed at end:
Alle wahren Vaterlandsfreunde.
    Another issue has title: Volksblatt ohne
Censur.
    In this edition, the last line on p.[1]
begins "Diebe wollen das Volk zur Unordnung
verleiten ..."

*GB8
V6755R
3.32.48

Volksblatt ohne Censur.
[Wien]Gedruckt bei Carl Gerold.[1848]
[2]p. 25x19.5cm.
Caption title; imprint on p.[2]; signed at end:
Alle wahren Vaterlandsfreunde.
Another issue has title: Volksblatt.
In this edition, the last line on p.[1]
begins "Diebe wollen das Volk zur Unordnung
verleiten ..."

*pGB8
V6755R
3.32.48

Weis, Johann Baptist, 1801-1862.
National-Garde, Pressfreiheit und Constitution,
oder: Was haben wir erhalten, und wie sollen wir
es benützen? Ein freies Wort zur Belehrung und
Beherzigung. Von J. B. Weis ...
[Wien]Gedruckt und zu haben bei Leop.Grund,am
Stephansplatze im Zwettelhofe.[1848]
[2]p. 41x25cm.

*GB8
V6755R
3.32.48

Volksblatt ohne Censur.
[Wien,1848]
[2]p. 25.5x19.5cm.
Caption title.
Another issue has imprint on p.[2].
In this edition, the last line on p.[1] reads
"Und auf den Nutzen müssen wir sehen."
Another edition has title: Volksblatt.

*GB8
V6755R
3.32.48

Ein Wort über die Liguorianer.
Wien,1848.Druck von U.Klopf sen.und A.Eurich,
Wollzeile 782.
folder([4]p.) 21x13cm.

*GB8
V6755R
3.32.48

Volksblatt ohne Censur.
[Wien]Gedruckt bei Carl Gerold.[1848]
[2]p. 25.5x20cm.
Caption title; imprint on p.[2].
Another issue is without imprint.
In this edition, the last line on p.[1] reads
"Und auf den Nutzen müssen wir sehen."
Another edition has title: Volksblatt.

*GB8
V6755R
3.32.48

Worte an das Volk zur gehörigen Würdigung der
Verhältnisse der Gegenwart.
Druck von U.Klopf sen.und A.Eurich in Wien,
Wollzeile Nr.782.[1848]
[2]p. 27.5x22cm.
Caption title; imprint on p.[2].
Printed on pink paper.

*GB8
V6755R
3.32.48

Volkslied. Nach der Melodie von "Gott erhalte"
zu singen.
[Wien]Gedruckt bei Carl Gerold.[1848]
broadside. 25.5x19.5cm.
Not recorded by Helfert (Wiener Parnass);
begins: Heil ihr Männer, Heil ihr Frauen/ In
dem ganzen Oesterreich./
Without the music.

*GB8
V6755R
3.32.48

[Zierrath, F   W   ]
Metternich's Glück und Ende in Oesterreich.
[Wien]Druck bei U.Klopf sen.und A.Eurich.[1848]
folder([4]p.) 20x13cm.
Caption title; imprint on p.[4].
Another issue is signed at end: F. W. Zierrath.

*GB8
V6755R
3.32.48

Weinberger, Rudolph.
Nur keine Juden-Emanzipation, oder der
geputzte Hans-Jörgel. Von Rud. Weinberger, Garde
im akad. Corps.
[Wien]Druck von U.Klopf sen.und Alex.Eurich,
Wollzeile 782.[1848]
folder([4]p.) 20.5x13.5cm.
Caption title; imprint on p.[4].
Against Hubert Müller's "Nur keine Juden-
Emanzipation!", here wrongly supposed to have
been written by the editor of "Hans-Jörgel",
J. B. Weis.

*GB8
V6755R
3.32.48

[Zierrath, F   W   ]
Metternich's Glück und Ende in Oesterreich.
[Wien]Druck bei U.Klopf sen.und A.Eurich.
[1848]
folder([4]p.) 20x13cm.
Caption title; imprint on p.[4]; signed at
end: F. W. Zierrath.
Another issue is unsigned.

*GB8
V6755R
3.32.48

II. [i.e. Zweites] Dreschen für nicht
constitutionelle Menschen. Grosse Viecharbeit
für Drescher oder Weltzopfreissen in Wien ...
[Wien,1848]

folder([4]p.) 26x21cm.
Illustration on t.-p.
Note at foot of t.-p. states "Das dritte
Dreschen erscheint bald"; no more published?

*GB8
V6755R
4.2.48

Die deutsche Fahne. Der Wiener Hochschule
gewidmet am 2. April 1848.
[Wien]Gedruckt in der k.k.Hof=Buchdruckerei
des L.Sommer(vorm.Strauss).[1848]

folder([4]p.) 21.5x14cm.
Helfert (Wiener Parnass) 762.
Caption title; imprint on p.[4].

*GB8
V6755R
4.1.48

Der härteste Eckstein aus der Brigittenau.
[Wien,1848]

folder(3p.) 19x12cm.
Caption title.
Dated in contemporary ms.: 1. April 848.
Antisemitic.

*GB8
V6755R
4.2.48

[Moering, Carl, 1810-1870]
Die drei Farben.
Wien bei Tendler & Comp.--Gedruckt bei Ferd.
Ullrich.[1848]

broadside. 26x20.5cm.
Helfert (Wiener Parnass) 760.
Dated & signed: Am 2. April 1848. Cameo
[pseud.].
Another edition has "F. Ullrich" in imprint.

*GB8
V6755R
4.1.48

[Spitzer, C Leopold]
Was weiter g'scheh'n soll.
[Wien]Gedruckt bei Josef Ludwig,in der
Josefstadt Florianigasse Nr.52.[1848]

folder(3p.) 22x14cm.
Caption title; imprint on p.3.
Dated & signed at end: Wien, den 1. April
1848. C. Leopold Spitzer.

*GB8
V6755R
4.2.48

[Moering, Carl, 1810-1870]
Die drei Farben.
Wien bei Tendler et Comp.Gedruckt bei F.
Ullrich.[1848]

broadside. 26.5x21cm.
Helfert (Wiener Parnass) 760.
Dated & signed: Am 2. April 1848. Cameo [pseud.]
Another edition has "Ferd. Ullrich" in
imprint.

*GB8
V6755R
4.1.48

Unterreiter, Friedrich, b.ca.1804.
Armenseelenlichtl für Jesuiten, Ligurianer
und Redemptoristen. Von Friedrich Unterreiter
... Fünfte Auflage.
[Wien]Gedruckt bei M.Lell,vormals Anna St.von
Hirschfeld,Jägerzeile,Weintraubengasse Nr.505.
[1848]

folder([4]p.) 23.5x15cm.

*pGB8
V6755R
4.2.48

Padovani, Matteo, b.1815.
Nationalgarde! Kameraden! Da etliche
Ehrenrührungen über mich im Umlauf sind, so
finde ich mich veranlasst, Folgendes zu
veröffentlichen ...
[Wien]Druck von U.Klopf sen.und Alex.Eurich,
Wollzeile Nr.782.[1848]

broadside. 40x26cm.
Quoting a letter from Count Hoyos, dated 2
April 1848, concerning Padovani's reinstatement
in the Nationalgarde.

*GB8
V6755R
4.1.48

·Vienna. Seidenzeugfabrikanten.
Bekanntmachung. Die Gefertigten bringen mit
Vergnügen zur allgemeinen Kenntniss, dass die
Verhandlungen und Besprechungen mit ihren
Arbeitern am 28. März in schönster Haltung,
Ordnung und Ruhe gepflogen, zu dem erfreulichen
Resultat führten ...
[Wien,1848]
broadside. 30x23.5cm.
Signed: Die Vorsteher und die Verhandlungs=
Commission der k. k. priv. und bürgl. Seidenzeug-
Fabrikanten in   Wien.
Dated in con-   temporary ms.: 1. April
848.

*GB8
V6755R
4.2.48

Parth, Peter.
Worte eines Bürgers an seine Mitbürger in
Betreff der geschmähten Liguorianer. Von Peter
Parth, Wiener Bürger.
[Wien]Gedruckt bei Carl Ueberreuter.[1848]

folder([4]p.) 26x22.5cm.
Concerns Friedrich Unterreiter's
Armenseelenlichtl für Jesuiten, Liguorianer
und Redemptoristen.

*pGB8
V6755R
4.2.48

Der 2. April ein grosser, ein herrlicher Tag!
[Wien,1848]

broadside. 47.5x30cm.
Signed: Von einem Vaterlandsfreunde.

---

*GB8
V6755R
4.4.48

[Hammerschmidt, J   B   ]
    Aufruf zur Begründung einer Wiener Studenten-
Warte.
    [Wien]Gedruckt bei Leopold Grund.[1848]

    [2]p. 26x16.5cm.
    Caption title; imprint on p.[2].
    Dated & signed at end: Wien den 4. April 1848.
Dr. Hammerschmidt.
    The proposed periodical did not appear.

---

*pGB8
V6755R
4.3.48

Oesterreicher, Leopold.
    Der deutsche Michel und die Juden.
[Wien]Gedruckt bei M.Lell.[1848]

broadside. 42x26cm.
Antisemitic.

---

*GB8
V6755R
4.4.48

[Hanausek, Richard]
    Unparteiische Beleuchtung zweier Flugschriften
über die Liguorianer nebst einer Bitte an die
Herren Redacteure der Wiener Zeitschriften.
    [Wien,1848]

    folder(4p.) 21x13cm.
    Caption title; signed & dated on p.3: Richard
Hanausek, Juristen im vierten Jahre,
Nationalgardisten der akademischen Legion.
Josephstadt Nr. 132. Wien am 4. April 1848.
                    (See next card)

---

*GB8
V6755R
4.3.48

Perissutti, G   M
    Oeffentliche Erwiderung. Jn einem erst am 1.
April d. J. durch die Stadtpost an mich
gelangten in französischer Sprache abgefassten
anonymen Briefe werden Zweifel über die
bisherige reele Verfahrungsweise bei den
Ziehungen der Güter=Lotterien ausgesprochen ...
    [Wien,1848]

    broadside. 28.5x22cm.
    Dated & signed: Wien am 3. April 1848. G. M.
Perissutti, k. k. pr. Grosshändler.
    Printed on yel-(low paper.

---

*GB8
V6755R
4.4.48

[Hanausek, Richard]   Unparteiische ... [1848]
                    (Card 2)

    Dealing with Friedrich Unterreiter's
"Armenseelenlichtl für Jesuiten, Liguorianer und
Redemptoristen" & Peter Parth's "Worte eines
Bürgers an seine Mitbürger".

---

*pGB8
V6755R
4.3.48

Vienna. Magistrat.
    Kundmachung. Da die durch den Patriotismus
mehrerer Einwohner von Wien hervorgerufene
Werbung von Freiwilligen aus der Bevölkerung
dieser Hauptstadt den günstigen Erfolg gehabt
hat, dass sich eine zureichende Anzahl dem
Dienste der Armee unterzogen hat ...
    [Wien,1848]

    broadside. 41x50cm.
    Signed & dated: Vom Magistrate der k. k.
Haupt= und Residenzstadt Wien den 3. April 1848.

---

*pGB8
V6755R
4.4.48

[Helfert, Joseph Alexander, freiherr von,
    1820-1910]
    Oesterreich's künftige Stellung. Sendschreiben
an die Männer von Wien.
    Wien 1848.Gedruckt bei Carl Gerold.
    [2]p. 43x27cm.
    Caption title; imprint on p.[2]; signed at
end: J. U. Dr. Helfert.

---

*pGB8
V6755R
4.4.48

Aufruf! Die Märztage haben grosse Opfer
gekostet, deren bedeutendste unersetzlich,
deren viele einer Abhilfe zugänglich sind ...
[Wien,1848]

broadside. 43x27cm.
Dated & signed: Wien am 4. April 1848.
Ferdinand Graf Colloredo=Mannsfeld. Rudolf v.
Arthaber. F. B. Geitler [& 5 others].

---

*GB8
V6755R
4.4.48

... Die Journale sprechen von der Insulte,
welche der österreichischen Botschaft in Rom
widerfahren ist ...
    [Wien](Gedruckt bei den Edlen von Ghelen'schen
Erben.)[1848]

    broadside. 27x21cm.
    At head: Wien, 4. April 1848.
    In this edition, the last line of text begins:
in Rom

*GB8
V6755R
4.4.48

... Die Journale sprechen von der Insulte, welche der österreichischen Botschaft in Rom widerfahren ist ...
[Wien](Gedruckt bei den Edlen von Ghelen'schen Erben.)[1848]

broadside. 27x21cm.
At head: Wien, 4. April 1848.
In this edition, the last line of text begins: chen Vorfall in Rom

---

*GB8
V6755R
4.4.48

Löschhörndl für das Armenseelenlichtl der Jesuiten, Ligurianer und Redemptoristen! von Friedrich Unterreiter ...
[Wien,1848]

folder([4]p.) 23.5x15cm.
Imprint on p.[4]: Gedruckt bei M. Lell, vormals Anna St. von Hirschfeld.
Also includes an address to Peter Parth concerning his "Worte eines Bürgers an seine Mitbürger".

---

*pGB8
V6755R
4.4.48

Vienna. Magistrat.
Kundmachung. Ueber Aufforderung der k. k. Militär=Verwaltung wird bekannt gemacht ...
[Wien,1848]

broadside. 44.5x28.5cm.
Signed & dated: Vom Magistrate der Stadt Wien, am 4. April 1848.

---

*GB8
V6755R
4.5.48

[Arthur, pseud.]
Ankunft des ersten Ligourianers aus Wien in der Hölle.
[Wien]Gedruckt bei Josef Ludwig Josefstadt Florianigasse Nr.52.[1848]

folder(4p.) 24x19.5cm.
Helfert (Wiener Parnass) 772.
Signed at end: Arthur.

---

*GB8
V6755R
4.5.48

Ausserordentlicher Courier aus dem Hauptquartiere des Feld=Marschalls Grafen Radetzky, mit übersichtlicher Darstellung der Operationen vom 19. bis 30. März ...
[Wien,1848]

folder(4p.) 25x19.5cm.
Imprint on p.4: Gedruckt und zu haben bei Leopold Grund, am Stephansplatze im Zwettelhofe, und am Hundsthurm im Schlossgebäude Nr. 1.

---

*GB8
V6755R
4.5.48

[Bowitsch, Ludwig, 1818-1881]
Germania: Italia.
[Wien]A.Dorfmeister's Buchdruckerei.[1848]

[2]p. 22x14cm.
Helfert (Wiener Parnass) 776.
Caption title; imprint on p.[2].
Signed at end: Ludwig Bowitsch.

---

*GB8
V6755R
4.5.48

[Scheibe, Theodor, 1820-1881]
Wider Seine Schein=Heiligkeit Papst Pius den IX. und für das Verheirathen der katholischen Geistlichen.
Wien,1848.Gedruckt und zu haben in der Josephstadt Langegasse Nr.58.

folder([4]p.) 26x20.5cm.
Signed at end: Theodor Scheibe.
Another edition has title reading "... für das Verheirathen katholischer Geistlichen."

---

*GB8
V6755R
4.5.48

[Scheibe, Theodor, 1820-1881]
Wider Seine Schein=Heiligkeit Pabst Pius den IX. und für das Verheirathen katholischer Geistlichen.
Wien,1848.Gedruckt und zu haben in der Josephstadt Langegasse Nr.58.

folder([4]p.) 25x20cm.
Signed at end: Theodor Scheibe.
Another edition has title reading "... für das Verheirathen der katholischen Geistlichen."

---

*GB8
V6755R
4.5.48

[Schick, Leopold]
... An meine Brüder Arbeiter!
[Wien](Zu haben in der Verlagshandlung des Franz Edlen v. Schmid,Seitenstättengasse Nr. 495.)[1848]

folder([4]p.) 23.5x16.5cm.
Caption title, with imprint above; at head of imprint: Dieses Blatt darf nicht theurer als für einen Kreuzer Wiener=Währung verkauft werden.
Signed at end: Leopold Schick, Nationalgardist
**Includes at end   a letter dated "Wien, den 5. April 1848" &   signed: Hofrath Baron Dercsényi.

---

*GB8
V6755R
4.5.48

[Ullmayer, Franz]
Wieder ein neues Hirschauerstückl! von einem Pfarrer. Wahre Begebenheit, welche sich in Ottakring zugetragen hat.
[Wien]Gedruckt bei M.Lell,Leopoldstadt, Weintraubengasse Nr.505.[1848]

folder([4]p.) 24x15cm.
Signed at end: F. Ullmayer.

*pGB8
V6755R
4.5.48

Vienna. Nationalgarde.
Euere Excellenz! Das Wort unseres
allergnädigsten konstitutionellen Kaisers hat
die Nationalgarde in's Leben gerufen, und
dadurch die ernste, heiligste Pflicht, die
Aufrechthaltung der Ruhe und gesetzlichen
Ordnung in unsere Hände gelegt ...
[Wien,1848]
[2]p. 42x26cm.
Caption title; dated at end: Wien, am 5. April
1848.
Addressed to (Pillersdorf.

*pGB8
V6755R
4.6.48

Bidschof, Franz Xavier.
Grosse Liguorianer Litanei.
[Wien]Gedruckt bei Josef Ludwig.[1848]

broadside. 38x24cm.

---

*pGB8
V6755R
4.6.48

Abschiedsworte an die abgezogenen Liguorianer.
[Wien]Gedruckt bei Josef Ludwig,Josefstadt
Florianigasse Nr.52.[1848]
[2]p. 38x24cm.
Caption title; imprint on p.[2]; signed at
end: F. W. Z.

*GB8
V6755R
4.6.48

[Gärtner, Wilhelm, 1811-1875]
Entgegnung an Herrn Dr. Fehr auf Fragen an den
Herrn Fürsterzbischof in Wien. Jm Namen seines
mundtodten Clerus von Dr. J. Fehr.
[Wien](Gedruckt bei den Edlen v.Ghelen'schen
Erben.)[1848]
[2]p. 27x21cm.
Caption title; imprint on p.[2]; signed at
end: Wilhelm Gärtner, Priester an der
Universitäts=Kirche.

---

*GB8
V6755R
4.6.48

Aufruf zur Wahl des Ober-Commandanten der
Nationalgarde.
Gedruckt bei J.P.Sollinger in Wien.[1848]

broadside. 29x22cm.
Dated & signed: Wien am 6. April 1848. Der
Verfasser des Rathschlags: "Wie muss eine
Nationalgarde exercirt werden?"
Suggesting Carl Moering as head of the
Nationalgarde.

*GB8
V6755R
4.6.48

[Leidesdorf, Eduard]
Die Ahnfrau im Liguorianerkloster zu Wien den
14. März 1848 um die Geisterstunde. Schlag 12
Uhr!
[Wien,1848]

broadside. 26.5x21.5cm.
Helfert (Wiener Parnass) 787.
Signed: Eduard Ldf.
This edition is without imprint or
"Nachschrift".

---

*pGB8
V6755R
4.6.48

Austria. Ministerium des Innern.
... An den Herrn Hauptmann der Nationalgarde
Ritter von Mitis.
[Wien,1848]

broadside. 42x26cm.
Dated & signed: Wien, am 6. April 1848.
Pillersdorff m/p.
At head: 488/M.J.
Replying to the address presented by the 2.
Compagnie of the Nationalgarde.

*GB8
V6755R
4.6.48

[Leidesdorf, Eduard]
Die Ahnfrau im Liguorianerkloster zu Wien
den 14. März 1848 um die Geisterstunde. Schlag 12
Uhr!
[Wien]Druck von U.Klopfsen.[!]und A.Eurich,
Wollzeile 287.[1848]

broadside. 21.5x12.5cm.
Helfert (Wiener Parnass) 787.
Signed: Eduard Ldf.
This edition has "Nachschrift" & imprint with
erroneous no. "287" for the printer's
address.

---

*pGB8
V6755R
4.6.48

Austria. Ministerium des Innern.
Kundmachung. Die Ruhe eines ehrwürdigen
Greises, dessen Leben ebenso reich an
Frömmigkeit, als an wohlthätigen Handlungen ist
... wurde durch verbrecherische Excesse gestört
...
[Wien,1848]

broadside. 44.5x57cm.
Dated & signed: Wien am 6. April 1848. Der
Minister des Inneren: Franz Freiherr von
Pillersdorff.

*GB8
V6755R
4.6.48

Neuestes aus Italien. Siegreicher Kampf der
treuen und heldenmüthigen österreichischen Armee
in Mailand und Venedig.
[Wien,1848]

folder([4]p.) 25x19.5cm.
Printer's imprint on p.[4]: Gedruckt und zu
haben bei Leop. Grund, am Hundsthurm Nr. 1.
Verlag: Stadt, Stephansplatz im Zwettelhofe.
Dated in contemporary ms.: 6. April 1848.

Vienna. Nationalgarde.
   Cameraden! Die Nationalgarden der zweiten
Compagnie des Schottenviertels haben sich
veranlasst gefunden, bei Seiner Excellenz
dem Herrn Minister des Innern, Freiherrn von
Pillersdorff, unter heutigem Tage eine Adresse
zu überreichen ...
   [Wien,1848]
      folder([4]p.) 38.5x26.5cm.
      Caption title; dated & signed on p.[1]: Wien,
am 6. April 1848. In Vertretung der gesammten
Compagnie: Ferdinand Ritter von
Mitis, Hauptmann.
                 (See next card)

*pGB8
V6755R
4.6.48

Vienna. Nationalgarde.   Cameraden ... [1848]
                         (Card 2)
   The text of the address, also printed separate-
ly from the same setting as a [2]p. broadside,
is found on p.[2-3]; p.[4] contains endorsed
direction: An die löbliche   Compagnie der
Nationalgarde.

*pGB8
V6755R
4.6.48

Die Studenten Wiens an die ungarische Nation.
[Wien,1848]
   broadside. 41.5x25cm.
   Dated: Wien den 7. April 1848.
   Ascribed in ms. to J. P. Lyser.

*pGB8
V6755R
4.7.48

Vienna. Nationalgarde.
   Cameraden! So wie wir uns für verpflichtet
hielten, Sie gestern von dem vollen Inhalte
der, Sr. Excellenz dem Herrn Minister des Innern
überreichten Adresse in Kenntniss zu setzen ...
   [Wien,1848]
      [2]p. 42x26cm.
      Dated & signed: Wien, am 7. April 1848. In
Vertretung der gesammten Compagnie: Ferdinand
Ritter von Mitis, Hauptmann.
      Giving the text of Pillersdorf's reply to the
                 (See next card)

*pGB8
V6755R
4.7.48

Vienna. Nationalgarde.   Cameraden ... [1848]
                         (Card 2)
   address of the 2. Compagnie.
      Endorsed direction on p.[2]: An die löbliche
Compagnie der Nationalgarde.

*pGB8
V6755R
4.7.48

Vienna. Nationalgarde.
   Dank-Adresse der Wiener National=Garden an
die National=Garde in Pesth.
   [Wien,1848]
      broadside. 52.5x34cm.
      Dated: Wien den 7. April 1848.

*pGB8
V6755R
4.7.48

Austria. Laws, statutes, etc., 1835-1848
   (Ferdinand I)
      Entwurf eines Statuts über die Organisation
der Nationalgarde in dem österreichischen
Kaiserstaate.
   [Wien,1848]
      8p. 45x28.5cm.
      Caption title; dated at end: Wien am 8.
April 1848.

*pGB8
V6755R
4.8.48

Austria. Ministerium des Innern.
   ... Kundmachung. Die Nationalgarde, eine der
festesten Stützen der constitutionellen
Einrichtungen, kann nur durch ein, von den
versammelten Abgeordneten aus allen Provinzen
zu berathendes Gesetz ihre definitive bleibende
Organisation erhalten ...
   [Wien,1848]
      broadside. 44.5x28cm.
      Reschauer-Smets II.71.
      Dated & signed: Wien am 8. April 1848. Der
                 (See next card)

*pGB8
V6755R
4.8.48

Austria. Ministerium des Innern.   ...
   Kundmachung ... [1848]   (Card 2)
Minister des Inneren: Franz Freiherr von
Pillersdorff.
   This issue has number at head: Ad Nro.
4597.

*pGB8
V6755R
4.8.48

Austria. Ministerium des Innern.
   Kundmachung. Die Nationalgarde, eine der
festesten Stützen der constitutionellen
Einrichtungen, kann nur durch ein, von den
versammelten Abgeordneten aus allen Provinzen
zu berathendes Gesetz ihre definitive bleibende
Organisation erhalten ...
   [Wien,1848]
      broadside. 44.5x29cm.
      Reschauer-Smets II.71.
      Dated & signed: Wien am 8. April 1848. Der
Minister des   Inneren: Franz Freiherr von
Pillersdorff.
      This issue is   without number at head.

*pGB8
V6755R
4.8.48

*pGB8
V6755R
4.8.48

Erklärung der Stände des Fürstenthums
Troppau und Jägerndorf an die versammelten
Ausschüsse der Provinzen.
[Wien,1848]

[2]p. 42x26cm.
Dated & signed: Troppau, den 8. April 1848.
Wilhelm Freiherr v. Badenfeld. Landeshauptmann.
Franz Freiherr v. Sedlnitzky. Carl Graf Arz
[& 8 others].

---

*pGB8
V6755R
4.8.48

... Reisepass für Pater Liguorian Teufelsohn,
Ritter der Furcht und des Tadels, Grossmeister
des Ordens der Säue an Gottes Tisch, und
Freiherrlicher Folterknecht des gesunden
Menschenverstandes.
[Wien,1848]

broadside. 42x26.5cm.
Printed within typographic border; at head:
Hauptstadt Mariasteg. Werbbezirk Wien.
Höllenreich Finsterniss.
Mock passport for the departure of the
Liguorians from   Vienna; dated: Ausgefertigt
... am 8. April   1848.

---

*GB8
V6755R
4.8.48

[Heidmayer, Carl]
Nur keine Spion=Prämie! Ein vertrautes Wort
neuester Zeit über den an allen Ecken
angeschlagenen Vorschlag des Herrn M. A. K.
Moravski (dd. 5. April d. J.) zu einer
Entdeckungs Prämie.
[Wien]Gedruckt bei M.Lell.[1848]

folder([4]p.) 24x15.5cm.
Caption title; imprint on p.[4].
Dated & signed at end: Wien, den 8. April
1848. Carl Heidmayer, Privatkanzellist.

---

*pGB8
V6755R
4.8.48

[Schmidbauer, Josef, edler von]
Das wahre Pressgesetz. Den Ministern des
österreichischen Kaiserstaates empfohlen.
[Wien,1848]

folder(4p.) 33.5x25.5cm.
Caption title; dated & signed at end:
Geschrieben den 8. April 1848. Jos. Edl. v.
Schmidbauer.

---

*GB8
V6755R
4.8.48

[Naske, Adolph Carl, 1814-1864]
Glück und Ende der Liguorianer in Wien. Eine
kurzgefasste Darstellung des Lebens und Wirkens
dieser am 6. April 1848 förmlich ausgewiesenen
Congregation, nebst einigen historischen Daten
über die nunmehr in das National=Eigenthum
übergegangene Kirche zu St. Maria am Gestade
(Maria Stiegen) in Wien.
[Wien]Zu haben bei dem Buchhändler Jakob Bader,
Stadt,Strobelgasse.Gedruckt bei Anton Benko.
[1848]

(See next card)

---

*pGB8
V6755R
4.8.48

Vienna. Magistrat.
Beschluss bei der am 6. und 7. April d. J.
Statt gehabten Abstimmung des gesammten Rathes
und prov. Bürger=Ausschusses über die Anträge
zur Constituirung eines Gemeinde=Ausschusses
der Stadt Wien.
[Wien,1848]

folder([3]p.) 36.5x22.5cm.
Caption title.
In this edition, line 14 on p.[2] has reading:
Prüfung der Wahlen ist dem Ansschusse [!]
vorbehalten.
(See next card)

---

*GB8
V6755R
4.8.48

[Naske, Adolph Carl, 1814-1864]   Glück
und Ende ... [1848]   (Card 2)

folder(4p.) 24.5x19.5cm.
Caption title; imprint on p.4.
Dated & signed at end: Wien am 8. April 1848.
Adolph Carl Naske.

---

*pGB8
V6755R
4.8.48

Vienna. Magistrat.   Beschluss ... [1848]
(Card 2)

"Ausweis über die Vertheilung der Gemeinde=
Ausschuss=Mitglieder in den Vorstädten":
p.[3].

---

*pGB8
V6755R
4.8.48

Partezettel. Ein freies Volk gibt für sich
als für alle andere freien Völker die höchst
erfreuliche Nachricht von dem mit allgemeinen
Jubel begleitenden Hinscheiden des Paters
Liguorian ...
Druck von U.Klopf sen.und A.Eurich in Wien.
[1848]

broadside. 25x32cm.
Mock obituary notice for the departure of the
Liguorians from Vienna on April 5-6, 1848.

---

*pGB8
V6755R
4.8.48

Vienna. Magistrat.
Beschluss bei der am 6. und 7. April d. J.
Statt gehabten Abstimmung des gesammten Rathes
und prov. Bürger=Ausschusses über die Anträge
zur Constituirung eines Gemeinde=Ausschusses
der Stadt Wien.
[Wien,1848]

folder([3]p.) 37x23cm.
Caption title.
In this edition, line 14 on p.[2] has reading:
Prüfung der Wähler ist dem Ausschusse
vorbehalten.
(See next card)

*pGB8
V6755R
4.8.48

Vienna. Magistrat.   Beschluss ... [1848]
                                (Card 2)
"Ausweis über die Vertheilung der Gemeinde=
Ausschuss=Mitglieder in den Vorstädten":
p.[3].

---

*GB8
V6755R
4.9.48

Frankl, Ludwig August, 1810-1894.
A Duna, von Ludwig August Frankl.
Pressburg.Gedruckt bei Franz Edlen v.Schmid
& J.J.Busch.Promenade Nr.749.[1848]

[2]p. 21.5x13.5cm.
Helfert (Wiener Parnass) 800.
Caption title; imprint on p.[2].
Dated at end: Am Bord des Schiffes "Johann" am
9. April 1848.

---

*pGB8
V6755R
4.8.48

Weitlof, Johann.
Ueber die Robotablösung.
[Wien,1848]

broadside. 43x26.5cm.
Dated: Wien, den 8. April 1848.

---

*GB8
V6755R
4.9.48

[Müller, Hubert, fl.1848]
Bittere Wahrheiten für die Juden und ihre
Vertheidiger. Eine Aufzählung actenmässig
constatirter Thatsachen zur Begründung und
Rechtfertigung der Juden=Vertreibungen in
neuerer Zeit, zugleich auch als Abfertigung für
alle gemietheten Juden=Vertheidiger.
[Wien]Zu haben bei dem Buchhändler Jakob
Bader,Stadt,Strobelgasse Nr.864.Gedruckt bei
Anton Benko.[1848]

folder(4p.) 27x21cm.
Caption title;   imprint on p.4.
Dated & signed   at end: Wien am 9. April
1848. Hubert   Müller.

---

*pGB8
V6755R
4.8.48

[Winkler, Jan, 1794-1874]
Sendschreiben an Herrn Doktor W. [i.e.
Wessely] Vertreter der Juden=Emancipation.
[Prague?,1848]

[2]p. 37x22.5cm.
Caption title; signed at end: J. Winkler.
A reply to an article by Wessely in "Bohemia",
6 April.

---

*GB8
V6755R
4.9.48

Reiselied für die Ligourianer am 9. April
1848.
[Wien]Verlag von J.Wenedikt.Gedruckt bei Franz
Edl.v.Schmid.[1848]

[2]p. 23x15cm.
Helfert (Wiener Parnass) 799.
Caption title; imprint on p.[2].

---

*GB8
V6755R
4.9.48

Buchheim, Carl Adolf, 1828-1900.
... Das sind die tapferen Magyaren! Von Adolf
Buchheim Student in Wien.
Pressburg,gedruckt bei Belnay's Erben.[1848]

broadside. 26.5x21cm.
Not recorded in Helfert (Wiener Parnass).
At head: Der hochherzigen ungarischen Nation
gewidmet!

---

*GB8
V6755R
4.9.48

Szentkirályi, Móricz, 1807-1882.
Erwiederungsrede des Herrn Moritz v.
Szentkirályi, Deputirten des Pester Comitats,
auf die durch Herrn Doctor Kálozdy im Namen der
Jugend der Wiener Universität am 9. April 1848
in der Unterhaussitzung vorgelesenen
Begrüssungsrede. Der Wiener Jugend gewidmet von
Anton Gyurits, Stenograph. (Aus dem Ungarischen
übersetzt.)
[Wien,1848]

[2]p. 21.5x13.5cm.
Caption title.

---

*GB8
V6755R
4.9.48

Daum, J   G
Aufruf an das freie und tapfere Volk der
Ungarn.
Gedruckt bei J.P.Sollinger in Wien.[1848]

broadside. 26.5x21cm.
Dated & signed: Wien, Sonntag den 9. April
1848. J. G. Daum, Nationalgarde und im Namen
vieler Brüder.

---

*GB8
V6755R
4.10.48

[Hilarius de Fonte acidulo, pseud.]
Allerneweste, heylsambe Predigt an das
Wienerische Volck. Von P. Abraham à S. Clara
[pseud.]. Oder: Wundersambe Historia, wie
solicher fürtrefflicher Ertz=Prediger, nach
100jähriger Rast sein Grab=Truhel in Maria=
Brunn vonwegen des grossmächtigen Getös, so die
guete Wien=Stadt in denen Merz=Tägen durch und
durch auffrebelliret, verlassen und abermalen
zu Rutz und Fromm aller gueten Geisteskinder,
wie auch zum Schröck= und Verderbnuss aller
murrischen Galgen=   Vögel sein salbungsreichen
Mund aufgethan.

                    (See next card)

*GB8
V6755R
4.10.48

[Hilarius de Fonte acidulo, pseud.]
Allerneweste ... [1848]   (Card 2)
Wien,Gedruckt bey Michael Lellius,Buchdruckern
am untern Werd.Verlegts alle Welt.[1848] Preiss:
5 gute Kreutzer.

    folder([4]p.) 26.5x21.5cm.
    Caption title; imprint on p.[4].
    Dated & signed at end: So geschrieben am 10.
Aprilis im Jahre des Heyls im ein tausend
achthundert vierzigsten und achten durch
Hilarium de Fonte   acidulo ...

---

*pGB8
V6755R
4.10.48

Vienna. Magistrat.
    Aufforderung. Am 14. d. M. Abends wird die
Aufnahme der Wähler behufs der bald
stattfindenden Wahl der Gemeinde=Ausschüsse für
die Stadt Wien geschlossen ...
    [Wien,1848]

    broadside. 44.5x57cm.

---

*GB8
V6755R
4.10.48

Das letzte Stündlein der Liguorianer!
[Wien,1848]
    folder([4]p.) 27.5x21.5cm.
    Woodcut illus. on t.-p.

---

*pGB8
V6755R
4.10.48

Vienna. Nationalgarde.
    ... An das Bezirks=Commando der Leopoldstadt!
In der Anlage theile ich dem Bezirks=Commando
in Bezug auf die unaufschiebbare Bewaffnung
und Uniformirung der National=Garde dasjenige
Resultat mit ...
    [Wien,1848]

    broadside. 42.5x26.5cm.
    Reschauer-Smets II.72.
    At head: Wien, den 10. April 1848.
    Signed: Hoyos, Feldmarschall=Lieutenant, Ober=
Commandant der   Nationalgarde.
    (See next card)

---

*GB8
V6755R
4.10.48

Das neue Orchester genannt die Katzenmusi.
[Wien]Gedruckt bei Josef Ludwig,Florianigasse
Nr.52.[1848]
    folder(4p.) 21x12.5cm.
    In the Viennese dialect.

---

*pGB8
V6755R
4.10.48

Vienna. Nationalgarde.   ... An das ... [1848]
                      (Card 2)
    Includes "Beschreibung der Montur und
Bewaffnung der National=Garde".
    Accompanied by a slightly abbreviated copy
of the text reproduced from manuscript.

---

*GB8
V6755R
4.10.48

[Schick, Leopold]
    ... Brüder Arbeiter! Habt acht! Nr. 2.
[Wien](Zu haben in der Verlagshandlung des
Franz Edlen v. Schmidt,Seitenstättengasse Nr.
495.)[1848]

    folder([4]p.) 23x16.5cm.
    Caption title, with imprint above; at head of
imprint: Das Blatt kostet einen Kreuzer Conv.
Mze.
    Signed at end: Leopold Schick, Nationalgardist.
    A continuation of his earlier An meine Brüder
Arbeiter!

---

*pGB8
V6755R
4.10.48

Vienna. Nationalgarde.
    Entwurf zu einer Geschäftsordnung für das
politische Central=Comite der gesammten Wiener
National=Garde.
    [Wien,1848]

    broadside. 46.5x29.5cm.
    Signed: Der zur Entwerfung dieser
Geschäftsordnung gewählte Ausschuss.—
Freiherr v. Dercsényi. Dr. Rosenfeld. Dr. Wilhelm
Taussig [& 3 others].

---

*pGB8
V6755R
4.10.48

Ullmayer, Franz.
    Das Kartenspiel, Ein Dreier in der k. k.
Haupt= und Residenzstadt Wien. Philosophische
Betrachtungen eines National=Gardisten über
die Vergangenheit, Gegenwart und Zukunft. Von
Franz Ullmayer.
    [Wien]Gedruckt bei M.Lell.[1848]

    broadside. 36.5x22cm.

---

*pGB8
V6755R
4.10.48

Vienna. Nationalgarde.
    Kundmachung vom 10. April 1848. Mit wahrem
Vergnügen übergebe ich hier der Oeffentlichkeit
die so eben von Sr. Excellenz dem Minister des
Innern, Freiherrn von Pillersdorff, erhaltenen
Grundzüge der Organisation der Nationalgarden
...
    [Wien,1848]

    2p. 44.5x28.5cm.
    Reschauer-Smets II.71.
    (See next card)

*pGB8
V6755R
4.10.48

Vienna. Nationalgarde.   Kundmachung ... [1848]
(Card 2)
Caption title; signed on p.2: Hoyos,
Feldmarschall-Lieutenant und Obercommandant
der Nationalgarde.
Giving the text of Pillersdorf's proclamation
of 8 April.

---

*pGB8
V6755R
4.10.48

Vienna. Nationalgarde.
Unter dem 6. dieses Monates hat es einem
gewissen Verfasser "des Rathschlages": "Wie
muss man Nationalgarden exerciren" beliebt, das
Publikum in einem Aufrufe zur Wahl eines neuen
Nationalgarden=Obercommandanten aufzufordern ...
[Wien,1848]

broadside. 44.5x57cm.
Reschauer-Smets II.71.
Dated & signed: Wien den 10. April 1848. Hoyos,
F. M. L. Obercommandant der Nationalgarden.
Refers to the anonymous "Aufruf zur Wahl
des Ober-Com-   mandanten der National-
garde".

---

*GB8
V6755R
4.10.48

400,000 Russen! oder die furchtbare Gefahr
Oesterreichs und unser einziges Rettungsmittel.
Wien.1848.Druck von J.N.Fridrich,Josephstadt
Nr.58.

folder([4]p.) 26x20.5cm.
Dated in contemporary ms.: 10. April 848.

---

*pGB8
V6755R
4.11.48

Austria. Sovereigns, etc., 1835-1848
(Ferdinand I)
Wir Ferdinand der Erste, von Gottes Gnaden
Kaiser von Oesterreich ... Ueber den Antrag
Unserer Nieder=Oesterreichischen Stände und nach
Anhörung Unseres Ministerraths haben Wir, in
der Absicht Unseren getreuen Unterthanen jede
mit dem Schutze der Eigenthums=Rechte vereinbare
Erleichterung zu gewähren, beschlossen ...
[Wien,1848]

folder([2]p.) 45x28.5cm.
(See next card)

---

*pGB8
V6755R
4.11.48

Austria. Sovereigns, etc., 1835-1848
(Ferdinand I)   Wir Ferdinand der Erste
... [1848]   (Card 2)
Caption title.
"Gegeben in Unserer kaiserlichen Haupt= und
Residenzstadt Wien, den eilften April, im
eintausend achthundert acht und vierzigsten ..."

---

*pGB8
V6755R
4.11.48

Dessauer, Joseph, 1798-1876.
Des Oesterreichers Vaterland. Von Joseph
Dessauer, Garde.
[Wien,1848]

broadside. 34x26cm.
Helfert (Wiener Parnass) 811.

---

*GB8
V6755R
4.11.48

Das Lebewohl der Freiwilligen an die Wiener,
ihre Aeltern und Geliebten.
[Wien]Gedruckt bei M.Lell.[1848]

broadside. 23x18.5cm.

---

*GB8
V6755R
4.11.48

Riedl, X
An die Handelslegion zur Einweihung der
Fahne.
[Wien,1848]

broadside. 23x15cm.
Helfert (Wiener Parnasse) 814.

---

*pGB8
V6755R
4.11.48

Vienna. Nationalgarde.
Cameraden! Das schöne Princip brüderlicher
Gleichheit und Einheit, ein Princip, welches
die Nationalgarde vor Allem unter sich aufrecht
erhalten sollte ...
[Wien,1848]

[2]p. 39.5x25cm.
Caption title; dated & signed at end: Wien, den
11. April 1848. Im Namen eines Nationalgarden=
Comité. Heinrich Graf von Wilczek,
Oberlieutenant der   Garde. Julius von Zerboni
di Sposetti,   ) Unterofficier der Garde.
Joseph Frank,   Garde.

---

*pGB8
V6755R
4.12.48

Austria, Lower. Landstländischer Ausschuss.
Einberufung einer Provinzial=Stände=
Versammlung in Oesterreich unter der Enns.
[Wien,1848]

[2]p. 44.5x28.5cm.
Caption title; dated & signed at end: Wien am
12. April 1848. Von dem provisorischen
niederösterreichisch-ständischen Ausschusse.

[Kaukasus, pseud.]
Schaudervolles aus Böhmen!! Eigenmächtiges
Volksstandrecht! Grässliche Hinrichtung einer
von der Nationalgarde gefangen genommenen
Proletarier=Bande mit ihrem Hauptmanne ohne
Galgen und Scharfrichter.
[Wien,1848]

*GB8
V6755R
4.12.48

folder([4]p.) 26.5x21cm.
Dated in contemporary ms.: 12. April.
Signed at end: Kaukasus.

[Janisch, Anton]
Vom Himmel gefallener Brief der Mariazeller
Mutter Gottes an die Oesterreicher und besonders
an die Wiener.
Wien,1848.Gedruckt in der Josephstadt,
Langegasse Nr.48.

*GB8
V6755R
4.13.48

folder([4]p.) 24x19cm.
Dated & signed at end: Wien, am 13. April 1848.
aufgefangen von Anton Janisch.
Discouraging pilgrimages to Mariazell.

Krzivanek, Joseph.
Einige Worte an die Herren Vorstadt=
Kaufleute.
[Wien]Gedruckt bei Edl.v.Schmidbauer und
Holzwarth.[1848]

*pGB8
V6755R
4.12.48

broadside. 42x25.5cm.
Dated: Wien, den 12. April 1848.
Protesting the proposed closing of shops on
Sunday.

Johann, archduke of Austria, 1782-1859.
Tyroler und Vorarlberger! Aus der Residenzstadt
Wien, wo die Kunde der Euerem Lande drohenden
Gefahr gekommen ist, sendet mich der Kaiser in
Euere Mitte ...
[Wien? 1848]

*pGB8
V6755R
4.13.48

broadside. 45x57cm.
Dated & signed: Innsbruck am 13. April 1848.
Erzherzog Johann.

Adresse der Polen aus Galizien und dem
Krakauer Kreise an Seine k. k. apostolische
Majestät Ferdinand I.
[Wien]Buchdruckerei St.Ulrich Nr.2.[1848]

*pGB8
V6755R
4.13.48

folder([3]p.) 39x24cm.
Caption title; imprint on p.[3].

Kaiser, Friedrich, 1814-1874.
Prolog zur Feier der Eröffnung des Theaters
an der Wien als National-Theater am 13. April
1848, gedichtet und gesprochen von Friedrich
Kaiser.
[Wien,1848]

*GB8
V6755R
4.13.48

folder(4p.) 22.5x14.5cm.
Helfert (Wiener Parnass) 820.
Caption title.

... Adresse der Polen aus Galizien und dem
Krakauer Kreise an Seine k. k. apostolische
Majestät Ferdinand I. Uebersetzt aus dem
Polnischen.
[Wien,1848]

*pGB8
V6755R
4.13.48

[2]p. 39x28.5cm.
Caption title; at head: Besondere Beilage zur
Wiener Zeitung Nr. 104 vom 13. April 1848.

[Naske, Adolph Carl, 1814-1864]
Die Wucher-Pest in Wien. Zeitgemässe
Darstellung des in Wien seit einigen Jahren
gleich einer Pestseuche grassirenden Wucher=
Unfuges und der hieraus entspringenden, immer
allgemeiner werdenden Verarmung unserer
Mitbürger.
[Wien]Zu haben bei dem Buchhändler Jakob Bader,
Stadt,Strobelgasse.Gedruckt bei Anton Benko.
[1848]

*GB8
V6755R
4.13.48

folder(4p.) 24x19.5cm.
(See next card)

Comfort, Richard, fl.1848.
Zu spät! Ein ernstes Wort zu seiner Zeit.
Von Richard Comfort, M. Dr.
Bei Schaumburg & Comp.in Wien.[1848]

*GB8
V6755R
4.13.48

folder([4]p.) 22.5x14.5cm.
Caption title; imprint on p.[4].
Dated at end: Wien, den 13. April 1848.

[Naske, Adolph Carl, 1814-1864]   Die Wucher-
Pest ... [1848]   (Card 2)

*GB8
V6755R
4.13.48

Caption title; imprint on p.4.
Dated & signed at end: Wien am 13. April
1848. Adolph Carl Naske.

*pGB8
V6755R
4.13.48

Vienna. Nationalgarde.
Aufforderung und Bitte zur vorläufigen
Einstellung der Debatten und Petitionen.Über
die Uniformirungs= und Bewaffnungs=Frage der
National=Garde.
.[Wien](Gedruckt bei den Edlen v.Ghelen'schen
Erben.)[1848]

broadside. 43x28cm.
Dated & signed: Wien, den 13. April 1848. Die
vierte Compagnie des Wimmer Viertels.

*pGB8
V6755R
4.14.48

Guter Rath wegen Zins! für die Einwohner
und Geschäfts-Inhaber Wiens!!!
[Wien]Gedruckt bei Edl.v.Schmidbauer und
Holzwarth.[1848]

broadside. 42x25.5cm.
Signed: Eine Stimme im Namen Vieler aus dem
Handels=Gremium.

*pGB8
V6755R
4.13.48

Vienna. Nationalgarde.
Vorschlag zur Ergänzung der am 10. April 1848
herausgegebenen Grundzüge der Organisation der
Nationalgarde.
[Wien](Gedruckt bei den Edlen v.Ghelen'schen
Erben.)[1848]

broadside. 43x27cm.
Dated & signed: Wien den 13. April 1848. L.
Breda, Bezirks=Chef, im eigenen und im Namen
der Officiere des VI. Bezirks.

*pGB8
V6755R
4.14.48

Vienna. Magistrat.
Bescheid des lbbl. Magistrates der k. k. Haupt=
und Residenzstadt Wien an das Mittel der
bürgerl. und befugten Weber.
[Wien,1848]

[2]p. 41x25cm.
Caption title; dated at end: Wien, den 14.
April 1848.

*pGB8
V6755R
4.13.48

Vienna. Stubenviertel (Polizeibezirk)
Verwaltungsrat.
An die National=Garden. Es ist zur Kenntniss
des Verwaltungsrathes im Bezirke Stubenviertel
gekommen, dass bei der Abstimmung über die zu
wählende Kopfbedeckung der Nationalgarde die
Stimmen nach Bezirken, und nicht nach Compagnien
gezählt worden seien ...
[Wien,1848]

broadside. 47x30cm.
Signed: Vom Bezirksverwaltungsrathe des
Stubenviertel.

*pGB8
V6755R
4.15.48

An die Nationalgarde. Kameraden! Nach dem Siege
des Volkes über die, bloss dem äusseren Scheine
nach geachteten Autoritäten, nach dem Siege der
Intelligenz über diese unintelligenten
Autoritäten ...
[Wien]Druck von U.Klopf sen.und Alex.Eurich,
Wollzeile Nr.782.[1848]

broadside. 46x29.5cm.
Signed: Ein Nationalgarde.

*pGB8
V6755R
4.13.48

Wien-Gloggnitzer Eisenbahn A.G.
Die Direction der k. k. priv. Wien=
Gloggnitzer Eisenbahn Actien=Gesellschaft an die
Arbeiter ihrer landesbefugten Maschinenfabrik.
[Wien,1848]

broadside. 44.5x29cm.
Dated: Wien den 13. April 1848.

*pGB8
V6755R
4.15.48

Aufruf an die Arbeiter.
[Wien,1848]

broadside. 36.5x22.5cm.
Dated: Wien am 14. April 1848.

*pGB8
V6755R
4.14.48

Aufruf an die ungarischen Bewohner Wiens.
[Wien,1848]

broadside. 40x25cm.
"Gegeben zu Pressburg am 14. April 1848, als am
4. Tage der neuen Wiedergeburt Ungarns."
Hungarian & German text in parallel columns.

*GB8
V6755R
4.15.48

Austria. Ministerium des Innern.
Kundmachung, betreffend die Verfassungs=
Urkunde Oesterreichs. Die Konstitutions=
Urkunde ist Sr. Majestät mit folgendem
alluntertthänigsten Vortrage des Ministers des
Innern zur Genehmigung vorgelegt worden:
.[Wien]Gedruckt bei Carl Gerold.[1848]

folder([4]p.) 26x19.5cm.
Caption title; imprint on p.[4].
Dated: Wien, den 15. April 1848.
At end: Verbreitet durch den kaufmännischen
Verein.

Austria. Ministerium des Innern.
Kundmachung. Ein heute erschienener Aufruf,
dessen Verfasser nicht genannt ist, aber
redlichen Willen und richtige Erkenntniss
verräth, enthält die beachtenswerthen Worte ...
[Wien,1848]

*pGB8
V6755R
4.15.48

broadside. 44.5x57cm.
Dated & signed: Wien am 15. April 1848. Der
Minister des Innern.

Bewohner Wien's! Es ist wohl Niemand unter uns,
der nicht über die grossen Beweise von Freund-
schaft, Anhänglichkeit und Brüderlichkeit
welche die hochherzigen Ungarn uns in der
letzten ereignissreichen Zeit gegeben haben,
begeistert wäre ...
[Wien,1848]

*pGB8
V6755R
4.15.48

broadside. 45x58.5cm.
Signed: Mehrere Wiener.
Printed on yellow paper.

Bidschof, Franz Xavier.
Die deutsche Bundesfahne und das Osterlamm.
Zwiegespräch der Bauer Hans=Jörgel und Michael.
Von F. X. Bidschof.
[Wien]Gedruckt bei Josef Ludwig,Josefstadt
Florianigasse Nr.52.[1848]

*pGB8
V6755R
4.15.48

broadside. 42x24.5cm.
In the Viennese dialect.

Buchheim, Carl Adolf, 1828-1900.
Abschied an die Tiroler Studenten! Von Adolph
Buchheim.
[Wien]Gedruckt bei M.Lell.[1848]

*GB8
V6755R
4.15.48

broadside. 23.5x15cm.
Helfert (Wiener Parnass) 837.

Castelli, Ignaz Franz, 1781-1862.
Wie weit geht denn die neue Freiheit, die wir
erst kriegt haben? Zweite Mittheilung für meine
lieben österreichischen Landsleute ausser Wien.
Von J. F. Castelli.
[Wien]Verlag und Eigenthum von Tendler et
Comp. Gedruckt bei F.Ullrich.[1848]

*pGB8
V6755R
4.15.48

[2]p. 36.5x22.5cm.
Caption title; imprint on p.[2].

Grundzüge der oesterreichischen Constitution
und die Bestimmungen zur Bildung eines Gemeinde=
Ausschusses für die Stadt Wien.
[Wien,1848]

*GB8
V6755R
4.15.48

folder([4]p.) 26x21cm.
Imprint on p.[4]: Gedruckt und zu haben bei L.
Grund, Hundsthurm, Schlossgebäude Nr. 1. Verlag
am Stephansplatze im Zwettelhofe.

Grundzüge der österreichischen Konstitution.
[Wien,1848]

*GB8
V6755R
4.15.48

folder([4]p.) 20x12.5cm.
Caption title.
'Separatabdruck aus der Zeitung "die neue
Zeit," redigirt von Dr. Siegf. Becher und
Seidlitz.'
"Auszug aus den Bestimmungen zur Bildung eines
Gemeinde=Ausschusses für die Stadt Wien":
p.[3-4].

Manifest des Kaisers von Russland an die Völker
von Oesterreich und Deutschland.
[Wien]Gedruckt bei Stöckholzer v.Hirschfeld.—
Zu haben in der Jägerzeil Nr.518 bei Ignaz
Singer.[1848]

*pGB8
V6755R
4.15.48

broadside. 43.5x27cm.
Signed: Nikolaus I. konstitutioneller
Selbstherrscher.
A satire.

Manifeste österreichischer Volkstribunen.
Wie steht unsere Nationalbank?
[Wien]Gedruckt bei Edl.v.Schmidbauer und
Holzwarth.[1848]

*GB8
V6755R
4.15.48

folder(4p.) 22.5x14cm.
Caption title; imprint on p.4.

Markbreiter, Moritz.
Geistliche und Juden. Ein Wort zu seiner Zeit.
Von Moritz Markbreiter.
[Wien]1848.

*GB8
V6755R
4.15.48

8p. 18.5x11.5cm.

Mehramt, Georg.
*GB8   Interessante Geständnisse eines sterbenden
V6755R Liguorianers auf der Flucht von Wien. Von
4.15.48 Georg Mehramt.
      Wien,1848.Gedruckt in der Josephstadt,
Langegasse Nr.58.[1848]

        folder([4]p.) 24x19.5cm.
        Illustrated t.-p.

Starnbacher, Wilhelm.
*pGB8 Aufruf. Bewohner Wiens! In den ruhmwürdigen
V6755R Tagen des 13. und 14. März sind aus dem ersten
4.15.48 Bürger=Regiment sechs hiesige Bürger verwundet
worden ...
      [Wien,1848]

        broadside. 26x34cm.
        Soliciting contributions for the wounded.

      National-Garde! Es wird Montags den 17. April
*pGB8 um 9 Uhr früh, eine Versammlung sämmtlicher
V6755R Kompagnien, im Sperl=Saale stattfinden ...
4.15.48 [Wien,1848]

        broadside. 35.5x21cm.
        Signed: Karl Ulbricht. Karl Neustädel. Josef
Uhl [& 20 andere].

Vienna. Nationalgarde.
*pGB8 Bekanntmachung für die Nationalgarde.
V6755R Diejenigen Herren Garden, welche die, an Se.
4.15.48 Excellenz den Herrn Minister des Innern zu
überreichende, bei sämmtlichen Herren Compagnie=
Commandanten aufliegende Adresse um Abänderung
der Uniformirungs=Vorschrift bezüglich der
Port-épées und bordirten Kragen zu unterzeichnen
gesonnen sind ...
      [Wien,1848]

                      (See next card)

      Das Neueste welches zu wissen nothwendig ist.
*GB8   [Wien]Gedruckt bei den Edlen von Ghelen'schen
V6755R Erben.[1848]
4.15.48

        folder(4p.) 28x22.5cm.
        Caption title; imprint on p.4; signed at end:
Ein Mann aus dem Volke.

Vienna. Nationalgarde.   Bekanntmachung ...
*pGB8 [1848]   (Card 2)
V6755R
4.15.48 broadside. 43x26.5cm.
        Signed: Jm Namen eines National-Garden-Comité:
Heinrich Graf von Wilczek ... Julius v.
Zerboni di Sposetti ... Joseph Frank ...

      Politisches Gespräch der Frau Rösl,
*GB8   Flugschriften=Verkäuferin, mit ihrer
V6755R Nachbarin der Frau Kathl.
4.15.48 Wien,1848.Gedruckt in der Josephstadt,
Langegasse Nr.58.

        folder([4]p.) 24x19cm.
        In the Viennese dialect.

Vienna. Nationalgarde.
*pGB8 Entwurf zu einer Geschäftsordnung für den
V6755R Verwaltungsrath der gesammten Wiener
4.15.48 Nationalgarde.
      [Wien,1848]

        folder(4p.) 44.5x28.5cm.
        Caption title.

Simić von Hohenblum, Joseph.
*pGB8 Vorschlag im Interesse aller jenen Gemeinden,
V6755R in deren Bezirk nach den Bestimmungen der
4.15.48 Kundmachung vom 10. April 1848 eine National=
Garde errichtet werden soll, zur gleichmässigen
Vertheilung der Organisirungs=Kosten der
National=Garde.
      [Wien,1848]

        broadside. 46x30.5cm.

      [Begins:] Die in Wien befindliche polnische
*pGB8 Deputation, anerkannt von allen Ständen in allen
V6755R Kreisen des Landes, anerkannt und huldreichst
4.16.48 aufgenommen von Seiner Majestät selbst,
erachtet für nöthig und dem allgemeinen Besten
des Landes angemessen, ihre Thätigkeit zu
theilen ...
      [Wien]Druck von A.Pichlers Witwe.[1848]
        broadside. 39x25cm.
        Dated: Gegeben in Wien, am 16. April 1848.

*GB8
V6755R
4.16.48

[Neumann, Josef, 1815-1878]
Anruf an einen sogenannten Herrn Dr. Schütte.
[Wien,1848]
folder(3p.) 26.5x22cm.
Caption title; dated & signed at end: Wien,
16. April 1848. Prof. D. Jos. Neumann.

*pGB8
V6755R
4.17.48

Vienna. Magistrat.
[Begins:] Die Nationalgarde und die
sämmtlichen derselben einverleibten Corps
richteten gestern an der Magistrat und Bürger=
Ausschuss der Stadt Wien, nachstehende mit
zahlreichen Unterschriften bedeckte Adresse: ...
[Wien,1848]
broadside. 45x57cm.
Signed & dated: Der Magistrat und
provisorische Bürger=Ausschuss der Stadt Wien
am 17. April 1848.

*pGB8
V6755R
4.16.48

Zang, August, 1807-1888.
Bescheidene Fragen.
[Wien,1848]
broadside. 43.5x53.5cm.
Dated: Wien, am 16. April 1848.

*pGB8
V6755R
4.17.48

Vienna. Universität.
Mitbürger! Am heutigen Tage im Universitäts=
Consistorial=Saale versammelte Abgeordnete der
Universität und der Nationalgarde haben mit
tiefer Entrüstung Kenntniss genommen von einem
Maueranschlage, welcher für heute Nachmittags
eine Volksversammlung im Odeon zu dem
ausgesprochenen Zwecke anberaumt, in dem
bisherigen Systeme der Zinsentrichtung eine
totale Aenderung einzuführen ...
[Wien,1848]
broadside. 45x57cm.
Reschauer-Smets II.89.

*pGB8
V6755R
4.17.48

An die Frauen in Wien. Nicht allein dem in
der Wiener=Zeitung vom 15. April an uns
ergangenen Aufrufe, sondern noch mehr der
Stimme des Herzens folgend ...
[Wien,1848]
[2]p. 43x28cm.
Caption title; dated: Wien, den 17. April
1848.
Long list of signatures of women pledging to
buy no goods of foreign make.

*pGB8
V6755R
4.18.48

An sämmtliche zinszahlende Partheien in der
Stadt und den Vorstädten Wiens! Formular einer
Erklärung der Partheien an ihre Hausherren
zum Georgytag, betreffend die Aufhebung der Zins=
Vorhineinzahlung und Herabsetzung desselben.
[Wien]Gedruckt bei Ant. Benko.[1848]
broadside. 41.5x26cm.
Reschauer-Smets II.88.
Asking for a reduction in rents and abolition
of the customary payment in advance.
Dated in contemporary ms.: 18. April 848.

*pGB8
V6755R
4.17.48

Gesellschaft der Volksfreunde, Vienna.
Manifest der Gesellschaft der Volksfreunde.
[Wien,1848]
broadside. 43x54cm.
Dated: Wien den 17. April 1848.

*pGB8
V6755R
4.18.48

[Arthur, pseud.]
Auf Georgi wird kein Zinns gezahlt. Frage!
Warum?-
[Wien]Gedruckt bei Josef Ludwig.[1848]
[2]p. 36x22.5cm.
Caption title; imprint on p.[2]; signed:
Arthur.

*GB8
V6755R
4.17.48

Hungary. Országgyülés.
Die Exmission der ungarischen Landtagsjugend
an den wackern Minister von Pillersdorf in Wien.
[Wien]Gedruckt bei Edl.v.Schmidbauer und
Holzwarth.[1848]
[2]p. 27x21.5cm.
Caption title; imprint on p.[2].
"Gesprochen Samstag den 15. April 1848 von
M. Herczegy."
Includes "Die feierliche Uebergabe der ersten
Fahne der ungarischen Nationalgarde in Wien",
dated "Gesprochen Montag den 17. April 1848
von M. Herczegy".

*pGB8
V6755R
4.18.48

Aufruf an sämmtliche Hauseigenthümer Wiens.
[Wien]Druck von U.Klopf sen.und Alex.Eurich,
Wollzeile Nr.782.[1848]
broadside. 42.5x26cm.
Signed: Mehrere Kaufleute und Bürger Wiens.
Proposing that rents be reduced by one quarter.

*pGB8
V6755R
4.18.48

Austria. Ministerium des Innern.
    Kundmachung. Da der Tag des allerhöchsten
Geburtsfestes Seiner Majestät unseres
allergnädigsten Kaisers heuer in die
Charwoche fällt ...
    [Wien,1848]
      broadside. 44.5x57cm.
      Dated & signed: Wien am 18. April 1848. Der
Minister des Inneren.
      Postponing the public celebration until the
25th of April.

---

*GB8
V6755R
4.18.48

Sprungmehr, Georg.
    Sturmglocke für alle Hausmeister in Wien,
als anerkannte Zinsvertheuerer und
privilegirte Blutegeln für die Parteien. Von
Georg Sprungmehr.
    [Wien]Gedruckt in der Josephstadt Langegasse
Nr.58.[1848]
      folder([4]p.) 26.5x20.5cm.
      Caption title; imprint on p.[4].

---

*GB8
V6755R
4.18.48

[Engländer, Leopold]
    Offener Brief an jene Hausherren, welche
unerschwingliche Zinsen verlangen ...
    [Wien]Gedruckt bei Franz Edlen von Schmid.
[1848]
      8p. 23.5x15cm.
      Signed at end: Leopold Engländer, bürgl.
Gastgeber, Alservorstadt, Nr, 275.

---

*pGB8
V6755R
4.18.48

Vienna. Magistrat.
    ... Kundmachung. Von dem Magistrate der k. k.
Haupt= und Residenzstadt wird zur Hintanhaltung
der bei dem Milchhandel theils durch den
unversteuerten Betrieb desselben ...
    [Wien,1848]
      broadside. 34x20.5cm.
      Dated: Wien, am 18. April 1848.
      At head: G. Z. 18665.

---

*GB8
V6755R
4.18.48

Mekhitarists. Vienna.
    An die Bürger und Bewohner Wiens! Von der
Mechitharisten=Congregation.
    [Wien,1848]
      folder([4]p.) 24.5x19.5cm.
      Caption title; dated & signed at end: Wien den
18. April 1848. Die Mechitharisten-Congregation.

---

*pGB8
V6755R
4.18.48

Vienna. Magistrat.
    ... Von dem Magistrate der k. k. Haupt= und
Residenzstadt Wien. In Folge der von den
Seidenzeugmachergesellen überreichten
Vorstellung um Abänderung des am 28. v. M. mit
den Herren Seidenzeugfabrikanten getroffenen
Übereinkommen, ist von beiden Theilen
einverständlich unter Genehmigung des Magistrates
Folgendes festgesetzt worden: ...
    [Wien,1848]
    [2]p. 39x25cm.
      Caption title; at head: G. Z. 20,281.
      Dated: Wien, am 18. April 1848.

---

*pGB8
V6755R
4.18.48

Mith, C
    Meine Brüder! Euer Zins ist ja schon gezahlt!
Erschreckt nicht von dem Georgi Tage, am welchem
Ihr Euren schwer verdienten Groschen nach dem
alten System zur Wucherbank Eurer Hausherren
habet tragen müssen ...
    [Wien,1848]
      broadside. 43x27cm.

---

*pGB8
V6755R
4.18.48

Vienna (Archdiocese) Clergy.
    An die Bürger, an die akademische Legion, das
technische Corps, und an alle Garden Wien's!
    [Wien]Druck von A.Pichler's Wittwe.[1848]
      broadside. 44.5x57cm.
      Signed & dated: Jm Namen der versammelten
Wiener=Geistlichkeit: Wien, am 18. April 1848.
Dr. Salzbacher, Domkustos. Dr. Brunner. Engel
[& 11 others].

---

*GB8
V6755R
4.18.48

Niederösterreichischer Gewerbe-Verein.
    An die Arbeiter! Brave Mitbürger und Freunde!
Ihr habt den betrüglichen Verlockungen
nichtswürdiger Aufwiegler, welche in Schafspelze
gehüllt, ihren schlechten Absichten bei Euch
Eingang verschaffen wollten, kein Gehör gegeben
    ...
    [Wien]Gedruckt bei Carl Gerold.[1848]
      broadside. 25.5x19.5cm.
      Dated: Wien, am 18. April 1848.

---

*GB8
V6755R
4.19.48

[Arthur, pseud.]
    Bei Gelegenheit des hohen und erfreulichen
Geburtsfestes Ihro Majestät Ferdinand I. Der
Rosenkranz in acht Vaterunser oder das Kaiser=
Gebet. Mit pflichtschuldiger Hochachtung und
gebührender Ehrfurcht unserm aller gnädigsten
Herrn und Kaiser gewidmet.
    [Wien]Gedruckt bei Josef Ludwig Josefstadt
Florianigasse Nr.52.[1848]
      folder(4p.) 26x21cm.
      Helfert (Wiener Parnass) 863.
      Signed at end: Arthur.

Engländer, Hermann.
*GB8 Der 55ste Geburtstag Kaiser Ferdinand I.
V6755R [Wien]Druck v.U.Klopf sen.u.A.Eurich,
4.19.48 Wollzeile Nr.782.[1848]

broadside. 26x21cm.
Helfert (Wiener Parnass) 861.

[Engländer, Hermann]
*GB8 Neues Volkslied für den Geburtstag des
V6755R glorreichen Kaisers am 19. April. Nach der
4.19.48 bestenhenden Melodie.
Wien.Druck von U.Klopf sen.und A.Eurich,
Wollzeile 782.[1848]

folder([4]p.) 21x14cm.
Helfert (Wiener Parnass) 865.
Signed at end: Hermann Engländer.
Without the music.

Herczeghy, Mór, 1815-1884.
*GB8 Dem Kaiser und König Ferdinand am 19. April
V6755R 1848, von Moritz Herczegy.
4.19.48 [Wien]Gedruckt bei Edl.v.Schmidbauer und
Holzwarth.[1848]

broadside. 25.5x16.5cm.
Helfert (Wiener Parnass) 866.

Mayer, Joseph, fl.1848.
*pGB8 Worte des Dankes zur allerhöchsten
V6755R Geburtsfeier Seiner Majestät unserem
4.19.48 constitutionellen grossen Kaiser Ferdinand
dem Ersten.
[Wien,1848]

broadside. 43.5x29cm.
Helfert (Wiener Parnass) 873.
Text printed in 24 lines, with the words
"constitutionellen grossen Kaiser Ferdinand
dem Ersten" (transcribed in title above) forming the
first & last letters of the words
beginning and end- ing each line.

Meisl, Karl, 1775-1853.
*GB8 Zur allerhöchsten Geburtstagsfeier Seiner
V6755R Majestät, unsers allergnädigsten Kaisers und
4.19.48 Herrn, Ferdinand, des I. constitutionellen
Kaisers von Oesterreich, Königs von Ungarn und
Böhmen etc. etc. den 19. April 1848. Von Carl
Meisl ...
[Wien]Gedruckt bei Josef Ludwig,Josefstadt
Florianigasse Nr.52.[1848]
folder([4]p.) 27x21cm.
Helfert (Wiener Parnass) 867.

Much, Adolf, b.1818.
*GB8 Rede des S. Stephans-Thurms an die Wiener.
V6755R Jm Jahre des wahren Heiles 1848. Von A. Much.
4.19.48 [Wien]Verlag von A.Wenedikt und gedruckt bei
Franz Edlem von Schmid.[1848]

folder(4p.) 23x15cm.
Caption title; imprint on p.4.
Dated in contemporary ms.: 19. April 848.

Rödl, Gottfried.
*GB8 Die deutschen Farben. (Bei Gelegenheit der
V6755R Geburtsfeier unsers konstitutionellen Kaisers.)
4.19.48 [Wien,1848]

broadside. 22.5x14.5cm.
Helfert (Wiener Parnass) 870.

Vienna. Nationalgarde. Akademische Legion.
*pGB8 Mitbürger! Ein wichtiges Faktum ist geschehen
V6755R ...
4.19.48 Druck von U.Klopf sen.und A.Eurich in Wien.
[1848]

broadside. 42.5x25.5cm.
Reschauer-Smets II.82.
Dated & signed: Wien den 19. April 1848. Die
gesammte akademische Legion.
Protesting the arrest and expulsion of Anton
Schütte.

An den Herrn Jnhaber des Privilegiums auf
Ankündigungs=Tafeln. Als Antwort auf die
*pGB8 Flugschrift, betitelt: Sturmglocke für alle
V6755R Hausmeister in Wien, als anerkannte Zins-
4.20.48 vertheuerer und priviligirte Blutegel für
die Partheien.
[Wien,1848]

broadside. 44.5x29cm.
Signed: Jm Namen aller Hausmeister Wiens. M.
Lestanov, J. Albert, Georg Müller.

Austria, Lower. Central-Comité für die Wahlen
zur constituirenden deutschen National-
*pGB8 Versammlung.
V6755R Aufruf zur Wahl der Abgeordneten zur deutschen
4.20.48 National-Versammlung in Frankfurt am Main.
[Wien,1848]

broadside. 45x57cm.
Dated: Wien am 20. April 1848.
In this folio sheet edition, the first line of
text ends: Ihre

*GB8
V6755R
4.20.48

Austria, Lower. Central-Comité für die Wahlen
zur constituirenden deutschen National-
Versammlung.
Aufruf zur Wahl der Abgeordneten zur
deutschen National=Versammlung in Frankfurt am
Main.
[Wien,1848]

broadside. 28.5x22cm.
Dated: Wien am 20. April 1848.
In this quarto sheet edition, the first line
of text ends: National=

---

*pGB8
V6755R
4.20.48

Bewohner Wiens. Man reizt euch von mancher
Seite auf, einen Theil des Miethzinses nicht
zu zahlen ...
[Wien,1848]

broadside. 43x26cm.
Dated: Wien, den 20. April 1848.

---

*pGB8
V6755R
4.20.48

Bidschof, Franz Xavier.
Zinns, Rock, Hemd, oder: die guten und
schlechten Hausherrn. Zweigespräch zwischen
den Bauer Hans=Jörgel und einen National-
gardisten. Von Franz X. Bidschof.
[Wien]Gedruckt bei Josef Ludwig,Josefstadt
Florianigasse Nr.52.[1848]

[2]p. 36x22cm.
Caption title; imprint on p.[2].

---

*pGB8
V6755R
4.20.48

[Czapka von Winstetten, Ignaz, 1792-1881]
Oeffentliche Erklärung.
[Wien,1848]

folder([4]p.) 42x26cm.
Caption title; signed at end: J. Czapka Ritter
von Winstetten, gewesener Bürgermeister.

---

*GB8
V6755R
4.20.48

Eggerth, Joseph.
Mitbürger! Mittwoch den 26. April haben wir die
Urwahlen zum deutschen Volkstag; die Männer,
welche aus dieser Wahl hervorgehen, versammeln
sich wieder am 3. Mai, um die Abgeordneten nach
Frankfurt zu wählen. Seid daher vorsichtig ...
[Wien,1848]
[2]p. 27x21cm.
Caption title; signed: Joseph Eggerth, bürgl.
Handelsmann und Badeinhaber, Laimgrube Nr. 123.

---

*pGB8
V6755R
4.20.48

Die fremden Aufwiegler. Mitbürger! Es treiben
sich Ausländer in unserer Mitte herum und suchen
Misstrauen und Aufwieglerey unter uns zu
verbreiten ...
[Wien,1848]

broadside. 48.5x39.5cm.

---

*pGB8
V6755R
4.20.48

Juridisch-politischer Leseverein, Vienna.
Mitbürger! Man hat euch auf heute zu einer
Massenversammlung berufen ...
[Wien,1848]

broadside. 37.5x45cm.
Printed on yellow paper.
Another edition has imprint of Klopf & Eurich.
In this edition, the first line of text ends:
Wer sind die Männer, die euch

---

*pGB8
V6755R
4.20.48

Juridisch-politischer Leseverein, Vienna.
Mitbürger! Man hat euch auf heute zu einer
Massenversammlung berufen ...
[Wien,1848]

broadside. 35x45cm.
Printed on yellow paper.
Another edition has imprint of Klopf & Eurich.
In this edition, the first line of text ends:
Wer sind die Männer, die euch berufen?

---

*pGB8
V6755R
4.20.48

Juridisch-politischer Leseverein, Vienna.
Mitbürger! Man hat euch auf heute zu einer
Massenversammlung berufen ...
[Wien]Druck von U.Klopf sen.und Alex.Eurich.
[1848]

broadside. 42.5x26.5cm.
Other editions are without imprint.

---

*GB8
V6755R
4.20.48

's Kleeblatt! G'schichten wie man sie in der
Vorstadt erzählt ...
[Wien]Gedruckt bei M.Lell,vormals Anna St.
von Hirschfeld.[1848]

[7]p. 18x12cm.
Charging officials of Leopoldstadt, and
particularly the priest Anton Wiesinger, with
corruption.

Neidl, Julius.
*GB8 Offener Brief an alle Hausherren in Wien.
V6755R Von Julius Neidl.
4.20.48 [Wien,1848]

folder([4]p.) 23.5x15.5cm.
Imprint on p.[4]: Druck von A. Pichler's
Witwe.

Oewel, J Maria.
*GB8 Er ist fort, der gefährliche Dr. Schütte! Eine
V6755R Triumphrede auf seinen Fortgang und der
4.20.48 Geschichte Rückgang. Von J. Maria Oewel.
[Wien]Bei Sallmayer & Comp.,Kärntnerstrasse Nr.
1044.[1848]

folder([4]p.) 22.5x15.5cm.
Caption title; imprint on p.[4].

[Schickh, M]
*GB8 Mitbürger! lenket Eure Aufmerksamkeit auf die
V6755R Wahlen für den Reichstag in Frankfurt so wie in
4.20.48 Wien ...
Wien,1848.Gedruckt bei Edl.v.Schmidbauer und
Holzwarth,und zu haben bei J.Wenedikt,Buch-
händler im Bürgerspital.

folder([4]p.) 22x13.5cm.
Signed at end: M. Schickh, Nationalgarde.

Vienna. Magistrat.
*pGB8 Der Magistrat und provisorische Bürger=
V6755R Ausschuss der Stadt Wien an seine Mitbürger!
4.20.48 Gedruckte Mauer=Anschläge und Flugblätter der
verschiedenartigsten Richtungen verkünden seit
einigen Tagen den Wohnungs=Parteien Wiens, dass
nicht nur in Zukunft, sondern auch schon für
die jetzige Georgi=Zinszahlung die Wohnungszinse
theils nur in willkürlich herabgesetzten
Beträgen, theils in anderen als den
vertragsmässig bedungenen und gesetzlich
(See next card)

Vienna. Magistrat. Der Magistrat ... [1848]
*pGB8 (Card 2)
V6755R
4.20.48 feststehenden Zahlungs=Terminen, theils gar
nicht gezahlt zu werden brauchen ...
[Wien,1848]

broadside. 45x57cm.
Reschauer-Smets II.90.
Dated: Wien am 20. April 1848.
Printed in 2 columns.
Establishing a Sicherheits-Comité for the
preservation of law and order.

Vienna. Magistrat.
*pGB8 Der Magistrat und provis. Bürger=Ausschuss
V6755R der Stadt Wien an seine Mitbürger! Gedruckte
4.20.48 Mauer=Anschläge und Flugblätter der
verschiedenartigsten Richtungen verkünden seit
einigen Tagen den Wohnungs=Parteien Wiens, dass
nicht nur in Zukunft, sondern auch schon für
die jetzige Georgi=Zinszahlung die Wohnungszinse
theils nur in willkürlich herabgesetzten
Beträgen, theils in anderen als den
vertragsmässig bedungenen und gesetzlich
(See next card)

Vienna. Magistrat. Der Magistrat und provis.
*pGB8 ... [1848] (Card 2)
V6755R
4.20.48 feststehenden Zahlungs=Terminen, theils gar
nicht gezahlt zu werden brauchen ...
[Wien,1848]
folder([3]p.) 44.5x29cm.
Reschauer-Smets II.90.
Caption title; dated at end: Wien am 20. April
1848.
Establishing a Sicherheits-Comité for the
preservation of law and order.

Vienna. Nationalgarde.
*GB8 Geschäftsordnung für den Verwaltungsrath
V6755R der gesammten Wiener Nationalgarde.
4.20.48 [Wien]Aus der k.k.Hof= und Staats=Druckerei.
[1848]

[2]p. 28.5x22cm.
Caption title; imprint on p.[2].

Vienna. Nationalgarde.
*pGB8 Tagsbefehl am 20.ten April 1848.
V6755R [Wien,1848]
4.20.48
folder(1l.) 38x24.5cm.
Reproduced from ms. copy; unsigned.

Die Zins-Remasurri im Odeon und der
Kapellmeister Marzikoter.
*GB8 [Wien]Gedruckt,bei M.Lell.[1848]
V6755R
4.20.48 8p. 19x12cm.
Woodcut illus. on t.-p.

*pGB8
V6755R
4.21.48

Austria, Lower. Central-Comité für die Wahlen zur
constituirenden deutschen National-
Versammlung.
Kundmachung. Ein wichtiger Moment naht seiner
Entscheidung. Die Abgeordneten zu der im Mai d.
J. in Frankfurt am Main zusammentretenden
deutschen National=Versammlung sollen gewählt
werden ...
[Wien]Gedruckt bey den Edlen v.Ghelen'schen
Erben.[1848]

broadside. 44x56.5cm.
Dated: Wien am ( ) 21. April 1848.

*GB8
V6755R
4.22.48

[Lamatsch, Ignaz]
Ein Geistlicher aus Österreich an die
Wahlmänner für Frankfurt am Main und für Wien.
[Wien]Gedruckt bei Carl Gerold.[1848]

[2]p. 28.5x22.5cm.
Caption title; imprint on p.[2].
Dated & signed at end: Retz, am 22. April 1848.
Ignaz Lamatsch ...

*GB8
V6755R
4.21.48

[Kaltenbaeck, Johann Paul, 1804-1861]
Schwarz und Gelb.
Zu haben bei Ignaz Klang,Buchhändler in Wien,
Dorotheergasse,1105.[1848]

[2]p. 23x14.5cm.
Helfert (Wiener Parnass) 882.
Caption title; imprint on p.[2].
Signed at end: J. P. Kaltenbaeck.
"Aus der constitutionellen Donau=Zeitung."

*GB8
V6755R
4.22.48

[Neumann, Josef, 1815-1878]
[Begins:] Der Verein, welcher angeregt wurde
durch den Gefertigten, besteht, entwickelt sich,
und will wirken unter den nachfolgenden
Bestimmungen. Er nennt sich: "Der Verein des
deutschen Hauses." ...
[Wien,1848]

folder([4]p.) 19.5x12cm.
Dated & signed on p.[4]: Wien, am 22. April
1848. Prof. Dr. Jos. Neumann.

*pGB8
V6755R
4.21.48

Literarischer Verein in Wien.
Zur Aufklärung der politischen Bedeutung der
bevorstehenden Wahlen zum deutschen Parlament in
Frankfurt am Main. Der unterzeichnete Literaten=
Verein hält es für seine Pflicht ...
[Wien,1848]

broadside. 47x29cm.
Dated: Wien, den 21. April 1848.

*pGB8
V6755R
4.22.48

Vienna. Magistrat.
Kundmachung. In Folge des hohen Ministerial=
Erlasses vom 12. d. M. ... sind alle
Staatsbürger an ihren bleibenden Wohnsitzen in
dem Alter von dem vollendeten 19. bis zum
vollstreckten 50. Jahre zum activen Dienste in
der Nationalgarde verpflichtet ...
[Wien,1848]

broadside. 36.5x22.5cm.
Signed & dated: Von dem Magistrate und prov.
Bürger=Ausschusse der Stadt Wien, am 22. April
1848.

*GB8
V6755R
4.21.48

Strampfer, Heinrich.
Die Nachtwache eines Nationalgardisten. Allen
Nationalgarden und der akademischen Legion der
Haupt- und Residenzstadt Wien gewidmet von ihrem
Kameraden Heinrich Strampfer. Zweite Auflage.
[Wien]Gedruckt bei Edl.v.Schmidbauer und
Holzwarth.[1848]

folder(4p.) 19.5x13cm.
Helfert (Wiener Parnass) 883.
Caption title; imprint on p.4.
Dated at end: Wien, den 21. April 1848.

*pGB8
V6755R
4.22.48

Vienna. Magistrat.
Kundmachung zum Behufe der Wahl von
Abgeordneten und Stellvertretern für die im
Mai d. J. nach Frankfurt am Main berufene
konstituirende deutsche National=Versammlung.
[Wien,1848]

[2]p. 36.5x22.5cm.
Caption title; signed at end: Von dem
Magistrate und prov. Bürgerausschusse der k. k.
Haupt= und Residenzstadt Wien.
This edition details the division of the inner
city into a single) voting district.

*pGB8
V6755R
4.22.48

Austria. Ministerium des Innern.
Kundmachung. Um den durch die eingetretenen
industriellen Stockungen zeitweise Erwerblosen
auch durch öffentliche Bauten einen Erwerb
auszumitteln ...
[Wien,1848]

broadside. 45x57cm.
Unterreiter III.36.
Dated & signed: Wien am 22. April 1848. Der
Minister des Innern: Franz Freiherr von
Pillersdorff.

*pGB8
V6755R
4.22.48

Vienna. Magistrat.
Kundmachung zum Behufe der Wahl von
Abgeordneten und Stellvertretern für die im Mai
d. J. nach Frankfurt am Main berufene
konstituirende deutsche National=Versammlung.
[Wien,1848]

folder([4]p.) 36.5x23cm.
Caption title; signed & dated at end: Von
dem Magistrate und prov. Bürger=Ausschusse der
k. k. Haupt= und Residenzstadt Wien am 22. April
1848.
This edition de- tails the division of the
suburbs into 6 voting districts.

*GB8
V6755R
4.23.48

Austria, Lower. Central-Comité fur die Wahlen
zur constituirenden deutschen National-
Versammlung.
An die Wahlmänner Oesterreichs!
[Wien,1848]

broadside. 29x21.5cm.
Dated & signed: Wien am 23. April 1848. Das
Central-Comité für die Wahlen zur
constituirenden deutschen National=Versammlung.

*GB8
V6755R
4.23.48

Huber, V
Ueber unsere Volkswahlen. Ein unentbehrlicher
Fingerzeig für alle Urwähler, Wahlmänner und
Wahlcandidaten. Von V. Huber.
Wien,1848.Gedruckt und zu haben bei J.P.
Sollinger,Stadt,Tuchlauben Nr.439,gegenüber
dem Musikvereins=Gebäude.

folder(3,[1]p.) 27x21.5cm.
Dated at end: Wien, den 23. April 1848.

*pGB8
V6755R
4.23.48

Bohemia. Landespräsidium.
So denken Fürsten, Grafen, Freiherren, Bürger,
Männer aus dem Volke und für das Volk, wenn sie
wahre Christen sind.
Buchdruckerei von J.St.v.Hirschfeld in Wien.
[1848]

broadside. 57x44.5cm.
Dated & signed: Prag am 23. April 1848. Vom
böhmischen k. k. Landespräsidium. Rudolf Graf
Stadion. Wilhelm Graf Wurmbrand [& 12 others].
Deploring antisemitism.
Printed on yel-   low paper.

*pGB8
V6755R
4.23.48

Schrenk von Notzing, Alois Joseph, abp.,
1802-1849.
So denkt und wirkt ein wahrer Christ und
Kirchenfürst! Bitte des Prager-Erzbischofs!
[Wien]Druck von U.Klopf sen.u.Alex.Eurich.
[1848]

broadside. 47x58cm.
Dated & signed: Prag, am Osterfeste den 23.
April 1848. Aloys Joseph, Erzbischof.
Printed within ornamental vine border.

*pGB8
V6755R
4.23.48

Dercsényi, János Lajos, báró, 1802-1863.
Osterwünsche.
[Wien]Gedruckt bei Carl Gerold.[1848]

broadside. 45x57cm.
Dated: Wien, am frühen Morgen des Ostersonntags
1848.

*pGB8
V6755R
4.24.48

Adresse an den Magistrat und an den
provisorischen Bürger=Ausschuss, so wie an das
verantwortliche Gesammt=Ministerium.
[Wien,1848]

folder(1l.) 43x27.5cm.
Caption title; dated: Wien, am 24. April 1848.

*GB8
V6755R
4.23.48

[Dercsényi, János Lajos, báró, 1802-1863]
... Osterwünsche.
[Wien]Gedruckt bei Carl Gerold.[1848]

folder([4]p.) 20.5x12.5cm.
Caption title; imprint on p.[4].
Dated & signed at end: Wien, am frühen Morgen
des Ostersonntags 1848. Johann Freiherr v.
Dercsényi.
At head of caption title: Dieses Blatt darf
nicht theurer als für 1 Kreuzer C. M. verkauft
werden.

*pGB8
V6755R
4.24.48

Born, Ernst Wilhelm.
Mitbürger! Durch den Erlass des Ministeriums
des Innern vom 23. 1. M. wurde ich von heute
an mit der Leitung der Geschäfte der Polizei=
Ober=Direction in ihrem vollen Umfange
provisorisch betraut ...
[Wien,1848]

broadside. 40.5x50cm.
Dated: Wien am 24. April 1848.

*GB8
V6755R
4.23.48

Die grässliche Juden-Verfolgung in Pressburg.
(Von einem Augenzeugen.)
[Wien,1848]

folder([4]p.) 26.5x21.5cm.
Printer's imprint on p.[4]: Gedruckt bei M.
Lell, Leopoldstadt, Weintraubengasse Nr.505.

*pGB8
V6755R
4.24.48
(A)

Der Deutsche Adler (Club), Vienna.
Der deutsche Adler an die deutschen Bewohner
aller Provinzen Oesterreichs.
[Wien]Gedruckt und zu haben bei U.Klopf sen.
und A.Eurich,Wollzeile Nr.782.[1848]

broadside. 52.5x68.5cm.
Dated & signed: Wien, am Abende des Oster-
montages 1848. Im Namen des Clubbs: "der
deutsche Adler".
Printed on white paper.

*pGB8
V6755R
4.24.48
(B)

Another copy. 55x76cm.
Printed on pink   paper.

*pGB8
V6755R
4.24.48

Grosse Gratulations=Litaney an alle Hausherrn.
[Wien]Gedruckt bei Josef Ludwig.[1848]

[2]p. 43x27cm.
Caption title; imprint on p.[2].
Signed at end: J. M. R.
Dated in contemporary ms.: 24. April 848.

---

*GB8
V6755R
4.24.48

[Weitlof, Johann]
Der Bauer und die landwirthschaftlichen
Zustände in Böhmen.
[Wien]Gedruckt bei den Edlen von Ghelen'schen
Erben.[1848]

folder([4]p.) 27x21.5cm.
Caption title; imprint on p.[4].
Dated & signed at end: Wien den 24. April
1848 am Ostermontag. J. Weitlof.

---

*GB8
V6755R
4.24.48

Johann, archduke of Austria, 1782-1859.
Rede, gesprochen von Sr. kaiserlichen Hoheit
Erzherzog Johann von Oesterreich zur ersten
ausrückenden Kompagnie des Innsbrucker
Universitätskorps bei Gelegenheit der Fahnenweihe
am 24. April 1848.
[Wien,1848]

broadside. 22x14.5cm.

---

*pGB8
V6755R
4.25.48

Austria. Constitution.
Wir Ferdinand der Erste, von Gottes Gnaden
Kaiser von Oesterreich ... Ueberzeugt, dass die
Staats=Institutionen den Fortschritten folgen
müssen, welche in der Cultur und Geistes=
Entwicklung der Völker eingetreten sind ... haben
Wir denselben durch Unser Patent vom 15. März d.
J. die Ertheilung einer Verfassung zugesichert
...[Wien,1848]
8p. 45x29cm.
Beschauer-Smets II.104; Helfert
(See next card)

---

*pGB8
V6755R
4.24.48

Juridisch-politischer Leseverein, Vienna.
An die Bewohner Wiens.
[Wien,1848]
broadside. 37.5x28.5cm.
Dated: Wien, den 24. April 1848.
Announcing morning and evening parades as part
of the festivities for the Emperor's birthday
celebration.

---

*pGB8
V6755R
4.25.48

Austria. Constitution.   Wir Ferdinand der
Erste ... [1848]   (Card 2)

(Geschichte) I.499ff.
Caption title.
"Verfassungs-Urkunde des österreichischen
Kaiserstaates": p.3-8.
"Gegeben in Unserer kaiserlichen Haupt= und
Residenzstadt Wien den fünf und zwanzigsten
April im eintausend achthundert acht und
vierzigsten ..."

---

*pGB8
V6755R
4.24.48

Vienna. Nationalgarde. Akademische Legion.
An die Gesammt=Bevölkerung Wiens. Mitbürger,
Brüder! Es wird von Böswilligen das Gerücht
ausgestreut, dass am 25. dieses Monats bei
Belegenheit der zur Geburtsfeier Sr. Majestät
des Kaisers am Josephstädter Glacis statt-
findenden Parade feindselige Angriffe gegen die
Studenten=Legion gemacht werden sollen ...
[Wien,1848]
broadside. 45x57cm.
Beschauer-Smets II.102.   (See next card)

---

*pGB8
V6755R
4.25.48

Austria. Ministerium des Innern.
Kundmachung. Seine k. k. Majestät haben
folgendes allerhöchste Cabinetschreiben an den
Minister des Inneren allergnädigst zu erlassen
geruhet ...
[Wien,1848]

broadside. 44.5x57cm.
Beschauer-Smets II.106.
Dated & signed: Wien den 25. April 1848. Der
Minister des Inneren: Franz Freiherr von
Pillersdorff m. p.

---

*pGB8
V6755R
4.24.48

Vienna. Nationalgarde. Akademische Legion.
An die Gesammt=Bevölkerung Wiens ... [1848]
(Card 2)

Dated: Wien am 24. April 1848.
Signed by 5 of the corps commanders; denying
the truth of the rumor.

---

*pGB8
V6755R
4.25.48

Austria, Lower. Central-Comité für die Wahlen zur
constituirenden deutschen National-
Versammlung.
Kundmachung. Morgen findet die Wahl der
Wahlmänner Statt, welche sodann am 3. Mai die
Abgeordneten nach Frankfurt zu wählen haben ...
[Wien]Gedruckt bei den Edlen v.Ghelen'schen
Erben.[1848]

broadside. 38x29cm.
Dated: Wien den 25. April 1848.

*pGB8
V6755R
4.25.48

Bundesstaat oder Staatenbund? Also Bundesstaat,
d. h. den Muth verlieren, die österreichische
Monarchie aufgeben und mit dem deutschen
Bruchtheile bettelnd nach Frankfurt flüchten? ...
[Wien,1848]

broadside. 38x29cm.
'Aus der "constitutionellen Donau=Zeitung."'
At end: Schwarz und Gelb, Gedicht von J. P.
Kaltenbaeck, ist im Verlage bei Ignaz Klang,
Dorotheergasse Nr. 1105, zu haben.

---

*GB8
V6755R
4.25.48

Hochleitner, Raimund.
Die Freimädchen, oder: Warum werden die Männer
den Frauen untreu? Ein Artikel für das weibliche
Geschlecht von ganz Europa ... Von Raimund
Hochleitner.
[Wien,1848]

8p. 26x21cm.

---

*pGB8
V6755R
4.25.48

Dringende Aufforderung an alle vaterländischen
Besitzer von Silber=Geräthschaften.
[Wien]Gedruckt bei U.Klopf sen.,u.Alex.Eurich.
[1848]

broadside. 61x46cm.
Signed: Mehrere Patrioten.

---

*pGB8
V6755R
4.25.48

[Leidenix, Ignaz, pseud.?]
Ein offenes Schreiben an den Ex-Bürgermeister
Ignaz Czapka über seine offene Erklärung. Von
einem Bürger Wien's.
Bei Jakob Bader,Buchhändler in Wien,Stadt,
Strobelgasse.[1848]

folder([4]p.) 46x31cm.
Caption title; imprint on p.[4].
Dated & signed at end: Wien, den 25. April
1848. Ignaz Leidenix.

---

*pGB8
V6755R
4.25.48

Endlich, Johann Quirin.
An sämmtliche Comite's zur Frankfurter
Abgeordneten Wahl.
[Wien,1848]

broadside. 54x42.5cm.
Dated: Wien, am 25. April 1848.

---

*GB8
V6755R
4.25.48

Leidesdorf, Eduard.
Constitutionelle Ostereier von verschiedener
Färbung.
[Wien]Druck von U.Klopf sen.und A.Eurich,
Wollzeile,Nr.782.[1848]

broadside. 27.5x19cm.
Printed on pink paper.

---

*GB8
V6755R
4.25.48

Gottwik, Sigmund.
Ein Wort über die Kleeblatt=Revolution in der
Leopoldstadt ... Von Sigmund Gottwik.
[Wien,1848]

folder([4]p.) 22.5x14cm.
Defending officials of Leopoldstadt, and
particularly the priest Anton Wiesinger, against
charges of corruption contained in the anonymous
pamphlet "'s Kleeblatt!"

---

*pGB8
V6755R
4.25.48

Möring, Carl, 1810-1870.
An die Urwähler und Wahlmänner des fünften
Hauptwahlbezirkes Neubau.
[Wien,1848]

broadside. 36x23cm.
"Diess ist das Programm Eures Candidaten für
die deutsche National=Versammlung zu Frankfurt
am Main."

---

*GB8
V6755R
4.25.48

Herczeghy, Mór, 1815-1884.
Zur geburtsfeierlichen Festivität Sr. Majestät
unsers Kaisers und Königs, verfasst von D[r].
M. Herczegy.
[Wien]Gedruckt bei Edl.v.Schmidbauer und
Holzwarth.[1848]

[2]p. 25x19.5cm.
Caption title; imprint on p.[2].
Dated: Wien, den 25. April 1848.

---

*pGB8
V6755R
4.25.48

Vienna. Magistrat.
Kundmachung. Ueber mehrseitig ausgesprochenen
Wunsch die Vornahme der Wahlen der Wahlmänner
für die deutsche National=Versammlung in Frank-
furt am Main wegen der nothwendigen vorläufigen
Besprechungen in den einzelnen Urwahlbezirken
noch einige Tage zu verschieben ...
[Wien,1848]

broadside. 45x57cm.
Dated & signed: Wien am 25. April 1848. Vom
Magistrate und prov. Bürgerausschusse.

*GB8
V6755R
4.25.48

Vollständige Auslegung der Constitution mit gleichzeitiger Beurtheilung des zwei Kammer-Systems. Gespräche in österreichischer Mundart. Nebst einem Anhange, das kaiserliche Patent vom 25. April 1848 und die Constitution (die Verfassungsurkunde des österreichischen Kaiserstaates enthaltend.)
[Wien]Gedruckt bei M.Lell,Leopoldstadt, Weintraubengasse Nr.505.[1848]

8p. 26x21cm.

---

*pGB8
V6755R
4.26.48

Austria. Sovereigns, etc., 1835-1848
(Ferdinand I)
Kundmachung. Lieber Freiherr von Pillersdorff! Den gestrigen Tag werde Ich stets zu denjenigen zählen, an welchem die Vorsehung Meinem Herzen die wohlthuendsten Eindrücke und die freudigsten Empfindungen geschenkt hat ...
[Wien,1848]

broadside. 45x57cm.
Reschauer-Smets II.108.
Dated & signed: Wien am 26. April 1848.
Ferdinand m. p.

---

*pGB8
V6755R
4.26.48

Buschman, Gotthard, freiherr von, 1810-1888.
An die Wahlmänner in der Frankfurter Wahlsache.
[Wien,1848]
broadside. 42x24.5cm.
Signed: Gotthard Freiherr v. Buschmann.
Large folio broadside, printed in one column; a small folio edition, with expanded text, is printed in two columns.

---

*GB8
V6755R
4.26.48

Buschman, Gotthard, freiherr von, 1810-1888.
An die Wahlmänner in der Frankfurter Wahlsache. Von Gotthard Freiherrn von Buschmann, Doctor der Rechte.
[Wien,1848]

broadside. 27x21.5cm.
Contemporary ms. note at head: 1000 Stk. 26 April 1848.

---

*GB8
V6755R
4.26.48

Löve, Paul.
Mitternächtliches Gespräch des Kaiser Joseph mit Kaiser Ferdinand in der Hofburg am 25/26 April 1848. Von Paul Löve.
[Wien,1848]

folder([4]p.) 23x14.5cm.
Printer's imprint on p.[4]: Gedruckt bei Franz Edlem [!] von Schmid.

---

*pGB8
V6755R
4.26.48

[Manussi, Ferdinand Carl]
Kameraden! Noch ganz von den Eindrücken des zur Feier des Allerhöchsten Geburtsfestes Sr. Majestät unsers allergnädigsten Kaisers Ferdinand des I. am Josephstädter Glacis statt gefundenen Verbrüderungsfestes ergriffen ...
[Wien,1848]

[2]p. 34.5x22cm.
Caption title; dated & signed on p.[2]: Wien am 26. April 1848. Ferdinand Carl Manussi ...

---

*pGB8
V6755R
4.26.48

Meisl, Karl, 1775-1853.
Wie sieht's in Italien aus? Von Karl Meisl.
[Wien]Gedruckt und zu haben bei Leop.Grund,am Hundsthurm Nr.1.Verlag:Stadt,im Zwettelhof.
[1848]

[2]p. 36.5x23cm.
Caption title; imprint on p.[2].
Dated in contemporary ms.: 26. April 848.

---

*pGB8
V6755R
4.26.48

Der 26. April! Auffallendes Zusammentreffen von Gewaltstreichen in Krakau, in Lemberg und in den Kreis=Städten von Galizien, am letzten Tage vor Ankunft der Verfassungs=Urkunde in Polen!
[Wien,1848]

broadside. 41.5x25.5cm.

---

*pGB8
V6755R
4.26.48

Simić von Hohenblum, Joseph.
Entgegnung auf den Aufruf der Comité des Clubbs der "deutsche Adler" an die deutschen Bewohner aller Provinzen Oesterreichs.
[Wien]Gedruckt bei Carl Ueberreuter, Alservorstadt,Hauptstrasse Nr.146.[1848]

broadside. 47x60cm.

---

*pGB8
V6755R
4.26.48

Vienna. Magistrat.
... Kundmachung. Jm Nachhange zur hierortigen Kundmachung vom 18. April d. J. Z. 18665 wird bekannt gemacht ...
[Wien,1848]

broadside. 42x26.5cm.
At head: G. Z. 23010.
Signed & dated: Von dem Magistrate der k. k. Haupt= und Residenzstadt Wien am 26. April 1848.
Concerning the distribution of milk.

*pGB8
V6755R
4.26.48

Vienna. Magistrat.
Kundmachung zum Behufe der Wahl von
Abgeordneten und Stellvertretern für die im Mai
d. J. nach Frankfurt am Main berufene
constituirende deutsche National=Versammlung.
[Wien,1848]

broadside. 44.5x57cm.
Dated & signed: Wien am 26. April 1848. Von dem
Magistrate und prov. Bürger=Ausschusse der
Stadt Wien.

---

*GB8
V6755R
4.28.48

[Miller, A   ]
Deutsches Bundeslied.
Wien 1848.Gedruckt bei Carl Gerold.

[2]p. 19.5x13cm.
Helfert (Wiener Parnass) 912.
Caption title; imprint on p.[2]; signed at
end: A. Miller.

---

*pGB8
V6755R
4.27.48

Poland. Landes-Deputation, 1848.
Protest der polnischen Deputation.
[Wien,1848]

broadside. 46x30cm.
Helfert (Geschichte) II.293-4; Reschauer-Smets
II.116.
Dated: Wien, am 27. April 1848.
Protesting provisions in the Verfassungsurkunde
relating to Galicia.

---

*pGB8
V6755R
4.28.48

Niederösterreichischer Gewerbe-Verein.
An den Clubb, welcher sich nennt: "Der
Deutsche Adler."
[Wien]Gedruckt bei den Edlen von Ghelen'schen
Erben.[1848]

broadside. 45x57cm.
Dated & signed: Wien, 28. April 1848. Der
Vorsteher und viele Mitglieder des n. ö.
Gewerbvereins.
Printed on green paper.

---

*pGB8
V6755R
4.27.48

Vienna. Magistrat.
Concurs-Ausschreibung. Der Magistrat und prov.
Bürgerausschuss der k. k. Haupt= und Residenz-
stadt Wien hat mit Genehmigung des Ministeriums
des Innern zur Aufrechthaltung der Ruhe,
Ordnung und Sicherheit innerhalb der Linien die
Einführung einer eigenen ...
[Wien,1848]

broadside. 41.5x26cm.
Dated: Wien am 27. April 1848.

---

*pGB8
V6755R
4.28.48

Vienna. Magistrat.
Kundmachung rücksichtlich der aus dem k. k.
Versatzamte unentgeltlich zu erfolgenden
Pfänder.
[Wien,1848]

broadside. 44x57cm.
Dated & signed: Wien am 28. April 1848.
Vom Magistrate und provisorischen Bürgeraus-
schusse.

---

*pGB8
V6755R
4.27.48

Vienna (Archdiocese) Archbishop, 1832-1853
(Vinzenz Eduard Milde)
Vincenz Eduard, von Gottes und des
apostolischen Stuhles Gnade der Kirche zu Wien
Fürsterzbischof ... Allen Gläubigen der Wiener=
Erzdiözese Heil und Segen! Nachdem die Constitu-
tion des Staates von Sr. k. k. Majestät am
25. April d. J. ertheilet und allgemein bekannt
gemacht worden ist ...
[Wien,1848]

folder([4]p.) 42x26cm.
Caption title;   dated on p.[4]: Aus meinem
Palais in Wien,   am 27. April 1848.

---

*GB8
V6755R
4.29.48

[Fesl, Michael Josef, 1788-1864]
An die Bewohner Wiens! Freiheit und Recht
sind so heilige Güter der Gesellschaft ...
[Wien]Gedruckt bey den Edlen von Ghelen'schen
Erben.[1848]

[2]p. 27x21.5cm.
Caption title; imprint on p.[2]; signed &
dated at end: Wien den 29. April 1848.
Professor M. J. Fesl ...
Defending Anton Wiesinger, rector of a church
in the Leopoldstadt, against charges of corruption.

---

*GB8
V6755R
4.28.48

[Janisch, Anton]
Vom Himmel gefallener Brief der Mariazeller
Mutter Gottes an die Oesterreicher und besonders
an die Wiener. Zweite Auflage.
Wien,1848.Gedruckt in der Josefstadt,Lang-
gasse Nr.58.

folder([4]p.) 24x19cm.
Dated & signed at end: Wien, am 28. April
1848 aufgefangen von Anton Janisch.
Discouraging pilgrimages to Mariazell.

---

*GB8
V6755R
4.29.48

Die Liguorianer wollen zurück! Feierlicher
Protest dagegen von Oesterreichs Völkern.
[Wien]Gedruckt bei Josef Ludwig.[1848]

folder([4]p.) 26x21cm.
Dated in contemporary ms.: 29. April 848.

Partl, ———.
An sämmtliche Herren Garden der VI. Comp.
des Bezirkes Wieden.
[Wien,1848]

*pGB8
V6755R
4.29.48

broadside. 38x23cm.
Contemporary ms. note at head: 100 Stück 29
April 1848.

Jelussig, ———
Die Herren Garden der 4. Compagnie des Stuben=
Viertels werden eingeladen, sich Dinstag den 2.
Mai 1848 Abends 7 Uhr in ihrem Versammlungslokale
im alten Fahrpostgebäude einzufinden ...
[Wien,1848]

*GB8
V6755R
4.30.48

broadside. 28.5x22.5cm.
Dated: Wien, den 30. April 1848.

Schick, Leopold.
Die jüngste Pressburger Judenverfolgung. Ein
Osterei als Beilage zum Humoristen ... von
Leopold Schick.
[Wien]Zu haben in der Verlagshandlung des
Franz Edlen v.Schmid.Seitenstättengasse N.495.
[1848]

*GB8
V6755R
4.29.48

folder([4]p.) 23x16cm.
Caption title; imprint on p.[4].

Kostner, Albert.
Aufforderung an die fünfzig Wahlmänner der zehn
Urwahlbezirke von Schottenfeld.
[Wien,1848]

*pGB8
V6755R
4.30.48

broadside. 37.5x26cm.
Signed: Jm Namen mehrerer Wahlmänner Albert
Kostner ... Jgnaz Gessmann ...

Austria, Lower. Laws, statutes, etc., 1835-1848
(Ferdinand I)
... Circulare der k. k. Landesregierung im
Erzherzogthume Oesterreich unter der Enns. In
Betreff des von dem k. k. Militär=Commando zu
Triest gegen die Stadt Venedig verfügten
Blockade=Zustandes.
[Wien,1848]

*pGB8
V6755R
4.30.48

broadside. 38x22cm.
At head: NO 22008. NO 52.
Dated: Wien am 30. April 1848.

Papst Pius IX. hat die Regierung niedergelegt.
Wort für Wort wahr.
[Wien,1848]

*GB8
V6755R
4.30.48

folder([4]p.) 24.5x20.5cm.
Imprint on p.[4]: Gedruckt und zu haben bei
Leopold Grund, am Stephansplatze im Zwettelhofe.
Title printed diagonally.

Der Deutsche Adler (Club), Vienna.
Der deutsche Adler. Als Abfertigung an seine
Gegner, ein für allemal.
Druck von U.Klopf sen.& Alex.Eurich,Wollzeile
782,in Wien.[1848]

*pGB8
V6755R
4.30.48

broadside. 53x42.5cm.
Dated & signed: Wien den 30. April 1848. Im
Namen des Clubbs: "der deutsche Adler."

Poland. Landes-Deputation, 1848.
Memorandum der polnischen Deputation an das
löbliche Central=Comité der Wiener National=
Garde.
[Wien,1848]

*pGB8
V6755R
4.30.48

.[10]p. 38x23.5cm.
Caption title; dated: Wien, am 30. April 1848.
Pages [3-10] contain Beilagen.

Die grässlichen Gräuelthaten oder der
Bauern=Aufstand in Szeret im Neutra=Comitat in
Ungarn.
[Wien]Gedruckt bei Josef Ludwig Josefstadt
Florianigasse Nr.52.[1848]

*GB8
V6755R
4.30.48

folder([4]p.) 26.5x21cm.
Account of a largely antisemitic insurrection
on 27 April.

Die Advokaten und ihre Solicitatoren. Von
Einem, der lange dabei war, und es wissen muss
...
[Wien,1848]

*GB8
V6755R
4.31.48

folder([4]p.) 25x19.5cm.
Signed on p.[4]: Fr. Jon***.

*GB8
V6755R
4.31.48

Allgemein rege gewordene Wünsche in Bezug
auf unsere National=Garde.
  Zu haben bei Schmidt & Leo in Wien, am Graben
Nr.1095.[1848]

  [2]p. 29x23cm.
  Caption title; imprint on p.[2]; signed at
end: Von mehreren Mitgliedern der National=Garde
und einem k. k. Officier.

---

*GB8
V6755R
4.31.48

Becker, Wilhelm, fl.1848.
  Für Wahrheit und Recht!
  Druck und Eigenthum von Hirschfeld in Wien.
[1848]

  broadside. 22x14.5cm.
  Helfert (Wiener Parnass) 634.

---

*GB8
V6755R
4.31.48

[Arthur, pseud.]
  Schnipp! Schnapp! Schnurr. Kilian von
Eipeldau ist wieder da, oder Wer weiss wozu
es gut ist? ...
  [Wien]Gedruckt bei Josef Ludwig,Josefstadt
Florianigasse Nr.52.[1848]

  folder([4]p.) 26.5x21cm.
  Dated & signed: Geschrieben zu Eipeldau im
Monat April 1848. Arthur.

---

*GB8
V6755R
4.31.48

[Bek, Henry Leo]
  Hoch Constitution!
  [Wien,1848]
  folder([4]p.) 22x13.5cm.
  Helfert (Wiener Parnass) 637.
  Printer's imprint on p.[4]: Druck und
Eigenthum von Hirschfeld in Wien.
  Signed at end: Henry Leo Bek, (K.........r).

---

*GB8
V6755R
4.31.48

Auf! nach Russland!
  [Wien,1848]
  broadside. 25.5x19cm.
  Helfert (Wiener Parnass) 981.
  Signed: J. M——r.

---

*pGB8
V6755R
4.31.48

[Bidschof, Franz Xavier]
  Der Bauer Hans=Jörgl, sein Weib, ihr
Beichtvater der Ligorianer Dickbauchius und der
provisorische Richter.
  [Wien]Gedruckt bei Jos.Ludwig,Josefstadt,
Florianigasse Nr.52.[1848]

  [2]p. 36x22cm.
  Caption title; imprint on p.[2]; signed: Franz
X. Bidschof.
  In the Viennese dialect.

---

*GB8
V6755R
4.31.48

Der aufgehängte Spitzel=Stock in der
Universität, oder: Kühne Vertheidigung eines
Studenten, der am Glacis Nachts von Schergen
vehmartig angefallen wurde.
  Wien,1848.Gedruckt in der Josephstadt,
Langegasse Nr.58.

  folder([4]p.) 24.5x19.5cm.
  Signed at end: Ein Nationalgarde.

---

*pGB8
V6755R
4.31.48

Bidschof, Franz Xavier.
  Des is a Unsin. Von Franz X. Bidschof.
  [Wien]Gedruckt bei Josef Ludwig,Josefstadt
Florianigasse Nr.52.[1848]

  broadside. 36x22cm.

---

*pGB8
V6755R
4.31.48

Der Beamten-Despotismus, oder: die Büreaukratie
in Oesterreich.
  [Wien]Gedruckt und zu haben bei J.B.
Wallishausser für 6 kr.C.M.[1848]

  [2]p. 39x25cm.
  Caption title; imprint on p.[2]; dated &
signed: Wien, im April 1848. Von einem Freunde
der Wahrheit und der Erfahrung.

---

*GB8
V6755R
4.31.48

[Bidschof, Franz Xavier]
  Die Frau von Mu und die Knechte.
  [Wien]Gedruckt bei Josef Ludwig,Josefstadt
Florianigasse Nr.52.[1848]

  folder([4]p.) 26.5x21.5cm.
  Signed at end: Fr. X. Bidschof.

*pGB8
V6755R
4.31.48

Bird, T   O'M
   Offenes Schreiben eines hier eingebürgerten
Engländers an seine Wiener Mitbürger.
[Wien]Gedruckt bei Carl Gerold.[1848]

   broadside. 44.5x57cm.

---

*pGB8
V6755R
4.31.48

"Den Juden schlägt man die Schädel ein?"
[Wien]Gedruckt bei M.Lell,Leopoldstadt,
Weintraubengasse Nro.505.[1848]

   broadside. 38x23cm.
   Signed: ein Jude.
   A reply to Franz Schmidt's Bittschrift der
Christensklaven an die Herren Juden.

---

*GB8
V6755R
4.31.48

Bowitsch, Ludwig, 1818-1881.
   Einladung. Die Sonne geht über eine neue
Erde auf! ...
[Wien,1848]

   broadside. 28x22.5cm.
   Dated & signed: Wien, im April 1848. Ludwig
Bowitsch. Cajetan Cerri.

---

*pGB8
V6755R
4.31.48

Denkwürdige Judenverfolgung des 19. Jahr-
hunderts, oder: Die neuesten Pressburger
Ereignisse.
[Wien]Druck v.U.Klopf sen.u.A.Eurich,Wollzeile
Nr.782.[1848]

   broadside. 42.5x26.5cm.
   Signed: R. W. [i.e. Rudolph Weinberger?]
   Printed within border of type-ornaments.
   Also issued with title: Schandmal des 19.
Jahrhunderts ...

---

*GB8
V6755R
4.31.48

[Caspar, Anton]
   An die Freiwilligen.
[Wien]Gedruckt bei Josef Ludwig.[1848]

   folder(4p.) 19x11.5cm.
   Helfert (Wiener Parnass) 942.
   Caption title; imprint on p.4; signed at end:
Anton Caspar.

---

*GB8
V6755R
4.31.48

Deutsch, Johannes, fl.1848.
   Es werde Licht. Nebst einem Anhange für meine
Brüder. Von Js. Deutsch.
[Wien]Zu haben bei Adalbert Praschack,bürgl,
Buchbinder in der Jägerzeile Nr.525.[1848]

   [2]p. 22x13.5cm.
   Caption title; imprint on p.[2].
   In verse; not in Helfert (Wiener Parnass).

---

*pGB8
V6755R
4.31.48

Castelli, Ignaz Franz, 1781-1862.
   Was ist die Constitution? und Was ist die
Constitution nicht? Dritte Mittheilung für
meine lieben österreichischen Landsleute ausser
Wien. Von J. F. Castelli.
   Verlag und Eigenthum von Tendler et Comp.in
Wien am Graben,Trattnerhof.Gedruckt bei
Ferdinand Ullrich.[1848]

   [2]p. 36.5x22.5cm.
   Caption title; imprint on p.[2].

---

*pGB8
V6755R
4.31.48

Dörflinger, J
   Die grosse Beichte der Hausherrn.
[Wien]Gedruckt bei Josef Ludwig,Josefstadt
Florianigasse Nr.52.[1848]

   broadside. 36x22cm.
   A satire.

---

*GB8
V6755R
4.31.48

Colombi, R
   La costituzione di Ferdinando I. imperatore
d'Austria.
[Vienna?,1848]

   broadside. 26x20.5cm.
   Signed: Dr. R. Colombi.
   In verse; not in Helfert (Wiener Parnass).

---

*pGP8
V6755R
4.31.48

Dominicus, Franz.
   Aufruf an Deutschland.
[Wien]Zu haben bei Schmidt & Leo,Buchhandlung
am Graben.[1848]

   broadside. 42.5x26.5cm.
   "NB. Das Manuscript wurde vor Kundmachung der
Frankfurter Volksversammlung dem Drucke
übergeben."

*GB8
V6755R
4.31.48

30 [i.e. Dreissig] polnische Deputirte
gehenkt in Petersburg.
[Wien,1848]

folder([4]p.) 26x20.5cm.
Imprint on p.[4]: Gedruckt bei M. Lell,
Leopoldstadt, Weintraubengasse Nr.505.

---

*pGB8
V6755R
4.31.48

Fein, Moritz.
Aufruf an die reichen Herren und Frauen.
[Wien]Druck von U.Klopf sen.und A.Eurich.
[1848]

broadside. 40x25cm.

---

*GB8
V6755R
4.31.48

[Dunkl, Anton]
Trost an die Lehrgehilfen.
[Wien]Druck von U.Klopf sen.und A.Eurich,
Wollzeile Nr.782.[1848]

[2]p. 26.5x21.5cm.
Helfert (Wiener Parnass) 965.
Caption title; imprint on p.[2]; signed at end:
Anton Dunkl.

---

*pGB8
V6755R
4.31.48

Felber, H
An die Arbeitsgeber in den Reihen der
Nationalgarde.
Druck von U.Klopf sen.und A.Eurich in Wien.
[1848]

broadside. 44.5x28cm.
Signed: Dr. H. Felber, Nationalgarde der VI.
Comp. Wieden.

---

*pGB8
V6755R
4.31.48

Der durchgeschossene Hut Nikolaus, Czaren
von Russland. Hört! was in Russland vorgeht!
[Wien]Gedruckt und zu haben bei Leop.Grund,
am Stephansplatz im neugebauten Zwettelhofe.
[1848]

[2]p. 37x23cm.
Caption title; imprint on p.[2]; signed at
end: K. R.

---

*GB8
V6755R
4.31.48

Frauentheilnahme.
[Wien]Druck von Ul.Klopf sen.und Alex.
Eurich,Wollzeile 782.[1848]

broadside. 22.5x15cm.
Helfert (Wiener Parnass) 623.
Signed: Eine Dame.

---

*GB8
V6755R
4.31.48
(A)

*GB8
V6755R
4.31.48
(B)

Eisele und Beisele als Ligorianer [!] und die
neue Dienstbothen-Herberge.
[Wien]Gedruckt bei M.Lell,Leopoldstadt,Wein-
traubengasse Nr.505.[1848]

8p. 22.5x14.5cm.
Illustrated t.-p.
Another copy. 21.5x13cm.
In this copy, the misspelling on t.-p. has
been corrected to Ligurianer.

---

*pGB8
V6755R
4.31.48

Freunde der constitutionellen Ordnung, Vienna.
Programm zur Bildung einer Gesellschaft,
genannt der Verein der Freunde der konstitutionellen Ordnung.
[Wien,1848]

[2]p. 43x26.5cm.
Caption title; p.[2] is headed: Subscriptions=
Bogen.

---

*GB8
V6755R
4.31.48

[Engländer, Hermann]
Pressfreiheit! Nationalgarde! Constitution!
[Wien]A.Dorfmeisters Druck und Verlag,Stadt,
Kühfussgasse Nr.575.[1848]

[2]p. 22.5x14.5cm.
Helfert (Wiener Parnass) 635.
Caption title; imprint on p.[2]; signed at
end: Hermann Engländer.

---

*GB8
V6755R
4.31.48

Der Garde-Hauptmann Murmon, verkleidet als
Leinwandhändler, Eroberer der 6,000,000
Zwanziger von italienischen Emissären.
[Wien]Gedruckt und zu haben bei Leopold Grund,
am Stephansplatze im Zwettelhofe.[1848]

folder([4]p.) 23x18cm.

*pGB8
V6755R
4.31.48

Gesellschaft der Volksfreunde, Vienna.
An die Bürger Wiens. Anonyme Denuncianten
haben sich erfrecht, Männer, die nur die
Freiheit und den Fortschritt auf dem Wege des
Rechtes wollen, als fremde Aufwiegler zu
verdächtigen ...
[Wien,1848]

broadside. 29x44.5cm.

---

*GB8
V6755R
4.31.48

Hört! Hört! was jetzt schauderhaftes in
Pressburg geschehen ist! Eine genaue und wahre
Beschreibung des furchtbaren Aufstandes und der
damit verbundenen grässlichen Judenverfolgung
am 23. und 24. April 1848 in Pressburg.
[Wien]Gedruckt bei Anton Benko.[1848]

[2]p. 24x24cm.
Caption title; imprint on p.[2]; signed at
end: J. U.

---

*GB8
V6755R
4.31.48

[Gustus, George]
Unserem vielgeliebten Kaiser Ferdinand.
Zu haben bei Teudler[!] & Comp.am Graben im
Trattnerhofe.Druck von Josef Stöckholzer v.
Hirschfeld in Wien.1848.

folder([4]p.) 26.5x22.5cm.
Helfert (Wiener Parnass) 693.
Signed at end: George Gustus.

---

*pGB8
V6755R
4.31.48

[Hrčka, Joseph]
Das ehrliche Wort eines Studenten an die
National-Garde und Bürger Wiens.
[Wien]Gedruckt und zu haben bei U.Klopf sen.und
A.Eurich.[1848]

[2]p. 40x25cm.
Caption title; imprint on p.[2]; signed at
end: Josef Hrczka, Mediziner.
"Der Reinertrag ist für die unglücklichen
Pressburger."

---

*GB8
V6755R
4.31.48

Hamböck, Alfons.
Das Wienerlied von Alfons Hamböck, National=
Gardist.
Eigenthum und Verlag bei Franz Barth in Wien,
Mariahilf,kleine Kirchengasse Nr.28.[1848]

folder(4p.) 17x11cm.
Helfert (Wiener Parnass) 670.
Caption title and imprint.

---

*GB8
V6755R
4.31.48

Joseph II. Stimme aus den elisäischen Feldern.
An sein biederes Volk.
[Wien,1848]

folder([4]p.) 22x14cm.
Helfert (Wiener Parnass) 702.
Printer's imprint on p.[4]: Gedruckt bei den
Edlen von Ghelen'schen Erben.

---

*GB8
V6755R
4.31.48

Hammerschmidt, J   B
Ligourianer-Briefe. Von J. B. Hammerschmidt.
[Wien]Gedruckt bei Franz Edlen von Schmid.
[1848]

folder([4]p.) 23x14.5cm.
Caption title; imprint on p.[4].
Dated in contemporary ms.: April 848.

---

*pGB8
V6755R
4.31.48

Der jüdische Spektakel.
[Wien]Gedruckt bei J.B.Wallishausser.[1848]

[2]p. 43x26.5cm.
Caption title; imprint on p.[2]; signed at end:
K.

---

*GB8
V6755R
4.31.48

[Hector, Vorbeller der Wiener Hunde, pseud.]
... Brief eines Wienerhundes an seinen Bruder
Frippon in Prag.
[Wien]Gedruckt bei Josef Ludwig,Josefstadt
Florianigasse Nr.52.[1848]

folder([4]p.) 22.5x18cm.
At head of title: Die Hundsversammlung am
Ostermontag betreffend.
Signed: Hector, Vorbeller der Wiener Hunde.

---

*GB8
V6755R
4.31.48

Junker, Friedrich.
Zeitgemässes Gespräch zwischen Maria Lichtmess
mit dem Herrn Georg, dem träumenden Herrn Jakob,
und dem einstweilen noch schlafenden Herrn
Michael. Ein Wort in jetziger Zeit angewendet
von Friedrich Junker.
[Wien,1848]

folder([4]p.) 26.5x21cm.
Imprint on p.[4]: Gedruckt bei M. Lell.

*GB8
V6755R
4.31.48

[Just, Wilhelm, fl.1848]
Feuer!
[Wien]Gedruckt bei J.B.Wallishausser.[1848]

[2]p. 19.5x12.5cm.
Helfert (Wiener Parnass) 697.
Caption title; imprint on p.[2]; signed at
end: W. Just, Techniker im 5. Jahre und
Nationalgardist.
Includes on p.[2] an "Acrostichon", the first
letters of the lines spelling out the word
"Nationalgarden".

*GB8
V6755R
4.31.48

[Krumhans, ———]
Das französische Volk an das Volk von
Oesterreich.
[Wien]Druck von J.N.Friedrich.[1848]

folder(1p.l.,2-3p.) 24x19cm.
Signed at end: Krumhans.

*GB8
V6755R
4.31.48

Just, Wilhelm, fl.1848.
Lied der National-Garde. Auf der Wachstube
gedichtet von Wilhelm Just, Techniker im 5.
Jahre.
[Wien]Gedruckt und zu baben[!] in der k.k.a.
pr.typo-geogr.Kunst-Anstalt,Leopoldstadt,
Herrngasse Nr.237.Stadt,Graben,Loosgewölbe beim
Trattnerhofe.[1848]

[2]p. 22.5x15cm.
Caption title; imprint on p.[2].
Not in Helfert (Wiener Parnass).

*GB8
V6755R
4.31.48

Langer, Anton, fl.1848.
Die Freimaurer in Oesterreich. Von Anton
Langer, Nationalgarde.
[Wien]Preis 3 kr.C.M. ... Franz Edl.v.Schmid,
Universitätsbuchdrucker.[1848]

folder(4p.) 23x15cm.

*GB8
V6755R
4.31.48

Keine Schwarzgelben mehr!
[Wien]Gedruckt bei Josef Ludwig.[1848]

folder(4p.) 21.5x13.5cm.
Caption title; imprint on p.4; signed at end:
Ein Unpartheiischer.

*GB8
V6755R
4.31.48

Langer, Anton, fl.1848.
Kasernen für die Arbeiter. Ein Wort an den
Minister der Arbeit. Von Anton Langer, National-
gardist.
[Wien]Preis 3 kr.C.M. ... Franz Edl.v.Schmid,
Universitätsbuchdrucker.[1848]

folder(4p.) 23.5x15cm.

*GB8
V6755R
4.31.48

Keppler, C
Prolog von C. Keppler, Garde der I.
Juristen-Compagnie.
[Wien]Druck von U.Klopf sen.und Alexander
Eurich.[1848]

[2]p. 26.5x21cm.
Helfert (Wiener Parnass) 608.
Caption title; imprint on p.[2].

*GB8
V6755R
4.31.48

[Leidesdorf, Eduard]
Dies Blatt gehört den Liguorianern!
[Wien,1848]

broadside. 27x21cm.
Dated & signed: Wien im ersten Jahre nach
Vertreibung der Liguorianer. Eduard Ldf.

*GB8
V6755R
4.31.48

[König, Ferdinand, fl.1848]
An die Freiwilligen Wien's im April 1848.
[Wien]A.Dorfmeister's Buchdruckerei.[1848]

[2]p. 23x14cm.
Not recorded in Helfert (Wiener Parnass).
Caption title; imprint on p.[2]; signed at
end: Ferdinand König.

*GB8
V6755R
4.31.48

[Leidesdorf, Eduard]
1 2 3 [i.e. Eins zwei drei] Marzi-Veigerl
herbei! Hier noch ein Marzi=Veigerl, da ein
Marzi=Veigerl, wieder ein Marzi=Veigerl und
glauben sie, ich habe keine Marzi=Veigerl mehr:—
so werden sie sehen, dass die Fortsetzung folgt.
[Wien]Druck von U.Klopf sen.und A.Eurich,
Wollzeile 782.[1848]

[2]p. 21x13cm.
Caption title; imprint on p.[2]; signed at end:
Eduard Leidesdorf.
A continuation of his "Zwei Dutzend
Marzi Veigerl".

*GB8
V6755R
4.31.48

[Leidesdorf, Eduard]
   Pressfreiheitiana.
[Wien]Druck von U.Klopf sen.und A.Eurich,
Wollzeile 782.[1848]

   [2]p. 21x12cm.
   Caption title; imprint on p.[2]; signed at end:
Eduard Leidesdorf.

---

*GB8
V6755R
4.31.48

Ligourianischer Vater unser.
[Wien,1848]

   broadside. 22.5x13cm.
   Helfert (Wiener Parnass) 930.
   Signed: Johann P.

---

*GB8
V6755R
4.31.48

[Leidesdorf, Eduard]
   Zwei Dutzend Marzi Veigerl, gebrockt im März
1848 auf dem Michälerplatze zu Wien.
[Wien,1848]

   [2]p. 21x13cm.
   Caption title; signed at end: Eduard Ldf.
Continued by his "1 2 3 Marzi-Veigerl herbei!"

---

*pGB8
V6755R
4.31.48

Die lobenswerthe Wiener National-Garde.
[Wien]Gedruckt bei Ullrich.[1848]

   broadside. 41x51.5cm.
   Signed: F. C.

---

*GB8
V6755R
4.31.48

Der letzte Spitzl! oder Wer war denn Alles
ein Spitzl? Das letzte Wort über die Spitzl.
[Wien,1848]

   folder([4]p.) 27.5x21.5cm.

---

*pGB8
V6755R
4.31.48

[Lonsetarf, A   ]
   Die gewaltsame Einnahme von Treviso. Die
freiwillige Ergebung von Padua. Die Flucht von
30,000 Italienern. Die Unterhandlungen von
Venedig. Die Todtenlegion und die mobile
Nationalgarde. Die Wiener-Civil-Brigade.
[Wien]Gedruckt und zu haben bei Leopold Grund,
am Stephansplatze im Zwettelhofe.[1848]

   [2]p. 36x23cm.
   Caption title; imprint on p.[2]; signed at end:
A. Lonsetarf.

---

*GB8
V6755R
4.31.48

Lied der Freiwilligen bei ihrem Ausmarsche
nach Italien. (Nach der Melodie: Fridolin.)
[Wien]Gedruckt bei M.Lell.[1848]

   broadside. 22.5x14cm.
   Not recorded in Helfert (Wiener Parnass).
   Without the music.

---

*GB8
V6755R
4.31.48

   Ein Lorberkranz für die Helden der k. k.
österreichischen Artillerie auf dem
Kriegsschauplatze in Italien.
Wien,1848.Gedruckt in der Josephstadt,
Langegasse Nr.58.

   folder([4]p.) 26.5x21cm.
   Illustration on t.-p.

---

*GB8
V6755R
4.31.48

Lied der Freiwilligen [!] Handelslegion nach
Italien.
[Wien]Gedruckt bei M.Lell.[1848]

   broadside. 23x14.5cm.
   Helfert (Wiener Parnass) 941; according to
Helfert also published with title: Lied der
Freiwilligen der Insel Leopoldstadt.

---

*GB8
V6755R
4.31.48

Ludwig, Johann, fl.1848.
   An Habsburg's hohen Sohn.
[Wien]Druck von U.Klopf sen.und A.Eurich.
[1848]

   broadside. 20x13cm.
   Helfert (Wiener Parnass) 690.

Maiss, P
*pGB8 Die grosse Zeugmacher Litanei. (gewöhnlich an
V6755R Samstagen nach dem Auszahln zu sprechen.)
4.31.48 [Wien]Gedruckt bei Josef Ludwig,Josefstadt
Florianigasse Nr.52.[1848]

broadside. 36x21.5cm.

Markbreiter, Moritz.
*GB8 Politisches Glaubensbekenntniss.
V6755R [Wien]Gedruckt und zu haben bei Leopold
4.31.48 Grund,am Stephansplatze im Zwettelhof.[1848]

broadside. 26.5x20cm.
Helfert (Wiener Parnass) 632.

Mand, J   E
*GB8 Die Polizei-Spitzeln als Menagerie=Vieher.
V6755R Halb Traum, halb Wirklichkeit, von J. E. Mand ...
4.31.48 [Wien,1848]

folder([4]p.) 25.5x20cm.
Imprint on p.[4]: Bei Jakob Bader, Buchhändler
in Wien, Stadt, Strobelgasse.

Mauthner, Joseph.
*GB8 Italien! Von Joseph Mauthner.
V6755R [Wien,1848]
4.31.48
folder([4]p.) 23x15cm.
Helfert (Wiener Parnass) 705.
Printer's imprint on p.[2]: Wien, gedruckt bei
Franz Edl. v. Schmid.

[Mantelmann, pseud.]
*GB8 Geschichte vom berüchtigten Carbonari=König
V6755R Carl Albert, welcher geschworen hat, binnen
4.31.48 drei Monaten, Wien in einen Schutthaufen zu
verwandeln.
Wien,1848.Gedruckt in der Josephstadt,
Langegasse Nr.58.

folder([4]p.) 23.5x19cm.

Signed at end: Mantelmann.
Also published with title: Wider den
berüchtigten   Carbonari=König Carl
Albert ...

Meisl, Karl, 1775-1853.
*GB8 Lied der wackeren Wiener=Freiwilligen,.die so
V6755R schnell und zahlreich dem Rufe: "Nach Italien"
4.31.48 gefolgt sind. Von Carl Meisl.
[Wien]Gedruckt und zu haben bei Leop.Grund,
am Rundsthurm Nr.1.Verlag:Stadt,Stephansplatz
im Zwettelhofe.[1848]

[2]p. 25x20cm.
Helfert (Wiener Parnass) 940.
Caption title; imprint on p.[2].

[Mantelmann, pseud.]
*GB8 Die Geschichte von dem braven und hochherzigen
V6755R Ober=Feuerwerker Pollet, der sich um das Vater-
4.31.48 land hochverdient gemacht hat.
Wien.Druck von Joh.Nep.Fridrich,Josephstadt
Langegasse Nr.58.[1848]

folder([4]p.) 26x21cm.
Signed at end: Der Mantelmann.

Moses und Christus halten Reichstag zusammen.
*pGB8 [Wien]Gedruckt bei M.Lell.[1848]
V6755R
4.31.48 [2]p. 38x22.5cm.
Caption title; imprint on p.[2]; signed at
end: L. L.

[Mantelmann, pseud.]
*GB8 Wider den berüchtigten Carbonari=König Carl
V6755R Albert, welcher geschworen hat, binnen drei
4.31.48 Monaten, Wien in einen Schutthaufen zu ver-
wandeln.
Wien,1848.Gedruckt in der Josephstadt,
Langegasse Nre [!] 58.

folder([4]p.) 25x20cm.
Signed at end: Mantelmann.
Also published with title: Geschichte vom
berüchtigten Carbonari=König Carl Albert ...

[Mugna, Pietro]
*GB8 Salmo composto pegl [!] avvenimenti de'giorni
V6755R nostri.
4.31.48 [Vienna]Libreria Tendler e comp.[1848]

folder(4p.) 21x13cm.
Caption title; imprint on p.4; signed at end:
Pietro Mugna.

*GB8
V6755R
4.31.48

Nettwald, Josef.
Erster Garden=Verein. (Landstrasse,
Hauptstrasse, Nr.64, neben dem Gasthause zur
goldenen Birne.)
[Wien,1848]

broadside. 28.5x22cm.

*GB8
V6755R
4.31.48

Die neueste Revolution in Krakau.
[Wien,1848]

folder([4]p.) 26x21cm.

*GB8
V6755R
4.31.48

[Niedopitalski, ———]
Der Papst kommt nach Wien.
[Wien]Gedruckt bei M.Lell,Leopoldstadt,
Weintraubengasse Nr.505.[1848]

folder([4]p.) 27x21.5cm.
Signed at end: Niedopitalski.

*pGB8
V6755R
4.31.48

Ein offener Brief an den Fürst=Erzbischof von
Wien.
. [Wien]Druck von U.Klopf sen.und A.Eurich,
Wollzeile 782.[1848]

[2]p. 42x26cm.
Caption title; imprint on p.[2]; signed at
end: Eine Stimme im Namen Vieler aus dem
Seminare!

*pGB8
V6755R
4.31.48

Offener Brief an die Hausherrn.
[Wien]Gedruckt bei Josef Ludwig,Josefstadt
Florianigasse Nr.52.[1848]

broadside. 41x25cm.
Signed: M. M. Garde der akadem. Legion.

*pGB8
V6755R
4.31.48

Petri, Hugo Jacques.
Ochsenwanderschaft wovon ein Kirchenvorsteher
der Führer ist.
[Wien]Druck von U.Klopf sen.und Alex.Eurich,
Wollzeile Nr.782.[1848]

broadside. 42x26.5cm.
On Archbishop Milde.

*pGB8
V6755R
4.31.48

[Petri, Hugo Jacques]
Petition der Ligourianer an die Wiener.
[Wien]Gedruckt bei Leop.Sommer.[1848]

broadside. 42x26cm.
Signed: Herausgeber: Hugo Jacques [pseud.].
Schottenfeld Nr. 484.
A satire.

*GB8
V6755R
4.31.48

[Petri, Hugo Jacques]
Ein Wort über die National=Garde.
[Wien,1848]

folder([4]p.) 21.5x13.5cm.
Signed at end: Hugo Jacques Petri.
Imprint on p.[4]: Druck und Eigenthum von
Hirschfeld in Wien.

*pGB8
V6755R
4.31.48

Pexa, L   J
...Woher ist Reaction zu fürchten? (Etwas
verspätet in Folge der von dem Herrn Generalen
der Volks=Freiheit ausgeübten Censur. Die ihm
misfälligsten Stellen habe ich, wie die
Censurlücken anzeigen, weggelassen.) Dieses
Plakat war es eigentlich, nicht aber jenes
betitelt "der Terrorismus" dessen Druck in der
v. Schmid'schen Buchdruckerei so ganz gegen alle
Pressfreiheit auf das Verlangen Häfners
hintertrieben ward.
                              (See next card)

*pGB8
V6755R
4.31.48

Pexa, L   J   ... Woher ist Reaction ...
[1848]   (Card 2)
[Wien]Gedruckt bei den Edlen von Ghelen'schen
Erben,und zu haben in der Buchhandlung des
Herrn Bader im Strobelgässchen ...[1848]

broadside. 45.5x58.5cm.
At head: Zweite Auflage mit verständlicheren
Censurlücken.

*GB8
V6755R
4.31.48

Pfeifer, Karl, fl.1848.
   Das Lied vom deutschen Mädchen. Dem gefeierten
Fräulein Mathilde Hellwig, Opernsängerin des
Nationaltheaters, als Zeichen der Verehrung
gewidmet von Karl Pfeifer.
   [Wien]Gedruckt bei Josef Ludwig,Josefstadt
Florianigasse Nr.52.[1848]

   [2]p. 20x12.5cm.
   Helfert (Wiener Parnass) 955.
   Caption title; imprint on p.[2].

---

*GB8
V6755R
4.31.48

Pfeifer, Karl, fl.1848.
   Unserem hochgeehrten Feldkaplan, dem
hochwürdigen Herrn Anton Füster, gewidmet von
Karl Pfeifer. National=Garden der akademischen
Legion.
   [Wien]Gedruckt bei Joseph Ludwig.[1848]

   [2]p. 21x13cm.
   Helfert (Wiener Parnass) 953.
   Caption title; imprint on p.[2].

---

*pGB8
V6755R
4.31.48

Podulak, Alexander.
   An die freien Wiener! Die vergessene
Geschichte vom 12. September 1683.
   [Wien,1848]

   broadside. 43x27cm.

---

*pGB8
V6755R
4.31.48

Populäre Darstellung des monarchisch=
konstitutionellen Lebens.
   [Wien,1848]

   broadside. 37x22.5cm.
   Signed: J. N. O., alte Wieden Nr. 437.

---

*GB8
V6755R
4.31.48

Radetzky's Sieg und der Schmähbrief aus
Mailand.
   [Wien]Gedruckt bei Leopold Grund,am
Hunsthurm[!],Schlossplatz Nr.1.[1848]

   folder([4]p.)
   Caption title; imprint on p.[4].

---

*GP8
V6755R
4.31.48

Radetzky's Truppen schreiten immer mehr
vorwärts. Modena und Ferrara.
   [Wien,1848]

   folder([4]p.) 23x18.5cm.
   Imprint on p.[4]: Gedruckt und zu haben bei
Leopold Grund, am Stephansplatze im Zwettelhofe.
Title printed vertically.

---

*pGB8
V6755R
4.31.48

Rede des Jesuiten=Generals, gehalten in einer
geheimen Sitzung zu Rom vor einer Versammlung
Jesuiten und Liguorianer. Aus dem Italienischen
ins Deutsche übersetzt.
   [Wien]Druck von J.Stöckholzer v.Hirschfeld.—Zu
haben im Bureau des "Omnibus," Stadt,
Liliengasse.Nr.898.[1848]

   [2]p. 34.5x26cm.
   Caption title; imprint on p.[2].
   A satire.

---

*GB8
V6755R
4.31.48

Revolution und Gegenrevolution.
   [Wien,1848]

   folder([4]p.) 20x13.5cm.
   Signed at end: S.
   Imprint on p.[4]: Druck von U. Klopf sen. und
A. Eurich, Wollzeile 782.

---

*GB8
V6755R
4.31.48

Die Revolutionen Europa's in Jahre 1848. Sturz
der verhassten Systeme. Neueste Nachrichten über
die Insurection des lombardisch=venetianischen
Königreiches. Aufstand von ganz Italien. Der
Weltfrieden in Gefahr.
   [Wien]Gedruckt bei Leop.Grund.[1848]

   [2]p. 26x21cm.
   Caption title; imprint on p.[2]; signed at
end: Zusammengestellt von F. W. Z.

---

*GB8
V6755R
4.31.48

[Rosental, Klemens, ascribed author]
   Politische Naturgeschichte für Freiheitskinder.
   [Wien]Verlag von J.Wenedikt.Gedruckt bei F.
E.v.Schmid.[1848]

   folder([4]p.) 22x14.5cm.
   Helfert (Wiener Parnass) 710.
   Caption title; imprint on p.[4]; signed
at end: K. R.

*GB8
V6755R
4.31.48

Rutta, Rudolf.
Antritts=Rede. Gesprochen von Rudolf Rutta,
bei seiner förmlichen Einreihung in die National=
Garde und Ernennung zum Feldwebel.
[Wien,1848]

broadside. 27.5x21cm.
Dated in contemporary ms.: April.

---

*GB8
V6755R
4.31.48

[Scherb, ———]
An die ausgewiesenen und alle Jesuiten!
[Wien,1848]

folder([4]p.) 26.5x21cm.
Signed on p.[3]: Scherb.
Imprint on p.[4]: K. k. Hof=Buchdruckerei des
L. Sommer (vormals Strauss).

---

*GB8
V6755R
4.31.48

[Schaffer, Franz Joseph, d.1880]
Des Wortes Macht.
[Wien]Ausgegeben von Tendler & Comp.[1848]

[2]p. 22.5x13.5cm.
Helfert (Wiener Parnass) 666.
Caption title; imprint on p.[2]; signed at
end: Fr. J. Schaffer.

---

*GB8
V6755R
4.31.48

Schickh, Joseph.
Patriotische Hymne, von Joseph Schickh. In
Musik gesetzt von Anton Diabelli.
[Wien]A.Dorfmeister's Buchdruckerei.[1848]

folder([3]p.) 16x10cm.
Helfert (Wiener Parnass) 681.
Without the music.

---

*pGB8
V6755R
4.31.48

Schandmal des 19. Jahrhunderts, oder: Die
neuesten Pressburger Ereignisse.
[Wien]Druck v.U.Klopf sen.u.A.Eurich,
Wollzeile Nr.782.[1848]

broadside. 42x25.5cm.
Signed: R. W. [i.e. Rudolph Weinberger?]
Printed within border of type-ornaments.
Also issued with title: Denkwürdige Judenver-
folgung des 19. Jahrhunderts ...

---

*GB8
V6755R
4.31.48

[Schild, Franz Josef, 1821-1889]
Die deutsche Eiche. (Melodie: Schier dreissig
Jahre bist du alt.)
[Wien]Gedruckt bei Josef Ludwig,Josefstadt
Florianigasse Nr.52.[1848]

[2]p. 21x13cm.
Caption title; imprint on p.[2]; signed at end:
Fr. Jos. Schild.
Not in Helfert (Wiener Parnass).
Without the music.

---

*GB8
V6755R
4.31.48

[Scheda, Julius]
Wien's wilde Studentenjagd.
[Wien]A.Dorfmeister's Druck und Verlag
(Stadt,Kühfussgasse Nr.575).[1848]

[2]p. 23x15cm.
Helfert (Wiener Parnass) 659.
Caption title; imprint on p.[2]; signed at
end: Julius Scheda, Jurist.

---

*pGB8
V6755R
4.31.48

Schinnagl, Maurus.
Liebe Mitbürger! Man verdächtiget uns
Geistliche als starre Anhänger des verhassten
früheren Knechtssystems; man nennt uns Feinde
der constitutionellen Verfassung; man
beschuldiget uns reactionärer Massregeln ...
[Wien]Gedruckt bei Ferd.Jahn,Zeughausgasse
Nr.179.[1848]

broadside. 40.5x50.5cm.

---

*GB8
V6755R
4.31.48

Scheidlin-Wenrich, Carolina von, b.1824.
Gruss an das Licht. Den tapfern Studenten der
Wiener Universität gewidmet von Carolina von
Scheidlin-Wenrich.
[Wien]Druck von U.Klopf sen.und A.Eurich,
Wollzeile 782.[1848]

[2]p. 20.5x13cm.
Helfert (Wiener Parnass) 656.
Caption title; imprint on p.[2].

---

*GB8
V6755R
4.31.48

[Schinnagl, Maurus]
Stimmen aus dem Clerus an Wien's Bevölkerung.
[Wien]Gedruckt bei den Edlen von Ghelen'schen
Erben.[1848]

[2]p. 27.5x21.5cm.
Caption title; imprint on p.[2]; signed at end:
Maurus Schinnagl, Priester des Benedictiner=
Stiftes zu den Schotten und Professor am k. k.
Gymnasium daselbst.

*pGB8
V6755R
4.31.48

Schleckerbartl! Sau d'Aristokraten alle,
endlich in der Mäusefalle!!
[Wien]Gedruckt bei M.Lell.[1848]

broadside. 38x24.5cm.
In verse, but printed as prose.

---

*GB8
V6755R
4.31.48

Schreckliche Raub= und Mord=Scenen in Szered
in Ungarn. Bei Gelegenheit der Juden=
Vertreibung.
[Wien,1848]

folder([4]p.) 1 illus. 30x24cm.

---

*pGB8
V6755R
4.31.48

Schmidt, Franz, fl.1848.
Bittschrift der Christensklaven an die
Herren Juden um Christen=Emancipation.
In Commission bei Jakob Bader,Buchhändler in
Wien,Stadt,Strobelgasse.[1848]

broadside. 52x41.5cm.
Antisemitic satire.

---

*pGB8
V6755R
4.31.48

[Seegen, Josef]
An die Studenten Wiens! Brüder! Der Kampf der
Märztage war der Kampf der Gesinnung und des
kräftig erwachten politischen Bewusstseins gegen
das System der Knechtung und Entgeistigung ...
[Wien]Gedruckt bei Edl.v.Schmidbauer und
Holzwarth.[1848]

[2]p. 42x26cm.
Caption title; imprint on p.[2]; signed: Med.
Dr. Josef Seegen. Heinrich Kern, Doctorand der
Rechte.
Proposing the establishment of a
reading-room and club for political discus-
sion.

---

*GB8
V6755R
4.31.48

[Schmidt, Franz, fl.1848]
Bittschrift der Christensklaven an die Herren
Juden um Christen=Emancipation.
In Commission bei Jakob Bader,Buchhändler in
Wien,Stadt,Strobelgasse.[1848]

[2]p. 25x20.5cm.
Caption title; imprint on p.[2]; signed at end:
Franz Schmidt.
Antisemitic satire.

---

*GB8
V6755R
4.31.48

[Seravalle, M   von]
An die Bürger von Wien. Vergangenheit,
Gegenwart und Zukunft.
[Wien]Gedruckt bei M.Lell,Leopoldstadt,
Weintraubengasse Nr.505.[1848]

folder(4p.) 21.5x13cm.
Caption title; imprint on p.4; signed at end:
M. von Seravalle, ehemaliger Kommandant der
Nationalgarde in Spanien.

---

*pGB8
V6755R
4.31.48

[Schön, Leopold]
Franz Schmidt der Judenfresser.
[Wien]Gedruckt bei Josef Ludwig.[1848]

[2]p. 1 illus. 43x27cm.
Caption title; imprint on p.[2]; signed at
end: Leopold Schön.

---

*GB8
V6755R
4.31.48

Sicheres Mittel zur Nichtzahlung des Georgi=
Zinses.
[Wien,1848]

folder([4]p.) 27x21.5cm.
Dated in contemporary ms.: April 1848.

---

*GB8
V6755R
4.31.48

Schrank, J   F
Deutschlands Freudentag. Gedicht von J. F.
Schrank.
[Wien]Gedruckt bei Josef Ludwig.[1848]

[2]p. 21.5x13cm.
Caption title; imprint on p.[2].

---

*pGB8
V6755R
4.31.48

Simić von Hohenblum, Joseph.
Vorschlag an die National-Garden, zur
Errichtung von Localitäten für jede Compagnie
behufs gemeinsamer Besprechungen.
[Wien]Gedruckt bei den Edlen von Ghelen'schen
Erben.[1848]

broadside. 43.5x26cm.

*pGB8
V6755R
4.31.48

So halten die Russen ihr Wort.
(Buchstäblich wahr).
[Wien]Druck von M.Lell.[1848]

[2]p. 38x23.5cm.
Caption title; imprint on p.[2].
A brief history of Graf Beniowski.

*pGB8
V6755R
4.31.48

Verein zur Beaufsichtigung der Kostkinder,
Vienna.
Anzeige für jene Eltern, welche ihre kleinen
Kinder in Kost zu geben genöthigt sind.
[Wien,1848]

broadside. 39x24cm.
Dated: Wien, im April 1848.

*GB8
V6755R
4.31.48

Der Soldat, der Student, der Bürger und der
Nationalgardist im Freudentaumel des
Entzückens.
[Wien]A.Dorfmeister's Druck und Verlag,Stadt,
Kühfussgasse Nr.575.[1848]

[2]p. 22.5x14cm.
Helfert (Wiener Parnass) 694.
Caption title; imprint on p.[2].

*pGB8
V6755R
4.31.48

[Vielweis, Liborius, pseud.]
Offener Brief an den Herrn Prälaten des
Klosters zu Heiligenkreuz. Von einem treuen
Unterthan.
[Wien]Gedruckt bei J.N.Fridrich.Herausgegeben
von Sammer.[1848]

[2]p. 42x26cm.
Caption title; imprint on p.[2]; signed at
end: Liborius Vielweis.

*GB8
V6755R
4.31.48

Stern, Max Emanuel, 1811-1873.
Aschenlied der Constitution. Von M. E. Stern.
[Wien,1848]

folder([4]p.) 22.5x15cm.
Helfert (Wiener Parnass) 611.
Imprint on p.[4]: Gedruckt bei Franz Edlen
von Schmid.

*GB8
V6755R
4.31.48

Vienna. Bürgergarde.
Die uniformirte Bürger-Garde Wien's an ihre
Cameraden Nationalgarden.
[Wien]Gedruckt bei Ferdinand Ullrich.[1848]

[2]p. 21.5x14.5cm.
Caption title; imprint on p.[2].
"Zur unentgeldlichen Ausgabe bestimmt."

*GB8
V6755R
4.31.48

Stern, Max Emanuel, 1811-1873.
Nationalgarden-Lied. Von M. E. Stern.
Componirt von Professor S. Sulzer.
[Wien,1848]

folder([3]p.) 23x14.5cm.
Helfert (Wiener Parnass) 640.
Printer's imprint on p.[3]: Gedruckt bei
Franz Edlen von Schmid.
Without the music.

*pGB8
V6755R
4.31.48

Vienna. Nationalgarde.
Beschreibung der Montur und Bewaffnung der
Nationalgarde.
[Wien,1848]

[2]p. 44.5x28.5cm.
Signed: Hoyos, Feldmarschall=Lieutenant und
Ober=Commandant der Bürger= und Nationalgarde.

*pGB8
V6755R
4.31.48

Eine Stimme aus der Nationalgarde.
[Wien]Gedruckt bei Ant.Benko.[1848]

broadside. 46x28.5cm.
On the outfitting of the Nationalgarde.

*GB8
V6755R
4.31.48

Vienna. Nationalgarde.
Entwurf einer Vorschrift über Urlaubs-
Bewilligungen in der Nationalgarde.
[Wien]Aus der k.k.Hof= und Staats=Druckerei.
[1848]

broadside. 29.5x22cm.

*pGB8
V6755R
4.31.48

Vienna. Universität. Ausschuss der Studierenden.
An die Nationalgarde. Die Studirenden Wiens,
lebhaft durchdrungen von dem Wunsch, in brüderlicher Eintracht und in herzlichem festen
Zusammenhalten mit dem übrigen Theile der
Nationalgarde gemeinschaftlich auf der von
ihnen betretenen Bahn der Freiheit
fortzuschreiten ...
[Wien,1848]

broadside. 58x48cm.
Signed: Von ⌠ dem Ausschusse der
Studirenden Wiens.⌡

*pGB8
V6755R
4.31.48

Zwei-Kammersistem.
[Wien]Gedruckt bei U.Klopf sen.u.Alex.Eurich.
[1848]

broadside. 42.5x26.5cm.
Explaining that the upper chamber need not be
restricted to the nobility.

---

*pGB8
V6755R
4.31.48

Vienna, Universität. Ausschuss der Studierenden.
Mitbürger! Nur durch Eintracht sind wir stark,
Zwietracht vernichtet uns, vernichtet die
Freiheit ...
[Wien]Aus der k.k.Hof= und Staatsdruckerei.
[1848]

broadside. 44.5x28.5cm.

*GB8
V6755R
4.31.48

Das zweite Vergismeinnicht über den Herrn
Pfarrer vom Lichtenthal.
[Wien]Gedruckt bei Josef Ludwig,Josefstadt
Florianigasse Nr.52.[1848]
folder([4]p.) 25.5x20.5cm.
Signed at end: A. M.

---

*GB8
V6755R
4.31.48

Vienna (Archdiocese) Clergy.
An den Clerus des österreichischen
Kaiserstaates von der Versammlung der Wiener-
Diöcesan-Geistlichkeit!
[Wien]Druck von A.Pichler's Witwe.[1848]
folder([3]p.) 27x21.5cm.
Caption title; imprint on p.[3]; signed at
end: Dr. Brunner. Joh. Engel. Ant. Gruscha
[& 9 others].

*GB8
V6755R
5.1.48

Die Antwort auf das Blatt: Die Freimädchen.
Oder die kann Gott danken, die einen braven
Mann hat. Ein Gleichniss für unsere Frauen, in
ganz Europa. Geschrieben von einer Französin!
[Wien]Gedruckt bei M.Lell,Weintraubengasse,Nr.
595.[1848]
folder([4]p.) 26.5x21cm.
"Die Freimädchen" is by Raimund Hochleitner.
Dated in contemporary ms.: 1. Mai 848.

---

*GB8
V6755R
4.31.48

Was die Schwalben in Wien Alles wissen, und
wie sie ganz unschönirt mitsammen plaudern.
[Wien]Gedruckt bei Anton Benko.[1848]
7,[1]p. 19.5x12cm.
Title vignette (swallow).
Imprint on p.7: Zu haben, in Gumpendorf,
untere Annagasse Nr. 507, zweiten Stock Thür
Nr. 9.
Anticlerical.

*pGB8
V6755R
5.1.48

Vienna. Magistrat.
Kundmachung. Die Zeit der Wahl für die
Abgeordneten und ihre Stellvertreter zur
deutschen National=Versammlung in Frankfurt am
Main wird, um Doppelwahlen möglichst zu
vermeiden, in nachstehender Weise vorgenommen ...
[Wien,1848]

broadside. 44.5x29cm.
Dated & signed: Wien am 1. Mai 1848. Vom
Magistrate und prov. Bürger-Ausschusse.

---

*GB8
V6755R
4.31.48

Was ist denn diese Nacht in der Leopoldstadt
schon wieder geschen'n!!! oder der Direktor Karl
und der Baron Schloissnig.
[Wien,1848]
folder([4]p.) 27.5x21.5cm.

*pGB8
V6755R
5.1.48

Vienna. Magistrat.
Kundmachung. Um dem mehrseitigen Wunsche zu
entsprechen, wird hiermit bekannt gemacht, dass
zwar nach der hierortigen Verlautbarung vom 13.
v. M. die Aufstellung von Markthütten und
Verkaufsständchen in der inneren Stadt für den
nächsten Jubilate=Markt zu unterbleiben hat ...
[Wien,1848]

broadside. 39.5x49.5cm.
Signed & dated: Vom Magistrate und prov.
Bürger=Ausschusse der Stadt Wien, am 1. Mai 1848.

1848 AUSTRIAN REVOLUTIONARY BROADSIDES AND PAMPHLETS

*pGB8
V6755R
5.1.48

Vienna. Nationalgarde. Akademische Legion.
Vorläufige Statuten für die National=
Liedertafel der akademischen Legion.
[Wien]Druck von U.Klopf senior und A.Eurich,
Wollzeile Nr.782.[1848]

broadside. 42x25.5cm.
Dated: Wien am 1. des Wonnemonats 1848.

*GB8
V6755R
5.3.48

Habt Acht, habt Acht! Die Liguorianer sind
schon wieder da! Aus der österr. deutschen
Zeitung nebst einem Anhang. Geheime Ordens=
Regeln der verjagten Ligouriauer [!].Wörtlich
übersetzt aus den vorgefnndenen [!] Papieren.
[Wien,1848]

folder([4]p.) 30x23cm.
Caption title.

*pGB8
V6755R
5.2.48

Liste der Candidaten für die Stelle eines
Abgeordneten zur deutschen National=
Versammlung in Frankfurt am Main.
[Wien,1848]

broadside. 44.5x28.5cm.
Includes the name of Friedrich Hebbel.

*pGB8
V6755R
5.3.48

... Habt Acht, habt Acht! Die Liguorianer sind
wieder da!
[Wien]Gedruckt bei Edl.v.Schmidbauer und
Holzwarth.[1848] Preis des einzelnen Blattes 3
kr.Conv.Minze.

[2]p. 34.5x26.5cm.
Caption-title; at head: Ausserordentliche
Beilage zur österreichisch=deutschen Zeitung ...
Zu N° 15. Wien, Mittwoch den 3. Mai. 1848.
Imprint on p.[2].

*pGB8
V6755R
5.2.48

Verein der Wiener Schriftsteller.
Wahlumtriebe! Die Wahlen zum deutschen Parla-
ment nach Frankfurt sind noch nicht vollendet,
und schon laufen von den verschiedensten
Punkten die bedenklichsten Nachrichten über
Umtriebe ein ...
[Wien]Druck von U.Klopf sen.und A.Eurich.
[1848]

broadside. 53x42cm.
Dated: Wien den 2. Mai 1848.

*pGB8
V6755R
5.3.48

Ignatz Rössler ein Polizey=Spitzel vom Bezirke
Wieden wird am 3. Mai 1848 vou [!] den Studenten
arretirt. Von einem Augenzeuge.
[Wien]Gedruckt bei M.Lell,Leopoldstadt,
Weintraubengasse Nr.505.[1848]

broadside. 43x26.5cm.
Another edition begins: Ignaz Rössler ...

*pGB8
V6755R
5.2.48

Vienna. Magistrat.
Von dem Magistrate der k. k. Haupt- und
Residenzstadt Wien. Auf Grundlage der von den
sämmtlichen Dienern der bürgerl. Kaffehsieder
in Wien überreichten Petition zur Regulirung
ihres Dienstverhältnisses ...
[Wien,1848]

[2]p. 40.5x25.5cm.
At head: G. Z. 24181.
Dated: Wien, am 2. Mai 1848.

*pGB8
V6755R
5.3.48

Ignaz Rössler ein Polizey=Spitzel vom
Bezirke Wieden wird am 3. Mai 1848 von den
Studenten arretirt. Von einem Augen=Zeuge.
[Wien]Gedruckt bei M.Lell,Leopoldstadt,
Weintraubengasse Nr.505.[1848]

broadside. 42.5x26cm.
Another edition begins: Ignatz Rössler ...

*pGB8
V6755R
5.3.48

Born, Ernst Wilhelm.
Kundmachung. Am heutigen Tage wurden
nacheinander zwei Individuen in und bei den
Hallen der Universität angehalten, weil sie
für Polizeispione gehalten wurden ...
[Wien,1848]

broadside. 40.5x50cm.
Dated: Wien am 3. Mai 1848.

*pGB8
V6755R
5.3.48

Philipp, pseud.
Der gefangene Liguorianer.
[Wien]Druck v.U.Klopf sen.u.A.Eurich,
Wollzeile Nr.782.[1848]

broadside. 42x26cm.
Refers to the "Katzenmusik" accorded the
Archbishop of Vienna on the night of May 2, 1848,
as a result of his having petitioned for the
return of the Liguorian order; cf. Reschauer-
Smets II.136 & Helfert (Geschichte) II.39.
(See next card)

87

*pGB8
V6755R
3.15.48

Philipp, pseud.   Der gefangene Liguorianer
... [1848]   (Card 2)
Another copy. 39x25cm.
Printed on the back of a copy of "Metternichs
Reisepass", dated 15 March 1848.

---

*pGB8
V6755R
5.4.48

Vienna. Kellner.
Petitionen der sämmtlichen Kellner zu Wien an
ihre Innungen.
[Wien]Druck von U.Klopf sen.und Alex.Eurich.
[1848]

  folder([3]p.) 42.5x27cm.
  Caption title; imprint on p.[3].
  Dated: Wien am 4. Mai 1848.

---

*pGB8
V6755R
5.4.48

Austria. Sovereigns, etc., 1835-1848
          (Ferdinand I)
  Proclamation. Die zu erngten Gefahren
führende Aufregung der Gemüther und die Wünsche
aller bei Aufrechthaltung der Ruhe und
Gesetzlichkeit betheiligten Bewohner Meiner
getreuen Haupt= und Residenzstadt fordern Mich
auf, einige eindringende Worte an Meine
geliebten Wiener zu richten ...
  [Wien,1848]
  broadside. 44.5x57cm.
  Reschauer-Smets   II.150.
  Dated & signed: Wien am 4. Mai 1848.
Ferdinand.

---

*pGB8
V6755R
5.4.48

Vienna. Magistrat.
  Grundzüge für den Sicherheits=Ausschuss der
Stadt Wien.
  [Wien,1848]

  broadside. 44.5x57cm.
  Dated & signed: Wien am 4. Mai 1848. Von dem
Magistrate und provisorischen Bürger-Ausschusse.

---

*pGB8
V6755R
5.4.48

Fuchs, Karl, fl.1848.
  Mitbürger und Bewohner der Gemeinde Windmühle!
[Wien]Gedruckt bei den Edlen von Ghelen'schen
Erbeu[!].[1848]

. broadside. 43x27.5cm.
  Dated: Wien am 4. Mai 1848.
  Proposing that individual citizens assume
the cost of providing uniforms for the Nationalgarde.

---

*pGB8
V6755R
5.4.48

Vienna. Magistrat.
  Kundmachung. Da nunmehr in der k. k. Haupt=
und Residenzstadt die Wahlen der Abgeordneten und
ihrer Stellvertreter zur deutschen National=
Versammlung in Frankfurt am Main beendiget sind
...
  [Wien,1848]

  broadside. 39.5x27.5cm.
  Dated & signed: Wien den 4. Mai 1848. Vom
Wiener Magistrate und prov. Bürgerausschusse.
  Announcing the names of the representatives
elected.

---

*pGB8
V6755R
5.4.48

Oesterreichischer Patrioten-Verein.
  Patrioten! Alle Zeitungen erheben ein
Geschrei und sagen, Oesterreich ist in grosser
Gefahr! ...
  [Wien,1848]

  [2]p. 44.5x31cm.
  Caption title.
  Dated & signed: Wien, den 4. Mai 1848. Vom
Österreichischen Patrioten=Verein.
  Another edition has imprint.
  Urging every inhabitant to contribute 1 gulden
to the support   of the state.

---

*pGB8
V6755R
5.4.48

Vienna. Magistrat.
  ... Von dem Magistrate der k. k. Haupt= und
Residenzstadt Wien. Über die Vorstellung der
Hutmachergesellen ...
  [Wien,1848]

  broadside.. 38x24cm.
  At head: G. Z. 20973.
  Dated: Wien, am 4. Mai 1848.

---

*pGB8
V6755R
5.4.48

Oesterreichischer Patrioten-Verein.
  Patrioten! Alle Zeitungen erheben ein Geschrei
und sagen, Oesterreich ist in grosser Gefahr! ...
  [Wien]Aus der k.k.Hof- und Staatsdruckerei.
[1848]

  [2]p. 44.5x28.5cm.
  Caption title; imprint on p.[2].
  Dated & signed: Wien den 4. Mai 1848. Vom
Österreichischen Patrioten-Verein.
  Another edition is without imprint.
  Urging every inhabitant to contribute 1 gulden
to the support   of the state.

---

*pGB8
V6755R
5.4.48

Vienna. Nationalgarde.
  Ganz Unberufene erlauben sich Aufrufe zu
Zusammenkünften und Petitionen zu stellen ...
  [Wien]Druck von Ulrich Klopf sen.und Alex.
Eurich.[1848]

  broadside. 42x26.5cm.
  Dated & signed: Wien, am 4. Mai 1848. Coloredo
Mannsfeld.

*GB8
V6755R
5.5.48

Rummelpuff, Max.
Nachträgliches Programm des Ministerium
Ficquelmont, von Max Rummelpuff.
[Wien]Druck von U.Klopf sen.und A.Eurich,
Wollzeile Nr.782.[1848]

folder(4p.) 21x13cm.
Caption title; imprint on p.4.

---

*pGB8
V6755R
5.5.48

Wimmer, Ignaz.
Mitbrüder, liebe Freunde! Zu meinem innigsten
Leide musste ich eine Demonstration gegen meine
Person erfahren, die nur ein böswilliges
Gerücht zu Folge hatte ...
[Wien,1848]

broadside. 34.5x22cm.
Dated: Matzleinsdorf am 5. Mai 1848.

---

*pGB8
V6755R
5.5.48

Vienna. Nationalgarde.
[Begins:] Der Bezirks=Verwaltungsrath besteht
aus dem Herrn Bezirks=Kommandanten als Präses,
dann aus den für jede der fünf Kompagnien
bereits gewählten drei Herren Deputirten ...
[Wien]Gedruckt bei Carl Gerold.[1848]

folder([4]p.) 39.5x25.5cm.
Caption-title; imprint on p.[4].
Dated & signed: Wien, am 5. Mai 1848. Von dem
Bezirks-Verwaltungsrathe des Kärntner-Viertels.

---

*pGB8
V6755R
5.6.48

Austria. Ministerium des Innern.
Kundmachung. Um den Arbeitern, welche durch
die jetzigen Zeitverhältniss brodlos werden
könnten, wieder Arbeit zu verschaffen ...
[Wien,1848]

broadside. 44.5x57cm.
Dated & signed: Wien am 6. Mai 1848. Der
Minister des Inneren: Freiherr von Pillersdorff.

---

*pGB8
V6755R
5.5.48

Vienna. Nationalgarde.
Die Ruhestörungen in den letzten Nächten haben
es nothwendig gemacht, dass zur Aufrechthaltung
der Sicherheit und Ordnung, so wie zur
Beseitigung aller Aufläufe von Seite der
sämmtlichen Nationalgarden kräftig eingewirkt
werde ...
[Wien,1848]

broadside. 44.5x56.5cm.
Dated & signed: Wien, am 5. Mai 1848. Vom
Ober-Commando sämmtlicher Garden.

---

*pGB8
V6755R
5.6.48

Vienna. Magistrat.
Kundmachung. In Folge der in den letzten
Nächten stattgefundenen Beunruhigungen findet
sich der Magistrat und provisorische Bürger=
Ausschuss veranlasst ...
[Wien,1848]

broadside. 40x52.5cm.
Dated & signed: Wien den 6. Mai 1848. Vom
Magistrate und prov. Bürger-Ausschusse.

---

*pGB8
V6755R
5.5.48

Vienna. Universität. Ausschuss der Studierenden.
Petition der Studierenden Wiens an den
Minister des Innern.
[Wien]Druck von U.Klopf sen.und A.Eurich,
Wollzeile Nr.782.[1848]

broadside. 42.5x26.5cm.
Reschauer-Smets II.152.
Signed & dated: Der Ausschuss der Studierenden
Wiens. Wien den 5. Mai 1848.

---

*pGB8
V6755R
5.6.48

Vienna. Nationalgarde.
Petition der Nationalgarde und des Bürger-Corps
von Wien an den Minister des Innern.
[Wien,1848]

broadside. 42.5x26.5cm.
Reschauer-Smets II.155.
Dated: Wien am 6. Mai 1848.

---

*pGB8
V6755R
5.5.48

Vienna. Universität. Ausschuss der Studierenden.
Die Studenten an die Einwohner Wiens!
[Wien]Druck von U.Klopf sen. und A.Eurich.
[1848]

broadside. 53x42cm.
Reschauer-Smets II.154.
Dated & signed: Wien den 5. Mai 1848. Im
Namen des Ausschusses [!] ...

---

*pGB8
V6755R
5.7.48

Entgegnung auf Dr. Knoth's Anklage gegen
Pietro di L. A. Galvagni.
[Wien,1848]

broadside. 42x26.5cm.
Dated & signed: Wien den 7. Mai 1848.
V.....i.

Knoth, Ludwig.
*pGB8   Mitbürger! Justitia regnorum fundamentum.
V6755R   Indem ihr jetzt für Freiheit und Vaterland so
5.7.48   vielfach in Anspruch genommen seid ...
     [Wien,1848]

     broadside. 41.5x53cm.
     Dated: Wien am 7. Mai 1848.

Vienna. Magistrat.
*pGB8   Aufruf an die mildthätigen Bürger und
V6755R   Bürgerinnen Wiens.
5.8.48   [Wien,1848]

     broadside. 44.5x57cm.
     Dated & signed: Wien am 8. Mai 1848. Vom
Magistrate und prov. Bürger-Ausschusse.

Vienna. Nationalgarde. Central-Comité.
*pGB8   Petition des Central=Comité's der gesammten
V6755R   Nationalgarde Wiens, an den Herrn Minister des
5.7.48   Innern.
     [Wien]Druck von U.Klopf sen.und Alex.Eurich
Wollzeile Nr.782.[1848]

     broadside. 40.5x25.5cm.
     Dated: Wien, am 7. Mai 1848.

Vienna. Magistrat.
*pGB8   Kundmachung. Mit allerhöchster Entschliessung
V6755R   vom 17. März d. J. wurde die Errichtung eines
5.8.48   Gemeinde=Ausschusses für die Stadt Wien
     bewilliget ...
     [Wien,1848]

     folder(4p.) 45x28.5cm.
     Caption title; dated & signed on p.2: Wien am
8. Mai 1848. Von dem Magistrate und provisorischen
Bürger-Ausschusse.
     In this edition, p.2 begins: 5. Die Wähler der
inneren Stadt ...

Vienna. Nationalgarde. Central-Comité.
*pGB8   Von dem politischen Central-Comité der
V6755R   gesammten National=Garde Wiens. An sämmtliche
5.7.48   Compagnien der National=Garde, des Bürger=Corps
und der akademischen Legion.
     [Wien,1848]

     broadside. 47x30cm.
     Dated: Wien am 7. Mai 1848.

Vienna. Magistrat.
*pGB8   Kundmachung. Mit allerhöchster Entschliessung
V6755R   vom 17. März d. J. wurde die Errichtung eines
5.8.48   Gemeinde=Ausschusses für die Stadt Wien
     bewilliget ...
     [Wien,1848]

     folder(4p.) 45x28.5cm.
     Caption title; dated & signed on p.4: Wien am
8. Mai 1848. Von dem Magistrate und prov.
Bürger-Ausschusse.
     In this edition, p.2 begins: 2. Die Wähler
vom Polizei=   Bezirk Wimmerviertel ...

Austria, Lower. Laws, statutes, etc., 1835-1848
*pGB8   (Ferdinand I)
V6755R   ... Von der k. k. n. ö. Landesregierung. In
5.8.48   der Absicht, die wohlthätigen Wirkungen unserer
Verfassungen recht bald im ausgedehntesten
Umfange sichtbar zu machen ...
     [Wien,1848]

     folder([3]p.) 37.5x23cm.
     Caption title; at head: N° 23117.
     Dated: Wien am 8. Mai 1848.

Vienna. Magistrat.
*pGB8   Kundmachung. Mit allerhöchster Entschliessung
V6755R   vom 17. März d. J. wurde die Errichtung eines
5.8.48   Gemeinde=Ausschusses für die Stadt Wien
     bewilliget ...
     [Wien,1848]

     folder(4p.) 45x28.5cm.
     Caption-title; dated & signed on p.3: Wien am
8. Mai 1848. Von dem Magistrate und prov.
Bürger-Ausschusse.
     In this edition, p.2 begins: 5. Die Wähler
in den 34.   Vorstadtgemeinden ...

Der Deutsche Adler (Club), Vienna.
*pGB8   Euer Excellenz! Das kaiserliche Wort Sr.
V6755R   Majestät hat uns am 15. März eine Constitution,
5.8.48   aus einer Volksberathung hervorgehend, in
Aussicht gestellt ...
     [Wien,1848]

     [2]p. 46x30cm.
     Caption title; dated & signed: Wien den 8. Mai
1848. Im Namen des Vereins: "Der deutsche
Adler".
     With several ms. signatures on p.[2].

Vienna. Nationalgarde.
*pGB8   An die Nationalgarden in Wien.
V6755R   [Wien,1848]
5.8.48

     broadside. 45x28.5cm.
     Dated & signed: Wien am 8. Mai 1848. Hoyos,
Ober=Commandant der Nationalgarden in Wien.

*pGB8
V6755R
5.8.48

Vienna. Universität. Ausschuss der Studierenden.
    Erklärung der Studenten Wiens.
    Druck von U.Klopf sen.und A.Eurich in Wien.
    [1848]

    broadside. 52.5x42.5cm.
    Dated & signed: Wien am 8. Mai 1848. Im Namen
des Ausschusses.

◐

---

*pGB8
V6755R
5.9.48

Austria. Ministerrat.
    Provisorische Wahlordnung zur Verfassungs=
Urkunde vom 25. April 1848.
    [Wien,1848]

    8p. 45x29cm.
    Caption title; dated: Wien am 9. Mai 1848.
    Regulations for the election of the
Reichstag.

◯

---

*pGB8
V6755R
5.9.48

Austria. Sovereigns, etc., 1835-1848
    (Ferdinand I)
    Wir Ferdinand der Erste, von Gottes Gnaden
Kaiser von Oesterreich ... Nach Genehmigung der,
unterm heutigen Tage erscheinenden provisorischen
Wahlordnung für den ersten Reichstag und nach
dem Antrage Unseres Ministerrathes finden Wir
den 26. Juni h. J. als den Tag der Eröffnung des
ersten Reichstages festzusetzen ...
    [Wien,1848]

    folder([2]p.) 45x29cm.
                        (See next card)

◐

---

*pGB8
V6755R
5.9.48

Austria. Sovereigns, etc., 1835-1848
    (Ferdinand I)   Wir Ferdinand der Erste
... [1848]   (Card 2)

    "Gegeben in Unserer kaiserlichen Haupt= und
Residenzstadt Wien den neunten Mai im eintausend
achthundert acht und vierzigsten ..."

◐

---

*pGB8
V6755R
5.9.48

Vienna. Gemeinde Alservorstadt.
    Mitbürger! In wenigen Tagen beginnt die Wahl
zum Gemeinde=Ausschusse der Haupt= und
Residenzstadt Wien ...
    [Wien,1848]

    broadside. 36.5x23cm.
    Dated: Wien, den 9. Mai 1848.

◐

---

*pGB8
V6755R
5.9.48

Vienna. Gemeinde Josephstadt.
    Mitbürger! In wenigen Tagen beginnt die Wahl
zum Gemeinde=Ausschusse der Haupt= und
Residenzstadt Wien ...
    [Wien,1848]

    broadside. 37x23cm.
    Dated: Wien, den 9. Mai 1848.

◯

---

*pGB8
V6755R
5.9.48

Vienna. Gemeinde Laimgrube.
    Mitbürger! In wenigen Tagen beginnt die Wahl
zum Gemeinde=Ausschusse der Haupt= und
Residenzstadt Wien ...
    [Wien,1848]

    broadside. 39x25cm.
    Dated: Wien, den 9. Mai 1848.

◯

---

*pGB8
V6755R
5.9.48

Vienna. Gemeinde Windmühle.
    Mitbürger! In wenigen Tagen beginnt die Wahl
zum Gemeinde=Ausschusse der Haupt= und
Residenzstadt Wien ...
    [Wien,1848]

    broadside. 39.5x25cm.
    Dated: Wien, den 9. Mai 1848.
    Contemporary ms. note in margin: 125 Stück
9 Mai 1848.

◯

---

*pGB8
V6755R
5.9.48

Vienna. Nationalgarde.
    Von der II. Compagnie des I. Stadtbezirkes der
National=Garde. An das politische Central=Comité
der National=Garde Wiens. An sämmtliche
Compagnien der National=Garde, des Bürger=Corps
und der akademischen Legion.
    [Wien,1848]

    broadside. 42x26cm.
    Dated & signed: Ueber Aufforderung und
Ermächtigung der Compagnie=Versammlung vom 9.
Mai 1848 im Namen aller Versammelten. Ferdinand
Ritter von Mitis, ◯ Hauptmann.

---

*pGB8
V6755R
5.10.48

Austria. Sovereigns, etc., 1835-1848
    (Ferdinand I)
    An das biedere Landvolk der Provinz Nieder-
Oesterreich.
    [Wien,1848]

    broadside. 44.5x29cm.
    Dated & signed: Wien den 10. Mai 1848.
Ferdinand.

➊

Oesterreichischer Patrioten-Verein.
   ... Patrioten! Alle Zeitungen erheben ein
Geschrei und sagen, Oesterreich ist in grosser
Gefahr! ...
   [Wien,1848]

   [2]p. 44.5x31cm.
   Caption title; at head: Beilage zur
"Allgemeinen oesterreichischen Zeitung" Nr.130,
10. Mai 1848.
   Dated & signed: Wien, den 4. Mai 1848. Vom
Oesterreichischen Patrioten-Verein.
   Printed from the same setting as the edition without imprint of 4 May.

*pGB8
V6755R
5.10.48

Vienna. Magistrat.
   Kundmachung. Mit Bezug auf den an die
Mildthätigkeit der Bürger und Bürgerinnen Wiens
erlassenen Aufruf vom 8. d. M. zur Einlieferung
von Wäsch= und Kleidungsstücken oder
Gewandstoffen für verarmte Arbeiter ...
   [Wien,1848]

   broadside. 44.5x29cm.
   Dated & signed: Wien am 10. Mai 1848. Vom
Magistrate und provisorischen Bürger-Ausschusse.

*pGB8
V6755R
5.10.48

Offener Brief an die Frau Fürstin Josefine
Wrede!
   [Wien,1848]

   broadside. 37x22cm.
   Dated & signed: Wien, den 10. Mai 1848. Eine
Bürgersfrau.

*pGB8
V6755R
5.10.48

Arthaber, Rudolf von, 1795-1867.
   Für die Herren Wahlmänner des Hauptwahlbezirkes
Klosterneuburg. Schreiben des Rudolph Arthaber
an Dr. Franz Schuselka.
   [Wien,1848]

   [2]p. 29.5x22.5cm.
   Caption title.
   Arthaber's letter is dated "Wien, am 1. Mai
1848"; "Antwort des Dr. Franz Schuselka"
(p.[2]) dated "Frankfurt a. M. 6. Mai 1848."
   In contemporary ms. at head: 1500 Stück. 11
Mai 1848.

*GB8
V6755R
5.11.48

[Poppenberger, Procop]
   Einige Worte an meine Landsleute im
Erzgebirge.
   [Wien]Druck von Ulrich Klopf sen.und Alex.
Eurich.[1848]

   [2]p. 40x24.5cm.
   Caption title; imprint on p.[2]; dated &
signed at end: Wien, den 10. Mai 1848. Procop
Poppenberger, junior.

*pGB8
V6755R
5.10.48

Bauernfreund, Joseph.
   Trauerrede für die am 25. April 1848
Gefallenen. Gehalten in der Nationalhalle in
Fünfhaus am 11. Mai 1848.
   [Wien]Gedruckt und zu haben bei U.Klopf sen.
und A.Eurich,Stadt,Wollzeile Nr.782.[1848]

   broadside. 40.5x25.5cm.
   A satire.

*pGB8
V6755R
5.11.48

[Told, Carl, fl.1848]
   Unterthänigste Erwiderung auf die Proklamation
vom 5. Mai 1848 Sr. Majestät des Kaisers
Ferdinand.
   [Wien]Gedruckt bei Franz Edlen von Schmid.
[1848]

   broadside. 37.5x26cm.
   Helfert (Wiener Parnass) 1070.
   Signed: Im Namen der österr. Nationalgarden.
C. T.

*pGB8
V6755R
5.10.48

Erste Gimpelversammlung in Wien, oder: Krieg
allen Spatzen ...
   [Wien]Zu haben bei dem Herausgeber,neue Wieden,
Beumühlgasse Nr.811,2.Stock,Thür Nr.14.[1848]

   folder([4]p.) 26.5x21.5cm.
   Dated at end: Wien, Donnerstag den 11. Mai
1848.
   "Von dieser Gimpelversammlung erscheint jeden
Donnerstag eine Fortsetzung und alle 4 Wochen
eine Hauptversammlung." No more appears to have
been published.

*GB8
V6755R
5.11.48

Triangel, J., pseud.
   Das Ganze der Katzen-Musik nach den neuesten
Fortschritten oder: theoretisch=praktische
Anleitung durch Selbstunterricht in kürzester
Zeit sich in dieser Kunst auszubilden. Von J.
Triangel ...
   [Wien,1848]

   folder([4]p.) 24x19cm.
   Woodcut illus, on t.-p.
   Imprint on p.[4]: Gedruckt bei Josef Ludwig.

*GB8
V6755R
5.10.48

Schlegl, Franziska.
   Kundmachung. Ich erkläre hiermit in meinem
Namen, dass eine "an den Minister des Innern und
provisorischen Ministerpräsidenten" gerichtete
Petition in Abwesenheit meines Gatten, daher
ohne seinem Wissen und Willen in meinem
Kaffeehause aufgelegt worden ist ...
   [Wien]Druck von U.Klopf sen.und A.Eurich
Stadt,Wollzeile Nr.782.[1848]

   broadside. 40.5x24cm.
   Dated: Wien am 11. Mai 1848.

*pGB6
V6755R
5.11.48

*GB8
V6755R
5.12.48

M. G. Saphir's ruchloses Treiben in Wien.
In Commission bei Jakob Bader, Buchhändler in
Wien, Stadt, Strobelgasse. [1848]

[2]p. 25.5x20cm.
Caption title; imprint on p.[2]; signed at end:
Eine Stimme aus dem Volke.

---

*pGB8
V6755R
5.13.48

Vienna. Nationalgarde.
Tagsbefehl für die Nationalgarde am 13. Mai
1848.
[Wien,1848]

broadside. 44.5x29cm.
Signed: Hoyos, Ober=Commandant der Nationalgarde in Wien.

---

*GB8
V6755R
5.12.48

Der Spitzel=Hauptmann in der Sepperl=Vorstadt,
genannt der Bluthund.
[Wien,1848]

folder([4]p.) 27.5x21.5cm.
Signed at end: J. R.
Woodcut illus. on t.-p.
Dated in contemporary ms.: 12. Mai 848.

---

*pGB8
V6755R
5.13.48

Vienna. Nationalgarde. Central-Comité.
An die National-Garde Wiens!
[Wien,1848]

broadside. 59x46.5cm.
Signed: Vom politischen Central=Comité der
Wiener National=Garde.
In this large folio broadside edition the last
line begins: nunmehr volle Beruhigung finden ...
Protesting the proposed dissolution of the
Central-Comité.

---

*GB8
V6755R
5.13.48

Hübsch, Eduard.
Sind das die Früchte der Pressfreiheit? Ist
das und nichts besseres der Erfolg dessen, da
wir unsere Meinungen dem Volke öffentlich
bekannt geben dürfen?
Druck von U.Klopf sen.und A.Eurich in Wien.
[1848]

broadside. 25x20cm.
Dated & signed: Wien am 13. Mai 1848. Eduard
Hübsch, aus Bitse im 1861. Trenchiner Comitat
in Ungarn gebürtig.

---

*pGB8
V6755R
5.13.48

Vienna. Nationalgarde. Central-Comité.
An die National-Garde Wiens!
[Wien,1848]

broadside. 44x26.5cm.
Signed: Vom politischen Central=Comité der
Wiener National=Garde.
In this small folio broadside edition the last
line begins: willkommen heissen werde.
Protesting the proposed dissolution of the
Central-Comité.

---

*pGB8
V6755R
5.13.48

Kraków (City) Inhabitants.
Protest der Krakauer Einwohner in Folge der in
den letzten Apriltagen d. J. von den Krakauer
Civil= und Militärbehörden verübten Gewaltthaten
und Machtübergriffe und die damit zusammen-
hängende Sr. Exzellenz dem provisorischen
Minister Präsidenten Baron von Pillersdorf
eingehändigte Anklageakte.
[Wien,1848]
folder([3]p.) 52.5x34.5cm.
Caption title; "Die Anklageakte" (p.[3])
dated: Wien den   13. Mai 1848.

---

*pGB8
V6755R
5.14.48

[Carl, Carl Bernbrunn, called, 1787-1854]
Carl an seine Mitbürger.
[Wien,1848]

broadside. 47x30cm.
Dated & signed: Den 14. Mai 1848. Carl.
Announcing his resignation from the National-
garde.

---

*pGB8
V6755R
5.13.48

Vienna. Magistrat.
Kundmachung. Nachdem die Abhaltung des
Jubilati=Marktes im Innern der Stadt aus
Rücksichten der öffentlichen Sicherheit
und Ruhe für die gegenwärtige Marktperiode nicht
zulässig erkannt wurde ...
[Wien,1848]

broadside. 38.5x23.5cm.
Signed & dated: Vom Magistrate und
provisorischen Bürger=Ausschusse der Stadt
Wien. Am 13. Mai 1848.

---

*GB8
V6755R
5.14.48

[Kopřiwa, J   N   ]
An die Wiener Freiwilligen nach der
Fahnenweihe in Wiener Neustadt am 14. Mai 1848.
[Wien,1848]

[2]p. 20x12.5cm.
Caption title; signed at end: J. N. Kopřiwa.

*pGB8
V6755R
5.14.48

Mitbürger! Seid auf Eurer Huth! Dass das Militär in gleicher Anzahl und Stärke mit der Nationalgarde zugleich alle Posten besetzt, ist nach den Ereignissen der letzten Tage keine hinreichende Bürgschaft, dass unsere Errungenschaften unangetastet bleiben ...
[Wien]Druck von U.Klopf sen.und Alex.Eurich. [1848]

broadside. 40x25cm.
Signed: Im Namen vieler Nationalgarden.

*pGB8
V6755R
5.15.48

Die Menschenrechte der Arbeiter.
[Wien,1848]

broadside. 59.5x47.5cm.
Signed: Ein Menschenfreund und Euer Mitbürger.

*pGB8
V6755R
5.14.48

Vienna. Nationalgarde.
Provisorisches Reglement für die National-Garde in Penzing.
[Wien,1848]

[2]p. 35x22.5cm.
Caption title; dated: Penzing, am 14. Mai 1848.

*GB8
V6755R
5.15.48

... Das Neueste von dem Versatzhaus! Etwas Gutes für die Wiener, und eine Adresse an den constitutionswidrigen Hausmeister aus dem Versatzamt.
Wien,1848.Gedruckt in der Josephstadt, Langegasse Nr.58.

folder([4]p.) 26.5x21.5cm.
At head of title: Der Mann des Volkes.
"Der Mann des Volkes" was a short-lived periodical; this may be an article reprinted from it.

*pGB8
V6755R
5.15.48

Austria. Ministerium des Innern.
Kundmachung. Das Ministerium hat in Erwägung der Pflichten, welche ihm gegen den Thron obliegen und um zur Beruhigung der aufgeregten Gemüther nach Kräften beizutragen die Zurücknahme des Tagsbefehles der Nationalgarde vom 13. Mai 1848 ...
[Wien,1848]
broadside. 44.5x57cm.
Reschauer-Smets II.191.
Dated & signed: Wien am 15. Mai 1848. Der Minister des   Innern Pillersdorff.

*GB8
V6755R
5.15.48

Die neuesten Nachrichten von unserm Feldmarschall Radetzky, und wie sich drei kaiserliche Grenadiere aus schmachtvoller Gefangenschaft selbst ranzionirt haben, und dafür vom Feldmarschall belohnt wurden. Von einem Augenzeugen erzählt.
[Wien]Gedruckt und zu haben bei Leopold Grund, am Stephansplatze im Zwettelhofe.[1848]

folder([4]p.) 25x20.5cm.

*GB8
V6755R
5.15.48

[Bidschof, Franz Xavier]
Die schwarze That in Venedig, oder die neue Geschichte von die [!] Mohren die sich weisz waschen wollen ...
[Wien]Gedruckt bei Josef Ludwig,Josefstadt Florianigasse Nr.52.[1848]

folder([4]p.) 24.5x19.5cm.
Signed at end: F. X. Bidschof.

*GB8
V6755R
5.15.48

Der politische Greissler aus der Leopoldstadt. Oder: Entgegnung auf die Flugschrift: Das magistratische Raubnest. Vom Verfasser der Spatzen.
[Wien]Gedruckt und zu haben bei U.Klopf sen. und Alex.Eurich.[1848]

folder([4]p.) 26x21cm.
Signed at end: R. R.
Dated in contemporary ms.: 15. Mai.

*GB8
V6755R
5.15.48

Freunde der constitutionellen Ordnung, Vienna.
Statuten zur Bildung des Vereines der Freunde der constitutionellen Ordnung und wahren Freiheit. Mit Zuziehung eines provisorischen Ausschusses entworfen von J. S. Hohenblum.
Wien,1848.Gedruckt bei Carl Ueberreuter.

7p. 22x13cm.
Dated at end: Wien, am 15. Mai 1848.

*GB8
V6755R
5.15.48

Fürkerth, Maximilian von.
Das Parlament.
[Wien,1848]

broadside. 26.5x21cm.
Dated: Wien am 15. Mai 1848.
Soliciting subscriptions for his newspaper Das Parlament.

*GB8
V6755R
5.15.48

Starke, Gustav.
  Offenes Schreiben an die Herren Nationalgarden
der sechsten Compagnie des ersten Bataillons
in Wien.
  [Wien,1848]

  broadside. 26x21cm.
  Dated & signed: Wien, am 15. Mai 1848. Gustav
Starke, Nationalgarde der sechsten Comp. ersten
Bataillons.

---

*pGB8
V6755R
5.16.48

Die Burg oder die Ereignisse in der Nacht
vom 15. auf den 16. Mai 1848.
  [Wien]Gedruckt und zu haben bei U.Klopf sen.
und Alex.Eurich,Wollzeile Nr.782.[1848]

  broadside. 39.5x24.5cm.
  Signed & dated: C. M., Garde der akad. Legion.
Geschrieben auf dem Trottoir-Pflaster am
Josefsplatz, am 15. Mai 1848, um 12 Uhr
Mitternachts.

---

*pGB8
V6755R
5.15.48

Vienna. Sicherheits-Comité.
  An die sämmtlichen Bewohner Wiens. Als der
Magistrat und provisorische Bürger-Ausschuss
sich bestimmt gefunden haben, einen Sicherheits-
Ausschuss zu berufen ...
  [Wien,1848]

  broadside. 45x57cm.
  Dated: Wien am 15. Mai 1848.

---

*pGB8
V6755R
5.16.48

... Das waren wieder die braven Studenten.
  [Wien]Druck von U.Klopf sen.und Alex.Eurich,
Wollzeile Nr.782.[1848]

  [2]p. 40x25.5cm.
  Caption title; at head: 15. Mai Nachts 2 Uhr.
  Imprint on p.[2]; signed at end: E. K.

---

*GB8
V6755R
5.15.48

Zerboni di Sposetti, Julius, 1805-1884.
  Zuruf an alle Völker des freien Oesterreichs.
Von Julius Zerboni di Sposetti. Herausgegeben
im Namen eines Vereines wahrer Vaterlandsfreunde.
  [Wien,1848]

  7p. 27.5x21.5cm.
  Dated at end: Wien am 15. Mai 1848.

---

*GB8
V6755R
5.16.48

Die grosse Revolution vom 15. May 1848. und
der noch grössere Volksbeglücker, unser gütiger
Kaiser Ferdinand.
  [Wien]Gedruckt bei Josef Ludwig Josefstadt
Florianigasse Nr.52.[1848]

  [2]p. 26.5x21cm.
  Caption title; imprint on p.[2].

---

*pGB8
V6755R
5.16.48

Austria. Sovereigns, etc., 1835-1848
      (Ferdinand I)
  Proclamation. Zur Beruhigung der am 15. Mai
1848 in Unserer Residenzstadt Wien entstandenen
Aufregung und zur Verhütung gewaltsamer
Ruhestörungen, wurde von Unserem Minister-Rathe
die Zurücknahme des für Unsere Nationalgarde am
13. Mai 1848 erlassenen Tagsbefehles in Betreff
der Vorgänge des politischen Central-Comités
beschlossen ...
  [Wien,1848]

  broadside. 44.5x57cm.   (See next card)

---

*pGB8
V6755R
5.16.48

Vienna. Magistrat.
  Kundmachung. Zur Hintanhaltung jeder
Feuersgefahr wird das Tabakrauchen in und
zwischen den Markthütten strenge untersagt ...
  [Wien,1848]

  broadside. 36x23cm.
  Signed & dated: Vom Magistrate der Stadt
Wien am 16. Mai 1848.

---

*pGB8
V6755R
5.16.48

Austria. Sovereigns, etc., 1835-1848
      (Ferdinand I)   Proclamation ... [1848]
                                  (Card 2)

  Reschauer-Smets II.195.
  Dated & signed: Wien am 16. Mai 1848.
Ferdinand.
  Reinforcing the similar proclamation of the
Ministerrat dated 15 May.

---

*GB8
V6755R
5.16.48

Was ist denn eigentlich gestern geschehen?
Was hat am 15. Mai 1848 das Volk errungen? dem
Volke erzählt, von einem seiner wahrsten
Freunde.
  [Wien]Bei Feichtinger,bürgerl.Buchbinder,
Josephstadt Florianigasse Nr.216,im Eckhause
am Glacis.[1848]

  [4]p. 26.5x19.5cm.
  Printer's imprint on p.[4]: Gedruckt bei
Franz Edlen von Schmid.

*GB8
V6755R
5.16.48

Die zweite und grösste Revolution in
Oesterreich am 15. Mai 1848.
[Wien]Druck von L.Sommer vormals Strauss.[1848]

[2]p. 26x21cm.
Caption title; imprint on p.[2]; dated at end:
Wien am 16. Mai 1848.

---

*pGB8
V6755R
5.17.48

Verein zur Beschäftigung brotloser Arbeiter,
Vienna.
... Bezirks= und Sections=Eintheilung der
innern Stadt, und Namen der Bezirks= und
Sections=Cassiere.
[Wien,1848]

broadside. 45x29cm.
At head: Verein zur Beschäftigung brotloser
Arbeiter.
Dated: Wien, den 17. Mai 1848.

---

*pGB8
V6755R
5.17.48

Austria. Ministerrat.
Kundmachung. Heute in der neunten Abendstunde
ist dem Ministerium die mündliche unerwartete
Mittheilung zugekommen, dass Se. Majestät der
Kaiser aus Gesundheits=Rücksichten in
Begleitung der Kaiserin und des durchlauchtigsten
Erzherzogs Franz Carl sammt seiner erlauchten
Gemahlin und drei Prinzen die Residenz verlassen,
und die Route nach Innsbruck eingeschlagen haben
...
[Wien,1848]

(See next card)

---

*pGB8
V6755R
5.17.48

Vienna. Magistrat.
Kundmachung. Mit Bezug auf den 4. Absatz
der Kundmachung vom 8. d. M., bezüglich der
Wahl der 100 Gemeinde=Ausschüsse für die Stadt
Wien wird nunmehr über die Art, die Zeit und den
Ort dieser Wahl Nachstehendes zur öffentlichen
Kenntniss gebracht ...
[Wien,1848]

folder([3]p.) 44.5x29cm.
Caption title; signed & dated at end: Vom
Magistrate und prov. Bürgerausschusse der Stadt
Wien am 17. Mai 1848.

---

*pGB8
V6755R
5.17.48

Austria. Ministerrat.   Kundmachung ... [1848]
(Card 2)

broadside. 44.5x57cm.
Reschauer-Smets II.210.
Dated & signed: Wien am 17. Mai 1848. Die
interimistischen Minister: Pillersdorff.
Sommaruga. Krauss. Latour. Doblhoff.
Baumgartner.

---

*pGB8
V6755R
5.18.48

Allgemeine oesterreichische Zeitung.
... Die Entführung unseres Kaisers aus
seiner Residenz.
[Wien]Leopold Sommer (vormals Strauss),
Dorotheergasse Nr.1108.[1848]

broadside. 42x26.5cm.
At head: Abdruck aus der Allgemeinen
oesterreichischen Zeitung.
Dated in contemporary ms.: 18. May 1848.
Abends.

---

*pGB8
V6755R
5.17.48

Der 15. Mai 1848, oder: die neueste Revolution
in Wien.
[Wien,1848]

[2]p. 41.5x26cm.
Caption title; dated & signed at end: Wien, am
17. Mai 1848. Ein Mediziner und Garde.

---

*pGB8
V6755R
5.18.48

Austria. Ministerrat.
Kundmachung. Die unerwartete Abreise Sr.
Majestät des Kaisers aus allerhöchst ihrer
Residenzstadt hat unter der treuen Bevölkerung
Wiens eben so tiefe Betrübniss, als
allgemeine Aufregung hervorgerufen ...
[Wien,1848]

broadside. 44.5x58cm.
Dated & signed: Wien am Nachmittage des 18.
Mai 1848. Die interimistischen Minister:
Pillersdorf. Sommaruga. Krauss. Latour. Doblhoff.
Baumgartner.

---

*pGB8
V6755R
5.17.48

Verein zur Beschäftigung brotloser Arbeiter,
Vienna.
Aufruf und Bitte an die biedern Einwohner
Wiens zur Betheiligung an dem Vereine zur
Beschäftigung brotloser Arbeiter.
[Wien,1848]

folder([3]p.) 44.5x29cm.
Caption title; dated at end: Wien, den 17. Mai
1848.

---

*pGB8
V6755R
5.18.48

Austria. Ministerrat.
Provisorische Verordnung gegen den Missbrauch
der Presse.
[Wien,1848]

folder(3p.) 45x29cm.
Caption title; dated & signed at end: Wien am
18. Mai 1848. Die interimistischen Minister:
Pillersdorff. Sommaruga. Krauss. Latour. Doblhoff.
Baumgartner.

*pGB8
V6755R
5.18.48

Austria. Ministerrat.
 Provisorische Verordnung über das Verfahren in
Presssachen.
 [Wien,1848]

 6p. 44.5x29cm.
Caption title; dated & signed at end: Wien
den 18. Mai 1848. Die interimistischen Minister:
Pillersdorff. Sommaruga. Krauss. Latour.
Doblhoff. Baumgartner.

---

*pGB8
V6755R
5.18.48

Austria, Lower. Regierungs-Präsident.
 Mitbürger. Es ist nicht leicht möglich, dass
unser heisser Wunsch, die Rückkehr unseres
geliebten Monarchen sich heute noch verwirkliche
...
 [Wien,1848]
 broadside. 44.5x57.5cm.
 Dated & signed: Wien am 18. Mai 1848. Der
Landespräsident Graf Montecuccoli.

---

*pGB8
V6755R
5.18.48

Austria, Lower. Regierungs-Präsident.
 Aufforderung. Im Interesse der öffentlichen
Ordnung und Sicherheit, mit deren Aufrecht-
haltung alle dazu berufenen Organe eifrigst
beschäftiget sind ...
 [Wien,1848]
 broadside. 44.5x57cm.
 Signed: Der Landespräsident Graf Montecuccoli.
Instituting a curfew.
 Dated in contemporary ms.: 18 Mai 848.

---

*GB8
V6755R
5.18.48

[Fischer, Johann, fl.1848]
 Hoch lebe Kaiser Ferdinand! sein Reich
bestehet, wann seine Völker hoch und einig leben!
 [Wien]Gedruckt bei Edl.v.Schmidbauer und
Holzwarth.[1848]

 folder([3]p.) 27x21.5cm.
 Signed at end: Johann Fischer ...
 Includes (p.[3]) a poem, "An Vater Ferdinand"
(Helfert, Wiener Parnass, 1101).

---

*pGB8
V6755R
5.18.48

Austria, Lower. Regierungs-Präsident.
 Kundmachung. Da es unter den obwaltenden
Verhältnissen als Gebot der Nothwendigkeit
erscheinet, ein besonderes Augenmerk auf die
zahlreichen Fremden zu richten, welche sich
ohne bestimmte Zwecke hier aufhalten ...
 [Wien,1848]

 broadside. 44.5x57.5cm.
 Dated & signed: Wien am 18. Mai 1848. Albert
Graf v. Montecuccoli-Laderchi, niederöoester.
Landmarschall und Regierungs=Präsidentens=
Stellvertreter.

---

*pGB8
V6755R
5.18.48

[Gugler, Josef, fl.1848]
 An die Gesammtbevölkerung des österreichischen
Kaiserstaates.
 [Wien]Gedruckt und zu haben bei U.Klopf sen.und
Alex.Eurich,Wollzeile Nr.782.[1848]

 [2]p. 42x26.5cm.
 Caption title; imprint on p.[2]; signed at
end: J. Gugler.

 A defense of the actions of the students
on 15 May.

---

*pGB8
V6755R
5.18.48

Austria, Lower. Regierungs-Präsident.
 Kundmachung. Die mannigfachen Aufforderungen,
welche unter verschiedenen Theilen der
Bevölkerung Wiens durch Ausrufung der Republik
zum gewaltsamen Umsturze der monarchischen
Verfassung verbreitet werden ...
 [Wien,1848]

 broadside. 44.5x57cm.
 Dated & signed: Wien am 18. Mai 1848. Vom
Landespräsidium in Niederösterreich.
Montecuccoli.
 Decreeing hang-   ing for those who commit
serious crimes.

---

*pGB8
V6755R
5.18.48

Der Kaiser auf seiner Flucht, angehalten
durch den Landsturm, bei St. Pölten.
 [Wien]Gedruckt in der Franz Edlen von
Schmid'schen Buchdruckerei.[1848]

 broadside. 40x25.5cm.

---

*pGB8
V6755R
5.18.48

Austria, Lower. Regierungs-Präsident.
 Kundmachung. Die so oft und besonders zur
Nachtszeit vorkommenden bedauerlichen Störungen
der öffentlichen Ruhe und Ordnung ...
 [Wien,1848]

 [2]p. 44.5x28.5cm.
 Reschauer-Smets II.219.
 Dated & signed: Wien am 18. Mai 1848. Albert
Graf Montecuccoli, niederösterr. Landmarschall
und Regierungs=Präsidentens=Stellvertreter.

---

*pGB8
V6755R
5.18.48

Der Kaiser und sein treues Volk.
 [Wien]Gedruckt bei M.Lell.[1848]

 broadside. 41.5x27cm.
 Signed: J. H.

*pGB8
V6755R
5.18.48

Der Kaiser und seine Familie fort!
[Wien]Druck von Ulrich Klopf sen.und Alex.
Eurich.[1848]

broadside. 53x42cm.
Signed: C. M., Akademiker.

---

*GB8
V6755R
5.18.48

Vienna. Nationalgarde.
Mitbürger! Das Central=Comité der National-
garde und akademischen Legion hat den Antrag ...
[Wien,1848]

broadside. 29.5x22.5cm.
Quarto broadside edition.
Signed: Dr. Hruby, prov. Präsident der
Nationalgarde.

---

*pGB8
V6755R
5.18.48

Knoth, Ludwig.
An den Herrn Advokaten Dr. Wildner Edlen von
Maithstein und V.....i.
[Wien,1848]

broadside. 42.5x52.5cm.
Dated: Wien, am 18. Mai 1848.

---

*pGB8
V6755R
5.18.48

Vienna. Nationalgarde.
Tagsbefehl am 18. Mai 1848.
[Wien,1848]

broadside. 44.5x57.5cm.
Signed: Auersperg, Feldmarschall-Lieutenant.

---

*pGB8
V6755R
5.18.48

Mitbürger! Das Vaterland ist in Gefahr. Se.
Majestät, wahrscheinlich den volksfeindlichen
Einflüsterungen der aristokratischen Parthei
nachgebend, hat seine treue Hauptstadt verlassen
...
[Wien,1848]

broadside. 54x43.5cm.
Reschauer-Smets II.211.
Dated & signed: Wien, den 18. Mai 1848. Dr. A.
J. Becher. Dr. Carl Tausenau. L. Ribarz. Mathias
Emanuel Löbenstein.

---

*pGB8
V6755R
5.18.48

Vienna. Nationalgarde. Central-Comité.
An die Bevölkerung Wiens! Mitbürger! Unser
geliebter Kaiser weilt seit zwölf Stunden
nicht mehr in unserer Mitte! ...
[Wien]Druck von U.Klopf sen.u.Alex.Eurich.
[1848]

broadside. 52.5x42cm.
Signed: Das Central-Comité (bestehend aus der
Nationalgarde, dem Bürgercorps und den
Studenten) und der Schriftstellerverein. Dr.
Hruby, prov. Präsident des Central=Comités.
Reschauer-Smets   II.218.

---

*pGB8
V6755R
5.18.48

Müller, Adolf, 1801-1886.
An das 18l. Bezirks-Commando Maria-Hilf.
[Wien,1848]

folder(2l.) 39.5x25cm.
Caption title; dated & signed: Wien, den 18.
Mai 1848. Adolph Müller, Capellmeister.
Endorsed title on verso of 2d leaf: An das 18bl
Bezirks=Commando Maria=Hilf. Das Musik-Corps
betreffend von Adolph Müller, Kapellmeister.
Contemporary ms. note at head: 20 Stück. 25
Mai 1848.

---

*pGB8
V6755R
5.18.48

Vienna. Sicherheits-Comité.
Aufforderung. Der Sicherheitsausschuss der
Stadt Wien fordert hiermit dringend die Herren
Hauseigenthümer oder Administratoren auf, in dem
mitfolgenden Bogen sämmtliche Jahres= und alle
Afterpartheien ohne Ausnahme mit genauer
Ausfüllung aller Rubriken auf das Verlässlichste
zu verzeichnen ...
[Wien,1848]

broadside. 36.5x23cm.
Signed & dated: Vom Sicherheits-Ausschusse
der Stadt Wien   am 18. Mai 1848.

---

*pGB8
V6755R
5.18.48

Vienna. Nationalgarde.
Mitbürger! Das Central=Comité der Nationalgarde
und akademischen Legion hat den Antrag ...
[Wien,1848]

broadside. 44.5x57cm.
Folio broadside edition.
Signed: Dr. Hruby, prov. Präsident der
Nationalgarde.
Dated in contemporary ms.: 18. May 1848.

---

*pGB8
V6755R
5.18.48

Vienna. Sicherheits-Comité.
Kundmachung. Die Bewohner der Residenz werden
hiemit benachrichtiget, dass der von dem
gesammten Ministerrathe genehmigte Sicherheits=
Ausschuss bereits seine Thätigkeit begonnen ...
[Wien,1848]

broadside. 42x26.5cm.
Signed & dated: Vom Sicherheits-Ausschusse
der Stadt Wien am 18. Mai 1848.

*GB8
V6755R
5.18.48

Wahre Nachricht der Ankunft Ihro Majestät des
Kaisers Ferdinand I. in Sichartskirchen, und
seine Abreise von da aus in 3 Wägen.
[Wien]Gedruckt bei Jos.Ludwig.[1848]

folder([4]p.) 26x21cm.

---

*pGB8
V6755R
5.19.48

Austria, Lower. Regierungs-Präsident.
Kundmachung ... [1848]   (Card 2)

Dated & signed: Wien am 19. Mai 1848. Albert
Graf Montecuccoli, niederösterr. Landmarschall
und Regierungs=Präsidentens=Stellvertreter.
Replacing his proclamation dated 18 May;
Reschauer-Smets II.219.

---

*pGB8
V6755R
5.18.48

[Weis, Johann Baptist, 1801-1862]
Aufruf an meine lieben Landsleute, Kameraden,
Brüder und Freunde!
[Wien]Gedruckt und zu haben bei Leop.Grund,
am Stephansplatze im neugebauten Zwettelhofe.
[1848]

[2]p. 36.5x23cm.
Caption title; imprint on p.[2]; dated &
signed at end: Wien am 18. Mai 1848. J. B. Weis.

---

*pGB8
V6755R
5.19.48

Austria, Lower. Regierungs-Präsident.
Kundmachung. Die so oft und besonders zur
Nachtszeit vorkommenden bedauerlichen
Störungen der öffentlichen Ruhe und Ordnung
machen es der Regierung zur Pflicht, die
nachstehenden, zur Wahrung der Sicherheit
unentbehrlichen Anordnungen nach Massgabe der
schon bestehenden Sicherheitsgesetze kund zu
machen ...
[Wien,1848]
[2]p. 44.5x29cm.   (See next card)

---

*pGB8
V6755R
5.18.48

Wiener Zeitung.
Ausserordentliche Beilage zur Wiener-Zeitung
vom 18. Mai 1848.
[Wien]Gedruckt bei den Edlen von Ghelen'schen
Erben.[1848]

broadside. 38x28.5cm.

---

*pGB8
V6755R
5.19.48

Austria, Lower. Regierungs-Präsident.
Kundmachung ... [1848]   (Card 2)

Caption title; dated & signed: Wien am 19. Mai
1848. Albert Graf Montecuccoli, niederösterr.
Landmarschall und Regierungs=Präsidentens=
Stellvertreter.
Replacing his proclamation dated 18 May;
Reschauer-Smets II.219.

---

*pGB8
V6755R
5.19.48

Austria. Ministerrat.
Bekanntmachung. Das Ministerium war seit der
Abreise Sr. Majestät eifrig bemüht, die
Regierungsgeschäfte mit sorgfältiger Rücksicht
auf die schwierige Lage der Residenz zu ordnen
...
[Wien,1848]

broadside. 44.5x57.5cm.
Dated & signed: Wien am 19. Mai 1848. Die
interimistischen Minister: Pillersdorff.
Sommaruga. Krauss. Latour. Doblhoff.
Baumgartner.

---

*pGB8
V6755R
5.19.48

Beer, Hieronymus, 1798-1873.
Abschiedsworte an die Herren Hörer der
gerichtlichen Medizin.
[Wien]Druck v.U.Klopf sen.und A.Eurich.[1848]

broadside. 39.5x25cm.
Dated: Wien, den 19. Mai 1848.

---

*pGB8
V6755R
5.19.48

Austria, Lower. Regierungs-Präsident.
Kundmachung. Die so oft und besonders zur
Nachtszeit vorkommenden bedauerlichen
Störungen der öffentlichen Ruhe und Ordnung
machen es der Regierung zur Pflicht, die
nachstehenden, zur Wahrung der Sicherheit
unentbehrlichen Anordnungen nach Massgabe der
schon bestehenden Sicherheitsgesetze kund zu
machen ...
[Wien,1848]

broadside. 44.5x57cm.
(See next card)

---

*pGB8
V6755R
5.19.48

... Die Deputation aus dem Königreiche Galizien
und dem Krakauer Kreise hat auf ihre Eingaben
folgende Zuschrift erhalten: ...
[Wien]K.K.Hofbuchdruckerei des L.Sommer
(vormals Strauss).[1848]

folder([4]p.) 42x26.5cm.
Caption title; at head: Beilage zur Allgemeinen
oesterreichischen Zeitung.
Imprint on p.[4].
Includes Pillersdorf's address "An die Herren
Deputirten aus dem Königreiche Galizien und dem
(See next card)

*pGB8
V6755R
5.19.48

... Die Deputation ... [1848]   (Card 2)

Krakauer=Kreise", dated "Wien den 19.
Mai 1848", followed by the deputation's
original petition.

---

*pGB8
V6755R
5.19.48

Vienna. Magistrat.
Provisorische Dienstes-Instruction der
städtischen Sicherheitswache.
[Wien,1848]

folder([3]p.) 42x26cm.
Caption title; signed & dated: Vom Magistrate
und prov. Bürger=Ausschusse der Stadt Wien am
19. Mai 1848.

---

*pGB8
V6755R
5.19.48

Der 15. Mai, geschildert von Freiherrn von
Pillersdorff.
[Wien]Gedruckt und zu haben bei U.Klopf sen.
und A.Eurich.[1848]

[2]p. 39.5x25cm.
Caption title; imprint on p.[2].
A news sheet, reprinting Pillersdorf's letter
to the editors of the Allgemeine oesterreichische
Zeitung, dated 19 May 1848; signed at end: Drei
Gardisten: V. & Tsch., Kärntner=Viertel, 1.
Comp. B., Stuben=Viertel, 2. Comp.

---

*pGB8
V6755R
5.19.48

Vienna. Nationalgarde. Central-Comité.
Vom Central=Comité der gesammten
Nationalgarde zur Aufrechthaltung der Ruhe,
Ordnung und Sicherheit.
[Wien,1848]

broadside. 45x57cm.
Dated: Wien am 19. Mai 1848.
Deploring a recent antisemitic broadside.

---

*pGB8
V6755R
5.19.48

Mitbürger. Es ist nicht leicht möglich, dass
unser heisser Wunsch, die Rückkehr unseres
geliebten Monarchen sich heute noch verwirkliche
...
[Wien,1848]

broadside. 44.5x57cm.

---

*pGB8
V6755R
5.19.48

Vienna. Sicherheits-Comité.
Kundmachung. Es ist gestern eine Kundmachung
ddo. 18. Mai 1848, mit Genehmigung des
Ministerrathes, von dem Grafen Montecuccoli ...
veröffentlicht worden ...
[Wien,1848]

broadside. 44.5x28.5cm.
Dated & signed: Wien den 19. Mai 1848. Vom
Sicherheits=Ausschuss der Stadt Wien.
Revoking Montecuccoli's proclamation of 18 May.

---

*pGB8
V6755R
5.19.48

Ruhe, Ordnung und Sicherheit waren gestern die
Losung des Tages, Vertrauen sei die heutige ...
[Wien,1848]

broadside. 44.5x57cm.
Dated & signed: Wien am 19. Mai 1848.
Mehrere Patrioten.

---

*GB8
V6755R
5.20.48

An die National=Garde. Wenn die Zeichen nicht
trügen, so ist der Augenblick nicht mehr fern,
in welchem der Ober=Commandant der Nationalgarde, Feldmarschall=Lieutenant Graf Hoyos, die
ihm in den denkwürdigen Märztagen angewiesene
Stellung wieder verlassen wird ...
Gedruckt bei J.P.Sollinger in Wien.[1848]

broadside. 25x16.5cm.

---

*pGB8
V6755R
5.19.48

Vienna. Magistrat.
Kundmachung. Bereits am 27. v. M. haben der
Magistrat und provisorische Bürgerausschuss
veröffentlicht, dass für die Stadt und
Vorstädte Wiens eine Sicherheitswache errichtet
werden soll ...
[Wien,1848]

broadside. 44.5x57cm.
Dated & signed: Wien den 19. Mai 1848. Vom
Magistrate und provisorischen Bürgerausschusse.

---

*pGB8
V6755R
5.20.48

Austria. Sovereigns, etc., 1835-1848
(Ferdinand I)
Manifest an Meine Völker.
[Wien,1848]

broadside. 45x57cm.
Unterreiter III.89; Helfert (Geschichte) II.241
Dated & signed: Innsbruck am 20. Mai 1848.
Ferdinand.
Explaining his reasons for leaving the capital
after the events of 15 May.

*pGB8
V6755R
5.20.48

Castelli, Ignaz Franz, 1781-1862.
Offener Brief an meine lieben Mitbürger über
eine unnöthige Furcht, von J. F. Castelli.
[Wien,1848]

[2]p. 44.5x28.5cm.
Caption title.
Attempting to allay fears that savings banks
and credit institutions were approaching
insolvency.

---

*pGB8
V6755R
5.20.48

Nachruf an unsern vielgeliebten Kaiser!
[Wien]Gedruckt bei M.Lell.[1848]

broadside. 41.5x26cm.
In this edition, the 4th line of text from
bottom ends: ausrufen mögen:

---

*GB8
V6755R
5.20.48

[Dietrich, Eduard, fl.1848]
... Religiöse Intoleranz in Wiener Neustadt.
[Wien,1848]

[2]p. 27x21.5cm.
Caption title (at head: Beilage zur Wiener
Kirchenzeitung); signed at end: Eduard Dietrich,
Pfarr=Curat zu Wiener=Neustadt.

---

*pGB8
V6755R
5.20.48

Nachruf an unsern vielgeliebten Kaiser.
[Wien]Gedruckt bei M.Lell.[1848]

broadside. 41x26.5cm.
In this edition, the 4th line of text from
bottom ends: rufen können:
Dated in contemporary ms.: 20/5/848.

---

*GB8
V6755R
5.20.48

[Brožka, Joseph]
Aufruf an die hochherzigen Frauen Wiens.
[Wien]Gedruckt bei Franz Edlen v.Schmid.[1848]

[2]p. 29.5x23cm.
Caption title; imprint on p.[2]; signed
at end: Joseph Brožka.
Dated in contemporary ms.: 20. Mai 848.

---

*pGB8
V6755R
5.20.48

FOR OTHER
COPIES SEE
UNION
CATALOGUE

Niederösterreichischer Gewerbe-Verein.
Die falschen Gerüchte, welche über den Werth
der Banknoten der priv. öster. National=Bank
verbreitet werden, glauben die unterzeichneten
Gremien und der niederöster. Gewerbsverein am
Besten thatsächlich dadurch zu widerlegen ...
[Wien,1848]

broadside. 44.5x57.5cm.
Dated & signed: Wien am 20. Mai 1848. Das
Gremium der k. k. priv. Grosshändler. Das k. k.
bürgerl. Handelsgremium. Der niederöster.
(See next card)

---

*pGB8
V6755R
5.20.48

Der Kaiser unter seinen Wiener Bürgern.
[Wien]Gedruckt und zu haben bei U.Klopf sen.
und A.Eurich.[1848]

broadside. 39.5x24cm.
Signed: B.
Printed within ornamental border.

---

*pGB8
V6755R
5.20.48

Niederösterreichischer Gewerbe-Verein. Die
falschen Gerüchte ... [1848]   (Card 2)

Gewerbsverein.
Stating that the exchange of bank-notes
will continue as usual, despite rumors to the
contrary.

---

*pGB8
V6755R
5.20.48

Leidesdorf, Eduard.
Wir wollen unsern Kaiser haben! Auf nach
Innsbruck!
[Wien]Druck von U.Klopf sen.und A.Eurich,
Wollzeile 782.[1848]

broadside. 39.5x25cm.
Dated & signed: Wien, den 20. Mai 1848. S. D.,
Garde der akad. Legion. Eduard Leidesdorf,
Garde der akademischen Legion.

---

*pGB8
V6755R
5.20.48

Oesterreichische Nationalbank.
Böswillige und unwahre Gerüchte werden über
den Werth der Banknoten der priv. österr.
Nationalbank verbreitet ...
[Wien,1848]

broadside. 44.5x57cm.
Dated & signed: Wien am 20. Mai 1848. Von der
Direction der priv. öst. Nationalbank.
Stating that the exchange of bank-notes will
continue as usual, despite rumors to the
contrary.

*pGB8 V6755R 5.20.48

Pädagogischer Verein, Vienna.
    Euere Majestät! Die Mitglieder des
pädagogischen Vereins, d. i. Schullehrer und
Freunde des Schulfachs, sind in tiefster
Bekümmerniss über die plötzliche Abreise Euerer
Majestät ...
    [Wien]Druck von U.Klopf sen.u.A.Eurich.[1848]
    broadside. 44.5x28cm.
    A petition for the Emperor's return to Vienna;
no names have been signed.

---

*GB8 V6755R 5.20.48

Perzini, pseud.
    An alle Gutgesinnten. Entdeckte Verschwörung
in Wien. Höchst wichtig für alle Juden,
Republikaner, Anarchisten und Wühler.
    [Wien]Gedruckt bei Josef Ludwig.[1848]
    [2]p. 30.5x23.5cm.
    Endorsed title; text begins: Freunde der Ruhe
und Ordnung! Mit Gefahr meines eigenen Lebens
ist es mir gelungen ...

---

*pGB8 V6755R 5.20.48

Vienna. Citizens.
    Eure Majestät! Die in tiefster Ehrfurcht
Unterzeichneten haben mit grösstem Schmerz
erfahren, dass Eure Majestät die Nachricht: dass
auch uniformirte Bürger= und National=Garden
sich der höchst illegalen undankbaren, ja! man
kann sagen, barbarischen Sturm=Petition vom 15.
d. M. angeschlossen--so sehr geschmerzt ...
    [Wien,1848]
    folder([4]p.) 42x26cm.
    Caption title; endorsed title on p.[4]: An
Seine Majestät   den Kaiser von
                    (See next card)

---

*pGB8 V6755R 5.20.48

Vienna. Citizens.   Eure Majestät ... [1848]
                (Card 2)
Oesterreich &c. &c. &c. allerunterthänigste
Adresse der Bürger- und National-Garden in Wien.
    Dated & signed on p.[2]: Wien, den 20. Mai
1848. allunterthänigst treugehorsamsten Bürger
und Garden Wiens.

---

*pGB8 V6755R 5.20.48

Vienna. Magistrat.
    Verzeichniss der für die Stadt Wien am 20. Mai
1848 gewählten 100 Gemeinde=Ausschüsse, und
zwar: in der innern Stadt 20 und in den
Vorstädten 80.
    [Wien]Aus der k.k.Staats=Druckerei.[1848]
    [2]p. 44.5x28.5cm.
    Caption title; imprint on p.[2].

---

*pGB8 V6755R 5.20.48

Vienna. Nationalgarde.
    Tagsbefehl vom 20. Mai 1848.
    [Wien,1848]
    broadside. 44.5x28.5cm.
    Signed: Sardagna, General=Major.
    This order contains 25 lines of text.

---

*pGB8 V6755R 5.20.48

Vienna. Nationalgarde.
    Tagsbefehl vom 20. Mai 1848.
    [Wien,1848]
    broadside. 44.5x29cm.
    Signed: Sardagna, General=Major.
    This order contains 10 lines of text.

---

*pGB8 V6755R 5.20.48

Vienna. Sicherheits-Comité.
    Kundmachung. Nachdem es erwiesen ist, dass
sich gegenwärtig in Wien eine Menge Fremde
aufhalten ...
    [Wien,1848]
    broadside. 44.5x57cm.
    Dated & signed: Wien den 20. Mai 1848. Vom
Sicherheits-Ausschusse der Stadt Wien.

---

*GB8 V6755R 5.20.48

Warum ist denn unser guter Kaiser fort?
[Wien]Gedruckt bei Josef Ludwig.[1848]
    folder([3]p.) 26.5x21cm.
    Signed at end: F., N. Garde.

---

*pGB8 V6755R 5.21.48

Montecuccoli, Albert Raimund Zeno, graf,
    1802-1852.
    Kundmachung. Wie bereits am Nachmittage des 18.
Mai zur öffentlichen Kenntniss gebracht wurde,
hat sich das politische Central=Comité der
Nationalgarde durch selbsteigenen Beschluss
aufgelöst ...
    [Wien,1848]
    broadside. 44.5x57cm.
    Reschauer-Smets II.238.
    Dated & signed: Wien am 21. Mai 1848.
Montecuccoli,   gewesener Präsident des
Central=Comités.

*pGB8
V6755R
5.21.48

FOR OTHER
COPIES SEE
UNION
CATALOGUE

Oesterreichische Nationalbank.
 Kundmachung. Bei Beginn der Unruhen in Italien
Ende Juni 1847 bestand der Bankschatz in
79,574.669 fl. ...
[Wien,1848]

 broadside. 44.5x57cm.
 Dated & signed: Wien am 21. Mai 1848. Mayer
Gravenegg, Bank=Gouverneur. Sina, Bank=Director.
 Announcing a temporary limitation on the
convertibility of bank-notes.

---

*pGB8
V6755R
5.22.48

Austria, Lower. Laws, statutes, etc., 1835-1848
 (Ferdinand I)
 Circulare der Nieder-Oester. Landesregierung
über die Verwechslung der Noten der öster.
Nationalbank, und deren Verwendung als
Zahlungsmittel.
[Wien,1848]

 broadside. 44.5x28.5cm.
 Dated & signed: Wien den 22. Mai 1848. Albert
Graf v. Montecuccoli-Laderchi, k. k. Nieder=
Oester. Landes=Präsident ...
 Ordering the acceptance of bank-notes
for all payments at their full value.

---

*pGB8
V6755R
5.21.48

[Scheibe, Theodor, 1820-1881]
 Keine Auflösung der Studenten-Legion, oder
Niederträchtigkeit der schwarzgelben Zöpfe.
 [Wien]Zu haben in der Stadt,Parisergasse Nr.
411,im Verkaufsgewölbe.Gedruckt bei U.Klopf sen.
und Alexander Eurich.[1848]

 [2]p. 1 illus. 39.5x25cm.
 Caption title; imprint on p.[2]; signed at
end: Scheibe.

---

*pGB8
V6755R
5.22.48

Austria, Lower. Laws, statutes, etc., 1835-1848
 (Ferdinand I)
 Circulare der Nieder-Oester. Landesregierung
über die Verwendung der Banknoten als
Zahlungsmittel.
[Wien,1848]

 broadside. 44.5x28.5cm.
 Dated & signed: Wien am 22. Mai 1848. Albert
Graf v. Montecuccoli-Laderchi, k. k. Nieder=
Oester. Landes=Präsident ...
 Supplementing the earlier directive of the same
day.

---

*pGB8
V6755R
5.21.48

Sporn, Moritz.
 Guter Rath an meine lieben Mitbürger wegen
der Sparcasse in Folge einer höchst unnöthigen
Belehrung des Herrn J. F. Castelli, von Moritz
Sporn.
 [Wien]Eigenthümer J.Sammer,Stadt,
Dorotheegasse.[1848]

 [2]p. 36.5x22cm.
 Caption title; imprint on p.[2].
 Warning of the increasing instability of banks
and credit institutions; directed against
Castelli's Offener Brief an meine lieben
Mitbürger.

---

*GB8
V6755R
5.22.48

Dunkel, Ernest.
 Lied der Arbeiter.
 [Wien]Gedruckt bei M.Lell.[1848]

 broadside. 23x14.5cm.
 Helfert (Wiener Parnass) 1110.
 Also published with title: Lied der Arbeiter
an der Regie zu Gumpendorf. Von Ernest Dunkel
und Anton Dirnberger, Arbeiter allda.

---

*pGB8
V6755R
5.21.48

Vienna. Magistrat.
 Kundmachung. Nachdem bereits alle öffentlichen
Bau= und Arbeitsplätze mit einer so grossen
Anzahl von Arbeitern übersetzt sind ...
[Wien,1848]

 broadside. 40x25cm.
 Signed & dated: Vom Magistrate und prov.
Bürger-Ausschusse. Wien am 21. Mai 1848.

---

*pGB8
V6755R
5.22.48

Leidesdorf, Eduard.
 Wir wollen unsern Kaiser haben! Auf, nach
Innsbruck!
 Druck von Fried.Eurich in Linz.(22.Mai 1848.)

 broadside. 36x23cm.
 Dated & signed: Wien, den 20. Mai 1848. S. D.,
Garde der akad. Legion. Eduard Leidesdorf, Garde
der akad. Legion.

---

*pGB8
V6755R
5.22.48

An die Wiener.
[Innsbruck? 1848]

 broadside. 40x24.5cm.
 Dated: Innsbruck, den 22. Mai 1848.
 Text begins: Ihr habt uns den Kaiser
geschickt ...

---

*pGB8
V6755R
5.22.48

Unser Kaiser auf der Reise.
 [Wien]Gedruckt und zu haben bei U.Klopf sen.
und A.Eurich,Wollzeile 782.[1848]

 [2]p. 39.5x25cm.
 Dated & signed: Wien den 22. Mai 1848. S. D.
 Includes the text of a proclamation to the
citizens of Linz by the President of Upper
Austria.

*pGB8
V6755R
5.22.48

Vienna. Sicherheits-Comité.
    Kundmachung. Da das immer mehr über Hand
nehmende Herumtreiben unterstandsloser
Individuen und Bettler ...
    [Wien,1848]

    broadside. 41.5x52cm.
    Signed & dated: Vom Sicherheits=Ausschusse der
Stadt Wien, am 22. Mai 1848.

---

*pGB8
V6755R
5.23.48

Knees, Joseph.
    Ehre dem Ehre gebührt! oder auch ein Wort
zur Vertheidigung der Wiener=Studenten.
    [Wien]Gedruckt bei M.Iell.[1848]

    broadside. 48x60.5cm.
    Dated & signed: Wien, den 23. Mai 1848. Joseph
Knees, Nationalgardist.

---

*pGB8
V6755R
5.23.48

Austria. Sovereigns, etc., 1835-1848
    (Ferdinand I)
    Wir Ferdinand der Erste, von Gottes Gnaden
Kaiser von Oesterreich ... Ueber den Antrag
Unserer getreuen Stände des Herzogthums Krain und
nach dem Vorschlage Unseres Ministerrathes ...
    [Wien,1848]

    folder([2]p.) 45x28.5cm.
    Caption title.
    "Gegeben in Unserer kaiserlichen Haupt= und
Residenzstadt Wien   den drei und zwanzigsten
Mai im eintausend   achthundert acht und
vierzigsten ..."

---

*pGB8
V6755R
5.23.48

Knees, Joseph.
    Ehre dem Ehre gebührt! oder auch ein Wort
zur Vertheidigung der Wiener=Studenten. Zweite
Auflage.
    [Wien]Gedruckt bei M.Iell.[1848]

    broadside. 47.5x57.5cm.
    Dated & signed: Wien, den 23. Mai 1848. Joseph
Knees, Nationalgardist.
    Printed on 1 side of a folio sheet; on the
other side is printed B. Knöpfelmacher's Das
Verbrüderungs=Fest im Odeon.

---

*pGB8
V6755R
5.23.48

Austria, Lower. Regierungs-Präsident.
    ... Kundmachung. Durch ein Versehen wurde bei
Ausfertigung des provisorischen Pressgesetzes
im Paragraphe 8 der Verordnung gegen den
Missbrauch der Presse die Beziehung auf den
Paragraph 4 weggelassen ...
    [Wien]Aus der k.k.Hof= und Staats=Druckerei.
[1848]

    broadside. 44x56.5cm.
    At head is the number "Ad Nro. 6219. 79";
another edition is without this.
                    (See next card)

---

*pGB8
V6755R
5.23.48

Naar, Wilhelm.
    Mein schönster Traum verwirklicht! Eine
Morgenerzählung dem Obercommandanten der Wiener-
Nationalgarde Herrn Pannasch freundlichst
gewidmet von Wilhelm Naar.
    [Wien]Gedruckt bei M.Iell.[1848]

    broadside. 40x50cm.
    Helfert (Wiener Parnass) 1114.

---

*pGB8
V6755R
5.23.48

Austria, Lower. Regierungs-Präsident.   ...
    Kundmachung ... [1848]   (Card 2)

    Dated & signed: Wien am 23. Mai 1848.
Albert Graf von Montecuccoli, k. k. n. ö.
Landes=Präsident.

---

*pGB8
V6755R
5.24.48

Austria. Ministerium des Innern.
    Zur Erläuterung des fünften Absatzes der
Kundmachung vom heutigen Tage wegen Schliessung
des akademischen Schuljahres ...
    [Wien]Aus der k.k.Hof= und Staats=Druckerei.
[1848]

    broadside. 44.5x57cm.
    Reschauer-Smets II.245.
    Dated & signed: Wien am 24. Mai 1848. Der
interimistische Minister des Inneren: Pillersdorff.

---

*pGB8
V6755R
5.23.48

Austria, Lower. Regierungs-Präsident.
    Kundmachung. Durch ein Versehen wurde bei
Ausfertigung des provisorischen Pressgesetzes
im Paragraphe 8 der Verordnung gegen den
Missbrauch der Presse die Beziehung auf den
Paragraph 4 weggelassen ...
    [Wien]Aus der k.k.Hof- und Staats-Druckerei.
[1848]

    broadside. 44.5x57.5cm.
    Dated & signed: Wien am 23. Mai 1848. Albert
Graf von Montecuccoli, k. k. n. ö. Landes=
Präsident.

---

*pGB8
V6755R
5.24.48

Austria. Ministerium für Cultus und Unterricht.
    Kundmachung. In Erwägung des billigen
Wunsches vieler Studierenden ...
    [Wien,1848]

    broadside. 44.5x57cm.
    Reschauer-Smets II.244.
    Dated & signed: Wien am 24. Mai 1848. Sommaruga,
Minister des Unterrichts.
    Announcing the closing of schools for the
remainder of the school year.

*pGB8
V6755R
5.24.48

Graf Bombelles. :Judas war ein Erzschelm.:
[Wien]Gedruckt bei Josef Ludwig.[1848]

broadside. 47x60cm.
Signed: B. L.
This edition begins "Jetzt endlich ist alles
entdeckt; Graf Bombelles soll es gewesen sein,
der den kaiserlichen Hof zu den unerhörten
Schritt Wien zu verlassen bewogen hat ..."; the
last line of text begins "würdiger Tag gewesen.--
So aber ging mit dem 15. Mai ..."

*GB8
V6755R
5.24.48

Die Studenten-Legionen lösen sich auf. Die
Studenten verlassen Wien?
[Wien]Gedruckt bei Jos.Ludwig.[1848]

folder([4]p.) 26x21.5cm.

*pGB8
V6755R
5.24.48

Graf Bombelles. :Judas war ein Erzschelm.:
[Wien]Gedruckt bei Josef Ludwig.[1848]

broadside. 47.5x60cm.
Signed: B. L.
This edition begins "Jetzt endlich ist alles
entdeckt; Graf Bombelles soll es gewesen sein,
der den kaiserlichen Hof zu den unerhörten
Schritt Wien zu verlassen bewogen hat ..."; the
last line of text begins "ging mit dem 15. Mai
eine neue Sonne für Oesterreich auf."

*pGB8
V6755R
5.24.48

Vienna. Nationalgarde.
Tagsbefehl vom 24. Mai 1848.
[Wien]Aus der k.k.Hof= und Staatsdruckerei.
[1848]

broadside. 44.5x28.5cm.
Signed: Vom Ober=Commando der Nationalgarde.
Sardagna, General=Major.

*pGB8
V6755R
5.24.48

Graf Bombelles oder Judas der Erzschelm.
(Auszug aus der Zeitschrift "der Volksfreund"
dd. 23. d. M.)
[Wien]Gedruckt bei Josef Ludwig.[1848]

broadside. 48x60cm.
This edition begins: Es ist heraus, der
Rädelsführer ist entdeckt; Graf Bombelles war es,
der den kaiserlichen Hof zu den unerhörten Schritt
einer Flucht von Wien bewogen hat ...

*pGB8
V6755R
5.24.48

Vienna. Nationalgarde.
Verwahrung der Wiener National=Garde.
[Wien]Druck von U.Klopf sen.und Alex.Eurich.
[1848]

broadside. 46x30cm.
Dated: Wien, den 24. Mai 1848.
Protesting statements to the effect that the
monarchy was doomed and that the Nationalgarde was guilty of high treason.

*pGB8
V6755R
5.24.48

[Hrczka, Joseph]
Das ist die Studentenschaft, die sich nennt:
die akademische Legion, die sich nennt: einen
Theil der Nationalgarde, die sich nennt: die
ganze Nation.
[Wien]Gedruckt und zu haben bei U.Klopf sen.und
Alex.Eurich,Wollzeile Nr.782.[1848]

[2]p. 42.5x26cm.
Caption title; imprint on p.[2]; signed &
dated at end: Josef Hrczka. Wien am 24. Mai 1848.

*pGB8
V6755R
5.24.48

Zeitung für die Wiener Nationalgarde,
herausgegeben vom Verwaltungsrathe derselben.
Programm.
[Wien]Aus der k.k.Hof= und Staats=Aerarial=
Druckerei.[1848]

broadside. 44.5x28cm.
Dated: Wien am 24. Mai 1848.
A prospectus; the periodical began publication
on 1 June 1848.

*pGB8
V6755R
5.24.48

Kaiser, Joseph, fl.1848.
An sämmtliche Compagnien der National=Garde.
[Wien,1848]

broadside. 44.5x28.5cm.
Dated & signed: Wien am 24. Mai 1848. Joseph
Kaiser, Garde der 4. Comp. des Bezirkes Wieden,
und Mitglied des Sicherheits=Ausschusses der
Stadt Wien.

*pGB8
V6755R
5.25.48

Austria. Ministerrat.
An alle Theilnehmer der akademischen Legion!
[Wien]Aus der k.k.Hof= und Staats=Druckerei.
[1848]

broadside. 47.5x61.5cm.
Reschauer-Smets II.254.
Dated & signed: Wien den 25. Mai 1848. Ueber
Auftrag des Ministerrathes: Albert Graf von
Montecuccoli ...
Dissolving the Akademische Legion as an
independent part of the Nationalgarde.

Austria. Sovereigns, etc., 1835-1848
*pGB8   (Ferdinand I)
V6755R   Wir Ferdinand der Erste, von Gottes Gnaden
5.25.48 Kaiser von Oesterreich ... Ueber den Antrag
Unserer getreuen Stände des Herzogthums
Kärnthen und nach dem Vorschlage Unseres
Ministerrathes haben Wir in Uebereinstimmung mit
den in Unserem Erlasse vom 25. April l. J.
getroffenen Anordnungen über die Einlösung
verschiedener auf Grund und Boden haftenden Lasten
und Leistungen Nachstehendes beschlossen ...
   [Wien,1848]
                                   (See next card)

Austria. Sovereigns, etc., 1835-1848
*pGB8   (Ferdinand I)   Wir Ferdinand der Erste
V6755R ... [1848]   (Card 2)
5.25.48 folder([2]p.) 44.5x29cm.
   Caption title; dated: Gegeben in Unserer
kaiserlichen Haupt= und Residenzstadt Wien am fünf
und zwanzigsten Mai im eintausend achthundert
acht und vierzigsten ...

Austria, Lower. Laws, statutes, etc., 1835-1848
*pGB8   (Ferdinand I)
V6755R Circulare der Nieder=Oester. Landesregierung
5.25.48 über die Einsammlung und die Abfuhr der zur
Bestreitung der Staatsbedürfnisse einfliessenden
freiwilligen Gelder.
   [Wien,1848]

   [2]p. 38x22.5cm.
   Caption title; dated at end: Wien den 25. Mai
1848.

[Brühl, Carl Bernhard, 1820-1899]
*pGB8   ... Wer ist schuld, dass der Kaiser fort ist?
V6755R Worte der Verständigung mit unsern Brüdern aus
5.25.48 dem Volke über den 15. und 18. Mai.
   [Wien]Gedruckt und zu haben bei U.Klopf sen.
und Alex.Eurich,Wollzeile 782.[1848]

   [2]p. 39.5x25cm.
   Caption title (at head: 2 Kreuzer Conv. Münze.);
imprint on p.[2]; signed: Brühl, Nationalgardist
des Stubenviertels für Hunderttausende von
Gleichgesinnten.

Minister=Katechismus. Was wir wollen und sie
*pGB8   sollen.
V6755R   [Wien]Gedruckt bei J.N.Fridrich,Josefstadt Nr.
5.25.48 58.[1848]

   [2]p. 38x23cm.
   Caption title; imprint on p.[2]; signed at
end: Der Mann des Volkes.
   "Der Mann des Volkes" was a short-lived
periodical; this is perhaps a reprint from it.

Oesterreichische Nationalbank.
*pGB8   Kundmachung. Mit Berufung auf die, von der
V6755R Bank=Direction erflossene Kundmachung vom 21. Mai
5.25.48 d. J. ... wird hiemit ein Formular der Banknoten
der priv. österr. Nationalbank zu 1 und zu 2
Gulden zur öffentlichen Kenntniss gebracht ...
   [Wien,1848]

   [2]p. illus. 44.5x29cm.
   Dated & signed: Wien am 25. Mai 1848. Mayer
Gravenegg, Bank=Gouverneur. Schloissnigg, Bank=
Director.
   Printed on yel-   low paper; the bank-notes
are pictured on   p.[2].

[Scheibe, Theodor, 1820-1881]
*GB8   ... Wer sein Vaterland liebt und retten will,
V6755R lese dieses Blatt! 300 Millionen Gulden!
5.25.48 [Wien]Gedruckt in der Josephstadt,
Langegasse Nr.58.[1848]

   folder([4]p.) 26x21cm.
   Caption title; imprint on p.[4]; signed at
end: Theodor Scheibe.
   At head of title: Der Mann des Volkes.
   "Der Mann des Volkes" was a short-lived
periodical edited   by Scheibe; this may be
a reprint from it.

Vienna. Nationalgarde.
*pGB8   An die Arbeiter! Studenten und Nationalgarden
V6755R haben sich brüderlich vereint ...
5.25.48 [Wien,1848]

   Broadside. 44.5x57cm.
   Signed: Dr. Bruby, prov. Präsident. Dr.
Taussig, prov. Secretär. Dr. Joh. Goldmark,
Hauptmann der akademischen Legion.

Vienna. Nationalgarde.
*pGB8   Tagsbefehl vom 25. Mai 1848.
V6755R [Wien]Aus der k.k.Staats=Druckerei.[1848]
5.25.48
   broadside. 45x29cm.
   Reschauer-Smets II.255.
   Repeating the 9 points of the proclamation
issued by the Ministerrat on 25 May dissolving
the Akademische Legion as an independent part
of the Nationalgarde.

Aufruf an alle Oesterreicher!
*GB8   [Wien]Gedruckt bei U.Klopf sen.und Alex.Eurich.
V6755R [1848]
5.26.48
   broadside. 25.5x21cm.
   Dated & signed: Wien, am 26. Mai 1848. Von
Eueren Brüdern in Wien.

Austria. Kriegsministerium.
Da eine Deputation die Besorgniss ausspricht,
es könne sich das böswillige Gerücht verwirk-
lichen ...
[Wien,1848]

*pGB8
V6755R
5.26.48

broadside. 44.5x28.5cm.
Reschauer-Smets II.275.
Dated & signed: Wien am 26. Mai 1848. Latour,
Feldzeugmeister.
Denying the rumor that 4 regiments of Bohemian
troops were marching on Vienna.

Austria. Ministerrat.
Die Unterzeichneten bestätigen, dass die
Truppen der Garnison sich bereits nach dem
Auftrage des Commandirenden in die Casernen
zurückgezogen haben ...
[Wien,1848]

*pGB8
V6755R
5.26.48

broadside. 45x57cm.
Reschauer-Smets II.275.
Dated & signed: Wien am 26. Mai 1848.
Pillersdorff. Latour.

Austria. Ministerium des Innern.
Kundmachung. Um falschen Gerüchten vorzubeugen,
als würden gegen die Studenten Gewaltmassregeln
angewendet, so erkläre ich hiermit ...
[Wien,1848]

*pGB8
V6755R
5.26.48

broadside. 45x57cm.
Signed: Der Minister des Inneren: Pillersdorff.

Austria. Ministerrat.
Die Zusicherungen des Kaisers vom 15. und 16.
Mai d. J. stehen in ihrer ganzen Ausdehnung
aufrecht. Die akademische Legion besteht
unverändert ...
[Wien,1848]

*pGB8
V6755R
5.26.48

broadside. 45x57cm.
Reschauer-Smets II.275.
Dated: Wien am 26. Mai 1848.

Austria. Ministerium des Innern.
Nach dem Wunsche der Herren Scherzer, Kalazdy,
Ranftl, Lechleitner und Habza nehme ich keinen
Anstand zu erklären ...
[Wien]Aus der k.k.Staatsdruckerei.[1848]

*pGB8
V6755R
5.26.48

broadside. 44.5x28.5cm.
Dated & signed: Wien am 26. Mai 1848.
Pillersdorff.
Stating that the instigators of the May 26th
uprising will be brought to justice.

Buchheim, Carl Adolf, 1828-1900.
Barrikaden-Lied.
[Wien]Gedruckt und zu haben bei U.Klopf sen.
und Alex.Eurich[1848]

*GB8
V6755R
5.26.48

broadside. 26.5x21cm.
Helfert (Wiener Parnass) 1130.
At end: Geschrieben auf einer Barrikade bei
der Wiener Universität am 26. Mai von Adolf
Buchheim. Student.

Austria. Ministerrat.
Kundmachung. Das Militär erhält hiermit den
Befehl, sogleich abzuziehen ...
[Wien]Aus der k.k.Hof= und Staats=Druckerei.
[1848]

*pGB8
V6755R
5.26.48

broadside. 44.5x28.5cm.
Reschauer-Smets II.275.
Dated: Wien den 26. Mai 1848.

[Ehrlich, Jakob, fl.1848]
Die Universität geschlossen oder Die
Verschwörung der 105 schwarzgelben Manichäer
gegen die Studenten. Eine wahre Geschichte zur
Warnung und Belehrung aller Rechtgläubigen.
[Wien]Gedruckt und zu haben bei Franz Edl.
von Schmid,Stadt,Seitenstättengasse Nr.495.
[1848]

*GB8
V6755R
5.26.48
(A)

[2]p. 30x22.5cm.
Caption title; imprint on p.[2]; signed at end:
Jakob Ehrlich.

(See next card)

Austria. Ministerrat.
Kundmachung. Der Ministerrath hat, um dem
dringenden Wunsche der Bevölkerung für die
Abwendung grösserer Gefahren und dem Begehren
der akademischen Legion zu entsprechen,
beschlossen, nicht auf der Vollziehung der
Auflösung und Vereinigung der Legion mit der
Nationalgarde zu beharren ...
[Wien]Aus der k.k.Staats=Druckerei.[1848]

*pGB8
V6755R
5.26.48

broadside. 45x57cm.
Reschauer-Smets II.274.
Dated: Wien am 26. Mai 1848.

[Ehrlich, Jakob, fl.1848]   Die Universität ...
[1848]   (Card 2)
In this copy, the first word of text ("Wie")
has an ordinary capital.

*GB8
V6755R
5.26.48
(B)

Another copy. 29.5x23cm.
In this copy, the first word of text has a
large black-letter capital.

*GB8
V6755R
5.26.48

Einstimmiger Ruf der Wiener nach den 26. May an ihren hochherzigen constitutionellen Kaiser Ferdinand.
[Wien]Gedruckt bei Josef Ludwig.[1848]

folder([4]p.) 26.5x21cm.
Signed: Einer für hunderttausende. F. National Garde.

---

*pGB8
V6755R
5.26.48

Patriotischer Verein zur Anschaffung von Waffen und Kleidung durch freiwillige Beiträge, Vienna.
Aufforderung. Mit Freuden wollte mancher brave österreichische Unterthan für sein Vaterland, für sein theures Oesterreich kämpfen ...
[Wien]Druck von U.Klopf sen.und A.Eurich.[1848]

broadside. 45x28cm.
Dated: Wien den 26. Mai 1848.

---

*pGB8
V6755R
5.26.48

Forderungen des Wiener-Volkes.
[Wien,1848]

broadside. 42x25.5cm.
Published on the 26th of May & listing 4 demands.

---

*GB8
V6755R
5.26.48

[Relstab, A   D   ]
Aufruf eines deutschen Patrioten an seine österreichischen Mitbürger.
[Wien]Gedruckt bei Ferdinand Ullrich.[1848]

folder([4]p.) 29x22cm.
Caption title; imprint on p.[4]; dated & signed at end: Wien den 26. Mai 1848. Dr. A. D. Relstab.

---

*pGB8
V6755R
5.26.48

Glaser, Moriz.
Was die Studenten dem guten Kaiser in Wien gethan haben. (Eine Mittheilung an meine österreichischen Landsleute ausser Wien). Von Moriz Glaser.
[Wien]Gedruckt und zu haben bei U.Klopf sen. und A.Eurich,Wollzeile 782.[1848]

[2]p. 37.5x25.5cm.
Caption title; imprint on p.[2]; dated at end: Wien, den 26. Mai 1848.

---

*pGB8
V6755R
5.26.48

So hat's kommen müssen! oder: Wer ist noch gegen die Studenten? Eine kurze Nachricht für die Bauern und Provinzbewohner. Geschrieben auf einer Barrikade Nachts am 26. Mai.
[Wien]Gedruckt bei M.Lell.[1848]

broadside. 41.5x26.5cm.
Signed: Ein Student.

---

*pGB8
V6755R
5.26.48

[Knöpfelmacher, Bernhard]
Die Barrikaden oder der 26. Mai.
[Wien]Gedruckt bei M.Lell.[1848]

broadside. 36.5x24cm.
Another issue has the author's name, "B. Knöpfelmacher", as last line of text.

---

*GB8
V6755R
5.26.48

Strampfer, Heinrich.
Ein Tag und eine Nacht des Mai im Jahre 1848. Ein Erinnerungsblättchen für alle Nationalgarden der Haupt= und Residenzstadt Wien; theils selbst erlebt, theils nacherzählt von Heinrich Strampfer.
[Wien]Gedruckt bei M.Lell[1848]

folder(4p.) 19x12cm.
Helfert (Wiener Parnass) 1127.
Caption title; imprint on p.4.

---

*pGB8
V6755R
5.26.48

Knöpfelmacher, Bernhard.
Die Barrikaden oder der 26. Mai.
[Wien]Gedruckt bei M.Lell.[1848]

broadside. 45.5x28.5cm.
"B. Knöpfelmacher" appears as the last line of text; another issue is without the name.

---

*GB8
V6755R
5.26.48

Die Vorgänge in Wien am 26. Mai.
[Wien]Druck von M.Klopf sen.und A.Eurich.[1848]

broadside. 22x17cm.
Signed: Bürger und Studenten Wiens.

*GB8
V6755R
5.26.48

Was wir wollen.
[Wien]Druck von U.Klopf sen.und A.Eurich.[1848]
broadside. 29x23cm.
Reschauer-Smets II.276.
Signed: Im Namen des Volkes.
Dated in contemporary ms.: Wien 26ten Mai 1848.

*GB8
V6755R
5.26.48

Worte eines Oesterreichers über den
Missbrauch der Presse.
Wien.26/5.1848.Gedruckt bei M.Lell.
[2]p. 25.5x20cm.
Helfert (Wiener Parnass) 1136; Helfert describes
this as a 2-leaf pamphlet, the first leaf in
prose beginning "Todesurtheil! wie viele arme
sündige und niederträchtige Flugschriften am 20.
Mai 1848 sind hingerichtet worden"; ascribed
to "Bik" (i.e. Johann Bernatzik).
Caption title; imprint on p.[2].

*pGB8
V6755R
5.27.48

Austria. Ministerrat.
Der Ministerrath erkennt die ausserordentlichen
Verhältnisse, welche es zu einem Gebote der
Nothwendigkeit gemacht haben, das sich ein
Ausschuss von Bürgern, Nationalgarden und
Studenten gebildet hat ...
[Wien]Aus der k.k.Hof= und Staats=Druckerei.
[1848]
broadside. 45x57cm.
Reschauer-Smets II.287.
Dated & signed: Wien den 27. Mai 1848. Im Namen
des Ministerrathes, Pillersdorff.

*pGB8
V6755R
5.27.48

Der Barikaden-Krieg in Neapel.
Gefangennehmung und Tod der Nationalgarde!
[Wien]Gedruckt bei M.Lell,Leopoldstadt,
Weintraubengasse Nr.505.[1848]
broadside. 43x27cm.
Dated: Augsburg am 27. Mai.

*pGB8
V6755R
5.27.48

Das grosse Barrieaden Manöver am 26. Mai 1848,
oder: Wie die Wiener Universität gesperrt wird!
[Wien]Gedruckt bei Josef Ludwig.[1848]
broadside. 44x55.5cm.
Signed: P. L.
Dated in contemporary ms.: 27. Mai 848.

*pGB8
V6755R
5.27.48

Herczeghy, Mór, 1815-1884.
An die braven Wiener Arbeiter.
[Wien]Gedruckt bei Edl.v.Schmidbauer und
Holzwarth.[1848]
broadside. 27x43cm.
Dated in contemporary ms.: 27. Mai 848.

*pGB8
V6755R
5.27.48

Pro memoria an Alle, die regieren wollen.
[Wien]Gedruckt bei M.Lell.[1848]
broadside. 45x57cm.
Signed: Ein Mann vom 26. Mai.

*pGB8
V6755R
5.27.48

[Swoboda, August, fl.1848]
Offener Brief an die vermöglichen Bewohner
Wiens.
[Wien]Gedruckt bei Edl.v.Schmidbauer und
Holzwarth.[1848]
[2]p. 43x26.5cm.
Caption title; imprint on p.[2]; signed at
end: August Swoboda.
The letter is dated: Wien, den 27. Mai 1848.

*pGB8
V6755R
5.27.48

Vienna. Sicherheits-Ausschuss.
In diesem dringenden Augenblicke haben sich
der Gemeinde-Ausschuss der Stadt Wien, die
Bürger, Nationalgarden und Studenten brüderlich
vereinigt, und einen provisorischen Ausschuss
gebildet ...
[Wien]Aus der k.k.Hof= und Staats=Druckerei.
[1848]
broadside. 44.5x57cm.
Reschauer-Smets II.280.
Dated & signed: Wien am 27. Mai 1848. Der
provisorische Ausschuss der Bürger,
Nationalgarden und Studenten.

*pGB8
V6755R
5.27.48

Vienna. Universität. Ausschuss der Studierenden.
Vom Studenten=Comite. In diesem Augenblicke,
in welchem es so nothwendig ist, mit vereinter
Kraft für die öffentliche Ordnung, Ruhe und
Sicherheit zu wirken ...
[Wien]Gedruckt bei U.Klopf sen.und A.Eurich.
[1848]
broadside. 42.5x53cm.
Dated: Wien, am 27. Mai 1848.
Concerning election of members of the
Akademische Legion to the Sicherheits-Ausschuss.

*pGB8
V6755R
5.27.48

Was haben wir noch zu thun?
[Wien]Gedruckt bei U.Klopf sen.und Alex.
Eurich.[1848]

broadside. 42.5x26.5cm.
Dated & signed: Wien am 27. Mai 1848. Im
Namen des Volkes.

---

*pGB8
V6755R
5.28.48

Austria, Lower. Laws, statutes, etc., 1835-1848
(Ferdinand I)
Circulare der Nieder=Oester. Landesregierung
über die Einsammlung und die Abfuhr der zur
Bestreitung der Staatsbedürfnisse einfliessenden
freiwilligen Gelder.
[Wien]Aus der k.k.Hof= und Staats=Druckerei.
[1848]

[2]p. 38x23.5cm.
Caption title; dated at end: Wien den 28. Mai
1848.
Text identical with the Circulare of 25
May.

---

*pGB8
V6755R
5.28.48

Die Arbeiter am 26. Mai.
[Wien]Gedruckt bei M.Lell.[1848]

broadside. 60.5x48cm.
Signed: J. R.
Includes at foot "Das ABC der Arbeiter", in
verse (Helfert, Wiener Parnass, 1128).

---

*pGB8
V6755R
5.28.48

Die Ereignisse den 26. May beim Rothen=
Thurmthor.
[Wien]Gedruckt bei Josef Ludwig.[1848]

broadside. 44x55.5cm.
Signed: Von einem Augenzeigen.

---

*pGB8
V6755R
5.28.48

Austria. Ministerium des Innern.
Da mit heutigem Ministerialbeschlusse ohnehin
alle die öffentliche Ruhe und Ordnung betreffenden Verfügungen unmittelbar anheim gestellt
worden sind ...
[Wien]Aus der k.k.Staats=Druckerei.[1848]

broadside. 45x57cm.
Dated & signed: Wien am 28. Mai 1848. Pillersdorff.
Another edition inserts the words "dem prov.
Ausschusse der Bürger, Nationalgarden und der
akademischen Legion" after
"unmittelbar".

---

*pGB8
V6755R
5.28.48

Geschichte der grossen Freiheits=Erhebung in
Wien.
[Wien]Gedruckt bei J.N.Fridrich.[1848]

broadside. 42x52.5cm.
Account of the events of 25-27 May.

---

*pGB8
V6755R
5.28.48

Austria. Ministerium des Innern.
Da mit heutigem Ministerialbeschlusse ohnehin
alle die öffentliche Ruhe und Ordnung
betreffenden Verfügungen unmittelbar dem prov.
Ausschusse der Bürger, Nationalgarden und der
akademischen Legion anheim gestellt worden sind
...
[Wien]Aus der k.k.Hof= und Staats=Druckerei.
[1848]

broadside. 45x57cm.
Dated & signed: Wien am 28. Mai 1848.
(See next card)

---

*GB8
V6755R
5.28.48

[Günther, Friedrich, fl.1848]
Andeutungen aus den politischen und staats=
ökonomischen Ansichten des gefertigten
Candidaten für eine Wahlmanns= und Deputirten=
Stelle bei dem kaiserl. österreichischen con-
stituirenden Reichstag.
[Wien]Gedruckt bei Ferdinand Ullrich.[1848]

folder([4]p.) 29x22cm.
Caption title; imprint on p.[4]; dated & signed
at end: Wien den 28. Mai 1848. Friedrich
Günther ...

---

*pGB8
V6755R
5.28.48

Austria. Ministerium des Innern. Da mit
heutigem ... [1848] (Card 2)

Pillersdorff.
Another edition omits the words "dem prov.
Ausschusse der Bürger, Nationalgarden und der
akademischen Legion" after "unmittelbar".

---

*pGB8
V6755R
5.28.48

[Leidesdorf, Eduard]
Wien und seine Barrikaden. Eine Schilderung
der älteren und neuesten Barrikaden, die
Wien aufzuweisen hat.
[Wien]Gedruckt und zu haben bei U.Klopf sen.
und Alex.Eurich.[1848]

[2]p. 39.5x25cm.
Caption title; imprint on p.[2]; dated & signed
at end: Wien am 28. Mai 1848. Eduard Leidesdorf,
Jurist.

*pGB8
V6755R
5.28.48

Wagner, Johann, 1820-1876.
Unser Feind und unsere Waffe.
[Wien]Druck von U.Klopf sen.und Alex.Eurich.
[1848]

broadside. 42.5x26.5cm.
Dated: Wien, den 28. Mai 1848.

*pGB8
V6755R
5.29.48

Vienna. Sicherheits-Ausschuss.
Durch Vermittlung des Ministerrathes wurden vom
Kriegsministerium der vereinigten Nationalgarde
und akademischen Legion 12 Geschütze auszufolgen
bewilliget ...
[Wien]Aus der k.k.Hof= und Staatsdruckerei.
[1848]

broadside. 44.5x57cm.
Dated & signed: Wien am 29. Mai 1848. Vom
Ausschusse der Bürger, Nationalgarde und
Studenten.

*pGB8
V6755R
5.29.48

Austria. Ministerrat.
Das Ministerium an die Bewohner der Residenz.
Die Handlungen des Ministeriums sind verschieden
beurtheilt worden ...
[Wien]Aus der k.k.Hof= und Staatsdruckerei.
[1848]

[2]p. 44.5x28.5cm.
Caption title; imprint on p.[2]; dated & signed
at end: Wien am 29. Mai 1848. Im Namen des
Ministerrathes: Pillersdorff.

*pGB8
V6755R
5.29.48

Vienna. Sicherheits-Ausschuss.
Kundmachung. Um beunruhigenden Gerüchten
vorzubeugen, beeilt sich der Ausschuss der
Bürger, der Nationalgarde und der Studenten,
das Publikum davon in Kenntniss zu setzen ...
[Wien]Aus der k.k.Staats=Druckerei.[1848]

broadside. 44.5x29cm.
Dated: Wien, am 29. Mai 1848.
Announcing the departure of Graf Nugent's
infantry regiment for Italy.

*pGB8
V6755R
5.29.48

Austria. Ministerrat.
Das Ministerium an die Bewohner Wiens. Die
Handlungen des Ministeriums sind verschieden
beurtheilt worden ...
[Wien]Gedruckt bei L.Sommer(vorm.Strauss).
[1848]

broadside. 41.5x26cm.
Dated: Wien, den 29. Mai 1848.
"Abdruck aus der Allgem. oesterr. Zeitung."

*pGB8
V6755R
5.30.48

Bauernschmid, Carl Eduard, 1801-1875.
Der 26. Mai 1848 in Wien.
[Wien]Gedruckt und zu haben bei U.Klopf sen.
und Alex.Eurich,Wollzeile Nr.782.[1848]

broadside. 40x25cm.
Dated: Wien, den 30. Mai 1848.

*pGB8
V6755R
5.29.48

Der neue Oberkommandant der Nationalgarde
Herr Anton Pannasch. Was wir ihm bringen und
was wir von ihm erwarten.
[Wien]Gedruckt und zu haben bei U.Klopf sen.und
A.Eurich.[1848]

[2]p. 40x25cm.
Caption title; imprint on p.[2]; dated &
signed at end: Wien am 29. Mai 1848 ... S. D.

*pGB8
V6755R
5.30.48

[Bernatzik, Johann]
Zum allerhöchsten Namensfeste unsers
konstitutionellen Kaisers heute am 30. Mai.
[Wien]Gedruckt bei M.Lell.[1848]

broadside. 38x24.5cm.
Not recorded in Helfert (Wiener Parnass).
Signed: Bik [pseud.].

*pGB8
V6755R
5.29.48

Vienna. Sicherheits-Ausschuss.
An die Arbeiter! Liebe Brüder, wackere
Freunde! Der Ausschuss der Bürger, der
Nationalgarde und der Studenten ist stolz
darauf ...
[Wien]Aus der k.k.Staats=Druckerei.[1848]

broadside. 45x29cm.
Dated: Wien am 29. Mai 1848.
Urging a return to work.

*pGB8
V6755R
5.30.48

Iwán, Theodor.
Courier wider den slavischen Konflikt.
Statistische Beantwortung der an mich Gefertigten
ergangenen Briefe ddo. Prag 25. April, ddo.
Carlstadt 30. April; ddo. Neusatz 19 Mai und
ddo. Wukovar 20. Mai 1848, über die, diesen
Parteien eingesandten 400 Broschuren für die
wissenschaftlich nicht gebildeten Slaven, zur
Einsicht der auch ihnen aus unserer Revolution
erwachsenen hochwichtigen Interessen.
[Wien,1848]
broadside. 60x47cm.
Dated: Wien, den 30. Mai 1848.

Knöpfelmacher, Bernhard.
Die Batterien, oder die Übergabe der Kanonen.
[Wien]Gedruckt und zu haben bei U.Klopf sen.
und Alex.Eurich.[1848]

*pGB8
V6755R
5.30.48

broadside. 40x25cm.
Dated: Wien den 30. Mai 1848.

[Knöpfelmacher, Bernhard]
Gedanken am allerhöchsten Namensfeste unsers
constitutionellen Kaisers heute am 30. Mai.
[Wien]Gedruckt und zu haben bei U.Klopf sen.
und A.Eurich.[1848]

*pGB8
V6755R
5.30.48

[2]p. 39.5x25cm.
Caption title; imprint on p.[2]; dated &
signed: Wien, den 30. Mai 1848. B. Knöpfelmacher.

[Relstab, A   D   ]
... Aufruf eines Deutschen an seine
Österreichischen Mitbürger. Inhalt: Ueber die
unwiderrufliche Errungenschaft, die Verbrüderung,
die Integrität und den Staatskredit Oesterreichs.
[Wien]Gedruckt bei Ferdinand Ullrich.[1848]

*GB8
V6755R
5.30.48

folder([4]p.) 28.5x22cm.
Caption title; imprint on p.[4]; dated &
signed at end: Wien den 30. Mai 1848. Dr. A. D.
Relstab.
At head of caption title: Dritte Auflage.

Sartorius, Friedrich.
Edle Züge von Menschlichkeit und Wohlthun!
Meine Herren Mitbürger und Kameraden! Es wird
wohl Einigen von Ihnen bekannt seyn, dass, als
in den Tagen nach Bekanntmachung der Abreise
Seiner Majestät ...
[Wien]Aus der k.k.Hof= und Staats=Druckerei.
[1848]

*pGB8
V6755R
5.30.48

broadside. 44.5x29cm.
Dated: Wien am 30. Mai 1848.
A later undated edition, though beginning with
the same words, is not the same text.
Asking for con-   tributions to the
Akademische   Legion.

Die Verbrüderung des Kärnthnerviertels mit
der akademischen Legion am Namenstage unsers
Kaisers am 30. Mai 1848.
[Wien]Gedruckt bei Josef Ludwig.[1848]

*pGB8
V6755R
5.30.48

broadside. 44x28cm.
Signed: C. M.

Vienna. Gemeinderat.
Der neugewählte Gemeinde=Ausschuss an die
Bevölkerung Wiens.
[Wien]Aus der k.k.Hof= und Staats=Druckerei.
[1848]

*pGB8
V6755R
5.30.48

broadside. 44.5x56.5cm.
Dated: Wien am 30. Mai 1848.

Vienna. Sicherheits-Ausschuss.
An die Bevölkerung Wiens! Täglich, ja
stündlich tauchen neue Gerüchte auf ...
[Wien]Aus der k.k.Hof= und Staats=Druckerei.
[1848]

*pGB8
V6755R
5.30.48

broadside. 44.5x57cm.
Dated: Wien am 30. Mai 1848.
Asking that unfounded rumors be ignored.

Vienna. Sicherheits-Ausschuss.
Von Seite des Ausschusses der Bürger,
Nationalgarden und Studenten für Aufrechthaltung
der Ruhe und Ordnung und für Wahrung der Rechte
des Volkes, sind die gegen den bisherigen
Obercommandanten der gesammten Nationalgarden
Herrn Grafen Hoyos aus Anlass der Vorgänge am
26. Mai vorgebrachten Beschwerdepunkte auf das
Genaueste untersucht worden ...
[Wien]Aus der k.k.Hof= und Staatsdruckerei.
[1848]

*pGB8
V6755R
5.30.48

broadside.   44.5x56.5cm.
Dated: Wien am   30. Mai 1848.

Knöpfelmacher, Bernhard.
Das Verbrüderungs=Fest im Odeon, oder: Der
überraschende Fackelzug mit Musik, gebracht dem
Pillersdorf, Pannasch, Füster.
[Wien]Gedruckt bei M.Lell.[1848]

*pGB8
V6755R
5.31.48

broadside. 48x60cm.
Another copy. 47.5x57.5cm.

*pGB8
V6755R
5.23.48

Printed on 1 side of a folio sheet; on the
other side is printed Joseph Knees, Ehre dem
Ehre gebührt! [23 May 1848]

Radetzky's grosser Sieg. Ausserordentliche
Staffette aus Italien vom Kriegsschauplatze.
[Wien]Gedruckt und zu haben bei L.Grund,
Stephansplatz im Zwettelhof.[1848]

*pGB8
V6755R
5.31.48

[2]p. 1 illus. 37x23cm.
Imprint on p.[2].

*pGB8
V6755R
5.31.48

[Schahrl, Hermann]
... An alle Feinde der Freiheit.
[Wien]Gedruckt und zu haben bei U.Klopf sen.
und A.Eurich.[1848]

[2]p. 40x25cm.
Caption title (price at head); imprint on p.[2];
dated & signed at end: Wien am 31. Mai 1848.
Hermann Schahrl, Nationalgarde.

○

*pGB8
V6755R
5.32.48

An alle Denkenden!
[Wien](Gedruckt bei den Edlen von Ghelen'schen
Erben.)[1848]

broadside. 43x26.5cm.
Signed: X. U. [pseud.]

○

*pGB8
V6755R
5.31.48

Vienna. Sicherheits-Ausschuss.
Arbeiter! Das Eigenthum ist heilig! war Euer
Ausspruch in den Tagen, wo Ihr mit muthigen und
edlen Herzen mit Eueren Leben für das
Fortbestehen der akademischen Legion für die
Freiheit Alle für Einen und Einer für Alle zum
Kampfe dagestanden seid ...
[Wien]Aus der k.k.Hof= und Staats=Druckerei.
[1848]

broadside. 45x57cm.

(See next card)

○

*pGB8
V6755R
5.32.48

An alle Denkenden! Nr.2.
[Wien]Gedruckt bei den Edlen v.Ghelen'schen
Erben.[1848]

broadside. 43x55cm.
Signed: X. U. [pseud.]

○

*pGB8
V6755R
5.31.48

Vienna. Sicherheits-Ausschuss.   Arbeiter ...
[1848]   (Card 2)

Dated & signed: Wien am 31. Mai 1848. Vom
Ausschusse der Bürger, Nationalgarden und
Studenten für Aufrechthaltung der Ruhe und
Ordnung und zur Wahrung der Rechte des Volkes.

○

*pGB8
V6755R
5.32.48

An die Arbeiter. Als Wien für die Freiheit
gekämpft, als es gesiegt hat, waret Ihr dabei,
Ihr hattet Euren Antheil an der Errungenschaft
...
[Wien]Gedruckt bei Leop.Sommer(vormals Strauss.)
[1848]

broadside. 45x60.5cm.
Perhaps a proofsheet.

○

*pGB8
V6755R
5.31.48

Vienna. Sicherheits-Ausschuss.
Kundmachung. Vom Freitage den 2. Juni d. J.
an, werden die Anweisungen zu den öffentlichen
Arbeiten ...
[Wien]Aus der k.k.Hof= und Staats=Druckerei.
[1848]

broadside. 44.5x57cm.
Dated & signed: Wien am 31. Mai 1848. Vom
Ausschusse der Bürger, Nationalgarden und
Studenten für Aufrechthaltung der Ruhe,
Sicherheit und Wahrung der Rechte des Volkes.

○

*pGB8
V6755R
5.32.48

An die Frauen Wiens!
[Wien]Gedruckt bei U.Klopf sen.und Alex.
Eurich,Wollzeile Nr.782.[1848]

broadside. 44.5x28.5cm.
Signed: Wilhelmine Heindörfer ... Caroline
Ostermayer ... Josepha Spiering [& 3 others].

○

*GB8
V6755R
5.32.48

Das 48ger Jahr wie no kan's da war.
Wien,1848.Gedruckt in der Josephstadt,
Langegasse Nr.58.

folder([4]p.) 24.5x19cm.
Helfert (Wiener Parnass) 923.
Signed at end: L. S.
Illustration on t.-p.

○

*pGB8
V6755R
5.32.48

An die Nationalgarden, Arbeiter und an die
akademische Legion. (Als Fortsetzung der
Vertheidigung der Wiener Studenten.)
[Wien]Gedruckt bei Edl.von Schmidbauer und
Holzwarth.[1848]

broadside. 68x52.5cm.
Signed: J. K.

○

*pGB8
V6755R
5.32.48

An die Wiener Garnison! Die Ereignisse der letzten Zeit haben uns in eine ernste Stellung zu Euch gebracht ...
   [Wien]Gedruckt bei Leop.Sommer(vormals Strauss).[1848]

   broadside. 52.5x42cm.
   Signed: Einer für Hunderttausend.

*GB8
V6755R
5.32.48

Bidschof, Franz Xavier.
   Die verborgenen Helden am 15. und 26. Mai 1848, oder die Ahndel, von Franz X. Bidschof ...
   [Wien]Gedruckt bei Josef Ludwig.[1848]

   folder([4]p.) 27x22cm.

*pGB8
V6755R
5.32.48

[Arthur, pseud.]
   Die Karten Auslegerin von Schottenfeld oder Ostereier der Frau Nanerl.
   [Wien]Gedruckt bei Josef Ludwig Josefstadt Florianigasse Nr.52.[1848]

   [2]p. 36x22.5cm.
   Helfert (Wiener Parnass) 992.
   Caption title; imprint on p.[2]; signed at end: Arthur.

*pGB8
V6755R
5.32.48

Bing, Johann.
   Guter Rath wie der Noth bei den Arbeitern vorzubeugen sei. Ein freundlicher Brief an die Arbeiter.
   [Wien]Gedruckt bei M.Lell,Leopoldstadt, Weintraubengasse Nr.505.[1848]

   broadside. 38x23cm.
   Signed: Johann Bing, Garde der akademischen Legion.

*pGB8
V6755R
5.32.48

Aufruf an die in Wien wohnenden Tiroler.
   [Wien,1848]

   broadside. 37x27.5cm.
   Signed: Joseph Polin. Thomas Kralinger. Johann Paul Fischer. Joseph Alois Schinnach.
   A call to arms against the Italians.

*pGB8
V6755R
5.32.48

Braucht Oesterreich eine Republik?
   [Wien]Gedruckt und zu haben bei Ulrich Klopf sen.und Alexander Eurich.[1848]

   [2]p. 39.5x25cm.
   Caption title; imprint on p.[2]; signed: H. L.

*pGB8
V6755R
5.32.48

Aufruf eines Wiener Bürgers an alle Patrioten unserer Monarchie.
   [Wien,1848]

   [2]p. 37.5x29cm.
   Caption title; signed: L. F.
   Calling for the contribution of old silver to aid the financial position of the state.

*GB8
V6755R
5.32.48

Buchheim, Carl Adolf, 1828-1900.
   Sie war bei den Studenten. Von Adolf Buchheim. Den hochherzigen Wienerinnen gewidmet.
   [Wien]Gedruckt und zu haben bei M.Lell.[1848]

   broadside. 30x21cm.
   Helfert (Wiener Parnass) 956.

*GB8
V6755R
5.32.48

[Beiser, Johann]
   Der Jude an die christlichen Freiheitskämpfer.
   [Wien,1848]

   [2]p. 21x13.5cm.
   Helfert (Wiener Parnass) 932.
   Caption title; signed on p.[2]: Drnd. Johann Beiser, Gardist.

*GB8
V6755R
5.32.48

Bürger! Die grossen Ereignisse der neuesten Zeit, die in die Entwicklungsgeschichte der Menschheit so tief eingreifende, so folgenreiche Erhebung der Nationen, hat unserm Blicke eine Zukunft eröffnet, die uns zu den schönsten Hoffnungen für das Wohl auch unseres Vaterlandes berechtigt ...
   [Wien,1848]

   folder([4]p.) 23.5x15cm.
   Signed at end: Ein Vaterlands-Freund.

Des Deutschen Lied.
[Wien]Druck von U.Klopf sen.und Alexander
Eurich.[1848]

*GB8
V6755R
5.32.48

broadside. 25x20cm.
Helfert (Wiener Parnass) 971.

Der Feldzeugmeister Graf Nugent in Italien
bedroht mit dem Kopfe seiner gefangenen Tochter
Gräfin D'Orsay.
[Wien]Gedruckt und zu haben bei Leopold Grund,
am Stephansplatze.[1848]

*GB8
V6755R
5.32.48

folder([4]p.) 23x18.5cm.
Signed at end: R.

Eichmann, Adolf, fl.1848.
Das Lied von den herrlichen Jungen. Meinen
hochherzigen Brüdern gewidmet von Adolf
Eichmann.
Wien,1848.Druck von U.Klopf sen.und A.Eurich.

*GB8
V6755R
5.32.48

folder([4]p.) 26.5x20.5cm.
Helfert (Wiener Parnass) 949.

[Fischer, Johann, fl.1848]
... Zopf und Perrücke in einer Sauce, oder:
eingesammelte Lorbeeren auf den Wiener
Barrikaden am 26. Mai 1848, nebst einem
andächtigen konstitutionellen deutschen
Unterthanen=Vater=Unser.
[Wien,1848]

*GB8
V6755R
5.32.48

folder([4]p.) 1 illus. 25x20cm.
Signed on p.[3]: Johann Fischer, Verfasser,
wohnhaft Erdberg Nr. 271.
At head of title: Guten Appetit zum Speisen,
(See next card)

Engel, Josef Friedrich.
Waffengruss der Universität.
Druck und Eigenthum von Hirschfeld in Wien.
[1848]

*GB8
V6755R
5.32.48

broadside. 22x14cm.
Helfert (Wiener Parnass) 950.

[Fischer, Johann, fl.1848]   ... Zopf und
Perrücke ... [1848]   (Card 2)
meine Herren!
Imprint on p.[4]: Gedruckt bei M. Lell,
Leopoldstadt, Weintraubengasse Nr. 505.

*GB8
V6755R
5.32.48

Euere Majestät! Wir nahen uns ehrfurchtsvoll
den Stufen des Thrones um Gnade flehend für
einen Biedermann und Bürger, dessen Leben in
Gefahr ist. Jacob Nitschner, Sohn eines Wiener
Bürgers ... ist vor ein Kriegsgericht gestellt
und angeklagt ...
[Wien,1848]

*pGB8
V6755R
5.32.48

broadside. 37.5x24cm.
A petition for clemency; no names have been
signed.

Fleischer, Johann, fl.1848.
... Warum keine Lotterie?!
[Wien]A.Dorfmeister's Druck und Verlag,Stadt,
Kühfussgasse Nr.575.[1848]

*pGB8
V6755R
5.32.48

broadside. 46x59cm.
At head: Preis: 2 kr. Conv. Mze.

F. M. G. v. [i.e. Feldmarschall Graf von]
Radetzky's grosser Sieg am 29. Mai bei Mantua.
[Wien,1848]

*GB8
V6755R
5.32.48

folder([4]p.) 25x20cm.
Imprint on p.[4]: Gedruckt und zu haben bei
Leopold Grund, am Stephansplatze im Zwettelhofe.
Woodcut illus. on t.-p.

[Frohner, Peter]
Der Riesenmüllergesell und seine Angabe.
Druck von U.Klopf sen.und A.Eurich,Wollzeile
Nro.782 in Wien.[1848]

*pGB8
V6755R
5.32.48

[2]p. 42x26.5cm.
Caption title; imprint on p.[2]; signed at
end: Peter Frohner, Müllergesell.

Funk, ——
*pGB8 Ja, was ist denn das wegen der Banknoten,
V6755R meine lieben Landleute.
5.32.48 [Wien]Gedruckt bei M.Lell.[1848]

broadside. 42x26cm.

Grausamer Raubmord an einer polnischen Familie
*GB8 verübt, durch acht donische Kosaken, fünf
V6755R Werste von Warschau.
5.32.48 [Wien,1848]

folder([4]p.) 24.5x19cm.
Imprint on p.[4]: Gedruckt bei M. Lell.

Gallbrunner, Leopold.
*GB8 Lied der Wiener Freiwilligen vom Jahre 1848.
V6755R [Wien]Gedruckt in der Josephstadt,Langegasse
5.32.48 Nr.58.[1848]

broadside. 21x13cm.
Helfert (Wiener Parnass) 936.

Die Grenadiere vom Getreidemarkt, oder:
*pGB8 Feierlicher Protest gegen die Stockprügel.
V6755R Gedruckt im Mai 1848 von Ulrich Klopf sen.
5.32.48 und Alex.Eurich in Wien.

broadside. 40x25cm.
Signed: Aus der Armee.

Glaser, Moriz.
*GB8 Das sind die braven Arbeiter!
V6755R [Wien]Druck von U.Klopf sen.und A.Eurich.
5.32.48 [1848]

broadside. 26.5x21.5cm.
Another issue has dated imprint.

Gugler, Josef, fl.1848.
*GB8 Der Studirenden Gruss, Dank und Bitte, an
V6755R die edlen deutschen Frauen und Mädchen Wiens.
5.32.48 Druck von U.Klopf sen.und A.Eurich in Wien.
[1848]

broadside. 30x23.5cm.
Helfert (Wiener Parnass) 957.
Printed on yellow paper.

Glaser, Moriz.
*GB8 Das sind die braven Arbeiter!
V6755R [Wien]Gedruckt im Mai 1848 von U.Klopf sen.
5.32.48 und A.Eurich.

broadside. 26x21.5cm.
Another issue does not have date in imprint.

Der Handschlag der Nationalgarde.
*pGB8 [Wien]Gedruckt bei J.N.Friedrich,Josephstadt,
V6755R Langegasse Nr.5S[!].[1848]
5.32.48
[2]p. 38.5x23cm.
Caption title; imprint on p.[2]; signed: E.
B****f. Nationalgarde des 12. Bezirks.

Glockenstimme gegen die Wucherer in Wien.
*GB8 [Wien]Gedruckt bei Josef Ludwig.[1848]
V6755R
5.32.48 folder([4]p.) 26.5x21cm.
Signed at end: C-L-J-N-K.
Dated in contemporary ms.: Mai 848.

Heilsames Pflaster für die Republikaner.
*pGB8 Frage: Ist eine Republik in Oesterreich
V6755R möglich? Antwort: Nein, abermals nein und
5.32.48 nochmals nein!
[Wien]Gedruckt bei Franz Edlen von Schmid.
[1848]
[2]p. 42x26.5cm.
Caption title; imprint on p.[2].

Herczeghy, Mór, 1815-1884.
    An alle treuen Wiener, welche es mit ihrem
Kaiser gut meinen.
    [Wien]Wird unentgeldlich ausgegeben.[1848]

    broadside. 44.5x27.5cm.
    Urging moderation; probably published after
the 26th of May.

*pGB8
V6755R
5.32.48

Klesheim, Anton, freiherr von, 1816?-1884.
    Frei-G'sangl von Schwarzblattl.
    [Wien,1848]

    broadside. 25.5x20cm.
    Helfert (Wiener Parnass) 924.

*GB8
V6755R
5.32.48

Hochlöblicher Ausschuss der Bürger, Nationalgarde und der akademischen Legion! Mit innigem
Bedauern vernehmen wir, dass der hochlöbliche
Ausschuss, der stets nur für das Wohl der
arbeitenden Classe bedacht war, gerade von
dieser in seinem löblichen Streben nach
Aufrechthaltung der Ordnung und Ruhe durch
unbillige Forderungen und Drohungen gestört
wird ...
    [Wien]Aus der k.k.Hof= und Staatsdruckerei.
[1848]

                    (See next card)

*pGB8
V6755R
5.32.48

[Knees, Joseph]
    Der Kampf zwischen den Wiener Teufeln und
Wiener Heiligen, oder die Vertheidigung der
Wienerstadt den Provinzen gegenüber; sammt
einem Anhange, wie der Nationalgarde=Dienst
erleichtert, wie die Milch=Pantscherei
beseitigt werden könne ...
    [Wien]Zu haben auf der Wieden, Heumühlgasse,in
der sogenannten Heumühle Nr.745,zu ebener Erde,
Thür Nr.8;dann in der Stadt,Brandstatt,in der
Lotto=Collectur;und in der Singerstrasse Nr.874,
                    (See next card)

*pGB8
V6755R
5.32.48

Hochlöblicher Ausschuss der Bürger ... [1848]
                    (Card 2)

    broadside. 45x28.5cm.
    Signed: Die gesammten Drucker und Formstecher
der Fabriken zu Sechshaus, Meidling, Penzing.

*pGB8
V6755R
5.32.48

[Knees, Joseph]   Der Kampf zwischen ...
    [1848]   (Card 2)
bei Ignaz Sterzinger,dem Gasthause zum
Reichsapfel gegenüber.[1848]

    8p. 34.5x24cm.
    Caption title; imprint on p.8.

*pGB8
V6755R
5.32.48

Irsa, Johann.
    In einer Zeit, wo Bosheit und Parteigehässig-
keit unablässig bemüht sind, alles nur
erdenkliche Schlechte und Entehrende dem
österreichischen Adel anzudichten ...
    [Wien]Gedruckt bei den Edlen von Ghelen'schen
Erben.[1848]

    broadside. 42x27.5cm.

*pGB8
V6755R
5.32.48

Langer, Anton, fl.1848.
    Oestreich als Republik, von Anton Langer.
Nationalgarde.
    [Wien]Preis 3 kr.C.M. ... Franz Edl.v.Schmid,
Universitätsbuchdrucker.[1848]

    folder([4]p.) 23x15cm.
    Caption title; imprint on p.[4].

*GB8
V6755R
5.32.48

    ... Keine Republik.
    [Wien]Gedruckt bei J.B.Wallishausser.[1848]

    folder(4p.) 29.5x23.5cm.
    Caption title (at head: Preis: 2 k.r C.M.);
imprint on p.4.

*GB8
V6755R
5.32.48

[Lindermann, J   ]
    Ein gutgemeintes Wort an unsere lieben
Landleute!
    [Wien]Gedruckt bei Franz Edlen von Schmid.
[1848]

    folder([4]p.) 23x14.5cm.
    Caption title; imprint on p.[4]; signed at
end: J. Lindermann.

*GB8
V6755R
5.32.48

*GB8
V6755R
5.32.48

Luise, pseud.
Eine zweite Marie, die Tochter der Universität.
[Wien]Gedruckt bei M.Iell,Leopoldstadt,
Weintraubengasse Nr.505.[1848]

broadside. 24.5x19cm.
Helfert (Wiener Parnass) 958.
Introductory note signed: D. Ph. Weiss.

*pGB8
V6755R
5.32.48

Offenes Schreiben eines Wieners an die
Bischöfe und Prälaten der österreichischen
Monarchie.
[Wien]A.Dorfmeister's Druck und Verlag.[1848]

broadside. 42.5x25.5cm.

*GB8
V6755R
5.32.48

Markl, Franz.
Hoch lebe Tyrol und dessen Einwohner.
[Wien]Gedruckt bei Josef Ludwig.[1848]

broadside. 22x13cm.
Helfert (Wiener Parnass) 947.

*GB8
V6755R
5.32.48

Oppenheimer, M   fl.1848.
An die braven Arbeiter.
[Wien,1848]

broadside. 23x14.5cm.
Helfert (Wiener Parnass) 1156.

*GB8
V6755R
5.32.48

Meineidige Priester, oder: Pfaffen und
Haushälterinnen.
[Wien,1848]

broadside. 30x20.5cm.

*GB8
V6755R
5.32.48

[Ottel, Michael]
Kaiser Ferdinand und sein Ministerium. Ein
historisch= politische Abhandlung über die
eigentlichen Motive der Abreise Sr. Majestät,
der Bewegungen des 15. Mai dieses Jahres, des
abzuhaltenden Reichstages, und der nothwendigen,
baldigen Rückkehr des Monarchen in Seine alte
Residenz.
Gedruckt im Mai 1848 von Ulrich Klopf sen.und
Alex.Eurich in Wien.

Tp. 26.5x21cm.
Signed on p.7:   Michael Ottel.

*GB8
V6755R
5.32.48

Müller, Adolf, 1801-1886.
Philister-Revolution. Gedicht von Adolf
Buchheim, in Musik gesetzt für eine Singstimme
mit Pianofortebegleitung von Adolf Müller ...
Wien,1848.K.k.Hofbuchdruckerei des L.Sommer,
(vormals Strauss.)

folder([3]p.) 22.5x14.5cm.
Helfert (Wiener Parnass) 989.

*GB8
V6755R
5.32.48

Politisches Gespräch eines Wiener Fiakers
mit einem alten Aristokraten über den Minister
des Innern Baron Pillersdorf und über die
Barricaden.
[Wien]Gedruckt bei Jos.Ludwig,Josefst.
Florianigasse Nr.52.[1848]

folder([4]p.) 28x22.5cm.
Signed at end: P. L.

*GB8
V6755R
5.32.48

Naar, Wilhelm.
So lob ich mir's, Commerce-Lied gewidmet den
freien Musensöhnen von Ihrem Mitkämpfer für
Freiheit und Recht!
[Wien]Gedruckt bei M.Iell,Leopoldstadt Nr.505.
[1848]

broadside. 23x27.5cm.
Helfert (Wiener Parnass) 952.

*pGB8
V6755R
5.32.48

Professor Hye oder: Auch Einer von denen!
oder: Keiner entgeht seinem Schicksal!
[Wien]Gedruckt bei M.Iell.[1848]
broadside. 38x24cm.
Signed: Einer seiner ehmaligen Schüler.

*GB8
V6755R
5.32.48

Purpurrosen.
[Wien]Druck von U.Klopf sen.und A.Eurich,
Wollzeile 782.[1848]

folder([4]p.) 20x13cm.
Helfert (Wiener Parnass) 976-977.
Two poems, "Oestreichs neues Wappen" &
"Kaisertreue", signed at end: S.

---

*GB8
V6755R
5.32.48

[Scheibe, Theodor, 1820-1881]
... Das neue Kapitel von dem schein=heiligen
Papste, oder der Carbonari am päpstlichen Stuhl.
Von dem Verfasser des in 10,000 Exemplaren
vergriffenen Flugblattes: "Wider Seine
Scheinheiligkeit Papst Pius IX."
Wien.1848.Gedruckt in der Josephstadt,
Langegasse Nr.58.
folder([4]p.) 25.5x21cm.
At head of title: (Der Mann des Volkes.)
"Der Mann des Volkes" was a short-lived
periodical edited by Scheibe; this would
appear to be a reprint from it.

---

*GB8
V6755R
5.32.48

Radetzky's Truppenvereinigung und das
Garnisons=Spital.
[Wien,1848]

folder([4]p.) 25.5x20cm.
Title within border of type-ornaments; imprint
on p.[4]: Gedruckt und zu haben bei Leopold
Grund, am Stephansplatze im Zwettelhofe.

---

*GB8
V6755R
5.32.48

[Scheibe, Theodor, 1820-1881]
... Wider die Nonnen=Klöster und nothwendige
Aufhebung dieser Schaudergefängnisse im
konstitutionellen Oesterreich.
Wien.1848.Gedruckt in der Josephstadt,
Langegasse Nr.58.
folder([4]p.) 26.5x21cm.
Signed at end: Theod. Scheibe.
At head of title: (Der Mann des Volkes.)
"Der Mann des Volkes" was a short-lived
periodical edited by Scheibe; this may be a
reprint from it.

---

*GB8
V6755R
5.32.48

Rosental, Klemens.
Der traurige Jude. Von Klemens Rosental.
[Wien]Gedruckt bei Leop.Grund,am Hundsthurm
Nr.1.—— Verlag: Stadt,Zwettelhof.[1848]

[2]p. 24.5x19.5cm.
Helfert (Wiener Parnass) 933.

---

*GB8
V6755R
5.32.48

Schickh, Joseph.
Marschlied für die Wiener Freiwilligen. Von
Joseph Schickh.
[Wien]A.Dorfmeister's Buchdruckerei.[1848]

broadside. 30x23cm.
Helfert (Wiener Parnass) 938.

---

*GB8
V6755R
5.32.48

Sachse, Anton.
An den Wohlthäter Herrn L. Schmid, Professor
an der Universität. Verfasst und gewidmet von
Anton Sachse, Arbeiter im Prater.
[Wien,1848]
[2]p. 19x12cm.
Caption title.
Not in Helfert (Wiener Parnass).

---

*pGB8
V6755R
5.32.48

Stremer, Leopold.
Ein Bauer an die unermüdeten Nationellen und
Studenten.
[Wien,1848]

broadside. 40x50cm.
Signed: Ein Bauer unter der Herrschaft
Jedlersdorf: Leopold Stremer.

---

*pGB8
V6755R
5.32.48

Scheibe, Theodor, 1820-1881.
Die Hofkamarilla. Wir wollen vergeben—
vergessen können wir nicht. Ernste Worte
zur Wiederkehr des Kaisers.
[Wien]Gedruckt bei Joh.N.Fridrich,Josephstadt,
Langegasse Nr.58.[1848]

broadside. 48x37.5cm.

---

*GB8
V6755R
5.32.48

Thom, J C
Was hört man denn jetzt Neues in Wien? Ein
Gelegenheitsgedicht mit Anmerkungen über die
Ereignisse und Begebenheiten in den Monaten
März und April 1848. Von J. C. Thom.
Wien 1848.Zu haben bei F.Klinkopf,National-
gardist,Maschinenaufseher in der Pichler'schen
Buchdruckerei,wohnhaft auf der neuen Wieden,
lange Gasse Nr.737,am Eck der Wehrgasse.
folder([4]p.) 30x23.5cm.
Helfert (Wiener Parnass) 927.
Printer's imprint on p.[4]: Druck von
A. Pichler's Witwe.

*pGB8
V6755R
5.32.48

[Tuvora, Joseph, 1811-1871]
Erklärung. Der Freiheit wiedergegeben, halten
wir es für unsere heiligste Pflicht uns dem
Publikum gegenüber offen und ehrlich
auszusprechen. Man hat schwere Beschuldigungen
auf unser Haupt gehäuft, sie sind ohne Grund ...
[Wien,1848]
[2]p. 46x29cm.
Caption title; signed at end: J. Tuvora, L.
Häfner.
Attempting to justify their attempt to incite
an overthrow of (the ministry on 18 May.

---

*GB8
V6755R
5.32.48

[Ullrich, ———]
Ein Promemoria für die Bischöfe.
Wien,1848.Gedruckt bei U.Klopf sen.und A.
Eurich,Wollzeile Nr.782.
folder([4]p.) 25.5x21cm.
Signed at end: Ullrich, Garde.

---

*pGB8
V6755R
5.32.48

Verein der Liberalen und Volksfreunde, Vienna.
Statuten des Vereins der Liberalen und
Volksfreunde.
[Wien]Gedruckt bei J.B.Wallishausser.[1848]
broadside. 33.5x25cm.

---

*pGB8
V6755R
5.32.48

Vienna. Gemeinderat.
Kundmachung. Der Gemeindeausschuss der Haupt=
und Residenzstadt Wien hat die Errichtung eines
Reichstags=Wahl=Comités für diese Hauptstadt
beschlossen ...
[Wien]Aus der k.k.Hof= und Staats=Druckerei.
[1848]
broadside. 44.5x57cm.
Signed: Vom Wahl-Comité des Gemeindeausschusses
der Haupt- und Residenzstadt Wien.

---

*pGB8
V6755R
5.32.48

Vienna. Nationalgarde.
An die Wiener Garnison und das gesammte k. k.
Heer! Soldaten! Brüder! die herzlichen
Sympathien, welche die gesammte Nationalgarde
Wiens für Euch empfindet, hat sie Euch schon zu
wiederholten Malen an den Tag gelegt ...
[Wien,1848]
broadside. 44.5x56.5cm.
Signed: Vom Verwaltungsrathe der gesammten
Nationalgarde Wiens.
Large folio broadside, without imprint.

---

*pGB8
V6755R
5.32.48

Vienna. Nationalgarde.
An die Wiener Garnison und das gesammte k. k.
Heer! Soldaten! Brüder! die herzlichen
Sympathien, welche die gesammte Nationalgarde
Wiens für Euch empfindet, hat sie Euch schon zu
wiederholten Malen an den Tag gelegt ...
[Wien]Aus der k.k.Hof= und Staats=Druckerei.
[1848]
broadside. 44.5x28.5cm.
Signed: Vom Verwaltungsrathe der gesammten
Nationalgarde Wiens.
Small folio (broadside, with imprint.

---

*pGB8
V6755R
5.32.48

Vienna. Nationalgarde.
Dank-Adresse der 13. Compagnie der Nationalgarde vom Bezirke Wieden, an die academische
Legion.
[Wien]Gedruckt und zu haben bei U.Klopf sen.
und A.Eurich.[1848]
broadside. 42.5x26.5cm.

---

*pGB8
V6755R
5.32.48

Vienna. Nationalgarde.
Verzeichniss der Compagnie=Vertreter der
sämmtlichen Nationalgarde.
[Wien,1848]
folder([3]p.) 44.5x28.5cm.
Caption title.

---

*pGB8
V6755R
5.32.48

Vienna. Sicherheits-Ausschuss.
An die Arbeiter. Einige Böswillige unter Euch
wagen es, durch unverschämte Forderungen und
Drohungen die Ruhe der Stadt zu stören ...
[Wien]Aus der k.k.Hof= und Staats=Druckerei.
[1848]
broadside. 44.5x57cm.
Signed: Vom Ausschusse der Bürger, National-
garde und Studenten, zur Aufrechthaltung der
Sicherheit und Ordnung und zur Wahrung der
Rechte des Volkes.

---

*pGB8
V6755R
6.1.48

Austria. Ministerium des Innern.
Kundmachung. Zur Ausführung der in der
Proclamation Sr. Majestät ddo. 16. Mai 1848
enthaltenen Bestimmung, dass die Verfassungs=
Urkunde vom 25. April 1848 vorläufig der
Berathung des Reichstages unterzogen ...
[Wien]Aus der k.k.Hof= und Staats=Druckerei.
[1848]
5p. 45x28.5cm.
Caption title; imprint on p.5.
Dated at end: Wien am 1. Juni 1848.
Procedures for (the election of repre-
sentatives to the (constitutional assembly.

Austria, Lower. Regierungs-Präsident.
Kundmachung. Die Nothwendigkeit schon dermal
einen Theil des deutschen Bundes-Contingentes
aufzustellen und der gegenwärtige Krieg in
Italien machen die möglichst schnelle Vermehrung
der k. k. Linien-Infanterie dringend nothwendig
...
[Wien]Aus der k.k.Hof= und Staats=Druckerei.
[1848]

*pGB8
V6755R
6.1.48

broadside. 45x57cm.
Dated & signed: Wien am 1. Juni 1848. Von der
k. k. Nieder-Oest.   Landesregierung. Anton
Raimund Graf v. (   ) Lamberg, k. k. Hofrath.

Vienna. Sicherheits-Ausschuss.
Kundmachung. Nach einer Mittheilung des
hiesigen k. k. Nieder=Oester. General=Commando
marschirt Morgen den 2. Juni dieses Jahres, ein
Bataillon des k. k. Infanterie=Regimentes
Nugent von hier nach Illyrien ab ...
[Wien]Aus der k.k.Hof= und Staats=Druckerei.
[1848]

*pGB8
V6755R
6.1.48

broadside. 44.5x28.5cm.
Dated & signed: Wien am 1. Juni 1848. Der
Ausschuss der Bürger, Nationalgarde und Studenten
zur Aufrechthaltung der Ruhe, Sicherheit und
Wahrung der (   ) Rechte des Volkes.

Die Böhmen haben sich angeschmiert! oder der
famose Nasenstüber aus Tirol.
[Wien]Gedruckt und zu haben bei U.Klopf sen.
und A.Eurich,Wollzeile 782.[1848]

*pGB8
V6755R
6.1.48

[2]p. 39.5x25cm.
Caption title; imprint on p.[2]; dated &
signed at end: Wien, den 1. Juni 1848. E. K.

Wagner, Johann, 1820-1876.
Ein ruhiges Wort in einer bewegten Zeit.
[Wien]Gedruckt und zu haben bei U.Klopf sen.
und A.Eurich.[1848]

*pGB8
V6755R
6.1.48

broadside. 53x42cm.
Dated: Wien, den 1. Juni 1848.

Eitelberger von Edelberg, Rudolf von, 1817-1885.
An die Herren Mitglieder des Gemeindeaus-
schusses von Wien.
[Wien,1848]

*pGB8
V6755R
6.1.48

broadside. 42x26cm.
Dated & signed: Wien den 1. Juni 1848. R.
Eitelberger v. Edelberg, Dozent der
Kunstgeschichte an der Wiener=Hochschule.

[Wagner, Richard, 1813-1883 (3)]
... Gruss aus Sachsen an die Wiener.
[Wien]Gedruckt bei L.Sommer(vormals Strauss).
[1848]

*GB8
V6755R
6.1.48

folder(4p.) 21x13cm.
Helfert (Wiener Parnass) 1202.
Caption title; imprint on p.4; dated & signed
at end: Dresden, 1. Juni 1848. Richard Wagner.
At head of caption title: Beilage zur
allgemeinen österreichischen Zeitung.

Der muthvolle Studenten=Feldpater, Freiheits=
Vertheidiger, Vaterlandsvertretter und Held
des Tages! Ein Lamartin Oesterreichs, der
bravste aller Geistlichen.
[Wien]Gedruckt bei J.N.Fridrich.[1848]

*pGB8
V6755R
6.1.48

broadside. 41.5x52cm.
In praise of Anton Füster.
Dated in contemporary ms.: 1. Juni 848.

Abschied an die hochherzigen Brünner-National-
garden.
[Wien]Gedruckt bei M.Lell.[1848]

*pGB8
V6755R
6.2.48

broadside. 38x22cm.

Vienna. Nationalgarde.
An sämmtliche Nationalgarden von Wien. Die
im Ober=Commando heute eingetretene Veränderung
löset das dienstliche Verhältniss ...
[Wien]Aus der k.k.Hof= und Staats=Druckerei.
[1848]

*pGB8
V6755R
6.1.48

broadside. 44.5x57cm.
Dated & signed: Wien am 1. Juni 1848.
Sardagna, General=Major.

Die Arbeiter gegenüber den Aristokraten, oder
wo ist edler Sinn und wo Verrätherei?
[Wien]Gedrukt und zu haben bei U.Klopf sen.und
Alex.Eurich.[1848]

*pGB8
V6755R
6.2.48

[2]p. 39.5x25cm.
Caption title; imprint on p.[2]; dated &
signed at end: Wien, 2. Juni 1848. L. H.

*pGB8
V6755R
6.2.48

Austria. Sovereigns, etc., 1835-1848
(Ferdinand I)
Wir Ferdinand der Erste, von Gottes Gnaden
Kaiser von Oesterreich ... In Erwägung der
dringenden Umstände, durch welche Unser
Ministerrath zu den einstweiligen, in den
Circularien Unserer Nieder=Oesterreichischen
Landes=Regierung vom 22. Mai 1848 enthaltenen
Verfügungen über die Verwechslung der Noten der
Österreichischen Nationalbank und deren
Verwendung als Zahlungsmittel bestimmt wurde ...
[Wien]Aus der k.k.Hof= und Staats=Druckerei.
[1848]

(See next card)

---

*pGB8
V6755R
6.2.48

Austria. Sovereigns, etc., 1835-1848
(Ferdinand I)   Wir Ferdinand der Erste
... [1848]   (Card 2)

[2]p. 44.5x28.5cm.
"Gegeben in Unserer kaiserlichen königlichen
Haupt= und Residenzstadt Wien am zweiten Juni
im eintausend achthundert acht und vierzigsten
..."

---

*pGB8
V6755R
6.2.48

Austria, Lower. Laws, statutes, etc., 1835-1848
(Ferdinand I)
... Circulare der k. k. Landesregierung im
Erzherzogthume Oesterreich unter der Enns. Wegen
der Abfuhr der bei den Depositen=Aemtern der
landesfürstlichen und der Patrimonial=Gerichte
erliegenden dort in künftighin in Aufbewahrung
kommenden baren Summen an die Depositen=Casse
des Staats=Tilgungs=Fondes.
[Wien]Aus der k.k.Hof= und Staatsdruckerei.
[1848]

(See next card)

---

*pGB8
V6755R
6.2.48

Austria, Lower. Laws, statutes, etc., 1835-1848
(Ferdinand I)   ... Circulare ... [1848]
(Card 2)

[2]p. 38x23cm.
Caption title; imprint on p.[2]; dated at
end: Wien am 2. Juni 1848.
At head of caption title: N° 27329.

---

*pGB8
V6755R
6.2.48

Brünn. Nationalgarde.
An die tapfern Vorkämpfer und Vertheidiger der
Freiheit.
[Wien]Gedruckt,bei Joseph Stöckholzer v.
Hirschfeld.[1848]

broadside. 46x28.5cm.

---

*pGB8
V6755R
6.2.48

Miller, Josef, fl.1848.
Dank=Adresse an die Herren Studenten und
Bürger Wiens. Dargebracht von den Arbeitern bei
St. Marx.
[Wien]Gedruckt und zu haben bei U.Klopf sen.
und A.Eurich.[1848]

broadside. 39.5x24.5cm.
Dated & signed: Wien am 2. Juni 1848. Josef
Miller, Ingenieur. Im Namen vieler hundert
Arbeiter.

---

*pGB8
V6755R
6.2.48

Vienna. Nationalgarde.
An den Herrn General=Major Baron Sardagna.
[Wien]Aus der k.k.Hof= und Staats=Druckerei.
[1848]

broadside. 44.5x54cm.
Dated & signed: Wien am 2. Juni 1848. Die
Nationalgarde.
This issue is printed on Whatman paper, the
text within a rule border.

---

*pGB8
V6755R
6.2.48

Vienna. Nationalgarde.
An den Herrn General=Major Baron Sardagna.
[Wien]Aus der k.k.Hof= und Staats=Druckerei.
[1848]

broadside. 45x57cm.
Dated & signed: Wien am 2. Juni 1848. Die
Nationalgarde.
This issue is printed on plain wove paper &
does not have a rule border around the text.

---

*pGB8
V6755R
6.2.48

Vienna. Sicherheits-Ausschuss.
An die Bevölkerung Wiens! Der Ausschuss der
Bürger, Nationalgarden und Studenten beeilt
sich, dem Publikum mitzutheilen, dass er in der
gestrigen Sitzung in Bezug auf Professor Hye und
seine Mitangeklagten folgende Beschlüsse
gefasst habe ...
[Wien]Aus der k.k.Hof= und Staats=Druckerei.
[1848]

broadside. 44.5x57cm.
Beschauer-Smets II.299.   (See next card)

---

*pGB8
V6755R
6.2.48

Vienna. Sicherheits-Ausschuss.   An die
Bevölkerung Wiens ... [1848]
(Card 2)

Dated & signed: Wien am 2. Juni 1848. Vom
Ausschusse der Bürger, Nationalgarden und
Studenten für Aufrechthaltung der Ruhe,
Sicherheit und Wahrung der Rechte des Volkes.

*pGB8
V6755R
6.2.48

Vienna. Sicherheits-Ausschuss.
Kundmachung. Vom Samstage den 3. Juni d. J. an,
werden die Anweisungen zu den öffentlichen
Arbeiten an die sich meldenden Arbeiter ...
[Wien]Aus der k.k.Hof= und Staats-Druckerei.
[1848]

broadside. 44.5x57cm.
Dated & signed: Wien am 2. Juni 1848. Vom
Ausschusse der Bürger, Nationalgarden und
Studenten für Aufrechthaltung der Ruhe, Sicherheit
und Wahrung der Rechte des Volkes.

*pGB8
V6755R
6.3.48

Pannasch, Anton, 1789-1855.
An die Nationalgarde. Meine Gesinnungen--meine
Ansichten; ausgesprochen als provisorischer
Chef der Nationalgarde.
[Wien]Aus der k.k.Hof= und Staats=Druckerei.
[1848]

broadside. 44.5x57.5cm.
Dated & signed: Wien am 3. Juni 1848.
Pannasch, Ober=Commandant der Nationalgarde.

*pGB8
V6755R
6.2.48

Vienna. Sicherheits-Ausschuss.
Liebe Mitbürger! Es ist wohl natürlich, dass
derjenige, der nichts empfängt, auch nichts
geben kann ...
[Wien]Aus der k.k.Hof= und Staats=Druckerei.
[1848]

broadside. 44.5x28.5cm.
Dated & signed: Wien den 2. Juni 1848. Vom
Ausschusse für Ruhe, Ordnung, Sicherheit und
Wahrung der Rechte des Volkes.
Calling for the enforcement of the consumer's
tax.

*pGB8
V6755R
6.3.48

Petri, Hugo Jacques.
Steckbrief, nachgesandt dem Grafen von
Bombello.
[Wien]Gedruckt und zu haben bei U.Klopf sen.
und Alex.Eurich,Wollzeile Nr.782.[1848]

broadside. 39.5x25cm.
Dated: Wien, 3. Juni 1848.
A satire.

*GB8
V6755R
6.3.48

An die braven Arbeiter. Am dritten Juni 1848.
[Wien]Gedruckt bei Josef Ludwig.[1848]
folder([4]p.) 30x23.5cm.
Signed at end: Ein wahrer Freund des Volkes,
der Arbeiter.

*pGB8
V6755R
6.3.48

[Resch, Christian]
Anzeige für Jeden, welchem daran gelegen ist,
sein und anderer Menschen Wohl zu begründen.
[Wien,1848]

[2]p. 40x25.5cm.
Caption title; dated & signed at end: Wien am
3. Juni 1848. Christian Resch, pens.
herrschaftlicher Beamter.
Ms. note at head: 450 Stk. 14 Juni 1848.

*pGB8
V6755R
6.3.48

Austria. Sovereigns,etc., 1835-1848
(Ferdinand I)
An die getreuen Einwohner Meiner Residenz.
[Wien]Aus der k.k.Hof= und Staats=Druckerei.
[1848]

broadside. 44.5x57cm.
Reschauer-Smets II.334.
Dated: Innsbruck den 3. Juni 1848.
Calling for peace and order in Vienna for the
opening of the Reichstag.

*GB8
V6755R
6.3.48

Rotter, Richard.
Worte des Abschieds an die Deputation der
Brünner Nationalgarde.
[Wien]Gedruckt bei Ant.Benko.[1848]

broadside. 22x13.5cm.
Helfert (Wiener Parnass) 1207.
Dated: Wien. Geschrieben am 3. Juni 1848 um
3 Uhr Morgens ...

*GB8
V6755R
6.3.48

Eckardt, Ludwig, 1827-1871.
Studentenlied vom deutschen Stürmer. Von L.
Eckard ...
[Wien]Gedruckt und zu haben bei U.Klopf sen.
und Alexander Eurich.[1848]

broadside. 25x19.5cm.
Helfert (Wiener Parnass) 1211.

*pGB8
V6755R
6.3.48

Vienna. Gemeinderat.
Adresse des Gemeinde=Ausschusses der Stadt
Wien an Seine Majestät den Kaiser.
[Wien,1848]

folder([3]p.) 44.5x28.5cm.
Caption title; dated at end: Wien, am 3. Juni
1848.
Asking the Emperor's return to Vienna.

1848 Austrian Revolutionary Broadsides and Pamphlets

Vienna. Nationalgarde.
Tagsbefehl am 3. Juni 1848.
[Wien]Aus der k.k.Staats=Druckerei.[1848]

*pGB8
V6755R
6.3.48

broadside. 45x29cm.
Signed: Vom Nationalgarde-Obercommando.
Pannasch, Obercommandant der Nationalgarde.

Verein der Deutschen aus Böhmen, Mähren und
Schlesien. Freunde.... [1848]
(Card 2)

*GB8
V6755R
6.4.48

folder([3]p.) 26x20.5cm.
Caption title; imprint on p.[3]; dated &
signed at end: Wien am 4. Juni 1848. Der Verein
der Deutschen aus Böhmen, Mähren und Schlesien,
zur Aufrechthaltung ihrer Nationalität.

Vienna. Sicherheits-Ausschuss.
An die Arbeiter. Liebe Brüder! Ihr habt uns
in den letzten Tagen herrliche Beweise Euerer
Ehrenhaftigkeit und Biederkeit gegeben ...
[Wien]Aus der k.k.Hof= und Staats=Druckerei.
[1848]

*pGB8
V6755R
6.3.48

broadside. 44.5x57cm.
Dated & signed: Wien am 3. Juni 1848. Vom
Ausschusse der Bürger, Nationalgarde und der
akademischen Legion zur Aufrechthaltung der
Ordnung, Sicherheit und Wahrung der Rechte des
Volkes.

Vienna. Sicherheits-Ausschuss.
An die Bevölkerung Wiens! Wiederholte
Anzeigen von sehr bedauerlichen Unglücksfällen
...
[Wien]Aus der k.k.Hof= und Staats=Druckerei.
[1848]

*pGB8
V6755R
6.4.48

broadside. 45x57cm.
Dated & signed: Wien am 4. Juni 1848. Vom
Ausschusse der Bürger, Nationalgarden und
Studenten für Aufrechthaltung der Ruhe, Sicher-
heit und Wahrung der Rechte des Volkes.

Vienna. Sicherheits-Ausschuss.
Kundmachung. Vaterlandsfreunde, welche
Vorschläge für öffentliche Arbeiten und zur
Verbesserung der Arbeiterszustände zu machen in
der Lage sind ...
[Wien]Aus der k.k.Hof= und Staats=Druckerei.
[1848]

*pGB8
V6755R
6.3.48

broadside. 45x28.5cm.
Dated & signed: Wien am 3. Juni 1848. Vom
Ausschusse der Bürger, Nationalgarden und
akademischen Legion.

Vienna. Sicherheits-Ausschuss.
Aufruf an das Landvolk! Die grossen
Ereignisse Wiens seit den Märztagen sind Euch
wohl durch Zeitungen, Flugschriften und
Erzählungen bekannt geworden ...
[Wien]Aus der k.k.Hof= und Staatsdruckerei.
[1848]

*pGB8
V6755R
6.4.48

[2]p. 44.5x29cm.
Caption title; imprint on p.[2]; dated &
signed at end: Wien am 4. Juni 1848. Der
Ausschuss der Bürger, Nationalgarden und
(See next card)

Vienna. Sicherheits-Ausschuss.
Verschiedene Fabrikanten, Professionisten und
Landleute haben sich beschwert, dass die Arbeiter
die Dienste ihrer Arbeitgeber verlassen ...
[Wien]Aus der k.k.Hof= und Staats Druckerei.
[1848]

*pGB8
V6755R
6.3.48

broadside. 44.5x57cm.
Dated & signed: Wien am 3. Juni 1848. Vom
Ausschusse der Bürger, Nationalgarde und
Studenten zur Aufrechthaltung der Ruhe,
Sicherheit und Wahrung der Rechte des Volkes.

Vienna. Sicherheits-Ausschuss. Aufruf ...
[1848]
(Card 2)

*pGB8
V6755R
6.4.48

Studenten zur Aufrechthaltung der Ordnung
und Sicherheit und für Wahrung der
Volksrechte.

Verein der Deutschen aus Böhmen, Mähren und
Schlesien.
Freunde und Landsleute! Durch zwei
überraschende Thatsachen haben wir in
letzterer Zeit das unglückselige, für uns
Deutsche hochgefährliche Streben der czechischen
Partei in Prag näher kennen und beurtheilen
gelernt: eine provisorische Regierung wurde
ernannt, und ein Slavencongress wurde eröffnet
...
[Wien]Gedruckt bei U.Klopf sen.und A.Eurich.
[1848]

*GB8
V6755R
6.4.48

(See next card)

Vienna. Sicherheits-Ausschuss.
Aufruf an die wackeren Städtebewohner der
Provinzen.
[Wien]Aus der k.k.Hof= und Staats=Druckerei.
[1848]

*pGB8
V6755R
6.4.48

[2]p. 44.5x29cm.
Dated & signed: Wien am 4. Juni 1848. Von dem
Ausschusse der Wiener Bürger, Nationalgarde und
akademischen Legion zur Aufrechthaltung der Ruhe
und Ordnung und Wahrung der Volksrechte.

124

*pGB8
V6755R
6.4.48

Vienna. Sicherheits-Ausschuss.
Prowolání na wenkowský lid.
[Wien]Aus der k.k.Hof= und Staats=Druckerei.
[1848]

[2]p. 44.5x28.5cm.
Caption title; imprint on p.[2]; dated &
signed at end: We Wídni 4. června 1848. Wýbor
městanů, národní stráže a študentů k zachowání
pořádku jistoty a národních práw.
Czech version of its Aufruf an das Landvolk.

---

*pGB8
V6755R
6.4.48

Wiener-Zeitung.
Extra Blatt zur Wiener=Zeitung vom 4. Juni
1848.
[Wien,1848]

broadside. 37.5x29cm.
Radetzky's war report from Mantua, 30 May
1848.

---

*pGB8
V6755R
6.5.48

Becher, Alfred Julius, 1803-1848.
Offener Brief des "Radikalen" an den Ausschuss
der Bürger, Nationalgarde und akademischen
Legion für Ordnung, Sicherheit und Wahrung der
Rechte des Volkes.
Gedruckt und zu haben bei U.Klopf sen.und A.
Eurich in Wien im Juni 1848.

broadside. 46x58cm.
Dated & signed: Wien am 5. Juni 1848. Der
verantwortliche Redakteur: Dr. A. J. Becher.
Becher's journal "Der Radikale" did not begin
publication until 16 June.

---

*pGB8
V6755R
6.5.48

Erklärung und Vorschlag an alle nur allein
durch Geburt, nicht aber durch Herz und Geist
Privilegirten.
[Wien]Druck aus A.Dorfmeister's Officin.[1848]

broadside. 39.5x24.5cm.
Signed: Ein Student im Geiste Vieler.

---

*GB8
V6755R
6.5.48

Kundmachung. Um die längst bestandenen Wünsche
der Bevölkerung Wiens zum Ziele zu führen, hat
sich eine Comitee gebildet, die nöthigen
Schritte bei den betreffenden Behörden zu thun,
um das längst bestandene in der Brigittenau
gefeierte Volksfest im k. k. Prater abzuhalten
...
[Wien,1848]

broadside. 19.5x20cm.
Signed: Alois Boynger. P. Calafati. G.
Fleischman [& 3 Andere].

---

*pGB8
V6755R
6.5.48

Paul, Johann Heinrich.
Rechtfertigung. Ich habe wahrgenommen, dass am
4. Juni wider mich ein unverschämter und
charakterloser Mann Lügenhaftes drucken und
veröffentlichen liess ...
[Wien]Gedruckt bei U.Klopf sen.und A.Eurich,
Wollzeile 782.[1848]

broadside. 42x26cm.
Dated: Währing, den 5. Juni 1848.

---

*pGB8
V6755R
6.5.48

Seitner, C C
Aufruf an die Bürger und Nationalgarden Wiens.
[Wien]Gedruckt und zu haben bei Ulrich Klopf
sen.und Alex.Eurich.[1848]

broadside. 39.5x25cm.
Dated & signed: Wien, 5. Juni 1848. C. C.
Seitner, Nationalgarde des 4. Bezirks 5.
Compagnie.
Proposing subscriptions for a marble memorial
to the role of the students in the March and May
revolutions.

---

*GB8
V6755R
6.5.48

Vienna. Nationalgarde.
Die Studenten und die Nationalgarde Wiens
an ihre Brüder auf dem Lande.
[Wien,1848]

folder([3]p.) 24.5x21.5cm.
Caption title.
Another issue has imprint on p.[3].
Signed at end: Die Nationalgarde und die
Studenten Wiens.

---

*GB8
V6755R
6.5.48

Vienna. Nationalgarde.
Die Studenten und die Nationalgarde Wiens an
ihre Brüder auf dem Lande.
[Wien]Druck von A.Pichler's Witwe.[1848]

folder([3]p.) 26.5x22cm.
Caption title; imprint on p.[3].
Another issue is without imprint.
Signed at end: Die Nationalgarde und die
Studenten Wiens.

---

*pGB8
V6755R
6.5.48

Vienna. Nationalgarde.
Tagsbefehl für die Nationalgarde. Am 5. Juni
1848.
[Wien]Aus der k.k.Hof= und Staats=Druckerei.
[1848]

broadside. 44.5x28.5cm.
In this edition, the text begins: Da sich
fort und fort Fälle ergeben ...

Vienna. Nationalgarde.

*pGB8
V6755R
6.5.48

Tagsbefehl für die Nationalgarde. Am 5. Juni 1848.
[Wien]Aus der k.k.Hof= und Staats=Druckerei. [1848]

broadside. 44.5x28.5cm.
In this edition, the text begins: Da sich in Betreff des Wachdienstes fort und fort Fälle ergeben ...

[Zerboni di Sposetti, Julius, 1805-1884]

*GB8
V6755R
6.5.48

Offene Antwort auf die gegen mich gerichteten Angriffe meiner politischen Gegner. [Wien,1848]

[2]p. 21x13cm.
Caption title; dated & signed at end: Wien, am 5. Juni 1848. Julius Zerboni ...

Vienna. Sicherheits-Ausschuss.

*pGB8
V6755R
6.5.48

An die Bewohner Wiens. Es haben sich beunruhigende Gerüchte über die Abdankung Sr. Majestät des Kaisers verbreitet ...
[Wien]Aus der k.k.Hof= und Staats=Druckerei. [1848]

broadside. 44.5x57cm.
Dated: Wien am 5. Juni 1848.
Denying rumors of the Emperor's abdication.

Austria. Sovereigns, etc., 1835-1848
(Ferdinand I)

*pGB8
V6755R
6.6.48

An Meine getreuen Nieder=Oesterreicher. Der Besuch bei Meinen biederen und treu ergebenen Tirolern, deren Empfang Mir unvergesslich bleiben wird ...
[Wien]Aus der k.k.Hof= und Staats=Druckerei. [1848]

broadside. 45x57cm.
Dated: Innsbruck den 6. Juni 1848.

Vienna. Sicherheits-Ausschuss.

*pGB8
V6755R
6.5.48

Es wird hiemit zur allgemeinen Kenntniss gebracht, dass ein Fuhrwesens=Transport, welcher von Prag über Wien geht ...
[Wien]Aus der k.k.Hof= und Staats=Druckerei. [1848]

broadside. 45x28cm.
Dated: Wien am 5. Juni 1848.

Engel, Arnold, fl.1848.

*pGB8
V6755R
6.6.48

An uns're lieb'n Steyrer Kameraden. Bei der zu Ehren der am 6. Juni l. J. nach Wien gekommenen steyrischen Deputation veranstalteten Festlichkeit im Sperl aus dem Stegreif gedichtet von A. Engel, National=Gardist.
Druck von Bl.Höfel in Wien.[1848]

broadside. 1 illus. 33.5x26cm.
Helfert (Wiener Parnass) 1223.
Printed within ornamental border.

Vienna. Sicherheits-Ausschuss.

*GB8
V6755R
6.5.48

Gemeinfasslicher Unterricht über Alles was in Bezug auf die Constitution und auf die Wahlen für den Reichstag zu wissen nothwendig ist. Veröffentlicht durch den Ausschuss der Wiener Bürger, Nationalgarde und Studenten zur Aufrechthaltung der Sicherheit und Ordnung, und zur Wahrung der Volksrechte ...
Wien,1848.Aus der k.k.Hof= und Staatsdruckerei.
7p. 23x15cm.
In this issue, the words "Gemeinfasslicher Unterricht" on the t.-p. are printed in 2 lines.

Pannasch, Anton, 1789-1855.

*pGB8
V6755R
6.6.48

Einige Erklärungen zu meinem am 2. Juni hinausgegebenen Programm, nebst einem Anschluss über meinen Tagsbefehl vom 5. Juni 1848.
[Wien]Aus der k.k.Hof= und Staatsdruckerei. [1848]

broadside. 44.5x57cm.

Vienna. Sicherheits-Ausschuss.

*GB8
V6755R
6.5.48

Gemeinfasslicher Unterricht über Alles was in Bezug auf die Constitution und auf die Wahlen für den Reichstag zu wissen nothwendig ist. Veröffentlicht durch den Ausschuss der Wiener Bürger, Nationalgarde und Studenten zur Aufrechthaltung der Sicherheit und Ordnung, und zur Wahrung der Volksrechte ...
Wien,1848.Aus der k.k.Hof= und Staatsdruckerei.

7p. 23x15cm.
In this issue, the words "Gemeinfasslicher Unterricht" on the t.-p. are printed in 1 line.

Die steyerische Fahne und die Gratzer Deputation.

*pGB8
V6755R
6.6.48

[Wien]Gedruckt und zu haben bei U.Klopf sen. und A.Eurich.[1848]

broadside. 46x58cm.
Dated & signed: Wien am 6. Juni 1848. Ein Akademiker.

*pGB8
V6755R
6.6.48

Vienna. Sicherheits-Ausschuss.
An die Arbeiter. Freunde! Durch frevelhafte
Auftritte, wie der gestern am 5. d. M. im
Gasthause des Sebastian Köpf, zu Währing Nr. 1
stattgehabte ...
[Wien]Aus der k.k.Hof= und Staats=Druckerei.
[1848]

broadside. 44.5x57cm.
Dated: Wien am 6. Juni 1848.

*pGB8
V6755R
6.6.48

Vienna. Sicherheits-Ausschuss.
Kundmachung. Zur Hintanhaltung jeder
Missdeutung wird zur öffentlichen Kenntniss
gebracht ...
[Wien]Aus der k.k.Hof= und Staats=Druckerei.
[1848]

broadside. 44.5x28.5cm.
Dated: Wien am 6. Juni 1848.
Announcing the departure of troops for Italy.

*pGB8
V6755R
6.6.48

Vienna. Sicherheits-Ausschuss.
Kundmachung an die Arbeiter. Durch unser
bisheriges Wirken ist es möglich geworden,
dass seit Freitag 3500 Euerer arbeitslosen
Brüder und Schwestern wirklich schon bei einer
Arbeit angestellt sind ...
[Wien]Aus der k.k.Hof und Staats=Druckerei.
[1848]

broadside. 44.5x57cm.
Dated: Wien am 6. Juni 1848.

*pGB8
V6755R
6.6.48

Ein Wort an Frau Cibini und Sturmfeder, Hof=
Kammerfrauen.
[Wien]Gedruckt bei M.Lell.[1848]

broadside. 38x24.5cm.
Signed: Ein Wiener.

*pGB8
V6755R
6.6.48

Vienna. Sicherheits-Ausschuss.
Kundmachung. Die Besorgniss erregende
Zunahme der Holzdiebstähle im Prater und in der
Brigittenau ...
[Wien]Aus der k.k.Hof= und Staats=Druckerei.
[1848]

broadside. 45x57cm.
Dated: Wien am 6. Juni 1848.

*pGB8
V6755R
6.7.48

Austria. Sovereigns, etc., 1835-1848
(Ferdinand I)
Wir Ferdinand der Erste, von Gottes Gnaden
Kaiser von Oesterreich ... Ueber den Antrag
Unserer getreuen Stände des Erzherzogthumes
Oesterreich ob der Enns und nach dem Vorschlage
Unseres Ministerrathes haben Wir in der Absicht,
Unsern Unterthanen jede mit dem Schutze des
Eigenthumsrechtes vereinbare Erleichterung zu
gewähren, beschlossen ...
[Wien]Aus der k.k.Hof= und Staats=Druckerei.
[1848]
(See next card)

*pGB8
V6755R
6.6.48

Vienna. Sicherheits-Ausschuss.
Kundmachung. Die nothwendige Errichtung von
Infanterie=Reserve=Bataillons in Böhmen, Mähren
und Inner=Oesterreich ...
[Wien]Aus der k.k.Hof= und Staats=Druckerei.
[1848]

broadside. 44.5x28.5cm.
Dated: Wien am 6. Juni 1848.

*pGB8
V6755R
6.7.48

Austria. Sovereigns, etc., 1835-1848
(Ferdinand I)   Wir Ferdinand der Erste
... [1848]   (Card 2)

folder([2]p.) 44.5x28.5cm.
Caption title; imprint on p.[2].
"Gegeben in Unserer kaiserlichen Haupt= und
Residenzstadt Wien den siebenten Juni im
eintausend achthundert acht und vierzigsten ..."

*pGB8
V6755R
6.6.48

Vienna. Sicherheits-Ausschuss.
Kundmachung. Zur Beruhigung des Publicums wird
hiermit bekannt gemacht ...
[Wien]Aus der k.k.Hof= und Staats=Druckerei.
[1848]

broadside. 45.5x28.5cm.
Dated: Wien am 6. Juni 1848.
Denying rumors of a bombardment of Prague.

*pGB8
V6755R
6.7.48

Vienna. Magistrat.
Kundmachung. Mit hohem Regierungs=Präsidial=
Dekrete vom 1. d. M. Zahl 1626, wurde mitgetheilt,
dass die konstituirende Reichsversammlung am 26.
d. M. hier in Wien eröffnet werde ...
[Wien]Gedruckt bei Leop.Grund,Hundsthurm Nr.1.
[1848]

broadside. 52x68cm.
Signed & dated: Vom Magistrate und Gemeinde=
Ausschusse der Stadt Wien, am 7. Juni 1848.
Voting regulations for the election of
representatives to the Reichstag.

*pGB8
V6755R
6.7.48

Vienna. Sicherheits-Ausschuss.
An die Arbeiter! Da der Ausschuss
benachrichtigt wurde, dass einzelne Arbeiter-
parteien mit Bier, Brod oder Geld betheilt
wurden ...
[Wien]Aus der k.k.Hof= und Staats=Druckerei.
[1848]

broadside. 44.5x28cm.
Dated: Wien am 7. Juni 1848.

---

*pGB8
V6755R
6.8.48

Klaus, Martin, fl.1848.
Die reuigen Kinder! Hoch der Beste der
Fürsten! Tausendfacher Segen über unsern
constitutionellen Kaiser Ferdinand!!
[Wien]Zu haben:bei Jakob Bader,Buchhändler,
Stadt,Strobelgasse Nr.864.[1848]

broadside. 40x24.5cm.
Dated: Wien, den 8. Juni 1848.

---

*pGB8
V6755R
6.7.48

Vienna. Sicherheits-Ausschuss.
An die Arbeiter! Liebe Freunde, Brüder! Es
wird Euch hiemit bekannt gegeben, dass das
Aufsammeln des Klaubholzes im Prater an jedem
Samstage Nachmittag, jedoch nur unter
gehöriger Aufsicht gestattet sei ...
[Wien]Aus der k.k.Hof= und Staatsdruckerei.
[1848]

broadside. 45x28.5cm.
Dated: Wien am 7. Juni 1848.

---

*pGB8
V6755R
6.8.48

Vienna. Magistrat.
Vom Magistrate und Gemeinde-Ausschusse der
Stadt Wien. Wie aus der anliegenden Kundmachung
ersehen werden wolle, sind die Uhrwähler dieser
Residenz eingeladen, zur Ausweisung ihres
Wahlrechtes zu der darin festgesetzten Zeit, und
an dem bestimmten Orte sich einzufinden ...
[Wien,1848]

folder(1l.) 41.5x25.5cm.
Caption title; dated: Wien am 8. Juni 1848.
Refers to a proclamation of the Lower
Austrian govern-   ment also dated 8 June.

---

*pGB8
V6755R
6.8.48

Armbruster, Heinrich.
Arbeiter und Brüder mit Willen Aller! Am
Pfingstmontage den 12. Juni geht ein Bittgang
mit Kreuz und Fahne nach Aspern an der Donau,
zwei Stunden von Wien, zum Throne Maria Hilf, um
dem dreieinigen Gott zu danken für den glücklich
errungenen Sieg der constitutionellen Freiheit
...
[Wien]Gedruckt bei Ulrich Klopf sen.und Alex.
Eurich.[1848]

broadside. 39.5x24.5cm.
Signed: Heinrich   Armbruster ... Johann
Heimbucher ...   Franz Miller ...

---

*pGB8
V6755R
6.8.48

Vienna. Sicherheits-Ausschuss.
Adresse der gesammten Einwohner Wiens an das
souveraine Parlament zu Frankfurt.
[Wien]Aus der k.k.Hof= und Staats=Druckerei.
[1848]

broadside. 44.5x28.5cm.
Dated & signed: Wien am 8. Juni 1848. Im
Namen der ganzen Bevölkerung Wiens: der
Ausschuss der Bürger, Nationalgarden und
Studenten für Ruhe, Ordnung, Sicherheit und
Wahrung der Rechte des Volkes.

---

*pGB8
V6755R
6.8.48

Austria, Lower.
Von dem k. k. n. ö. Landes-Regierungs-
Präsidium! Bei den nun eingeleiteten Wahlen
für den konstituirenden Reichstag ...
[Wien,1848]

folder([3]p.) 39.5x25cm.
Caption title; dated at end: Wien am 8. Juni
1848.
Addressed: An die Herren Vorsteher des
Gemeinde=Ausschusses der Stadt Wien.

---

*pGB8
V6755R
6.8.48

Vienna. Sicherheits-Ausschuss.
Kundmachung. Am 5. Juni d. J. sind drei bei
den Dammbauten in der Brigittenau beschäftigte
Arbeiter durch unvorsichtiges Baden in der
Donau verunglückt ...
[Wien]Aus der k.k.Hof= und Staatsdruckerei.
[1848]

broadside. 44.5x28.5cm.
Dated: Wien am 8. Juni 1848.

---

*GB8
V6755R
6.8.48

Grillparzer, Franz, 1791-1872.
Feldmarschall Radetzky.
(Aus der constitutionellen Donauzeitung Nr.68;
zu haben bei Ignaz Klang in Wien,Dorotheergasse
Nr 1105.)[1848]

broadside. 22x14.5cm.
Helfert (Wiener Parnass) 1234.

---

*pGB8
V6755R
6.8.48

Vienna. Sicherheits-Ausschuss.
Kundmachung an die Arbeiter. Um dem
augenblicklichen Mangel der vielen brotlos
gewordenen Arbeiter abzuhelfen, sind so schnell
als möglich grossartige Bau= und Erdarbeiten
in Angriff genommen ...
[Wien]Aus der k.k.Hof= und Staats=Druckerei.
[1848]

broadside. 44.5x28.5cm.
Dated: Wien am 8. Juni 1848.

*pGB8
V6755R
6.8.48

Vienna. Sicherheits-Ausschuss.
Kundmachung. Aus Anlass einer am Schlusse des gestrigen Verbrüderungs=Festes im Universum stattgehabten wiederholten Abfeuerung von Böllerschüssen ...
[Wien]Aus der k.k.Hof= und Staatsdruckerei.
[1848]

broadside. 44.5x28cm.
Dated: Wien am 8. Juni 1848.

*pGB8
V6755R
6.10.48

Colloredo-Mannsfeld, Ferdinand, graf, 1777-1848.
An die akademische Legion Ihr ehemaliger Anführer.
[Wien]Gedruckt bei Carl Gerold.[1848]

broadside. 44.5x57.5cm.
Signed: Colloredo-Mannsfeld.
Reschauer-Smets II.305.

*pGB8
V6755R
6.9.48

Kaltenbrunner, Carl Adam, 1804-1867.
D' Wedner an d' Grazer. (Oberösterreichisch.)
[Wien,1848]

broadside. 33.5x26cm.
Helfert (Wiener Parnass) 1236.
Dated: Wien, den 9. Juni 1848.

*pGB8
V6755R
6.10.48

Josef Lusk Handelsmann am Braunhirschengrund der thätigste Reaktionär der Menschenquälerei.
[Wien]Gedruckt bei M.Lell.[1848]

broadside. 40x24.5cm.
Signed: Von einem Volksfreunde und unpartheiischen Augenzeugen.

*GB8
V6755R
6.9.48

[Patatschny, Franz]
Des Wiener Waisenhauses schönster Freudentag durch Beschluss des hochherzigen Bürger= Ausschusses, am 9. Juni 1848.
[Wien]Gedruckt bei U.Klopf sen.und Alexander Eurich.[1848]

folder(3p.) 24.5x19.5cm.
Caption title; imprint on p.3; signed at end:
Franz Patatschny, k. k. Staatsbeamter und National=Garde.

*pGB8
V6755R
6.10.48

[Knotzer, Johann Nepomuk]
Die Aufhebung der Klöster, oder die dicken und die dünnen Pfaffen. Nebst einer gründlichen Darstellung von der Entstehung und Fortpflanzung der Klöster ... I. Auflage.
[Wien]Buchdruckerei des L.Sommer (vormals Strauss).[1848]Nur zu haben beim Verfasser.

[2]p. 42x26cm.
Caption title; imprint on p.[2]; signed at end: Joh. Nep. Knotzer.
Includes a partial reprint of Anastasius Grün's poem "Die Dicken und die Dünnen"; Helfert (Wiener Parnass) 1552.

*pGB8
V6755R
6.9.48

Vienna. Sicherheits-Ausschuss.
Kundmachung. Ueber die an den Ausschuss gelangte Anzeige, als sei gestern am 8. Juni ein Mann in den, dem polytechnischen Institute gegenüber gelegenen Canal gekrochen ...
[Wien]Aus der k.k.Hof= und Staatsdruckerei.
[1848]

broadside. 44.5x28.5cm.
Dated: Wien am 9. Juni 1848.

*GB8
V6755R
6.10.48

Radetzky's jetzige Stellung in Italien.
[Wien,1848]
folder([4]p.) 23x18.5cm.
Imprint on p.[4]: Gedruckt und zu haben bei Leop. Grund, am Stephansplatze im Zwettelhofe.

*pGB8
V6755R
6.10.48

Austria. Post-Kurs-Bureau.
... Circulare an sämmtliche Beamte und Practikanten des k. k. Hofpostamtes.
[Wien]Aus der k.k.Hof= und Staats=Druckerei.
[1848]

folder([2]p.) 39x23cm.
Caption title (at head: H. P. A.); imprint on p.[2]; dated at end: Wien am 10. Juni 1848.
Directed against employees' attempting to excuse absenteeism by pleading National guard duty.

*GB8
V6755R
6.10.48

[Richter, Theodor Franz Johann]
Wohlgemeinte Worte an die P. T. Herren Wähler des Bezirkes Laimgrube, bevor sie zur Deputirten=Wahl für den ersten Reichstag schreiten.
[Wien,1848]
[2]p. 29.5x22.5cm.
Caption title; signed at end: Dr. Th. Franz Joh. Richter, emerit. philosophischer Professor der Geschichte, geistlicher Rath, mehrerer gelehrten Gesellschaften Mitglied, und Wahlmann.

*pGB8
V6755R
6.10.48

Vienna. Gemeinderat.
    Kundmachung. Der Gemeinde-Ausschuss beeilt
sich, die ihm gewordene nachstehende Mittheilung
des Herrn Minister des Innern zur Kenntniss
des Publikums zu bringen ...
    [Wien]Aus der k.k.Staats=Druckerei.[1848]

    broadside. 44.5x57cm.
    Dated: Wien am 10. Juni 1848.
    Relates to the election of representatives
to the Reichstag.

*pGB8
V6755R
6.10.48

Vienna. Magistrat.
    Kundmachung. Nach der am 18. Mai d. J.
erlassenen provisorischen Verordnung über das
Verfahren in Presssachen und mit Rücksicht auf
die Bevölkerung dieser Residenz ...
    [Wien,1848]

    broadside. 39x24.5cm.
    Signed & dated: Vom Magistrate und Gemeinde=
Ausschusse der Stadt Wien am 10. Juni 1848.
    Providing for the election of jurymen.

*pGB8
V6755R
6.10.48

Vienna. Nationalgarde.
    Nur jenen Herren der Nationalgarde, welche
sich als, von Seite ihrer respectiven Compagnie
zur Deputation nach Gratz gewählt, ausgewiesen
haben, erhalten die Fahr=Anweisungen für die
Eisenbahnen ...
    [Wien,1848]

    broadside. 36.5x52cm.
    Dated: Wien, am 10. Juni 1848.
    Contemporary ms. note at head: 100 Stk. 11
Juni 1848.

*pGB8
V6755R
6.10.48

Vienna. Sicherheits-Ausschuss.
    An die Bevölkerung Wiens. Durch Kundmachung
dieses Ausschusses vom 2. d. M. wurde dem
Publikum eröffnet, dass man die Untersuchung
gegen den Herrn Professor Hye und seine
Mitangeklagten der competenten Gerichtsbehörde
mitgetheilt habe ...
    [Wien]Aus der k.k.Hof= und Staats=Druckerei.
[1848]

    broadside. 44.5x56.5cm.
    Dated: Wien am 10. Juni 1848.

*pGB8
V6755R
6.11.48

Vienna. Magistrat.
    Kundmachung. In der behufs der Wahl der
Abgeordneten zur constituirenden Reichs-
versammlung erlassenen Kundmachung vom 7. d.
M. wurde für die Urwähler in den zwei
Wahlbezirken in der Stadt ...
    [Wien,1848]

    broadside. 37x45.5cm.
    Signed & dated: Vom Magistrate und Gemeinde-
Ausschusse der Stadt Wien am 11. Juni 1848.

*pGB8
V6755R
6.11.48

Vienna. Sicherheits-Ausschuss.
    An die Arbeiter! Das Ministerium des Innern
hat mittelst Erlasses vom 10. Juni 1. J. an
den gefertigten Ausschuss erklärt: dass
selbstständige Arbeiter, wenn sie das 24. Jahr
zurückgelegt haben ... als Wähler auftreten
dürfen ...
    [Wien]Aus der k.k.Hof= und Staatsdruckerei.
[1848]

    broadside. 44.5x28.5cm.
    Dated: Wien am 11. Juni 1848.

*pGB8
V6755R
6.12.48

Heidmayer, Carl.
    Hoch lebe Pillersdorf! Auch die Arbeiter
dürfen als Wähler der Abgeordneten zum
konstituirenden Reichstag auftreten. Ein
populäres aber aufrichtiges Wort des Dankes
für die durch den Gemeindeausschuss der Stadt
Wien kundgemachte Mittheilung des Herrn Ministers
des Innern, ddto. 10. Juni d. J.
    [Wien]Gedruckt bei Ulrich Klopf sen.und Alex.
Eurich.[1848]

    broadside. 41x53cm.
    Dated: Wien den   12. Juni 1848.

*pGB8
V6755R
6.12.48

Vienna. Magistrat.
    Ueber die Wahl der Geschwornen.
    [Wien,1848]

    broadside. 36.5x23cm.
    Signed & dated: Vom Magistrate und Gemeinde-
Ausschusse der Stadt Wien am 12. Juni 1848.

*pGB8
V6755R
6.12.48

Vienna. Sicherheits-Ausschuss.
    Kundmachung an die Arbeitsuchenden. Nachdem
schon an 20.000 Arbeiter aus öffentlichen
Fonden beschäftiget sind, und täglich noch mehr
bei den öffentlichen Bauten Verdienst suchen ...
    [Wien]Aus der k.k.Hof= und Staatsdruckerei.
[1848]

    broadside. 44.5x28.5cm.
    Dated: Wien am 12. Juni 1848.

*pGB8
V6755R
6.12.48

Vienna. Sicherheits-Ausschuss.
    Kundmachung. Von mehreren Seiten wird dem
unterzeichneten Ausschusse die Anzeige gemacht,
dass durch das öffentliche Baden in den
Bewässern innerhalb der Linien, wobei Personen
beiderlei Geschlechtes unbekleidet am Ufer
umhergehen ...
    [Wien]Aus der k.k.Hof= und Staats=Druckerei.
[1848]

    broadside. 44.5x28.5cm.
    Dated: Wien am   12. Juni 1848.

*pGB8
V6755R
6.13.48

Austria, Lower. Laws, statutes, etc., 1835-1848
(Ferdinand I)
... Circulare der k. k. Landesregierung im
Erzherzogthume Oesterreich unter der Enns.
Bestrafung derjenigen, welche unbefugt die
Uniform, einen Theil der Uniform, oder ein
Abzeichen der aus der akademischen Legion, den
alt uniformirten Bürger=Corps und der neu
uniformirten Garde bestehenden National=Garde
tragen.
[Wien]Aus der k.k.Hof= und Staatsdruckerei.
[1848]

(See next card)

---

*pGB8
V6755R
6.13.48

Austria, Lower. Laws, statutes, etc., 1835-1848
(Ferdinand I)   ... Circulare ... [1848]
(Card 2)

broadside. 37.5x23cm.
At head: № 29136.
Dated: Wien am 13. Juni 1848.

---

*GB8
V6755R
6.13.48

Blutige Scenen in Prag. Am 12. Juni.
[Wien]Gedruckt bei Josef Ludwig.[1848]

folder([4]p.) 27.5x21.5cm.

---

*GB8
V6755R
6.13.48

Schwarz, Johann, fl.1848.
Was ist ein Beamter? "Ein trauriger Scherz!"
Von Johann Schwarz.
[Wien,1848]

folder([3]p.) 23x15cm.
Helfert (Wiener Parnass) 1253.
Imprint on p.[3]: A. Dorfmeister's Druck und
Verlag.

---

*pGB8
V6755R
6.13.48

Smreker, A
Gruss und Kuss den freien Wiener Brüdern!
[Graz,1848]

broadside. 39x24.5cm.
Dated: Gratz, am 13. Juni 1848.

---

*pGB8
V6755R
6.13.48

Vienna. Gemeinderat.
Kundmachung. Zur Unterstützung arbeitsunfähiger
mittelloser Individuen und solcher Arbeiter,
welche eine zahlreiche Familie zu erhalten haben
...
[Wien]Aus der k.k.Hof= und Staatsdruckerei.
[1848]

broadside. 44.5x28.5cm.
Dated & signed: Wien am 13. Juni 1848. Vom
Sammlungs=Comité des Gemeinde= und Sicherheits=
Ausschusses.
Soliciting contributions for the relief
of the needy.

---

*pGB8
V6755R
6.13.48

Vienna. Sicherheits-Ausschuss.
An die Arbeiter! Es ist vielfach über den
Unfug geklagt worden, dass sich betrügerische
Leute unter Euch begeben, um Euch zum Spiel,
vorzüglich zum sogenannten Mariandelspiel zu
verleiten ...
[Wien]Aus der k.k.Hof= und Staatsdruckerei.
[1848]

broadside. 44.5x28cm.
Dated: Wien am 13. Juni 1848.

---

*pGB8
V6755R
6.13.48

Vienna. Sicherheits-Ausschuss.
Aufforderung. Die von dem Magistrate und
Gemeinde=Ausschusse der Stadt Wien in Bezug auf
die bevorstehenden Wahlen für den constituirenden
Reichstag erlassene Kundmachung ...
[Wien]Aus der k.k.Hof= und Staats=Druckerei.
[1848]

broadside. 44.5x57cm.
Dated: Wien am 13. Juni 1848.
Urging voter registration.

---

*pGB8
V6755R
6.13.48

Vienna. Sicherheits-Ausschuss.
Vor einigen Tagen hat sich eine grössere
Anzahl czechischer Studenten und Swornostmänner
aus Prag ohne irgend einen offen ausgesprochenen
Zweck in Wien eingefunden ...
[Wien]Aus der k.k.Hof= und Staats=Druckerei.
[1848]

broadside. 45x57cm.
Dated: Wien den 13. Juni 1848.

---

*GB8
V6755R
6.14.48

Aufklärung über das unglückliche Ereigniss in
Carlowicz in Syrmien am 12. Juni 1848.
[Wien? 1848]

[2]p. 28.5x22.5cm.
Caption title; dated & signed at end:
Carlowicz den 14. Juni 1848. Die serbische
Nation.

Wiener Zeitung.
Aus der Wiener Zeitung vom 13. Juni 1848.
[Wien,1848]

*GB8
V6755R
6.14.48

[2]p. 27.5x20cm.
Caption title.
A reprint of Pillersdorf's proclamation of 9
June.

Böhmen droht Oesterreich zu verschlingen.
Hört! Hört! Oesterreich's grösste und nächste
Gefahr, und Wiens gedrohter Untergang.
[Wien,1848]

*GB8
V6755R
6.15.48

[2]p. 24x18.5cm.
Caption title.
"Extrablatt zum österreichischen Landboten."
Includes an extract from Nr.32 of the Wiener
Sonntagsblätter, signed: Dr. Schilling.

[Zerboni di Sposetti, Julius, 1805-1884]
Constitutionelle Staatsbürger!
[Wien,1848]

*GB8
V6755R
6.14.48

folder(3p.) 26x21cm.
Caption title; dated & signed on p.3: Wien,
den 14. Juni 1848. Julius Zerboni di Sposetti.
Urging his election as a member of the
constitutional assembly.

Das fürchterliche Blutbad in Prag und die
Bombardirung der Stadt durch Fürst
Windischgrätz. Von einem Augenzeugen.
[Wien]Gedruckt im Juni von U.Klopf sen.und
A.Eurich.[1848]

*pGB8
V6755R
6.15.48

broadside. 47x26.5cm.

Audiatur et altera pars!
[Wien]Gedruckt bei den Edlen von Ghelen'schen
Erben.[1848]

*pGB8
V6755R
6.15.48

[2]p. 43x26.5cm.
Caption title; imprint on p.[2]; dated &
signed at end: Am 15. Juni 1848. Ein Aristokrat
für Hunderte.

Die letzten Revolutionen in Prag, Pesth und
Brünn.
[Wien]Druck und Verlag bei Leopold Grund,am
Stephansplatze im Zwettelhofe.[1848]

*GB8
V6755R
6.15.48

folder([4]p.) 22.5x18.5cm.

Aufruf an die Wähler vom Neubau.
[Wien,1848]

*pGB8
V6755R
6.15.48

broadside. 47x30cm.
Dated: Wien, am 15. Juni 1848.
Urging the election of Carl Möring to the
constitutional assembly.

Neueste ausführliche Prager Revolutions=
Geschichte und der Aufstand der böhmischen
Sensenmänner.
[Wien]Gedruckt und zu haben bei Joh.N.
Fridrich,Josephstadt,Langegasse Nr.58.[1848]

*pGB8
V6755R
6.15.48

broadside. 48.5x38.5cm.
Signed: Der Mann des Volkes.
"Der Mann des Volkes" was a short-lived
Viennese newspaper edited by Theodor Scheibe, who
may here be using the name as a pseudonym.
Dated in contemporary ms.: 15. Juni 848.

Austria, Lower. Landstände.
Der Ausschreibung des Landtages für die
Provinz Nieder=Oesterreich, auf welchem die
Constituirung der Provinzial=Stände verhandelt
werden soll ...
[Wien]Aus der k.k.Hof= und Staatsdruckerei.
[1848]

*pGB8
V6755R
6.15.48

broadside. 44.5x28.5cm.
Dated & signed: Wien am 15. Juni 1848. Franz
Graf von Beroldingen, N. Oest Landmarschalls=
Stellvertreter.

[Niedopitalski, ————]
Der grosse Sieg bei Vicenza.
[Wien,1848]

*GB8
V6755R
6.15.48

folder([4]p.) 23x18.5cm.
Signed at end: Niedopitalski.
Title printed vertically; imprint on p.[4]:
Druck und Verlag von Leopold Grund, am
Stephansplatze im Zwettelhofe.

*GB8
V6755R
6.15.48

[Niedopitalski, ———]
Die Wiedereroberung von Italien.
[Wien,1848]
folder([4]p.) 23x18cm.
Signed at end: Niedopitalski.
Imprint on p.[4]: Gedruckt und zu haben bei
Leopold Grund, am Stephansplatze im Zwettelhofe.

---

*pGB8
V6755R
6.15.48

Scheibe, Theodor, 1820-1881.
Die Rebellen auf dem Schutthaufen in Prag.
Haben sie capitulirt? Heiliger Kreuzzug der
Wiener gegen die slavischen Meuchelmörder.
[Wien]Gedruckt und zu haben bei Joh.N.
Fridrich,Josephstadt,Langegasse Nr.58.[1848]
broadside. 49x38.5cm.

---

*GB8
V6755R
6.15.48

Oesterreichs Zustand. Ein dringendes Wort
an die Wähler zum Reichstag.
[Wien]Gedruckt bei Josef Ludwig.[1848]
folder([4]p.) 27x21.5cm.
Caption title; imprint on p.[4]; signed at end:
Ein Garde der akademischen Legion.

---

*pGB8
V6755R
6.15.48

Vienna. Gemeinderat.
Bekanntmachung. Es wird hiemit zur öffentlichen
Kenntniss gebracht, dass die Anfertigung der
Wähler=Listen zur Reichstags=Versammlung ...
[Wien]Aus der k.k.Hof= und Staatsdruckerei.
[1848]
broadside. 44.5x28cm.
Dated & signed: Wien am 15. Juni 1848. Von dem
Gemeinde-Ausschusse der Stadt Wien.

---

*pGB8
V6755R
6.15.48

Padovani, Matteo, b.1815.
Programm. Der Unterzeichnete tritt im
Vertrauen auf jene Nachsicht seiner Landsleute,
die sie ihm einige Jahre vorher als er sich
nämlich in Odessa in der Eigenschaft eines
General=Agenten und Correspondenten des
österreichischen Lloyd befand, als Hauptredakteur
einer Zeitschrift auf, welche den Namen: La
Guardia nazionale führen wird ...
[Wien]Gedruckt bei U.Klopf sen.und Alex.
Eurich.[1848]
(See next card)

---

*pGB8
V6755R
6.15.48

Vienna. Sicherheits-Ausschuss.
An die Arbeiter bei den öffentlichen Bauten.
Ihr wisst es alle selbst, mit welchen
ungeheueren Opfern wir bemüht sind, Euch eure
Existenz nach Kräften zu sichern ...
[Wien]Aus der k.k.Hof= und Staatsdruckerei.
[1848]
broadside. 44.5x57cm.
Dated: Wien am 15. Juni 1848.

---

*pGB8
V6755R
6.15.48

Padovani, Matteo.   Programm ... [1848]
(Card 2)
[2]p. 39.5x24.5cm.
Caption title; text in Italian on p.[2]
begins: Programma. Il sottoscritto, fidando in
quel compatimento ...
The proposed newspaper did not appear.

---

*pGB8
V6755R
6.15.48

Vienna. Sicherheits-Ausschuss.
Kundmachung. Da in dieser Woche nach dem
Feiertage sogleich ein Regentag folgte ...
[Wien]Aus der k.k.Hof= und Staatsdruckerei.
[1848]
broadside. 44x28.5cm.
Dated: Wien am 15. Juni 1848.

---

*GB8
V6755R
6.15.48

Radetzky liefert ein siegreiches Gefecht vor
Verona. Der Heldenmuth seiner kais. Hoheit des
Erzherzogs Franz Joseph. Treviso hat kapitulirt.
[Wien]Gedruckt und zu haben bei Leopold Grund,
am Stephansplatze.[1848]
folder([4]p.) 24.5x20cm.
Caption title; imprint on p.[4].

---

*pGB8
V6755R
6.15.48

Vienna. Sicherheits-Ausschuss.
Kundmachung. Morgen den 16. Juni kömmt mittelst
Eisenbahn ein Ergänzungs=Transport von 81
Mann des 12. Jäger=Bataillons ...
[Wien]Aus der k.k.Hof= und Staats=Druckerei.
[1848]
broadside. 44.5x57cm.
Dated: Wien am 15. Juni 1848.

*pGB8
V6755R
6.15.48

Wiener Zeitung.
Ausserordentliches Beilage zur Wiener-Zeitung vom 14. Juni 1848. Der F. M. L. Baron Welden hat aus Conegliano vom 12. Juni mittelst Courier so eben dem Kriegsministerium die Copie jener Nachrichten eingesendet ...
[Wien,1848]

broadside. 38x28.5cm.
In this edition, line 1 of the 1st column of text ends: aus Coneg■

(

*pGB8
V6755R
6.16.48

Enthoffer, Josef.
Aufforderung an die Urwähler des X. Wahl-districts von Nr.545 bis 587 zur constituirenden Reichsversammlung.
[Wien]Druck aus A.Dorfmeister's Officin.[1848]

broadside. 39x25cm.
Dated: Wien, am 16. Juni 1848.

(

*pGB8
V6755R
6.15.48

Wiener Zeitung.
Ausserordentliche Beilage zur Wiener Zeitung vom 15. Juni 1848. Der F. M. L. Baron Welden hat aus Conegliano vom 12. Juni mittelst Courier so eben dem Kriegs■Ministerium die Copie jener Nachrichten eingesendet ...
[Wien,1848]

broadside. 37.5x29cm.
In this edition, line 1 of the 1st column of text ends: aus Conegliano

(

*GB8
V6755R
6.16.48

Die Ermordung des böhmischen Herzogs und die Amazonen. Wahre Schilderung der schreklichen Begebenheiten in Prag.
[Wien]Gedruckt bei Josef Ludwig.[1848]

folder([4]p.) 26.5x21.5cm.

(

*pGB8
V6755R
6.15.48

Windischgrätz und das Bombardement in Prag.
[Wien]Gedruckt bei M.Lell.[1848]

broadside. 40x25cm.
Signed: Ein Ungar, der mit Leib und Seele an den deutschen Wienern hängt.

(

*GB8
V6755R
6.16.48

Das grosse Ereigniss in Prag.
[Wien]Gedruckt und zu haben bei Leop.Grund,am Stephansplatze im Zwettelhofe.[1848]

folder([4]p.) 22.5x18cm.
Caption title; imprint on p.[4].

(

*GB8
V6755R
6.16.48

Allgemeine oesterreichische Zeitung.
Ausserordentliches Bulletin zur Allgemeinen oesterreichischen Zeitung vom 16. Juni 1848 Nr. 76.
[Wien]Gedruckt bei Leop.Sommer(vorm.Strauss).[1848]

broadside. 30.5x22cm.
Announcing the resignation of Windisch-Grätz.

(

*pGB8
V6755R
6.16.48

Vienna. Sicherheits-Ausschuss.
An die Arbeiter! Ihr habt Arbeit verlangt, wir haben alle unsere Kräfte aufgeboten, Euch dieselbe zu verschaffen ...
[Wien]Aus der k.k.Hof■ und Staats■Druckerei.[1848]

broadside. 44.5x28.5cm.
Dated: Wien, am 16. Juni 1848.

(

*pGB8
V6755R
6.16.48

Austria. Sovereigns, etc., 1835-1848
(Ferdinand I)
Proclamation. Ich habe in Meinem Manifeste vom 3. Juni d. J. die Absicht ausgedrückt, den in Wien abzuhaltenden Reichstag in eigener Person zu eröffnen ...
[Wien]Aus der k.k.Hof■ und Staats■Druckerei.[1848]

broadside. 44.5x57cm.
Dated: Innsbruck den 16. Juni 1848.
Announcing his inability to undertake the journey from (Innsbruck to Vienna for reasons of health.

*pGB8
V6755R
6.16.48

Wiener Zeitung.
Extra■Blatt zur Wiener-Zeitung vom 16. Juni 1848.
[Wien,1848]

broadside. 37x29cm.
Announcing the resignation of Windisch-Grätz.

(

Austria. Kriegsministerium.
*pGB8   Zuschrift des Kriegsministeriums an den
V6755R   Verwaltungsrath der Nationalgarde zu Wien ddo.
6.17.48 17. Juni 1848, Nr.2598-M.K.
         [Wien]Aus der k.k.Hof= und Staatsdruckerei.
         [1848]

         broadside. 44.5x57cm.
         Signed: Graf Latour F. Z. M.

Austria. Ministerium des Innern.   Kundmachung
*pGB8   ... [1848]   (Card 2)
V6755R
6.17.48   Another issue is dated & signed: Wien den
         17 Juni 1848. Der Minister des Inneren:
         Pillersdorff.
            Announcing the indisposition of the Emperor
         and the appointment of the Archduke Franz Carl
         as his deputy.

Austria. Ministerium des Innern.
*pGB8   Aufruf an die Bewohner der Hauptstadt Prag.
V6755R   [Wien]Aus der k.k.Hof= und Staatsdruckerei.
6.17.48 [1848]

         broadside. 44.5x28.5cm.
         Dated: Wien am 17. Juni 1848.
         Czech and German in parallel columns.

Austria. Ministerium des Innern.
*pGB8   Kundmachung. Der lebhafte Wunsch der
V6755R   Bevölkerung Wiens und die Sorge für den
6.17.48 regelmässigen Gang der Regierungsgeschäfte
         fordert gleichmässig die baldige Rückkehr des
         Kaisers in seine Residenz ...
         [Wien]Aus der k.k.Hof= und Staatsdruckerei.
         [1848]

            broadside. 44.5x57cm.
            Dated & signed: Wien den 17. Juni 1848. Der
                                   (See next card)

Austria. Ministerium des Innern.
*pGB8   Aufruf an die Stadt= und Landbewohner
V6755R   Böhmens.
6.17.48 [Wien]Aus der k.k.Hof= und Staatsdruckerei.
         [1848]

         broadside. 44.5x29cm.
         Dated: Wien am 17. Juni 1848.
         Czech and German in parallel columns.

Austria. Ministerium des Innern.   Kundmachung
*pGB8   ... [1848]   (Card 2)
V6755R   Minister des Inneren: Pillersdorff.
6.17.48   Announcing the indisposition of the Emperor
         and the appointment of the Archduke Franz Carl
         as his deputy.
            Another issue is undated & is signed:
         Pillersdorff.

Austria. Ministerium des Innern.
*pGB8   Heute und Morgen ist der letzte Termin zur
V6755R   Einzeichnung der Urwähler in die Wählerlisten
6.17.48 ...
         [Wien]Aus der k.k.Hof= und Staatsdruckerei.
         [1848]

         broadside. 44.5x57cm.
         Dated: Wien den 17. Juni 1848.

Austria. Ministerium des Innern.
*pGB8   Kundmachung. Die Erwiederung der tele-
V6755R   graphischen Anzeige des Prager Bürgermeisters
6.17.48 konnte gestern nicht mehr auf demselben Wege
         nach Prag gelangen ...
         [Wien]Aus der k.k.Hof= und Staats=Druckerei.
         [1848]

            broadside. 44.5x57cm.
            Dated & signed: Wien am 17. Juni 1848. Der
         Minister des Inneren: Pillersdorff.

Austria. Ministerium des Innern.
*pGB8   Kundmachung. Der lebhafte Wunsch der
V6755R   Bevölkerung Wiens und die Sorge für den
6.17.48 regelmässigen Gang der Regierungsgeschäfte
         fordert gleichmässig die baldige Rückkehr des
         Kaisers in Seine Residenz ...
         [Wien]Aus der k.k.Hof= und Staatsdruckerei.
         [1848]

            broadside. 44.5x57cm.
            Signed: Pillersdorff.

                          (See next card)

Boschan, Alessandro.
*pGB8   Concittadini constitutionali. Nel giorno
V6755R   26 corr. si aprirà la Dicta [!] constituente ...
6.17.48 [Vienna,1848]

            broadside. 40x24cm.
            Dated: Vienna 17. giugno 1848.

1848 AUSTRIAN REVOLUTIONARY BROADSIDES AND PAMPHLETS

*pGB8
V6755R
6.17.48

Vienna. Gemeinderat.
Die Herren Urwähler des achten Wahl=
Districtes, zweiten Wahlbezirkes in der Stadt
von den Häusern Nr.979 bis 1052 werden
eingeladen ...
[Wien]Aus der k.k.Hof= und Staatsdruckerei.
[1848]

broadside. 44.5x57cm.
Dated: Wien den 17. Juni 1848.

*pGB8
V6755R
6.17.48

Vienna. Sicherheits-Ausschuss.
Kundmachung. Es sind mehrere Fälle vorgekommen,
dass Plakate des gefertigten Ausschusses
besudelt, zerfetzt oder von den Anschlagplätzen
herabgerissen wurden ...
[Wien]Aus der k.k.Hof= und Staats-Druckerei.
[1848]

broadside. 44.5x28.5cm.
Dated: Wien am 17. Juni 1848.

*pGB8
V6755R
6.17.48

Vienna. Gemeinderat.
Kundmachung. Zu Folge des hohen Ministerial=
Erlasses vom 17. Juni 1848, Z. 1119-167, wurde
anher bekannt gegeben, dass die Anwendung des
Paragraphes 29 der provisorischen Wahlordnung ...
[Wien]Aus der k.k.Hof= und Staats=Druckerei.
[1848]

broadside. 44.5x29cm.
Dated: Wien am 17. Juni 1848.

*pGB8
V6755R
6.17.48

Vienna. Sicherheits-Ausschuss.
Kundmachung über die Wahlen. Dem
unterzeichneten Ausschusse ist so eben
nachstehender Erlass des hohen Ministeriums des
Inneren zugekommen ...
[Wien]Aus der k.k.Hof= und Staats-Druckerei.
[1848]

broadside. 45x57cm.
Dated: Wien den 17. Juni 1848.

*pGB8
V6755R
6.17.48

Vienna. Magistrat.
Kundmachung. Es wird zur öffentlichen
Kenntniss gebracht, dass die Wahl der Wahlmänner
zur Ernennung der Abgeordneten der Stadt
Wien für die constituirende Reichsversammlung
...
[Wien]Aus der k.k.Hof= und Staats=Druckerei.
[1848]

broadside. 45x28.5cm.
Dated: Wien am 17. Juni 1848.

*pGB8
V6755R
6.18.48

Vienna. Gemeinderat.
Der Gemeinde=Ausschuss beeilt sich
nachstehenden Ministerial=Erlass zur allgemeinen
Kenntniss zu bringen: ...
[Wien]Aus der k.k.Hof= und Staats-Druckerei.
[1848]

broadside. 44.5x29cm.
Dated: Wien am 18. Juni 1848.

*pGB8
V6755R
6.17.48

Vienna. Sicherheits-Ausschuss.
An die Arbeiter! Der unterzeichnete Ausschuss
ist bei allen Bestimmungen und Anordnungen,
welche derselbe hinsichtlich der öffentlichen
Bauten bisher getroffen hat, stets nur von dem
Gefühle der Menschlichkeit und den Rücksichten
der Billigkeit geleitet worden ...
[Wien]Aus der k.k.Hof= und Staats=Druckerei.
[1848]

broadside. 44.5x28.5cm.
Dated: Wien den 17. Juni 1848.

*pGB8
V6755R
6.18.48

Vienna. Nationalgarde.
Kundmachung. Zuschrift Sr. Excellenz des
hierlands commandirenden Herrn Generalen,
k. k. F. M. L. Grafen von Auersperg, an das
gefertigte Nationalgarde=Ober=Commando. Wien am
18. Juni 1848, Praes. Nro. 246-P.
[Wien]Aus der k.k.Hof= und Staats=Druckerei.
[1848]

broadside. 44.5x28.5cm.
Signed: Pannasch, provisorischer Ober=
Commandant der Nationalgarde.

*pGB8
V6755R
6.17.48

Vienna. Sicherheits-Ausschuss.
An die Bewohner der Residenz! Um die
zahlreichen, durch das Darniederliegen aller
Gewerbe brotlos gewordenen Arbeiter zu
ernähren und zu beschäftigen, bringen Staat
und Stadt tagtäglich die grössten Opfer ...
[Wien]Aus der k.k.Hof= und Staatsdruckerei.
[1848]

broadside. 44.5x57cm.
Dated: Wien am 17. Juni 1848.

*pGB8
V6755R
6.18.48

Vienna. Sicherheits-Ausschuss.
Kundmachung an die Arbeiter. Der unterzeichnete
Ausschuss kann heute nur wiederholen was er
Euch Samstag schon bekannt gegeben hat: Arbeiter
können und dürfen nur für wirklich geleistete
Arbeit bezahlt werden ...
[Wien]Aus der k.k.Hof= und Staats=Druckerei.
[1848]

broadside. 44.5x57cm.
Dated: Wien den 18. Juni 1848.

136

*pGB8
V6755R
6.18.48

Vienna. Sicherheits-Ausschuss.
Kundmachung. Morgen den 19. findet bei dem
k. k. Invalidenhause, wie alljährig, ein
feierliches Hochamt mit den üblichen Salven
statt ...
[Wien]Aus der k.k.Hof= und Staats=Druckerei.
[1848]

broadside. 44.5x28.5cm.
Dated: Wien am 18. Juni 1848.

---

*pGB8
V6755R
6.19.48

Vienna. Eisengiessereien und Maschinen-
werkstätten. Löblicher ... [1848]
(Card 2)

broadside. 44.5x29cm.
Dated & signed: Wien am 19. Juni 1848. Die
Arbeiter der Eisengiessereien und Maschinen-
werkstätten Wiens.

---

*pGB8
V6755R
6.18.48

Wiener Zeitung.
Extra=Blatt zur Wiener=Zeitung vom 18. Juni
1848. Das Kriegs=Ministerium theilt nachstehenden,
ihm so eben zugekommenen Bericht des F. M. L.
Baron Welden aus Treviso vom 15. d. M. wörtlich
mit ...
[Wien,1848]

broadside. 37x29cm.

---

*pGB8
V6755R
6.19.48

Vienna. Gemeinderat.
Da wegen Consignirung der Garden die Wahlen
heute nicht vollendet werden können ...
[Wien]Aus der k.k.Hof= und Staats=Druckerei.
[1848]

broadside. 44.5x29cm.
Dated: Wien, am 19. Juni 1848.

---

*pGB8
V6755R
6.19.48

Austria, Lower. Laws, statutes, etc., 1835-1848
(Ferdinand I)
Circulare der Nieder=Oesterreichischen
Landesregierung über die ausserordentliche
Besteuerung einiger Bezüge und Arten des
Einkommens.
[Wien]Aus der k.k.Hof= und Staats=Druckerei.
[1848]

[2]p. 35.5x21cm.
Caption title; imprint on p.[2]; dated at end:
Wien am 19. Junius 1848.

---

*pGB8
V6755R
6.19.48

Zay, Joseph.
Brüder! Cameraden! Die Abgeordneten der Wiener
Nationalgarde bringen Euch von den Brüdern in
Gratz die heissesten Wünsche für das Gedeihen
der errungenen Freiheit ...
[Wien]Aus der k.k.Hof= und Staats=Druckerei.
[1848]

broadside. 45x28.5cm.
Dated: Wien den 19. Juni 1848.

---

*pGB8
V6755R
6.19.48

Pannasch, Anton, 1789-1855.
Worte der Erwiederung, gesprochen von dem
Nationalgarde=Ober=Commandanten Pannasch, bei
Gelegenheit der feierlichen Uebernahme einer
Fahne, welche von den hochherzigen Söhnen
Steiermarks als Beweis der innigsten Verbrüderung
den Wiener Nationalgarden am 19. Juni 1848
überbracht worden ist.
[Wien]Aus der k.k.Hof= und Staatsdruckerei.
[1848]

broadside. 44.5x28.5cm.

---

*pGB8
V6755R
6.19.48

Zay, Joseph.
Einladung. Nächsten Mittwoch den 21. Juni d.
J. um 10 Uhr Vormittags wird die feierliche
Uebergabe der von der Gratzer Nationalgarde ...
[Wien]Aus der k.k.Hof= und Staats=Druckerei.
[1848]

broadside. 44.5x28.5cm.
Dated: Wien den 19. Juni 1848.

---

*pGB8
V6755R
6.19.48

Vienna. Eisengiessereien und Maschinen-
werkstätten.
Löblicher Sicherheits=Ausschuss der Wiener
Bürger, Nationalgarden und Studenten. Die
unterzeichneten Arbeiter unterstehender Fabriken
erklären in Ihrem Namen, und dem aller Ihrer
Kameraden, von denen sie bevollmächtigt sind,
Ihre höchste Unzufriedenheit über das undankbare
pflichtvergessene Benehmen der bei den
öffentlichen Bauten beschäftigten Arbeiter ...
[Wien]Aus der k.k.Hof= und Staats=Druckerei.
[1848]

(See next card)

---

*GB8
V6755R
6.20.48

An die Wähler vom Hauptwahlbezirke Neubau.
[Wien,1848]

[2]p. 29.5x22.5cm.
Caption title; dated & signed at end: Wien, am
20. Juni 1848. F.
Urging the election of Carl Möring to the
constitutional assembly.

*pGB8
V6755R
6.20.48

[Friedrich, Johann, fl.1848]
Offener Brief an Seine kaiserliche Hoheit
Herrn Erzherzog Johann!
Gedruckt und zu haben bei Ulrich Klopf sen.und
Alexander Eurich in Wien.[1848]

[2]p. 40x25cm.
Caption title; imprint on p.[2]; signed at
end: Johann Friedrich.

*GB8
V6755R
6.20.48

[Wimmer, Ferdinand]
Die Wahl des Reichstags-Deputirten in Staatz
und Zistersdorf.
[Wien]Gedruckt bei Franz Ed.v.Schmid.[1848]

[2]p. 22.5x13.5cm.
Caption title; imprint on p.[2]; signed at end:
Ferdinand Wimmer.
Concerns Egid Fritsch.

*pGB8
V6755R
6.20.48

Neuer blutiger Bürgerkrieg! 50,000 Rebellen.
Ihr Sieg über die Ungarn. Einfall der türkischen
Räuber, und Withen der Cholera.
[Wien]Gedruckt bei Leop.Sommer.Zu haben im
Verlagsgewölbe in dem Durchhause am Haarmarkt
Nr.730.[1848]

broadside. 41.5x26cm.

*pGB8
V6755R
6.21.48

Wiener Zeitung.
Extra=Blatt zum Abendblatte der Wiener Zeitung
vom 21. Juni 1848. Die jüngsten Ereignisse in
Prag.
[Wien,1848]

broadside. 38x29cm.

*pGB8
V6755R
6.20.48

Prag in Feuer und Flammen oder die Illumina-
tion des General Windischgrätz in Prag, welches
jetzt in Schutthaufen begraben liegt.
[Wien]Gedruckt bei J.N.Fridrich.[1848]

broadside. 52.5x42cm.

*pGB8
V6755R
6.22.48

Vienna. Gemeinderat.
An die Herren Armen=Instituts=Vorsteher der
Pfarrbezirke Wiens.
[Wien,1848]

broadside. 40x25cm.
Dated: Wien, am 22. Juni 1848.

*GB8
V6755R
6.20.48

[Riedl, J]
Hut ab, der von Wien spricht! oder Vertrauen
weckt Vertrauen. Erwiederung auf das Audiatur
et altera pars der Aristokraten.
[Wien]Gedruckt von U.Klopf sen.und Alexander
Eurich.[1848]

[2]p. 25x19.5cm.
Caption title; imprint on p.[2]; signed at
end: J. Riedl.

*pGB8
V6755R
6.24.48

Vienna. Sicherheits-Ausschuss.
An alle Staatsbürger der österreichischen
Monarchie. Die Wahl der Abgeordneten zum
Reichstage ist für jeden Staatsbürger eine
der wichtigsten Aufgaben ...
[Wien]Aus der k.k.Hof= und Staatsdruckerei.
[1848]

broadside. 44x28.5cm.
Dated: Wien den 24. Juni 1848.

*pGB8
V6755R
6.20.48

Vivat Erzherzog Johann der wackere Tiroler=
Hanns.
[Wien]Gedruckt bei M.Lell,Leopoldstadt,Nr.505.
[1848]

[2]p. 38x24.5cm.
Caption title; imprint on p.[2].

*pGB8
V6755R
6.24.48

Vienna. Sicherheits-Ausschuss.
Kundmachung. Mehrseitige Klagen über die
Nichtbeachtung der bei den unentgeltlichen
Badeanstalten am Tabor und Schüttel bestehenden
Badeordnungen ...
[Wien]Aus der k.k.Hof= und Staatsdruckerei.
[1848]

broadside. 37.5x22.5cm.
Dated: Wien am 24. Juni 1848.

Grüner, C
Va banque! Extra=Blatt des Wiener
Bürgerblatt!
[Wien]Gedruckt bei J.B.Wallishausser.[1848]
*GB8
V6755R
6.25.48

broadside. 26x21cm.

Habt Acht, Wiener! Die Böhmen flüchten sich
zu uns!
[Wien]Gedruckt und zu haben bei U.Klopf sen.
und A.Eurich,Wollzeil Nr.782.[1848]
*pGB8
V6755R
6.25.48

[2]p. 39.5x24cm.
Caption title; imprint on p.[2].
At end: Die Meinung eines Rechtsfreundes.

Johann, archduke of Austria, 1782-1859.
Proclamation. Se. Majestät der Kaiser hat mich
in Anbetracht Seines noch andauernden
Unwohlseins zu Seinem Stellvertreter ernannt ...
[Wien]Aus der k.k.Hof= und Staatsdruckerei.
[1848]
*pGB8
V6755R
6.25.48

broadside. 44.5x57cm.
Dated in contemporary ms.: 25 Juni.

Oesterreichs Stern der Erzherzog Johann ist
angekommen.
[Wien]Gedruckt bei M.Lell,Leopoldstadt,Nr.505.
[1848]
*pGB8
V6755R
6.25.48

[2]p. 38x24cm.
Caption title; imprint on p.[2].

Vienna. Sicherheits-Ausschuss.
Kundmachung in Bezug auf die verbotenen Spiele.
[Wien]Aus der k.k.Hof= und Staatsdruckerei.
[1848]
*pGB8
V6755R
6.25.48

broadside. 44.5x28.5cm.
Dated: Wien am 25. Juni 1848.

Reil, Benno.
Liebe Pfarrgemeinde! Da sich gestern ein
Gerücht verbreitete, was meine Ehre tief
verletzt, so sehe ich mich bewogen zu erklären,
dass ich von einer Sammlung der Lehrjungen zur
Musik bei dem Frohnleichnams=Umgange, von der
gesammelten Summe und der Verwendung gar
nichts wusste ...
[Wien,1848]
*pGB8
V6755R
6.26.48

broadside. 47x30.5cm.
Dated: Wien, St. Ulrich den 26. Juni 1848.

Vienna. Magistrat.
Kundmachung rücksichtlich der aus dem k. k.
Versatzamte unentgeltlich zu verabfolgenden
weiterer Pfänder.
[Wien]Aus der k.k.Hof= und Staats=Druckerei.
[1848]
*pGB8
V6755R
6.26.48

broadside. 44.5x57cm.
Dated & signed: Wien den 26. Juni 1848. Vom
Gemeinde-Ausschusse und Magistrate der Stadt
Wien.

Vienna. Sicherheits-Ausschuss.
Warnung gegen Holzfrevel. In letzter Zeit
hat im Prater, in der Brigittenau und den
umliegenden Forst=Revieren der Unfug, Bäume und
grünes Holz zu fällen und wegzuschleppen, so
sehr überhand genommen ...
[Wien]Aus der k.k.Hof= und Staatsdruckerei.
[1848]
*pGB8
V6755R
6.26.48

broadside. 38x23cm.
Dated: Wien am 26. Juni 1848.

[Neuwall, Albert, ritter von]
An die Herren Wahlmänner der Abgeordneten
zum constituirenden österreichischen Reichstage.
Wien 1848.Gedruckt bei Carl Gerold.
*pGB8
V6755R
6.27.48

[2]p. 43x27cm.
Caption title; imprint on p.[2]; dated &
signed at end: Wien, den 27. Juni 1848. Albert
Ritter von Neuwall.

Allgemeine oesterreichische Zeitung.
Ausserordentliches Bulletin zur Allgemeinen
oesterreichischen Zeitung vom 28. Juni 1848.
Nr. 87. Estaffette der Redaction aus Cöln.
[Wien]Gedruckt bei Leop.Sommer (vormals
Strauss),Dorotheergasse Nr.1108.[1848]
*GB8
V6755R
6.28.48

broadside. 29.5x22cm.

*pGB8
V6755R
6.28.48

Austria. Ministerium für öffentliche Arbeiten.
... Kundmachung. Um Gleichmässigkeit und
Regelmässigkeit bei allen öffentlichen Arbeiten
zu erzielen, wird folgende Arbeiter-Ordnung,
welche vom 3. Juli 1848 angefangen zur
allgemeinen Richtschnur zu dienen hat, hiermit
bekannt gemacht.
[Wien,1848]

broadside. 42x54cm.
At head: Nro. 8580.
Dated & signed: Wien den 28. Juni 1848. Der
(See next card)

---

*pGB8
V6755R
6.28.48

Austria. Ministerium für öffentliche Arbeiten.
... Kundmachung ... [1848] (Card 2)
Minister der öffentlichen Arbeiten A.
Baumgartner.
Another edition is without number at head
& has imprint.

---

*pGB8
V6755R
6.28.48

Austria. Ministerium für öffentliche Arbeiten.
Kundmachung. Um Gleichmässigkeit und
Regelmässigkeit bei allen öffentlichen Arbeiten
zu erzielen, wird folgende Arbeiter-Ordnung,
welche vom 3. Juli 1848 angefangen zur
allgemeinen Richtschnur zu dienen hat, hiermit
bekannt gemacht.
[Wien]Aus der k.k.Hof= und Staats=Druckerei.
[1848]

broadside. 44.5x57cm.
Dated & signed: Wien den 28. Juni 1848. Der
Minister der   öffentlichen Arbeiten A.
Baumgartner.
Another edition   has number at head & is with-
out imprint.

---

*GB8
V6755R
6.28.48

... Des Bürgers Zukunft. Auszug aus dem
"Unparteiischen" aus Nr. 26.
[Wien]Gedruckt bei Carl Gerold.[1848]

folder([4]p.) 20x13cm.
Caption title (at head: Preis: 1 kr.);
imprint on p.[4].

---

*GB8
V6755R
6.28.48

Löbenstein, Mathias Emanuel.
Die Kaiserin Mutter. Auszug aus dem
"Unparteiischen" aus Nr. 26, Mittwoch, den 28.
Juni 1848. Redigirt von: Mathias Emanuel
Löbenstein.
[Wien]Gedruckt bei Carl Gerold.[1848]

folder([4]p.) 20x13cm.
Caption title; imprint on p.[4].

---

*pGB8
V6755R
6.28.48

Vienna. Nationalgarde.
Tagsbefehl für die Nationalgarde. Am 28.
Juni 1848.
[Wien]Aus der k.k.Hof= und Staats=Druckerei.
[1848]

broadside. 44.5x28.5cm.

---

*pGB8
V6755R
6.29.48

Austria, Lower. Laws, statutes, etc., 1835-1848
(Ferdinand I)
... Circulare der k. k. Landesregierung im
Erzherzogthume Oesterreich unter der Enns.
Abänderungen in den bestehenden Strafgesetzen.
[Wien]Aus der k.k.Hof= und Staatsdruckerei.
[1848]

folder([3]p.) 38x23cm.
Caption title (at head: Nº 31285); imprint
on p.[3]; dated at end: Wien den 29. Juni 1848.

---

*pGB8
V6755R
6.30.48

Lackner, Johann, fl.1848.
Erzherzog Johann als deutsches Reichs=
Oberhaupt und die Deputation der Frankfurter
National-Versammlung.
[Wien,1848]

broadside. 34x26cm.

---

*pGB8
V6755R
6.30.48

[Teigaff, Elias]
Grosse Katzenmusik und kleines Brot, oder die
lustigen Leopoldstädter. Neueste Begebenheit,
mitgetheilt von einem constitutionellen Jodl.
[Wien]Gedruckt bei M.Lell,Leopoldstadt,
Weintraubengasse Nr.505.[1848]

[2]p. 38x24cm.
Caption title; imprint on p.[2]; signed at
end: Elias Teigaff, Jodel, Dichter und Demokrat.

---

*pGB8
V6755R
6.30.48

Vienna. Sicherheits-Ausschuss.
An die Bewohner Wiens! Seit einigen Tagen wird
abermals die Nachtruhe, namentlich in den
Vorstädten vielfältig durch lärmende
Volks=Zusammenläufe, sogenannte Katzenmusiken,
gestört ...
[Wien]Aus der k.k.Hof= und Staatsdruckerei.
[1848]

broadside. 45x57cm.
Dated: Wien am 30. Juni 1848.
Providing for the putting down of night
disturbances by   the Nationalgarde.

*pGB8
V6755R
6.31.48

Abenteuer eines Juden-Polizeikommissärs.
[Wien,1848]

broadside. 33.5x26cm.
Printed on one side of a small folio sheet;
on the other side is printed "Der Liberale und
der Reaktionär".

---

*pGB8
V6755R
6.31.48

Austria. Sovereigns, etc., 1835-1848
(Ferdinand I)
Antwort Kaiser Ferdinand von Oesterreich auf
das Sendschreiben des Papsten Pius IX. Zur
besseren Verständlichkeit der weiter folgenden
Antwort folgt hier zwar nicht Wort= aber
Jnhaltgetreu das Sendschreiben Pius des IX. an
den Kaiser von Oesterreich.
[Wien]Gedruckt und zu haben bei Leopold Grund
am Stephansplatze im Zwettelhofe.[1848]
[2]p. 36.5x22cm.
Caption title; imprint on p.[2].

---

*pGB8
V6755R
6.31.48

Alberti, C
Offener Brief an den Freiherrn von Rothschild.
[Wien]Gedruckt im Juni von U.Klopf sen.und
Alex.Eurich.[1848]

broadside. 39.5x25cm.
Signed: C. Alberti, freier Bürger Wiens.

---

*pGB8
V6755R
6.31.48

Brenner, Johann Nepomuk.
Ein neues Ministerium.
[Wien]Gedruckt bei M.Lell.[1848]

broadside. 38x23.5cm.
Protesting the suggested replacement of
Pillersdorf by Stadion.

---

*pGB8
V6755R
6.31.48

An den Minister des Innern und provisorischen
Ministerpräsidenten.
[Wien,1848]

broadside. 40x25cm.
"Diese Petition liegt zur Unterzeichnung auf
in Schlegel's Kaffeehaus am Graben."
Requesting changes in the proposed constitution.

---

*GB8
V6755R
6.31.48

Buchheim, Carl Adolf, 1828-1900.
Sie wollen die Studenten vertreiben. Von
Adolph Buchheim, Student.
[Wien]Druck von U.Klopf sen.u.Alex.Eurich.
[1848]

broadside. 25.5x20.5cm.
Helfert (Wiener Parnass) 1155.

---

*pGB8
V6755R
6.31.48

An die geliebten Bewohner der Stadt Brünn.
[Wien]Josef Stöckholzer v.Hirschfeld'sche
Officin.[1848]

broadside. 46x29cm.
Dated & signed: Wien im Juni 1848. Die
Deputation der Bürger, Nationalgarde und
Studenten von Wien.

---

*pGB8
V6755R
6.31.48

[Clother, ———]
Der Aristokrat, der Pestdoktor und die
Hebamme. (Der Ort der Handlung ist Ischl.)
Unser Doktor aber ist auch nicht so dubios als
grandios, und wieder nicht so grandios als
burschikos.
[Wien]Gedruckt bei M.Lell.[1848]
[2]p. 38x22.5cm.
Caption title; imprint on p.[2]; signed at
end: Clother.
A mock drama.

---

*GB8
V6755R
6.31.48
(A)

*GB8
V6755R
6.31.48
(B)

Auspitz, Moravia.
Den Bürgern, Nationalgarden und der
akademischen Legion in Wien, von ihren
Auspitzer Brüdern.
[Wien?,1848]

broadside. 28.5x22cm.
Another copy. 27.5x21.5cm.
Printed on pink paper.

---

*GB8
V6755R
6.31.48

Der edlen kroatischen Nation. Gewidmet von
einem alten Husaren.
[Wien,1848]

broadside. 14x10cm.
In verse; not in Helfert (Wiener Parnass).

*GB8
V6755R
6.31.48

Des Doctor Eisele und seines Zöglings des
Baron Beisele Wanderung durch die Wiener Stadt
am 26. Mai 1848.
Wien im Juni 1848.Gedruckt von U.Klopf sen.und
Alex.Eurich.
folder([4]p.) 19.5x12.5cm.

---

*GB8
V6755R
6.31.48

Grüner, C
... Nur mit Gewalt!
[Wien,1848]
broadside. 26x21cm.
At head of title: Extra=Blatt zum Wiener
demokratischen Bürgerblatt.

---

*pGB8
V6755R
6.31.48

Der Deutsche Adler (Club), Vienna.
Der deutsche Adler über Wiens gegenwärtige
Lage.
[Wien]Gedruckt im Juui[!] 1848 bei U.Klopf sen.
und Alex.Eurich.
broadside. 46x58cm.

---

*GB8
V6755R
6.31.48

[Halbhuber, Johann]
Streit zwischen Greissler und Minister, oder:
wie steht's mit der Judenemancipation.
Gewidmet dem Hans=Jörgel.
[Wien,1848]
folder([4]p.) 21.5x13.5cm.
Helfert (Wiener Parnass) 1169.
Signed at end: Johann Halbhuber,
verabschiedeter Unteroffizier, dermalen
Greissler.
Printer's imprint on p.[4]: Druck von U. Klopf
sen. und Alex.   Eurich, Wollzeile 782.

---

*pGB8
V6755R
6.31.48

Die Dienstbothen=Tirannin.
[Wien]Gedruckt,bei M.Lell,Leopoldstadt,
Weintraubengasse,Nr.505.[1848]
broadside. 38x24cm.
Signed: Katharina E.

---

*pGB8
V6755R
6.31.48

Hartinger, Johann.
Ein Wort an das Militär!
[Wien]Gedruckt bei Ullrich.[1848]
broadside. 42x26cm.

---

*pGB8
V6755R
6.31.48

Eckardt, Ludwig, 1827-1871.
Ungarn hat einen König, wir wollen einen
Erzherzog haben! Von L. Eckardt ...
[Wien,1848]
broadside. 42.5x26.5cm.
Printed within ornamental border.

---

*GB8
V6755R
6.31.48

[Hennig, Josef Heinrich, ascribed author]
Hört! Hört! den Kriegsschauplatz in Italien
betreffend.
[Wien]Druck und Verlag bei Leopold Grund,am
Stephansplatze im Zwettelhofe.[1848]
folder([4]p.) 25x20.5cm.
Signed at end: J. H. H.——g., National=Garde.

---

*pGB8
V6755R
6.31.48

Ehrnstell, Leopold.
An die Wahlmänner Wiens! Ihr habt die schöne
aber schwierige Aufgabe, die Abgeordneten zum
Reichstage zu wählen ...
[Wien]Gedruckt bei U.Klopf sen.und Alexander
Eurich,Wollzeil Nr.782.[1848]
broadside. 39.5x25.5cm.
Dated: Wien im Juni 1848.

---

*pGB8
V6755R
6.31.48

Herczeghy, Mór, 1815-1884.
Ein ernstes Wort an die Wiener Arbeiter.
[Wien]Gedruckt von U.Klopf und sen.[!]
A.Eurich.[1848]
broadside. 46x58cm.
Remonstrating against wage demands.

*pGB8
V6755R
6.31.48

Die Hochverräther, welche für 7 Millionen
Rubel Oesterreich an Kaiser von Russland
verkaufen wollten.
[Wien]Zu haben in der Kölnerhofgasse Nr.740.
Gedruckt bei Leop.Sommer(vorm.Strauss).[1848]

broadside. 41.5x26.5cm.

---

*pGB8
V6755R
6.31.48

Kugler, Franz, fl.1848.
Antwort auf das Placat, das der hochlöbl.
Sicherheit=Ausschuss für gut gefunden hat gegen
die Bäcker, Fleischhauer &c. zu erlassen.
[Wien]Gedruckt bei U.Klopf senior und
Alexander Eurich.[1848]

broadside. 66x52.5cm.
Signed: Franz Kugler, 8. Bezirk, 1. B. 4.
Compagnie, Bürger und Garde.

---

*pGB8
V6755R
6.31.48

[Klaus, Martin, fl.1848]
Wer sollte Wiens' Erzbischof sein? oder: "Ich
will keine Stunde länger leben, wenn je ein
Priester sein heiliges Gelübde der Keuschheit
hielt."
[Wien]Gedruckt bei M.Lell.[1848]

[2]p. 38x23cm.
Caption title; imprint on p.[2]; signed at end:
Mart. Klaus.
The quotation is from a speech made by Anton
Füster.

---

*pGB8
V6755R
6.31.48

Der Liberale und der Reaktionär.
[Wien,1848]

broadside. 33.5x26cm.
Printed on one side of a small folio sheet;
on the other is printed "Abenteuer eines Juden-
Polizeikommissärs".

---

*GB8
V6755R
6.31.48

Knöpfelmacher, Bernhard.
Wir haben sie begleitet, und haben froh
geweint. Von Bernhard Knöpfelmacher, Mediziner.
[Wien]A.Dorfmeister's Buchdruckerei.[1848]

folder([4]p.) 22.5x15cm.
Helfert (Wiener Parnass) 1172.
Caption title on p.[3]; imprint on p.[4]; on
p.[1]: Unsern biedern Deputirten nach Frankfurt
am Main. Hoch!

---

*pGB8
V6755R
6.31.48

Löve, Paul.
Die Befestigung von Wien gegen anrükende
Feinde.
[Wien]Gedruckt bei Josef Ludwig,Josefstadt.
[1848]

broadside. 55.5x44cm.

---

*pGB8
V6755R
6.31.48

Der Koch von Fiquelmont eingefangen, wie er
ist unter die Arbeiter gegangen.
[Wien]Gedruckt bei M.Lell.[1848]

broadside. 38x24cm.

---

*pGB8
V6755R
6.31.48

Malek, Anton.
Aufruf an die Arbeiter von ihren Mitbrüdern!
Gedruckt im Juni 1848 von Ulrich Klopf sen.und
Alex.Eurich in Wien.

broadside. 39.5x25cm.
Signed: Anton Malek, Arbeiter im Prater. Alois
Pasching und Josef Pasching, Arbeiter auf der
Regie.

---

*pGB8
V6755R
6.31.48

... Der Kreuzzug der Provinzen gegen Wien.
[Wien]Gedruckt bei Leop.Sommer (vormals
Strauss),Dorotheergasse Nr.1108.[1848]

broadside. 41.5x26.5cm.
At head: Abdruck aus der Abendbeilage Nr.54
der Allgemeinen oesterreichischen Zeitung
redigirt von Ernst von Schwarzer.

---

*pGB8
V6755R
6.31.48

[Naske, Adolph Carl, 1814-1864]
Die Todsünden der Bureaukratie verurtheilt
vom Richterstuhle der öffentlichen Meinung.
Bei Jakob Bader,Buchhändler in Wien,Stadt,
Strobelgasse.[1848]

folder([4]p.) 39x25cm.
Caption title; imprint on p.[4]; dated &
signed at end: Wien, im Juni 1848. Adolf Carl
Naske.

*pGB8
V6755R
6.31.48

Neue grosse Lotterie! Mit hoher Bewilligung
der gesammten Bevölkerung gewinnt man auf den
ersten Ruf des hohen Reichstages das höchste Gut
des Österreichers die Rückkehr Sr. Maj. des
Kaisers ...
[Wien]Gedruckt bei M.Lell.[1848]

broadside. 37.5x22.5cm.
Printed within border of type-ornaments.
A satire.

*pGB8
V6755R
6.31.48

Die schöne schlanke Dame in Ketten soll frei
werden!
[Wien]Gedruckt im Juni von U.Klopf sen.und A.
Eurich.[1848]

broadside. 42.5x26cm.
Signed: Ein Mann aus dem Volke im Namen
Tausender.
Asking that the toll for the use of the
Kettenbrücke be abolished.

*pGB8
V6755R
6.31.48

Das neue slavische Kaiserreich und der grosse
Völkerbund von 80 Millionen Slaven. Zur
Entlarvung der drohenden Gespenstes, welches die
Kluft zwischen den verschiedenen Nationen
Oesterreichs immer weiter öffnet, und in
neuester Zeit in mannigfacher Gestalt unter
dem Volke circulirt.
[Wien]Gedruckt im Juni von U.Klopf sen.und
Alex.Eurich.[1848]
[2]p. 39.5x25cm.
Caption title; imprint on p.[2]; signed at
end: C. M. [i.e.   Carl Möring?]

*pGB8
V6755R
6.31.48

[Schwarz, Wenzel, fl.1848]
Vorschlag über die Aufhebung der
Verzehrungssteuer von Lebensmitteln und zur
Errichtung eines Getreide-Monopoles.
[Wien]Buchdruckerei des Leop.Sommer (vormals
Strauss).[1848]

folder([4]p.) 42x26cm.
Caption title; imprint on p.[4]; dated & signed
at end: Wien im Juni 1848. Wenzel Schwarz,
Handelsmann und Inhaber mehrerer k. k. ausschl.
priv. Parfümerie-Erzeugnissen ...

*pGB8
V6755R
6.31.48

Pietznigg, Franz, 1802-1856.
Einige Worte an meine Landsleute bei der Wahl
ihrer Vertreter zum kommenden Reichstage.
[Wien]Zu haben in der Mechitharisten
Congregations Buchhandlung.[1848]

broadside. 60x47cm.
Dated: Wien, im Juni 1848.

*pGB8
V6755R
6.31.48

Tory, S
Der Kaiservertreter und was die Wiener von
Johann dem Deutschen zu erwarten haben.
[Wien]Gedruckt bei Josef Ludwig.(Zu haben in
der Stadt,Kölnerdofgasse[!]Nr.740.)[1848]

broadside. 43x52cm.

*pGB8
V6755R
6.31.48

Scheibe, Theodor, 1820-1881.
Der Croaten und Slavaken-Krieg mit Ungarn,
Hochverrath des königlichen Staathalters Baron
Jellachich.
[Wien]Gedruckt im Juni und zu haben bei J.N.
Fridrich,Josefstadt,Langegasse Nr.58.[1848]

broadside. 48x38cm.

*GB8
V6755R
6.31.48

Verein der Deutschen aus Böhmen, Mähren und
Schlesien.
Deutsche Brüder in Böhmen! Um Euch, wenn ein
Beweis von der Ungesetzlichkeit und Ungültigkeit
der provisorischen Regierung zu Prag nöthig
wäre, diesen zu geben, theilen wir Euch den
Erlass des hiesigen Ministeriums darüber mit ...
[Wien,1848]
broadside. 21x13cm.
Signed: Der Verein der Deutschen aus Böhmen,
Mähren und Schlesien, zur Aufrechthaltung ihrer
Nationalität.

*pGB8
V6755R
6.31.48

[Scheibe, Theodor, 1820-1881]
Rebellische Geistliche gegen die Constitution,
auf welche Weise sind sie unschädlich zu
machen? und Beantwortung der Frage: Wie lange
werden noch die Liguorianer in Wien spuken?
[Wien]Gedruckt im Juni bei J.N.Friedrich.
[1848]

[2]p. 38x24.5cm.
Caption title; imprint on p.[2]; signed at
end: Theodor Scheibe.

*pGB8
V6755R
6.31.48

Vienna. Citizens.
Die Bürger, Nationalgarde und Studenten von
Wien an ihre Brüder in Brünn!
[Wien]Gedruckt bei Franz Gastl,Postgasse Nr.
446.[1848]

broadside. 37x22.5cm.

*pGB8
V6755R
6.31.48

Vienna. Sicherheits-Ausschuss.
Kundmachung. Ueber die jetzt so häufig vorgekommenen Klagen, dass einige Bäcker, Fleischhauer und Victualienhändler, theils durch schlechtes Gewicht, theils aber auch durch Verkauf von schlechten, der Gesundheit nachtheiligen Lebensmitteln, das Publikum beeinträchtigen ...
[Wien]Aus der k.k.Hof= und Staats=Druckerei. [1848]
broadside. 44.5x57cm.

*GB8
V6755R
6.31.48

Wisst ihr wohl, Kameraden, wie die National= Garde entstanden ist? Ein Beitrag zur Zeitgeschichte.
Gedruckt im Juni 1848 von Ulrich Klopf sen. und Alex.Eurich in Wien.
folder([4]p.) 26x20.5cm.
Signed at end: Ein alter Nationalgardist.

*pGB8
V6755R
6.31.48

Vienna. Sicherheits-Ausschuss.
Liebe Freunde Arbeiter! Die eingetretene Störung der heutigen Werbung zeigt, dass ein Theil von Euch in offenbarem Irrthum ist ...
[Wien]Aus der k.k.Hof= und Staats=Druckerei. [1848]
broadside. 45x28cm.
Signed: Der Ausschuss der Bürger, National- garden und Studenten.

*GB8
V6755R
6.31.48

Zwei gräfliche Volks=Verräther in Linz, oder reactionäres Treiben in den Provinzen.
[Wien]Gedruckt im Juni bei J.N.Fridrich, Josephstadt Langegasse Nr.58.[1848]
folder([4]p.) 24.5x19cm.
Caption title; imprint on p.[4]; signed at end: D. C.
On Montecuccoli & Breuner.

*pGB8
V6755R
6.31.48

Vienna. Sicherheits-Ausschuss.
Programm des Central-Wahl-Comités für den bevorstehenden constituirenden Reichstag.
[Wien]Aus der k.k.Hof= und Staats=Druckerei. [1848]
broadside. 44.5x57cm.
Dated: Wien im Juni 1848.

*pGB8
V6755R
7.1.48

Des Pabsten Sohn (eine Satyre).
[Wien]Gedruckt bei M.Lell,Leopoldstadt, Weintraubengasse,Nr.505.[1848]
broadside. 40x24cm.

*pGB8
V6755R
6.31.48

Vienna. Sicherheits-Ausschuss.
Programm des Central=Wahl=Comité's für den bevorstehenden constituirenden Reichstag.
[Wien]Aus der k.k.Hof= und Staatsdruckerei. [1848]
[2]p. 44.5x28.5cm.
Caption title; imprint on p.[2]; dated at end: Wien im Juni 1848.

*pGB8
V6755R
7.1.48

Vienna. Magistrat.
Kundmachung. Zur Handhabung der bestehenden allgemeinen Marktvorschriften und zur Abstellung aller dagegen überhand genommenen Unfüge wird Folgendes in Erinnerung gebracht ...
[Wien,1848]
broadside. 39.5x24.5cm.
Signed & dated: Vom Magistrate der Stadt Wien, am 1. Juli 1848.

*pGB8
V6755R
6.31.48

Die weibliche Nationalgarde in Wien. Buchstäblich wahr.
[Wien]Gedruckt bei Leop.Sommer.[1848]
broadside. 41.5x26cm.
Signed: F. B.

*pGB8
V6755R
7.1.48

Vienna. Nationalgarde. Akademische Legion.
An die Herren Garden der V. Abtheilung der akademischen Legion! Da nach dem von dem Ministerium des Inneren ausgesprochenen Grundsätzen jeder Staatsbürger verpflichtet ist, sich in die Nationalgarde einreihen zu lassen ...
[Wien]Aus der k.k.Hof= und Staats=Druckerei. [1848]
broadside. 44.5x57cm.
Dated & signed: Wien, den 1. Juli 1848.
Aigner, Com-   mandant.

*pGB8
V6755R
7.1.48

Vienna. Sicherheits-Ausschuss.
... An die Landleute! Ihr habt den Wienern in herzlichen Worten gedankt für das, was sie in den März= und Maitagen für ganz Oesterreich, und insbesondere auch für Euch gethan ...
[Wien]Aus der k.k.Hof= und Staatsdruckerei. [1848]

broadside. 38x22.5cm.
Dated: Wien den 1. Juli 1848.
At head: Der Ausschuss der Bürger, National-garden und Studenten zur Aufrechthaltung der Ruhe und Ordnung (und zur Wahrung der Rechte des Volkes.(

*pGB8
V6755R
7.3.48

Vienna. Sicherheits-Ausschuss.
Kundmachung. Am 4. dieses Monats wird in Folge Mittheilung des k. k. N. Oest. General= Commando das 1. Landwehrbataillon von Prinz Emil Infanterie ... in Wien eintreffen ...
[Wien]Aus der k.k.Hof= und Staatsdruckerei. [1848]

broadside. 38x22.5cm.
Dated: Wien am 3. Juli 1848.

*pGB8
V6755R
7.1.48

Vienna. Sicherheits-Ausschuss.
Kundmachung. An einem der nächsten Tage wird das Infanterie=Regiment Erzherzog Leopold Nr. 53 auf seinem Durchmarsche nach Italien hier eintreffen ...
[Wien]Aus der k.k.Hof= und Staatsdruckerei. [1848]

broadside. 37.5x23cm.
Dated: Wien am 1. Juli 1848.

*pGB8
V6755R
7.3.48

Vienna. Sicherheits-Ausschuss.
Kundmachung. Gemäss einer Eröffnung des k. k. N. Oest. General=Commando kömmt von Böhmen ein Fuhrwesens=Mannschaft= und. Pferde=Transport hier an ...
[Wien]Aus der k.k.Hof= und Staatsdruckerei. [1848]

broadside. 44.5x28.5cm.
Dated: Wien am 3. Juli 1848.

*pGB8
V6755R
7.1.48

Vienna. Sicherheits-Ausschuss.
Landleute, Brüder! Die Nachrichten, welche wir aus vielen Gegenden des Landes erhalten, machen uns sehr traurig ...
[Wien]Aus der k.k.Hof= und Staatsdruckerei. [1848]

broadside. 37.5x22.5cm.
Dated: Wien den 1. Juli 1848.

*pGB8
V6755R
7.4.48

Vienna. Sicherheits-Ausschuss.
Kundmachung. Morgen den 5. Juli Vormittags wird ein gemischter Militär=Transport ... auf der k. k. priv. Nordbahn ankommen ...
[Wien]Aus der k.k.Hof= und Staatsdruckerei. [1848]

broadside. 38x23cm.

*pGB8
V6755R
7.2.48

Ruft es aus in alle Winde! Erzherzog Johann von Oesterreich ist Bundeshaupt des einigfreien deutschen Volkes.
[Wien]Gedruckt bei Josef Ludwig.[1848]

broadside. 46x58cm.
Signed: L. P. Garde.

*pGB8
V6755R
7.5.48

Haffner, Karl, 1804-1876.
Carl Haffner an die ehemaligen Mitglieder des Josefstädter Theaters, und deren Ausschuss.
[Wien,1848]

broadside. 42x53cm.
Dated: Wien, den 5. Juli 1848.
This large folio broadside is printed in 2 columns.

*pGB8
V6755R
7.2.48

Vienna. Magistrat.
Kundmachung. Mit Bezug auf die hierortige Kundmachung vom 7. v. M. in Betreff der Wähleraufnahme und der Wahl der Wahlmänner rücksichtlich der constituirenden Reichsver-sammlung, wird nun über die Wahl der Abgeordneten selbst, Folgendes bekannt gemacht ...
[Wien]Gedruckt bei Leopold Grund,am Bundsthurm Nr.1.[1848]

broadside. 52x66.5cm.
Signed & dated: (Vom Magistrate der Stadt Wien am 2. Juli (1848.

*pGB8
V6755R
7.5.48

Haffner, Karl, 1804-1876.
Carl Haffner an die ehemaligen Mitglieder des Josefstädter Theaters, und deren Ausschuss.
[Wien,1848]

broadside. 34.5x22cm.
Dated: Wien, den 5. Juli 1848.
This small folio broadside is printed in 1 column.

*pGB8
V6755R
7.5.48

Pokorny, Franz, d.1850.
  Direktor Pokorny an das Publikum, in Betreff
des Ausschusses der ehemaligen Josefstädter
Theater=Gesellschaft.
  [Wien,1848]
    broadside. 38x46cm.
    Dated: Wien, den 5. Juli 1848.
    This large folio broadside is printed in 2
columns.

*GB8
V6755R
7.5.48

Pokorny, Franz, d.1850.
  Direktor Pokorny an das Publikum, in Betreff
des Ausschusses der ehemaligen Josefstädter
Theater=Gesellschaft.
  [Wien,1848]
    broadside. 22x18cm.
    Dated: Wien, den 5. Juli 1848.
    This small quarto broadside is printed in 1
column.

*pGB8
V6755R
7.5.48

Vienna. Gemeinderat.
  Kundmachung. Die unterzeichneten Ausschüsse
veranstalten zur Feier des Tages, heute den 5.
Juli Abends um 9 Uhr einen grossen Fackelzug
mit Serenade ...
  [Wien]Aus der k.k.Hof= und Staats=Druckerei.
[1848]
    broadside. 48x64.5cm.
    Dated & signed: Wien am 5. Juli 1848. Der
Gemeinde=Ausschuss. Der vereinigte Ausschuss der
Bürger, Nationalgarde und Studenten.

*pGB8
V6755R
7.5.48

Vienna. Sicherheits-Ausschuss.
  Kundmachung. Zu Folge eines heute, den 5. Juli,
aus Prag eingelangten Berichtes wird ein
Artillerie=Fuhrwesens=Transport ... morgen den
6. d. hier anlangen ...
  [Wien]Aus der k.k.Hof= und Staatsdruckerei.
[1848]
    broadside. 45x28.5cm.

*pGB8
V6755R
7.6.48

Austria, Lower. Laws, statutes, etc., 1835-1848
    (Ferdinand I)
  ... Circulare der k. k. Landesregierung im
Erzherzogthume Oesterreich unter der Enns.
Betreffend die Mauthbefreiung aller Fuhren mit
Baumaterialien zur Wiedererbauung eines durch
irgend ein Elementar=Ereigniss zerstörten Hauses.
  [Wien]Aus der k.k.Hof= und Staatsdruckerei,
[1848]
    broadside. 38x23cm.
    At head: Nº   32312.
    Dated: Wien am   6. Juli 1848.

*pGB8
V6755R
7.6.48

Johann, archduke of Austria, 1782-1859.
  Proclamation. Die deutsche National=
Versammlung in Frankfurt hat mich zum
Reichsverweser erwählt ...
  [Wien]Aus der k.k.Hof- und Staats=Druckerei.
[1848]
    broadside. 44.5x57cm.
    Dated: Wien am 6. Juli 1848.

*pGB8
V6755R
7.6.48

Lackner, Johann, fl.1848.
  Nur ein Deutschland! Feierlicher Empfang und
Einzug der Frankfurter Deputirten.
  [Wien,1848]
    broadside. 34.5x26cm.

*GB8
V6755R
7.6.48

[Swiedack, Karl, 1815-1888]
  Ein Gottesgericht. Ballade von Carl Elmar
[pseud.]. Zur Feier der Anwesenheit der
Deputirten aus Frankfurt an den Reichsverweser
Erzherzog Johann. Am 6. Juli 1848, im National-
theater an der Wien gesprochen von Frl. Amalie
Weissbach.
  [Wien,1848]
    [2]p. 22.5x14.5cm.
    Helfert (Wiener Parnass) 1389.
    Caption title.
    Printed on pink   paper.

*pGB8
V6755R
7.6.48

Vienna. Ausschuss der Wiener National-Arena.
  Der Ausschuss der Wiener National=Arena
an das Publikum, betreffs des Herrn Directors
Pokorny.
  [Wien]Gedruckt bei Carl Ueberreuter.[1848]
    broadside. 62.5x47cm.
    Dated: Wien, am 6. Juli 1848.

*GB8
V6755R
7.7.48

Kaiser Joseph's Feier, von der akademischen
Legiou [!] veranstaltet. Aus L. A. Frankl's
"Sonntagsblättern" besonders abgedruckt.
  [Wien]Druck von Josef Stöckholzer v.Hirschfeld.
--Papier aus der Imster=Fabrik[!].[1848]
    folder([4]p.) 26.5x17cm.
    Caption title; imprint on p.[4].
    Includes 2 poems (Helfert, Wiener Parnass,
1394-95) by J. N. Vogl & Friedrich Kaiser.

Moor, ——.
*pGB8   Hütet Euch! Kaufet ja nicht das Tageblatt die
V6755R   "Presse."
7.7.48   [Wien]Druck der M.Lell'schen Offizin.[1848]

broadside. 38.5x24cm.

Gross, Johann, fl.1848.
*pGB8   ... Offener Brief an den Redacteur des
V6755R   "Unpartheiischen" Hrn. Löbenstein.
7.8.48   [Wien](Gedruckt bei Franz Edlen v.Schmid.)
[1848]

broadside. 42.5x53cm.
Dated: Salzburg am 8. Juli 1848.
A defense of the Queen Mother.

Vienna. Ausschuss der Wiener National-Arena.
*pGB8   An Herrn Haffner, ehemaligen Sekretär des
V6755R   Josephstädter Theaters.
7.7.48   [Wien,1848]

[2]p. 44.5x26cm.
Caption title; dated at end: Wien, am 7. Juli
1848.

Haffner, Karl, 1804-1876.
*pGB8   Carl Haffner an den Ausschuss der Arena=
V6755R   Unternehmung.
7.8.48   [Wien,1848]

broadside. 53.5x43.5cm.
Dated: Wien, den 8. Juli 1848.
This large folio broadside is printed in 2
columns.

Die Constitution, Vienna.
*GB8   ... Extrablatt zur Constitution. Wien am 8.
V6755R   Juli 1848, 2 Uhr Nachmittags. Das Ministerium
7.8.48   hat abgedankt!
[Wien]Gedruckt bei Franz Edlen von Schmid.
[1848]

broadside. 29x22cm.
Price at head.
In this edition, last line of text begins:
niss vor einem ...

Haffner, Karl, 1804-1876.
*pGB8   Carl Haffner an den Ausschuss der Arena=
V6755R   Unternehmung.
7.8.48   [Wien,1848]

broadside. 36x20.5cm.
Dated: Wien, den 8. Juli 1848.
This small folio broadside is printed in 1
column.

Die Constitution, Vienna.
*GB8   ... Extrablatt zur Constitution. Wien am 8.
V6755R   Juli 1848, 2 Uhr Nachmittags. Das Ministerium
7.8.48   hat abgedankt!
[Wien]Gedruckt bei Franz Eelen[!] von Schmid.
[1848]

broadside. 29.5x23.5cm.
Price at head.
In this edition, last line of text begins:
sind wir auch ...

Johann, archduke of Austria, 1782-1859.
*pGB8   Abschiedsworte des verehrten Reichsverwesers
V6755R   Johann an die Deputation des Ausschusses der
7.8.48   Bürger, Nationalgarde und Studenten.
[Wien]Gedruckt bei Edl.v.Schmidbauer und
Holzwarth.[1848]

broadside. 43x27cm.
Reported & signed by J. H. Singer.

Die Constitution, Vienna.
*GB8   ... Extrablatt zur Constitution. Wien am 8.
V6755R   Juli 1848, 2 Uhr Nachmittags. Das Ministerium hat
7.8.48   abgedankt!
Wien gedruckt bei Franz Edlen von Schmid.
[1848]

broadside. 29.5x22.5cm.
Price at head.
In this edition, last line of text begins:
rium Stadion ...

... Das Ministerium Pillersdorf gestürzt!!
*pGB8   (mit Ausnahme Doblhoff's) und Absetzung des
V6755R   Gouverneurs von Tirol Grafen Brandeis.
7.8.48   [Wien]Gedruckt bei M.Lell.[1848]

broadside. 38.5x22.5cm.
At head: Allerneuestes.

*GB8
V6755R
7.8.48

Schmidt, Wilhelm Gottfried.
Nachricht für die P. T. Herren Pränumeranten
der "Versuche eines deutschen Beranger."
[Wien,1848]

broadside. 23x29cm.
Announcing that the first 7 numbers will be
ready on 10 July.

---

*pGB8
V6755R
7.10.48

Austria. Reichstag, 1848-1849.
Protokoll der ersten vorberathenden Sitzung
der constituirenden Reichs=Versammlung am 10.
Juli 1848.
[Wien]Aus der k.k.Hof= und Staatsdruckerei.
[1848]

broadside. 44.5x28.5cm.

---

*GB8
V6755R
7.8.48

Der Sturz des Ministeriums Pillersdorf. Das
Ministerium Doppelhof. Alle Besorgnisse
wenigstens vor der Hand beseitigt.
Unzweckmässige Allarmgerüchte vieler Blätter.
Die Unruhe in Gratz.
[Wien]Gedruckt bei Josef Ludwig.[1848]

folder([4]p.) 24.5x20cm.

---

*pGB8
V6755R
7.10.48

Austria. Reichstag, 1848-1849.
Provisorische Geschäfts-Ordnung.
[Wien]Aus der k.k.Hof= und Staatsdruckerei.
[1848]

[2]p. 44.5x28cm.
Caption title; imprint on p.[2].

---

*pGB8
V6755R
7.8.48

Vienna. Nationalgarde.
An die gesammte Nationalgarde Wiens. So eben
erhalte ich das beifolgende Dankschreiben der
Herren Deputirten von Frankfurt und beeile mich,
selbes hiemit zur Kenntniss der gesammten
Nationalgarde zu bringen ...
[Wien]Aus der k.k.Hof= und Staats=Druckerei.
[1848]

broadside. 38x23cm.
Dated & signed: Wien den 8. Juli 1848. Pannasch
Ober=Commandant der Nationalgarde.

---

*pGB8
V6755R
7.10.48

Austria. Reichstag, 1848-1849.
Verzeichniss der bis zum 10. Juli 1848 sich
gemeldeten Abgeordneten zum constituirenden
Reichstage.
[Wien]Aus der k.k.Hof= und Staatsdruckerei.
[1848]

[8]p. 36.5x22cm.
Caption title; imprint on p.[8].

---

*pGB8
V6755R
7.8.48

Vienna. Universität. Ausschuss der Studierenden.
Kundmachung. Der Ausschuss der Studenten hat
in Bezug auf die Organisirung, der die
Studentenschaft Wiens betreffenden
Geldangelegenheiten ... Folgendes zu veröf-
fentlichen beschlossen ...
[Wien]Gedruckt bei U.Klopf sen.und Alexander
Eurich.[1848]

broadside. 53.5x42cm.
Dated: Wien am 8. Juli 1848.

---

*pGB8
V6755R
7.10.48

Croatia-Slavonia. Sabor.
Repräsentation des Landtags der vereinten
Königreiche an Se. Majestät den Kaiser und
König in Bezug auf die künftigen Verhältnisse
der Militärgrenze. (Aus der Nationalsprache).
[Wien?1848]

folder([4]p.) 37x23cm.
Caption title; dated & signed at end: Agram
den 10. Juli 1848. Der Landtag der vereinten
Königreiche Croatien Slavonien und Dalmatien.

---

*pGB8
V6755R
7.9.48

Vienna. Sicherheits-Ausschuss.
Kundmachung. Es haben sich aus Anlass, dass
an die hier einquartirte Mannschaft des Prinz
Leopold Infanterie=Regiments scharfe Munition
vertheilt wurde, verschiedene beunruhigende
Gerüchte in der Bevölkerung verbreitet ...
[Wien]Aus der k.k.Hof= und Staatsdruckerei.
[1848]

broadside. 44.5x28.5cm.
Dated: Wien, am 9. Juli 1848.

---

*pGB8
V6755R
7.10.48

Endlich, Johann Quirin.
Der Sicherheitsausschuss unmöglich.
[Wien]Gedruckt bei A.Dorfmeister.[1848]

broadside. 46.5x31cm.
Signed: Die Gebrüder Endlich.
Denouncing the Committee's vote of no confi-
dence in the Pillersdorf ministry on July 8th;
includes antisemitic statements.

Haffner, Karl, 1804-1876.

*pGB8
V6755R
7.10.48

Carl Haffner, Dichter des National=Theaters
an der Wien. An die Herren Just, Fröhlich,
Langer und Denemi.
. [Wien,1848]

· [2]p. 36x21.5cm.
Caption title; dated at end: Wien, den 10.
Juli 1848.

Haffner, Karl, 1804-1876.

*pGB8
V6755R
7.10.48

Carl Haffner, Sekretär des National=Theaters
an der Wien. An die Herren Just, Fröhlich,
Langer und Denemi.
[Wien,1848]

broadside. 52.5x42cm.
Dated: Wien, den 10. Juli 1848.

Kraus, M

*pGB8
V6755R
7.10.48

Wie die Aula und der Professor Füster
aufgesessen sind, oder Wie die Versammlung am 7.
d. M. in der Aula und Prof. Füster hinters
Licht geführt wurde, oder die Schweinfurter
Juden, welche New=York nie gesehen haben,
schenken als Deputirte aus Amerika den Studenten
30 fl. und versprachen 8000 Dollars.
[Wien]Gedruckt bei M.Lell.[1848]
broadside. 38x22.5cm.
Another issue is unsigned.

[Kraus, M   ]

*pGB8
V6755R
7.10.48

Wie die Aula und der Professor Füster
aufgesessen sind, oder Wie die Versammlung am 7.
d. M. und Prof. Füster hinters
Licht geführt wurde, oder die Schweinfurter
Juden, welche New=York nie gesehen haben,
schenken als Deputirte aus Amerika den Studenten
30 fl. und versprachen 8000 Dollars.
[Wien]Gedruckt bei M.Lell.[1848]
broadside. 38x23cm.
Another issue   is signed: M. Kraus.

---

*GB8
V6755R
7.10.48

Radetzky und die grosse Feierlichkeit in
Verona.
[Wien,1848]

folder([4]p.) 23x19cm.
Imprint on p.[4]: Gedruckt und zu haben bei
Leopold Grund, am Stephansplatz im Zwettelhofe.

---

*pGB8
V6755R
7.10.48

Radetzky und sein heldenmüthiger Machtspruch.
[Wien]Gedruckt und zu haben bei Leopold Grund
am Stephansplatze im Zwettelhofe.[1848]

[2]p. 36.5x22.5cm.
Caption title; imprint on p.[2].

Vienna. Sicherheits-Ausschuss.

*pGB8
V6755R
7.10.48

Kundmachung. Da neuerdings von mehreren Seiten
angezeigt wurde, dass bei mehreren Fabrikanten,
Handwerkern und Gewerbetreibenden Arbeiter und
Arbeiterinnen benöthiget werden ...
[Wien]Aus der k.k.Hof= und Staats=Druckerei.
[1848]

broadside. 44.5x29cm.
Dated: Wien am 10. Juli 1848.

Vienna. Sicherheits-Ausschuss.

*pGB8
V6755R
7.10.48

Verordnung. Aus Anlass der am heutigen Tage
stattgefundenen sehr bedauerlichen Störungen der
Accordarbeiter im Prater bei Verrichtung ihrer
Arbeit ...
[Wien]Aus der k.k.Hof= und Staatsdruckerei.
[1848]

broadside. 44.5x29cm.
Dated: Wien am 10. Juli 1848.

Austria. Reichstag, 1848-1849.

*pGB8
V6755R
7.11.48

Protokoll der zweiten vorberathenden Sitzung
der constituirenden Reichs=Versammlung am 11.
Juli 1848.
[Wien]Aus der k.k.Hof= und Staatsdruckerei.
[1848]

broadside. 38x23cm.

Kossuth, Lajos, 1802-1894.

*GB8
V6755R
7.11.48

Kossuth's begeisterungsvolle Rede, gehalten am
11. Juli 1848 im Unterhause vor den zahlreich
versammelten Repräsentanten.
Pressburg,1848.Gedruckt bei Franz Edlen v.
Schmid.

folder([3]p.) 31.5x21cm.
Caption title; imprint on p.[3].

*pGB8
V6755R
7.11.48

Vienna. Sicherheits-Ausschuss.
Kundmachung. Am 13. d. M. wird ein nach
Galizien bestimmter Chargen-Transport von
Koudelka Infanterie in Wien eintreffen ...
[Wien]Aus der k.k.Hof= und Staatsdruckerei.
[1848]

broadside. 44.5x28.5cm.
Dated: Wien am 11. Juli 1848.

---

*pGB8
V6755R
7.12.48

Vienna. Nationalgarde.
Der Verwaltungsrath an die gesammte
Nationalgarde Wiens.
[Wien]Aus der k.k.Hof= und Staatsdruckerei.
[1848]

broadside. 44.5x28.5cm.
Dated & signed: Wien den 12. Juli 1848. Vom
Verwaltungsrathe der Wiener Nationalgarde.

---

*pGB8
V6755R
7.12.48

Austria. Reichstag, 1848-1849.
Protokoll der dritten vorberathenden Sitzung
der constituirenden Reichs=Versammlung am 12.
Juli 1848.
[Wien]Aus der k.k.Hof= und Staatsdruckerei.
[1848]

broadside. 38x23cm.

---

*pGB8
V6755R
7.12.48

Vienna. Sicherheits-Ausschuss.
Kundmachung. Zur Verstärkung der Armee in
Italien werden über Anordnung des k. k. Kriegs=
Ministeriums nachbenannte galizische erste
Landwehr=Bataillons ... in Wien ... eintreffen
...
[Wien]Aus der k.k.Hof= und Staatsdruckerei.
[1848]

broadside. 44.5x28.5cm.
Dated: Wien am 12. Juli 1848.

---

*pGB8
V6755R
7.12.48

Haffner, Karl, 1804-1876.
Bekanntmachung. Bezüglich aller Punkte des am
7 d. M. gegen mich gerichteten Maueranschlags
...
[Wien,1848]

broadside. 38x46cm.
Dated: Wien, den 12. Juli 1848.
Large folio sheet.

---

*pGB8
V6755R
7.13.48

Vienna. Nationalgarde.
Berichtigung. Es hatte sich eine Schaar
zusammen gefunden, welche beabsichtigte,
sich mit dem Abzeichen eines Todtenkopfes als
Todtenkopf=Legion zu organisiren ...
[Wien]Aus der k.k.Hof= und Staatsdruckerei.
[1848]

broadside. 38x23cm.
Dated & signed: Wien den 13. Juli 1848.
Pannasch, Ober=Commandant der Nationalgarde.

---

*GB8
V6755R
7.12.48

Haffner, Karl, 1804-1876.
Bekanntmachung. Bezüglich aller Punkte des
am 7. d. M. gegen mich gerichteten
Maueranschlags ...
[Wien,1848]

broadside. 21x18cm.
Dated: Wien, den 12. Juli 1848.
Small quarto sheet.

---

*pGB8
V6755R
7.13.48

Vienna. Nationalgarde.
Kundmachung. Die Eröffnung des Reichstages
rückt heran ...
[Wien]Aus der k.k.Hof= und Staatsdruckerei.
[1848]

broadside. 44.5x57cm.
Dated & signed: Wien den 13. Juli 1848.
Pannasch, Ober=Commandant der Nationalgarde.

---

*pGB8
V6755R
7.12.48

Tory, S
Ausserordentliches Blatt! Entdeckte
Verrätherei der Rebellen Windischgrätz. Seine
Drohung mit einer 20,000 Mann starken Armee.
Schaudervolle Aufschlüsse aus den hinter-
lassenen Akten des gestürzten Ministers.
[Wien]Zu haben im Verschleissgewölbe,Stadt,
Kölnerhofgasse Nr.730.Gedruckt bei Leop.Sommer.
[1848]

broadside. 42x26cm.
Dated in contemporary ms.: 12 July 848.

---

*pGB8
V6755R
7.13.48

Vienna. Nationalgarde.
Nachtrag zum Tagsbefehle vom 13. Juli 1848.
[Wien]Aus der k.k.Hof= und Staatsdruckerei.
[1848]

broadside. 38x23cm.
Signed: Pannasch, Ober=Commandant der
Nationalgarde.

*pGB8
V6755R
7.13.48

Vienna. Sicherheits-Ausschuss.
An die Bevölkerung Wiens. Die Verletzungen
der öffentlichen Sittlichkeit, so wie die
Aufreizung und Beunruhigung der Gemüther
durch Placate und Flugschriften ...
[Wien]Aus der k.k.Hof= und Staatsdruckerei.
[1848]

broadside. 38.5x23.5cm.
Dated: Wien den 13. Juli 1848.

---

*pGB8
V6755R
7.13.48

Vienna. Sicherheits-Ausschuss.
Zur Kundmachung vom 23. Juni 1848
anzuschliessen.
[Wien]Aus der k.k.Hof= und Staatsdruckerei.
[1848]

broadside. 38x23cm.
Dated: Wien am 13. Juli 1848.

---

*pGB8
V6755R
7.13.48

Vienna. Sicherheits-Ausschuss.
Kundmachung. Da das auf den 16., 17. und 18.
d. M. angekündigte Constitutions=Fest im Prater
nur eine Privat=Speculation ... beabsichtigt
war ...
[Wien]Aus der k.k.Hof= und Staats=Druckerei.
[1848]

broadside. 44.5x57cm.
Dated: Wien am 13. Juli 1848.

---

*pGB8
V6755R
7.14.48

Austria. Armee. Wiener Garnison.
Bewohner Wien's! Gerüchte werden ausgestreut,
dass wir einen Schlag gegen die junge Freiheit
zu führen beabsichtigen ...
[Wien]Gedruckt und daselbst unentgeldlich zu
haben bei U.Klopf sen.und Alexander Eurich,in
der Wollzeile Nr.782.[1848]

broadside. 39.5x24.5cm.
Dated & signed: Am 14. Juli 1848. Die Garnison
von Wien.

---

*pGB8
V6755R
7.13.48

Vienna. Sicherheits-Ausschuss.
Kundmachung. Nach den bestehenden Satzungs=
Vorschriften ist den Fleischhauern nur dann
die Hintangabe einer Zugabe erlaubt, wenn
die Quantität des auf Einmal an eine Partei
verkauften Fleisches das Gewicht von zwei
Pfunden übersteigt ...
[Wien]Aus der k.k.Hof= und Staatsdruckerei.
[1848]

broadside. 44.5x57cm.
Dated: Wien am 13. Juli 1848.

---

*pGB8
V6755R
7.14.48

Haffner, Karl, 1804-1876.
An das Publikum. Ich habe in meinen
Maueranschlägen nie über Bücherführung und
Gebahrung der Aktien-Gelder gegen die Herren
Denemy, Langer, Just und Fröhlich gesprochen ...
[Wien,1848]

broadside. 38x46cm.
Dated: Wien, den 14. Juli 1848.

---

*pGB8
V6755R
7.13.48

Vienna. Sicherheits-Ausschuss.
Kundmachung. Um die bei den gegenwärtigen
Zeitverhältnissen unumgänglich nöthige
Ergänzung und Vermehrung der Armee ...
[Wien]Aus der k.k.Hof= und Staatsdruckerei.
[1848]

broadside. 38x23cm.
Dated: Wien den 13. Juli 1848.

---

*pGB8
V6755R
7.14.48

Lichtenstern, Ludwig.
Nur Wahrheit!
[Wien]Aus der k.k.Hof= und Staatsdruckerei.
[1848]

broadside. 38x23cm.
Dated in contemporary ms. on verso: 14
Juli 848.

---

*pGB8
V6755R
7.13.48

Vienna. Sicherheits-Ausschuss.
Kundmachung. Zur Beruhigung des Publikums,
welches in den letzten Tagen durch Gerüchte der
aufregendsten Art, namentlich aber über
Truppen=Concentrirungen in feindlicher Absicht
...
[Wien]Aus der k.k.Hof= und Staatsdruckerei.
[1848]

broadside. 44.5x29cm.
Dated: Wien am 13. Juli 1848.

---

*GB8
V6755R
7.14.48

[Patatschny, Franz]
Verbrüderung der Generalität des Stabs- und
Ober-Offiziers-Corps der gesammten Wiener
Garnison, als Jubeltag der ruhmgekrönten
Kaiserstadt am Morgen des 14. Juli 1848.
[Wien]Josef Stöckholzer v.Hirschfeld'sche
Officin.[1848]

folder([4]p.) 21.5x14cm.
Signed at end: Franz Patatschny ...
Printed on pink paper.

*pGB8
V6755R
7.14.48

Vienna. Gemeinderat.
An die Bewohner Wiens. Mehr als je machen sich seit einigen Tagen Uebelwollende zum Geschäfte durch künstlich erzeugte und verbreitete Gerüchte die Gemüther zu beängstigen und zu verwirren ...
[Wien]Gedruckt bei Leopold Grund,Hundsthurm Nr.1.[1848]

broadside. 40x50cm.
Signed & dated: Vom Gemeinde-Ausschusse der Stadt Wien, am 14. Juli 1848.

---

*pGB8
V6755R
7.15.48

Austria. Reichstag, 1848-1849.
Protokoll der vierten vorberathenden Sitzung der constituirenden Reichs=Versamlung am 15. Juli 1848. Gegenwärtig 217 Mitglieder.
[Wien]Aus der k.k.Hof= und Staatsdruckerei. [1848]

folder([4]p.) 38.5x23cm.
Caption title; imprint on p.[4].

---

*pGB8
V6755R
7.14.48

Vienna. Nationalgarde.
Tagsbefehl am 14. Juli 1848.
[Wien]Aus der k.k.Hof= und Staatsdruckerei. [1848]

broadside. 44.5x28.5cm.
Dated & signed: Wien am 14. Juli 1848.
Pannasch, Ober=Commandant der Nationalgarde.

---

*pGB8
V6755R
7.15.48

Endlich, Johann Quirin.
Wahrheiten für den Sicherheitsausschuss.
Jn Commission bei J.Bader,Buchhändler in Wien, Stadt,Strobelgasse.Preis: 4 kr.Conv.Münze.
Gedruckt bei A.Dorfmeister.[1848]

broadside. 52.5x42cm.
Signed: J. Q. Endlich.
Antisemitic; refers to his earlier broadside "Der Sicherheitsausschuss unmöglich".

---

*pGB8
V6755R
7.14.48

Vienna. Sicherheits-Ausschuss.
An sämmtliche Compagnien der Nationalgarde, der akademischen Legion und des Bürger=Corps.
[Wien]Aus der k.k.Hof= und Staatsdruckerei. [1848]

broadside. 38x23cm.
Dated: Wien am 14. Juli 1848.

---

*GB8
V6755R
7.15.48

[Fischbach, Jakob Bernhard]
Ehrenvolle Auszeichnung.
[Wien,1848]

folder([3]p.) 29x22.5cm.
Caption title; signed at end: J. B. Fischbach.
Reprinted from nos.188 & 190 of the Wiener Zeitung, 9 & 11 July 1848.
In praise of Franz Dafner's work with the deaf and dumb.

---

*pGB8
V6755R
7.14.48

Vienna. Sicherheits-Ausschuss.
Kundmachung. Vom k. k. niederösterr. General= Commando ist uns eben folgende Mittheilung zugekommen: ...
[Wien]Aus der k.k.Hof= und Staatsdruckerei. [1848]

broadside. 38x23cm.
Dated: Wien am 14. Juli 1848.

---

*GB8
V6755R
7.15.48

[Tirka, D   ]
... Mit Bedauern sehe ich, dass alle meine Vorstellungen und Ersuchen, sich dem National- garde=Dienst mit grösserem Eifer zu unterziehen, bei einem Theil der Compagnie bisher fruchtlos blieben ...
[Wien,1848]

folder([2]p.) 27x22.5cm.
Text begins without caption; at head: IV. Bezirk. 6. Compagnie.
Dated & signed on p.[2]: Wien, den 15. Juli 1848. D. Tirka,   Hauptmann.
In contemporary   ms. at head: 220 Stück. 15. Juli 1848.

---

*pGB8
V6755R
7.15.48

Austria. Reichstag, 1848-1849.
Geschäfts-Ordnung für den constituirenden Reichstag.
[Wien]Aus der k.k.Hof= und Staats=Druckerei. [1848]

12p. 37x22cm.
Caption title; imprint on p.12.

---

*pGB8
V6755R
7.15.48

Vienna. Nationalgarde.
Wien, 1848. 13., 14., 15. März, 13., 14., 15. Juli. Garnison verbrüdert mit der Nationalgarde.
[Wien]Aus der k.k.Hof= und Staatsdruckerei. [1848]

broadside. 38x23cm.
Signed: Vom Ober-Commando der Nationalgarde.

Wiener demokratischer Verein.
*pGB8   Manifest des Wiener demokratischen Vereins.
V6755R   [Wien]Druck von U.Klopf sen.und Alexander
7.15.48   Eurich.[1848]

     broadside. 42x25.5cm.
     Dated: Wien, den 15. Juli 1848.
     Printed within ornamental border.

Vienna. Nationalgarde.
*pGB8   Kundmachung. Es haben mehrere Compagnien der
V6755R   Wiener Nationalgarden Ausweise über unbemittelte
7.17.48   Garden behufs ihrer Betheilung mit Beiträgen
     von eingegangenen Uniformirungsgeldern
     eingegeben ...
     [Wien]Aus der k.k.Hof= und Staatsdruckerei.
     [1848]

     broadside. 38x23cm.
     Dated & signed: Wien am 17. Juli 1848. Vom
     Verwaltungsrathe der Wiener Nationalgarde.

Vienna. Nationalgarde.
*pGB8   Kundmachung. Die gestern vom Ober=Commando
V6755R   erlassene Kundmachung in Betreff der Eröffnung
7.16.48   des Reichstages darf keineswegs beunruhigen ...
     [Wien]Aus der k.k.Hof= und Staatsdruckerei.
     [1848]

     broadside. 44.5x28.5cm.
     Dated & signed: Wien den 16. Juli 1848.
     Pannasch, Ober=Commandant der Nationalgarde.

Vienna. Sicherheits-Ausschuss.
*pGB8   Auf, zum Kampfe! An die freien Patrioten
V6755R   Oesterreichs.
7.17.48   [Wien]Aus der k.k.Hof= und Staatsdruckerei.
     [1848]

     broadside. 44.5x57cm.
     Dated & signed: Wien am 17. Juli 1848. Von
     der Werb-Commission, zusammengesetzt aus dem
     Sicherheits- und Gemeinde-Ausschusse, dann dem
     k. k. Militär.
     Seeking recruits for the war in Italy.

Austria. Reichstag, 1848-1849.
*pGB8   Protokoll der fünften vorberathenden Sitzung
V6755R   der constituirenden Reichs=Versammlung am 17.
7.17.48   Juli 1848.
     [Wien]Aus der k.k.Hof= und Staatsdruckerei.
     [1848]

     folder([3]p.) 38.5x23cm.
     Caption title; imprint on p.[3].

Vienna. Sicherheits-Ausschuss.
*pGB8   Kundmachung. Da dem seit einiger Zeit
V6755R   überhandnehmenden Bettler=Unfuge kräftigst
7.17.48   gesteuert werden muss ...
     [Wien]Aus der k.k.Hof= und Staatsdruckerei.
     [1848]

     broadside. 38x22.5cm.
     Dated: Wien am 17. Juli 1848.

Austria, Lower. Laws, statutes, etc.,
*pGB8   1835-1848 (Ferdinand I)
V6755R   ... Circulare der k. k. Landesregierung im
7.17.48   Erzherzogthume Oesterreich unter der Enns.
     Bestimmung des Postrittgeldes für den zweiten
     Semester 1848.
     [Wien]Aus der k.k.Hof= und Staatsdruckerei.
     [1848]

     broadside. 38x23cm.
     At head: Nr.34282.
     Dated: Wien am 17. Juli 1848.

Austria. Reichstag, 1848-1849.
*pGB8   Protokoll der sechsten vorberathenden
V6755R   Sitzung der constituirenden Reichs=
7.18.48   Versammlung am 18. Juli 1848.
     [Wien]Aus der k.k.Hof= und Staatsdruckerei.
     [1848]

     broadside. 38.5x23.5cm.

[Sammer, Joachim]
*pGB8   Zur Wahrung der Menschenrechte! Zeitgemässer
V6755R   Vorschlag. Dem hohen Reichs=Parlamente zur
7.17.48   Berücksichtigung unterbreitet.
     [Wien]Gedruckt bei Anton Benko.[1848]

     [2]p. 39.5x25cm.
     Caption title; imprint on p.[2]; dated & signed
     at end: Wien, am 17. July 1848. Joachim Sammer,
     m/p. Privilegiums-Inhaber, Josephstadt Nr.57.

Austria, Lower.
*pGB8   Kundmachung. Da von dem hohen Ministerium des
V6755R   Innern im Einverständnisse mit dem Kriegs-
7.18.48   ministerium eine freiwillige Werbung für die
     Linientruppen angeordnet worden ist ...
     [Wien]Aus der k.k.Hof= und Staatsdruckerei.
     [1848]

     broadside. 45x57cm.
     Dated & signed: Wien am 18. Juli 1848. Von
     der k. k. niederöster. Landesregierung.

*pGB8
V6755R
7.18.48

Erzherzog Johann und der Gruss Deutschlands.
[Wien]Gedruckt bei M.Lell.[1848]

broadside. 38x23cm.

---

*pGB8
V6755R
7.18.48

Johann, archduke of Austria, 1782-1859.
An die Bewohner Wiens. In der Stunde des
Scheidens aus euerer Mitte in dem Augenblicke
wo eine unabweisliche Pflicht mich an den
Antritt meines Amtes als deutscher Reichsverwerer
mahnt ...
[Wien]Aus der k.k.Staatsdruckerei.[1848]

broadside. 44.5x56.5cm.

---

*GB8
V6755R
7.18.48

[Mautner, Josef]
Feierlicher Empfang der erlauchten Gemalin
Sr. k. k. Hoheit des Erzherzogs Johann, am 18.
Juli 1848.
[Wien]Gedruckt bei J.B.Wallishausser.[1848]

[2]p. 26.5x21cm.
Caption title; imprint on p.[2]; signed at
end: Josef Mautner, Garde der 3. Comp. 1. Bez.

---

*pGB8
V6755R
7.18.48

... Offenes Sendschreiben an den Kaiser
von Oesterreich.
[Wien]Druck von U.Klopf sen.und Alexander
Eurich.[1848]

[2]p. 39.5x25cm.
Caption title; imprint on p.[2]; at head of
title: Auszug aus den politischen literarischen
Tagsblatte Nr. 3 Gold und Larve.
Dated & signed at end: Wien, im fünften Monate
der Befreiung. Ein Mann aus dem Volke.
Asking the Emperor's return to Vienna.

---

*pGB8
V6755R
7.18.48

Vienna. Gemeinderat.
An die Bewohner Wiens. Durchdrungen von der
Nothwendigkeit, die zur Wahrung der Sicherheit
der Person und des Eigenthumes berufenen Behörden
auf volksthümliche Art in Wirksamkeit zu setzen
...
[Wien]Aus der k.k.Hof= und Staatsdruckerei.
[1848]

broadside. 44.5x56.5cm.
Dated: Wien am 18. Juli 1848.
Another edition has number at head & is
without imprint.

---

*pGB8
V6755R
7.18.48

Vienna. Gemeinderat.
... An die Bewohner Wiens. Durchdrungen von
der Nothwendigkeit, die zur Wahrung der
Sicherheit der Person und des Eigenthumes
berufenen Behörden auf volksthümliche Art
in Wirksamkeit zu setzen ...
[Wien,1848]

broadside. 38x46.5cm.
At head: Zu Nro. 10628.
Dated: Wien am 18. Juli 1848.
Another edition is without number at head &
has imprint.

---

*pGB8
V6755R
7.19.48

Alter Ego, pseud.
Minister des Cultus. Prof. Füster.
[Wien]Gedruckt bei M.Lell.[1848]

broadside. 38.5x23cm.
Signed: Alter Ego.

---

*pGB8
V6755R
7.19.48

Austria. Reichstag, 1848-1849.
Protokoll der siebenten Sitzung der
constituirenden Reichs=Versammlung am 19.
Juli 1848.
[Wien]Aus der k.k.Hof= und Staatsdruckerei.
[1848]

[2]p. 38x23cm.
Caption title; imprint on p.[2].

---

*pGB8
V6755R
7.19.48

Austria. Reichstag, 1848-1849.
Zweites Verzeichniss der bis 19. Juli 1848
sich gemeldeten Abgeordneten zum
constituirenden Reichstage.
[Wien]Aus der k.k.Hof= und Staatsdruckerei.
[1848]

folder([3]p.) 37.5x23cm.
Caption title; imprint on p.[3].

---

*pGB8
V6755R
7.19.48

Vienna. Magistrat.
Kundmachung. Durch den Austritt eines für
das Stubenviertel gewählten Gemeinde-
Ausschusses der Stadt Wien ist die neue Wahl
eines solchen Mitgliedes nothwendig geworden ...
[Wien,1848]

broadside. 39.5x25cm.
Signed & dated: Vom Magistrate der Stadt
Wien am 19. Juli 1848.

1848 AUSTRIAN REVOLUTIONARY BROADSIDES AND PAMPHLETS

*pGB8
V6755R
7.19.48

Vienna. Magistrat.
Kundmachung. Durch den Austritt eines für die Gemeinde Alservorstadt gewählten Gemeinde-Ausschusses der Stadt Wien ist die neue Wahl eines solchen Mitgliedes nothwendig geworden ...
[Wien,1848]

broadside. 40x25cm.
Signed & dated: Vom Magistrate der Stadt Wien am 19. Juli 1848.

*pGB8
V6755R
7.20.48

Austria. Reichstag, 1848-1849.
Protokoll der achten Sitzung der constituirenden Reichs-Versammlung am 20. Juli 1848.
[Wien]Aus der k.k.Hof- und Staatsdruckerei. [1848]

[2]p. 38x23cm.
Caption title; imprint on p.[2].

*pGB8
V6755R
7.19.48

Vienna. Nationalgarde.
Der Verwaltungsrath an die gesammte Nationalgarde Wiens. Dem Verwaltungsrathe wurde die Mittheilung gemacht, dass einige Bezirks-Chefs der Nationalgarde die Absicht hegen, bleibende Abzeichen für sämmtliche Garden eingeführt zu sehen ...
[Wien]Aus der k.k.Hof- und Staatsdruckerei. [1848]

broadside. 38x22.5cm.
Dated: Wien am 19. Juli 1848.

*pGB8
V6755R
7.20.48

Letztes Wort an den Kaiser!
[Wien]Gedruckt und zu haben bei U.Klopf sen. und Alexander Eurich.[1848]
[2]p. 40x25cm.
Caption title; imprint on p.[2]; signed at end: C. M., Akademiker.
Page [1] printed within border of type-ornaments.

*pGB8
V6755R
7.19.48

Vienna. Sicherheits-Ausschuss.
Kundmachung. In Folge einer Mittheilung des General-Commando's kann die Artillerie-Division Nr. 113 erst am 20. d. M. von Prag mittelst Eisenbahn in Marsch gesetzt werden ...
[Wien]Aus der k.k.Hof- und Staatsdruckerei. [1848]

broadside. 38x23cm.
Dated: Wien am 19. Juli 1848.

*pGB8
V6755R
7.20.48

Scheibe, Theodor, 1820-1881.
Minister Schwarzer, ehemaliger Kipfelbäcker und seine Todfeinde.
[Wien]Zu haben im Verlagsgewölbe in der Stadt Parisergasse,Nro.411.[1848]

broadside. 39x25cm.

*pGB8
V6755R
7.19.48

Vienna. Sicherheits-Ausschuss.
Kundmachung. Nachdem von den Arbeitsplätzen, und zwar vorzüglich aus dem Prater und der Brigittenau, wiederholt von ehrenwerthen Arbeitern diesem Ausschusse Anzeigen zugekommen sind, welche theils Beschwerden wegen des unbefugten Verkaufes von Branntwein enthalten ...
[Wien]Aus der k.k.Hof- und Staatsdruckerei. [1848]

broadside. 38x23cm.
Dated: Wien am 19. Juli 1848.

*pGB8
V6755R
7.20.48

Vereinigung der hohen und höchsten Generalität des ganzen Officiercorps und der gesammten Mannschaft, mit den Bürgern, Nationalgarden und Studenten, wodurch wir eine der grössten Schlachten gewonnen haben.
[Wien]Gedruckt und zu haben bei U.Klopf sen.und Alexander Eurich.[1848]
[2]p. 40x25cm.
Caption title; imprint on p.[2].

*GB8
V6755R
7.19.48

Waldschütz, Johann Nepomuk.
An meinen Kameraden Herrn Ignaz Höbert, bei Ueberreichung eines Ehrensäbels am 19. Juli 1848.
[Wien,1848]

broadside. 22x13.5cm.
Helfert (Wiener Parnass) 1458.

*pGB8
V6755R
7.20.48

Vienna. Sicherheits-Ausschuss.
Kundmachung. Von Seite des gefertigten Ausschusses wird bekannt gegeben, dass ein für den 13. und 14. August durch Herrn Eckstein angekündetes "Wiener Brigittenauer Volksfest" ...
[Wien]Aus der k.k.Hof- und Staatsdruckerei. [1848]

broadside. 38x23cm.
Dated: Wien am 20. Juli 1848.

*pGB8
V6755R
7.21.48

Austria. Reichstag, 1848-1849.
Programm der feierlichen Reichstags-Eröffnung.
[Wien]Aus der k.k.Hof= und Staatsdruckerei.
[1848]

broadside. 44.5x28.5cm.

*pGB8
V6755R
7.22.48

Johann, archduke of Austria, 1782-1859.
Die feierliche Eröffnung des Reichstages am
22. Juli 1848, die Thronrede des Erzherzog
Johann und die Antwort des Präsidenten des
constituirenden Reichstages.
[Wien]Gedruckt bei U.Klopf sen.und Alexander
Eurich,in der Wollzeile Nr.782.[1848]
[2]p. 39.5x25cm.
Caption title; imprint on p.[2].

*GB8
V6755R
7.21.48

Freunde der constitutionellen Ordnung, Vienna.
Tendenz des Vereins der Freunde der
gesetzlichen Ordnung und wahren Freiheit im
constitutionellen Staatsleben, unter dem
Titel: Freunde der constitutionellen Ordnung.
[Wien,1848]
[2]p. 26.5x22cm.
Caption title; dated & signed at end: Wien,
den 21. Juli 1848. J. S. Hohenblum und Dr. Joh.
Hoffer, als Gründer des Vereins.

*pGB8
V6755R
7.22.48

Johann, archduke of Austria, 1782-1859.
Thronrede Seiner k. k. Hoheit des
Erzherzogs Johann bei Eröffnung des
constituirenden Reichstages am 22. Juli 1848.
[Wien]K.k.Hofbuchdruckerei des Leop.Sommer.
[1848]
broadside. 44.5x28.5cm.

*pGB8
V6755R
7.21.48

Vienna. Sicherheits-Ausschuss.
Kundmachung. Vorfälle sehr betrübender Art
und freier Männer völlig unwürdig haben am
gestrigen Tage und Nachts darauf Statt gefunden
...
[Wien]Aus der k.k.Hof= und Staatsdruckerei.
[1848]
broadside. 38x23cm.
Dated: Wien am 21. Juli 1848.

*pGB8
V6755R
7.22.48

Johann, archduke of Austria, 1782-1859.
... Die Thronrede, womit Erzherzog Johann
den constituirenden Reichstag eröffnet hat,
und die Antwortsrede des Präsidenten.
[Wien]Gedruckt bei Franz Edlen von Schmid.
[1848]
broadside. 45.5x29cm.
At head: Extra=Beilage zur Constitution am
22. Juli 1848.

*pGB8
V6755R
7.22.48

Austria. Reichstag, 1848-1849.
Protokoll der Sitzung am 22. Juli 1848 zur
Eröffnung des constituirenden Reichstages.
[Wien]Aus der k.k.Hof= und Staatsdruckerei.
[1848]
folder([4]p.) 38x23cm.
Caption title; imprint on p.[4].

*pGB8
V6755R
7.22.48

Programm zu der am 24ten d. M. abzuhaltenden
Fahnenweihe der Bezirke N.° 1,2,3,4, und N.° 12,
dann der National Garde Cavallerie Division II.
[Wien,1848]
folder([3]p.) 37.5x23cm.
Caption title.
Reproduced from ms. copy.

*GB8
V6755R
7.22.48

Johann, archduke of Austria, 1782-1859.
Feierliche Eröffnung des ersten
österreichischen constituirenden Reichstages,
Thronrede Sr. kaiserl. Hoheit des
Stellvertreters Sr. Majestät des Kaisers,
Erzherzog Johann, Reichsverweser von Deutschland.
[Wien]Gedruckt und zu haben bei Leop.Grund,
am Stephansplatz im Zwettelhofe.[1848]
[2]p. 29.5x17cm.
Caption title; imprint on p.[2].
Includes (p.[2]) the reply to the Archduke's
speech by Franz Schmitt, president of the
Reichstag.

*pGB8
V6755R
7.22.48

Wiener demokratischer Verein.
Adresse des Wiener demokratischen Vereines an
die Gemeinden des V. U. M. B. Hausleiten,
Wolfpassing, Seizersdorf, Goldgeben,
Königsbrunn, Unterabtsdorf, Hippersdorf,
Mitterstockstall, Unterstockstall,
Zaustenberg, Inkersdorf und Stetteldorf.
[Wien,1848]
broadside. 39.5x25cm.
Dated: Wien den 22. Juli 1848.

*pGB8
V6755R
7.23.48

Vienna. Sicherheits-Ausschuss.
Kundmachung. Laut Anzeige des niederöster.
General=Commando wird am 27. d. M. ein nach
Italien bestimmter Ergänzungs=Transport ...
hierorts eintreffen ...
[Wien]Aus der k.k.Hof= und Staatsdruckerei.
[1848]

broadside. 38x23cm.
Dated: Wien am 23. Juli 1848.

*pGB8
V6755R
7.25.48

Scheibe, Theodor, 1820-1881.
Der Siegeskourier! Radetzky's glänzender Sieg
bei Mantua nebst der Trauerpost: die
Gefangennehmung des kühnen Fürsten
Liechtenstein's.
[Wien]Im Verlagsgewölbe,Kölnerhofgasse Nr.730.
Gedruckt bei Leop.Sommer.[1848]

broadside. 42x26cm.

*pGB8
V6755R
7.24.48

Austria. Reichstag, 1848-1849.
Begründung zu dem Gesetzes=Entwurfe I[-II].
[Wien]Aus der k.k.Hof= und Staatsdruckerei.
[1848]

folder([3]p.) 41x25cm.
Caption title; imprint on p.[3]; dated on p.
[2]: Wien am 24. Juli 1848.

*pGB8
V6755R
7.25.48

Vienna. Sicherheits-Ausschuss.
Dank=Adresse an die Bürgerschaft und Nationalgarde von Nikolsburg.
[Wien]Aus der k.k.Hof= und Staatsdruckerei.
[1848]

broadside. 38x23cm.
Dated: Wien am 25. Juli 1848.

*pGB8
V6755R
7.24.48

Austria. Reichstag, 1848-1849.
Protokoll der Sitzung der constituirenden
Reichs=Versammlung am 24. Juli 1848.
[Wien]Aus der k.k.Hof= und Staatsdruckerei.
[1848]

folder([4]p.) 37.5x23cm.
Caption title; imprint on p.[4].

*pGB8
V6755R
7.26.48

Austria. Reichstag, 1848-1849.
Protokoll der Sitzung der constituirenden
Reichs=Versammlung am 26. Juli 1848.
[Wien]Aus der k.k.Hof= und Staatsdruckerei.
[1848]

folder([3]p.) 38x23cm.
Caption title; imprint on p.[3].

*GB8
V6755R
7.24.48

Rolletschek, Ignaz.
Worte, gesprochen bei der Fahnen=Weihe des
ersten Bataillons achten Bezirks am 24. Juli
1848. Von Ignaz Rolletschek ...
Wien,1848.K.k.Hof=buchdruckerei des L.Sommer
(vorm.Strauss).

folder([4]p.) 28x22.5cm.

*pGB8
V6755R
7.27.48

Andenken zur Fahnen-Weihe des XI. Bezirks
Alservorstadt Donnerstag den 27. Juli 1848.
K.k.Hofbuchdruckerei des Leop.Sommer in Wien.
[1848]

broadside. 41x29cm.
Helfert (Wiener Parnass) 1497.
According to Helfert, also published with
title: Der hohen deutschen Frau Baronin Anna von
Brandhof als Fahnenmutter ...

*pGB8
V6755R
7.25.48

Austria. Reichstag, 1848-1849.
Protokoll der Sitzung der constituirenden
Reichs=Versammlung am 25. Juli 1848.
[Wien]Aus der k.k.Hof= und Staatsdruckerei.
[1848]

[5]p. 37x22.5cm.
Caption title; imprint on p.[5].

*pGB8
V6755R
7.27.48

Austria. Reichstag, 1848-1849.
Protokoll der Sitzung der constituirenden
Reichs=Versammlung am 27. Juli 1848.
[Wien]Aus der k.k.Hof= und Staatsdruckerei.
[1848]

folder([3]p.) 38x23cm.
Caption title; imprint on p.[3].

*pGB8
V6755R
7.27.48

Der blessirte Student und das hohe deutsche
Ehepaar.
Wien,Gedruckt im Juli 1848 bei J.N.Fridrich,
Josephstadt Langegasse Nr.58.

[2]p. 38x23cm.
Caption title; imprint on p.[2]; signed:
F. B...f.
Description of the ceremonies attending the
reception of Archduke Johann and his wife in
Schönbrunn.

---

*pGB8
V6755R
7.28.48

Der Aufstand und Feuerlärm im Strafhause.
[Wien]Gedruckt bei M.Lell.[1848]

broadside. 38x23cm.
Signed: Das Strafhaus=Aufsichtspersonale.

---

*GB8
V6755R
7.27.48

Scheibe, Theodor, 1820-1881.
... Baronin Brandhof als Erzherzogin Anna von
Oestreich, oder: Was die gestrige Nacht in
Schönbrunn und Hietzing statt gefunden hat.
[Wien]Gedruckt bei Leop.Sommer.[1848]
broadside. 26x21cm.
Signed: Im Verlagsgewölbe, Kölnerhofgasse Nr.
730. Scheibe.
At head: Extra=Blatt!

---

*pGB8
V6755R
7.28.48

Austria. Ministerium für öffentliche Arbeiten.
Kundmachung. Um Gleichmässigkeit und
Regelmässigkeit bei allen öffentlichen Arbeiten
zu erzielen, wird folgende Arbeiter-Ordnung,
welche vom 3. Juli 1848 angefangen zur
allgemeinen Richtschnur zu dienen hat, hiermit
bekannt gemacht.
[Wien]Aus der k.k.Hof= und Staats=Druckerei.
[1848]

broadside. 45x29cm.
Dated: Wien den 28. Juli 1848.
A republication of the proclamation of
28 June.

---

*pGB8
V6755R
7.27.48

Vienna. Magistrat.
Kundmachung. Nachdem durch den Austritt eines
für das Schottenviertel in der Stadt gewählten
Gemeinde=Ausschusses die neue Wahl eines solchen
Mitgliedes ...
[Wien,1848]
folder([3]p.) 42x26cm.
Caption title; signed & dated: Vom Magistrate
der Stadt Wien am 27. Juli 1848.

---

*pGB8
V6755R
7.28.48

Austria. Reichstag, 1848-1849.
Protokoll der Sitzung der constituirenden
Reichs=Versammlung am 28. Juli 1848.
[Wien]Aus der k.k.Hof- und Staatsdruckerei.
[1848]

broadside. 38x22.5cm.

---

*pGB8
V6755R
7.27.48

Vienna. Magistrat.
Kundmachung. Nachdem durch den Austritt eines
für das Wimmerviertel in der Stadt gewählten
Gemeinde=Ausschusses die neue Wahl eines solchen
Mitgliedes ...
[Wien,1848]
folder([3]p.) 41x26cm.
Caption title; signed & dated: Vom Magistrate
der Stadt Wien am 27. Juli 1848.

---

*pGB8
V6755R
7.28.48

Croatia-Slavonia. Vienna deputies, 1848.
Die Kroaten und Slawonier an die Voelker
Oesterreichs.
[Wien,1848]
folder([4]p.) 39x24.5cm.
Caption title; dated & signed at end: Wien,
im Juli 1848. Die kroatisch-slawonischen
Deputirten.
In contemporary ms. at head: Den 28 July 1848
aus der Hand des Herrn Banus Jélachich erhalten.

---

*pGB8
V6755R
7.27.48

Vienna. Sicherheits-Ausschuss.
Bewohner Wiens! Der gefertigte Ausschuss hat
beschlossen, in dem Augenblicke, wo die
Abgeordneten aller österreichischen Völker hier
im Reichstage versammelt sind, eine weihevolle
Todtenfeier für die in den Märztagen gefallenen
Vorkämpfer unserer Freiheit abzuhalten ...
[Wien]Aus der k.k.Hof= und Staatsdruckerei.
[1848]

broadside. 44.5x57cm.
Dated: Wien am 27. Juli 1848.

---

*pGB8
V6755R
7.28.48

[Feldschreier, X   ]
Radetzky, Liechtenstein und Susan. Die
letzten Siege in Italien bei Rivoli,
Sommacampagna, Vallegio, Pastrengo Castelnuovo
&c. &c.
[Wien]Gedruckt und zu haben bei L.Grund,
Stephansplatz im Zwettelhof.[1848]

[2]p. 1 illus. 36.5x22.5cm.
Caption title; imprint on p.[2]; signed at end:
X. Feldschreier.

*pGB8
V6755R
7.28.48

Füster, Anton, 1808-1881.
   Rede am Trauerfeste für die in den Märztagen
Gefallenen. Gehalten von Professor Dr. Anton
Füster am 28. Juli 1848.
   [Wien]Gedruckt bei Leop.Sommer(vormals Strauss).
[1848]
    [2]p. 41.5x26cm.
    Caption title; imprint on p.[2].

---

*pGB8
V6755R
7.28.48

Vienna. Sicherheits-Ausschuss.
   Bewohner Wiens! Die Feinde der neuen Gestaltung
der Dinge, durch die Fruchtlosigkeit der früheren
Versuche zur Herbeiführung eines gesetzlosen
Zustandes nicht eingeschüchtert, suchen in
letzterer Zeit auf die mannigfaltigste Art
Misstrauen und Hass gegen einen Theil unserer
Mitbürger, die Juden, zu säen ...
   [Wien]Aus der k.k.Hof= und Staatsdruckerei.
[1848]
    broadside. 44.5x57cm.
    Dated: Wien am   28. Juli 1848.

---

*pGB8
V6755R
7.28.48

Scheibe, Theodor, 1820-1881.
   ... Wiens nächtliche Aufregung am 28. Juli
und die Kathastrofe des grossen slavischen
Fackelzuges zu Ehren Jellachichs.
   [Wien]Gedruckt bei Leop.Sommer.[1848]
    broadside. 42x26.5cm.
    Signed: Im Verlagsgewölbe, Kölnerhofgasse Nr.
730. Scheibe.
    At head: Extra=Blatt!

---

*pGB8
V6755R
7.28.48

Vienna. Sicherheits-Ausschuss.
   Brave Arbeiter! Liebe Mitbürger! In einer, in
mehrfacher Beziehung ungesetzlichen, gedruckten
Einladung hat ein uns Unbekannter den männlichen
Theil der hiesigen Arbeiter auf den 30. Juli d.
J. zu einer Versammlung im Freien zusammen-
berufen ...
   [Wien]Aus der k.k.Hof= und Staatsdruckerei.
[1848]
    broadside. 38x23cm.
    Dated: Wien den 28. Juli 1848.

---

*pGB8
V6755R
7.28.48

Vienna. Nationalgarde.
   Der Verwaltungsrath an die gesammte Nationalgarde Wiens. Der Verwaltungsrath wurde durch
das Ober=Commando am 26. July in Kenntniss
gesetzt: dass der Sicherheits=Ausschuss eine
Todtenfeier für die in den Märztagen Gefallenen
auf den 28. Juli angeordnet habe ...
   [Wien]Aus der k.k.Hof= und Staatsdruckerei.
[1848]
    broadside. 45x57cm.
    Large folio edition, with imprint.
    Dated: Wien am   28. Juli 1848.

---

*GB8
V6755R
7.29.48

Ausserordentliche telegraphische Depesche an
das Kriegsministerium. Wien, am 29. Juli,
Nachmittags 2 Uhr. Grosser Sieg der
österreichischen Armee unter dem Feldmarschall
Radetzky, über den treulosen König Albert.
   [Wien]Druck von J.Stöckholzer v.Hirschfeld.--
Zu haben im Bureau des Stad[!] "Omnibus",
Liliengasse,Nr.898.[1848]
    broadside. 30x24cm.

---

*pGB8
V6755R
7.28.48

Vienna. Nationalgarde.
   Der Verwaltungsrath an die gesammte National-
garde Wiens. Der Verwaltungsrath wurde durch das
Ober=Commando am 26. Juli in Kenntniss gesetzt:
dass der Sicherheits=Ausschuss eine Todtenfeier
für die in den Märztagen Gefallenen auf den 28.
Juli angeordnet habe ...
   [Wien,1848]
    broadside. 37.5x29cm.
    Small folio edition, without imprint.
    Dated: Wien am 28. Juli 1848.
    Printed on the other side of this sheet is a
    (See next card)

---

*pGB8
V6755R
7.29.48

Austria. Reichstag, 1848-1849.
   Protokoll der Sitzung der constituirenden
Reichs=Versammlung am 29. Juli 1848 Abends.
   [Wien]Aus der k.k.Hof= und Staats=Druckerei.
[1848]
    [2]p. 38x23cm.
    Caption title; imprint on p.[2].

---

*pGB8
V6755R
7.29.48

Vienna. Nationalgarde.   Der Verwaltungsrath ...
   [1848]   (Card 2)
"Kundmachung" of Anton Pannasch, dated 29 July
1848.

Another copy. 37.5x29cm.

---

*pGB8
V6755R
7.29.48

Austria, Lower.
   Kundmachung. Die freiwillige Werbung für die
Linientruppen wird unter den in der
Bekanntmachung vom 18. Juli kundgemachten
Bedingungen Montag, den 31. Juli ...
fortgesetzt werden.
   [Wien]Aus der k.k.Hof= und Staatsdruckerei.
[1848]
    broadside. 44.5x57cm.
    Dated & signed: Wien am 29. Juli 1848. Von der
k. k. niederöster. Landesregierung.

*pGB8
V6755R
7.29.48

Pannasch, Anton, 1789-1855.
Kundmachung. Es ist zur Oeffentlichkeit gelangt, dass ich in Folge der Aufforderung des vereinigten Ausschusses abgedankt hätte ...
[Wien]Aus der k.k.Hof= und Staatsdruckerei. [1848]
broadside. 44.5x57cm.
Dated: Wien den 29. Juli 1848.
Large folio edition, with imprint.

*pGB8
V6755R
7.30.48

Füster, Anton, 1808-1881.
Predigt. Vorgetragen von Professor Dr. Anton Füster beim feierlichen Feldgottesdienste der sämmtlichen Erdarbeiter Wiens am 30. Juli 1848.
[Wien]Gedruckt bei Leop.Sommer(vorm.Strauss). [1848]
[2]p. 41.5x26cm.
Caption title; imprint on p.[2].

*pGB8
V6755R
7.29.48

Pannasch, Anton, 1789-1855.
Kundmachung. Es ist zur Oeffentlichkeit gelangt, dass ich in Folge der Aufforderung des vereinigten Ausschusses abgedankt hätte ...
[Wien,1848]
broadside. 37.5x29cm.
Dated: Wien, den 29. Juli 1848.
Small folio edition, without imprint.
Printed on the other side of this sheet is "Der Verwaltungsrath an die gesammte Nationalgarde Wiens", dated 28 July 1848.

*pGB8
V6755R
7.28.48

Another copy.   37.5x29cm.

*pGB8
V6755R
7.30.48

Pannasch, Anton, 1789-1855.
Tagsbefehl. Am 27. wurde ich durch eine Deputation der Nationalgarde zum Ober= Commandanten erwählt ...
[Wien]Aus der k.k.Hof= und Staatsdruckerei. [1848]
broadside. 44.5x56.5cm.
Submitting his resignation.

*pGB8
V6755R
7.29.48

Vienna. Gemeinderat.
Der Gemeinde=Ausschuss der Stadt Wien an die tapfere österreichische Armee in Italien und ihren Feldherrn.
[Wien,1848]
broadside. 46x57cm.
Signed & dated: Vom Gemeinde-Ausschusse der Haupt- und Residenzstadt Wien, am 29. Juli 1848.
In this edition, without imprint, line 15 of the text has reading "des Deutschen, des Magyaren und Slaven Blut".

*pGB8
V6755R
7.30.48

Scheibe, Theodor, 1820-1881.
Die Abdankung des Nationalgarden-Oberkommandanten Pannasch, welchen das Kind der Revolution besiegte.
[Wien]Gedruckt bei Leop.Sommer.[1848]
broadside. 42x26cm.
Signed: Im Verlagsgewölbe, Kölnerhofgasse Nr. 730. Scheibe.

*pGB8
V6755R
7.29.48

Vienna. Gemeinderat.
Der Gemeinde=Ausschuss der Stadt Wien an die tapfere österreichische Armee in Italien und ihren Feldherrn.
[Wien]Gedruckt bei Leopold Grund,Hundsthurm Nr.1.[1848]
broadside. 46x57cm.
Signed & dated: Vom Gemeinde-Ausschusse der Haupt- und Residenzstadt Wien, am 29. Juli 1848.
In this edition, with imprint, line 15 of the text has reading "des Deutschen, des Magyaren, Slaven und Romanen Blut".

*pGB8
V6755R
7.31.48

Austria. Reichstag, 1848-1849.
Protokoll der Sitzung der constituirenden Reichs=Versammlung am 31. Juli 1848.
[Wien]Aus der k.k.Hof= und Staatsdruckerei. [1848]
[5]p. 37.5x22.5cm.
Caption title; imprint on p.[5].

*pGB8
V6755R
7.30.48

Austria. Reichstag, 1848-1849.
Protokoll der Sitzung der constituirenden Reichs=Versammlung am 30. Juli 1848.
[Wien]Aus der k.k.Hof= und Staatsdruckerei. [1848]
folder([4]p.) 38.5x23cm.
Caption title; imprint on p.[4].

*GB8
V6755R
7.31.48

[Fraporta, F   A   J   ]
Das biedere Wort der vereinten Brünner National-Garde als diese der Wiener-Bürger-National-Garde und Akad. Legion die Schwesterfahne der Verbrüderung überreichte.
Jn Verlag bei Fr.Wimmer in Brünn.[1848]
folder([4]p.) 20.5x13.5cm.
At end: Verlautet von F. A. J. Fraporta, Garde der 1. Comp. II. Bat. der Brünner National=Garde.
Printer's imprint on p.[2]: Druck von C. Winiker.
In contemporary   ms. at head of title: 31. Juli 848.

*pGB8
V6755R
7.31.48

[Freund, Josef, fl.1848]
... Die Juden werden immer zudringlicher!
Hüthet, und aber und abermals hüthet Euch vor der
Juden=Herrschaft!!!
[Wien]Gedruckt bei M.Lell.[1848]
[2]p. 38x23cm.
Dated & signed at end: Wien am 31. Juli 1848.
Josef Freund.
At head: Zu haben bei Jakob Bader, Buchhändler,
Stadt Strobelgasse, Nr. 864. Preis 2 Kr.CM.

*pGB8
V6755R
7.32.48

Austria. Reichstag, 1848-1849.
Der Reichstags-Saal in Wien im Jahre 1848.
[Wien,1848]
broadside. illus.(plan) 44.5x56cm.
Plan of the chamber, with names of the
delegates printed in 6 columns.

*pGB8
V6755R
7.32.48

Aller Neuestes. Der Kaiser kommt——nicht!
Wien,Gedruckt im Juli 1848 bei J.N.Fridrich,
Josephstadt Langegasse Nr.48.
[2]p. 38x23cm.
Caption title; imprint on p.[2].
"Auszug aus dem Demokraten."

*pGB8
V6755R
7.32.48

Beschreibung des Reichstag=Saales in Wien,
und der Ordnung in welcher die Verhandlungen
vorkommen, oder: Was haben wir von dem
Reichstage zu erwarten.
[Wien]Druck von J.Stöckholzer v.Hirschfeld.—
Zu haben im Bureau des "Omnibus,"Stadt,
Liliengasse,Nr.898.[1848]
[2]p. 1 illus. 47.5x30cm.
Caption title; imprint on p.[2].

*pGB8
V6755R
7.32.48

An sämmtliche Herrn der bürgerlichen
Artillerie.
Gedruckt bei Ulrich Klopf sen.und Alexander
Eurich in Wien.[1848]
broadside. 39.5x24.5cm.
Signed: Carl Teich, Ignaz Hafer, Johann Klein
[& 7 others].

*pGB8
V6755R
7.32.48

Brod den Arbeitern, oder die absichtliche
Schwäche des Ministeriums.
[Wien]Gedruckt und zü[!] haben bei U.Klopf
sen.und Alex.Eurich,Wollzeile Nr.782.[1848]
broadside. illus. 40.5x25cm.

*GB8
V6755R
7.32.48

Ausserordentliche Siegesnachricht aus Italien.
[Wien]Druck von J.Stöckholzer v.Hirschfeld.—
Zu haben im Bureau des "Omnibus",Stadt,
Liliengasse,Nr.698.[1848]
broadside. 30.5x24cm.

*pGB8
V6755R
7.32.48

Brunner, ———.
Die Menschenrechte des Arbeiters.
[Wien]Gedruckt bei J.N.Fridrich.[1848]
broadside. 38x23.5cm.
Signed: Brunner, Arbeiter.

*pGB8
V6755R
7.32.48

Austria. Armee. Wiener Garnison.
An den löblichen Verwaltungsrath der
gesammten Nationalgarde Wiens.
[Wien]Aus der k.k.Hof= und Staats=Druckerei.
[1848]
broadside. 44.5x57cm.
Signed by Maximilian von Auersperg as commandant; includes an authorization to publish
signed by Anton Pannasch.

*GB8
V6755R
7.32.48

Der ersten deutschen Frau, Gemahlin des
deutschen Reichsverwesers. Der erhabenen
Fahnenmutter des I. Bataillons, VIII. Bezirkes,
der Wiener Nationalgarde.
[Wien]Gedruckt bei J.P.Sollinger.[1848]
broadside. 30.5x22.5cm.
Helfert (Wiener Parnass) 1326.
Addressed to Baronin Brandhof.

Deutsch, Ignaz, 1808-1881.
*pGB8 ... Ueber die gegenwärtige Gewerbs- und
V6755R Arbeiterfrage und über die Mittel zur
7.32.48 gänzlichen Tilgung der Staatsschuld, gerichtet
an die hohe Reichsversammlung von Ignaz Deutsch,
Fabrikant in Wien.
[Wien,1848].

folder([4]p.) 38.5x29cm.
Caption title; at head: Besondere Beilage zur
Wiener=Zeitung.

○

Fuchsenlied.
*GB8 [Wien]Druck von U.Klopf sen.und Alexander
V6755R Eurich.[1848]
7.32.48
broadside. 21x26cm.
Helfert (Wiener Parnass) 1554.

○

Die Deutsche Flagge (Club), Vienna.
*pGB8 Allgemeine Statuten des Vereines: "Die
V6755R deutsche Flagge."
7.32.48 [1848]Aus der k.k.Hof= und Staatsdruckerei.
[1848]

broadside. 44,5x57cm.
Signed: Die Gründer des Vereines: "Die
deutsche Flagge."

○

Die Geschichte: wie unser Kaiser zum
*pGB8 Deputirten ist gewählt worden. Etwas Lustiges
V6755R in unserer traurigen Zeit, und die
7.32.48 babilonische Sprachenverwirrung am Wiener
Reichstage.
[Wien]Zu haben im Verschleissgewölbe,Stadt,
Kölnerhofgasse Nr.730.Gedruckt bei Leop.Sommer.
[1848]

broadside. 42x26cm.

○

Die Deutsche Flagge (Club), Vienna.
*pGB8 Aufruf zum Vereine: Die deutsche Flagge.
V6755R [Wien]Druck von U.Klopf sen.und Alexander
7.32.48 Eurich.[1848]

broadside. 42x53cm.
Signed: Die Gründer des Vereines: "Die deutsche
Flagge."
On the other side of the sheet is printed
"Provisorische Statuten des Vereines: Die
deutsche Flagge."

○

[Giftnigl, Jeremias, pseud.]
*GB8 Ueber was sich ein ehrlicher Wiener in einem
V6755R Tag 60 Mal giften muss.
7.32.48 [Wien]Druck von J.N.Friedrich Josefstadt,
9angngasse[!] Nr.58.[1848]

folder([4]p.) 27x21cm.
Caption title; imprint on p.[4]; signed at end:
Jeremias Giftnigl.

○

Die Deutsche Flagge (Club), Vienna.
*pGB8 Provisorische Statuten des Vereines: Die
V6755R deutsche Flagge.
7.32.48 [Wien]Gedruckt bei U.Klopf sen.und Alexander
Eurich.[1848]

broadside. 42x53cm.
Signed: Die Gründer des Vereines: "Die deutsche
Flagge."
On the other side of the sheet is printed
"Aufruf zum Vereine: Die deutsche Flagge."

○

Der Graf aus der Fremde. Ein Zeitgedicht.
*pGB8 Nach Schiller's "Mädchen aus der Fremde".
V6755R [Wien]Druck aus A.Dorfmeister's Officin.[1848]
7.32.48
broadside. 39x25cm.
Helfert (Wiener Parnass) 1323.
Signed: Ein Student.
On Bombelles?

○

[Frei, Hanns, pseud.?]
*pGB8 Brief eines Freien an Se. Maj. den
V6755R constitutionellen Bürgerkaiser.
7.32.48 [Wien]Gedruckt bei M.Lell,Leopoldstadt Nr.505.
[1848]

[2]p. 38x23cm.
Caption title; imprint on p.[2]; signed:
Hanns Frei.

○

[Guthfeldberg, ———]
*pGB8 Die Flucht des Königs von Sardinien und die
V6755R Auflösung von 62,349 Italienern.
7.32.48 [Wien]Gedruckt bei U.Klopf sen.und Alexander
Eurich.[1848]

[2]p. 40x25cm.
Caption title; imprint on p.[2]; signed at end:
Guthfeldberg.

○

*pGB8
V6755R
7.32.48

Haas, Georg Emanuel, 1821-1895.
    Triumfbogen jüdischer Nation. Gesetzt von
Georg Emmanuel Haas.
    [Wien]Gedruckt bei M.Lell.[1848]
    [2]p. 38x23cm.
    Caption title; imprint on p.[2].

---

*pGB8
V6755R
7.32.48

Lackner, Johann, fl.1848.
    Was mit einem kais. Kammerdiener in Innsbruck
wegen einem Brief geschehen ist.
    [Wien]Gedruckt bei Franz Edlen von Schmid.
[1848]

    broadside. 34x26cm.

---

*GB8
V6755R
7.32.48

Karschin, Gustav.
    Oestreichs Held. Gedicht von Gustav Karschin,
Musik vom Capellmeister August Pütz. Vorgetragen
von der akademischen National=Liedertafel.
    [Wien,1848]

    broadside. 23x15cm.
    Helfert (Wiener Parnass) 1335.
    On Radetzky.
    Without the music.

---

*pGB8
V6755R
7.32.48

    Der letzte Streich der Camarilla in Innsbruck
    (feindlich gesinnten Hofparthei), und uns're
Schutzwehr!!
    [Wien]Gedruckt bei Josef Ludwig.[1848]

    [2]p. 38x23cm.
    Caption title; imprint on p.[2].

---

*pGB8
V6755R
7.32.48

Krenn, Julius.
    Was müssen wir thun, wenn der Kaiser nicht
kommen will? Eine höchst wichtige Zeitfrage.
    [Wien]Zu haben im Redactions-Locale des
Omnibus:Stadt,Liliengasse Nr.898.Gedruckt bei A.
Dorfmeister.[1848]

    broadside. 42x26.5cm.

---

*pGB8
V6755R
7.32.48

[Meier, ————]
    Erster Theil der neuesten Nachrichten der
braven Wiener Freiwilligen, nebst dem
Schlachtliede des im Kampfe gefallenen Georg
Schwarz, und dem Namens=Verzeichnisse jener
Heldenjünglinge, die sich besonders ausgezeichnet
haben.
    [Wien]Schnellpressendruck von Jos.Stöckholzer
von Hirschfeld.Zu haben im Redaktions=Bureau des
"Omnibus," Stadt,Liliengasse Nr.898.[1848]
    broadside. 47.5x30cm.
                              (See next card)

---

*GB8
V6755R
7.32.48

[Kumenecker, Josef]
    Die ganz neue Beschreibung von der
schrecklichen Mordthat! oder wie einige National=
Gardisten den jüdischen Zeitungsschreiber
Mahler so schaudervoll umgebracht haben.
Offenes Schreiben an das ganze Publikum
insbesonders aber an die h. h. National=Garden
Wiens.
    [Wien]Gedruckt bei Josef Ludwig.[1848]
    folder([4]p.) 24.5x19.5cm.
    Caption title; imprint on p.[4]; signed at end:
Josef Kumenecker   (junior.) National=Garde.

---

*pGB8
V6755R
7.32.48

[Meier, ————]   Erster Theil ... [1848]
                              (Card 2)
    The "Schlachtlied" (5 stanzas at foot) is
recorded by Helfert (Wiener Parnass) 1532.
    A "Zweiter Theil" is signed: Meier.
    On the Italian campaign.
    Dated in contemporary ms.: Juli 848.

---

*pGB8
V6755R
7.32.48

[Lackner, Johann, fl.1848]
    Eine Jesuiten=Predigt aus Innsbruck. Wortgetreu
erzählt durch einen von dort hier Angekommenen.
    [Wien]Gedruckt bei M.Lell.[1848]

    [2]p. 38x24.5cm.
    Caption title; imprint on p.[2]; signed at
end: Johann Lackner, Josefstadt Nr.45.

---

*pGB8
V6755R
7.32.48

Meier, ————.
    Zweiter Theil der neuesten Nachrichten der
braven Wiener Freiwilligen, nebst dem Namens=
Verzeichnisse jener Heldenjünglinge, die sich
besonders ausgezeichnet haben.
    [Wien]Schnellpressendruck von Jos.Stöckholzer
von Hirschfeld.Zu haben im Redaktions=Bureau des
"Omnibus," Stadt,Liliengasse Nr.898.[1848]

    broadside. 43x27cm.
    This part is signed "Meier"; an "Erster Theil"
is unsigned.
    On the Italian   campaign.
    Dated in con-   temporary ms.: Juli 848.

Mihlböck, ———.
*GB8   Weihe eines National=Gardisten.
V6755R   Druck und Eigenthum von Hirschfeld in Wien.
7.32.48   [1848]

    broadside. 22.5x14.5cm.
    Helfert (Wiener Parnass) 1339.

Paul, Ignaz.
*pGB8   Ist Böhmen ein deutsches oder ein slavisches
V6755R   Land? Zur Beherzigung für die Czechen und zur
7.32.48   Aufklärung für Diejenigen, welche nicht
Gelegenheit haben, sich mit Geschichtsstudien zu
befassen. Von Ignaz Paul.
    [Wien]Gedruckt bei Leop.Sommer (vorm.Strauss).
[1848]

    [2]p. 37.5x28.5cm.
    Caption title; imprint on p.[2].
    'Abdruck aus der Zeitschrift "Der Demokrat".'

Napoléon I, emperor of the French, 1769-1821.
*pGB8   Ein historisch=ehrenvolles Document des Kaisers
V6755R   Napoleon an die P. T. Bewohner Wiens.
7.32.48   [Wien]Druck von U.Klopf sen.u.Alex.Eurich.
[1848]

    broadside. 41x26cm.
    Reprinting a proclamation dated "Schönbrunn
den 6ten Nivos Jahr 14" (i.e. 26 Dec. 1805);
preceded & followed by commentary.

[Puff, Ferdinand]
*pGB8   A steirischer Woaldbaua über'n Prinz Hanns'l.
V6755R   A Briaf a seini liaw'n Londsleut.
7.32.48   Zu haben bei Jakob Bader,Buchhändler in Wien,
Stadt,Strobelgasse.Druck aus A.Dorfmeister's
Officin.[1848]

    [2]p. 35x25cm.
    Caption title; imprint on p.[2]; signed at
end: Ferdinand Puff.

[Niedopitalski, ———-]
*GB8   Die Italiener sind schon am Hermarsche nach
V6755R   Wien.
7.32.48   [Wien]Druck und Verlag von Leopold Grund,am
Stephansplatze im Zwettelhofe.[1848]

    folder([4]p.) 23x18cm.
    Signed at end: Niedopitalsky.

Purschke, Carl.
*GB8   An die National-Garde.
V6755R   Druck von Hirschfeld in Wien.[1848]
7.32.48

    broadside. 30.5x23.5cm.
    Helfert (Wiener Parnass) 1340.
    Printed within ornamental border.

Nürnberger, A   L
*GB8   Oesterreich's Nacht und Morgenröthe.
V6755R   Patriotisches Gedicht von A. L. Nürnberger,
7.32.48   gewidmet Sr. k. k. Hoheit dem erhabenen
Reichsverweser Erzherzog Johann.
    [Wien]Druck von Josef Stöckholzer v.Hirschfeld.
[1848]

    folder([4]p.) 24x15cm.
    Caption title; imprint on p.[4].
    Helfert (Wiener Parnass) 1329.

Der Reichstag oder Aristokraten und Dummköpfe.
*pGB8   Wien.Gedruckt im Juli 1848,bei J.N.Fridrich,
V6755R   Josephstadt Langegasse Nr.58.
7.32.48

    [2]p. 38x22cm.
    Caption title; imprint on p.[2]; signed at end:
H. B.

Offenes Sendschreiben an Sr. k. k. Hoheit
*pGB8   Erzherzog Johann.
V6755R   [Wien]Druck von U.Klopf sen.und Alexander
7.32.48   Eurich.[1848]

    broadside. 39.5x24.5cm.

Ein ruhiges Wort, das Vertrauen fordert und
*GB8   Vertrauen verdient.
V6755R   [Wien,1848]
7.32.48

    folder(4p.) 25.5x20cm.
    Caption title; signed at end: Ein wahrer
Demokrat.

*pGB8
V6755R
7.32.48

Sartorius, Friedrich.
Edle Züge von Menschlichkeit und Wohlthun!
Meine Herren Mitbürger und Kameraden! Es wird
wohl Einigen von Ihnen bekannt seyn, dass, als
in den Tagen nach Bekanntmachung der Abreise
Seiner Majestät ...
[Wien]Aus der k.k.Hof= und Staats=Druckerei.
[1848]
broadside. 44.5x28.5cm.
An earlier edition, dated 30 May 1848, though
beginning with the same words, is not the same
text.
Asking for con-   tributions to the
Akademische Legion.

*pGB8
V6755R
7.32.48

[Scheibe, Theodor, 1820-1881]
Etwas neues von dem hinterlistigen Papst. Wie
er den Kaiser durch Cardinal Marichini zu
einem schmählichen Frieden verleiten will.
[Wien]Gedruckt im Juli 1848 bei J.N.Fridrich,
Josefstadt,Langegasse Nr.48.
[2]p. 36.5x23.5cm.
Caption title; imprint on p.[2]; signed at
end: Th. Scheibe.

*pGB8
V6755R
7.32.48

Sendschreiben an die Nationalgarde.
[Wien]Gedruckt bei Leop.Sommer (vorm.Strauss.)
[1848]
broadside. 52.5x68cm.
Signed: B., k. k. Premier=Rittmeister.
"Abgedruckt aus der allgemeinen
Oesterreichischen Zeitung."

*pGB8
V6755R
7.32.48

[Steinbach, F   X   ]
Frische Judenkirschen.
[Wien]Gedruckt bei M.Lell.[1848]
[2]p. 38.5x25cm.
Caption title; imprint on p.[2]; signed at
end: F. X. Steinbach, Neubau Nr.321.
Antisemitic.

*pGB8
V6755R
7.32.48

Stern, Max Veitel, pseud.
Die jüdischen Feder=Helden oder: Das
politisch=literarische Schabesgärtle in Wien,
von Max Veitel Stern.
[Wien]Gedruckt bei M.Lell.[1848]
[2]p. 38x22.5cm.
Caption title; imprint on p.[2].

*pGB8
V6755R
7.32.48

Stix, A   Fr
Reichstagsgebet eines schwarzgelben
Hausherrn mit Anmerkungen seines radikalen
Hausmeisters! Ein tragi=komisches Lebensbild von
A. Fr. Stix.
[Wien]Gedruckt und zu haben bei U.Klopf sen.
und Alexander Eurich,Wollzeile Nr.782.[1848]
[2]p. 39.5x25cm.
Caption title; imprint on p.[2].

*pGB8
V6755R
7.32.48

Studenten, Bürger, Arbeiter! Vertraut dem
Reichstage!
[Wien]Gedruckt bei Edl.v.Schmidbauer und
Holzwarth.[1848]
broadside. 43x27cm.

*GB8
V6755R
7.32.48

[Thaller, Joseph]
Oesterreich's Manifest! ein teutscher Sinn.
Wien,gedruckt im Juli bei U.Klopf sen.und
Alexander Eurich.[1848]
[2]p. 25x20cm.
Helfert (Wiener Parnass) 1534.
Caption title; imprint on p.[2]; signed at end:
Jos. Thaller.
The first letters of the lines of the poem form
an acrostic of the title.

*GB8
V6755R
7.32.48

Ullmayer, Franz.
Der unentschlossene Wiener, oder welches
Geschäft ist in unserer constitutionellen Zeit
das einträglichste. Eine humoristische Zeitfrage
von F. Ullmayer, Verfasser der Wiener Spatzen.
Wien.Gedruckt im Juli 1848 bei J.N.Fridrich,
Josephstadt,Langegasse Nr.48.
folder([4]p.) 26x21cm.
Caption title; imprint on p.[4].

*pGB8
V6755R
7.32.48

Verzeichniss der zur Bildung des Geschwornen=
Gerichtes in der Stadt und in den Vorstädten
gewählten Geschwornen.
[Wien]Gedruckt bei Leopold Grund.[1848]
folder([3]p.) 58x45cm.
Caption title; imprint on p.[3].
Dated in contemporary ms.: Soffer 1848.

*pGB8
V6755R
7.32.48

Victoria! unser guter Kaiser kommt.
Wien,Gedruckt im Juli 1848 bei J.N.Fridrich.
[2]p. 38x22.5cm.

*pGB8
V6755R
8.1.48

Arnold, Johann, fl.1848.
Wie soll man den Kaiser empfangen.
[Wien]Druck von J.Stöckholzer v.Hirschfeld.-
Zu haben im Bureau des "Omnibus,"Stadt,
Liliengasse,Nr.898.[1848]

broadside. 45x28.5cm.

*pGB8
V6755R
7.32.48

Vienna. Ausschuss zur Wahrung der Volksrechte.
Aufruf! Da der unterzeichnete Ausschuss den
Process gegen die Urheber der Vorgänge am 26.
Mai dem Reichstag zu übergeben beschloss, hat
er unter Einem aus seiner Mitte eine Commission
niedergesetzt ...
[Wien]Aus der k.k.Hof= und Staatsdruckerei.
[1848]

broadside. 45x57cm.
Signed: Der Ausschuss der Bürger, Nationalgarden und Studenten zur Wahrung der Volksrechte.

*pGB8
V6755R
8.1.48

Austria. Reichstag, 1848-1849.
Drittes Verzeichniss der bis 1. August 1848
sich gemeldeten Abgeordneten zum constituirenden
Reichstage.
[Wien]Aus der k.k.Hof= und Staats=Druckerei.
[1848]

[2]p. 38x23cm.
Caption title; imprint on p.[2].

*pGB8
V6755R
7.32.48

Wie ein falscher Kaiser Ferdinand mit dem
wilden Windischgrätz zum König Ludwig von
Baiern kommt, um den kleinen Napoleon wegen
den Russen um Rath zu fragen. (Nicht Phantasie,
sondern Wahrheit.)
[Wien]Gedruckt bei J.N.Fridrich.[1848]

[2]p. 38x24.5cm.
Caption title; imprint on p.[2]; signed at
end: J. K.

*pGB8
V6755R
8.1.48

Austria. Reichstag, 1848-1849.
Protokoll der Sitzung der constituirenden
Reichs=Versammlung am 1. August 1848.
[Wien]Aus der k.k.Hof= und Staatsdruckerei.
[1848]

folder([3]p.) 38x23cm.
Caption title; imprint on p.[3].

*pGB8
V6755R
7.32.48

Wie es in Innsbruck ausschaut!!!
[Wien]Schnellpressendruck von Jos.Stöckholzer
von Hirschfeld.Zu haben im Redaktions-Bureau
des "Omnibus," Stadt,Liliengasse Nr.898.[1848]

broadside. 47x30cm.
Signed: B.

*pGB8
V6755R
8.1.48

Der Bürgerkrieg in den österreichischen
Staaten.
[Wien]Gedruckt bei M.Lell.[1848]
[2]p. 38x22.5cm.
Caption title; imprint on p.[2]; dated & signed
at end: Wien am 1. August 1848. F. W——r.

*GB8
V6755R
7.32.48

[Witlačil, ——]
... An die gesammten arbeitenden Volksklassen
in Wien und der Umgebung.
[Wien]Gedruckt bei Ant.Benko.[1848]
folder([4]p.) 22.5x15.5cm.
Caption title (at head: 1 Kreuzer C.M.);
imprint on p.[4]; signed at end: Dr. Witlácil,
Garde der akademischen Legion, Stadt,
Kumpfgasse Nr.826.

*pGB8
V6755R
8.1.48

[Heinisch, Constantin]
Ausserordentliches Blatt!!! Nach Privat-
nachrichten von Innsbruck, den 1. August. Wie
es die Pfaffen und Aristokraten mit dem Kaiser
in Innsbruck getrieben haben!
[Wien]Zu haben bei der Redaction der
Studentenzeitung,Altlerchenfeld Nr.5.Druck von
Franz Edlen von Schmid.[1848]

[2]p. 42.5x26.5cm.
Caption title; imprint on p.[2]; signed at
end: Constantin Heinisch, Jurist.

*GB8
V6755R
8.1.48

[Montecuccoli, Albert Raimund Zeno, graf, 1802-1852]
  Hohe Reichsversammlung! Es ist eine bekannte Thatsache, dass mein Name seit dem 26. Mai auf die schmählichste Weise verunglimpft ...
  [Wien,1848]
    folder([3]p.) 22.5x14.5cm.
    Caption title; dated & signed on p.[3]:
Verona, den 1. August 1848. Albert Graf Montecuccoli.

*pGB8
V6755R
8.2.48

[Windisch-Grätz, Alfred, fürst zu, 1787-1862]
  Kundmachung. Die Ereignisse der Pfingstwoche hatten mir die Verpflichtung auferlegt, die damalen in Prag zur That gewordenen revolutionären Umtriebe und ohne die mindeste Veranlassung von Seite des Militärs erfolgten thätlichen Angriffe gegen daselbe mit Gewalt der Waffen zu bekämpfen ...
  [Wien? 1848]
    folder([4]p.) 35x21cm.
    Caption title; dated & signed at end: Prager Schloss am 2. August 1848. Alfred Fürst Windischgrätz.

*GB8
V6755R
8.1.48

Eine Regentschaft in Oesterreich, wenn der Kaiser nicht kommen will! (Besondere Abdrücke aus dem Radikalen Nr.38, vom 1. August 1848.)
  [Wien]Gedruckt bei Carl Ueberreuter.[1848]
    [2]p. 31x21.5cm.
    Caption title; imprint on p.[2].

*GB8
V6755R
8.3.48

Altlechner, ———.
  Aufforderung. Jndem ich nun mehrseitig aufgefordert wurde, einen der Jetzt= und Folgezeit nützlichen und zweckmässigen Arbeiterverein in das Leben zu rufen ...
  [Wien,1848]
    broadside. 21.5x25.5cm.
    Dated: Wien, den 3. August 1848.

*pGB8
V6755R
8.2.48

Austria. Reichstag, 1848-1849.
  Protokoll der Sitzung der constituirenden Reichs=Versammlung am 2. August 1848.
  [Wien]Aus der k.k.Hof= und Staatsdruckerei. [1848]
    [5]p. 38x23cm.
    Caption title; imprint on p.[5].

*pGB8
V6755R
8.3.48

An die National=Garde! Cameraden! Es gibt im Bereiche dieser Residenzstadt und ihrer Umgebungen noch viele Tausende, die, wahrscheinlich weil sie im Fall eines ausbrechenden Kampfes den Pulvergeruch nicht gut vertragen zu können glauben ...
  [Wien]Gedruckt bei Josef Ludwig.[1848]
    broadside. 43x54cm.
    Dated & signed: Wien den 3. August 1848. Ein Garde des XI. Bezirkes.

*pGB8
V6755R
8.2.48

Vienna. Sicherheits-Ausschuss.
  An die Bevölkerung Wiens. Abermals ist in den letztverflossenen Tagen in mehreren Vorstädten Wiens die Nachtruhe und der Friede der Bevölkerung durch sogenannte "Katzenmusiken" auf das bedauerlichste gestört worden ...
  [Wien]Aus der k.k.Hof= und Staatsdruckerei. [1848]
    broadside. 44.5x57cm.
    Dated: Wien am 2. August 1848.

*pGB8
V6755R
8.3.48

Austria. Reichstag, 1848-1849.
  Protokoll der Sitzung der constituirenden Reichs=Versammlung am 3. August 1848.
  [Wien]Aus der k.k.Hof= und Staatsdruckerei. [1848]
    folder([4]p.) 38x23cm.
    Caption title; imprint on p.[4].

*pGB8
V6755R
8.2.48

Vienna. Sicherheits-Ausschuss.
  Kundmachung. Es hat sich das falsche Gerücht verbreitet, der vereinigte Ausschuss für Ordnung, Sicherheit und Wahrung der Volksrechte sei der von der Stadthauptmannschaft angeordneten Confiscation der Flugschrift "Was müssen wir thun, wenn der Kaiser nicht kommen will" durch seinen Beschluss entgegengetreten ...
  [Wien]Aus der k.k.Hof= und Staatsdruckerei. [1848]
    broadside. 38x23cm.
    Dated: Wien am 2. August 1848.

*pGB8
V6755R
8.3.48

Vienna. Nationalgarde.
  Tagsbefehl. Bei den in den letzten Tagen häufig vorgekommenen Ruhestörungen durch sogenannte Katzenmusiken hat es sich leider gezeigt, dass selbst einzelne Herren der Nationalgarde als Beschützer derselben auftraten ...
  [Wien]Aus der k.k.Hof= und Staatsdruckerei. [1848]
    broadside. 44.5x57cm.
    Dated & signed: Wien den 3. August 1848.
Streffleur General=Adjutant und Ober=Commandant= Stellvertreter.

*pGB8
V6755R
8.4.48

Austria. Reichstag, 1848-1849.
    Adresse des hoh. Reichstages an Sr. Maj. den
Kaiser, um ihn zur Rückkehr in die Burg seiner
Väter zu bestimmen.
    [Wien]Gedruckt und zu haben bei Ulrich Klopf
sen.und Alexander Eurich.[1848]
    [2]p. 40x25cm.
    Caption title; imprint on p.[2].

*pGB8
V6755R
8.4.48

Vienna. Universität. Ausschuss der Studierenden.
    Die Studenten an die Bewohner Wiens. Seit
einigen Tagen durchschleichen beängstigende
Gerüchte unsere gut gesinnte Stadt ...
    [Wien]Aus der k.k.Hof= und Staatsdruckerei.
[1848]
    broadside. 44.5x57cm.
    Dated & signed: Wien den 4. August 1848.
Dr. Florian Heller, Schriftführer. Dr. Goldmark,
Vorsitzer.

*pGB8
V6755R
8.4.48

Austria. Reichstag, 1848-1849.
    Protokoll der Sitzung der constituirenden
Reichs=Versammlung am 4. August 1848.
    [Wien]Aus der k.k.Hof= und Staatsdruckerei.
[1848]
    [5]p. 38x23cm.
    Caption title; imprint on p.[5].

*pGB8
V6755R
8.5.48

Austria. Reichstag, 1848-1849.
    Protokoll der Sitzung der constituirenden
Reichs=Versammlung am 5. August 1848.
    [Wien]Aus der k.k.Hof= und Staatsdruckerei.
[1848]
    folder([3]p.) 38x23cm.
    Caption title; imprint on p.[3].

*pGB8
V6755R
8.4.48

Füster, Anton, 1808-1881.
    Offene Erklärung. Ein böswillig erfundenes
Gerücht über gefährliche Absichten, welche
meiner Person zur Last gelegt werden, durchläuft
die Stadt ...
    [Wien]Gedruckt bei Ulrich Klopf sen.und
Alexander Eurich.[1848]
    broadside. 40x50cm.
    Dated: Wien, den 4. August 1848.

*pGB8
V6755R
8.5.48

Bardach, D
    Was sollen wir thun, wenn der Kaiser kommt?
[Wien]Gedruckt bei M.Lell.[1848]
    broadside. 1 illus. 40x24.5cm.
    Signed: D. Bardach, Mitglied der akademischen
Legion.

*GB8
V6755R
8.4.48

    Die Verschwörung gegen das jetzige Ministerium,
die akademische Legion, den Sicherheitsausschuss
und die Nationalgarde. (Besonderer Abdruck aus
dem Radikalen Nr.41, vom 4. August 1848.)
    [Wien]Zu haben im Comptoir des Radikalen,
Dorotheergasse Nr.1119.Gedruckt bei Carl
Ueberreuter.[1848]
    [2]p. 31.5x21cm.
    Caption title; imprint on p.[2].

*pGB8
V6755R
8.5.48

Polák, F
    Wie unser brave alte Feldherr Marschall
Radetzky beschimpft wurde, und eine Aufklärung
über das republikanische Treiben!
    Jm Commission bei J.Bader,Buchhändler in Wien,
Stadt,Strobelgasse.[1848]
    broadside. 42x52.5cm.
    Signed & dated: F. Polák mit einem Wiener
Bürger. Wien, den 5. August 1848.

*pGB8
V6755R
8.4.48

Vienna. Nationalgarde.
    Protest der gefertigten Nationalgarde=
Kompagnien an das hohe Ministerium des Jnnern
über die von Seite des Verwaltungsrathes der
sämmtlichen Nationalgarden Wiens durch mehrere
ihm nicht zustehende Beschlüsse und erlassene
allgemein bindende Normen erfolgte Ueberschreitung
seines gesetzlichen Wirkungskreises.
    [Wien]Gedruckt bei Carl Ueberreuter.[1848]
    folder(4p.) 40x25cm.
    Caption title; imprint on p.4; dated & signed:
Wien, den 4. August 1848, Jm Namen und in
Ermächtigung der Nationalgarde, 2. Comp.,
Wimmer Viertel.

*GB8
V6755R
8.5.48

Scheibe, Theodor, 1820-1881.
    Extra=Blatt! Neuester Bericht aus Innsbruck.
Warum der Kaiser nicht kommt.
    [Wien]Im Verlagsgewölbe,Kölnerhofgasse Nr.730.
Gedruckt bei Leop.Sommer.[1848]
    broadside. 26x21cm.

*pGB8
V6755R
8.5.48

Vienna. Sicherheits-Ausschuss.
An die Bewohner Wiens! Die jetzt verbreiteten
Gerüchte, als sollte in einigen Tagen hier die
Republik ausgerufen werden, entbehrten eines
jeden stichhältigen Grundes ...
[Wien]Aus der k.k.Hof= und Staats=Druckerei.
[1848]

broadside. 45x57cm.
Dated: Wien am 5. August 1848.

---

*pGB8
V6755R
8.6.48

Der Hochverräther Ebersberg.
[Wien]Gedruckt bei Josef Ludwig.[1848]
[2]p. 38x23cm.
Objecting to the contents of no.122 of
Ebersberg's periodical "Wiener Zuschauer".
Caption title; imprint on p.[2].

---

*pGB8
V6755R
8.5.48

Vienna. Sicherheits-Ausschuss.
Kundmachung. Aus Anlass einer Zuschrift des
hierländigen 18bl. General=Commando, ddo. 5.
August 1848, Z.4171, sieht sich der gefertigte
Ausschuss zu der Veröffentlichung veranlasst:
"dass für die Spitäler der Armee in Italien weder
Weiber noch Mädchen zur Krankenpflege oder
Wäschreinigung aufgenommen werden, noch jemahls
aufgenommen worden sind." ...
[Wien]Aus der k.k.Hof= und Staatsdruckerei.
[1848]
broadside. 45x28cm.
Dated: Wien am 5. August 1848.

---

*pGB8
V6755R
8.6.48

Komödien aus der Unterwelt.
[Wien]Preis des Blattes 1 kr.Conv.Minze.
Schnellpressendruck von Jos.Keck & Sohn.[1848]

[2]p. 40.5x24.5cm.
Caption title; imprint on p.[2].
Contents: Brief des Hrn. Spitzelius
Constitutionalis [pseud.] an Hrn. Paphnuzius
Pankratius Onuphrius Paracelsus [pseud.].--
Scenen aus der Unterwelt.
The "Brief" is dated: Unterwelt, den 6. August
1848.
A satire on Stadion and
Montecuccoli.

---

*pGB8
V6755R
8.5.48

Vienna. Universität. Ausschuss der Studierenden.
An die Bewohner Wiens! Der sechste August war
bis jetzt ein Trauertag für jedes deutsche Herz
...
[Wien]Gedruckt bei U.Klopf sen.und Alexander
Eurich,Wollzeile Nr.782.[1848]
broadside. 46x58cm.
Dated & signed: Wien den 5. August 1848. Vom
Ausschuss der Studenten Wiens.

---

*pGB8
V6755R
8.7.48

Austria. Reichstag, 1848-1849.
Protokoll der Sitzung der constituirenden
Reichs=Versammlung am 7. August 1848.
[Wien]Aus der k.k.Hof= und Staatsdruckerei.
[1848]
folder([4]p.) 38x23cm.
Caption title; imprint on p.[4].

---

*pGB8
V6755R
8.5.48

Vienna. Universität. Ausschuss der Studierenden.
Die Studenten an die Bewohner Wiens. Seit
einigen Tagen durchschleichen beängstigende
Gerüchte unsere gutgesinnte Stadt ...
[Wien]Gedruckt bei L.Sommer.[1848]
broadside. 44.5x30cm.
Dated & signed: Wien am 5. August 1848. Vom
Ausschuss der Studenten in Wien.
A reprint of the previous day's proclamation.

---

*pGB8
V6755R
8.8.48

Aufgepasst! Schnell gekauft, bevor dieses
Blatt konfiszirt wird!!! Partezettel der
Camarilla.
[Wien]Zu haben im Redaktions=Bureau des
"Omnibus" Stadt,Liliengasse Nr.898.[1848]Druck
von Hirschfeld.

broadside. 1 illus. 29.5x47cm.
Mock obituary.

---

*pGB8
V6755R
8.6.48

Austria. Weberinnung.
Löblicher Gemeinde-Ausschuss! Jnhalt der
Puncte. 1. Einreihung der Perchtoldsdorfer=
Freiweber zu der hiesigen Jnnung. 2.
Gleichstellung der Meister und Befugten ...
[Wien,1848]
folder([4]p.) 44.5x29cm.
Caption title; dated & signed at end: Wien,
den 6. August 1848. Barthol. Entres,
Obervorsteher.
Proposing the strengthening of union regula-
tions and control of illegal textile
imports.

---

*pGB8
V6755R
8.8.48

Austria. Ministerium des Innern.
Se. Majestät der Kaiser haben am 5. d. M. die
Reichstags=Deputation empfangen und derselben
folgende Antwort ertheilt ...
[Wien]Aus der k.k.Hof= und Staatsdruckerei.
[1848]

broadside. 45x57cm.
Dated & signed: Wien am 8. August 1848. Der
Minister des Jnneren: Doblhoff.
Announcing that the Emperor will return to
Vienna on the 12th.

*pGB8
V6755R
8.8.48

Austria. Reichstag, 1848-1849.
    Protokoll der Sitzung der constituirenden
Reichs=Versammlung am 8. August 1848.
[Wien]Aus der k.k.Hof= und Staatsdruckerei.
[1848]

    folder([3]p.) 38.5x23cm.
    Caption title; imprint on p.[3].

---

*GB8
V6755R
8.8.48

Palme, Alois, 1793-1864.
    Garden-Lied der akademischen Legion. (Nach der
Melodie von Proch's "Garden=Lied.")
[Wien,1848]

    broadside. 24x15cm.
    Helfert (Wiener Parnass) 1635.
    Without the music.

---

*pGB8
V6755R
8.8.48

    Des Kaisers Abreise aus Jnnsbruck erfolgte
auf den Ruf des Volkes.
[Wien]Gedruckt bei Leopold Sommer,
Alservorstadt.[1848]

    [2]p. 42x26.5cm.
    Caption title; imprint on p.[2].
    Includes a reprint of Doblhoff's proclamation
of 8 August, beginning: Se. Majestät der Kaiser
haben am 5. d. M. ...

---

*pGB8
V6755R
8.8.48

Die Reaktion ohne Kopf, oder Zum Teuxel ist
der Zopf!
[Wien]Schnellpressendruck von Jos.Stöckholzer
von Hirschfeld.Zu haben im Redaktions=Bureau des
"Omnibus," Stadt,Liliengasse Nr.898.[1848]

    broadside. 46x28.5cm.
    Dated in contemporary ms.: 8 August.

---

*pGB8
V6755R
8.8.48

Oesterreichischer Patrioten-Verein.
    Aufforderung an die P. T. Herren Hausbesitzer
oder deren Stellvertreter!
[Wien]Aus der k.k.Hof= und Staatsdruckerei.
[1848]

    broadside. 38x23cm.
    Dated & signed: Wien den 8. August 1848. Vom
Ausschusse des österreichischen Patrioten-
Vereines zur Einhebung der freiwilligen
Beisteuer.

---

*pGB8
V6755R
8.8.48

Vienna. Nationalgarde.
    Tagsbefehl vom 8. August 1848.
[Wien]Aus der k.k.Hof= und Staatsdruckerei.
[1848]

    broadside. 38x22.5cm.
    Signed: Streffleur, General=Adjutant und
Ober=Commandant=Stellvertreter.

---

*pGB8
V6755R
8.8.48

Oesterreichischer Patrioten-Verein.
    Aufruf an die Patrioten Oesterreichs!
[Wien]Aus der k.k.Hof= und Staats=Druckerei.
[1848]

    broadside. 44x57cm.
    Dated & signed: Wien den 8. August 1848. Vom
österreichischen Patrioten-Vereine zur
Einhebung der freiwilligen Beisteuer.
    Urging financial contributions for the support
of the state.

---

*pGB8
V6755R
8.8.48

Vienna. Sicherheits-Ausschuss.
    An die Bewohner Wiens! Der gefertigte
Ausschuss beeilt sich folgenden Auszug aus dem
Protokolle seiner Nachtpermanenz vom 7. d. M.
zur allgemeinen Kenntniss zu bringen ...
[Wien]Aus der k.k.Hof= und Staatsdruckerei.
[1848]

    broadside. 38x23cm.
    Dated: Wien am 8. August 1848.
    Announcing that the Emperor will return to
Vienna on the 12th.

---

*pGB8
V6755R
8.8.48

Oesterreichischer Patrioten-Verein.
    Aufruf an die Patrioten Oesterreichs!
[Wien]Aus der k.k.Hof= und Staats=Druckerei.
[1848]

    [2]p. 44.5x28cm.
    Caption title; imprint on p.[2]; dated & signed
at end: Wien den 8. August 1848. Vom
österreichischen Patrioten-Vereine zur Einhebung
der freiwilligen Beisteuer.
    Urging financial contributions for the support
of the state.

---

*pGB8
V6755R
8.9.48

Austria. Reichstag, 1848-1849.
    Protokoll der Sitzung der constituirenden
Reichs=Versammlung am 9. August 1848.
[Wien]Aus der k.k.Hof= und Staatsdruckerei.
[1848]

    folder([3]p.) 38x23cm.
    Caption title; imprint on p.[3].

*pGB8
V6755R
8.9.48

Viktoria, der Kaiser hat Innsbruck verlassen!!!
oder Bombelles und Cibini ziehen mit langen
Nasen ab, und die Tyroler Pfaffen werden sich
schön hintern Ohren kratzen!
[Wien]Schnellpressendruck von Jos.Stöckholzer
von Hirschfeld.Zu haben im Redaktions=Bureau[!]
des "Omnibus," Stadt,Liliengasse Nr.898.[1848]

broadside. 47.5x30cm.

---

*pGB8
V6755R
8.10.48

... Der Kaiser kommt! Der Kaiser kommt auf den
Ruf des Volkes.
[Wien]Gedruckt und zu haben bei L.Sommer,
Alservorstadt Nr.147.[1848]

broadside. 41.5x26.5cm.
At head: Neueste Nachricht aus Innsbruck.

---

*pGB8
V6755R
8.9.48

Wiener Zeitung.
Extra=Blatt zur Wiener Zeitung vom 9.
August 1848.
[Wien,1848]

broadside. 38.5x29cm.
Announcing the occupation of Milan.

---

*pGB8
V6755R
8.10.48

[Löve, Paul]
Gespräch eines alten Tirolers mit dem guten
Kaiser Ferdinand in Insbruck. Victoria! der
Kaiser kommt!
[Wien]Gedruckt bei Josef Ludwig.[1848]

[2]p. 42x26cm.
Caption title; imprint on p.[2]; signed at end:
P. Löve.

---

*pGB8
V6755R
8.10.48

Ausserordentliches Bulletin aus Mailand
von der österreichischen Armee.
[Wien]Gedruckt und zu haben bei L.Grund,
Stephansplatz im Zwettelhof.[1848]

[2]p. 36.5x23cm.
Caption title; imprint on p.[2].

---

*pGB8
V6755R
8.10.48

Scheibe, Theodor, 1820-1881.
Die Wiederkehr unsers Kaisers! Die Aufnahme der
Deputirten.—Des Kaisers Worte.—Seine Reise
nach Wien!
[Wien]Verlagsgewölb:Stadt,Parisergasse.
Gedruckt bei U.Klopf sen.und Alexander Eurich.
[1848]

broadside. 42x26.5cm.

---

*pGB8
V6755R
8.10.48

Austria. Reichstag, 1848-1849.
Protokoll der Sitzung der constituirenden
Reichs=Versammlung am 10. August 1848.
[Wien]Aus der k.k.Hof= und Staatsdruckerei.
[1848]

folder([3]p.) 38.5x23cm.
Caption title; imprint on p.[3].

---

*pGB8
V6755R
8.10.48

Verein zur Beschäftigung brotloser Arbeiter,
Vienna.
Der Verein zur Beschäftigung brotloser
Arbeiter an seine Mitbürger.
[Wien]Aus der k.k.Hof= und Staats=Druckerei.
[1848]

broadside. 44x57cm.
Dated: Wien den 10. August 1848.

---

*pGB8
V6755R
8.10.48

Austria. Reichstag, 1848-1849.
Reise-Protokoll der Reichstags=Deputation nach
Innsbruck.
[Wien]Aus der k.k.Hof= und Staatsdruckerei.
[1848]

7,[1]p. 38.5x23cm.
Caption title; imprint on p.[8].
Report of the deputation sent to persuade the
Emperor to return to Vienna.

---

*pGB8
V6755R
8.10.48

Verein zur Beschäftigung brotloser Arbeiter,
Vienna.
Der Verein zur Beschäftigung brotloser
Arbeiter an seine Mitbürger.
[Wien]Aus der k.k.Hof= und Staats=Druckerei.
[1848]

[2]p. 44.5x28cm.
Caption title; imprint on p.[2]; dated at end:
Wien den 10. August 1848.

Victoria. Die Oesterreicher sind in Mailand eingerückt.
*pGB8
V6755R
8.10.48
[Wien]Gedruckt bei U.Klopf sen.und Alexander Eurich.[1848]

broadside. 40x25cm.

Vienna. Gemeinderat.
Programm für die Feier des Empfanges Sr.
*pGB8
V6755R
8.11.48
Majestät des Kaisers.
[Wien]Aus der k.k.Hof= und Staatsdruckerei.
[1848]

broadside. 45x57cm.
Dated: Wien am 11. August 1848.

Vienna. Nationalgarde.
*pGB8
V6755R
8.10.48
Spalier zum Empfange Seiner Majestät am 12ten
dieses Monats von Nussdorf bis Schönbrunn.
[Wien,1848]

[2]p. 38x25cm. and plan. 46x55.5cm.
Reproduced from handwritten copy.
Caption title; signed at end: Streffleur.

Vienna. Magistrat.
Kundmachung. Die erst in neuester Zeit wieder
*pGB8
V6755R
8.11.48
vorgekommenen Fälle, dass Menschen durch Hunde
angefallen und verletzt wurden ...
[Wien,1848]

broadside. 40.5x25cm.
Dated: am 11. August 1848.
Ordering dogs to be muzzled.

Austria. Justizministerium.
*pGB8
V6755R
8.11.48
... Verordnung des Ministeriums der Justiz.
Ueber vorläufiges Einvernehmen mit dem
Ministerium des Innern werden hiemit sämmtliche
Gerichtsbehörden in dem Sprengel der Senate des
k. k. obersten Gerichtschofes angewiesen ...
[Wien,1848]

broadside. 38.5x23cm.
At head: Zahl 2261.
Dated: Wien am 11. August 1848.
Directing the use of "Herr" and "Frau" as
forms of address   without distinction of
rank.

Vienna. Nationalgarde.
*pGB8
V6755R
8.11.48
An die Bürger, Nationalgarde und Studenten
Brünns! Kameraden! Brüder! Wenn schon von
jeher die Schwesterstädte Wien und Brünn
in der Geschichte unseres schönen, blühenden
Vaterlandes so manches herrliche Beispiel
inniger wechselseitiger Liebe gegeben haben ...
[Wien]Aus der k.k.Hof= und Staatsdruckerei.
[1848]

broadside. 44.5x56.5cm.
Dated & signed: Wien am 11. August 1848. Der
Verwaltungsrath im   Namen der gesammten
Nationalgarde   Wiens.

Austria. Reichstag, 1848-1849.
*pGB8
V6755R
8.11.48
Protokoll der Sitzung der constituirenden
Reichs=Versammlung am 11. August 1848.
[Wien]Aus der k.k.Hof= und Staatsdruckerei.
[1848]

[2]p. 38x23cm.
Caption title; imprint on p.[2].

Vienna. Nationalgarde.
*pGB8
V6755R
8.11.48
Der Verwaltungsrath an die gesammte
Nationalgarde Wiens. Dem Verwaltungsrathe wurde
ein Protest, ausgehend von der zweiten Compagnie
Wimmerviertel mit dem Bemerken vorgelegt, dass
Unterschriften in der Nationalgarde für
denselben geworben werden ...
[Wien]Aus der k.k.Hof= und Staatsdruckerei.
[1848]

broadside. 38x22.5cm.
Dated: Wien am 11. August 1848.

Endlich, Johann Quirin.
*pGB8
V6755R
8.11.48
Die Anarchie auf dem Lande.
In Commission bei J.Bader,Buchhändler in Wien,
Stadt,Strobelgasse.[1848]

broadside. 45x56cm.
Dated: Wien am, 11. August 1848.

Austria. Reichstag, 1848-1849.
*pGB8
V6755R
8.12.48
Protokoll der Sitzung der constituirenden
Reichs=Versammlung am 12. August 1848.
[Wien]Aus der k.k.Hof= und Staatsdruckerei.
[1848]

[2]p. 38x23cm.
Caption title; imprint on p.[2].

*GB8
V6755R
8.12.48

Die Feierlichkeiten bei der Ankunft des
Kaisers. Samstag, den 12. August 1848.
[Wien]Gedruckt bei Franz Edlem von Schmid.
[1848]
[2]p. 29x23cm.
Caption title; imprint on p.[2].

*pGB8
V6755R
8.12.48

[Patatschny, Franz]
Kaiser Ferdinands Einzug in die immer getreue
Residenz den 12. August 1848.
[Wien]Gedruckt und zu haben bei Leopold Grund,
am Stephansplatz im Zwettelhofe.[1848]
[2]p. illus.(port.) 41.5x26cm.
Caption title; imprint on p.[2]; signed at
end: Franz Patatschny.
This issue is without a list of honor-guards
on p.[2].

*GB8
V6755R
8.12.48

[Lyser, Johann Peter, 1803-1870]
Dem guten Kaiser Ferdinand I. von Oesterreich
bei Seiner Rückkehr nach Wien dargebracht von
seinem treuen Volke, am 12. August 1848.
Wien.[1848]
folder([4]p.) 26x21cm.
Helfert (Wiener Parnass) 1661.
Signed at end: J. P. Lyser.
Printer's imprint on p.[4]: Gedruckt bei Leop.
Sommer (vormals Strauss).

*pGB8
V6755R
8.12.48

[Patatschny, Franz]
Kaiser Ferdinands Einzug in die immer getreue
Residenz den 12. August 1848.
[Wien]Gedruckt und zu haben bei Leopold
Grund,am Stephansplatz im Zwettelhofe.[1848]
[2]p. illus.(port.) 40x25cm.
Caption title; imprint on p.[2]; signed at
end: Franz Patatschny.
This issue contains a list of honor-guards
on p.[2].

*pGB8
V6755R
8.12.48

Meisl, Karl, 1775-1853.
Wien, seinem rückkehrenden geliebten Kaiser
Ferdinand I. am 12. August 1848.
[Wien]Gedruckt und zu haben bei Leopold Grund,
am Stephansplatz im Zwettelhofe.[1848]
broadside. 40x25cm.
Helfert (Wiener Parnass) 1652.

*pGB8
V6755R
8.12.48

Programm des festlichen Einzuges Sr. Majestät
des Kaisers in Wien am 12. August 1848.
[Wien,1848]
broadside. 38x29.5cm.

*pGB8
V6755R
8.12.48

Miller, Carl, fl.1848.
Unser Kaiser kommt zurück! Haltet aber Ordnung
und Sicherheit! Edles österreichisches Volk! Die
zwei Seligkeit bringenden Worte: Ordnung und
Sicherheit liegen in Deiner Hand!
[Wien]Druck von Ulrich Klopf sen.und Alex.
Eurich.[1848]
broadside. 58x46cm.
Signed: Carl Miller, Literat, Garde d. akad.
Legion, 2. Comp.

*pGB8
V6755R
8.12.48

Schweickhardt, Franz Xavier Joseph, b.1794.
Beschreibung der feierlichen Ankunft Ihrer k.
k. Majestäten in Wien, zwischen 3 und 4 Uhr
Nachmittags. Von Schweickhardt.
[Wien]Mechitharisten-Buchdruckerei.[1848]
broadside. 34x26cm.

*GB8
V6755R
8.12.48

Ottel, Michael.
Danklied. Niedergelegt am Altare des Vaterlandes. Den tapfern akademischen Vorkämpfern und
den edlen Bürgern Wiens hochachtungsvoll
geweiht von Michael Ottel.
Wien 1848.Gedruckt bei Ferdinand Ullrich.
folder([4]p.) 22x14.5cm.
Helfert (Wiener Parnass) 469.
Dated in contemporary ms.: 12. August 848.

*pGB8
V6755R
8.12.48

Volks- und National-Comödie Wien's. Unter
persönlicher Leitung der geehrten Frauen:
Freiheit, Ordnung und Gleichheit! Heute
Sonnabend den 12. August 1848 zum Vortheile des
österreichischen Volkes zum ersten Male: Die
Rückkehr des Kaisers oder: Der Triumph der
Demokratie.
[Wien]Zu haben im Redaktions=Bureau des
"Omnibus" Stadt,Liliengasse Nr.898.[1848]
Schnellpressendruck von Jos.Stöckholzer v.
Hirschfeld.
broadside. 47.5x30.5cm.
A mock playbill.

*pGB8
V6755R
8.13.48

Austria. Post-Kurs-Bureau. Kondukteure.
  Petition. Die k. k. Postkondukteure haben
nachstehende Petition der Reichsversammlung
überreicht:
  [Wien]Gedruckt bei M.Lell.[1848]
  folder([3]p.) 40x25cm.
  Caption title; imprint on p.[3]; dated at end:
Wien am 13. August 1848.
  Asking for improved working conditions and
compensation.

*pGB8
V6755R
8.14.48

Austria. Reichstag, 1848-1849.
  Protokoll der Sitzung der constituirenden
Reichs=Versammlung am 14. August 1848.
[1848]
  folder([3]p.) 38x23cm.
  Caption title; imprint on p.[3].

*pGB8
V6755R
8.13.48

Austria. Sovereigns, etc., 1835-1848
  (Ferdinand I)
  An Meine getreuen Wiener! Der gestrige Tag,
an welchem Ich in Eure Mitte zurückkehrend, die
schönsten Beweise Eurer alten unveränderlichen
Liebe erntete ...
  [Wien]Aus der k.k.Hof= und Staatsdruckerei.
[1848]
  broadside. 44.5x56cm.
  Dated: Wien am 13. August 1848.

*pGB8
V6755R
8.14.48

Remay, C., pseud.
  Man dreht den Mantel nach dem Wind, oder der
grosse Herr Saphir, als Schildknappe der
berühmten Herrn Ebersberg, Endlich, Landsteiner
und Raudnitz, oder Die ersten Waffenthaten
eines Badener National=Gardisten als Polizeimann;
engagirt--wahrscheinlich bei Herrn Saphir--
und gennant Herr (?) Handl junior.
  Charaktergemälde in Abtheilungen, welche noch
nicht bestimmt anzugeben sind. Verfasst von C.
Remay, Opfer des Schildknappen und Polizeimanns
...
                              (See next card)

*pGB8
V6755R
8.13.48

Radetzky, Josef Wenzel, graf, 1766-1858.
  Dankschreiben des Feldmarschall Radetzky an den
löblichen Magistrat der Stadt Steyr!
  [Wien]Aus der Buchdruckerei des Friedrich
Eurich.[1848]
  broadside. 38x25cm.
  Dated: Hauptquartier Mailand, am 13. August
1848.

*pGB8
V6755R
8.14.48

Remay, C., pseud.   Man dreht ... [1848]
                       (Card 2)
  [Wien]Gedruckt bei Franz Edlen von Schmid.
[1848]
  [2]p. 42x26.5cm.
  Caption title; imprint on p.[2]; dated &
signed: Baden, am 14. August 1848. Remay,
Regisseur am Stadttheater in Baden.

*GB8
V6755R
8.13.48

Stimme zur Zeit der Fahnen-Weihe der National-
Garde in der l. f. Stadt Korneuburg am 13.
August 1848.
  [Korneuburg,Austria?1848]
  folder([3]p.) 25x19.5cm.
  Caption title.
  In verse.

*pGB8
V6755R
8.14.48

Walter, Ferdinand Ulrich.
  An die Juden Wien's. Wohlmeinende Worte eines
Christen.
  Zu haben bei J.Bader,Buchhändler in Wien,Stadt,
Strobelgasse.[1848] Preis: 3 kr.C.M.
  broadside. 42x53cm.
  Dated: Wien, am 14. August 1848.

*pGB8
V6755R
8.13.48

Wiener Zeitung.
  Extra=Blatt zur Wiener Zeitung. 13. August
1848.
  [Wien,1848]
  broadside. 29x29.5cm.
  Despatches concerning the war in Italy.
  Torn at bottom, perhaps removing imprint.

*pGB8
V6755R
8.15.48

[Komorny, Joseph]
  Ungarns Verlangen der Kaiser soll nach Pest
reisen.
  [Wien]Zu haben in der Stadt,Sterngasse Nr.452,
im Hofmagazin.Gedruckt bei Leopold Grund.[1848]
  [2]p. 36.5x23cm.
  Caption title; imprint on p.[2]; signed at
end: Herausgegeben von Joseph Komorny, neue
Wieden, Hauptstrasse Nr.667.

1848 AUSTRIAN REVOLUTIONARY BROADSIDES AND PAMPHLETS

[Ohms, Ferdinand, ritter von]
Circular-Schreiben der k. k. österreichischen
Agentie für die geistlichen Angelegenheiten an
sämmtliche nicht-italienische erzbischöfliche
und bischöfliche Ordinariate der k. k.
Monarchie.
*pGB8 [Wien,1848]
V6755R folder([4]p.) 35.5x22.5cm.
8.15.48 Caption title; dated & signed on p.[4]: Rom,
den 15. August 1848. Ferdinand Ritter von Ohms,
k. k. Botschaftsrath und zeitweiliger Agent für
(See next card)

[Ohms, Ferdinand, ritter von]   Circular-
Schreiben ... [1848]   (Card 2)
*pGB8
V6755R die geistlichen Angelegenheiten am heiligen
8.15.48 Stuhle.
In contemporary ms. at top of p.[1]: 180
Stück 16 Septbr 1848.

Radetzky und der geschlossene Waffenstillstand.
[Wien]Gedruckt und zu haben bei Leopold Grund,
*pGB8 am Stephansplatz im Zwettelhofe.[1848]
V6755R [2]p. 1 illus. 37x23cm.
8.15.48 Imprint on p.[2].

Vienna. Sicherheits-Ausschuss.
An dürftige Gewerbsleute Wiens. Der
*pGB8 gefertigte Ausschuss hat einen öffentlichen
V6755R Aufruf erlassen, und zu Beiträgen zur
8.15.48 Unterstützung hilfsbedürftiger Gewerbsleute
aufgefordert.
[Wien]Aus der k.k.Hof= und Staatsdruckerei.
[1848]
broadside. 44.5x57cm.
Dated: Wien am 15. August 1848.

Austria. Armee.
Waffenstillstands=Convention zwischen der k. k.
*pGB8 österreichischen und königl. sardinischen Armee
V6755R als Voreinleitung der Negotiationen zu einem
8.16.48 Friedensschluss.
Druck von Friedrich Eurich in Linz.(16.August
1848.)
[2]p. 44.5x29cm.
Caption title; imprint on p.[2]; dated &
signed at end: Jnnsbruck, am 12. August 1848.
Radetzky m.p., Feldmarschall.

Austria. Reichstag, 1848-1849.
Protokoll der Sitzung der constituirenden
*pGB8 Reichs=Versammlung am 16. August 1848.
V6755R [Wien]Aus der k.k.Hof= und Staatsdruckerei.
8.16.48 [1848]
[2]p. 38x23cm.
Caption title; imprint on p.[2].

Austria. Reichstag, 1848-1849. Finanz-Ausschuss.
Hohe Versammlung! Der von Jhren Abtheilung
*pGB8 gewählte Ausschuss zur Prüfung der Anträge des
V6755R Ministeriums über die noch vor der Feststellung
8.16.48 des nächsten Staatsvoranschlages erforderlichen
Finanz=Massregeln hat vor Allem die
Nothwendigkeit erkannt ...
[Wien]Aus der k.k.Hof und Staatsdruckerei.
[1848]
6p. 38x23cm.
Caption title; imprint on p.6; dated at end:
Wien am 16. August 1848.

Buchheim, Carl Adolf, 1828-1900.
Dank für unsere Befreiung.
*pGB8 [Wien]Schnellpressendruck von Jos.Keck &
V6755R Sohn.[1848]
8.16.48
broadside. 34.5x27cm.
Signed: Adolf Buchheim, Oskar Falke,
Redakteure des "politischen Studenten=Couriers."
Dated in contemporary ms.: 16 August 1848.

Feyertag, Johann.
Dankes- und Jubel-Worte beim Empfange der
*pGB8 Fahnen, welche Ihre Durchlaucht die Frau Fürstin
V6755R Wilhelmine von Auersperg und die Frau Magdalena
8.16.48 Seelig den unter dem Kommando des Herrn Fürsten
Vinzenz von Auersperg stehenden National-Garden
des X. Bezirks gespendet. Verfasst von Johann
Feyertag ... Wien, den 16. August 1848.
[Wien]Mechitharisten-Buchdruckerei.[1848]
folder([4]p.) 31.5x25.5cm.
Helfert (Wiener Parnass) 1689.

Männer-Gesang-Verein, Vienna.
Einladung an die Herren ausübenden Mitglieder
*pGB8 des Männer=Gesang-Vereines. Der löbliche
V6755R Gemeinde=Ausschuss der Stadt Wien veranstaltet
8.16.48 Donnerstag den 16. August 1848 zur Feier der
Rückkehr Seiner Majestät des Kaisers im k. k.
Lustschlosse zu Schönbrunn einen Fackelzug in
Verbindung mit einer Serenade ...
[Wien]Aus der k.k.Hof= und Staats=Druckerei.
[1848]
broadside. 45x57cm.
Dated & signed: Wien den 16. August 1848. Die
Direction des   Männer-Gesang-Vereines.

Niglas, Johann Nepomuk.
*GB8 Rede, gesprochen bei dem feierlichen
V6755R Gottesdienste vor Einweihung der Fahnen des
8.16.48 X. Bezirkes der National=Garde am 16. August
1848. Von Johann Nep. Niglas ...
Wien.Gedruckt bei Carl Ueberreuter.[1848]
folder([4]p.) 29.5x23cm.

Reitter, Gustav.
*GB8 Zur Fahnen-Weihe, des 10. Nationalgarde=
V6755R Bezirkes (Josephstadt), am 16. August 1848,
8.16.48 gewidmet von Gustav Reitter, Garde des XI.
Bezirkes, 4. Compagnie.
[Wien,1848]
broadside. 30x23.5cm.
Helfert (Wiener Parnass) 1688.

Scheibe, Theodor, 1820-1881.
*pGB8 Eine neue Religion in Wien! und entdeckte
V6755R Verruchtheit Metternichs.
8.16.48 [Wien]Zu haben im Verlagsgewölbe:Parisergasse
411.Gedruckt bei U.Klopf sen.und Alexander
Eurich.[1848]
broadside. 42x26.5cm.
Listing the tenets of the "German-Catholic
religion" of Johannes Ronge, introduced into
Vienna in August of 1848. Ronge had been denied
entrance into Austria by Metternich.

Vienna. Sicherheits-Ausschuss.
*pGB8 Kundmachung. Der gefertigte Ausschuss muss
V6755R wiederholt auf das Ungesetzliche und
8.16.48 Verwerfliche der sogenannten Katzenmusiken und
auf die dagegen ergriffenen energischen
Massregeln hinweisen ...
[Wien]Aus der k.k.Hof= und Staatsdruckerei.
[1848]
broadside. 44.5x57cm.
Dated: Wien am 16. August 1848.

Austria. Reichstag, 1848-1849.
*pGB8 Protokoll der Sitzung der constituirenden
V6755R Reichs=Versammlung am 17. August 1848.
8.17.48 [Wien]Aus der k.k.Hof= und Staatsdruckerei.
[1848]
folder([4]p.) 38x23cm.
Caption title; imprint on p.[4].

Gärtner, Wilhelm, 1811-1875.
*pGB8 Ueber die sogenannte "neue Religion" in Wien.
V6755R [Wien]Gedruckt bei Carl Gerold.[1848]
8.17.48 broadside. 39x25.5cm.
Dated: Wien, den 17. August 1848.
'Entnommen der № 7 des "Sprechers für Staat
und Kirche", im Verlage bei C. Gerold.'
Suggesting a debate on the principles of the
Catholic faith with Hermann Pauli, who had
introduced the "German-Catholic religion" of
Johannes Ronge into Vienna.

Austria. Reichstag, 1848-1849.
*pGB8 Protokoll der Sitzung der constituirenden
V6755R Reichs-Versammlung am 18. August 1848.
8.18.48 [Wien]Aus der k.k.Hof= und Staatsdruckerei.
[1848]
[2]p. 38x22.5cm.
Caption title; imprint on p.[2].

Keine neue Religion sondern die uralte! Ein
*pGB8 Wort an die Deutsch=Katholiken, ihre Freunde und
V6755R Feinde.
8.18.48 [Wien]Zu haben im Redactions=Bureau des
"Omnibus" Stadt,Liliengässchen Nr.898.Druck v.
Jos.St.v.Hirschfeld.[1848]
broadside. 43x27cm.
Signed: K. Mr.

Austria. Reichstag, 1848-1849.
*pGB8 Protokoll der Sitzung der constituirenden
V6755R Reichs=Versammlung am 19. August 1848.
8.19.48 [Wien]Aus der k.k.Hof= und Staatsdruckerei.
[1848]
[2]p. 38x23cm.
Caption title; imprint on p.[2].

Hirschberg und Pauli im Odeon oder: Was Alles
*pGB8 dort geschehen ist!
V6755R [Wien]Gedruckt bei M.Lell.[1848]
8.19.48 broadside. 38x23cm.
Account of a meeting on 18 August.

*pGB8
V6755R
8.19.48

Klaus, Martin, fl.1848.
　Hecker, der Republikaner in Wien!
[Wien]Gedruckt bei Josef Ludwig.[1848]

broadside. 43x26.5cm.

---

*pGB8
V6755R
8.20.48

[Alterego, pseud.]
　Dr. Schütte als Prophet! Unglaublich, aber
doch wahr! (Nach seiner eigenen Aussage in
der Aula am 16. August 1848.)
[Wien]Gedruckt bei U.Klopf sen.und Alexander
Eurich.[1848]

[2]p. 40x25cm.
Caption title; imprint on p.[2]; signed at end:
Alterego.

---

*pGB8
V6755R
8.20.48

Joh. [i.e. Johannes] Ronge. Ein Wort zu
seiner Zeit.
[Wien]Gedruckt bei M.Lell.[1848]

broadside. 38.5x23cm.

---

*pGB8
V6755R
8.20.48

Scheibe, Theodor, 1820-1881.
　Was 12 Millionen Menschen von der Wiener
Reichsversammlung verlangen.
　[Wien]Zu haben im Verlagsgewölbe in der Stadt,
Parisergasse Nr.411,Druck von U.Klopf sen.und
Alexander Eurich.[1848]

broadside. 48x65.5cm.

---

*pGB8
V6755R
8.21.48

Austria. Justizministerium.
　... Provisorische Vorschrift über den
Wirkungskreis des Justiz=Ministeriums.
[Wien,1848]

folder(4p.) 38x23cm.
Caption title; at head: Ad $\frac{2545}{J.M.}$
Dated: Wien am 21 August 1848.

---

*pGB8
V6755R
8.21.48

Austria. Ministerium für öffentliche Arbeiten.
　Kundmachung. Das Ministerium der öffentlichen
Arbeiten hat im Einvernehmen mit dem Ministerium
des Jnnern den Beschluss gefasst, von der mit dem
Erlasse vom 18. d. M. verfügten Ermässigung des
Taglohnes bei öffentlichen Arbeiten, und zwar
auf 15 kr. C.M. für Weiber und auf 10 kr. C.M.
für Personen unter 15 Jahren in keinem Falle
abzugehen ...
　[Wien]Aus der k.k.Hof= und Staatsdruckerei.
[1848]

broadside. 45x57cm.
Dated: Wien am 21. August 1848.

---

*pGB8
V6755R
8.21.48

Austria. Reichstag, 1848-1849.
　Protokoll der Sitzung der constituirenden
Reichs=Versammlung am 21. August 1848.
[Wien]Aus der k.k.Hof= und Staatsdruckerei.
[1848]

folder([4]p.) 38x23cm.
Caption title; imprint on p.[4].

---

*pGB8
V6755R
8.21.48

Austria. Reichstag, 1848-1849.
　Protokoll der Sitzung der constituirenden
Reichs=Versammlung am 21. August 1848
Nachmittags.
[Wien]Aus der k.k.Hof= und Staatsdruckerei.
[1848]

folder([3]p.) 38x23cm.
Caption title; imprint on p.[3].

---

*pGB8
V6755R
8.21.48

Die schwarzgelben Studenten. Ein Warnungswort
an Wiens Bürger.
[Wien]Gedruckt bei Edl.v.Schmidbauer und
Holzwarth.[1848]

broadside. 43x26.5cm.
Defending the Akademische Legion.

---

*pGB8
V6755R
8.21.48

Vienna. Gemeinderat.
　Kundmachung. Aus Anlass der heutigen Bewegung
findet sich der Gemeinde=Ausschuss veranlasst,
alle gutgesinnten Einwohner Wiens zu ersuchen,
nicht aus müssiger Neugierde die aufgeregten
Massen zu vermehren ...
　[Wien]Aus der k.k.Hof= und Staatsdruckerei.
[1848]

broadside. 38x46cm.
Dated: Wien den 21. August 1848.

Austria. Reichstag, 1848-1849.
*pGB8
V6755R
8.22.48
Protokoll der Sitzung der constituirenden
Reichs=Versammlung am 22. August 1848.
[Wien]Aus der k.k.Hof= und Staatsdruckerei.
[1848]

[6]p. 38x23cm.
Caption title; imprint on p.[6].

Wiener demokratischer Verein.
*pGB8
V6755R
8.22.48
Arbeiter! Der demokratische Verein,dessen
Gesinnungen gegen Euch gewiss nicht bezweifelt
werden können, ist tief betrübt durch die
Ereignisse des gestrigen Tages ...
[Wien]Druck von Jos.Keck & Sohn.[1848]

broadside. 50x40cm.
Dated: Wien, den 22. August 1848.

Vienna. Gemeinderat.
*pGB8
V6755R
8.22.48
An die Bevölkerung der Stadt Wien! Mit
Beziehung auf ein angeblich von dem
Ausschusse des demokratischen Vereines
herrührendes Placat vom heutigen Tage ...
[Wien,1848]

broadside. 36.5x48cm.
Dated: Wien am 22. August 1848.
Trimmed at bottom, perhaps removing imprint.

Austria. Reichstag, 1848-1849.
*pGB8
V6755R
8.23.48
Protokoll der Sitzung der constituirenden
Reichs=Versammlung am 23. August 1848.
[Wien]Aus der k.k.Hof= und Staatsdruckerei.
[1848]

folder([4]p.) 38x23cm.
Caption title; imprint on p.[4].

Vienna. Gemeinderat.
*pGB8
V6755R
8.22.48
An die Nationalgarde Wiens! Der Gemeinde=
Ausschuss der Stadt Wien fühlt sich
verpflichtet, der Nationalgarde für ihre
energische und erfolgreiche Mitwirkung zur
Aufrechthaltung der neuerlich gefährdeten Ruhe
der Hauptstadt seinen lebhaften Dank
auszusprechen ...
[Wien]Aus der k.k.Hof= und Staatsdruckerei.
[1848]

broadside. 44.5x28.5cm.
Dated: Wien am   22. August 1848.

Klaus, Martin, fl.1848.
*pGB8
V6755R
8.23.48
Blutiger Kampf der Arbeiter im Prater.
[Wien]Gedruckt bei M.Lell.[1848]

broadside. 38x23cm.

Vienna. Nationalgarde.
*pGB8
V6755R
8.22.48
Tagsbefehl vom 22. August 1848.
[Wien]Aus der k.k.Hof= und Staatsdruckerei.
[1848]

broadside. 44.5x28.5cm.

Vienna. Gemeinderat.
*pGB8
V6755R
8.23.48
An die steuerpflichtigen Bewohner Wiens! Das
Jahr 1848, durch die erzielten Errungenschaften
für jeden patriotisch gesinnten Staatsbürger
unvergesslich, hat von der Stadtgemeinde Wien
bedeutende Geldopfer erheischt und neue
Erfordernisse hervorgerufen ...
[Wien]Aus der k.k.Hof= und Staatsdruckerei.
[1848]

broadside. 42.5x28.5cm.
Dated: Wien am 23. August 1848.

Vienna. Sicherheits-Ausschuss.
*pGB8
V6755R
8.22.48
Mitbürger! Der Drang der Gefahren, das
Drohen hereinbrechender Anarchie, und in Folge
dessen Auflösung aller bestehenden Bande
der Staatsgesellschaft, waren es, die als
Rettungsmittel dem Ausschusse sein Leben gaben
...
[Wien]Aus der k.k.Hof= und Staatsdruckerei.
[1848]

broadside. 44.5x28.5cm.
In contemporary ms. at foot: Aufgelöst 24
August 848,   ausgegeben 22 August 848.

Vienna. Gemeinderat.
*pGB8
V6755R
8.23.48
Kundmachung. Es werden böswillige Gerüchte
ausgestreut, dass bei den am 21. d. M. Statt
gefundenen tumultuarischen Bewegungen
bedeutende, ja sogar tödtliche Verletzungen
durch das Einschreiten der Sicherheitswache
vorgefallen seien ...
[Wien]Aus der k.k.Hof= und Staatsdruckerei.
[1848]

broadside. 44.5x28.5cm.
Dated: Wien am 23. August 1848.

*pGB8
V6755R
8.23.48

Vienna. Sicherheits-Ausschuss.
Volk von Wien! Die Ereignisse der
letztverflossenen Tage haben den gefertigten
Ausschuss veranlasst, seine freiwillige
Auflösung mit der feierlichen Erklärung
auszusprechen, dass er an den Ursachen und
Wirkungen der Arbeiter=Unruhen durchaus keinen
Theil habe ...
[Wien]Aus der k.k.Hof= und Staats=Druckerei.
[1848]
    broadside. 44.5x57cm.
    Dated: Wien am 23. August 1848.
                    (See next card)

---

*pGB8
V6755R
8.23.48

Vienna. Sicherheits-Ausschuss.   Volk von
Wien ... [1848]   (Card 2)

Includes "Copie des Ministerial-Erlasses
über das Auflösungsgesuch des vereinten
Ausschusses", also dated 23. August 1848.

---

*pGB8
V6755R
8.24.48

Arbeiter=Aufstand, Einschreiten der National-
garde und Sicherheitswache, dann schrecklicher
Meuchelmord eines wehrlosen Bürgers in der
Leopoldstadt.
Wien.Gedruckt im August 1848 bei J.N.Fridrich.
[2]p. 38.5x23cm.
Caption title; imprint on p.[2].

---

*pGB8
V6755R
8.24.48

Die Arbeiter=Unruhen oder die Kämpfe am 19.
und 23. August und die Zerwürfnisse der
Nationalgarden und der Studenten-Legion.
[Wien]Gedruckt bei Franz Edlen von Schmid.
[1848]
    [2]p. 39.5x25cm.
    Caption title; imprint on p.[2].
    At end: Wien, den 24. August 1848.
    Verantwortlich die Redaktion der
    Studentenzeitung.
                    (See next card)

---

*pGB8
V6755R
8.24.48

Die Arbeiter=Unruhen ... [1848]
                    (Card 2)

Another issue has "am 21. und 23. August"
in title & "Verantwortlich Paul Löve,
Redacteur der Studentenzeitung" at end.

---

*pGB8
V6755R
8.24.48

Die Arbeiter=Unruhen oder die Kämpfe am 21.
und 23. August und die Zerwürfnisse der
Nationalgarden und der Studenten-Legion.
[Wien]Gedruckt bei Franz Edlen von Schmid.
[1848]
    [2]p. 39.5x25cm.
    Caption title; imprint on p.[2].
    At end: Wien, den 24. August 1848.
    Verantwortlich Paul Löve, Redacteur der
    Studentenzeitung.
    Another issue has "am 19. und 23. August" in
    title & "Verantwortlich die Redaktion der
    Studentenzeitung"   at end.

---

*pGB8
V6755R
8.24.48

Austria. Ministerrat.
    Kundmachung. Seit einigen Tagen ist die Stadt
Wien und ihre Umgebung durch die Excesse der bei
öffentlichen Bauten beschäftigten Arbeiter in
beständige Unruhe und Aufregung versetzt ...
    [Wien]Aus der k.k.Hof= und Staats=Druckerei.
[1848]
    broadside. 44.5x57cm.
    Dated: Wien am 24. August 1848.
    Another edition has number at head & is
without imprint.

---

*pGB8
V6755R
8.24.48

Austria. Ministerrat.
    ... Kundmachung. Seit einigen Tagen ist die
Stadt Wien und ihre Umgebung durch die Excesse
der bei öffentlichen Bauten beschäftigten
Arbeiter in beständige Unruhe und Aufregung
versetzt ...
    [Wien,1848]
    broadside. 38x46.5cm.
    At head: Zu Nro.10706.-149. Nro.2.
    Dated: Wien am 24. August 1848.
    Another edition is without number at head
& has imprint.

---

*pGB8
V6755R
8.24.48

Austria. Ministerrat.
    Kundmachung. Um der zur Aufrechthaltung der
Ruhe, Ordnung und Sicherheit einschreitenden
Nationalgarde den gebührenden gesetzlichen
Schutz zu sichern, wird hiermit verordnet ...
    [Wien]Aus der k.k.Hof= und Staats=Druckerei.
[1848]
    broadside. 45x57cm.
    Dated: Wien am 24. August 1848.
    Another edition has number at head & is
without imprint.

---

*pGB8
V6755R
8.24.48

Austria. Ministerrat.
    ... Kundmachung. Um der zur Aufrechthaltung
der Ruhe, Ordnung und Sicherheit einschreitenden
Nationalgarde den gebührenden gesetzlichen
Schutz zu sichern, wird hiemit verordnet ...
    [Wien,1848]
    broadside. 38x47cm.
    At head: Zu Nro.10706.-149. Nro.3.
    Dated: Wien den 24. August 1848.
    Another edition is without number at head &
has imprint.

*pGB8
V6755R
8.24.48

Austria. Reichstag, 1848-1849.
    Protokoll der Sitzung der constituirenden
Reichs=Versammlung am 24. August 1848.
    [Wien]Aus der k.k.Hof= und Staatsdruckerei.
[1848]

        folder([4]p.) 38x23cm.
        Caption title; imprint on p.[4].

---

*pGB8
V6755R
8.24.48

Vienna. Nordbahnhof. Arbeiter.
    Kundmachung. Wir sämmtliche Arbeiter des
Wiener Bahnhofes der Kaiser Ferdinands Nordbahn
sehen uns veranlasst, den wirklichen Thatbestand
des am 23. d. M. vorgefallenen Confliktes
zwischen uns und der Sicherheitswache, der
Wahrheit getreu, zur Widerlegung ganz falscher
Gerüchte und zur Rechtfertigung unseres stets
bewiesenen Strebens, für die Aufrechthaltung der
Ruhe, Sicherheit und Ordnung, zur
Veröffentlichung zu bringen ...
                        (See next card)

---

*pGB8
V6755R
8.24.48

Der blutige Kampf wegen der Arbeiter im Prater
und der Brigittenau.
    [Wien]Gedruckt bei Franz Edlen von Schmidt.
[1848]

        broadside. 42x26cm.
        Dated: Monat August 1848.
        In this edition, last line of text reads: Man
sagt bis jetzt von 20 Todten und über 100
Verwundeten.
        In contemporary ms. at head: 24. August 848.

---

*pGB8
V6755R
8.24.48

Vienna. Nordbahnhof. Arbeiter.   Kundmachung
    ... [1848]   (Card 2)

    [Wien,1848]

        broadside. 60.5x47.5cm.
        Dated: Wien, am 24. August 1848.

---

*pGB8
V6755R
8.24.48

Der blutige Kampf wegen der Arbeiter im Prater
und der Brigittenau.
    [Wien]Gedruckt bei Franz Edlen von Schmidt.
[1848]

        broadside. 41.5x26.5cm.
        In this (undated) edition, last line of text
reads: Man spricht von 58 Todten und gegen
200 Verwundeten.

---

*GB8
V6755R
8.24.48

[Waldschütz, Johann Nepomuk]
    Zur Namensfeier des verehrten National=Garde=
Hauptmanns des IX. Bezirks III. Compagnie
Herrn Bartholomäus Moschigg. Dargebracht am 24.
August 1848.
    [Wien]Gedruckt bei Leop.Sommer.[1848]
        [2]p. 22.5x14.5cm.
        Caption title; imprint on p.[2]; signed at end:
J. U. [i.e.N.] Waldschütz, Garde des IX.
Bezirkes, 3. Comp.
        Helfert (Wiener Parnass)1721.

---

*pGB8
V6755R
8.24.48

Klaus, Martin, fl.1848.
    Der Sicherheits=Ausschuss ist gestorben den
Tod des Gerechten.
    [Wien]Gedruckt bei M.Lell.[1848]

        broadside. 37.5x23cm.

---

*pGB8
V6755R
8.25.48

Austria. Reichstag, 1848-1849.
    Protokoll der Sitzung der constituirenden
Reichs=Versammlung am 25. August 1848.
    [Wien]Aus der k.k.Hof= und Staatsdruckerei.
[1848]

        [2]p. 37.5x22.5cm.
        Caption title; imprint on p.[2].

---

*pGB8
V6755R
8.24.48

Vienna. Comité zur Unterstützung mitteloser
        Gewerbsleute.
    An die Gewerbetreibenden Wiens! Um den tief
darniederliegenden Gewerbestand der Haupt= und
Residenzstadt Wien nach Möglichkeit zu heben,
hat über Aufforderung des hohen Ministeriums
sich ein Comité gebildet ...
    [Wien]Aus der k.k.Hof= und Staats=Druckerei.
[1848]

        broadside. 45x57cm.
        Dated: Wien am 24. August 1848.

---

*pGB8
V6755R
8.25.48

Vienna. Gemeinderat.
    An die Bevölkerung Wiens! Seit einigen Tagen
werden die schändlichsten Lügen über die
Wirksamkeit des Gemeinde=Ausschusses der Stadt
Wien offenbar in der Absicht, die Massen gegen
denselben aufzuregen und seine Thätigkeit zu
lähmen, im Publikum verbreitet ...
    [Wien]Aus der k.k.Hof= und Staatsdruckerei.
[1848]

        broadside. 45x57cm.
        Dated: Wien den 25. August 1848.

*pGB8
V6755R
8.25.48

Vienna. Nationalgarde.
Vom Nationalgarde-Ober-Commando. Der Herr
Minister des Jnneren hat über das Verhalten der
Herren Nationalgarden am 23. d. M. folgendes
Schreiben an das Nationalgarde=Ober=Commando
erlassen: ...
[Wien]Aus der k.k.Hof= und Staatsdruckerei.
[1848]

broadside. 44.5x28.5cm.
Dated: Wien am 25. August 1848.

---

*pGB8
V6755R
8.26.48

[Pexa, L   J   ]   Erwiederung ...
[1848]   (Card 2)
näher kennen wollt, der Verfasser der
Broschüre: Belehrung über das Wesen eines
Schwurgerichtes in Strafsachen.
A later edition is signed with the author's
name.

---

*pGB8
V6755R
8.26.48

Austria. Reichstag, 1848-1849.
Protokoll der Sitzung der constituirenden
Reichs=Versammlung am 26. August 1848.
[Wien]Aus der k.k.Hof= und Staatsdruckerei.
[1848]

folder([4]p.) 38x23cm.
Caption title; imprint on p.[4].

---

*pGB8
V6755R
8.26.48

Pexa, L   J
... Erwiederung auf die schändlichen
Ausfälle gegen die Nationalgarde von Seiten der
"Prostitution" Tagblatt für anarchisches
Volkstreiben und Volksverführung," fälschlich
"Constitution," Tagblatt für constitutionelles
Volksleben und Belehrung, genannt.
[Wien]Gedruckt und zu haben bei Carl
Ueberreuter,Stadt,Dorotheergasse Nr.1111.[1848]

broadside. 44x52cm.
At head: Dritte Auflage.
Dated & signed: Wien, den 26. August 1848.
L. J. Pexa, Garde   des XI. Bezirkes ...

---

*pGB8
V6755R
8.26.48

Hört und richtet uns! Ein Vertheidigungswort
von den Arbeitern.
[Wien]Gedruckt bei M.Lell.[1848]

broadside. 38.5x23cm.
Signed & dated: Jm Namen vieler gutgesinnten
Arbeiter. Am 26. August 1848.
In this edition, the last full line of text
ends: sehr kurzer Zeit,

---

*pGB8
V6755R
8.26.48

Vienna. Nationalgarde.
An die gesammte Nationalgarde. Jn Befolgung des
so eben erhaltenen hohen Ministerial=Auftrages
beeilt sich das provisorische Ober=Commando
der Nationalgarde das nachstehende, an den
Herrn Minister des Jnneren herabgelangte
allerhöchste Handschreiben Seiner Majestät vom
25. August d. J. zur Kenntniss der Nationalgarde
zu bringen ...
[Wien]Aus der k.k.Hof= und Staatsdruckerei.
[1848]

(See next card)

---

*pGB8
V6755R
8.26.48

Hört uud [!] richtet uns! Ein
Vertheidigungswort von den Arbeitern.
[Wien]Gedruckt bei M.Lell.[1848]

broadside. 35x23cm.
Signed & dated: Jm Namen vieler gutgesinnten
Arbeiter. Am 26. August 1848.
In this edition, the last full line of text
ends: in sehr kurzer

---

*pGB8
V6755R
8.26.48

Vienna. Nationalgarde.   An die gesammte ...
[1848]   (Card 2)
broadside. 45x29cm.
Dated: Wien am 26. August 1848.
Ferdinand's letter is dated: Schönbrunn den
25. August 1848.

---

*pGB8
V6755R
8.26.48

[Pexa, L   J   ]
Erwiederung auf die schändlichen Ausfälle
gegen die Nationalgarde von Seiten des
Tagesblattes "Prostitution für anarchisches
Treiben und Volksverführung," armassenderweise
"Constitution für Volksbelehrung," genannt.
[Wien]Gedruckt und zu haben bei Carl
Ueberreuter,Stadt,Dorotheergasse Nr.1111.[1848]

broadside. 44.5x52cm.
Dated & signed: Wien, den 26. August 1848.
Ein Garde des XI. Bezirkes, und wenn ihr ihn
                    (See next card)

---

*pGB8
V6755R
8.26.48

Vienna. Nationalgarde.
Tagsbefehl. vom 26. August 1848.
[Wien]Druck von Jos.Keck & Sohn.[1848]

broadside. 40x25cm.

Johannes, pseud.
Des Sicherheitsausschusses Glück und Ende.
*pGB8 [Wien]Jm Verlag bei J.Bader,Stadt,
V6755R Stroblgasse.[1848]
8.27.48

broadside. 42x26.5cm.
Dated & signed: Wien am 27. August 1848.
Johannes.

Austria. Reichstag, 1848-1849.
Protokoll der Sitzung der constituirenden
*pGB8 Reichs=Versammlung am 29. August 1848.
V6755R [Wien]Aus der k.k.Hof= und Staatsdruckerei.
8.29.48 [1848]

[5]p. 38x23cm.
Caption title; imprint on p.[5].

Siegl, W
Grosses Leichenbegängniss der Wiener=
*pGB8 Arbeiter. für ihre am 26. August gefallenen
V6755R Brüder.
8.27.48 [Wien]Gedruckt bei Josef Ludwig,Josephstadt
Nr.52.[1848]

broadside. 38.5x24.5cm.
Dated: Wien am 27. August 1848.

Die letzten Worte eines sterbenden Arbeiters
im Spital und dessen Testament.
*pGB8 [Wien]Gedruckt bei Franz Ed.v.Schmid.[1848]
V6755R
8.29.48 [2]p. 39.5x25cm.
Caption title; imprint on p.[2].
Dated & signed: Wien, am 29. August 1848.
Verantwortlich die Redaktion der
Studentenzeitung. Altlerchenfeld, Nr.5.

Vienna. Magistrat.
Kundmachung. Um die irrigen oder böswilligen
*pGB8 Angaben mehrerer Zeitungsblätter zu widerlegen,
V6755R welche gestern einen angeblichen Bericht der
8.27.48 Stadthauptmannschaft über die Anzahl der bei
dem Zusammenstosse der Arbeiter mit der
bewaffneten Macht am 23. d. M. Gefallenen und
Verwundeten veröffentlichten ...
[Wien]Aus der k.k.Hof= und Staatsdruckerei.
[1848]
broadside. 45x57cm.
Dated & signed: Wien am 27. August 1848. Von
der Stadthauptmannschaft.

Vienna. Gemeinderat.
Kundmachung. Der Gemeinde=Ausschuss der Stadt
*pGB8 Wien hat in der Sitzung vom 24. d. M. mit
V6755R Rücksicht auf die besonderen obwaltenden
8.29.48 Umstände den einstimmigen Beschluss gefasst,
sogleich den in den Entwurf der neuen Gemeinde=
Ordnung aufzunehmenden Wahlmodus zu berathen ...
[Wien,1848]
[3]p. 42x26cm.
Caption title; signed & dated at end: Vom
Gemeinde-Ausschusse der Stadt Wien am 29. August
1848.
Another edition has imprint on p.[3].

Berger, A   W
An die ehrenhaften und gutgesinnten Bürger
*pGB8 Wien's.
V6755R Zu haben bei J.Bader,Buchhändler in Wien,Stadt,
8.28.48 Strobelgasse.[1848] Preis:3 kr.C.M.

broadside. 42.5x53cm.
Dated: Wien, am 28. August 1848.

Vienna. Gemeinderat.
Kundmachung. Der Gemeinde=Ausschuss der
*pGB8 Stadt Wien hat in der Sitzung vom 24. d. M.
V6755R mit Rücksicht auf die besonderen obwaltenden
8.29.48 Umstände den einstimmigen Beschluss gefasst,
sogleich den in den Entwurf der neuen Gemeinde=
Ordnung aufzunehmenden Wahlmodus zu berathen
...
[Wien]Gedruckt bei Leopold Grund,Hundsthurm
Nr.1.[1848]

(See next card)

Vienna. Comité zur Unterstützung mittelloser
Gewerbsleute.
*pGB8 An die Gewerbetreibenden Wiens! Das im
V6755R Auftrage des hohen Ministeriums gebildete
8.28.48 Comité zur Unterstützung mittelloser
Gewerbsleute in Wien, hat bei der zu Folge
Kundmachung vom 24. d. M. abgehaltenen
öffentlichen Sitzung am 28. d. M. die
Ueberzeugung gewonnen ...
[Wien]Aus der k.k.Hof= und Staats=Druckerei.
[1848]
broadside.   45x57cm.
Dated: Wien am   28. August 1848.

Vienna. Gemeinderat.   Kundmachung ... [1848]
(Card 2)
*pGB8
V6755R
8.29.48 folder([3]p.) 40.5x26cm.
Caption title; imprint on p.[3]; signed &
dated at end: Vom Gemeinde-Ausschuss der
Stadt Wien am 29. August 1848.
Another edition is without imprint.

*pGB8
V6755R
8.30.48

Austria. Finanzministerium.
    Auf Grundlage des durch reichstäglichen
Beschluss vom 21. d. M. dem Finanz=Ministerium
eröffneten Credits hat sich dasselbe zur
Hinausgabe von fünfpercentigen Cassa=
Anweisungen bestimmt gefunden ....
    [Wien]Aus der k.k.Hof= und Staatsdruckerei.
[1848]

    broadside. 44.5x28.5cm.
    Dated: Wien am 30. August 1848.

*pGB8
V6755R
8.31.48

Austria. Reichstag, 1848-1849.
    Protokoll der Sitzung der constituirenden
Reichs=Versammlung am 31. August 1848.
    [Wien]Aus der k.k.Hof= und Staats=Druckerei.
[1848]

    [6]p. 38x23cm.
    Caption title; imprint on p.[6].

*pGB8
V6755R
8.30.48

Austria. Reichstag, 1848-1849.
    Protokoll der Sitzung der constituirenden
Reichs=Versammlung am 30. August 1848.
    [Wien]Aus der k.k.Hof= und Staatsdruckerei.
[1848]

    [6]p. 38x23cm.
    Caption title; imprint on p.[6].

*pGB8
V6755R
8.31.48

Vienna. Nationalgarde.
    Der Verwaltungsrath an die gesammte
Nationalgarde Wiens. Um ein richtiges
Verständniss über den Verwaltungsrath der
Wiener Nationalgarde und dessen Wirksamkeit zu
erzielen ...
    [Wien]Aus der k.k.Hof= und Staats=Druckerei.
[1848]

    folder([4]p.) 45x29cm.
    Caption title; imprint on p.[4].
    Dated: Wien am 31. August 1848.

*pGB8
V6755R
8.30.48

Gritzner, Maximilian C
    An Wien. Der politische Himmel ist düster, die
Luft ist drückend schwül ...
    [Wien]Gedruckt bei Franz Edlen v.Schmid.[1848]

    broadside. 58.5x46cm.
    Dated & signed: Wien, am 30. August 1848.
    Gritzner, im Namen der Redaktion und
sämmtlicher Mitarbeiter der Constitution.

*pGB8
V6755R
8.32.48

    ... Aerzte, schafft Aerzte für die Armee und
die Feldspitäler. Aufhebung der Josefs=Akademie.
Dringendes Wort an die hohe Reichsversammlung
und an das Ministerium des Krieges in Sachen
der österr. Militär-Aerzte.
    [Wien,1848]

    [2]p. 44x27.5cm.
    Caption title; at head: Beilage zum österr.
Courier.
    "Dieser Aufsatz ist auch einzeln, im Comptoir
dieser Zeitung, für 6 kr. C. M. zu haben."
    Dated at end: Wien, im August 1848.

*pGB8
V6755R
8.30.48

    ... Die letzten Worte eines sterbenden
Arbeiters im Spital und dessen Testament.
    [Wien]Gedruckt bei Franz Ed.v.Schmid.[1848]

    [2]p. 39.5x25cm.
    Caption title; at head, "(Zweite Auflage.)";
imprint on p.[2]; dated & signed at end: Wien,
am 30. August 1848. Verantwortlich die
Redaktion der Studentenzeitung. Altlerchenfeld,
Nr.5.

*pGB8
V6755R
8.32.48

Austria. Justizministerium.
    Bericht über den Entwurf eines Gesetzes für
Ehrengerichte der Nationalgarde.
    [Wien]Aus der k.k.Hof= und Staatsdruckerei.
[1848]

    9p. 38.5x23cm.
    Caption title; imprint on p.8.
    "Entwurf einer Vorschrift für Ehrengerichte
der Nationalgarde": p.4-8.
    In contemporary ms. at head: August.

*pGB8
V6755R
8.31.48

    Ausserordentliches Extrablatt. Die erste
goldene Frucht des Reichstages! Kein Robot!
Kein Zehnt mehr!
    [Wien]Gedruckt bei Franz Edlen von Schmid.
[1848]

    [2]p. 39.5x25cm.
    Caption title; imprint on p.[2]; dated &
signed at end: Wien, am 31. August 1848.
Verantwortlich die Redaction der Studentenzeitung

*pGB8
V6755R
8.32.48

    Blutiger Kampf! Die projectirte Belagerung von
Pesth. Unerhörte Gräuelscenen und die
Befürchtung: "Ungarn ist verloren."
    [Wien]Zu haben im Verlagsgewölbe:Parisergasse,
Nr.411.Druck von U.Klopf sen.und Alexander
Eurich.[1848]

    broadside. 39.5x25cm.
    Signed: T.

Bodnár, L

*pGB8
V6755R
8.32.48

Relation über die am 23. August 1848 stattgehabten Begebenheiten, in Bezug des VI. Bezirkes Landstrasse, gegenüber der aufgewiegelten Arbeiter.
[Wien]Aus der k.k.Hof= und Staats-Druckerei. [1848]

broadside. 44.5x57cm.
Signed: L. Bodnár, Commandant des 1. Bataillons, VI. Bezirkes.

Fischer, J   E   fl.1848.

*GB8
V6755R
8.32.48

Wiener deutsches Lied. (Nach der Melodie des Fuchs=Liedes) und zum Trommelschlag der National=Garde.
[Wien]Druck von U.Klopf sen.und Alexauder [!] Eurich,[1848]

broadside. 25x19.5cm.
Helfert (Wiener Parnass) 1559.
Another edition has "und Alex. Eurich." in imprint.
Without the music.

Die Deutsch=Katholiken im Odeon.

*pGB8
V6755R
8.32.48

[Wien]Markl,Gumpendorf Nr.396.—Gedruckt bei Leop.Grund.[1848]

[2]p. 36.5x23cm.
Caption title; imprint on p.[2].

Fischer, J   E   fl.1848.

*GB8
V6755R
8.32.48

Wiener deutsches Lied. (Nach der Melodie des Fuchs=Liedes) und zum Trommelschlag der National=Garde.
[Wien]Gedruckt von U.Klopf sen.und Alex. Eurich.[1848]

broadside. 25x19cm.
Helfert (Wiener Parnass) 1559.
Another edition has "und Alexauder [!] Eurich," in imprint.
Without the music.

[Dominicus, Franz]

*pGB8
V6755R
8.32.48

An deutsche Männer und Helden!
Wien,1848.Bei Schmidt & Leo,Buchhandlung am Graben.Druck v.U.Klopf sen.u.A.Eurich,Wollzeile Nr.782.

[2]p. 42.5x28cm.
Caption title; imprint on p.[2]; signed at end: Franz Dominicus.

Der Frauenaufruhr im Volksgarten oder: Die Waschanstalt der Wienerdamen.

*pGB8
V6755R
8.32.48

[Wien]Gedruckt bei M.Lell.[1848]

broadside. 38.5x23cm.

Dominicus, Franz.

*GB8
V6755R
8.32.48

Wer sind die Radikalen? Widmung den Brüdern unter der schwarz-roth-goldenen Fahne. (Aus der Nacht durch Blut zum Licht.) Von Franz Dominicus.
[Wien]Zu haben bei Schmidt und Leo,Buchhandlung am Graben.[1848]

[2]p. 26.5x21cm.
Helfert (Wiener Parnass) 1749.
Caption title; imprint on p.[2].

Frieden mit Italien, Kriegsrüstungen in Russland. Ein Verein der Civilisirten Europas gegen die Ungebildeten.

*pGB8
V6755R
8.32.48

[Wien]Druck und Verlag von Leopold Grund, am Stephansplatze im Zwettelhofe.[1848]

[2]p. 36.5x23cm.
Caption title; imprint on p.[2].

Engel, Arnold, fl.1848.

*GB8
V6755R
8.32.48

An die 10. Compagnie des 5. Bezirks. Jmpromptu in östreich'scher Mundart. von Arnold Engl, Garde.
[Wien,1848]

.broadside. 23x15cm.
Helfert (Wiener Parnass) 1752.

Die Geheimnisse von Wien. Sedlnitzky, der Mädchenverführer.

*pGB8
V6755R
8.32.48

Wien.Gedruckt im August 1848,bei J.N. Fridrich.

[2]p. 38x23.5cm.
Caption title; imprint on p.[2]; signed at end: C. S.

*pGB8
V6755R
8.32.48

Grab=Rede für die am 23. August gefallenen
Arbeiter. Gesprochen von einem Mann aus dem
Volke.
[Wien]Gedruckt bei Franz Ed.v.Schmid.[1848]

[2]p. 39.5x25cm.
Caption title; imprint on p.[2]; dated at end:
Monat August 1848.

---

*pGB8
V6755R
8.32.48

Manifest im Namen der kroatisch-slavonischen
Nation gegen das unter demselben Namen in
Agram erschienene Manifest gerichtet.
[Wien]Gedruckt bei Franz Edlen von Schmid.
[1848]

8p. 39.5x25cm.
Caption title; imprint on p.8; dated & signed
at end: Wien, im August 1848. Jm Namen der
kroatisch=slavonischen Nation ihre freien Söhne.

---

*pGB8
V6755R
8.32.48

Die Leichenkammer im Spital und das Lazareth
bei den Barmherzigen als Folge der blutigen
Ereignisse wegen der Arbeiter am Tabor, in
der Brigittenau und Prater.
[Wien]Gedruckt bei F.Schmid.[1848]
[2]p. 39.5x25cm.
Caption title; imprint on p.[2]; dated at end:
Wien im August.
In this edition, line 14 on p.[2] begins:
allein es war keine Metzelei bloss um
Menschenleben zu opfern ...

---

*pGB8
V6755R
8.32.48

Metternich, Mörder des jungen Napoleon.
Wien.Gedruckt im August 1848 bei J.N.Fridrich.
[2]p. 37.5x23cm.
Caption title; imprint on p.[2]; signed at
end: L. S.
"Obige Daten sind einem Buche entnommen,
welches betitelt ist: Briefe eines Verstorbenen
[von Pückler-Muskau], und welches zu
Sedlnitzkys Zeiten stark verpönt war, weil es
die Wahrheit enthielt."
Accusing Metternich of having poisoned not
only the King of Rome but Napoléon
Bonaparte as well.

---

*pGB8
V6755R
8.32.48

Die Leichenkammer im Spital und das Lazareth
bei den Barmherzigen als Folge der blutigen
Ereignisse wegen der Arbeiter am Tabor, in der
Brigittenau und Prater.
[Wien]Gedruckt bei F.Schmid.[1848]

[2]p. 40x25cm.
Caption title; imprint on p.[2]; dated at end:
Wien im August 1848.
In this edition, line 14 on p.[2] begins: es
war eine Metzelei und Menschen fielen als
Opfer ...

---

*pGB8
V6755R
8.32.48

Die Pressfreiheit unter der glorreichen
Regierung des Kaiser Joseph.
[Wien]Gedruckt bei Franz Edlen von Schmid.
[1848]

broadside. 46x29cm.
Dated at end: Monat August 1848.

---

*GB8
V6755R
8.32.48

Ein Lied ganz neu, von der alten Polizei!
Von einem bussfertigen und reuevollen Spitzel,
nach der beliebten Melodie des Fuchsliedes.
[Wien]Gedruckt bei M.Lell.[1848]

[2]p. 21.5x13.5cm.
Helfert (Wiener Parnass) 1560.
Caption title; imprint on p.[2].
Without the music.

---

*pGB8
V6755R
8.32.48

Radetzky als Schustermeister.
[Wien]Schnellpressendruck von Jos.
Stöckholzer v.Hirschfeld.—Zu haben im Büreau
des "Omnibus",Stadt,Liliengasse Nr.898.[1848]

broadside. 1 illus. 43x27cm.

---

*GB8
V6755R
8.32.48

Man soll Herrn Saphir durchaus nicht
vertheidigen!
[Wien]Druck von U.Klopf sen.und A.Eurich.
[1848]

broadside. 25x20cm.
Signed: Buchheim, Phil. Dr. Hammerschmidt. Ed.
Leidesdorf, Jurist [& 4 andere].

---

*GB8
V6755R
8.32.48

Scheibe, Theodor, 1820-1881.
Extra=Blatt! Wie in Wien heute Nacht der
demokratische Klubb gesprengt worden ist.
[Wien]Im Verlagsgewölbe,Kölnerhofgasse Nr.730.
Gedruckt bei Leop.Sommer.[1848]

broadside. 26x20.5cm.

*GB8
V6755R
8.32.48

[Schmidt, Wilhelm Gottfried]
    Des Burschen Liebe! aut Studiosus de arte
amandi!
    [Wien,1848]

    folder([3]p.) 24x19cm.
    Helfert (Wiener Parnass) 1795.
    Caption title; signed at end: W. G. Schmidt,
Bürger und Garde der VI. Komp. XII. Bezirks.

○

*GB8
V6755R
8.32.48

[Schmidt, Wilhelm Gottfried]
    ... Das Taubenpaar. Ein Wahrheits=Gedicht.
    [Wien,1848]

    [2]p. 23.5x18.5cm.
    Helfert (Wiener Parnass) 1771.
    Caption title; signed at end: W. G. Schmidt,
Bürger und Garde. XII. Bez. 6. Compagnie
Lichteutal [!] Nr. 9.
    Dedication at head of title: Ihro Kais.
Hoheiten Erzherzog Franz Carl und Erzherzogin
Sophie.

○

*pGB8
V6755R
8.32.48

Schneider, Leopold, fl.1848.
    Das Lied der ersten Compagnie im ersten
Bezirk (Schottenviertel) gewidmet vom Kameraden
Leopold Schneider.
    [Wien,1848]

    broadside. 46x29cm.
    Helfert (Wiener Parnass) 1756.
    "In Musik gesetzt von Ferdinand Nikolaus
Schmidtler." Without the music.

○

*pGB8
V6755R
8.32.48

Seling, C   A
    Der Adel Oesterreichs. Von C. A. Seling.
    [Wien]Druck von M.Lell's Offizin.[1848]

    [2]p. 38x21cm.
    Caption title; imprint on p.[2].

○

*pGB8
V6755R
8.32.48

[Swoboda, August, fl.1848]
    Plan. Bei der Annahme, dass mindestens
30000 steuerpflichtige Gewerbsleute in diesem
Augenblicke durch ein Darlehen von 50 bis
350 fl. C.M. an jeden Einzelnen, in den Stand
gesetzt werden würden, die ihre jetzige
Existenz bedrohliche Periode zu überstehen,
—wäre ein Kapital von 6 Millionen nothwendig ...
    [Wien]Gedruckt bei Edl.v.Schmidbauer und
Holzwarth.[1848]
    [2]p. 43x27cm.
    Caption title; imprint on p.[2]; signed at end:
August Swoboda.
    In contemporary ○ ms. at head: August.

*GB8
V6755R
8.32.48

Uhl, Friedrich, 1825-1906.
    Lied der fünften Kompagnie, von Friedrich Uhl.
    [Wien]Druck von U.Klopf sen.und Alex.Eurich,
Wollzeile 782.[1848]

    broadside. 21x13cm.
    Helfert (Wiener Parnass) 1755.

○

*GB8
V6755R
8.32.48

Uhl, Friedrich, 1825-1906.
    Lied der fünften Kompagnie, von Friedrich Uhl.
    [Wien]Druck von U.Klopf sen.und Alex.Eurich,
Wollzeile 782.[1848]

    broadside. 20x13cm.
    Helfert (Wiener Parnass) 1755.
    At foot: Dritte Auflage.

○

*pGB8
V6755R
8.32.48

Was 100000 Proletarier vom Wiener Reichstag
verlangen, oder: Wien's furchtbarster Feind,
welcher die Stadt zu verderben droht.
    [Wien]Gedruckt bei J.N.Fridrich.[1848]

    broadside. 42.5x52.5cm.

○

*pGB8
V6755R
8.32.48

Wer trägt die Schuld an dem Arbeiter-
Aufstande vom 23. August, und dem dabei
vergossenen Blute?
    [Wien]Druck von Hirschfeld.[1848]

    broadside. 43x27cm.
    Signed: L....m.

○

*pGB8
V6755R
8.32.48

Wir haben gehört--Gott wird richten.
Entgegnung auf Hört und richtet uns!
    [Wien]Gedruckt bei Franz Edlen von Schmid.
[1848]

    [2]p. 39.5x25cm.
    Caption title; imprint on p.[2]; dated &
signed at end: Wien, im August 1848. Einer
für Viele.

○

*pGB8
V6755R
9.1.48

Austria. Ministerium des Innern.
Es sind dem Ministerium des Jnnern wiederholte Anzeigen zugekommen, dass in letzterer Zeit der Sicherheitswache in Vollziehung ihrer Dienstpflichten Widerstand geleistet, und dieselbe sogar thätlich angegriffen und insultirt wurde ...
[Wien]Aus der k.k.Hof= und Staats=Druckerei. [1848]

broadside. 45x57cm.
Dated: Wien am 1. September 1848.

---

*pGB8
V6755R
9.1.48

Grosses Blutbad in Ungarn oder Gräulthaten der besiegten Magyaren.
[Wien](Zu haben in der Wenedikt'schen Buch-handlung am Lobkowitzplatze Nr.1100.)[1848] Gedruckt bei Franz Ed.v.Schmid.
[2]p. 39.5x25cm.
Caption title; imprint on p.[2]; dated & signed at end: Wien am 1. September 1848. X.

---

*pGB8
V6755R
9.1.48

Austria. Ministerium des Innern.
Gegenüber den in den hiesigen Tageblättern und Flugschriften enthaltenen, den wahren Sachverhalt entstellenden Berichten über die Ereignisse des 21. und 23. August ...
[Wien]Aus der k.k.Hof= und Staats=Druckerei. [1848]

broadside. 45x57cm.
Dated: Wien am 1. September 1848.

---

*pGB8
V6755R
9.1.48

[Rath, J   M   ]
Aristokratie-Parthei-Wuth gegen einem fünfzehnjährigen Mädchen im Prater, und Namens= Verzeichniss und Verwundungs=Angabe derjenigen Arbeiter und Arbeiterinnen, welche am 23. August 1848 in das Spital zu den Barmherzigen gebracht wurden.
[Wien]Gedruckt bei Joseph Ludwig,Josephstadt Florianigasse Nr.52.[1848]

[2]p. 33.5x26cm.
Caption title; imprint on p.[2]; dated & signed: Wien im   Monath September 1848. J. M. Rath.

---

*pGB8
V6755R
9.1.48

Austria. Reichstag, 1848-1849.
Protokoll der Sitzung der constituirenden Reichs=Versammlung am 1. September 1848.
[Wien]Aus der k.k.Hof= und Staatsdruckerei. [1848]

folder([4]p.) 38x23cm.
Caption title; imprint on p.[4].

---

*pGB8
V6755R
9.1.48

Sonntags, den 3. September Nachm. 4 Uhr grosse Leichenfeier für die am 23. August gefallenen Arbeiter.
[Wien]Gedruckt bei Franz Edlen von Schmid. [1848]

broadside. 39.5x25cm.
Dated & signed: Wien, im September 1848.
Verantwortlich die Redaktion der Studentenzeitung.

---

*pGB8
V6755R
9.1.48

Der Bauer ist frei. Kein Zehent, keine Robot mehr, beschlossen und mit allgemeine Stimmenmehrheit angenommen durch die hohe Reichsversammlung, am 30. und 31. August 1848.
[Wien]Gedruckt bei Franz Edlen von Schmid. [1848]

broadside. 52.5x42cm.
Dated: Wien am 1. September 1848.

---

*pGB0
V6755R
9.1.48

Vienna. Nationalgarde.
Dienstvorschriften für die akademische Legion.
[Wien]Gedruckt bei U.Klopf sen.und Alexander Eurich.[1848]

broadside. 42x27cm.
Dated: Wien, den 1. September 1848.

---

*pGB8
V6755R
9.1.48

Friedeborn, Ad   Gust
Auch ein Wort im Jnteresse der subalternen Staatsbeamten.
Zu haben bei J.Bader,Buchhändler in Wien, Stadt,Strobelgasse.[1848] Preis:3 kr.C.M.

broadside. 42.5x53cm.
Dated: Wien, am 1. September 1848.

---

*pGB8
V6755R
9.2.48

Austria. Reichstag, 1848-1849.
Protokoll der Sitzung der constituirenden Reichs=Versammlung am 2. September 1848.
[Wien]Aus der k.k.Hof= und Staatsdruckerei. [1848]

10p. 38.5x23cm.
Caption title; imprint on p.10.

*pGB8
V6755R
9.2.48

Gritzner! auch deine Stunde schlägt!
[Wien]Gedruckt bei M.Lell.[1848]

broadside. 38x23cm.
Signed: A. M., Garde des 5. Bezirkes.
Another edition is dated 2 September 1848.

---

*pGB8
V6755R
9.2.48

Vienna. Chirurgen.
Die Wundärzte Wiens theilen hiermit ihren
Kollegen der Gesammt=Monarchie zur gefälligen
Kenntnissnahme die Petition mit, welche sie
gegen die laut Hauptblattes der Wiener Zeitung
vom 26. August d. J. mittelst Erlasses des
Unterrichts=Ministeriums verordnete Aufhebung
des niederen chirurgischen Studiums der hohen
Reichsversammlung unterbreitet haben ...
[Wien,1848]
[2]p. 38x27.5cm.
Caption title;   dated on p.[2]: Wien am
2. September   1848.

---

*pGB8
V6755R
9.2.48

Gritzner! auch deine Stunde schlägt!
[Wien]Gedruckt bei M.Lell.[1848]

broadside. 38x23cm.
Dated & signed: Wien am 2. September 1848. A.
M. Garde des 5. Bezirkes.
Another edition is undated.

---

*GB8
V6755R
9.3.48

Bernstein, Joseph, fl.1848.
Gewidmet zur Fahnenweihe in Unter-Sievering
am 3. September 1848.
[Wien,1848]

broadside. 32.5x23.5cm.
Helfert (Wiener Parnass) 1816.
Printed within ornamental border.

---

*pGB8
V6755R
9.2.48

[Jude, pseud.]
Jud bleibt Jud. Offenes Sendschreiben an alle
Juden die Minister werden wollen.
Wien,2.Sept.1848.Gedruckt bei Franz Edlen von
Schmid.
[2]p. 39.5x25cm.
Caption title; imprint on p.[2]; signed & dated
at end: Jude. Geschrieben am 4. Tage des Monats
Aelul im 5208 Jahr--das ist am 2. August 1848.

---

*pGB8
V6755R
9.3.48

Vienna. Gemeinderat.
Kundmachung. Mit Bezug auf die hierortige
Kundmachung vom 29. v. M., womit die mit h.
Ministerialdekrete vom 27. v. M. Z.2389
genehmigte Wahlordnung für die Wahl des neuen
Gemeinderathes zur allgemeinen Kenntniss
gebracht wurde ...
[Wien]Gedruckt bei Leop.Grund,am Hundsthurm Nr.
1.[1848]

broadside. 48x66cm.
Signed & dated: Vom Gemeinde=Ausschusse der
Stadt Wien, am   3. September 1848.

---

*pGB8
V6755R
9.2.48

Neuestes aus Jtalien! Blutiger Kampf in
Venedig und die Ermordung der
Oesterreichischgesinnten durch die Republikaner
und die Friedensbedingungen, welche Radetzky den
Jtalienern stellt.
[Wien]Gedruckt bei U.Klopf sen.und Alexander
Eurich.[1848]
[2]p. 39.5x25cm.
Caption title; imprint on p.[2]; dated & signed
at end: Wien, den 2. September 1848. S. T.

---

*pGB8
V6755R
9.4.48

Austria. Sovereigns, etc., 1835-1848
(Ferdinand I)
... Manifest des Kaisers Ferdinand an den
Banus von Kroatien.
[Wien]Gedruckt bei Franz Edlen v.Schmid.[1848]
broadside. 39.5x25cm.
At head: Ausserordentliches Extrablatt der
Agramer Zeitung vom 7. September 1848.
Dated: Schönbrunn, 4. September 1848.

---

*pGB8
V6755R
9.2.48

Oesterreichischer Patrioten-Verein.
... Erste Kundmachung über jene freiwilligen
Beiträge, welche die Einwohner von Wien ihrer
volksthümlichen constitutionellen
Staatsregierung zur Bestreitung der
ausserordentlichen Staatsbedürfnisse gegeben
haben.
[Wien]Aus der k.k.Hof= und Staatsdruckerei.
[1848]

broadside. 44.5x28cm.
Dated: Wien den 2. September 1848.

---

*pGB8
V6755R
9.4.48

Frieser, J
Trauer=Rede zur grossen Leichenfeier für die
am 23. August gefallenen Arbeiter. Am Grabe
unserer Brüder!
[Wien]Gedruckt im Monat September 1848.
Druck von Hirschfeld.

broadside. 43x27cm.
The service was held on 3 September.

*pGB8
V6755R
9.4.48

[Pichler, P   ]
   Des Kaisers Gespräch in Schönbrunn mit dem
Bauer Nikolaus B... aus G... der ihm über das
gewordene Geschenk der Robot= und der Zehent=
Aufhebung dankend zu den Füssen fallen wollte.
[Wien]Gedruckt bei Franz Edlen von Schmid.
[1848]
   [2]p. 40x25.5cm.
   Caption title; imprint on p.[2]; dated &
signed at end: Wieu [!] am 4 September 1848. P.
Pichler.

*pGB8
V6755R
9.5.48

   Die Geheimnisse des hochwürdigsten Wiener
Consistoriums oder das geistliche Kleeblatt:
Erzbischof, Weihbischof und Kanzleidirektor.
[Wien]Gedruckt bei Stöckholzer v.Hirschfeld.--
Zu haben in der Liliengasse Nro.898.[1848]
   broadside. 52.5x68.5cm.
   Dated & signed: Wien, im September 1848. J. F.

*pGB8
V6755R
9.4.48

Prague. Citizens.
   Protest der Bürger und Juristen Prags gegen die
in der "Kundmachung" des Fürsten Windischgrätz
vom 2. August 1848 ausgesprochene Beschuldigung
einer weitverzweigten Verschwörung und die in
Folge derselben ergriffenen Massregeln.
   Druck von Friedrich Eurich in Linz.(4.Sept.
1848.)
   folder(4p.) 38x25cm.
   Caption title; imprint on p.4.

*pGB8
V6755R
9.5.48

Hungary. Honvédelmi minisztérium.
   Statuten des Frei-Corps nach Ungarn.
[Wien]Gedruckt bei U.Klopf sen.und Alexander
Eurich.[1848]
   broadside. 35.5x22cm.
   Dated: Wien, den 5. September 1848.

*pGB8
V6755R
9.4.48

Vienna. Nationalgarde. Akademische Legion.
   Beschluss der Plenar-Sitzung des Studenten=
Ausschusses und der Commandanten und
Hauptleute der akademischen Legion.
[Wien]Aus der k.k.Hof= und Staatsdruckerei.
[1848]
   [2]p. 44.5x28.5cm.
   Caption title; imprint on p.[2]; dated at end:
Wien am 4. September 1848.

*GB8
V6755R
9.5.48

Vienna. Comité zur Unterstützung mittelloser
   Gewerbsleute.
   Statuten für das Comité zur Unterstützung
mittelloser Gewerbsleute in Wien.
[Wien]Aus der k.k.Hof= und Staats=Druckerei.
[1848]
   folder([4]p.) 27x19.5cm.
   Caption title; imprint on p.[4]; dated at end:
Wien am 5. September 1848.

*GB8
V6755R
9.4.48

Wiener allgemeiner Arbeiter-Verein.
   Arbeiterausschuss aller Gewerbe. Der Wiener
Arbeiter=Verein hat sich die Aufgabe gestellt,
eine Versammlung ins Leben zu rufen, bestehend
aus Arbeitern aller Gewerbe, wozu jede Jnnung
oder jedes Gewerbe drei aus ihrer Mitte
gewählte Deputirte zu senden hat ...
[Wien]Gedruckt bei Franz Edlen v.Schmid.[1848]
   broadside. 23x14.5cm.
   Dated: Wien, am 4. September 1848.

*pGB8
V6755R
9.6.48

Austria. Ministerium des Innern.
   Bekanntmachung. Der unterm 5. d. M.
ergangene Nationalgarde-Ober-Commando-Befehl
könnte zur Missdeutung Anlass geben, dass
Niemand gesetzlich zum Gardedienste
verpflichtet sei ...
[Wien]Aus der k.k.Hof= und Staats=Druckerei.
[1848]
   broadside. 44.5x57cm.
   Dated: Wien am 6. September 1848.

*pGB8
V6755R
9.5.48

Austria. Reichstag, 1848-1849.
   Protokoll der Sitzung der constituirenden
Reichs=Versammlung am 5. September 1848.
[Wien]Aus der k.k.Hof= und Staatsdruckerei.
[1848]
   7p. 38x23cm.
   Caption title; imprint on p.7.

*pGB8
V6755R
9.6.48

Austria. Reichstag, 1848-1849.
   Protokoll der Sitzung der constituirenden
Reichs=Versammlung am 6. September 1848.
[Wien]Aus der k.k.Hof= und Staatsdruckerei.
[1848]
   6p. 38x23cm.
   Caption title; imprint on p.6.

*pGB8
V6755R
9.6.48

Oesterreichischer Patrioten-Verein.
... Zweite Kundmachung über die freiwilligen Beiträge, welche die Einwohner von Wien ihrer volksthümlichen constitutionellen Staatsregierung zur Bestreitung der ausserordentlichen Staatsbedürfnisse gegeben haben.
[Wien]Aus der k.k.Hof= und Staats=Druckerei. [1848]

broadside. 44.5x28.5cm.
Dated: Wien den 6. September 1848.

---

*pGB8
V6755R
9.7.48

Austria. Sovereigns, etc., 1835-1848
(Ferdinand I)
Wir Ferdinand der Erste, constitutioneller Kaiser von Oesterreich ... haben über Antrag Unseres Ministerrathes in Uebereinstimmung mit dem constituirenden Reichstage beschlossen und verordnen, wie folgt: Erstens. Die Unterthänigkeit und das schutzobrigkeitliche Verhältniss ist sammt allen diese Verhältnisse normirenden Gesetzen aufgehoben ...
[Wien]Aus der k.k.Hof= und Staatsdruckerei. [1848]

(See next card)

---

*pGB8
V6755R
9.6.48

Der Redelsführer des berichtigten Vereins zur Auflösung der akademischen Legion. Dr. Rudolph Vivenot!!???
[Wien]Gedruckt bei Franz Ed.v.Schmid.[1848]
[2]p. 40x25cm.
Caption title; imprint on p.[2]; dated & signed at end: Wien, am 6. September 1848. H. L.

---

*pGB8
V6755R
9.7.48

Austria. Sovereigns, etc., 1835-1848
(Ferdinand I)   Wir Ferdinand der Erste
... [1848]   (Card 2)
folder([3]p.) 44.5x28.5cm.
Caption title; imprint on p.[3].
"Gegeben in Unserer kaiserlichen Haupt= und Residenzstadt Wien, den siebenten September im Eintausend acht Hundert acht und vierzigsten ..."

---

*pGB8
V6755R
9.6.48

Ungarn muss siegen, oder Oesterreich ist verloren.
Wien,gedruckt im September 1848,bei U.Klopf sen.und Alexander Eurich.

broadside. 58.5x46cm.

---

*pGB8
V6755R
9.7.48

Politische Gedanken eines Esels,
Geheimschreiben eines Demokraten an alle Gutgesinnten.
[Wien]Gedruckt bei Franz Edlen von Schmidt. [1848]
[2]p. 51.5x33cm.
Endorsed title on p.[2]; imprint at foot of text on p.[1]; dated & signed: Wien den 7. September 1848. F. W. Z.
Text has heading: Die politischen Jahreszeiten.

---

*pGB8
V6755R
9.6.48

Warum sind die 200 ungarischen Reichstagsdeputirten in Wien?
[Wien]Gedruckt bei Franz Edlen von Schmid. [1848]
[2]p. 39.5x25cm.
Caption title; imprint on p.[2]; signed & dated at end: J. Sch. Wien, am 6. September 1848.

---

*pGB8
V6755R
9.7.48

Vienna. Nationalgarde.
Tagsbefehl vom 7. September 1848.
[Wien]Druck von Jos.Keck & Sohn.Zu haben: Stadt,am Hohenmarkt Nr.446.[1848]

broadside. 39x24.5cm.

---

*pGB8
V6755R
9.7.48

Austria. Reichstag, 1848-1849.
Protokoll der Sitzung der constituirenden Reichs=Versammlung am 7. September 1848.
[Wien]Aus der k.k.Hof= und Staatsdruckerei. [1848]

5,[1]p. 38x23cm.
Caption title; imprint on p.[6].

---

*pGB8
V6755R
9.7.48

Vienna. Nationalgarde. Akademische Legion.
... Corps=Befehl.
[Wien]Aus der k.k.Hof= und Staatsdruckerei. [1848]

broadside. 44.5x57cm.
At head: Akademische Legion. Techniker-Corps.
Dated: Wien am 7. September 1848.

*pGB8
V6755R
9.7.48

Weltner, Josef, fl.1848.
An den feigen Verläumder des
fürsterzbischöflichen Consistoriums und
anonymen Scribler J. F.
Jn Commission bei J.Bader,Buchhändler in Wien,
Stadt,Strobelgasse.[1848]

broadside. 42.5x53cm.
Dated: Wien, am 7. September 1848.
An attack on Die Geheimnisse des hochwürdigsten
Wiener Consistoriums.

---

*pGB8
V6755R
9.9.48

[Pichler, **Adolf**, 1819-1900]
Der Redacteur der schwarzgelben Geissel. Die
schwarzgelbe Fahne. Zusammenlauf. Entrüstung
wegen diesem Reactions=Versuche.
Wien,den 9.September.Gedruckt bei Franz Edlen
von Schmid.[1848]

broadside. 34.5x26cm.
Another issue has the more correct reading
"wegen dieses Reactions=Versuches" in heading.
Signed: A. P.
Occasioned by J. F. Böhringer (editor of "Die
Geissel") displaying the Austrian flag from his
office window.

---

*pGB8
V6755R
9.8.48

Constitutioneller Verein, Vienna.
Programm des constitutionellen Vereines.
[Wien]Gedruckt bei J.P.Sollinger.[1848]

broadside. 44x28cm.
Dated: Wien, am 8. September 1848.

*pGB8
V6755R
9.22.48

**Another copy. 44x27.5cm.
Printed on the other side of the sheet is
"Aufruf des Wiener constitutionellen Vereines",
dated 22 Sept. 1848.**

---

*pGB8
V6755R
9.9.48

[Pichler, **Adolf**, 1819-1900]
Der Redacteur der schwarzgelben Geissel. Die
schwarzgelbe Fahne. Zusammenlauf. Entrüstung
wegen dieses Reactions=Versuches.
Wien,den 9.September.Gedruckt bei Franz Edlen
von Schmid.[1848]

broadside. 34x25.5cm.
Another issue has the dialect reading "wegen
diesem Reactions=Versuche" in heading.
Signed: A. P.
Occasioned by J. F. Böhringer (editor of "Die
Geissel") display- ing the Austrian flag
from his office window.

---

*pGB8
V6755R
9.8.48

Nur so fort 5 Kreuzer täglich.
[Wien]Gedruckt bei M.Lell.[1848]

broadside. 38x23cm.
Dated: 8/9.48.

---

*pGB8
V6755R
9.9.48

Die schwarzgelbe Fahne ausgesteckt vom
Fenster des Redaktions=Bureau der "Geissel."
[Wien]Gedruckt bei M.Lell.[1848]

broadside. 24.5x40cm.
Dated & signed: 9/9.48. C....

---

*pGB8
V6755R
9.8.48

Oesterreich ist nicht verloren, wenn auch
Ungarn nicht siegt! Antwort auf die Flugschrift:
Ungarn muss siegen od. Osterreich [!] ist
verloren.
[Wien]Gedruckt bei Frauz[!]Edlen von Schmid.
[1848]

broadside. 50x39.5cm.
Dated & signed: Wien am 8. September 1848.
Ein Deutscher.

---

*pGB8
V6755R
9.10.48

Jelačić, Josip, grof, 1801-1859.
Manifest. Als in den Märztagen die laute
Stimme des Volkes nach Befreiung von dem
Jahrhunderte langen Drucke des alten Systems
rief ...
Wien im September 1848.Gedruckt bei Carl
Gerold.

broadside. 44x57.5cm.

---

*pGB8
V6755R
9.9.48

Constitutioneller Verein, Vienna.
Aufforderung an alle constitutionell=
monarchisch Gesinnten.
[Wien]Gedruckt bei J.P.Sollinger.[1848]

broadside. 52x67.5cm.
Dated: Wien, den 9. September 1848.

---

*pGB8
V6755R
9.10.48

Koch, Mathias, b.1797.
Schwarz und Gelb. Diese Farben und der
Doppeladler sind die Abzeichen des
österreichischen Kaiserreichs ...
Jn Commission bei J.Bader,Buchhändler in Wien,
Stadt,Strobelgasse.[1848]

broadside. 42x52.5cm.
Dated & signed: Wien, den 10. September 1848.
Matthias Koch [&] Joh. Quirin Endlich.
Urging the patriotic display of the Austrian
flag.

*pGB8
V6755R
9.10.48

Mit unserer Freiheit steht's wirklich
miserabel! Ein ernstes Wort an alle
gutgesinnten Wiener.
  Jn Commission bei J.Bader,Buchhändler in Wien,
Stadt,Strobelgasse.[1848]

  broadside. 42x27cm.
  Dated & signed: Wien, den 10. September 1848.
Ein Bürger Wien's im Namen aller
Gutgesinnten.

---

*pGB8
V6755R
9.11.48

Austria, Lower. Laws, statutes, etc., 1835-1848
  (Ferdinand I)
  ... Circulare der k.k. Landesregierung im
Erzherzogtume Oesterreich unter der Enns.
Provisorische Vorschrift über den Wirkungskreis
des Justiz=Ministeriums.
  [Wien]Aus der k.k.Hof= und Staatsdruckerei.
[1848]

  folder([4]p.) 38x23cm.
  Caption title (at head: № 43232); imprint
on p.[4].
  Dated: Wien am   11. September 1848.

---

*pGB8
V6755R
9.10.48

Ein neuer Papst oder die grosse Kirchen=
Revolution in Rom.
  [Wien]Zu haben im Verlagsgewölbe:Stadt,
Parisergasse Nr.411.Gedruckt bei U.Klopf sen.
und Alexander Eurich.[1848]

  broadside. 42x26cm.
  Dated & signed: Wien, am 10. September 1848.
S. T. [i.e. Tory?]

---

*pGB8
V6755R
9.11.48

Jelačić, Josip, grof, 1801-1859.
  An die ungarische Nation.
  Wien im September 1848.Gedruckt bei Carl
Gerold.

  broadside. 44.5x57.5cm.
  Dated: Von der Drave im September 1848.
  Announcing his invasion of Hungary (11 Sept.).

---

*pGB8
V6755R
9.10.48

Ungarn und sein gutes Recht.
  Wien im September 1848.Gedruckt bei Franz
Edlen von Schmid.

  broadside. 45.5x51.5cm.
  Signed: Ein Ungar.

---

*pGB8
V6755R
9.11.48

Vienna. Nationalgarde.
  Tagsbefehl vom 11. September 1848.
  [Wien]Druck von Jos.Keck & Sohn.Zu haben:
Stadt,am Hohenmarkt Nr.446.[1848]

  broadside. 39x25cm.

---

*pGB8
V6755R
9.10.48

Wie schaut's mit Oesterreich aus. Ungarn in
Gefahr, Kossuth als Patriot und Beöthi,
Diktator von Ungarn, also Republik. Jellachich
der Magyarenfresser. Borrosch der edle
Volksmann und der Deputirte Graf Stadion in
Anklagestand versetzt.
  [Wien]Gedruckt bei Franz Ed.1[!]v.Schmid.
[1848]

  broadside. 52.5x42cm.
  Dated & signed: Wien den 10. September 1848. Z.

---

*pGB8
V6755R
9.12.48

Austria. Ministerium des Innern.
  Kundmachung. Der von dem Herrn Swoboda
gegründete Actien=Verein kann nur als eine
Privat=Unternehmung angesehen, und daher
Niemand verhalten werden, die durch ihn
ausgegebenen Actien als bares Geld anzunehmen ...
  [Wien]Aus der k.k.Hof= und Staatsdruckerei.
[1848]

  broadside. 45x57cm.
  Dated: Wien den 12. September 1848.

---

*pGB8
V6755R
9.11.48

Austria. Reichstag, 1848-1849.
  Protokoll der Sitzung der constituirenden
Reichs=Versammlung am 11. September 1848.
  [Wien]Aus der k.k.Hof= und Staatsdruckerei.
[1848]

  [7]p. 38x23cm.
  Caption title; imprint on p.[7].

---

*pGB8
V6755R
9.12.48

Austria. Ministerium des Innern.
  Kundmachung. Die Störung der öffentlichen
Ordnung durch der Zusammenlauf so vieler Menschen
erregt die Besorgniss der Bevölkerung,
untergräbt den Credit und wirkt verderblich auf
den Erwerb ...
  [Wien]Aus der k.k.Hof= und Staatsdruckerei.
[1848]
  broadside. 44.5x57cm.
  Dated: Wien den 12. September 1848.
  Refers to the riot in the Judenplatz on the
night of September 11.

Austria. Ministerrat.
*pGB8   Kundmachung. Die vorgekommenen Störungen der
V6755R   öffentlichen Ruhe und Ordnung machen es dem
9.12.48   Ministerium zur Pflicht, die nachstehenden, zur
Wahrung der Sicherheit unentbehrlichen
Anordnungen nach Massgabe der schon bestehenden
Sicherheitsgesetze kund zu machen ...
[Wien]Aus der k.k.Hof= und Staatsdruckerei.
[1848]

    broadside. 44.5x57cm.
    Dated: Wien am 12. September 1848.

Jn Bezug auf den Swoboda'schen Aushülfsverein.
*pGB8   [Wien]Gedruckt bei Franz Edlen v.Schmid.
V6755R   [1848]
9.12.48
    broadside. 50x40.5cm.
    Dated & signed: Wien, 12. September 1848.
    Mehrere Geschäftsleute Wiens.

Fürst, D   P   F
*pGB8   1000 Stück, schreibe eintausend Stück k. k.
V6755R   vollgewichtige Dukaten in Gold werden von dem
9.12.48   Gefertigten Demjenigen bezahlt, welcher
innerhalb 4 Monaten durch Beibringung einer
Richtiganerkennungserklärung seines Beweises von
Seite der Justiz=Ministerien Oesterreichs,
Frankreichs und Englands ... beweiset, dass die
Wechselseitigkeit bei Vereinen in der
möglichsten Ausdehnung nicht zu den festesten
Grundlagen gehöre.
             (See next card)

Kossuth, Lajos, 1802-1894.
*pGB8   Kossuth's letzte Aufforderung an die Ungarn.
V6755R   [Wien]Sept.1848.Gedruckt bei M.Lell.
9.12.48
    broadside. 38x46cm.
    Printed within border of type-ornaments.

Fürst, D   P   F   1000 Stück ...
*pGB8   [1848]   (Card 2)
V6755R   [Wien]Gedruckt bei U.Klopf Senior und
9.12.48   Alexander Eurich,Wollzeile Nr.782.[1848]
    broadside in 2 sheets. 25.5x38cm.
    Dated & signed: Wien, am 12. September 1848.
    D. P. F. Fürst, Vorstand des wechselseitigen
allgemeinen Credit=Vereines.
    The 2d sheet has been pasted to the fore-edge
of the 1st.
    Also imposed as a folder of [4]p.

Der Krawall am Judenplatz bei der
    Ministerial-Kanzlei, wegen der Aktiengesellschaft
*pGB8   des Herrn Swoboda.
V6755R   [Wien]Gedruckt bei Franz Edlen v.Schmid.
9.12.48   [1848]
    [2]p. 40.5x25cm.
    Caption title; imprint on p.[2]; signed &
dated at end: S. Wien den 12. September 1848.

[Fürst, D   P   F   ]
*pGB8   1000 Stück, schreibe eintausend Stück k. k.
V6755R   vollgewichtige Dukaten in Gold werden von dem
9.12.48   Gefertigten Demjenigen bezahlt, welcher
innerhalb 4 Monaten durch Beibringung einer
Richtiganerkennungserklärung seines Beweises von
Seite der Justiz=Ministerien Oesterreichs,
Frankreichs und Englands ... beweiset, dass die
Wechselseitigkeit bei Vereinen in der
möglichsten Ausdehnung nicht zu den festesten
Grundlagen gehöre.
             (See next card)

Vienna. Nationalgarde.
*pGB8   Tagsbefehl vom 12. September 1848.
V6755R   [Wien]Druck von Jos.Keck & Sohn.Zu haben:
9.12.48   Stadt,am Hohenmarkt Nr.446.[1848]

    broadside. 39x25cm.

[Fürst, D   P   F   ]   1000 Stück ...
*pGB8   [1848]   (Card 2)
V6755R   [Wien]Gedruckt bei U.Klopf Senior und
9.12.48   Alexander Eurich,Wollzeile Nr.782.[1848]
    folder([4]p.) 31x25cm.
    Caption title; imprint on p.[4]; dated &
signed at end: Wien, am 12. September 1848.
    D. P. F. Fürst, Vorstand des wechselseitigen
allgemeinen Credit=Vereines.
    Also imposed as a 2-sheet broadside.

Austria. Ministerrat.
*pGB8   Kundmachung. Jm Nachhange zu der Kundmachung
V6755R   des Ministers des Jnneren vom 12. d. M. wird
9.13.48   hiemit zur öffentlichen Kenntniss gebracht,
dass die Commission zur Liquidirung der bis 11.
d. ausgegebenen, und noch im Besitze der
ursprünglichen Empfänger befindlichen Actien des
vom Herrn Swoboda gegrüneten Privat=Anleihen=
Vereines ...
[Wien]Aus der k.k.Hof= und Staatsdruckerei.
[1848]
    broadside.   45x57cm.
    Dated: Wien am   13. September 1848.

*pGB8
V6755R
9.13.48

Austria. Ministerrat.
Mitbürger! Die gesetzliche Ordnung ist heute
abermals auf höchst betrübende Weise gestört
worden ...
[Wien]Aus der k.k.Hof= und Staatsdruckerei.
[1848]

broadside. 45x57cm.
Dated: Wien, am 13. September 1848.

*pGB8
V6755R
9.14.48

Die Ereignisse des gestrigen Tages (13.
September) in Wien.
[Wien]Gedruckt bei Franz Edlen v.Schmid.[1848]

broadside. 36x24cm.
Dated & signed: Wien, am 14. September 1848.
Z.

---

*pGB8
V6755R
9.13.48

Constitutioneller Verein, Vienna.
Anzeige für alle constitutionell=monarchisch
Gesinnten.
[Wien]Gedruckt bei J.P.Sollinger.[1848]

broadside. 51x66cm.
Dated: Wien den 13. September 1848.
In contemporary ms. at head: 300 Stück. 14
Septbr. 1848.

*pGB8
V6755R
9.14.48

Frieser, J
Bürgerkrieg in Wien.
[Wien]Gedruckt bei Stöckholzer von Hirschfeld.
—Zu haben Stadt,Liliengasse Nro.898.[1848]

broadside. 43.5x27cm.
Dated: Wien, im September 1818 [i.e.1848].
Printed within border of type-ornaments.
Refers to the events of 13 September.

---

*pGB8
V6755R
9.13.48

Ehrenfeld, Adolf, fl.1848.
Wieder eine brennende Lunte zwischen Bürger,
Nationalgarde und akademische Legion.
[Wien]Gedruckt bei den Edlen von Ghelen'schen
Erben.[1848]

broadside. 45.5x58cm.
Signed: Adolf Ehrenfeld, Jurist der ak. Legion,
Augen= und Ohrenzeuge.
Dated in contemporary ms.: 13. September 848.

*pGB8
V6755R
9.14.48

[Koller, Alexander, freiherr von, 1813-1890]
Zuschrift an die akademische Legion.
[Wien]Aus der k.k.Hof= und Staatsdruckerei.
[1848]

[2]p. 38x23cm.
Caption title; imprint on p.[2]; dated &
signed at end: Wien am 14. September 1848.
Koller.
Announcing his resignation as commander
of the Legion.

---

*pGB8
V6755R
9.13.48

Vienna. Universität. Ausschuss der Studierenden.
Bürger von Wien! Es hat sich in der Stadt
das höchst beunruhigende, und für die
Universität entehrende Gerücht verbreitet, als
wäre in der Aula der Beschluss gefasst worden,
die hohe Reichsversammlung zu sprengen und das
Ministerium zu stürzen ...
[Wien]Druck von U.Klopf sen.und Alexander
Eurich.[1848]

broadside. 40x25.5cm.
Dated: Wien, am 13. September 1848.

*pGB8
V6755R
9.14.48

[Pichler, Adolf, 1819-1900]
Mittwoch, den 13. September. Was wir wollen?
[Wien]Gedruckt bei Franz Edlen von Schmid.
[1848]

[2]p. 40.5x25cm.
Caption title; imprint on p.[2]; dated &
signed at end: Wien, 14. September 1848. A. P.
Calling for the reëstablishment of the
Sicherheits-Ausschuss.

---

*pGB8
V6755R
9.14.48

Ausserordentliches Extrablatt!!!
Umständlicher und wahrheitsgetreuer Bericht über
die gestrigen und heutigen Begebenheiten in Wien,
oder: Was ist denn alles Neues im Reichstage,
Ministerium und auf der Aula geschehen und was
haben wir nach diesen Vorfällen für eine
Zukunft zu erwarten?
[Wien]Gedruckt bei Stöckholzer v.Hirschfeld.--
Zu haben Stadt Liliengasse Nr.898.[1848]

[2]p. 43.5x27cm.
Caption title; imprint on p.[2]; dated &
signed at end: Wien, am 14. September 1848.
J. F.

*pGB8
V6755R
9.14.48

Scheibe, Theodor, 1820-1881.
Die Sturm=Glocke an der Universität, der
kühne Held Wutschel und die 36 Studenten, welche
sich um die Freiheit des Vaterlandes hoch
verdient gemacht haben. Zur Zeit als man gegen
die jugendlichen Freiheitskämpfer die Kanonen
richtete.
Wien,gedruckt im September 1848,bei U.Klopf
sen.und Alexander Eurich,Wollzeile Nr.782.
Verlagsgewölbe:Stadt Parisergasse Nr.411.
broadside. 39.5x50cm.
Refers to the events of 13 September.

*pGB8
V6755R
9.14.48

Die Sturm=Bewegung mit ihren Ereignissen und
Ursachen am 13. September in Wien.
[Wien]Gedruckt bei Franz Edlen von Schmid.
[1848]

broadside. 50x40.5cm.
Dated & signed: Wien, am 14. September 1848.
s.

---

*pGB8
V6755R
9.14.48

Wiener Legion für Ungarn.
Auf! zum Kampfe nach Ungarn. Auf ihr
Musensöhne, Brüder der akademischen Legion, auf,
auf, ihr Jünger der Freiheit, auf Brüder zum
Kampfe!
[Wien]Gedruckt bei Franz Edlen von Schmid.
[1848]

broadside. 40.5x25cm.
Dated & signed: Wien, am 14. Sept. 1848. Von
dem Kommissariate des freien Eliten-Korps der
Wiener Legion für Ungarn.

---

*pGB8
V6755R
9.14.48

Vienna. Comité zur Unterstützung mittelloser
       Gewerbsleute.
Kundmachung. Das unterzeichnete Comité
befindet sich nunmehr in der Lage, den
unbemittelten producirenden Gewerbsleuten jene
Unterstützungen zukommen zu lassen, die es in
seiner ersten Kundmachung veröffentlichte ...
[Wien]Aus der k.k.Hof= und Staatsdruckerei.
[1848]

broadside. 44.5x57cm.
Dated: Wien den 14. September 1848.

---

*pGB8
V6755R
9.15.48

Austria. Handelsministerium.
Kundmachung. Der hohe Reichstag hat zu Folge
seines gestern gefassten Beschlusses dem
Ministerium die Ausführung der geeigneten
Massregeln überlassen, um den Gewerbetreibenden
der Stadt Wien und der zum Polizeibezirke Wien
gehörigen Ortschaften in ihrer gegenwärtigen
bedrängten Lage mit Hilfe des zu diesem Ende
eröffneten Credites aufzuhelfen ...
[Wien]Aus der k.k.Hof= und Staatsdruckerei.
[1848]

(See next card)

---

*pGB8
V6755R
9.14.48

Vienna. Nationalgarde.
Kameraden Bürger und Nationalgarden! Der
gestrige Tag hat uns offen gezeigt, wer seit
langer Zeit die Ruhestörungen jeder Art
genährt und geleitet hat, und welcher Zweck
hierbei heimlich verfolgt wurde ...
[Wien,1848]

broadside. 47x30cm.
Dated & signed: Wien, den 14. September 1848.
Die 6. Compagnie des IX. Bezirkes der Wiener
Nationalgarde.

---

*pGB8
V6755R
9.15.48

Austria. Handelsministerium.   Kundmachung ...
[1848]   (Card 2)

broadside. 45x57cm.
Dated & signed: Wien den 15. September 1848.
Hornbostel, Minister für Ackerbau, Gewerbe und
Handel.

---

*pGB8
V6755R
9.14.48

Vienna. Nationalgarde.
Tagsbefehl vom 14. September 1848.
[Wien]Druck von Jos.Keck & Sohn.Zu haben:
Stadt,am Hohenmarkt Nr.446.[1848]

broadside. 39x25cm.
"Mittwoch den 13. September wurde kein
Tagsbefehl ausgegeben."

---

*pGB8
V6755R
9.15.48

Austria. Ministerrat.
Kundmachung an das Landvolk. Durch das im
constitutionellen Wege erflossene Gesetz vom
7. September 1848 ist das Unterthänigkeits=
Verhältniss sammt den daraus entspringenden
Lasten aufgehoben worden ...
[Wien]Aus der k.k.Hof= und Staatsdruckerei.
[1848]

broadside. 44.5x28.5cm.
Dated: Wien den 15. September 1848.
Signed by the Interior, Justice, & Finance
ministers.

---

*GB8
V6755R
9.14.48

[Wiener, Wilhelm, fl.1848]
Flüchtige Beleuchtung der Vorgänge am 13.
September.
[Wien]Gedruckt bei Stöckholzer v.Hirschfeld.
[1848]

[2]p. 30x24cm.
Caption title; imprint on p.[2]; dated &
signed: Wien, im September 1848. Wilhelm Wiener,
Garde der akademischen Legion III. Compagnie
Jur.

---

*pGB8
V6755R
9.15.48

Austria. Ministerrat.
Kundmachung an das Landvolk. Durch das im
constitutionellen Wege erflossene Gesetz vom 7.
September 1848 ist das Unterthänigkeits=
Verhältniss sammt den daraus entspringenden
Lasten aufgehoben worden ...
[Wien]Aus der k.k.Hof= und Staatsdruckerei.
[1848]

[2]p. 38x23cm.
Caption title; imprint on p.[2]; dated: Wien
den 15. September 1848.
Signed by the   Interior, Justice, &
Finance ministers.

*pGB8
V6755R
9.15.48

Austria. Ministerrat.
    Kundmachung an die Patrimonial=Behörden und
Beamten. Jn dem Gesetze vom 7. September 1848
über die Aufhebung des Unterthänigkeitsverbandes
...
    [Wien]Aus der k.k.Hof= und Staatsdruckerei.
[1848]
    broadside. 44.5x28.5cm.
    Dated: Wien am 15. September 1848.
    Signed by the Interior, Justice, & Finance
ministers.

---

*pGB8
V6755R
9.15.48

Die Schwarzgelben sollen leben! Vivat Hoch.
    [Wien]Gedruckt bei Franz Edlen von Schmid.
[1848]
    [2]p. 40x25cm.
    Caption title; imprint on p.[2]; dated &
signed at end: Wien, am 15. September 1848.
Z.

---

*pGB8
V6755R
9.15.48

Austria. Ministerrat.
    Kundmachung an die Patrimonial=Behörden und
Beamten. Jn dem Gesetze vom 7. September 1848
über die Aufhebung des Unterthänigkeitsverbandes
...
    [Wien]Aus der k.k.Hof= und Staatsdruckerei.
[1848]
    [2]p. 38x23cm.
    Caption title; imprint on p.[2]; dated: Wien
am 15. September 1848.
    Signed by the Interior, Justice, & Finance
ministers.

---

*GB8
V6755R
9.15.48

Wiener Legion für Ungarn.
    Freie, deutsche Männer der akademischen
Legion und Nationalgarde! Wer der deutschen
Sache hold, und sich scharren will um das
Panier der Freiheit und des Rechtes, möge
eintreten rasch und entschlossen in das sich
bildende Freie Eliten=Korps der Wiener Legion
für Ungarn ...
    [Wien]Gedruckt bei Franz Edlen v.Schmid.[1848]
    broadside. 22.5x29cm.
    Signed & dated: Von der Bildungs=Kommission des
freien Eliten=Korps   der Wiener Legion für
Ungarn. Wien den ( )15. September 1848.

---

*GB8
V6755R
9.15.48

Bergmann, Emmanuel.
    Neue Nasenstüber für den "Stern". Von Em.
Bergmann.
    [Graz]Gedruckt in der Kienreich'schen
Buchdruckerei.[1848]
    8p. 21.5x13.5cm.
    Caption title; imprint on p.8.
    Apparently a reply to an article in
Oesterreichs Stern.

---

*pGB8
V6755R
9.16.48

Austria. Reichstag, 1848-1849.
    Protokoll der Sitzung der constituirenden
Reichs=Versammlung am 16. September 1848.
    [Wien]Aus der k.k.Hof= und Staatsdruckerei.
[1848]
    [3]p. 38x23cm.
    Caption title; imprint on p.[3].

---

*pGB8
V6755R
9.15.48

Constitutioneller Verein, Vienna.
    Bekanntmachung für die constitutionell=
monarchisch Gesinnten. Da das Zuströmen zu
dem "constitutionellen Vereine" aus allen
Volksklassen so bedeutend ist ...
    [Wien]Gedruckt bei J.P.Sollinger.[1848]
    broadside. 51x66.5cm.
    Dated: Wien den 15. September 1848.
    In contemporary ms. at head: 300 Stück. 15
Septbr. 1848.

---

*pGB8
V6755R
9.16.48

Constitutioneller Verein, Vienna.
    Bekanntmachung für die constitutionell=
monarchisch Gesinnten. Da in Folge des so
erfreulichen Andranges zu der Einzeichnung in
den "constitutionellen Verein" ...
    [Wien]Gedruckt bei J.P.Sollinger.[1848]
    broadside. 44x58cm.
    Dated: Wien den 16. September 1848.

---

*pGB8
V6755R
9.15.48

Oesterreichischer Patrioten-Verein.
    ... Dritte Kundmachung über die freiwilligen
Beiträge, welche die Einwohner von Wien ihrer
volksthümlichen constitutionellen
Staatsregierung zur Bestreitung der
ausserordentlichen Staatsbedürfnisse gegeben
haben.
    [Wien]Aus der k.k.Hof= und Staats=Druckerei.
[1848]
    [6]p. 44.5x28.5cm.
    Caption title; imprint on p.[6]; dated at end:
Wien den 15.   September 1848.

---

*pGB8
V6755R
9.16.48

Constitutioneller Verein, Vienna.
    Bekanntmachung für die constitutionell=
monarchisch Gesinnten. Um den, von böswilligen
Parteien, welche alles nur Erdenkliche
aufbieten ...
    [Wien]Gedruckt bei J.P.Sollinger.[1848]
    broadside. 43.5x58cm.
    Dated: Wien den 16. September 1848.

*pGB8
V6755R
9.16.48

Hütet Euch vor den schwarz-gelben Bändern.
[Wien]Gedruckt bei Franz Edlen von Schmid.
[1848]

broadside. 37.5x47cm.
Dated & signed: Wien, am 16. September 1848. J.
W.

*pGB8
V6755R
9.17.48

Vienna. Universität. Ausschuss der Studierenden.
An die Mitglieder der akadem. Legion.
[Wien]Gedruckt bei U.Klopf sen.und Alexander
Eurich.[1848]

broadside. 39x25cm.
Dated & signed: Wien, den 17. September 1848.
Vom Ausschusse der Studenten.

*pGB8
V6755R
9.16.48

... Der Kampf um die schwarzgelben Bänder oder:
Wer ist eigentlich ein Schwarzgelber?
[Wien]Gedruckt bei Franz Edlen von Schmid.
[1848]

broadside. 50x40cm.
At head: Für Jedermann zu wissen nothwendig!
Dated & signed: Wien, am 16. September 1848.
J. B. M.

*GB8
V6755R
9.17.48

Zur Fahnenweihe der Nationalgarde des III.
Bataillons VII. Bezirk.
[Wien,1848]

[2]p. 22.5x15cm.
Helfert (Wiener Parnass) 1858.
Caption title; dated at end: Wien, am 17.
September 1848.

*pGB8
V6755R
9.17.48

Böhmischer Handwerksverein.
Offenes Schreiben der Deputirten des
böhmischen Handwerksvereins an das Wiener
Central=Gremium und Jnnungs=Comitee, und an alle
Jnnungen Wiens.
[Wien,1848]

broadside. 44.5x29cm.
Dated & signed: Wien den 17. September 1848.
Franz Niksic, Geschäftsleiter und Deputirter.
Josef Fluom, Josef Niemetz ...
Printed on yellow paper.

*pGB8
V6755R
9.18.48

Austria, Lower.
... Vom k. k. Nieder. Oester. Landes-Präsidium.
Ueber die provisorische Versehung der
Gerichtsbarkeit und der politischen
Amtsverwaltung durch die bisher bestandenen
Patrimonial=Behörden auf Kosten des Staates.
[Wien]Aus der k.k.Hof= und Staatsdruckerei.
[1848]

broadside. 38x23.5cm.
At head: Z.545-P.
Dated: Wien am 18. September 1848.

*pGB8
V6755R
9.17.48

Constitutioneller Verein, Vienna.
Kundmachung für alle constitutionell=
monarchisch Gesinnten. Das Abendblatt der Wiener
Zeitung vom 16. d. M., enthält folgenden
Artikel eines Ungenannten ...
[Wien,1848]

broadside. 52x67cm.
Dated: Wien den 17. September 1848.

*pGB8
V6755R
9.18.48

Austria, Lower. Laws, statutes, etc., 1835-1848
(Ferdinand I)
Circulare der k. k. Landesregierung im
Erzherzogthume Oesterreich unter der Enns.
Wegen Ausgabe neuer Scheidemünze.
[Wien]Aus der k.k.Hof= und Staatsdruckerei.
[1848]

broadside. illus. 40.5x25cm.
Dated: Wien am 18. September 1848.

*pGB8
V6755R
9.17.48

Vienna. Nationalgarde. Akademische Legion.
Bekanntmachung. Die Herren Garden der
akademischen Legion werden auf das Bestimmteste
aufgefordert, bei Allarmirungen sich auf ihren
Sammelplätzen mit Gewehren einzufinden ...
[Wien]Gedruckt bei U.Klopf sen.und A.Eurich.
[1848]

broadside. 40x50.5cm.
Dated & signed: Wien, den 17. September 1848.
Aigner, provisorischer Legions=Commandant.

*pGB8
V6755R
9.18.48

Constitutioneller Verein, Vienna.
Bekanntmachung für die Mitglieder des
constitutionellen Vereines. Um durch ein
schnelles, kräftig=organisirtes Zusammentreten
...
[Wien]Gedruckt bei J.P.Sollinger.[1848]

broadside. 52x68cm.
Dated & signed: Wien den 18. September 1848.
Von dem prov. Comité des constitutionellen
Vereines.
Large folio edition, with imprint.

Constitutioneller Verein, Vienna.
*pGB8   Bekanntmachung für die Mitglieder des
V6755R   constitutionellen Vereines. Um durch ein
9.18.48   schnelles, kräftig=organisirtes Zusammentreten
       ...
       [Wien,1848]

       broadside. 44x28cm.
       Dated & signed: Wien, den 18. September 1848.
    Vom prov. Comité des constitutionellen Vereines.
    Small folio edition, without imprint.

Austria. Reichstag, 1848-1849.
*pGB8   Protokoll der Sitzung der constituirenden
V6755R   Reichs=Versammlung am 19. September 1848.
9.19.48   [Wien]Aus der k.k.Hof= und Staatsdruckerei.
    [1848]

       folder([4]p.) 38x23cm.
       Caption title; imprint on p.[4].

Fiedler, ———.
*GB8   ... Erwiederung auf eine verleumderische
V6755R   Stelle in der Beilage zum "österreichischen
9.18.48   Courier" Nr.222 in Bezug auf Militärärzte.
    [Wien,1848]

       broadside. 28x22cm.
       At head: Beilage zum österr. Courier.
       Dated & signed: Wien, am 18. September 1848.
    Einer der fünf Oberärzte, suppl. Professoren, Dr.
    Fiedlers, Prosector.

Constitutioneller Verein, Vienna.
*pGB8   Bekanntmachung an die constitutionell=
V6755R   monarchischen Gesinnten. Die Einschreibungen in
9.19.48   den "constitutionellen Verein" ...
    [Wien]Gedruckt bei J.P.Sollinger.[1848]

       broadside. 44.5x57cm.
       Dated & signed: Wien den 19. September 1848.
    Von dem prov. Comité des constitutionellen
    Vereines.

Vienna. Gemeinderat.
*pGB8   Kundmachung. Mit Bezug auf die hierortigen
V6755R   Kundmachungen vom 29. v. M. und 3. d. M.
9.18.48   betreffend die Wahl des neuen Gemeinderathes
    für die Stadt Wien, wird nunmehr über die Art,
    die Zeit und den Ort dieser Wahl Nachstehendes
    zur öffentlichen Kenntniss gebracht ...
    [Wien]Gedruckt bei Leop.Grund,am Hundsthurm
    Nr.1.[1848]

       broadside. 47.5x66cm.
       Signed & dated: Vom Gemeinde=Ausschusse der
    Stadt Wien am   18. September 1848.

Constitutioneller Verein, Vienna.
*pGB8   Bekanntmachung an die Mitglieder des
V6755R   constitutionellen Vereines. Seit zwei tagen
9.19.48   erhalten mehrere Mitglieder des
    constitutionellen Vereines schriftliche
    Aufforderungen ...
    [Wien]Gedruckt bei J.P.Sollinger.[1848]

       broadside. 52x67.5cm.
       Dated & signed: Wien den 19. September 1848.
    Von dem prov. Comité des constitutionellen
    Vereines.

Vienna. Nationalgarde.
*pGB8   Mitbürger! Seit acht Tagen herrscht eine
V6755R   beklagenswerthe Aufregung unter uns ...
9.18.48   [Wien]Gedruckt bei Leop.Sommer (vorm.Strauss).
    [1848]

       broadside. 45x56cm.
       Dated & signed: Wien den 18. September 1848.
    Die 4. Compagnie die XI. Bezirkes der Wiener
    Nationalgarde.

Constitutioneller Verein, Vienna.
*pGB8   Kundmachung für alle constitutionell=
V6755R   monarchisch Gesinnten. Wegen der im Zuge
9.19.48   stehenden Organisation des constitutionellen
    Vereines ...
    [Wien]Gedruckt bei J.P.Sollinger.[1848]

       broadside. 44.5x58cm.
       Dated & signed: Wien den 19. September 1848.
    Von dem prov. Comité des constitutionellen
    Vereines.

Ausserordentliches Extrablatt. Neuestes
*pGB8   vom ungarischen Kriegsschauplatze.
V6755R   Schändlicher Verrath des Grafen Adam Teleky.
9.19.48   Erzherzog Stephan vertheidigt mit seinen
    letzten Blutstropfen das Land.
    [Wien]Gedruckt bei Franz Edlen von Schmid.
    [1848]

       [2]p. 46x29cm.
       Caption title; imprint on p.[2]; dated &
    signed: Wien, den 19. Sept. 1848. B.

László, ———.
*pGB8   Die Magyaren nehmen Abschied von ihren
V6755R   deutschen Brüdern in Wien. — Vielleicht für
9.19.48   immer. Von einem Magyaren, der das schöne
    Oesterreich eben so wie seine Heimat liebt und
    verehrt!
    [Wien]Sollinger'sche Buchdruckerei.[1848]

       broadside. 44x55.5cm.
       Signed: László. Leopoldstadt Nr. 133.
    In contemporary ms.: 1000 Stück 19 Septbr 1848.

*pGB8
V6755R
9.19.48

Revolution des Militärs in Berlin und das
Dankschreiben der Soldaten an die National-
versammlung.
[Wien]Gedruckt bei Franz Edlen von Schmid.
[1848]

broadside. 40x24.5cm.
Dated & signed: Wien am 19. September 1848.
Z.

---

*pGB8
V6755R
9.20.48

Memento mori. Barthe=Zettel [i.e.Parte-Zettel]
der Schwarzgelben.
[Wien]Gedruckt bei Franz Edlen von Schmid.
[1848]

broadside. 25x40cm.
Dated: Wien am 20. Septbr. 1848.
Satirical obituary.

---

*pGB8
V6755R
9.19.48

Die ungarischen Deputirten überreichen dem
öster. Reichstag ein sechs Monate altes Kind
zum Schutz.
[Wien]Gedruckt bei Franz Edlen von Schmid.
[1848]

broadside. 50x40cm.
Dated & signed: Wien, den 19. September 1848.
O. H.

---

*pGB8
V6755R
9.20.48

Die Riesen=Versammlung im Odeon. Verbrüderung
der freiheitsbegeisterten Nationalgarden und
Studenten.
[Wien]Gedruckt bei Franz Edlen v.Schmid.[1848]

broadside. 40.5x25cm.
Dated & signed: Wien, im Septbr. 1848. Z.

---

*pGB8
V6755R
9.19.48

Vienna. Comité zur Unterstützung mittelloser
Gewerbsleute.
Kundmachung. Um den begründeten Anforderungen
der vielen mittellosen Gewerbsleute nach
Möglichkeit und in kurzer Zeit, dabei auch
streng gewissenhaft nachkommen zu können ...
[Wien]Aus der k.k.Hof= und Staatsdruckerei.
[1848]

broadside. 45x57cm.
Dated: Wien am 19. September 1848.

---

*pGB8
V6755R
9.20.48

Verein der mit der akademischen Legion
sympathisirenden Nationalgarden und
Bürger Wiens.
Der Verein der mit der akademischen Legion
sympathisirenden National=Garden und Bürger Wiens
und der nächsten Umgebung. Zufolge der im
Odeon=Saale am 18. September dieses Jahres
stattgefundenen Versammlung findet die
Einschreibung am 21. bis inclusive 29. d. M. ...
statt ...

(See next card)

---

*pGB8
V6755R
9.20.48

Brandler, A
Der neueste Triumph der akademischen Legion.
Rede des Herrn A. Brandler, gehalten am 18.
September 1848 im Odeon, bei Gelegenheit der
ersten Versammlung der Bürger, Nationalgarde und
Studenten.
[Wien]Gedruckt bei U.Klopf sen.und Alexander
Eurich.[1848]

[2]p. 39.5x25cm.
Caption title; imprint on p.[2]; dated: Wien,
am 20. September 1848.

---

*pGB8
V6755R
9.20.48

Verein der mit der akademischen Legion
sympathisirenden Nationalgarden und
Bürger Wiens.   Der Verein ... 1848.
(Card 2)

Wien,gedruckt im September 1848,bei U.Klopf
sen.und Alexander Eurich.

broadside. 46x60cm.
Printed on green paper.

---

*pGB8
V6755R
9.20.48

Kossuth, der Freund Oesterreichs!
[Wien,1848]

broadside. 43x53.5cm.
Quoting passages from Kossuth's speech to the
Hungarian Parliament on 15 September 1848.
Dated & signed: Wien, im September 1848. Ein
treuer Bürger des österr. Gesammtstaates.

---

*GB8
V6755R
9.20.48

Vienna. Comité zur Unterstützung mittelloser
Gewerbsleute.
Instruktion für die Vertrauensmänner der
freien Gewerbe.
[Wien]Aus der k.k.Hof= und Staatsdruckerei.
[1848]

folder([3]p.) 23x19cm.
Caption title; imprint on p.[3]; dated &
signed: Wien am 20. September 1848. Vom
Comité zur Unterstützung mittelloser
Gewerbsleute in Wien.

*pGB8
V6755R
9.20.48

Welche Farben sollen wir Oesterreicher
tragen? Oder der Farben= und Bänder=Krieg in
Wien.
    Wien,gedruckt im September 1848,bei U.Klopf
sen.und Alexander Eurich.

    broadside. 39x24.5cm.
    Helfert (Wiener Parnass) 1869.
    Signed: F. G. H...l...g.

○

*pGB8
V6755R
9.20.48

Wer will den Reichstag sprengen? und warum
sind die ungarischen Deputirten nicht
vorgelassen worden? Der Fackelzug der Demokraten
für die Deputirten.
    [Wien]Gedruckt bei Franz Edlen von Schmid.
[1848]

    broadside. 50x40cm.
    Dated & signed: Wien im Septbr. 1848. Z.

○

*pGB8
V6755R
9.21.48

    Fürchterliches Schicksal eines Schwarzgelben
in Neulerchenfeld. Grosser Strassenkrawall und
Katzenmusik bei Herrn Fleischhauer Wöss.
    [Wien]Gedruckt bei Franz Edlen v.Schmid.[1848]

    [2]p. 40.5x25.5cm.
    Caption title; imprint on p.[2]; dated &
signed: Wien, im Sept. 1848. J.

○

*GB8
V6755R
9.21.48

[Glax, Heinrich]
    An die Herren Wähler des IV. Wahlbezirkes in
Wien.
    [Wien,1848]

    folder([3]p.) 22x14.5cm.
    Caption title; dated & signed on p.[3]: Wien,
am 21. September 1848. Heinrich Glax.

○

*pGB8
V6755R
9.21.48

[Schleichert, J   M   ]
    Das Ministerium wird in Anklagestand versetzt.
Entschiedene Thatsachen liegen gegen dasselbe
am Tage, die von vielen Zeugen beschworen
werden. Streffleur der Zweizüngler.
    [Wien]Gedruckt bei Franz Edlen von Schmid.
[1848]

    [2]p. 46x29cm.
    Caption title; imprint on p.[2]; dated &
signed: Wien, am 21. Septbr. 1848. J. M.
Schleichert, Jurist.

○

*pGB8
V6755R
9.21.48

    Der Windischgrätz ist da.
    [Wien]Gedruckt bei Franz Edlen von Schmid.
[1848]

    [2]p. 40x25cm.
    Caption title; imprint on p.[2]; dated &
signed: Wien am 21. September 1848. J.

○

*pGB8
V6755R
9.22.48

Austria. Reichstag, 1848-1849.
    Protokoll der Sitzung der constituirenden
Reichs=Versammlung am 22. September 1848
Vormittags.
    [Wien]Aus der k.k.Hof= und Staatsdruckerei.
[1848]

    folder([3]p.) 38x23cm.
    Caption title; imprint on p.[3].

○

*pGB8
V6755R
9.22.48

Austria. Reichstag, 1848-1849.
    Protokoll der Sitzung der constituirenden
Reichs=Versammlung am 22. September 1848
Abends.
    [Wien]Aus der k.k.Hof= und Staatsdruckerei.
[1848]

    folder([4]p.) 38x23cm.
    Caption title; imprint on p.[4].

○

*pGB8
V6755R
9.22.48

Constitutioneller Verein, Vienna.
    Aufruf des Wiener constitutionellen Vereines
an sämmtliche Provinzen, in Bezug auf die
Bildung von Filial-Vereinen.
    [Wien]Gedruckt bei J.P.Sollinger.[1848]

    broadside. 43.5x28cm.
    Dated & signed: Wien, am 22. September 1848.
Vom prov. Comité des constitutionellen Vereines.

*pGB8
V6755R
9.22.48

Another copy. 44x27.5cm.
    Printed on the other side of the sheet is
"Programm des constitutionellen Vereines",
dated 8 Sept.   1848.
    In contemporary ( ) ms. at head: 1000 Stk. 7
Octob. 1848.

*pGB8
V6755R
9.22.48

    Jn Frankfurt Republik ausgerufen, der
Reichstag gesprengt, Barrikaden gebaut.
    [Wien]Gedruckt bei Franz Edlen v.Schmid.
[1848]

    [2]p. 40x25cm.
    Caption title; imprint on p.[2]; dated &
signed: Wien im Septbr. 1848. J. S.
    In contemporary ms. at head: 22. September 848.

○

*pGB8
V6755R
9.22.48

Vienna. Comité zur Unterstützung mittelloser
Gewerbsleute.
Kundmachung. Das gefertigte Comité bringt
hiemit zur Kenntniss sämmtlicher Herren Nationalgarden, dass es die hiesige Kleidermacher=
Jnnung zur Unterstützung und Beschäftigung
unbemittelter Kleidermacher beauftragen ...
[Wien]Aus der k.k.Hof= und Staatsdruckerei.
[1848]

broadside. 45x57cm.
Dated: Wien am 22. September 1848.

*pGB8
V6755R
9.23.48

Oesterreichischer Patrioten-Verein.
... Vierte Kundmachung über die freiwilligen
Beiträge, welche die Einwohner von Wien ihrer
volksthümlichen constitutionellen Staatsregierung
zur Bestreitung der ausserordentlichen
Staatsbedürfnisse gegeben haben.
[Wien]Aus der k.k.Hof= und Staats=Druckerei.
[1848]

folder([3]p.) 45x29cm.
Caption title; imprint on p.[3]; dated: Wien
den 23. September 1848.

*pGB8
V6755R
9.22.48

[Zierrath, F W]
Blatt bestimmt zur Confiscation! Wien ein
grossartiger Narrenthurm. Reaction u.
Liberalismus.
[Wien]Gedruckt bei Franz Edlen v.Schmid.[1848]

[2]p. 40.5x24.5cm.
Caption title; imprint on p.[2]; dated &
signed: Wien im September 1848. Zierrath.

*pGB8
V6755R
9.23.48

Offenes Sendschreiben an den Herrn Erzbischof
von Wien. Gegeben in unserem europäisch
berühmten Flugschriften=Verschleiss, Stadt,
Liliengasse Nr.898.
[Wien]Buchdruckerei in der Leopoldstadt Nr.
656.[1848]

broadside. 43x27cm.
In contemporary ms. at head: 23. September 848.

*pGB8
V6755R
9.23.48

Austria, Lower.
Vom k. k. Nieder-Oester. Landes-Präsidium.
Wegen der Eröffnung einer provisorischen
montanistischen Lehranstalt in Vordernberg.
[Wien]Aus der k.k.Hof= und Staats=Druckerei.
[1848]

broadside. 44.5x29cm.
Dated: Wien den 23. September 1848.

*pGB8
V6755R
9.23.48

Vienna. Gemeinderat.
Kundmachung. Jn Folge eines vom h. Ministerium
des Jnnern so eben herabgelangten Auftrages
dto. 22. d. M. Z. 2549 hat Behufs der Wahl
des Gemeinderathes für die Stadt Wien noch eine
nachträgliche Ausweisung des Wahlrechtes ...
[Wien]Gedruckt bei Leop.Grund,am Hundsthurm Nr.
1.[1848]

broadside. 48x66cm.
Signed & dated: Vom Gemeinde-Ausschusse der
Stadt Wien, am 23. September 1848.

*pGB8
V6755R
9.23.48

Katzenmusik bei den reichen Holzdieben in
Lichtenthal oder der Sieveringer Wald.
[Wien]Gedruckt bei Franz Edlen v.Schmid.[1848]

[2]p. 40.5x25cm.
Caption title; imprint on p.[2]; dated &
signed: Wien, im Sept. 1848. J.

*pGB8
V6755R
9.24.48

Das deutsche Volk in Frankfurt hat gesiegt!
Erzherzog Johann ist in Gefahr!
[Wien]Gedruckt bei Franz Edlen v.Schmid.[1848]

[2]p. 40x24.5cm.
Caption title; imprint on p.[2]; dated &
signed: Wien im September 1848. J.
In contemporary ms. at head: 24. September 848.

*pGB8
V6755R
9.23.48

[Komorny, Joseph]
Gott erhalte die Wiener Studenten, denn sie
sind das Recht, die Gerechtigkeit selbst.
Wien,gedruckt im September 1848,bei U.Klopf
sen.und Alexander Eurich.

[2]p. 39.5x25cm.
Caption title; imprint on p.[2]; signed at end:
Komorny. Zu haben in der Stadt, Sterngasse Nr.
452, im Hofmagazin.
In contemporary ms. at head: 2000 23 Sept.

*pGB8
V6755R
9.24.48

Extrablatt! Republik in Frankfurt a. M.
[Wien]Septemb.1848.Gedruckt bei M.Lell.
broadside. 38x22.5cm.

*pGB8
V6755R
9.24.48

Höchst wichtige Depesche. Erzh. Johann aus
Frankfurt geflüchtet! Blutiger Kampf der
Republikaner in Frankfurt! Die deutsche
Republik!
[Wien]Gedruckt bei Franz Edlen von Schmid.
[1848]

[2]p. 40.5x25cm.
Caption title; imprint on p.[2]; dated & signed:
Wien im September 1848. A. Sch.

---

*pGB8
V6755R
9.24.48

Vienna. Nationalgarde.
Nachtrag zum Tagsbefehle vom 24. September
1848.
[Wien]Aus der k.k.Hof= und Staats=Druckerei.
[1848]

broadside. 44.5x29cm.

---

*GB8
V6755R
9.24.48

Holzapfel, Joseph, 1815-1854.
Fest-Rede, gesprochen von Joseph Holzapfel,
Priester im deutschen Ritter-Orden, bei der
Fahnen- und Estandarten-Weihe der vier
Stadtbezirke und des XII. Bezirkes, so wie der
National=Garde=Cavallerie=Division.
[Wien]Am 24.September 1848.

folder([4]p.) 28.5x22cm.
Printer's imprint at end: Gedruckt bei J.P.
Sollinger.

---

*pGB8
V6755R
9.25.48

Austria. Justizministerium.
... Kundmachung. Seine Majestät haben nach
Antrag Jhres Justiz=Ministeriums nachfolgende
Anordnung zu genehmigen geruht: Da das in Wien
niedergesetzte Comité zur Unterstützung
mittelloser Gewerbsleute ...
[Wien]Aus der k.k.Hof= und Staatsdruckerei.
[1848]

broadside. 44.5x28cm.
At head: 3522/J.M.
Dated: Wien am 25. September 1848.

---

*pGB8
V6755R
9.24.48

Perger, Aloys von.
Fahnen-Hymne zur Feier der Estandarten=Weihe
der Nationalgarde-Cavallerie Wiens am 24.
September 1848; gedichtet von Alois v. Perger,
in Musik gesetzt von Rudolf v. Vivenot ...
[Wien]Druck von U.Klopf sen.und Alexander
Eurich.[1848]

folder(2l.) 46x31cm.
Helfert (Wiener Parnass) 1884.
Title within ornamental border.
Without the music.

---

*pGB8
V6755R
9.25.48

Austria. Sovereigns, etc., 1835-1848
(Ferdinand I)
An Meine Armee in Ungarn.
[Wien]Aus der k.k.Hof= und Staatsdruckerei.
[1848]

broadside. 45x29cm.
Dated & signed: Gegeben in Meiner Haupt= und
Residenzstadt Wien den fünf und zwanzigsten
September eintausend achthundert acht und
vierzig. Ferdinand.

---

*pGB8
V6755R
9.24.48

Vienna. Comité zur Unterstützung mittelloser
Gewerbsleute.
Kundmachung. Das gefertigte Comité für
Unterstützung mittelloser Gewerbsleute beeilt
sich dem gewerblichen Publikum zu eröffnen, dass
in Folge der Verwendung eines hohen
Ministeriums für Ackerbau, Gewerbe und Handel,
ddo. 16. September d. J., nach dem Beschlusse
im hohen Ministerrathe alle Minuendo-
Versteigerungen für die Dauer des Nothstandes
suspendirt bleiben ...
[Wien]Aus der   k.k.Hof= und Staats-
druckerei.[1848]
(See next card)

---

*pGB8
V6755R
9.25.48

Erster Wiener Privat-Anlehen-Verein.
Das Comité des ersten Wiener Privat=Anlehen=
Vereines an die sämmtlichen Ausschüsse und
Mitglieder desselben.
[Wien,1848]

broadside. 45x57cm.
Dated & signed: Wien den 25. September 1848.
Das Comité des ersten Wiener Privat-Vereines.
August Swoboda. Joseph Gutmann. Franz Reim.

---

*pGB8
V6755R
9.24.48

Vienna. Comité zur Unterstützung mittelloser
Gewerbsleute.   Kundmachung ... [1848]
(Card 2)

broadside. 45x57cm.
Dated: Wien am 24. September 1848.

---

*pGB8
V6755R
9.25.48

Erzherzog Stephan ist in Wien. Jelasich ist
in Pesth.
[Wien]Gedruckt bei Franz Edlen v.Schmid.[1848]

[2]p. 40x25cm.
Caption title; dated & signed: Wien, am 25.
September 1848. J.

*pGB8
V6755R
9.25.48
Der grosse Fackelzug der dankbaren Landleute aus allen Provinzen und die Reden der Reichstagsdeputirten am 24. September in Wien.
[Wien]Gedruckt bei Franz Edlen v.Schmid.[1848]
[2]p. 40.5x24.5cm.
Caption title; imprint on p.[2]; dated & signed: Wien im September 1848. J. S.

*pGB8
V6755R
9.25.48
Vienna. Comité zur Unterstützung mittelloser Gewerbsleute.   Kundmachung ... [1848]
(Card 2)
[Wien]Aus der k.k.Hof= und Staatsdruckerei. [1848]

broadside. 45x57cm.
Refers to the "Instruktion" of 20 September.

*GB8
V6755R
9.25.48
Katholiken-Verein für Glauben, Freiheit und Gesittung, Vienna.
Katholiken=Verein für Glauben, Freiheit und Gesittung. Die neue Verfassung, der wir vertrauensvoll entgegen sehen, sichert allen Staatsbürgern jedenfalls zwei unschätzbare Güter zu: die Glaubensfreiheit und das Recht der Association ...
Druck von A.Pichler's Witwe in Wien.[1848]
folder([3]p.) 26.5x21.5cm.
Caption title; imprint on p.[3].
Announcing the   organization of the Verein.

*pGB8
V6755R
9.25.48
Vienna. Nationalgarde.
... Bezirksbefehl vom 25. September 1848.
[Wien]Druck von Jos.Keck & Sohn.Zu haben: Stadt,am Hohenmarkt Nr.446.[1848]
broadside. 44x29cm.
At head: Nationalgarde. III. Bezirk.
Includes "Tagsbefehl vom 24. September 1848."

*pGB8
V6755R
9.25.48
Mahler, Georg, fl.1848.
Um Gotteswillen emancipirt die Juden! Geschrieben von einem, welchem nichts dafür bezahlt wurde.
Jm Verlage bei J.Bader,Buchhändler in Wien, Stadt,Strobelgasse.[1848]
broadside. 42x53cm.
Dated: Wien den 25. September 1848.

*pGB8
V6755R
9.25.48
Vienna. Nationalgarde.
Tagsbefehl vom 25. September 1848.
[Wien]Druck von Jos.Keck & Sohn.Zu haben: Stadt,am Hohenmarkt Nr.446.[1848]
broadside. 39x24cm.

*pGB8
V6755R
9.25.48
Pexa, L   J
Terrorismus. (Schreckens=System.)
[Wien]Gedruckt und zu haben bei M.Lell dann in der Buchhandlung bei Herrn Bader in dem Strobelkopfgässchen,und in den beiden Lotto-Collekt[uren],Bräunerstrasse und Schauflergasse. Septemben[!]1848.
broadside. 47.5x60cm.
Printed within border of type-ornaments.
A few letters in the imprint have failed to print.

*pGB8
V6755R
9.25.48
Vienna. Stubenviertel (Polizeibezirk)
Verwaltungsrat.
Aufforderung. Jene Herren des Bezirkes Stubenviertel, welche mit der Legitimationskarte zur Wahl des Gemeinderathes versehen sind ...
[Wien,1848]
broadside. 25.5x31cm.

*pGB8
V6755R
9.25.48
Vienna. Comité zur Unterstützung mittelloser Gewerbsleute.
Kundmachung. In der Instruction für die Vertrauensmänner der Gewerbs-Corporationen, und in den an alle Vertrauensmänner der Innungen und freien Beschäftigungen hinausgegebenen Gesuchs-Formularien hat die Bemerkung: "Dass die Deckung für die zu ertheilenden Vorschüsse durch Werthspapiere, Sparkassebüchel, Wechsel, Personalbürgschaft u.s.w." geleistet werden kann, zu Missverständnissen Veranlassung gegeben ...
(See next card)

*pGB8
V6755R
9.26.48
Ausserordentliches Extrablatt. Auszug aus dem gestern erschienenen Manifest Sr. Majestät des Kaisers an die ungarische Nation.
Gedruckt bei Franz Edlen von Schmid in Wien, [1848]
[2]p. 40.5x25cm.
Caption title; imprint on p.[2]; dated & signed: Wien, im September 1848. J.
A news report only.

*pGB8
V6755R
9.26.48

Austria. Reichstag, 1848-1849.
Protokoll der 56. Sitzung der constituirenden
Reichs=Versammlung am 26. September 1848
Vormittags.
[Wien]Aus der k.k.Hof= und Staatsdruckerei.
[1848]

folder([3]p.) 38x23cm.
Caption title; imprint on p.[3].

---

*pGB8
V6755R
9.26.48

Eine höchst merkwürdige Prophezeihung auf das
Jahr 1848 und 1849.
Wien,gedruckt im September[1848]bei U.Klopf
sen.und Alexander Eurich.

broadside. 42x27cm.
Signed: X.
In contemporary ms. at head: 26 Sept.

---

*pGB8
V6755R
9.26.48

Austria. Reichstag, 1848-1849.
Protokoll der 57. Sitzung der constituirenden
Reichs=Versammlung am 26. September 1848
Nachmittags.
[Wien]Aus der k.k.Hof= und Staatsdruckerei.
[1848]

broadside. 38x23cm.

---

*pGB8
V6755R
9.26.48

Der Joh. Garber'sche Krawall. Katzenmusik=
Revolution! in Gumpendorf.
[Wien]Gedruckt bei Franz Edlen von Schmid.
[1848]

[2]p. 40x24.5cm.
Caption title; imprint on p.[2]; dated: Wien,
im September 1848.

---

*pGB8
V6755R
9.26.48

Austria, Lower.
... Von der k. k. n. ö. Landesregierung. Das
hohe Ministerium des Ackerbaues, Handels und der
Gewerbe findet, laut Dekretes vom 10. d. M. ...
bei der gegenwärtigen Stockung des Verkehrs ...
[Wien,1848]

folder([2]p.) 34.5x22cm.
Caption title; at head: Z.45862. M. Z. 60163.
Dated: Wien den 26. September 1848.

---

*pGB8
V6755R
9.27.48

Knoth, Ludwig.
Volks=Vertreter!
[Wien]Gedruckt und zu haben bei U.Klopf sen.
und Alexander Eurich.[1848]

broadside. 42x53cm.
Dated: Wien, am 27. September 1848.

---

*pGB8
V6755R
9.26.48

Constitutioneller Verein, Vienna.
Kundmachung für alle Mitglieder des
constitutionellen Vereines.
[Wien]Gedruckt bei J.P.Sollinger.[1848]

broadside. 51.5x67.5cm.
Dated: Wien den 26. September 1848.

---

*pGB8
V6755R
9.27.48

Der Militär=Krawall in der Gumpendorfer=
Kaserne wegen 25 Stockschläge.
[Wien]Gedruckt bei Franz Edlen von Schmid.
[1848]

broadside. 40.5x25cm.
Dated & signed: Wien, im September 1848. Z.

---

*pGB8
V6755R
9.26.48

Garber, Johann, fl.1848.
Edle Mitbürger! Wenn ich Jemanden aus Eurer
Mitte beleidigt habe, so geschah es gewiss nicht
absichtlich, sondern im Augenblicke der
Leidenschaft ...
[Wien]Gedruckt bei U.Klopf sen.und Alexander
Eurich.[1848]

broadside. 39x50cm.
Dated: Wien, am 26. September 1848.

---

*pGB8
V6755R
9.27.48

Die Republik im Grossherzogthum Baden.
Struves zweiter republikanischer Einfall.
[Wien]Gedruckt bei Franz Edlen von Schmid.
[1848]

[2]p. 40x25.5cm.
Caption title; imprint on p.[2]; dated &
signed: Wien den 27. September 1848. L.

*pGB8
V6755R
9.27.48

Was geht im Reichstag vor? Die Linke verlässt die Sache der Volksfreiheit. Wehe uns! [Wien]Gedruckt bei Franz Edlen v.Schmid.[1848]

broadside. 40.5x25cm.
Dated & signed: Wien, am 27. Septbr. 1848. Z.

---

*pGB8
V6755R
9.28.48

[Löve, Paul]
Warnungsruf eines Patrioten über Katzenmusiken. [Wien]Gedruckt bei Franz Edlen v.Schmid.[1848]

[2]p. 40.5x25cm.
Caption title; imprint on p.[2]; dated & signed: Wien, am 28. Septbr. 1848. Paul Löve, Redakteur des Stürmers.

---

*pGB8
V6755R
9.28.48

Aigner, Joseph Matthäus, 1818-1886.
Cameraden! Mein Herz erglüht vor Freude und Stolz, über die mir erwiesene Ehre, Euer Führer sein zu dürfen! ...
[Wien]Gedruckt bei U.Klopf sen.und Alexander Eurich.[1848]

broadside. 39x25cm.
Dated: Wien, den 28. Sept. 1848.
Aigner had been elected commander of the Academic Legion.

---

*pGB8
V6755R
9.28.48

Vienna. Comité zur Unterstützung mittelloser Gewerbsleute.
Kundmachung. Das Comité zur Unterstützung mittelloser Gewerbsleute in Wien beabsichtiget mehrere Tausend Ellen mohrengraues, 7/4 breites, gut eingegangenes Tuch ...
[Wien]Aus der k.k.Hof- und Staatsdruckerei. [1848]

broadside. 44.5x28.5cm.
Dated: Wien am 28. September 1848.

---

*pGB8
V6755R
9.28.48

"Der constitutionelle Verein" hat sich eines Verbrechens schuldig gemacht, weil er binnen den ersten 8 Tagen seines Bestehens bereits 25,000 Mitglieder zählt!
Wien,im September 1848.Gedruckt bei Carl Gerold.

broadside. 39.5x25.5cm.
Signed: Mehrere Bürger Wiens im Namen aller Gutdenkenden.
In contemporary ms. at head: 28. September 848.

---

*pGB8
V6755R
9.28.48

Vienna. Comité zur Unterstützung mittelloser Gewerbsleute.
Kundmachung. Seine Majestät haben nach Antrag Jhres Justiz-Ministeriums nachfolgende Anordnung zu genehmigen geruht: ...
[Wien]Aus der k.k.Hof- und Staatsdruckerei. [1848]

broadside. 44.5x28.5cm.
Dated: Wien am 28. September 1848.

---

*pGB8
V6755R
9.28.48

Dank=Adresse, welche unterm 18. Juli d. J. an Se. Durchlaucht, dem Herrn kommandirenden Generalen von Böhmen, Feldmarschall=Lieutenant Fürst zu Windischgrätz, von Wien übersendet, und von Sr. Durchlaucht dankbar angenommen wurde.
Wien,am 28.September 1848.

broadside. 42x52cm.
Signed: P. S. ein alt erprobter Patriot.

---

*pGB8
V6755R
9.28.48

Vienna. Comité zur Unterstützung mittelloser Gewerbsleute.
Kundmachung. Zur Beruhigung derjenigen Gewerbsleute, welche Unterstützungsgesuche bei dem gefertigten Comité eingereicht haben ...
[Wien]Aus der k.k.Hof- und Staatsdruckerei. [1848]

broadside. 45x57cm.
Dated: Wien am 28. September 1848.

---

*pGB8
V6755R
9.28.48

[Langer, Anton, fl.1848]
Die Vorstadt=Hausmeister dürfen nicht um 9 Uhr sperren. Das ist gewiss seinen Groschen werth. Dem freien Wien, zum Michaelystage 1848. gewidmet.
[Wien]Gedruckt bei Josef Ludwig,Josefstadt Florianigasse,Nr.52.[1848]

[2]p. 38.5x23.5cm.
Caption title; imprint on p.[2]; dated & signed: Geschrieben am 28. September, 1848. Anton Langer, verantwortlicher Schreiber.

---

*pGB8
V6755R
9.28.48

Vienna. Gemeinderat.
Kundmachung. Mit Bezug auf die hierortigen Kundmachungen vom 29. v. M., 3. und 23. d. M. betreffend die Wahl des neuen Gemeinderathes für die Stadt Wien, wird nunmehr über die Art, die Zeit und den Ort dieser Wahl Nachstehendes zur öffentlichen Kenntniss gebracht: ...
[Wien]Gedruckt bei Leop.Grund,am Hundsthurm Nr.1.[1848]

broadside. 53x69cm.
Signed & dated: Vom Gemeinde=Ausschusse der Stadt Wien am 28. September 1848.

*pGB8
V6755R
9.28.48

Vienna. Gemeinderat.
    Kundmachung. Mit Bezug auf die hierortigen
Kundmachungen vom 29. v. M. und 3. d. M.
betreffend die Wahl des neuen Gemeinderathes
für die Stadt Wien, wird nunmehr über die Art,
die Zeit und den Ort dieser Wahl Nachstehendes
zur öffentlichen Kenntniss gebracht: ...
    [Wien]Gedruckt bei Leopold Grund,Hundsthurm
Nr.1.[1848]
    broadside. 52x68cm.
    Signed & dated: Vom Gemeinde=Ausschusse der
Stadt Wien am 28.   September 1848.

*pGB8
V6755R
9.29.48

Lichnowsky's und Auerswald's Mörder sind
nur erschreckt, nicht entwaffnet!
    Zu haben bei J.Bader,Buchhändler in Wien,
Stadt,Stroblgasse.[1848]
    broadside. 42.5x26.5cm.
    Dated & signed: Wien, den 29. September 1848.
Ein Mensch.

*pGB8
V6755R
9.28.48

Wien fliegt in die Luft oder werden
Windischgrätz, Jellasich und Radetzky die
Residenz belagern? Beantwortung dieser
Zeitfrage.
    [Wien]Gedruckt bei Franz Edlen von Schmid.
[1848]
    [2]p. 40x25cm.
    Caption title; imprint on p.[2]; dated &
signed: Wien am 28. September 1848. Z.

*pGB8
V6755R
9.30.48

An Se. kais. königl. Majestät Ferdinand I.
Die Güterbesitzer der Provinzen Steiermark und
Niederösterreich bitten wiederholt und auf das
allerdringendste um hohe Veranlassung ...
    [Wien,1848]
    folder([4]p.) 42x26cm.
    Endorsed title on p.[4]; text on p.[1] begins:
Eure kaiserl. königl. Majestät! Der ganz
verzweiflungsvolle Zustand, in welchem die
steiermärkischen Güter und Giltenbesitzer seit
der Proclamation der Constitution versetzt
wurden, hat sie   gezwungen ...
    Dated: Den   letzten September 1848.

*pGB8
V6755R
9.29.48

Austria. Reichstag, 1848-1849.
    Protokoll der 59. Sitzung der constituirenden
Reichs=Versammlung am 29. September 1848.
    [Wien]Aus der k.k.Hof= und Staatsdruckerei.
[1848]
    [2]p. 38x22.5cm.
    Caption title; imprint on p.[2].

*pGB8
V6755R
9.30.48

Die Aufhebung der Klöster eine Speculation
für Kapitalisten!! Eine Prise für Auflöser des
christlichen Kreuzes.
    [Wien]Druck von A.Pichler's Witwe.[1848]
    broadside. 58x45cm.
    Dated & signed: Wien, am letzten September
1848. Ein Mitglied des Katholiken=Central=
Vereins.

*pGB8
V6755R
9.29.48

Berichtigung eines Druckfehlers. Jn dem
gestern erschienenen Placate des provisorischen
Comités der mit der akademischen Legion
sympathisirenden Nationalgarden und Bürger Wiens
und nächster Umgebung: Etwas für Alle! hat sich
ein Druckfehler eingeschlichen. Es soll heissen:
Alles für Etwas!
    [Wien]Aus Jakob Bader's Buchhandlung,Stadt,
Strobelgasse.[1848]
    broadside. 42.5x53cm.
    Dated: Wien den   29. September 1848.

*pGB8
V6755R
9.30.48

Austria. Reichstag, 1848-1849.
    Protokoll der 60. Sitzung der constituirenden
Reichs=Versammlung am 30. September 1848.
    [Wien]Aus der k.k.Hof= und Staatsdruckerei.
[1848]
    folder([3]p.) 38x23cm.
    Caption title; imprint on p.[3].

*pGB8
V6755R
9.29.48

Die Klöster müssen aufgehoben werden.
Entgegnung an Jene, welche eine Petition an den
Reichstag zur Bewahrung der Klostergüter
beabsichtigen.
    Gedruckt bei Franz Edlen von Schmid in Wien,
[1848]
    broadside. 50x40cm.
    Dated & signed: Wien, im September 1848. J. S.

*GB8
V6755R
9.30.48

Extra-Blatt. Staffete von Pesth. Einmarsch
der kaiserlichen Truppen.
    Zu haben im Verlagsgewölbe:Stadt,Parisergasse
Nr.411.(Wien,gedruckt im Sept.1848,bei U.Klopf
Senior und A.Eurich.)
    broadside. 26.5x21cm.

*pGB8
V6755R
9.30.48
Grässlicher Meuchelmord. Entsetzen
durchschauert die menschliche Brust ...
[Wien]Aus Jakob Bader's Buchhandlung,Stadt,
Strobelgasse.[1848]

   broadside. 42.5x53cm.
   Dated & signed: Wien, den 30. September 1848.
Ein Mensch.
   On the murder of Lamberg, 28 September 1848.

*pGB8
V6755R
9.31.48
Ausserordentliches Extrablatt. Radetzky und
fünfmalhunderttausend Russen.
[Wien]Gedruckt bei Franz Edlen von Schmid.
[1848]

   [2]p. 40.5x25cm.
   Caption title; imprint on p.[2]; dated &
signed: Wien im September 1848. Z.

*pGB8
V6755R
9.30.48
Thaten der Frankfurter Republikaner, welche
sich Freiheitsmänner nennen.
Zu haben bei J.Bader,Buchhändler in Wien,
Stadt,Strobelgasse.[1848] Preis: 1 kr.C.M.
   broadside. 42.5x53cm.
   Dated & signed: Wien, den 30. September 1848.
J. M.
   On the murder of Lichnowsky and Auerswald.

*pGB8
V6755R
9.31.48
Bruno, Karl, fl.1848.
   Ausserordentliches, noch nie dagewesenes
Extrablatt!!! Schauderhafte politische Prüfung
des Professors Gelbschwarz mit seinem Schüler
Heckerl=Eisenfresser.
   [Wien]Gedruckt bei Stöckholzer von Hirschfeld.
—Zu haben Stadt,Liliengasse Nro.898.[1848]

   broadside. 43.5x54cm.
   Dated: Wien, im September 1848.

*pGB8
V6755R
9.31.48
Ausserordentliches Blatt! Der Krieg in Jtalien
bricht wieder los. Die 9 Hinrichtungen in
Mailand. Neue blutige Revolutionen.
Zusammenkunft des Helden Radetzky und der
berüchtigten Prinzessin Belgiojoso.
   [Wien]Verlagsgewölbe,Stadt,Parisergasse Nr.411.
Gedruckt bei Franz Edlen von Schmid.[1848]

   [2]p. 40x25.5cm.
   Caption title; imprint on p.[2]; dated &
signed: Wien im September 1848. S. T. [i.e.
Tory?]

*pGB8
V6755R
9.31.48
Bruno, Karl, fl.1848.
   Das Tagebuch des Schneiders Zwirn im Jahre
1847 und 1848 oder: Was haben die Wiener
Geschäftsleute von den Errungenschaften
profitirt?
   [Wien]Gedruckt bei Stöckholzer v.Hirschfeld.--
Zu haben in der Liliengasse Nr.898.[1848]

   broadside. 29.5x47.5cm.
   Dated: Wien, im September 1848.

*pGB8
V6755R
9.31.48
Ausserordentliches Blatt. Versuchter
Meuchlmord an Feldmarschall Radetzky und die
Franzosen in Triest.
[Wien]Zu haben im Verlagsgewölbe:Stadt,
Parisergasse 411.Gedruckt im September 1848 bei
U.Klopf sen.und Alexander Eurich.

   [2]p. 39x25cm.
   Caption title; imprint on p.[2]; signed: T. R.

*pGB8
V6755R
9.31.48
Constitutioneller Verein, Vienna.
   Entwurf zu einer Geschäftsordnung für die
prov. dirig. Commission des constitutionellen
Vereins.
   [Wien,1848]

   folder([4]p.) 45.5x27.5cm.
   Caption title.

*pGB8
V6755R
9.31.48
Ausserordentliches Extrablatt aus Pesth.
Wahrhafte Beschreibung eines Augenzeugen der
schauderhaften Ermordung des Grafen Lamberg.
Kossuth an der Spitze des Landsturmes.
   [Wien]Gedrnckt[!]bei Franz Edlen von Schmid.
[1848]

   [2]p. 40x26cm.
   Caption title; imprint on p.[2]; dated &
signed: Wien im Septbr. 1848. J.

*pGB8
V6755R
9.31.48
Cordier, Philippe, & Dutertre, firm, publishers,
   Paris.
   Das Heil der Welt, oder die grösste Entdeckung,
— die der Wahrheit und des Glückes für alle
Menschen. Le livre de l'époque.
   [Wien]Gedruckt bei J.B.Wallishausser.[1848]

   folder(4p.) 33.5x24cm.
   A prospectus for Léger Noël's "Le livre de
l'époque", signed & dated "Philippe Cordier &
Dutertre, éditeurs, rue du Ponceau, 24. à Paris.
Paris den 4. September 1848." The prospectus
                              (See next card)

*pGB8
V6755R
9.31.48

Cordier, Philippe, & Dutertre, firm, publishers,
   Paris.   Das Heil der Welt ... [1848]
                  (Card 2)
is probably translated into German by Noël, with
a French poem by him at end, "A ma lectrice
inconnue", signed & dated: Léger Noël, professeur
de langue française, Wickenburggasse, 11.
Vienne, 25. September 1848.
   Caption title; imprint on p.4.

---

*pGB8
V6755R
9.31.48

Freiligrath, Ferdinand, 1810-1876.
   Das von der preussischen Regierung verbotene
Gedicht von F. Freiligrath: Die Todten an die
Lebenden.
   Wien,im September 1848.Gedruckt bei Franz
Edlen von Schmid.

   broadside. 29x46cm.
   Helfert (Wiener Parnass) 1908.

---

*GB8
V6755R
9.31.48

Denkschrift der Künstler Wiens an die hohe
constituirende Reichs-Versammlung.
   Wien,im September 1848.

   6p. 30x23.5cm.
   Imprint on p.6: Aus der k.k. Hof= und
Staatsdruckerei.

---

*pGB8
V6755R
9.31.48

[Frieser, J   ]
   Haderlump! Haderlump! Altes Eisen, Messing,
Blei, Glasscherben. Politische Betrachtungen
eines Lumpensammlers.
   [Wien]Gedruckt bei Stöckholzer von Hirschfeld.
  —Zu haben Liliengasse Nro.898.[1848]

   broadside. 1 illus. 43.5x27cm.
   Dated & signed: Wien, im September 1848. J. F.
Printed within border of type-ornaments.

---

*GB8
V6755R
9.31.48

Deutschkatholisches Rheinleid. Allen
freisinnigen deutschen Katholiken gewidmet.
   [Germany?1848]
   folder([4]p.) 17x12cm.
   Helfert (Wiener Parnass) 1763 ("Wie mir
scheint, ausser-österreichischen Ursprungs").

---

*pGB8
V6755R
9.31.48

[Frieser, J   ]
   Das Neueste aus Schönbrunn!! oder: Was die
Viecher in der grossen Menagerie mit einander
plauschen.
   [Wien]Gedruckt bei Stöckholzer von Hirschfeld.
  —Zu haben Liliengasse Nro.898.[1848]

   broadside. illus. 43x27cm.
   Dated & signed: Wien, im September 1848. J.F.
Printed within border of type-ornaments.

---

*pGB8
V6755R
9.31.48

[Floda, ————]
   Jelaciç vor Pesth, oder die Ultra-Magyaren
verlieren den Kopf. Letzter Act des historischen
Schauspiels: "Der bestrafte Uebermuth der
Magyaren".
   [Wien]Gedruckt bei Josef Ludwig,Josefstadt,
Florianigasse,Nro.52.[1848]

   [2]p. 38.5x23cm.
   Caption title; imprint on p.[2]; dated &
signed: Wien im Monat September 1848. Floda.

---

*pGB8
V6755R
9.31.48

Die gänzliche Niederlage der Kroaten.
Jellachich hängt!!! Camarilla capores!
   [Wien]Gedruckt bei Franz Edlen von Schmid.
[1848]

   [2]p. 40x24.5cm.
   Caption title; imprint on p.[2]; dated &
signed: Wien im September 1848. Z.

---

*pGB8
V6755R
9.31.48

[Foglár, Adolf, 1822-1900, ascribed author]
   Früh= und Abend=Gebet aller Schwarzgelben.
   Wien,Gedruckt im September 1848 bei J.N.
Fridrich,Josephstadt Langegasse Nr.58.

   broadside. 37.5x23cm.
   Apparently a variant of Helfert (Wiener
Parnass) 1910, which is described as signed "A.
F."; Helfert suggests the initials may be those
of Adolf Foglár.
   Also published with title: Das Vater Unser
der Aristokraten und Fürstenknechte.

---

*GB8
V6755R
9.31.48

[Gnanth, Anton]
   Das Juden-Turnier beim Schottnern am Stein.
   [Wien]Gedruckt bei M.Lell,vormals Anna St.
von Hirschfeld.[1848]

   folder(4p.) 20x12.5cm.
   Helfert (Wiener Parnass) 1766.
   Signed at end: Anton Gnanth.
   Woodcut illus. on t.-p.
   A poem in the Viennese dialect.

*pGB8
V6755R
9.31.48

Haas, Georg Emanuel, 1821-1895.
    Gedicht gegen Freiligrath von Georg Emanuel
Haas. Die Lebendigen an die Todten.
    Wien,im September 1848.Gedruckt bei Franz
Edlen von Schmid.

    broadside. 25.5x40.5cm.
    Helfert (Wiener Parnass) 1909.

---

*pGB8
V6755R
9.31.48

Krieg der Schwarzgelben mit den Schwarz-Roth-
Goldnen.
    [Wien]Gedruckt bei Franz Edlen von Schmid.
[1848]

    broadside. 37x24cm.
    Dated & signed: Wien im September 1848. J. S.

---

*pGB8
V6755R
9.31.48

Häfner, General der Volksfreiheit und
Gritzner sein Adjutant.
    [Wien]Gedruckt bei Franz Edlen von Schmid.
[1848]

    broadside. 50x40cm.
    Dated & signed: Wien, im Septbr. 1848. Z.
    The 2 men were editors of "Die Constitution".

---

*GB8
V6755R
9.31.48

[Lagout, ———]
    Wenn das so ginge, brauchten die Pfarrer
freilich keine Köchinnen. Oder Ein geistlicher
Herr behauptete: das Recht der ersten Nacht
bei "neuvermählten" Weibern nach dem
angenommenen Herkommen zu besitzen.
    [Wien]Gedruckt bei Josef Ludwig,Josefstadt,
Florianigasse,Nro.52.[1848]

    [2]p. 29.5x23cm.
    Caption title; imprint on p.[2]; dated &
signed: Wien im September 1848. Lagout.

---

*pGB8
V6755R
9.31.48

Jelačić, Josip, grof, 1801-1859.
    Aufgefangene Briefe des Banus von Kroatien an
hochgestellte Personen in Wien. Officiell
veröffentlicht laut k. ungar. Reichstagsbeschluss.
    Wien in Septbr.1848.Gedruckt bei Franz Edlen
v.Schmid.

    broadside. 30x40cm.
    Two letters, the first addressed to Latour,
the second (dated 23 Sept. 1848) to Baron
Kulmer.

---

*GB8
V6755R
9.31.48

Lange, Wilhelm, fl.1848.
    Rede gehalten bei der feierlichen
Fahnenweihe des IX. Bezirks, gesprochen von
Wilhelm Lange, Bezirks-Chef.
    [Wien]Mechitharisten=Buchdruckerei.[1848]

    broadside. 30x21.5cm.

---

*pGB8
V6755R
9.31.48

Der Kaiser mit dem deutschen Band in
Schönbrunn und die Schwarzgelben in der
Stadt.
    [Wien]Gedruckt bei Franz Edlen von Schmid.
[1848]

    [2]p. 40x25cm.
    Caption title; imprint on p.[2]; dated &
signed: Wien im September 1848. J. S.

---

*pGB8
V6755R
9.31.48

Lothar, pseud.
    Grosses Naturalien=Cabinet der Riesenzöpfe
Wiens im Jahre der Freiheit und des Heils 1848.
    [Wien]Druck von Hirschfeld.—Zu haben in der
Liliengasse.Nro.898.[1848]

    broadside. 43x27cm.

---

*GB8
V6755R
9.31.48

Katholiken-Verein für Glauben, Freiheit und
    Gesittung, Vienna.
    Statuten des Katholiken=Vereines für Glauben,
Freiheit und Gesittung.
    [Wien,1848]

    folder([4]p.) 23x15cm.
    Caption title.

---

*pGB8
V6755R
9.31.48

Der Minister als Aschenmann.
    [Wien]Zu haben in der Stadt,Liliengasse,Nr.
898.Buchdruckerei in der Leopoldstadt Nr.656.
[1848]

    broadside. 1 illus. 47.5x30cm.
    Dated & signed: Wien, im Monat September 1848.
J. F. J.
    A satire on Metternich.

*pGB8
V6755R
9.31.48

Mosen, Hary.
   Das Wort, das man nicht sagen darf! oder:
Nieder mit der R.......!
   [Wien,1848]
      broadside. 40x25cm.
      Dated: Wien, im Septemberi [!].
      At end: Nieder mit der Republik!
      Printed on the other side of the sheet is A.
   Pichler's Nieder mit der Reaktion!

---

*pGB8
V6755R
9.31.48

Parte=Zettel und schauerliches Ende der
   ehrsamen, tugendhaften, allgemein verehrten
Jungfer Cibinerl.
   [Wien]Sept.1848.Gedruckt bei M.Lell.
      broadside. illus. 30x47cm.
      Satire in the form of a mock obituary.
      Signed: v. K.

---

*pGB8
V6755R
9.31.48

Neue Constitution. Entwurf der Grundrechte.
   Vom Constitutionsausschusse dem Reichstage
vorgelegt.
   [Wien]Gedruckt bei Franz Edlen v.Schmid.[1848]
      [2]p. 40x25cm.
      Caption title; imprint on p.[2]; dated: Wien,
   im September 1848.

---

*pGB8
V6755R
9.31.48

Patriotischer Verein der Freunde der
      konstitutionellen Ordnung, Vienna.
   An Oesterreich's Helden, die Armee und ihren
Führer in Jtalien!
   [Wien]Gedruckt bei Carl Ueberreuter im
September 1848.
      broadside. 40x25.5cm.
      Signed: Vom patriotischen Vereine der Freunde
   der konstitutionellen Ordnung. Dr. Hoffer, als
   Vorstand, im Folge einstimmigen Beschlusses der
   General=Versammlung vom 23. August 1848.
      Printed on pale green paper.

---

*pGB8
V6755R
9.31.48

Neuestes, ausserordentliches Blatt aus
   Deutschland!! Metternich an der
Spitze des deutschen Landsturms. Die gefallenen
Oesterreicher auf den Barrikaden. Der
unglückliche Reichsverweser Johann. Ermordung
von Reichstags=Deputirten.
   Zu haben im Verlagsgewölbe:Stadt,Parisergasse
Nr.411.Wien,gedruckt im September 1848,bei U.
Klopf sen.und Alex.Eurich.

   [2]p. 39x25cm.
      Caption title; imprint on p.[2]; signed: T. R.

---

*pGB8
V6755R
9.31.48

Pichler, Adolf, 1819-1900.
   An den Herrn Justiz-Minister Bach!
   [Wien]Gedruckt bei Franz Ed.v.Schmid.[1848]
      [2]p. 40x25cm.
      Endorsed title on p.[2]; dated & signed: Wien
   im September 1848. A. Pichler.

---

*pGB8
V6755R
9.31.48

Offener Brief an Madame Strunz.
   Wien.Gedruckt im September 1848,bei J.N.
Fridrich.
      broadside. 38.5x23cm.
      Signed: —— t. Mediciner.

---

*pGB8
V6755R
9.31.48

[Pichler, Adolf, 1819-1900]
   Der kluge Arbeiter und der gute Kaiser!
Eine wahre Begebenheit.
   [Wien]Gedruckt bei Franz Edlen von Schmid.
[1848]
      [2]p. 40x25cm.
      Caption title; imprint on p.[2]; dated &
   signed: Wien, im September 1848. A. Pichler.

---

*pGB8
V6755R
9.31.48

Der Papst Pius heirathet! Wir gratuliren zu
   Ihrer Heiligkeit der Frau Päpstin.
   [Wien]Gedruckt und zu haben bei U.Klopf sen.und
Alexander Eurich.[1848]
      broadside. 39.5x25.5cm.
      Includes a 3-stanza poem beginning "Auf Erden
   ist kein Wunder ..."; Helfert (Wiener Parnass)
   1761.
      A satire.

---

*pGB8
V6755R
9.31.48

Pichler, Adolf, 1819-1900.
   Nieder mit der Reaktion! (obgleich man's
sagen darf.)
   [Wien]Gedruckt bei Franz Edlen von Schmid.
[1848]
      broadside. 40x25cm.
      Dated: Wien, im September 1848.
      Printed on the other side of the sheet is
   Hary Mosen's Das Wort, das man nicht sagen
   darf!

*GB8
V6755R
9.31.48

Die politisirenden Schusterbuben.
[Wien]9.48[i.e.September 1848].Gedruckt bei
M.Lell.

    [2]p. 1 illus. 30x23.5cm.
Caption title; woodcut illus. at head;
imprint on p.[2].

[Steiner, Friedrich, fl.1848]
De neue Jüden-Bürger-Miliz. Zweite Auflage.
[Wien,1848]

    folder([4]p.) 21x13cm.
Helfert (Wiener Parnass) 1767.
Signed at end: Friedrich Steiner.
Printer's imprint on p.[4]: Gedruckt bei M.
Lell, Leopoldstadt, Weintraubengasse Nr.505.
Eigenthumsrecht und Verlag, Gumpendorf
Gärtnergasse Nr. 545, im zweiten Stock.
Woodcut illus. on t.-p.
A poem in the   Viennese dialect.

*GB8
V6755R
9.31.48

---

*pGB8
V6755R
9.31.48

Professor Füster hat geheirathet und ein
Findelkind angenommen.
[Wien]Gedruckt bei Stöckhalzer[!]v.Hirschfeld.
—Zu haben Liliengasse Nr.898.[1848]

    broadside. 43x27cm.
Dated & signed: Wien im September 1848.
J. E. J.
Printed within border of type-ornaments.

[Steiner, Friedrich, fl.1848]
De neue Jüden-Bürger-Miliz. Dritte Auflage.
[Wien,1848]

    folder([4]p.) 20.5x13cm.
Helfert (Wiener Parnass) 1767.
Signed at end: Friedrich Steiner.
Printer's imprint on p.[4]: Gedruckt bei M.
Lell, Leopoldstadt, Weintraubengasse Nr.505.
Eigenthumsrecht und Verlag, Gumpendorf
Gärtnergasse Nr.545, im zweiten Stock.
Woodcut illus. on t.-p.
A poem in the   Viennese dialect.

*GB8
V6755R
9.31.48

---

*pGB8
V6755R
9.31.48

Stanzl, ———
Liener Zeissl-Bauern Revolution bey der
Lerchenfelder Linie.
[Wien,1848]

    broadside. 39.5x24cm.
In the Viennese dialect.

Verein der demokratisch-monarchisch-Gesinnten
    auf der Landstrasse.
Offene Erklärung des Vereins der Liberalen auf
der Landstrasse.
Wien im Monat September 1848,gedruckt bei
Joseph Ludwig.

    broadside. 44.5x58cm.

*pGB8
V6755R
9.31.48

---

*GB8
V6755R
9.31.48

[Stanzl, ———]
Der wahnsinnige Jude.
[Wien]Gedruckt bei Josef Ludwig,Josefstadt
Florianigasse Nr.52.[1848]

    folder([4]p.) 22.5x15cm.
Caption title; imprint on p.[4]; signed:
Stanzl.
Helfert (Wiener Parnass) 1769.
Poem in the Viennese dialect.

Vienna. Nationalgarde.
Hoher Reichstag! Es war am 14. März. d. J.,
wo die Bevölkerung Wiens mit begeistertem Jubel
nach dem Zeughause eilte, um Waffen zu
erlangen ...
[Wien]Aus der k.k.Hof- und Staatsdruckerei.
[1848]

    [2]p. 40.5x24.5cm.
Caption title; imprint on p.[2]; signed at
end: Im Namen des Verwaltungsrathes der Wiener
Nationalgarde. Klucky, Präsident.
    Protesting the   weakening of the National-
garde.

*pGB8
V6755R
9.31.48

---

*GB8
V6755R
9.31.48

[Steiner, Friedrich, fl.1848]
De neue Jüden-Bürger-Miliz.
[Wien,1848]

    folder([4]p.) 23.5x15cm.
Helfert (Wiener Parnass) 1767.
Signed at end: Friedrich Steiner.
Printer's imprint on p.[4]: Gedruckt bei M.
Lell, Leopoldstadt, Weintraubengasse Nr.505.
Eigenthumsrecht und Verlag, Gumpendorf
Gärtnergasse Nr.545, im zweiten Stock.
A poem in the   Viennese dialect.

Wie die alte Frau Baberl, über die Freiheit
lamentirt.
[Wien]Druck von J.N.Fridrich,im September
1848.Zu haben in der Leopoldstadt,anfangs der
Jägerzeil Nr.525.

    [2]p. 38x22.5cm.
Caption title; imprint on p.[2].

*pGB8
V6755R
9.31.48

*pGB8
V6755R
10.1.48

Austria. Armee.
Jn dem "Abendblatte der allgemeinen
österreichischen Zeitung" vom 30. September
wird gemeldet, dass dumpfe Gerüchte die Stadt
durchziehen, es werde Montag das Militär auf
dem Glacis ein Lager aufschlagen ...
[Wien]Aus der k.k.Hof= und Staatsdruckerei.
[1848]
broadside. 44.5x57cm.
Dated & signed: Wien am 1. Oktober 1848.
Feldmarschall-Lieutenant Graf Auersperg,
commandirender General.

*pGB8
V6755R
10.1.48

Austria. Reichstag, 1848-1849.
Kundmachung. Nachstehende Eingabe wird mit
dem Beifügen zur allgemeinen Kenntniss
gebracht, dass deren Jnhalt vom Reichstage zur
wohlgefälligen Kenntniss genommen wurde.
[Wien]Aus der k.k.Hof= und Staatsdruckerei.
[1848]
broadside. 44.5x57cm.
Includes a petition from the Wiener
allgemeiner Arbeiter-Verein.
In contemporary ms. at head: 1 Oktober.

*pGB8
V6755R
10.1.48

... Erfreuliche Nachrichten. Jelachich mit
2000 Mann in Schwandorf. Aufforderung an den
Commandant Auersberg. Die Deputation von Prag.
Die Deputation von Brünn. Nachrichten aus Gratz.
Gedruckt bei Franz Edl v.enSchmid[!]in Wien.
[1848]
[2]p. 40x25cm.
Caption title; at head: Verantwortlich die
Redaktion des Stürmers; imprint on p.[2].
Dated & signed: Wien im October 1848. L.

*pGB8
V6755R
10.1.48

Extra=Post aus Pesth. Die Ungarn siegen.
Graf Zichy wurde aufgehängt.
[Wien]Gedruckt bei Franz Edlen von Schmid.
[1848]
broadside. 40x25cm.
Dated & signed: Wien im Oktober 1848. Z.

*pGB8
V6755R
10.1.48

[Heinisch, Constantin]
... Der böhmische Parteigänger Pater Urban. Ein
verrätherischer Helfershelfer des Ban
Jellachich (aus aufgefangenen Briefen).
[Wien]Gedruckt bei Franz Edlen v.Schmid.[1848]
[2]p. 40.5x25cm.
Caption title; at head: Ausserordentliche
Beilage zum Stürmer (Studentenzeitung); imprint
on p.[2].
Dated & signed: Wien im Oktober 1848. Heinisch.

*pGB8
V6755R
10.1.48

Jellasich in Raab, Ludwig Kossuth erschossen!
[Wien]Gedruckt bei Franz Edlen v.Schmid.[1848]
[2]p. 40x24.5cm.
Caption title; imprint on p.[2]; dated &
signed: Wien im Oktober 1848. Z.
Deploring false rumors.

*pGB8
V6755R
10.1.48

... Neuester Courier aus Ungarn. General
Kempen mit den Kroaten vor Pesth. Niederlage der
Ungarn. Kossuth und das Revolutions-Tribunal.
Schreckliche Anarchie. Zehntausend Flüchtlinge.
Wien,gedruckt im Oct.1848,bei U.Klopf sen.und
Alexander Eurich.
[2]p. 39.5x25cm.
Caption title (Austrian arms at head); imprint
on p.[2].

*pGB8
V6755R
10.1.48

Oesterreichischer Patrioten-Verein.
... Fünfte Kundmachung über die freiwilligen
Beiträge, welche die Einwohner von Wien ihrer
volksthümlichen constitutionellen
Staatsregierung zur Bestreitung der
ausserordentlichen Staatsbedürfnisse gegeben
haben.
[Wien]Aus der k.k.Hof= und Staats=Druckerei.
[1848]
folder([3]p.) 45x28.5cm.
Caption title; imprint on p.[3].
Dated: Wien im October 1848.

*pGB8
V6755R
10.1.48

Die Presse, Vienna.
Der konstitutionelle Verein. Die "Presse" vom
30. September enthält folgenden Artikel: "Der
konstitutionelle Verein": ...
Zu haben bei J.Bader,Buchhändler in Wien,
Stadt,Stroblgasse.[1848]
broadside. 46x29.5cm.
Dated: Wien, den 1. Oktober 1848.

*pGB8
V6755R
10.1.48

Unglaublich und doch wahr. Fürchterlicher
Kampf der Wiener Studenten gegen Wiener
Studenten und der k. k. Soldaten gegen k. k.
Soldaten am ungarisch=croatischen Schlachtfelde.
[Wien]Gedruckt bei Franz Edlen von Schmid.
[1848]
[2]p. 40x25cm.
Caption title; imprint on p.[2]; dated &
signed: Wien im Oktober 1848. J.

*pGB8
V6755R
10.1.48

Verein der Deutschen in Oesterreich.
An die hohe Reichsversammlung in Wien! Jn
der 40. Sitzung des Reichstages vom 11.
September, rief ein Vertreter des östreichischen
Volkes, nachdem er zuvor den deutschen Stamm in
Minorität erklärt hatte, der hohen Versammlung
die ungemessenen Worte entgegen: "Wir Slaven
sind bei weitem die grösste Macht des Staates
...
Wien,im Oktob.1848,gedruckt bei U.Klopf Senior
und Alexander Eurich,Wollzeile Nr.782.
(See next card)

*pGB8
V6755R
10.3.48

Austria. Reichstag, 1848-1849.
Protokoll der 61. Sitzung der constituirenden
Reichsversammlung am 3. October 1848 Vormittags.
[Wien,1848]

folder([4]p.)   38x23cm.
Caption title.

*pGB8
V6755R
10.1.48

Verein der Deutschen in Oesterreich.   An die
hohe ... 1848.   (Card 2)

[2]p. 44.5x28.5cm.
Caption title; imprint on p.[2]; dated &
signed: Jm September 1848. Der Verein der
Deutschen in Oestreich.

*pGB8
V6755R
10.3.48

Austria. Reichstag, 1848-1849.
Protokoll der 62. Sitzung der constituirenden
Reichsversammlung am 3. October 1848 Abends.
[Wien]Aus der k.k.Hof= und Staatsdruckerei.
[1848]

broadside. 38x23cm.

*pGB8
V6755R
10.2.48

Austria. Ministerrat.
Kundmachung. Jn Folge der Kundmachung des
Ministeriums vom 13. September 1848 sind von
der Commission zur Liquidirung der bis 11.
September d. J. ausgegebenen, und im Besitze der
ursprünglichen Empfänger befindlichen Actien des
vom Herrn Swoboda gegründeten Privat=Darleihens=
Vereines bereits eine bedeutende Anzahl solcher
Actien unter den in der erwähnten Kundmachung
des Ministeriums vorgezeichneten Modalitäten
eingelöst worden ...
(See next card)

*pGB8
V6755R
10.3.48

Austria. Sovereigns, etc., 1835-1848
(Ferdinand I)
Manifest an die Ungarn. Wir Ferdinand der
Erste, constitutioneller Kaiser von Oesterreich
u. s. w. ...
[Wien]Gedruckt bei Franz Edlen von Schmid.
[1848]
[2]p. 41x26cm.
Caption title; imprint on p.[2]; dated: Gegeben
zu Schönbrunn den 3. October 1848.
(See next card)

*pGB8
V6755R
10.2.48

Austria. Ministerrat.   Kundmachung ... [1848]
(Card 2)
[Wien]Aus der k.k.Hof= und Staatsdruckerei.
[1848]

broadside. 45x57cm.
Dated: Wien am 2. October 1848.

*pGB8
V6755R
10.3.48

Austria. Sovereigns, etc., 1835-1848
(Ferdinand I)   Manifest an die Ungarn ...
[1848]   (Card 2)

Also published with imprint of the Staats-
druckerei with text beginning: Wir Ferdinand der
Erste ...
Dissolving the Hungarian parliament and placing
all Hungarian troops under the command of
Jelačič.

*pGB8
V6755R
10.2.48

Hungary. Országgyűlés.
Proklamation der Ungarn an den hohen
constituirenden Reichstag in Wien, und an die
gesammte Bevölkerung Oesterreichs! Die
ungarische Nation, im heiligen Kampfe für ihre
Freiheit und ihr gutes Recht ...
Wien im Oktober[1848],gedruckt bei Franz
Edlen von Schmid.
broadside. 40x50cm.
Dated & signed: Pesth, im Oktober 1848. B.
Sigmund Perenyi,   Vicepräses der
Magnatentafel.   Johann Pallfi, Vicepräses
des Repräsentanten   hauses.

*pGB8
V6755R
10.3.48

Austria. Sovereigns, etc., 1835-1848
(Ferdinand I)
Wir Ferdinand der Erste, constitutioneller
Kaiser von Oesterreich ... Ungarns, des
Grossfürstenthums Siebenbürgen, so wie aller
Nachbarländer Reichsbaronen, kirchlichen und
weltlichen Würdenträgern, Magnaten und
Repräsentanten, die auf dem von Uns in der
königl. Freistadt Pesth zusammenberufenen
Reichstage versammelt sind, Unsern Gruss und
Unser Wohlwollen ...
(See next card)

Austria. Sovereigns, etc., 1835-1848
*pGB8   (Ferdinand I)   Wir Ferdinand der Erste
V6755R   ... [1848]   (Card 2)
10.3.48

[Wien]Aus der k.k.Hof= und Staatsdruckerei.
[1848]

    folder([2]p.) 45x28.5cm.
    Caption title; imprint on p.[2]; dated:
Gegeben zu Schönbrunn den 3. October 1848.
    Another edition is without imprint; and another,
with imprint of Schmid, has title: Manifest
an die Ungarn.
    Dissolving the Hungarian parliament and
placing all Hungarian troops under the
command of Jelačić.

Austria. Sovereigns, etc., 1835-1848
*pGB8   (Ferdinand I)
V6755R   Wir Ferdinand der Erste, constitutioneller
10.3.48   Kaiser von Oesterreich ... Ungarns, des
Grossfürstenthums Siebenbürgen, so wie aller
Nachbarländer Reichsbaronen, kirchlichen und
weltlichen Würdenträgern, Magnaten und
Repräsentanten, die auf dem von Uns in der k.
Freistadt Pesth zusammenberufenen Reichstage
versammelt sind, Unsern Gruss und Unser
Wohlwollen ...
                 (See next card)

Austria. Sovereigns, etc., 1835-1848
*pGB8   (Ferdinand I)   Wir Ferdinand der Erste
V6755R   ... [1848]   (Card 2)
10.3.48   [Wien,1848]

    folder([2]p.) 44.5x28.5cm.
    Caption title; dated: Gegeben zu Schönbrunn den
3. October 1848.
    Another edition has imprint of the Staats-
druckerei; and another, with imprint of Schmid,
has title: Manifest an die Ungarn.
    Dissolving the Hungarian parliament and placing
all Hungarian troops under the command
of Jelačić.

Freude für alle Schwarzgelben. Noch haben die
*pGB8   Waffen der Freiheit nicht gesiegt. Neuestes vom
V6755R   ungarischen Kriegsschauplatz.
10.3.48   [Wien]Gedruckt bei Franz Edlen v.Schmid.[1848]

    [2]p. 40x25.5cm.
    Caption title; imprint on p.[2]; dated: Wien
im Oktober 1848.

Vienna. Universität. Medizinische Fakultät.
*pGB8   Die Herren Mitglieder der medicinischen
V6755R   Facultät werden hiemit eingeladen, Freitag den
10.3.48   13. October l. J. Abends 5 Uhr im Universitäts=
Consistorialsale zur Plenar=Versammlung zu
erscheinen ...
    [Wien]Aus der k.k.Hof= und Staatsdruckerei.
[1848]

    broadside. 36x21.5cm.
    Dated: Wien am 3. October 1848.

Austria. Reichstag, 1848-1849.
*pGB8   Protokoll der 63. Sitzung der constituirenden
V6755R   Reichsversammlung am 4. October 1848.
10.4.48   [Wien]Aus der k.k.Hof= und Staatsdruckerei.
[1848]

    [7]p. 38x23cm.
    Caption title; imprint on p.[7].

      ... Die Fahnenweihe.
*pGB8   [Wien,1848]
V6755R
10.4.48   broadside. 46.5x29.5cm.
    At head of title: Besonderer Abdruck aus der
Beilage der Wiener Zeitung. N⁰ 274. 4. October
1848.
    Describing the presentation of colors on 24
September.

Austria. Reichstag, 1848-1849.
*pGB8   Protokoll der 64. Sitzung der constituirenden
V6755R   Reichsversammlung am 5. October 1848.
10.5.48   [Wien]Aus der k.k.Hof= und Staatsdruckerei.
[1848]

    [5]p. 38x23.5cm.
    Caption title; imprint on p.[5].

    Selbst die Hölle hasst den Zopf!
*GB8   [Wien]Zu haben beim Herausgeber,Breitenfeld
V6755R   Nr.6.Druck der a.p.Kunstanst.Leopoldstadt Nr.
10.5.48   237,Oktob.1848.

    [2]p. 1 illus. 29x22.5cm.
    Caption title; imprint on p.[2].
    News reports, one of them dated: Wien, 4.
October.
    Dated in contemporary ms.: 5. Oktober 848.

Austria. Ministerium des Innern.
*pGB8   An die Nationalgarde. Nach dem mir von dem
V6755R   hohen Reichstage ausgedrückten Wunsche sehe
10.6.48   ich mich in Anbetracht der eingetretenen
ausserordentlichen Umstände zur möglichst
schleunigen Herstellung der gesetzlichen Ordnung
bestimmt, den Herrn Abgeordneten Scherzer als
provisorischen Ober=Commandanten der Nationalgarde von Wien und Umgebung zu ernennen ...
    [Wien]Aus der k.k.Hof= und Staatsdruckerei.
[1848]
                 (See next card)

*pGB8
V6755R
10.6.48

Austria. Ministerium des Innern.   An die
Nationalgarde ... [1848]   (Card 2)

broadside. 44.5x29cm.
Dated: Wien den 6. October 1848.
Lyser (Wiener-Ereignisse) p.17.

---

*pGB8
V6755R
10.6.48

Austria. Ministerrat.
An die Bevölkerung Wiens. Bei dem für heute
früh angeordneten Abmärsche eines Theiles der
hiesigen Garnison haben sich bei einen Theile
dieser Truppen meuterische Bewegungen gegen
diesen Befehl gezeigt ...
[Wien]Aus der k.k.Hof= und Staatsdruckerei.
[1848]
broadside. 44.5x57cm.
Dated: Wien am 6. October 1848.
Lyser (Wiener-Ereignisse) p.14.

---

*pGB8
V6755R
10.6.48

Austria. Ministerrat.
Nationalgarde! Das Ministerium hat mit dem
schmerzlichsten Bedauern vernommen, dass
Nationalgarden gegen Nationalgarden, dass Bürger
gegen Bürger im Kampfe stehen ...
[Wien]Aus der k.k.Hof= und Staatsdruckerei.
[1848]
broadside. 44.5x28.5cm.
Dated: Wien am 6. October 1848.
Lyser (Wiener-Ereignisse) p.15.

---

*pGB8
V6755R
10.6.48

Austria. Reichstag, 1848-1849.
Kundmachung. Der Reichstag beschliesst, der
Direction der Nordbahn zu befehlen, dass dafür
zu sorgen sei, dass kein Militär auf der
Nordbahn hieher geführt werde ...
[Wien]Aus der k.k.Hof= und Staatsdruckerei.
[1848]
broadside. 44.5x28.5cm.
Dated: Wien am 6. October 1848.
Lyser (Wiener-Ereignisse) p.14.

---

*pGB8
V6755R
10.6.48

Austria. Reichstag, 1848-1849.
Kundmachung. Der Reichstag beschliesst, der
Direction der Südbahn zu befehlen, dass dafür
zu sorgen sei, dass kein Militär auf der
Südbahn hieher geführt werde ...
[Wien]Aus der k.k.Hof= und Staatsdruckerei.
[1848]
broadside. 45x29cm.
Dated: Wien am 6. October 1848.
Lyser (Wiener-Ereignisse) p.16.

---

*pGB8
V6755R
10.6.48

Austria. Reichstag, 1848-1849.
Kundmachung. Der Reichstag hat beschlossen,
Seiner Majestät die Bildung eines volksthümlichen,
das Vertrauen der Bevölkerung geniessenden
Ministeriums, an welchem die bisherigen Minister
Doblhoff und Hornbostel Theil zu nehmen hätten,
als ein unerlässliches Bedürfniss zur
Herstellung der Ordnung zu bezeichnen ...
[Wien]Aus der k.k.Hof= und Staatsdruckerei.
[1848]

(See next card)

---

*pGB8
V6755R
10.6.48

Austria. Reichstag, 1848-1849.   Kundmachung
... [1848]   (Card 2)

broadside. 44.5x29cm.
Dated: Wien den 6. October 1848.
Lyser (Wiener-Ereignisse) p.16.

---

*pGB8
V6755R
10.6.48

Austria. Reichstag, 1848-1849.
Kundmachung. Um irrigen Gerüchten zu begegnen,
als ob ein Theil der Mitglieder des Reichstages
an seinen Sitzungen nicht Theil nehmen würde ...
[Wien]Aus der k.k.Hof= und Staatsdruckerei.
[1848]
broadside. 44.5x28.5cm.
Dated: Wien am 6. October 1848.
Lyser (Wiener-Ereignisse) p.14.

---

*pGB8
V6755R
10.6.48

Austria. Reichstag, 1848-1849.
Proclamation. Der Reichstag bringt hiemit
zur öffentlichen Kunde, dass er eben in
Berathung über die Massregeln sei, das Militär
aus dem Bezirke der Stadt zu entfernen ...
[Wien]Aus der k.k.Hof= und Staatsdruckerei.
[1848]
broadside. 45x28cm.
Dated: Wien am 6. October 1848.
Lyser (Wiener-Ereignisse) p.15.

---

*pGB8
V6755R
10.6.48

Austria. Reichstag, 1848-1849.
Proclamation. Der Reichstag, von den
verhängnissvollen Ereignissen benachrichtigt,
die diese Hauptstadt erschüttert haben, hat sich
versammelt ...
[Wien]Aus der k.k.Hof= und Staats=Druckerei.
[1848]
broadside. 45x28.5cm.
Dated: Wien am 6 October 1848.
Lyser (Wiener-Ereignisse) p.15-16.

*pGB8
V6755R
10.6.48

Austria. Reichstag, 1848-1849.
    Protokoll der 65. Sitzung der constituirenden
Reichs=Versammlung am 6. October 1848.
    [Wien,1848]

    [7]p. 38x23cm.
    Caption title.

O

*pGB8
V6755R
10.7.48

Austria. Reichstag, 1848-1849.
    Kundmachung. Der Reichstag hat beschlossen,
dass der neugewählte Gemeinderath der Stadt
Wien sogleich zusammen zu treten ...
    [Wien]Aus der k.k.Hof= und Staatsdruckerei.
[1848]

    broadside. 45x28.5cm.
    Dated: Wien am 7. October 1848.

O

*pGB8
V6755R
10.6.48

Austria, Lower. Laws, statutes, etc., 1835-1848
        (Ferdinand I)
    ... Circulare der k. k. Landesregierung im
Erzherzogthume Oesterreich unter der Enns. Die
Bewilligung eines General Pardon für alle
Deserteurs der k. k. Armee, vom Feldwebel und
Wachtmeister abwärts, betreffend.
    [Wien]Aus der k.k.Hof= und Staatsdruckerei.
[1848]

    broadside. 44.5x29cm.
    At head of title: NO 45905.
    Dated: Wien am 6. October 1848.

O

*pGB8
V6755R
10.7.48

Austria. Reichstag, 1848-1849.
    Kundmachung. Der Reichstag hat zufolge
gestrigen Beschlusses Militär=Zuzüge auf der
Nordbahn verboten ...
    [Wien]Aus der k.k.Hof= und Staats=Druckerei.
[1848]

    broadside. 44.5x29cm.
    Dated: Wien den 7. October 1848.
    Lyser (Wiener-Ereignisse) p.28.

O

*pGB8
V6755R
10.6.48

Der blutige Kampf in der Stephanskirche.
    [Wien]Gedruckt bei Franz Edlen v.Schmid.[1848]

    broadside. 40x25cm.
    Dated & signed: Wien, im October 1848. J.

O

*pGB8
V6755R
10.7.48

Austria. Reichstag, 1848-1849.
    Kundmachung. Zur Beruhigung wird Nachfolgendes,
vom Ministerrathe dem hohen Reichstage
mitgetheiltes Schreiben des Commandirenden
Grafen Auersperg zur öffentlichen Kenntniss
gebracht ...
    [Wien]Aus der k.k.Hof= und Staatsdruckerei.
[1848]

    broadside. 44.5x57cm.
    Dated: Wien am 7. October 1848.
    Lyser (Wiener-Ereignisse) p.29-30.

O

*pGB8
V6755R
10.6.48

Die Ermordung des Grafen Lambert auf der
Pesther Brücke, des von Sr. Majestät dem Kaiser
eingesetzten Generalissismus [!] der königlich=
ungarischen und kroatischen Truppen. Jellachich
von den tapferen Magyaren auf's Haupt geschlagen
bei Killity. Kriegsminister Theodor Baillet de
Latour hat abgedankt.
    [Wien]Gedruckt bei Franz Edlen von Schmid.
[1848]

    broadside. 40.5x25cm.
    Dated & signed: Wien, im Oktober 1848. Z.

O

*pGB8
V6755R
10.7.48

Austria. Reichstag, 1848-1849.
    Nationalgarden! Der Reichstag hat das Wohl
und die Freiheit des Vaterlandes, die
Unverletzlichkeit des constitutionellen Thrones
und des Reichstages unter den Schutz der
Nationalgarde gestellt ...
    [Wien]Aus der k.k.Hof= und Staatsdruckerei.
[1848]

    broadside. 44.5x28.5cm.
    Dated: Wien den 7. October 1848.
    Lyser (Wiener-Ereignisse) p.28.

O

*pGB8
V6755R
10.6.48

Vienna. Universität. Ausschuss der Studierenden.
    Mitbürger! Unsere Winsche, die Jhr theilen
werdet, sind: ...
    Wieu[!],gedruckt im Oktober 1848,bei U.Klopf
sen.und Alexander Eurich.

    broadside. 42x26.5cm.
    Dated & signed: Wien, den 6. October 1848.
    Vom Studenten=Comitée.

O

*pGB8
V6755R
10.7.48

Austria. Reichstag, 1848-1849.
    Protokoll der 66. Sitzung der constituirenden
Reichsversammlung von $8\frac{1}{2}$ Uhr Morgens bis $9\frac{3}{4}$ Uhr
Nachts am 7. October 1848.
    [Wien]Aus der k.k.Hof= und Staatsdruckerei.
[1848]

    [7]p. 38x23cm.
    Caption title; imprint on p.[7].

O

*pGB8
V6755R
10.7.48

Austria. Reichstag, 1848-1849.
Der Reichstag gibt hiermit den ausdrücklichen
Befehl die Localitäten des Zeughauses gänzlich
zu schliessen ...
[Wien]Aus der k.k.Hof= und Staats=Druckerei.
[1848]

broadside. 45x28cm.
Dated: Wien am 7. October 1848.
Lyser (Wiener-Ereignisse) p.27.

*pGB8
V6755R
10.7.48

Vienna. Nationalgarde.
Liebe Landsleute! Unsere Freiheit ist in
Gefahr -- die Stadt ist von Soldaten umringt --
ein Theil der Soldaten ist zu uns übergegangen,
aber neues Militär zieht gegen uns heran ...
[Wien,1848]

broadside. 42x25.5cm.
Dated & signed: Wien, den 7. Oktober 1848.
Dir [!] Nationalgarde und die freisinnige
Bevölkerung Wiens.

*pGB8
V6755R
10.7.48

Austria. Reichstag, 1848-1849.
Völker Oesterreichs! Die Folgen
verhängnissvoller Ereignisse drohen den kaum
begonnenen Grundbau unseres neuen Staatsgebäudes
zu erschüttern ...
[Wien,1848]

broadside. 38.5x47cm.
Dated: Wien am 7. Oktober 1848.
Lyser (Wiener-Ereignisse) p.31-32.
Large folio broadside edition.

*pGB8
V6755R
10.7.48

Vienna. Nationalgarde.
Mitbürger! Man sucht unter Euch Uneinigkeit
zu streuen ...
[Wien]Aus der k.k.Hof= und Staats=Druckerei.
[1848]

broadside. 44.5x29cm.
Dated & signed: Wien am 7. October 1848. Vom
provisorischen Ober-Commando. Scherzer.
Lyser (Wiener-Ereignisse) p.30-31.

*pGB8
V6755R
10.7.48

Austria. Reichstag, 1848-1849.
Völker Oesterreichs! Die Folgen
verhängnissvoller Ereignisse drohen den kaum
begonnenen Grundbau unseres neuen
Staatsgebäudes zu erschüttern ...
[Wien,1848]

broadside. 44.5x28.5cm.
Dated: Wien am 7. October 1848.
Lyser (Wiener-Ereignisse) p.31-32.
Small folio broadside edition.

*pGB8
V6755R
10.7.48

Vienna. Nationalgarde. Akademische Legion.
Bekanntmachung. Um böswilligen Gerüchten zu
begegnen, wird hiemit auf das Bestimmteste
erklärt, dass die Sicherheitswache bei den
Bewegungen am 6. und 7. October durchaus keine
Partei nahm ...
[Wien]Aus der k.k.Hof- und Staatsdruckerei.
[1848]

broadside. 45x29cm.
Dated & signed: Wien am 7. October 1848. Der
Ausschuss der akademischen Legion.

*pGB8
V6755R
10.7.48

Die Ereignisse des sechsten Oktobers.
Latour's Hinrichtung.
[Wien]Gedruckt bei Franz Edlen v.Schmid.[1848]

broadside. 39.5x25.5cm.
Dated & signed: Wien im October 1848. Z.

*pGB8
V6755R
10.8.48

Austria. Reichstag, 1848-1849.
An die Nationalgarde. Jn Eurer Hand, Männer der
Volkswehr liegt zum grossen Theile die Zukunft
des Vaterlandes ...
[Wien]Aus der k.k.Hof= und Staats-Druckerei.
[1848]

broadside. 45x29cm.
Dated: Wien am 8. October 1848.

*pGB8
V6755R
10.7.48

Vienna. Nationalgarde.
An die gesammte National- und Bürgergarde und
akademische Legion der Haupt- und Residenzstadt
Wien. Cameraden! Berufen durch das Vertrauen
der hohen Reichsversammlung ...
[Wien]Aus der k.k.Hof= und Staatsdruckerei.
[1848]

broadside. 44.5x28.5cm.
Dated & signed: Wien am 7. October 1848. Vom
provisorischen Ober=Commando: Scherzer.
Lyser (Wiener-Ereignisse) p.30.

*pGB8
V6755R
10.8.48

Austria. Reichstag, 1848-1849.
Euere Majestät! Der Reichstag, welcher unter
den verhängnissvollen Ereignissen der letzten
Tage es als eine seiner ersten Pflichten
erkannte ...
[Wien,1848]

broadside. 38x47.5cm.
Dated: Wien am 8. Oktober 1848.
Large folio edition, without imprint.

Austria. Reichstag, 1848-1849.
*pGB8   Euere Majestät! Der Reichstag, welcher unter
V6755R   den verhängnissvollen Ereignissen der letzten
10.8.48   Tage es als eine seiner ersten Pflichten
    erkannte ...
    [Wien]Aus der k.k.Hof= und Staatsdruckerei.
    [1848]

    broadside. 44.5x28.5cm.
    Dated: Wien am 8. October 1848.
    Small folio edition, with imprint.

Der Kaiser in Sieghartskirchen und Jelachich
*pGB8   mit der croatischen Armee im Marsche gegen Wien,
V6755R   und die Ungarn kommen in 48 Stunden!
10:8.48   Wien,gedruckt im October 1848,bei U.Klopf sen.
    und Alexander Eurich.

    [2]p. 39.5x25cm.
    Caption title; imprint on p.[2].

Austria. Reichstag, 1848-1849.
*pGB8   Protokoll der 67. Sitzung der constituirenden
V6755R   Reichs=Versammlung am 8. October 1848.
10.8.48   [Wien]Aus der k.k.Hof= und Staatsdruckerei.
    [1848]

    folder([4]p.) 38x23cm.
    Caption title; imprint on p.[4].

Vienna. Nationalgarde.
*pGB8   Erklärung. Da sich gestern das falsche
V6755R   Gerücht verbreitete, als habe eine Abtheilung des
10.8.48   ersten Bezirkes aus dem k. k. Zeughause auf das
    Volk gefeuert ...
    [Wien]Aus der k.k.Hof= und Staats=Druckerei.
    [1848]

    broadside. 44.5x57cm.
    Dated & signed: Wien am 8. October 1848.
    Leszczynski, Bezirks=Commandant.

Austria. Reichstag, 1848-1849.
*pGB8   Der Reichstags=Ausschuss hat an das Ober=
V6755R   Commando der Nationalgarde den Befehl ertheilt,
10.8.48   dass der Austausch und das Wegtragen der Waffen
    im k. k. Zeughause sogleich einzustellen sei ...
    [Wien]Aus der k.k.Hof= und Staats=Druckerei.
    [1848]

    broadside. 44.5x28.5cm.
    Dated: Wien am 8. October 1848.

Vienna. Nationalgarde.
*pGB8   Nationalgarden! Kameraden! Ich brauche Euch
V6755R   nicht erst die Gefahren, von denen wir umringt
10.8.48   sind, zu schildern! ...
    [Wien]Aus der k.k.Hof= und Staats=Druckerei.
    [1848]

    broadside. 44.5x28.5cm.
    Dated & signed: Wien am 8. October 1848. Braun,
    provisorischer Ober-Commandant.

Der Bruder=Kampf oder was ist jetzt in Wien
*pGB8   geschehen -- seit 6. October.
V6755R   [Wien]Druck u.Verlag der k.k.p.a.t.g.
10.8.48   Kunstdruckerei.--Leopoldstadt,Herrengasse,Nr.
    237.--Franz Raffelsperger,Geograph.[1848]

    [2]p. 1 illus. 41x26cm.
    Caption title; imprint on p.[2].
    News reports, 6-8 October.

Vienna. Nationalgarde.
*pGB8   Die Stadtgarden an ihre Cameraden. Die
V6755R   traurigen Ereignisse der jüngsten Zeit haben
10.8.48   eine gefährliche Spaltung zwischen akademischer
    Legion, Garde und Bürger=Corps derart
    hervorgerufen ...
    [Wien][A]us der k.k.Hof= und Staatsdruckerei.
    [1848]

    broadside. 44.5x29cm.
    Dated & signed: Wien am 8. October 1848 ...
    Scherzer, provis. Ober-Commandant.

Erstes Verzeichniss der Gefallenen und
*pGB8   Blessirten am 6. und 7. Oktober.
V6755R   [Wien]Oktober 1848.Gedruckt bei M.Lell.
10.8.48

    broadside. 38x23cm.

Vienna. Universität. Ausschuss der Studierenden.
*pGB8   Der Ausschuss der Studenten beeilt sich seinen
V6755R   Mitbrüdern folgende Zuschrift des hohen
10.8.48   Reichstages kund zu geben ...
    [Wien]Aus der k.k.Hof= und Staats=Druckerei.
    [1848]

    broadside. 44.5x29cm.
    Dated: Wien, am 8. October 1848.

*pGB8
V6755R
10.8.48

Wien's Schreckens=Tag oder der 6. Oktober
1848. Dargestellt von einem Augenzeugen.
[Wien]Oktob.1848.Gedruckt bei M.Lell.

[2]p. 38x24cm.
Caption title; imprint on p.[2].

*pGB8
V6755R
10.9.48

Austria. Reichstag, 1848-1849.
Protokoll der 69. Sitzung der constituirenden
Reichsversammlung am 9. October 1848 Abends.
[Wien]Aus der k.k.Hof= und Staatsdruckerei.
[1848]

folder([3]p.) 38x23cm.
Caption title; imprint on p.[3].

*pGB8
V6755R
10.9.48

Austria. Ministerium des Innern.
Kundmachung. Jn Erwägung der Erkrankung des
provisorischen Ober=Commandanten der Nationalgarde von Wien und der Umgebung, Herrn
Abgeordneten Scherzer ...
[Wien]Aus der k.k.Hof= und Staatsdruckerei.
[1848]

broadside. 45x29cm.
Dated: Wien am 9. October 1848.

*pGB8
V6755R
10.9.48

Austria, Lower. Mercantil- und Wechselgericht.
Kundmachung. Ueber Ansuchen der k. k.
privilegirten Nationalbank und in Folge des am
8. diess gefassten Beschlusses des
Ministerrathes ...
[Wien]Aus der k.k.Hof= und Staatsdruckerei.
[1848]

broadside. 45x29cm.
Dated: Wien den 9. October 1848.

*pGB8
V6755R
10.9.48

Austria. Reichstag, 1848-1849.
An die Bewohner Wiens. Mitbürger! Verschiedene
aufregende Gerüchte durchirren die Stadt,
erhitzen die Gemüther, und erfüllen die
Bewohner mit einer Aengstlichkeit und
Bangigkeit ...
[Wien]Aus der k.k.Hof= und Staatsdruckerei.
[1848]

broadside. 45x57cm.
Dated: Wien am 9. October 1848.

*pGB8
V6755R
10.9.48

Vienna. Nationalgarde.
Kundmachung. Nachdem der hohe Reichstag die
Siegel bei dem k. k. Zeughause angelegt hat ...
[Wien]Aus der k.k.Hof= und Staats=Druckerei.
[1848]

broadside. 44.5x28.5cm.
Dated: Wien am 9. October 1848.

*pGB8
V6755R
10.9.48

Austria. Reichstag, 1848-1849.
Kundmachung. Der nachfolgende Beschluss der
hohen Reichs=Versammlung in der Sitzung vom
8. October 1848 wird hiemit kundgemacht ...
[Wien]Aus der k.k.Hof= und Staats=Druckerei.
[1848]

broadside. 45x28.5cm.
Dated: Wien am 9. October 1848.
Defining the organization and function of the
Reichstag.

*pGB8
V6755R
10.9.48

Vienna. Nationalgarde.
Tagsbefehl am 9. October 1848.
[Wien]Aus der k.k.Hof= und Staats=Druckerei.
[1848]

broadside. 44.5x28.5cm.

*pGB8
V6755R
10.9.48

Austria. Reichstag, 1848-1849.
Protokoll der 68. Sitzung der constituirenden
Reichsversammlung am 9. October 1848 Mittags.
[Wien]Aus der k.k.Hof= und Staatsdruckerei.
[1848]

folder([3]p.) 38x23cm.
Caption title; imprint on p.[3].

*pGB8
V6755R
10.9.48

Vienna. Universität. Ausschuss der Studierenden.
Brüder, Mitbürger. Manch edles Blut ist
geflossen, bis wir Waffen aus dem k. k.
Zeughaus errungen hatten ...
[Wien]Gedruckt bei Franz Edlen von Schmid.
[1848]

broadside. 49.5x40.5cm.
Dated: Wien am 9. October 1848.

*pGB8
V6755R
10.9.48

Vienna. Universität. Ausschuss der Studierenden.
Hochherziges Volk von Wien! Die Art und Weise,
mit der man das freie Ungarvolk verfolgte, die
Errungenschaften unserer Freiheitskämpfe zu
vernichten suchte ...
Wien,gedruckt im Oct.1848,bei U.Klopf sen.
und Alexander Eurich.

broadside. 39.5x50.5cm.
Dated: Wien, den 9. Oetober [!] 1848.

---

*pGB8
V6755R
10.10.48

Austria. Reichstag, 1848-1849.
Protokoll der 71. Sitzung der constituirenden
Reichsversammlung am 10. October 1848 Abends.
[Wien]Aus der k.k.Hof= und Staatsdruckerei.
[1848]

[5]p. 38x23cm.
Caption title; imprint on p.[5].

---

*pGB8
V6755R
10.10.48

Austria. Reichstag, 1848-1849.
Kundmachung. Der Gemeinderath der Stadt
Wien bringt den Erlass des permanenten
Reichstags=Ausschusses vom 10. October 1848 zur
Kenntniss.
[Wien]Aus der k.k.Hof= und Staats=Druckerei.
[1848]

broadside. 45x29cm.
Stating that the defense of the city is the
sole responsibility of the Gemeinderat and the
Nationalgarde.

---

*pGB8
V6755R
10.10.48

Grazer demokratischer Verein.
Jhr lieben Wiener. Vernehmt, wie es in
Steiermark zugeht! Als die Kunde von Eurem
heldenmüthigen Kampfe am 6. Oktober nach Gratz
kam ...
[Wien]Gedruckt bei Franz Edlen von Schmid.
[1848]

broadside. 50x40.5cm.
Dated & signed: Wien, am 10. Oktober 1848.
Joseph Leopold Stiger, Vorsitzer des Gratzer
demokratischen Vereins.
Includes a second proclamation dated & signed:
Gratz, am 8. Oktober 1848. Vom
demokratischen verein.

---

*pGB8
V6755R
10.10.48

Austria. Reichstag, 1848-1849.
Kundmachung. So eben hat der Reichstags-
Ausschuss eine Commission an den Grafen
Auersperg abgeschickt ...
[Wien]Aus der k.k.Hof= und Staatsdruckerei.
[1848]

broadside. 44.5x28cm.
Dated: Wien den 10. October 1848.

---

*pGB8
V6755R
10.10.48

Hungary. Országgyülés.
An den hohen constituirenden Reichstag in Wien!
Die ungarische Nation, im heiligen Kampfe für
ihre Freiheit und ihr gutes Recht ...
[Wien]Aus der k.k.Hof= und Staatsdruckerei.
[1848]

broadside. 45x57cm.
Dated & signed: Pesth am 10. October 1848. Des
ungarischen Reichstages Oberhauses Vice=
Präsident: B. Sigmund v. Perény. Unterhauses
erster Vice=Präsident: Johann Pálffy.

---

*pGB8
V6755R
10.10.48

Austria. Reichstag, 1848-1849.
Popoli dell'Austria! La dieta chiamata dalla
vostra fiducia a fondare con mezzi pacifici la
nostra libertà venne per la forza degli
avvenimenti tutto ad un tratto posta in mezzo
alla lotta attuale ...
[Vienna,1848]

broadside. 44.5x28.5cm.
Dated & signed: Vienna il 10. ottobre 1848.
Dall'Assemblea costituente.

---

*pGB8
V6755R
10.10.48

Hungary. Országgyülés.
An den hohen constituirenden Reichstag in
Wien! Die ungarische Nation, im heiligen Kampfe
für ihre Freiheit und ihr gutes Recht ...
Wien,gedruckt im Oktober 1848,bei U.Klopf sen.
und A.Eurich.

broadside. 39x50cm.
Dated & signed: Pest, am 10. Oktober 1848.
B. Sigmund Perényi, Vicepräses der Magnatentafel.
Johann Pálffi, Vicepräses des Repräsentanten-
hauses.

---

*pGB8
V6755R
10.10.48

Austria. Reichstag, 1848-1849.
Protokoll der 70. Sitzung der constituirenden
Reichsversammlung am 10. October 1848 Vormittags.
[Wien]Aus der k.k.Hof= und Staatsdruckerei.
[1848]

folder([3]p.) 38x23cm.
Caption title; imprint on p.[3].

---

*pGB8
V6755R
10.10.48

Jelačić, Josip, grof, 1801-1859.
Der Ban Jelachich an die Wiener! Volk von
Wien! So eben erfahre ich, dass ihr in der
grössten Sorge lebt wegen den ungarischen
Angelegenheiten, wo die Ruhe durch meine Schuld
so betrübend gestört wird ...
Wien,im Oktober 1848.Gedruckt bei Joseph
Ludwig,Josephstadt,Florianigasse Nr.52.

[2]p. 38x23cm.
Caption title; imprint on p.[2].

[Johne, G Ferdinand]

*pGB8
V6755R
10.10.48

Freie Aeusserungen eines Wieners über die Flucht des Kaisers von Oesterreich. [Wien]Gedruckt bei Joseph Luwig[!],Josephstadt, Florianigasse Nr.52.[1848]

[2]p. 44.5x29cm.
Caption title; imprint on p.[2]; dated & signed: Wien im Ocober [!] 1848. G. Ferdinand Johne.

Vienna. Universität. Ausschuss der Studierenden.

*pGB8
V6755R
10.10.48

Brüder, Landleute! Die traurige Lage, in der wir uns jetzt befinden, welche vielleicht bald Euere persönliche Gegenwart und Mithilfe nöthig machen wird ...
[Wien]Druck von U.Klopf sen.und Alexander Eurich.[1848]

broadside. 25.5x39.5cm.
Dated: Wien, den 10. October 1848.
Asking for contributions of food.

[Link, ————]

*pGB8
V6755R
10.10.48

Jellachich vor Wien. Was der Jellachich für Augen macht, wie er an der Spitze seiner Horden den Heldensitz Wien anglotzt.
[Wien]Gedruckt bei Franz Edlen von Schmid. [1848]

[2]p. 1 illus. 40.5x24.5cm.
Caption title; imprint on p.[2]; dated & signed: Wien im Oktober 1848. Link.

Vienna. Universität. Ausschuss der Studierenden.

*pGB8
V6755R
10.10.48

Hoher Reichstag! Blutige Ereignisse haben stattgefunden; die reaktionäre Politik des gegenwärtigen Ministerums [!] hat den traurigsten Bürgerkrieg in den Strassen Wiens ... veranlasst ...
[Wien]Gedruckt bei Franz Edlen von Schmid,am 10.Oktober 1848.

broadside. 40.5x25cm.
Signed by representatives of the Studenten-Ausschuss & of the Demokratischer Verein.

Vienna. Comité zur Unterstützung mittelloser Gewerbsleute.

*pGB8
V6755R
10.10.48

Die Geschäfts=Erledigungen dieses Comites werden für heute wegen Uebersiedlung in die neuen Locale am Ballplatze, altes Regierungs= Gebäude, unterbrochen ...
[Wien,1848]

broadside. 44.5x57cm.
Dated: Wien am 10. October 1848.

Von einem Soldaten an seine Kameraden!
Gedruckt bei Franz Edlen v.Schmid in Wien.
[1848]

*pGB8
V6755R
10.10.48

broadside. 40x50cm.
Two addresses, one dated "Wien am 7. Oktober 1848", the other "Wien, am 10. Oktober 1848".

Vienna. Gemeinderat.

*pGB8
V6755R
10.10.48

Mitbürger! Der Gemeinderath der Stadt Wien hat eine ernste Pflicht darin gesehen, über die gegenwärtig in Umlauf befindlichen Gerüchte, insbesondere über die Absichten des Herrn Commandirenden von Wien, Grafen von Auersperg, dann des Ban von Croatien, Jellachich erprobte Nachrichten einzuholen ...
[Wien,1848]

broadside. 46x58cm.
Dated: den 10. Oktober 1848.

A Wörtl an den Kaiser!
[Wien]Gedruckt bei Franz Edlen von Schmid. [1848]

*pGB8
V6755R
10.10.48

[2]p. 1 illus. 40.5x25cm.
Caption title; imprint on p.[2]; dated & signed: Im Oktober 1848. Ein Garde der akademischen Legion.

Vienna. Nationalgarde.

*pGB8
V6755R
10.10.48

An die Bevölkerung Wiens. Nach einem von dem Comité des hohen Reichstages zur Erhaltung der Ruhe, Ordnung und Sicherheit genehmigten Beschlusse des Verwaltungsrathes der gesammten Nationalgarde ...
[Wien]Aus der k.k.Hof= und Staatsdruckerei. [1848]

broadside. 45x28cm.
Dated: Wien den 10. October 1848.
Concerning arrangements for burial of those killed in the up- rising of 6-7 October.

Austria. Reichstag, 1848-1849.

*pGB8
V6755R
10.11.48

Der Gemeinderath der Stadt Wien von mehreren Seiten aufgefordert, den Anmarsch der ungarischen Truppen anzuordnen ...
[Wien]Aus der k.k.Hof= und Staatsdruckerei. [1848]

broadside. 45x57cm.
Dated: Wien am 11. October 1848.
Lyser (Wiener-Ereignisse) p.36.

*pGB8
V6755R
10.11.48

Austria. Reichstag, 1848-1849.
Kundmachung. Alle k. k. von Conducteuren geleiteten Postwägen sind ungehindert passiren zu lassen ...
[Wien]Aus der k.k.Hof= und Staatsdruckerei. [1848]

broadside. 44.5x28.5cm.
Dated: Wien am 11. October 1848.
Lyser (Wiener-Ereignisse) p.37.

*pGB8
V6755R
10.11.48

Vienna. Gemeinderat.
Der Gemeinderat der Stadt Wien hat beschlossen, wie folgt: "Die Gemeinde übernimmt die Versorgung aller im Dienste derselben erwerbsunfähig gewordenen und mittellosen Personen, sowie ihrer Hinterbliebenen, so ferne für deren anderweitige Versorgung nicht schon durch die bereits bestehenden Gesetze vorgedacht ist ...
[Wien]Aus der k.k.Hof= und Staats-Druckerei. [1848]

(See next card)

*pGB8
V6755R
10.11.48

Austria. Reichstag, 1848-1849.
Kundmachung. Es hat sich in der Stadt das Gerücht verbreitet, dass der Reichstag den ungarischen Truppen verboten habe, die österreichische Gränze zu überschreiten ...
[Wien]Aus der k.k.Hof= und Staatsdruckerei. [1848]

broadside. 45x28.5cm.
Dated: Wien am 11. October 1848.
Lyser (Wiener-Ereignisse) p.34.
Denying the rumor.

*pGB8
V6755R
10.11.48

Vienna. Gemeinderat.   Der Gemeinderath ...
[1848]   (Card 2)

broadside. 45x57cm.
Dated: Wien am 11. October 1848.
Lyser (Wiener-Ereignisse) p.35.

*pGB8
V6755R
10.11.48

Austria. Reichstag, 1848-1849.
Protokoll der 72. Sitzung der constituirenden Reichsversammlung am 11. October 1848, von 12 Uhr Mittags bis 2 Uhr Nachmittags.
[Wien]Aus der k.k.Hof= und Staatsdruckerei. [1848]

folder([4]p.) 38.5x23cm.
Caption title; imprint on p.[4].

*pGB8
V6755R
10.11.48

Vienna. Gemeinderat.
Kundmachung. Die brauchbaren Waffen, welche sich im kaiserlichen Zeughause befanden, sind bereits alle an die Bezirks=Commandanten der Nationalgarde ausgetheilt worden ...
[Wien]Aus der k.k.Hof= und Staatsdruckerei. [1848]

broadside. 45x29cm.
Dated: Wien den 11. October 1848.
Lyser (Wiener-Ereignisse) p.37.

*pGB8
V6755R
10.11.48

Austria. Reichstag, 1848-1849.
Protokoll der 73. Sitzung der constituirenden Reichsversammlung am 11. October 1848 Abends.
[Wien]Aus der k.k.Hof= und Staatsdruckerei. [1848]

[2]p. 38x23cm.
Caption title; imprint on p.[2].

*pGB8
V6755R
10.11.48

Vienna. Gemeinderat.
Kundmachung. Die gegenwärtigen ausserordentlichen Verhältnisse und die Nothwendigkeit, für die hinlängliche Approvisionirung der Stadt Wien die möglichste Sorge zu tragen ...
[Wien]Aus der k.k.Hof= und Staats-Druckerei. [1848]

broadside. 44.5x29cm.
Dated: Wien am 11. October 1848.
Lyser (Wiener-Ereignisse) p.38.

*pGB8
V6755R
10.11.48

Vienna. Gemeinderat.
Aufruf. Alle gutgesinnten Bewohner Wiens, welche in den jüngsten Tagen Waffen erhalten haben und nicht in die Nationalgarde eingereiht sind ...
[Wien]Aus der k.k.Hof= und Staats=Druckerei. [1848]

broadside. 38x23cm.
Dated & signed: Wien am 11. October 1848. Vom Gemeinderathe der Stadt Wien im Einvernehmen mit dem Nationalgarde-Ober-Commando.
Lyser (Wiener- Ereignisse) p.38.

*pGB8
V6755R
10.11.48

Vienna. Gemeinderat.
Mitbürger! Es sind leider Fälle vorgekommen, dass Personen welche sich in jetziger drohender Zeit von Wien wegzubegeben beabsichtigten, gewaltsam aufgehalten wurden ...
[Wien]Aus der k.k.Hof= und Staats=Druckerei. [1848]

broadside. 45x28.5cm.
Dated: Wien den 11. Oktober 1848.
Lyser (Wiener-Ereignisse) p.35.

Vienna. Gemeinderat.
*pGB8
V6755R Mitbürger! Jm Jnteresse der öffentlichen
10.11.48 Sicherheit der Stadt Wien sieht sich der
Gemeinderath verpflichtet, alle bewaffneten und
nicht bewaffneten Bewohner dieser Stadt auf die
Gefahr aufmerksam zu machen ...
[Wien]Aus der k.k.Hof= und Staats=Druckerei.
[1848]
    broadside. 45x28.5cm.
    Dated: Wien, am 11. October 1848.
    Lyser (Wiener-Ereignisse) p.37.

(

Vienna. Gemeinderat.
*pGB8
V6755R Note. Damit die Aprovisionirung der Stadt
10.11.48 Wien keine Störung erleide, hat der Gemeinderath
beschlossen, das löbl. Nationalgarde=Ober=
Commando zu ersuchen, die Bäcker durch Tagsbefehl
vom Dienste zu entheben ...
[Wien]Aus der k.k.Hof= und Staatsdruckerei.
[1848]
    broadside. 44.5x28.5cm.
    Dated: Wien am 11. October 1848.
    Lyser (Wiener-Ereignisse) p.36.

(

Vienna. Nationalgarde.
*pGB8
V6755R Kundmachung. 1. Jm Einverständnisse mit dem
10.11.48 Ober=Commando werden alle Neubewaffneten
aufgefordert, sich bei dem zuständigen Compagnie=
Commando zu melden ...
[Wien]Aus der k.k.Hof= und Staats=Druckerei.
[1848]
    broadside. 45x28.5cm.
    Dated: Wien am 11. October 1848.

(

Vienna. Universität. Ausschuss der Studierenden.
*pGB8
V6755R Brüder, Landleute! Die traurige Lage, in der
10.11.48 wir uns jetzt befinden, welche vielleicht bald
Euere persönliche Gegenwart und Mithilfe
nöthig machen wird ...
Wien,gedruckt im Oct.1848,bei U.Klopf sen.und
Alexander Eurich.
    broadside. 25.5x39.5cm.
    Dated: Wien, den 11. October 1848.
    A repetition of the previous day's appeal for
contributions of food.

(

Wiener demokratischer Verein.
*pGB8
V6755R Steiermärker! Der von der Camarilla besoldete
10.11.48 Jellachich, der Feind unserer jungen Freiheit,
der unter dem eitlen Vorwande der Nationalität
die edeln Magyaren überfiel, flüchtete sich mit
seinen beutelustigen Horden ...
[Wien]Gedruckt bei Franz Edlen von Schmid.
[1848]
    broadside. 40x25cm.
    Dated & signed: Wien am 11. Oktober 1848. Der
Central=Ausschuss aller demokratischen Vereine
                    (See next card)

(

Wiener demokratischer Verein.   Steiermärker
*pGB8
V6755R ... [1848]   (Card 2)
10.11.48 Wiens.
Warning that Jelačić might attempt to flee
to Croatia by way of the Steiermark.

(

Austria. Reichstag, 1848-1849.
*pGB8
V6755R Kundmachung. Die hohe constituirende
10.12.48 Reichsversammlung hat beschlossen: Unter den
gegenwärtigen Verhältnissen erscheint es zur
Aufrechthaltung der Ordnung und Sicherheit
erforderlich ...
[Wien]Aus der k.k.Hof= und Staatsdruckerei.
[1848]
    broadside. 45x28.5cm.
    Dated: Wien, den 12. October 1848.
    Lyser (Wiener-Ereignisse) p.41.

(

Austria. Reichstag, 1848-1849.
*pGB8
V6755R Kundmachung. Jn Folge Reichstags=
10.12.48 Beschlusses vom heutigen Tage werden die so
überaus wichtigen Jnstitute der National=Bank
und der niederösterr. Spar=Casse als unter den
Schutz des Reichstages gestellt, erklärt ...
[Wien]Aus der k.k.Hof= und Staats=Druckerei.
[1848]
    broadside. 45x57cm.
    Dated: Wien am 12. October 1848.
    Lyser (Wiener-Ereignisse) p.40.

(

Austria. Reichstag, 1848-1849.
*pGB8
V6755R Protokoll der 74. Sitzung der constituirenden
10.12.48 Reichsversammlung am 12. October 1848 Vormittags.
[Wien]Aus der k.k.Hof= und Staatsdruckerei.
[1848]
    [5]p. 38.5x23cm.
    Caption title; imprint on p.[5].

(

Austria. Reichstag, 1848-1849.
*pGB8
V6755R Protokoll der 75. Sitzung der constituirenden
10.12.48 Reichsversammlung am 12. October 1848 Abends.
[Wien]Aus der k.k.Hof= und Staatsdruckerei.
[1848]
    folder([3]p.) 38.5x23.5cm.
    Caption title; imprint on p.[3].

(

1848 AUSTRIAN REVOLUTIONARY BROADSIDES AND PAMPHLETS

*pGB8
V6755R
10.12.48

Nachricht. Die Aerzte des vierten Bezirkes der National=Garde haben in Berücksichtigung der jetzigen Verhältnisse sich bewogen gefunden ...
[Wien]Druck von Carl Gerold und Sohn.[1848]

broadside. 39x25cm.
Dated: Wien, am 12. Oktober 1848.

---

*pGB8
V6755R
10.12.48

Styria. Deputies, 1848.
Die Steiermärker an die Wiener. Liebe Wiener! So eben ist wieder eine neue Deputation aus Gratz angekommen, um die noch immer verzögerte Absetzung Wickenburgs zu bewirken ...
[Wien]Gedruckt bei Franz Edlen v.Schmid.[1848]

broadside. 40.5x25cm.
Dated & signed: Wien am 12. Oktober 1848.
Jm Namen der steiermärkischen Deputirten: Jos. Leop. Stiger, Dr.   Emperger, Joseph Pregl, Anton Retz.

---

*pGB8
V6755R
10.12.48

Vienna. Gemeinderat.
Erklärung des Gemeinderathes in Wien. Der Gemeinderath der Stadt Wien hat am 10. d. M. der k. k. Nieder=Oester. Landesregierung mitgetheilt ...
[Wien]Aus der k.k.Hof= und Staatsdruckerei. [1848]

broadside. 41x25.5cm.
Another issue has document number at head.
Dated: Wien am 12. October 1848.

---

*pGB8
V6755R
10.12.48

Vienna. Gemeinderat.
... Erklärung des Gemeinderathes in Wien. Der Gemeinderath der Stadt Wien hat am 10. d. M. der k. k. Nieder=Oester. Landesregierung mit-getheilt ...
[Wien]Aus der k.k.Hof= und Staatsdruckerei. [1848]

broadside. 40.5x24.5cm.
At head: Nro.12990.195.
Dated: Wien am 12. October 1848.

---

*pGB8
V6755R
10.12.48

Vienna. Gemeinderat.
Der Gemeinderath von Wien hat für die Dauer der jetzigen ausnahmsweisen Zustände beschlossen, wie folgt: Diejenigen wehrfähigen Jndividuen, welche, ohne Nationalgarden oder zum National-garde=Dienste verpflichtet zu seyn ...
[Wien]Aus der k.k.Hof= und Staats=Druckerei. [1848]

broadside. 44.5x28.5cm.
Dated: Wien den 12. October 1848.
Lyser (Wiener-Ereignisse) p.41.

---

*pGB8
V6755R
10.12.48

Vienna. Gemeinderat.
Kundmachung. Der Gemeinderath der Stadt Wien hat beschlossen, dass in Anbetracht der gegenwärtigen Verhältnisse die jetzige Ausziehzeit um 14 Tage verlängert ...
[Wien,1848]

broadside. 41.5x25.5cm.
Dated: am 12. Oktober 1848.

---

*pGB8
V6755R
10.12.48

Vienna. Gemeinderat.
Kundmachung. Mit Beziehung auf die Kundmachung vom 11. d. M. betreffend die Freizügigkeit wird als Richtschnur Folgendes vorgezeichnet: ...
[Wien]Aus der k.k.Hof= und Staats-Druckerei. [1848]

broadside. 45x28.5cm.
Dated: Wien den 12. October 1848.

---

*pGB8
V6755R
10.12.48

Vienna. Gemeinderat.
Mitbürger! Laut einer von Seite des Herrn Commandirenden, Grafen v. Auersperg, an das hohe Ministerium gelangten Zuschrift, hat der Erstere seine bisherige Stellung im Belvedere verlassen und mit seinen Truppen sich nach Jnzersdorf zurückgezogen ...
[Wien]Aus der k.k.Hof= und Staats=Druckerei. [1848]

broadside. 45x57cm.
Dated: Wien den 12. October 1848.
Lyser (Wiener-Ereignisse) p.40.

---

*pGB8
V6755R
10.12.48

Vienna. Nationalgarde.
... Vom Commando der 1. Nationalgarde= Cavallerie=Division wird hiemit der Befehl ertheilt, dass der Stadt=Zug und jener aus der Leopoldstadt permanent in der kaiserlichen Stallburg versammelt seyn sollen ...
[Wien]Aus der k.k.Hof= und Staatsdruckerei. [1848]

broadside. 44.5x28cm.
At head: Nationalgarde 1. Cavallerie-Division.
Dated: Wien den 12. October 1848.
Lyser (Wiener-Ereignisse) p.39.

---

*GB8
V6755R
10.12.48

Vienna. Ordinances, etc.
Provisorisches Statut über die Dienst- und Disciplinar-Verhältnisse der Bürgerwehr in Wien, sammt den zum Polizei=Bezirke der Stadt gehörenden Ortschaften.
[Wien]Aus der k.k.Hof= und Staats-Druckerei. [1848]

8p. 22.5x14.5cm.
Caption title; imprint on p.8; dated at end: Wien den 12. October 1848.

225

Vienna. Universität. Medizinische Fakultät.
*pGB8   Die medicinische Facultät hat die Anordnung
V6755R   der ärztlichen Dienstes für sämmtliche
10.12.48 Verwundete übernommen ...
          [Wien]Aus der k.k.Hof= und Staats=Druckerei.
[1848]

          broadside. 45x28.5cm.
          Dated: Wien, am 12. October 1848.

Deutsche constitutionelle Zeitung.
*GB8   Extra-Beilage zur Nummer 275 der Deutschen
V6755R   constitutionellen Zeitung. Neuestes aus Wien.
10.13.48 Verlag der C.A.Fahrmbacher'schen Buchhandlung
          in Augsburg.Redigirt unter deren Verantwortlich-
keit.[1848]

          [2]p. 30.5x22cm.
          Caption title; imprint on p.[2].
          Dated: München, den 13. Oktober 1848.

          Zur Nachricht. Es wird hiemit bekannt gegeben,
*pGB8   dass nach gemachter Anzeige des löbl.
V6755R   Gemeinderathes im Fürst Lichtenstein'schen
10.12.48 Hause, Herrengasse, unter Bereitwilligkeit des
          Herrn Secretärs ein Spital ... in ordentlichen
          Stand gesetzt wurde ...
          [Wien]Aus der k.k.Hof= und Staatsdruckerei.
[1848]

          broadside. 45x57cm.
          Dated: Wien am 12. October 1848.
          Lyser (Wiener-Ereignisse) p.39.

          Endlich, Johann Quirin.
*pGB8   Theuere Mitbürger! Die traurige Katastrofe,
V6755R   welche wir schon lange gefürchtet, ist endlich
10.13.48 eingetreten. Wien ist vom Militär umlagert ...
          Gedruckt bei Heinrich Liebergesell.in Wr.
Neustadt.[1848]

          broadside. 38.5x23.5cm.
          Dated: Wien am 13. Oktober 1848.

          Austria. Reichstag, 1848-1849.
*pGB8   Kundmachung. Alle öffentlichen Cassen, alle
V6755R   Wohlthätigkeitsfonde und Jnstitute, überhaupt
10.13.48 alles öffentliche und Privat-Eigenthum ist mit
          völliger Beruhigung dem in den schwierigsten
          Verhältnissen so glänzend bewährten Edelsinn des
          Wiener Volkes anvertraut ...
          [Wien]Aus der k.k.Hof= und Staatsdruckerei.
[1848]

          broadside. 45x28.5cm.
          Dated: Wien den 13. October 1848.

          Sarejanni, Demeter Alexander.
*GB8   An das hohe k. k. Ministerium des Jnnern in
V6755R   Wien. Gesuch des Demeter Alexander Sarejanni aus
10.13.48 Triest ...
          [Wien,1848]
          folder(4p.) 26x21cm.
          Dated at end: Wien, den 13. Oktober 1848.
          Concerning the entail of the estate of
          Demetrius Carciotti.

          Austria. Reichstag, 1848-1849.
*pGB8   Kundmachung. Die hohe Reichsversammlung hat
V6755R   beschlossen, jeden der Reichstags=Abgeordneten
10.13.48 mit einer Medaille von Kupfer zu versehen ...
          [Wien]Aus der k.k.Hof= und Staatsdruckerei.
[1848]

          broadside. 45x28.5cm.
          Dated: Wien den 13. October 1848.
          Lyser (Wiener-Ereignisse) p.44.

          Vienna. Chirurgen.
*pGB8   An die Bevölkerung Wiens. Die bürgerlichen
V6755R   Wundärzte hierorts machen sich's zur Ehre,
10.13.48 hiemit anzuzeigen: dass ihre öffentlichen
          Officinen ... allen Verwundeten und plötzlich
          Verunglückten als Zufluchtsort und
          Rettungsanstalt zu dienen ... mit grösster
          Bereitwilligkeit offen stehen ...
          [Wien]Aus der k.k.Hof= und Staatsdruckerei.
[1848]

          broadside. 44.5x28.5cm.
                                    (See next card)

          Austria, Lower.
*pGB8   Kundmachung des kaiserlich-königlichen
V6755R   niederösterreichischen Landes-Präsidiums. Die
10.13.48 hohe Reichsversammlung hat vermöge einer an
          das Ministerium des Jnnern gelangten Eröffnung
          des Reichstags=Vorstandes in der heute
          abgehaltenen Sitzung folgende Beschlüsse
          gefasst: ...
          [Wien]Aus der kaiserlich=königlichen Hof=
          und Staatsdruckerei.[1848]
          broadside. 45x57cm.
          Dated: Wien am   13. October 1848.
          Asserting the   authority of the
Reichstag.

          Vienna. Chirurgen.   An die Bevölkerung Wiens
*pGB8   ... [1848]   (Card 2)
V6755R   Dated & signed: Wien am 13. October 1848.
10.13.48 Jm Namen aller hiesigen bürgl. Wundärzte: Der
          Vorstand des wundärztlichen Gremiums.

*pGB8
V6755R
10.13.48

Vienna. Gemeinderat.
Mitbürger! Es verlautet, dass von Seite der Garden ein Angriff auf die vor den Linien stehenden Truppen beabsichtiget werde ...
[Wien]Aus der k.k.Hof= und Staatsdruckerei. [1848]

broadside. 45x57cm.
Dated: Wien am 13. October 1848.
Lyser (Wiener-Ereignisse) p.41.

*pGB8
V6755R
10.13.48

Vienna. Gemeinderat.
Vom Gemeinderathe der Stadt Wien. Mitbürger! Es ist vorgekommen, dass einzelne Mitglieder der Municipalgarde von Seiten des Volkes verhöhnt worden sind ...
[Wien,1848]

broadside. 42x26.5cm.
Dated: Wien, den 13. Oktober 1848.

*pGB8
V6755R
10.13.48

Vienna. Nationalgarde.
An die gesammte Volkswehr der Stadt Wien und Umgebung. Cameraden! Durch Ministerial=Erlass vom 12. d. [!] bin ich im Einverständnisse mit dem Reichstags=Ausschusse zum provisorischen Nationalgarde=Ober=Commandanten für Wien und die Umgebung ernannt worden ...
[Wien]Aus der k.k.Hof= und Staats=Druckerei. [1848]

broadside. 45.5x57cm.
Dated & signed: Wien am 13. October 1848.
W. Messenhauser, prov. Ober-Commandant.
Lyser (Wiener-Ereignisse) p.43.

*pGB8
V6755R
10.13.48

Vienna. Nationalgarde.
An sämmtliche Bezirke der Nationalgarde. Um eine Gleichförmigkeit bei Auszahlung und Verrechnung jener Beträge zu erzielen, welche auf Anordnung des hohen Finanz=Ministeriums an jene mittellosen Garden mit 20 kr. pr. Kopf zu verabreichen sind ...
[Wien]Aus der k.k.Hof- und Staatsdruckerei. [1848]

broadside. 44.5x28.5cm.
Dated: Wien den 13. October 1848.

*pGB8
V6755R
10.13.48

Vienna. Nationalgarde.
Bekanntmachung. Um den häufigen Nachfragen um Waffen und Munition, welche angeblich im Schottenstift niedergelegt seyn sollen, zu begegnen ...
[Wien]Aus der k.k.Hof= und Staats=Druckerei. [1848]

broadside. 44.5x28cm.
Dated: Wien den 13. October 1848.
Lyser (Wiener-Ereignisse) p.45.

*pGB8
V6755R
10.14.48

Austria. Reichstag, 1848-1849.
An Seine Excellenz den Banus von Croatien, Baron Jelachich. Auf die am heutigen Tage von Euer Excellenz und dem Grafen Auersperg unterzeichnete Zuschrift, lässt der constituirende Reichstag durch seinen permanenten Ausschuss Folgendes erklären: ...
[Wien]Aus der k.k. Hof= und Staatsdruckerei. [1848]

broadside. 45x57cm.
Dated: Wien den 14. October 1848.
Lyser (Wiener-Ereignisse) p.45.

*pGB8
V6755R
10.14.48

Austria. Reichstag, 1848-1849.
Kundmachung. Jm Namen des Reichstages wird hiemit erklärt, dass der k. k. General=Major und Stadt=Commandant von Wien, Herr Matauscheck, sammt allen ihm unterstehenden k. k. Officieren ... unter den Schutz des Reichstages und des Volkes von Wien gestellt ist ...
[Wien]Aus der k.k.Hof= und Staatsdruckerei. [1848]

broadside. 45x28.5cm.
Dated: Wien am 14. October 1848.

*pGB8
V6755R
10.14.48

Vienna. Gemeinderat.
Der Gemeinderath der Stadt Wien hat zur kräftigen Unterstützung der, von der löblichen Wiener medicinischen Facultät angeordneten Massregeln für Heilung und Pflege der Verwundeten angeordnet ...
[Wien]Aus der k.k.Hof= und Staatsdruckerei. [1848]

broadside. 44.5x28.5cm.
Dated: Wien den 14. October 1848.

*pGB8
V6755R
10.14.48

Vienna. Gemeinderat.
Kundmachung. Damit das Publikum unter den gegenwärtigen Umständen so wenig als möglich in plötzliche Beunruhigung gerathen möge ...
[Wien,1848]

broadside. 42x27cm.
Dated: Wien den 14. Oktober 1848.
Suspending the ringing of church bells for the duration of the crisis.

*pGB8
V6755R
10.14.48

Vienna. Gemeinderat.
Kundmachung. Der Gemeinderath der Stadt Wien, überzeugt von der Dürftigkeit der meisten Nationalgarden ...
[Wien]Aus der k.k.Hof= und Staatsdruckerei. [1848]

broadside. 44.5x28cm.
Dated: Wien am 14. October 1848.
Providing for compensation according to length of duty.

Vienna. Nationalgarde.
*pGB8 Bekanntmachung. Alle Personen, welche die
V6755R Linien Wiens zu passiren wünschen, haben sich
10.14.48 in der Kanzlei der Feldadjutantur des Ober=
Commando's der Nationalgarde mit einem
Geleitschein zu versehen ...
[Wien]Aus der k.k.Hof= und Staats=Druckerei.
[1848]
broadside. 44.5x28.5cm.
Dated: Wien am 14. October 1848.

Vienna. Nationalgarde.
*pGB8 Kundmachung. Der Gemeinderath der Stadt Wien
V6755R hat es für rätlich erkannt, dass zur
10.14.48 Sicherung der Approvisionirung der Stadt
Wien die hiesigen bürgerlichen Fleischer ...
von dem Dienste in der Nationalgarde befreit
sind ...
[Wien]Aus der k.k.Hof= und Staatsdruckerei.
[1848]
broadside. 44.5x28.5cm.
Dated & signed: Wien am 14. October 1848. Vom
Nationalgarde-Ober- Commando.

Vienna. Nationalgarde.
*pGB8 Bekanntmachung. Der Ober=Commandant der
V6755R Nationalgarde Wiens und der Umgebung gibt an die
10.14.48 Garden und mobilen Corps, so wie dem Publikum
die erfreuliche Nachricht, dass ... General=
Lieutenant Bem ihm in Leitung der strategischen
Angelegenheiten zur Seite stehen wird ...
[Wien]Aus der k.k.Hof= und Staatsdruckerei.
[1848]
broadside. 44.5x57cm.
Dated: Wien am 14. October 1848.

Vienna. Nationalgarde.
*pGB8 Kundmachung der Personen und Leiter meines
V6755R Hauptquartiers. Mein Hauptquartier bleibt
10.14.48 nach wie vor in den Localitäten der Stallburg ...
[Wien]Aus der k.k.Hof= und Staats=Druckerei.
[1848]
broadside. 44.5x28.5cm.
Dated & signed: Wien am 14. October 1848.
Messenhauser, provisorischer Ober=Commandant.

Vienna. Nationalgarde.
*pGB8 Kundmachung. Auf Anordnung des Nationalgarde=
V6755R Ober=Commandanten Herrn Messenhauser errichtet
10.14.48 der Gefertigte das dritte Bataillon der
Mobilgarde ...
[Wien]Aus der k.k.Hof= und Staats=Druckerei.
[1848]
broadside. 44.5x57cm.
Dated & signed: Wien den 14. October 1848. Franz
Wutschel m. p., Hauptmann im Juristen-Corps.
Lyser (Wiener-Ereignisse) p.47.

Vienna. Nationalgarde.
*pGB8 Kundmachung der Vorstände und Leiter, behufs
V6755R der Vertheidigung der Stadt Wien sammt
10.14.48 Vorstädten.
[Wien]Aus der k.k.Hof= und Staats=Druckerei.
[1848]
broadside. 44.5x28.5cm.
Dated & signed: Wien am 14. October 1848.
Messenhauser, provisor. Ober=Commandant.

Vienna. Nationalgarde.
*pGB8 Kundmachung. Betreffs des St. Stephansthurms.
V6755R [Wien]Aus der k.k.Hof= und Staats=Druckerei.
10.14.48 [1848]
broadside. 44.5x28.5cm.
Dated & signed: Wien am 14. October 1848.
Messenhauser, provisorischer Ober=Commandant.

Vienna. Nationalgarde.
*pGB8 Kundmachung für alle Garden und Glieder
V6755R mobiler Corps.
10.14.48 [Wien]Aus der k.k.Hof= und Staatsdruckerei.
[1848]
broadside. 44.5x28.5cm.
Dated: Wien am 14. October 1848.

Vienna. Nationalgarde.
*pGB8 Kundmachung. Das fortwährende Schiessen und
V6755R Plänkeln auf den Basteien und Glacis, welches die
10.14.48 Sicherheit der Passanten bereits zu
wiederholten Malen ernsthaft gefährdet hat ...
wird abermals streng untersagt ...
[Wien]Aus der k.k.Hof= und Staatsdruckerei.
[1848]
broadside. 44.5x57cm.
Dated & signed: Wien am 14. October 1848.
Messenhauser, provisorischer Ober=Commandant.
Lyser (Wiener- Ereignisse) p.45.

Vienna. Nationalgarde.
*pGB8 Kundmachung in Betreff des Artilleriewesens.
V6755R Die gesammte Artillerie zerfällt, wie bekannt,
10.14.48 in die zwei Abtheilungen: ...
[Wien]Aus der k.k.Hof= und Staatsdruckerei.
[1848]
broadside. 44.5x29cm.
Dated: Wien am 14. October 1848.

*pGB8
V6755R
10.14.48

Vienna. Nationalgarde.
Kundmachung. Ueber die vom löblichen Ober=
Commando gestellte Anfrage hat der Verwaltungsrath beschlossen, sogleich zur Zusammensetzung
des Ehren= und Disciplinar=Gerichtes auf
Grundlage des prov. Statuts vom 12. October d. J.
zu schreiten ...
[Wien]Aus der kaiserlich=königlichen Hof=
und Staatsdruckerei.[1848]

broadside. 44.5x28.5cm.
Dated: Wien den 14. October 1848.

---

*pGB8
V6755R
10.14.48

Vienna. Nationalgarde.
Kundmachung. Um jedem weiteren Andrange zum
kaiserl. Zeughause vorzubeugen ...
[Wien]Aus der k.k.Hof= und Staatsdruckerei.
[1848]

broadside. 44.5x57cm.
Dated: Wien am 14. October 1848.

---

*pGB8
V6755R
10.14.48

Vienna. Nationalgarde.
Tagsbefehl vom 14. October, Abends 9 Uhr.
[Wien]Aus der k.k.Hof= und Staats=Druckerei.
[1848]

broadside. 44.5x29cm.

---

*pGB8
V6755R
10.14.48

Vienna. Universität. Ausschuss der Studierenden.
Höchst wichtig! Mitbürger! Die Augenblicke
sind dringend. Unsere gegenwärtige ungewisse
Lage ist für länger unerträglich ...
[Wien]Aus der k.k.Hof= und Staats=Druckerei.
[1848]

broadside. 44.5x28.5cm.
Dated: Wien am 14. October 1848.
Lyser (Wiener-Ereignisse) p.47.

---

*pGB8
V6755R
10.15.48

Austria. Post-Kurs-Bureau.
Kundmachung. Damit während der Dauer der
gegenwärtigen Verhältnisse die abgehenden Posten
noch vor Einbruch der Dämmerung die Linien und
die nächste Umgebung Wiens passieren können ...
[Wien]Aus der k.k.Hof= und Staatsdruckerei.
[1848]

broadside. 45x57cm.
Dated & signed: Wien am 15. October 1848.
Vom k. k. Hofpostamte.

---

*pGB8
V6755R
10.15.48

Austria. Reichstag, 1848-1849.
Kundmachung. Die Mitglieder der gesammten
Volkswehr, auf deren gutem Geiste, Eintracht
und Ordnung das Schicksal Wiens und Oesterreichs
ruht ...
[Wien]Aus der k.k.Hof= und Staatsdruckerei.
[1848]

broadside. 45x29cm.
Dated: Wien den 15. October 1848.
Lyser (Wiener-Ereignisse) p.54.

---

*pGB8
V6755R
10.15.48

Austria. Sovereigns, etc., 1835-1848
(Ferdinand I)
An meine Völker! Angekommen in Olmütz, wo ich
vor der Hand zu verweilen gesonnen bin, ist es
meinem väterlichen Herzen Bedürfniss, die
wohlthuenden Beweise treuer Anhänglichkeit,
welche ich auf meiner Hieherreise von dem Volke
allenthalben erhalten habe, anzuerkennen ...
[Olmütz?,1848]

broadside. 44x28cm.
Dated & signed: Olmütz am 15. Oktober 1848.
Ferdinand.
                    (See next card)

---

*pGB8
V6755R
10.15.48

Austria. Sovereigns, etc., 1835-1848
(Ferdinand I)   An meine Völker ... [1848]
(Card 2)

Cut of the royal arms at foot.
Lyser (Wiener-Ereignisse) p.48 records an
edition dated "Wien, am 15. October 1848."

---

*pGB8
V6755R
10.15.48

Vienna. Gemeinderat.
An die Arbeiter der öffentlichen Bauplätze.
Es hat sich ereignet, dass einige bisher bei
den öffentlichen Bauten beschäftigten Arbeiter,
welche gegenwärtig in der mobilen Nationalgarde
dienen ...
[Wien,1848]

broadside. 41.5x26.5cm.
Signed & dated: Vom Gemeinderathe der Stadt
Wien den 15. Oktober 1848.

---

*pGB8
V6755R
10.15.48

Vienna. Nationalgarde.
An Se. Exc. den Banus von Kroatien, Baron
Jellachich.
[Wien]Aus der k.k.Hof= und Staatsdruckerei.
[1848]

broadside. 45x57cm.
Dated & signed: Wien am 15. October 1848.
Messenhauser, provisorischer Ober=Commandant.
Lyser (Wiener-Ereignisse) p.49.

Vienna. Nationalgarde.
*pGB8
V6755R
10.15.48
Dringende Kundmachung. Es schmerzt mich zu
vernehmen, dass aus dem Umstande, weil gestern
Abends um 10 Uhr von St. Stephan Raketen=Signale
aufstiegen, beunruhigende Gerüchte Wurzel
fassen konnten ...
[Wien]Aus der k.k.Hof= und Staats=Druckerei.
[1848]
broadside. 45x29cm.
Dated: Wien am 15. October 1848.
Lyser (Wiener-Ereignisse) p.54.

Vienna. Nationalgarde.
*pGB8
V6755R
10.15.48
Tagsbefehl. Es ist in der letzten Zeit
vorgekommen, dass Unterthanen auswärtiger Mächte
zum Waffendienste aufgefordert und verhalten
wurden ...
[Wien]Aus der k.k.Hof= und Staatsdruckerei.
[1848]
broadside. 45x29cm.
Signed: Messenhauser, provisor. Ober=
Commandant.

Vienna. Nationalgarde.
*pGB8
V6755R
10.15.48
Kundmachung. Die Nacht ist ruhig verflossen.--
Es wird auch am Tage keine Verletzung unseres
Weichbildes versucht werden ...
[Wien]Aus der k.k.Hof= und Staatsdruckerei.
[1848]
broadside. 44.5x28.5cm.
Dated: Wien am 15. October 1848.
Lyser (Wiener-Ereignisse) p.53.

Vienna. Universität. Ausschuss der Studierenden.
*pGB8
V6755R
10.15.48
Bürger von Wien! Seit einer Zeit, jener
traurigen, unglücklichen Zeit, wo sich zuerst ein
unheilvoller Zwiespalt durch die höllischen
Mittel der Reaktion in Mitten der Nationalgarde
eingeschlichen ...
[Wien]Gedruckt bei U.Klopf Senior und Alex.
Eurich.[1848]
broadside. 25.5x39.5cm.
Dated: Wien, den 15. Oktober 1848.

Vienna. Nationalgarde.
*pGB8
V6755R
10.15.48
Kundmachung. Die Verpflegung aller
waffentragenden Mittellosen betreffend.
[Wien]Aus der k.k.Hof= und Staats=Druckerei.
[1848]
broadside. 45x29cm.
Dated: Wien den 15. October 1848.
Lyser (Wiener-Ereignisse) p.48 (wrongly
dated 14 Oct.).

Vienna. Universität. Ausschuss der Studierenden.
*pGB8
V6755R
10.15.48
Bürger von Wien! Unsere Sache ist der
Entscheidung nahe! Die Magyaren, diese tapfern
Freiheitskämpfer haben sich mit uns vereinigt ...
[Wien]Gedruckt bei U.Klopf sen.und Alexander
Eurich.[1848]
broadside. 25.5x39.5cm.
Dated: Wien, am 15. Oktober 1848.

Vienna. Nationalgarde.
*pGB8
V6755R
10.15.48
Kundmachung. Nach einer mir vom Gemeinderathe
zugekommenen Mittheilung sollen bewaffnete
Arbeiter und Garden hin und wieder herumziehen
...
[Wien]Aus der k.k.Hof= und Staats=Druckerei.
[1848]
broadside. 44.5x29cm.
Dated: Wien am 15. October 1848.
Lyser (Wiener-Ereignisse) p.52.

Austria. Sovereigns, etc., 1835-1848
*pGB8
V6755R
10.16.48
(Ferdinand I)
An das souveräne Volk von Wien! Der Central=
Ausschuss der demokratischen Vereine Wiens
übergiebt dem freien Volke Wiens ein Aktenstück
der Ollmützer Hofpartei, welches den
öffentlichen Verrath derselben an die durch die
März= und Mairevolution errungenen Rechte
zeigt ... An Meine Völker! Als mich die zu
Wien am 6. October verübten Frevelthaten
bewogen, eine Stadt zu verlassen ...
[Wien]Gedruckt   bei Franz Edlen v.Schmid.
[1848]
(See next card)

Vienna. Nationalgarde.
*pGB8
V6755R
10.15.48
Kundmachung über die Plakate von Seite des
gegenwärtigen Ober=Commando's.
[Wien]Aus der k.k.Hof= und Staatsdruckerei.
[1848]
broadside. 44.5x29cm.
Dated: Wien am 15. October 1848.
Complaining that announcements are not being
posted in the main squares of Vienna.

Austria. Sovereigns, etc., 1835-1848
*pGB8
V6755R
10.16.48
(Ferdinand I)   An das souveräne ...
[1848]   (Card 2)
broadside. 40x50cm.
Dated & signed: Ollmütz, den 16. October 1848.
Ferdinand m. p.
Announcing that he is sending troops against
Vienna to put down the insurrection.
Published by the Demokratischer Verein with the
ironic question: Das ist also die väterliche
Fürsorge des Monarchen?

1848 Austrian Revolutionary Broadsides and Pamphlets

Austria. Sovereigns, etc., 1835-1848
(Ferdinand I)
*pGB8   An meine Völker! Als Mich die zu Wien am 6.
V6755R October verübten Frevelthaten bewogen, eine
10.16.48 Stadt zu verlassen, welche der Tummelplatz der
wildesten und verworfensten Leidenschaften
geworden war ...
Gedruckt bei Ignaz Alois Kleinmayr in Laibach.
[1848]

broadside. 39.5x24cm.
Lyser (Wiener-Ereignisse) p.55.
(See next card)

Austria. Sovereigns, etc., 1835-1848
(Ferdinand I)   An Meine Völker! ...
*pGB8   [1848]   (Card 2)
V6755R
10.16.48 Dated & signed: Olmütz den 16. Oktober 1848.
Ferdinand m. p.
Announcing that he is sending troops against
Vienna to put down the insurrection.

Austria. Sovereigns, etc., 1835-1848
(Ferdinand I)   An meine Völker! ... [1848]
*pGB8   (Card 2)
V6755R
10.16.48 Dated & signed: Olmütz, den 16. October
1848. Ferdinand m. p.
Announcing that he is sending troops against
Vienna to put down the insurrection.

Demokratischer Bürgerwehrverein, Berlin.
Folgende herzliche Zuschriften aus unserer
*pGB8   Schwesterstadt Berlin sind uns soeben
V6755R zugekommen ... An die akad. Legion und die
10.16.48 Nationalgarde zu Wien. Brüder! Unser Verein,
ergriffen von dem rühmlichen Kampfe, den Jhr
siegreich gegen die Despotie begonnen ...
Wien 1848, gedruckt bei U.Klopf Senior und
Alex.Eurich.

broadside. 42x53cm.
Preliminary statement dated & signed "Wien,
(See next card)

Austria. Sovereigns, etc., 1835-1848
(Ferdinand I)
*pGB8   An meine Völker! Als Mich die zu Wien am 6.
V6755R Oktober verübten Frevelthaten bewogen, eine
10.16.48 Stadt zu verlassen, welche der Tummelplatz der
wildesten und verworfensten Leidenschaften
geworden war ...
Skarnitzl's Buchdruckerei in Olmütz.[1848]
broadside. 45.5x58cm.
Lyser (Wiener-Ereignisse) p.55.
Dated & signed: Olmütz den 16. Oktober 1848.
(See next card)

Demokratischer Bürgerwehrverein, Berlin.
Folgende herzliche ... 1848.
*pGB8   (Card 2)
V6755R
10.16.48 den 16. October 1848. Vom Ausschuss der
Studenten"; the 2 Berlin addresses are dated
& signed: Berlin, den 13. October 1848. Der
demokratische Bürgerwehrverein.

Austria. Sovereigns, etc., 1835-1848
(Ferdinand I)   An meine Völker! ...
*pGB8   [1848]   (Card 2)
V6755R
10.16.48 Ferdinand m./p.
Announcing that he is sending troops against
Vienna to put down the insurrection.

Plattensteiner, ———.
Mitbürger! Ich hätte nie gedacht, meine
*pGB8   Gesinnungen, die ich so oft im Angesichte der
V6755R gesammten Nationalgarde in und ausser dem
10.16.48 Bezirke in Wort und That offen kund gab, und
die ich über jeden Verdacht erhaben glaubte,
nochmals öffentlich aussprechen zu müssen ...
[Wien]Gedruckt bei A.Dorfmeister.[1848]

broadside. 42.5x52.5cm.
Dated & signed: Wien, am 16. Oktober 1848.
Plattensteiner, Bezirks-Chef der Landstrasse.

Austria. Sovereigns, etc., 1835-1848
(Ferdinand I)
*pGB8   An Meine Völker! Als Mich die zu Wien am 6.
V6755R Oktober verübten Frevelthaten bewogen, eine
10.16.48 Stadt zu verlassen, welche der Tummelplatz der
wildesten und verworfensten Leidenschaften
geworden war ...
Gedruckt bei Heinrich Liebergesell in Wr.
Neustadt.[1848]

broadside. 38.5x46.5cm.
Lyser (Wiener-Ereignisse) p.55.
(See next card)

Telegraphische Depesche von Olmütz nach
Floridsdorf.
*pGB8   [Wien]Aus der k.k.Hof- und Staats-Druckerei.
V6755R [1848]
10.16.48
broadside. 45x47.5cm.
Dated: Floridsdorf am 16. October 1848,
Nachmittags 2 Uhr.
Reporting the Emperor's reply to an address
of the Reichstag.

231

Vienna. Nationalgarde.
*pGB8
V6755R
10.16.48

... An Seine Excellenz den Herrn Feldmarschall=
Lieutenant Grafen von Auersperg. Der
Unterzeichnete hat die Ehre, Euer Excellenz
eine Abschrift Desjenigen zu übersenden, was er
dem Herrn Banus von Croatien im Laufe dieses
Vormittags mitzutheilen, länger keinen
Augenblick mehr säumen konnte ...
[Wien]Aus der k.k.Hof= und Staats=Druckerei.
[1848]

broadside. 45x57.5cm.

(See next card)

Vienna. Nationalgarde.
*pGB8
V6755R
10.16.48

Kundmachung. Ich erweitere meinen
diessfallsigen Befehl betreffs der
Dienstleistung des berühmten Herrn General=
Lieutenant Bem dahin ...
[Wien]Aus der k.k.Hof= und Staats=Druckerei.
[1848]

broadside. 45x29cm.
Lyser (Wiener-Ereignisse) p.60.
Dated & signed: Wien den 16. October 1848.
Messenhauser, provisorischer Ober=Commandant.

Vienna. Nationalgarde. ... An Seine
*pGB8
V6755R
10.16.48

Excellenz ... [1848] (Card 2)

Lyser (Wiener-Ereignisse) p.57.
Dated & signed: Wien am 16. October 1848.
Messenhauser, provisorischer Ober=Commandant.
At head: (Nr. 19.)

Vienna. Nationalgarde.
*pGB8
V6755R
10.16.48

Kundmachung. Ich habe gestern die Postirung
der Lagertruppen und deren Unterbringung in
Augenschein genommen ...
[Wien]Aus der k.k.Hof= und Staats=Druckerei.
[1848]

broadside. 44.5x29cm.
Lyser (Wiener-Ereignisse) p.61.
Dated & signed: Wien den 16. October 1848.
Messenhauser, provisorischer Ober=Commandant.

Vienna. Nationalgarde.
*pGB8
V6755R
10.16.48

Kundmachung an alle Nationalgarden der
Umgebung von Wien. Mitbürger und Waffenbrüder!
Eure Lage ist eine peinliche ...
[Wien]Aus der k.k.Hof= und Staats=Druckerei.
[1848]

broadside. 45.5x29cm.
Lyser (Wiener-Ereignisse) p.57.
Dated & signed: Wien am 16. October 1848.
Messenhauser, provisorischer Ober=Commandant.

Vienna. Nationalgarde.
*pGB8
V6755R
10.16.48

Kundmachung. Zwei kroatische Officiere, die
ihrer Krankheit halber zum Gebrauche der Bäder
nach Baden zu reisen die Absicht hatten, sind von
den Vorposten ergriffen, und in das
Hauptquartier gebracht worden ...
[Wien]Aus der k.k.Hof= und Staats=Druckerei.
[1848]

broadside. 45x29cm.
Lyser (Wiener-Ereignisse) p.60.
Dated & signed: Wien den 16. October 1848.
Messenhauser, provisorischer Ober-
Commandant.

Vienna. Nationalgarde.
*pGB8
V6755R
10.16.48

... Kundmachung. Auf Befehl des hohen General=
Commando im Belvedere wird der Herr Hauptmann
und Bezirks=Chef Steydle beauftragt, den Garden
des dortigen Bezirkes Herrn Dr. Julius C.
Reyer zum Werbungs=Commissär für die Mobile=
Garde des Carolinen=Viertels ungesäumt zu
verwenden ...
[Wien]Aus der k.k.Hof= und Staats=Druckerei.
[1848]

broadside. 45x29cm.
Dated: Wien den 16. October 1848.
At head: (Nr. 23.)

Vienna. Universität. Ausschuss der Studierenden.
*pGB8
V6755R
10.16.48

Freunde vom Lande! Ihr werdet doch die
letzten Tage viel, sehr viel von Wien gehört
haben ...
[Wien]Gedruckt bei U.Klopf sen.und Alexander
Eurich.[1848]

broadside. 39.5x50cm.
Dated: Wien, den 16. Oktober 1848.

Vienna. Nationalgarde.
*pGB8
V6755R
10.16.48

... Kundmachung. Die ungarische Armee, unter
den Feldherren Czanyi und Moga hat heute
die Gränze überschritten ...
[Wien]Aus der k.k.Hof= und Staats=Druckerei.
[1848]

broadside. 45x58cm.
Lyser (Wiener-Ereignisse) p.59.
Dated & signed: Wien am 16. October 1848
Abends. W. Messenhauser, prov. Ober=Commandant.
At head: (Nr. 20.)

---

*pGB8
V6755R
10.16.48

Warum kommen die Bauern nicht? Ihr Landleute
und Brüder um Wien! Trotz Raketen und Plakaten,
Sturmläuten und ausgeschickten Deputirten hat
sich der Landsturm bisher nur zum Theile
erhoben ...
[Wien]Gedruckt bei Franz Edlen von Schmid.
[1848]

broadside. 40x25cm.
Dated: Wien, am 16. Oktober 1848.

Zergollern, Johann von.
*pGB8   Berichtigung. Um die Gerüchte über die
V6755R   Behandlung der in Gefangenschaft befindlichen
10.16.48   Herren croatischen Officiere zu widerlegen,
folgt hier die eigenhändige Bestätigung der
beiden Herren, das Original befindet sich im
Studenten-Ausschusse ...
   [Wien]Aus der k.k.Hof- und Staats=Druckerei.
[1848]
     broadside. 45x58cm.
           (See next card)

Zergollern, Johann von.   Berichtigung ...
*pGB8   [1848] .   (Card 2)
V6755R
10.16.48   Signed: Johann von Zergollern ... Joseph
Jovellic ...
   The two men were taken into custody on 16
October.
   Lyser (Wiener-Ereignisse) p.67.

Austria. Armee.
*pGB8   ... Antwort Sr. Exc. des Herrn Grafen von
V6755R   Auersperg. An das löbl. Nationalgarden=
10.17.48   Commando der Hauptstadt Wien. Haupt-Quartier
Inzersdorf den 17. October 1848.
   [Wien]Aus der k.k.Hof- und Staatsdruckerei.
[1848]
     broadside. 45x57.5cm.
     Lyser (Wiener-Ereignisse) p.62.
     At head: Vom Ober=Commando.

Vienna. Nationalgarde.
*pGB8   An den hohen constituirenden Reichstag!
V6755R   Es haben sich bei der Nationalgarde Wiens
10.17.48   Zweifel erhoben, ob das hohe Reichstag die
Verantwortlichkeit der Vertheidigung der Haupt=
und Residenzstadt gegen die k. k. Armee bei
Seiner Majestät dem Kaiser übernehme ...
   [Wien,1848]
     broadside. 45x28cm.
     Signed by 14 district commanders of the
Nationalgarde.

Vienna. Nationalgarde.
*pGB8   ... Aufruf vom Nationalgarde-Ober-Commando. Der
V6755R   Anmarsch der ungarischen Armee bemüssiget mich
10.17.48   zur Deckung der Ost= und Südseite der Stadt das
Lager vom Belvedere beziehen zu lassen ...
   [Wien]Aus der k.k.Hof= und Staatsdruckerei.
[1848]
     broadside. 45x29cm.
     Lyser (Wiener-Ereignisse) p.65.
     At head: (Nr. 22.)
     Dated & signed: Wien am 17. October 1848.
Messenhauser,   provisorischer Ober=
Commandant.

Vienna. Nationalgarde.
*pGB8   Edle, hochherzige Bewohner der Vorstadtgründe
V6755R   St. Ulrich, Spittelberg, Neubau und
10.17.48   Schottenfeld. Nachdem in den herannahenden Tagen
der Gefahr in Folge Auftrag des Gemeinderathes
der Stadt Wien ein zeitweiliges Spital für
Verwundete im Gebäude der k. ungarischen
Leibgarde errichtet worden ist ...
   [Wien,1848]
     broadside. 47x60.5cm.
     Dated & signed: Wien, am 17. Oktober 1848. Jm
Namen mehrer Garden des IX. Bezirkes.

Vienna. Nationalgarde.
*pGB8   ... Kundmachung. Auf Befehl des Nationalgarde-
V6755R   Ober-Commando wird die Werbung für das mobile
10.17.48   Corps der Nationalgarde des Karolinen-Viertels
im deutschen Hause in der Singerstrasse
fortgesetzt ...
   [Wien]Aus der k.k.Hof= und Staats=Druckerei.
[1848]
     broadside. 45x29cm.
     At head: (Nr. 24.)
     Dated & signed: Wien den 17. October. 1848.
Julius Reyer, Werb=Commissär.

Vienna. Nationalgarde.
*pGB8   Kundmachung. Der Verwaltungsrath der Wiener=
V6755R   Nationalgarde fordert, durch die Dringlichkeit
10.17.48   der Umstände veranlasst, für die unbemittelten
und verwundeten Garden zu Beiträgen an Geld und
Lebensmitteln in und um Wien Alle Jene auf ...
   [Wien]Aus der k.k.Hof= und Staats=Druckerei.
[1848]
     broadside. 45x29.5cm.
     Dated & signed: Wien am 17. October 1848. Vom
Verwaltungsrathe der Wiener Nationalgarde.

Vienna. Nationalgarde.
*pGB8   Kundmachung wegen Alarmirung. Jn den
V6755R   Vorstädten erfolgt ein Alarm durch die Herren
10.17.48   Districts= und Bezirks=Chefs ...
   [Wien]Aus der k.k.Hof= und Staatsdruckerei.
[1848]
     broadside. 44.5x28.5cm.
     Dated & signed: Wien am 17. October 1848.
Messenhauser, prov. Ober=Commandant.

Vienna. Nationalgarde.
*pGB8   Tagsbefehl [17. October 1848].
V6755R   [Wien]Aus der k.k.Hof= und Staatsdruckerei.
10.17.48 [1848]
     broadside. 45x57.5cm.
     Another issue has number at head.
     Lyser (Wiener-Ereignisse) p.63.
     Dated & signed: Wien am 17. October 1848.
Messenhauser, provisorischer Ober=Commandant.

Vienna. Nationalgarde.
    ... Tagsbefehl [17. October 1848].
*pGB8 [Wien]Aus der k.k.Hof= und Staatsdruckerei.
V6755R [1848].
10.17.48

    broadside. 44.5x57.5cm.
    At head: (Nr. 25.)
    Lyser (Wiener-Ereignisse) p.63.
    Dated & signed: Wien am 17. October 1848.
    Messenhauser, provisorischer Ober=Commandant.

Austria, Lower. Laws, statutes, etc., 1835-1848
    (Ferdinand I)
*pGB8 Circulare der Nieder=Oesterreichischen
V6755R Regierung über eine Disciplinar-Verordnung der
10.18.48 Nationalwehre.
    [Wien]Aus der k.k.Hof= und Staatsdruckerei.
    [1848]

    broadside. 45x29cm.
    Lyser (Wiener-Ereignisse) p.67.
    Dated: Wien am 18. October 1848.

Vienna. Nationalgarde.
    ... Vom Nationalgarde-Ober=Commandanten an die
*pGB8 Bevölkerung der Stadt Wien und Umgebung.
V6755R Mitbürger! Waffenbrüder! Jhr habt gestern
10.17.48 Morgens meine erste Note an den Banus gelesen
    ...
    [Wien]Aus der k.k.Hof= und Staats-Druckerei.
    [1848]

    broadside. 45x58cm.
    At head: (Nr. 21).
    Dated & signed: Wien am 17. October 1848.
    Messenhauser,   provisorischer Ober=
    Commandant.

Csernátony, Lajos, 1823-1901.
    Eine Stimme aus Ungarn, an das edle Volk
*pGB8 Wiens! Brüder im heiligen Freiheitskampfe,
V6755R Männer! erprobt durch die höchsten
10.18.48 patriotischen Tugenden! An Euch wende ich mich
    im Namen einer ganzen Nation ...
    Wien,gedruckt im Oct.1848,bei U.Klopf sen.und
    A.Eurich.

    broadside. 40x50.5cm.
    Dated & signed: Am 18. Oktober 1848. Ludwig
    Csernátoni, Mitredacteur des radikalen Blattes
    Mazczius'   tizenötdikc und Kossuth=
    Gardist.

Vienna. Universität. Medizinische Fakultät.
    Kundmachung. Von der medicinischen
*pGB8 Facultät wird hiemit bekannt gegeben, dass
V6755R bereits nachfolgende Aushilfs=Spitäler für
10.17.48 Verwundete organisirt worden sind ...
    [Wien]Aus der k.k.Hof= und Staats-Druckerei.
    [1848]

    broadside. 45x58cm.
    At head: (F. Z. 962.)
    Dated: Wien, den 17. October 1848.

Vienna. Gemeinderat.
    Berichtigung. Der Gemeinderath der Stadt Wien
*pGB8 bringt zur Kenntniss seiner Mitbürger, dass der
V6755R Herr Ober=Commandant der Nationalgarde, nicht,
10.18.48 wie es in seiner heutigen Kundmachung enthalten
    ist, sich mit seinem Gesuche betreffs der
    ungarischen Armee an den Gemeinderath wendete
    ...
    [Wien]Aus der k.k.Hof= und Staatsdruckerei.
    [1848]

    broadside. 45x28.5cm.
    Dated: Wien am 18. October 1848.

Vienna. Zivilgericht.
    Kundmachung. Das hohe Justiz=Ministerium hat
*pGB8 sich laut Erlasses vom 16. Oktober 1848 Zahl
V6755R 4130 durch die gegenwärtigen Verhältnisse
10.17.48 veranlasst gefunden ...
    [Wien,1848]

    broadside. 42x26cm.
    Signed & dated: Vom Civilgerichte der Stadt
    Wien am 17. Oktober 1848.

Vienna. Gemeinderat.
    Der Gemeinderath der Stadt Wien hat in seiner
*pGB8 Plenar-Sitzung vom 18. October die Absendung
V6755R einer Deuptation an Se. Majestät beschlossen,
10.18.48 welche bereits am 19. d. M. abgegangen ist,
    und nachstehende Adresse zu überreichen hat: ...
    [Wien]Aus der k.k.Hof= und Staatsdruckerei.
    [1848]

    broadside. 44.5x58cm.
    Dated: Wien am 18. October 1848.

Austria. Reichstag, 1848-1849.
    Euere Majestät! Jn der Antwort, welche Euere
*pGB8 Majestät auf die Adresse des constituirenden
V6755R Reichstages von 13. October 1848 zu ertheilen
10.18.48 geruhten, haben Euere Majestät die Absicht
    geäussert, Alles aufbiethen zu wollen, um
    die Ruhe und Sicherheit in der Hauptstadt
    wieder herzustellen ...
    [Wien]Aus der k.k.Hof= und Staats=Druckerei.
    [1848]
    broadside. 45x57.5cm.
    Lyser (Wiener-Ereignisse) p.71.
    Dated: Wien, am 18. October 1848.

Vienna. Gemeinderat.
    Kundmachung. Von Seite des Verwaltungsrathes
*pGB8 und Ober=Commandos der Wiener Nationalgarde
V6755R wurden an mehrere Mitglieder jener Commission,
10.18.48 welche beauftragt ist, alle in Wien vorhandenen
    Munitions= und Waffenvorräthe zu eruiren,
    Vollmachten ausgestellt ...
    [Wien]Aus der k.k.Hof= und Staatsdruckerei.
    [1848]

    broadside. 45x28.5cm.
    Lyser (Wiener-Ereignisse) p.73.
    Dated: Wien am 18. October 1848.

*pGB8
V6755R
10.18.48

Vienna. Nationalgarde.
Aufforderung. Jeder Waffenfähige, welcher sich
dem dritten Bataillon der Mobil=Garde
einreihen will ...
[Wien]Aus der k.k.Hof= und Staatsdruckerei.
[1848]

broadside. 45x58cm.
In contemporary ms. at head: 18 Okt.

---

*pGB8
V6755R
10.18.48

Vienna. Nationalgarde.   ... Neueste Nachricht
... [1848]   (Card 2)
Lyser (Wiener-Ereignisse) p.72.
At head: Vom Ober=Commando.
Dated & signed: Wien, den 18. October 1848
Abends. Messenhauser, provisorischer Ober=
Commandant.

---

*pGB8
V6755R
10.18.48

Vienna. Nationalgarde.
Kundmachung. Das Ober=Commando hat bereits
mittelst Tagsbefehl bekannt gegeben, dass
diejenige Verordnung des Gemeinderathes, welche
Garden für ihre aussergewöhnliche Dienstleistung
40 Kreuzer Conv. Minze bestimmt ...
[Wien]Aus der k.k.Hof= und Staats=Druckerei.
[1848]

broadside. 45x28.5cm.
Dated & signed: Wien am 18. October 1848.
Messenhauser, provisorischer Ober=Commandant.

---

*pGB8
V6755R
10.18.48

Vienna. Nationalgarde.
Ober=Commando=Befehl. Der Herr Chef des
Generalstabes Haug hat das Hauptquartier zu
organisiren ...
[Wien]Aus der k.k.Hof= und Staats=Druckerei.
[1848]

broadside. 45x29cm.
Dated & signed: Wien am 18. October 1848.
Messenhauser, prov. Ober=Commandant.

---

*pGB8
V6755R
10.18.48

Vienna. Nationalgarde.
Kundmachung. Die Casse des National=Garde=
Ober=Commando's befindet sich im Haupt=Quartier
des Ober=Commandanten im fürstlich
Schwarzenberg'schen Palais am Rennweg ...
[Wien]Aus der k.k.Hof= und Staatsdruckerei.
[1848]

broadside. 45x29cm.
Dated & signed: Wien den 18. October 1848.
Von der Central-Kanzlei des Nationalgarde-Ober-
Commando's.

---

*pGB8
V6755R
10.18.48

Vienna. Nationalgarde.
... Ueber den Verkauf von Waffen.
[Wien]Aus der k.k.Hof= und Staatsdruckerei.
[1848]

broadside. 45x28.5cm.
Dated & signed: Wien den 18. October 1848.
Messenhauser, provisorischer Ober=Commandant.
At head: Nr. 26.

---

*pGB8
V6755R
10.18.48

Vienna. Nationalgarde.
Kundmachung. Gestern Abends hat der Ober=
Commandant den ersten Bericht des Herrn General=
Lieutenants Bem entgegengenommen ...
[Wien]Aus der k.k.Hof= und Staats=Druckerei.
[1848]

broadside. 45x58cm.
Lyser (Wiener-Ereignisse) p.72.
Dated & signed: Wien am 18. October 1848.
Messenhauser, provisorischer Ober=Commandant.

---

*pGB8
V6755R
10.18.48

Vienna. Nationalgarde. Akademische Legion.
Aufruf an die akademische Legion! Sämmtliche
Herren Wehrmänner der akademischen Legion werden
hiemit aufgefordert, sich unverzüglich in der
Heumarkt=Caserne einzufinden ...
[Wien]Aus der k.k.Hof= und Staats=Druckerei.
[1848]

broadside. 45x29cm.
Dated: Wien am 18. October 1848.

---

*pGB8
V6755R
10.18.48

Vienna. Nationalgarde.
... Neueste Nachricht. Heute ist dem Ober=
Commandanten die Nachricht zugekommen, dass der
hohe Reichstag von Ungarn den Beschluss
gefasst habe, die ungarische Armee unter
Czianyi und Moga würde, obwohl sie bereits die
Landesgränze überschritten, nur dann vorrücken
...
[Wien]Aus der k.k.Hof= und Staats=Druckerei.
[1848]

broadside. 45x57cm.

(See next card)

---

*pGB8
V6755R
10.18.48

Vienna. Universität. Ausschuss der Studierenden.
An das deutsche Volk! Brüder! Jhr wisst,
welch' grossartiger Kampf unter den Mauern Wiens
gekämpft wird ...
[Wien]Gedruckt bei U.Klopf sen.und A.Eurich.
[1848]

broadside. 39.5x25cm.
Dated: Wien, den 18. Oktober 1848.

*pGB8
V6755R
10.18.48

Vienna. Universität. Ausschuss der Studierenden.
An die Bevölkerung Wiens. Brüder, Freunde!
Der Tag des Jahres 1813 ist gekommen, der Tag,
an dem bei Leipzig die Fesseln unseres Vater-
landes abgeschüttelt ...
[Wien]Gedruckt bei U.Klopf sen.und Alexander
Eurich.[1848]

broadside. 39.5x24.5cm.
Dated: Wien, am 18. October 1848.

*pGB8
V6755R
10.19.48

Austria. Sovereigns, etc., 1835-1848
(Ferdinand I)   Wir Ferdinand ... [1848]
(Card 2)

broadside. 45.5x58.5cm.
Lyser (Wiener-Ereignisse) p.74.
"Gegeben in Unserer k. Hauptstadt Olmütz den
19. Oktober 1848."
Announcing the temporary transfer of the seat
of government to Olmütz and proclaiming martial
law.

*pGB8
V6755R
10.18.48

Was ist mit dem Erzherzog Stefan geschehen?
[Wien]Gedruckt bei Franz Edlen v.Schmid.[1848]

broadside. 40x25cm.
Dated & signed: Wien, den 18. Oktober 1848.
Dr. *.

*pGB8
V6755R
10.19.48

Germany. Reichskommission nach Oesterreich, 1848.
Jm Namen des deutschen Reichsverwesers. Der
Reichsverweser von Deutschland, Erzherzog
Johann von Oesterreich, in Betracht seiner
Pflicht, über die Sicherheit und Wohlfahrt in
allen deutschen Landen zu wachen, sendete uns,
die Unterzeichneten, als Reichscommissäre nach
Oesterreich ...
[Wien]Aus der k.k.Hof= und Staatsdruckerei.
[1848]

broadside. 45x57cm.
(See next card)

*pGB8
V6755R
10.19.48

Austria. Sovereigns, etc., 1835-1848
(Ferdinand I)
Wir Ferdinand der Erste, constitutioneller
Kaiser von Oesterreich, König von Ungarn &c. &c.
entbieten Unseren getreuen Völkern Unseren väterlichen Gruss. Durch die blutigen Ereignisse,
welche seit dem 6. dieses Unsere Haupt= und
Residenzstadt Wien in einen Schauplatz
anarchischer Wirren umgewandelt haben ...
[Wien]Aus der k.k.Hof= und Staatsdruckerei.
[1848]

(See next card)

*pGB8
V6755R
10.19.48

Germany. Reichskomission nach Oesterreich, 1848.
Jm Namen ... [1848]   (Card 2)
Lyser (Wiener-Ereignisse) p.69 (recorded as
dated 18 October).
Dated & signed: Passau, den 19. October 1848.
Die Reichscommission.Welcker. Mosle.

*pGB8
V6755R
10.19.48

Austria. Sovereigns, etc., 1835-1848
(Ferdinand I)   Wir Ferdinand der Erste
... [1848]   (Card 2)

broadside. 45x57cm.
Lyser (Wiener-Ereignisse) p.74.
"Gegeben in Unserer k. Hauptstadt Olmütz den
19. October 1848."
Announcing the temporary transfer of the seat
of government to Olmütz and proclaiming martial
law.

*pGB8
V6755R
10.19.48

Hungary. Hondvédség.
Erklärung der ungarischen Armee. Dem National-
garde=Ober=Commando ist soeben das nachstehende
Document zugekommen ... Die ungarische Nation
ist seit Jahrhunderten durch die innigsten
Bruderbande mit dem Volke Oesterreichs
verknüpft ...
[Wien]Aus der k.k.Hof= und Staatsdruckerei.
[1848]

broadside. 45x57cm.
Lyser (Wiener-Ereignisse) p.75.
Dated: Aus dem   ungarischen Feldlager den
19.October 1848.

*pGB8
V6755R
10.19.48

Austria. Sovereigns, etc., 1835-1848
(Ferdinand I)
Wir Ferdinand der Erste constitutioneller
Kaiser von Österreich, König von Ungarn &c. &c.
entbieten Unseren getreuen Völkern Unseren
väterlichen Gruss. Durch die blutigen Ereignisse,
welche seit dem 6. dieses Unsere Haupt= und
Residenzstadt Wien in einen Schauplatz
anarchischer Wirren umgewandelt haben ...
Jm Auftrage gedruckt von H.Liebergesell in Wr.
Neustadt.[1848]Aus der k.k.Hof= und
Staatsdruckerei.

(See next card)

*pGB8
V6755R
10.19.48

Vienna. Bürgergarde.
Cameraden! Ich bringe Euch den herzlichsten
Gruss und den brüderlichsten Händedruck der uns
zu Hilfe geeilten Brüder aus Ungarn ...
[Wien]Aus der k.k.Hof= und Staats=Druckerei.
[1848]

broadside. 45x28.5cm.
Dated & signed: Wien den 19. October 1848.
Leszczynski,Commandant des ersten Bezirkes der
Volkswehr.

Vienna. Gemeinderat.
*pGB8
V6755R
10.19.48
Kundmachung von Seite der Approvisionirungs-Commission des Gemeinderathes der Stadt Wien. Um das Verpflegswesen sowohl für die Herren National=, als die Mobilgarden, in strenge Ordnung zu bringen ...
[Wien,1848]
broadside. 45x57cm.
Dated: Wien den 19. October 1848.

Vienna. Nationalgarde.
*pGB8
V6755R
10.19.48
Kundmachung. Die Herren Fleischhauer, Bäcker und sonstige Partheien werden ersucht, nur gegen Anweisung des gefertigten Bezirks=Commando an einzelne Garde=Abtheilungen Fleisch, Brot, Holz, Stroh &c. auszufolgen ...
[Wien,1848]
broadside. 43x27cm.
Dated & signed: Wien den 19. Oktober 1848.
Vom National-Garde-Bezirks-Commando Wieden.

Vienna. Mobilgarde.
*pGB8
V6755R
10.19.48
An das mobile Universitäts=Corps. Kammeraden! Jhr habt Euch der Universität angeschlossen und wollt unter ihrer Fahne kämpfen ...
Wien 1848,gedruckt bei Ulrich Klopf sen.und A.Eurich.
broadside. 38.5x50.5cm.
Dated & signed: Wien den 19. October 1848. Habrowsky, Corps=Commandant.

Austria. Armee.
*pGB8
V6755R
10.20.48
An die Bewohner Wiens! Von Seiner Majestät dem Kaiser beauftragt, und mit allen Vollmachten ausgerüstet, um dem in Wien dermalen herrschenden gesetzlosen Zustande ohne Zeitverlust ein Ziel zu setzen ...
[Wien,1848]
broadside. 45.5x30cm.
Lyser (Wiener-Ereignisse) p.78.
Dated & signed: Lundenburg den 20. Oktober 1848. Fürst zu Windisch-Grätz, Feldmarschall. Another edition has number at head, and another has title: Wien im Belagerungszustand.

Vienna. Mobilgarde.
*pGB8
V6755R
10.19.48
Kundmachung. Da Gefertigter zur Errichtung einer Compagnie der Universitäts=Mobilgarde zur Vervollständigung des 1. Bataillons beauftragt ist ...
[Wien]Aus der k.k.Hof= und Staatsdruckerei.
[1848]
broadside. 45x57cm.
Dated & signed: Wien am 19. October 1848. Carl Schöltzel, Hauptmann der 2. Compagnie Techniker=Corps.

Austria. Armee.
*pGB8
V6755R
10.20.48
... An die Bewohner Wiens! Von Sr. Majestät dem Kaiser beauftragt, und mit allen Vollmachten ausgerüstet, um dem in Wien dermalen herrschenden gesetzlosen Zustande ohne Zeitverlust ein Ziel zu setzen ...
[Wien,1848]
broadside. 38x24cm.
Lyser (Wiener-Ereignisse) p.78.
At head: Nro. 13373.
Dated & signed: Lundenburg den 20. Oktober 1848.
(See next card)

Vienna. Nationalgarde.
*pGB8
V6755R
10.19.48
... An den Herrn Commandanten des Uhlanen-Vorpostens jenseits von Floridsdorf.
[Wien]Aus der k.k.Hof= und Staatsdruckerei.
[1848]
broadside. 44.5x28.5cm.
Lyser (Wiener-Ereignisse) p.76.
Dated & signed: Wien den 19. October 1848. Messenhauser, provisorischer Ober=Commandant.
At head: Vom Nationalgarde-Ober-Commando.

Austria. Armee.   ... An die Bewohner Wiens! ...
*pGB8
V6755R
10.20.48
[1848]   (Card 2)
Fürst zu Windisch=Grätz, Feldmarschall.
Another edition is without number at head, and another has title: Wien im Belagerungszustand.

Vienna. Nationalgarde.
*pGB8
V6755R
10.19.48
Bekanntmachung. Da sich wiederholt Fälle ereignet haben, dass mit vom Nationalgarde=Ober=Commando ausgestellten Geleitscheinen versehene Jndividuen von Wach=Commandanten an den Linien zurückgewiesen und sogar insultirt worden sind ...
[Wien]Aus der k.k.Hof= und Staatsdruckerei.
[1848]
broadside. 45x28.5cm.
Dated & signed: Wien am 19. October 1848. Messenhauser,   provisorischer Ober=Commandant.

Austria. Armee.
*pGB8
V6755R
10.20.48
Bekanntmachung. Die höchst unzweckmässig gebauten Barrikaden in der Stadt und den Vorstädten, welche quer über die Strassen gebaut sind ...
[Wien]Aus der k.k.Hof= und Staatsdruckerei.
[1848]
broadside. 45x28.5cm.
Lyser (Wiener-Ereignisse) p.80.
Dated & signed: Wien am 20. October 1848. Jn Verhinderung des Chefs des Generalstabs, die Stellvertreter: Fenneberg ... Endhofer ...

Austria. Armee.

*pGB8
V6755R
10.20.48

... Wien im Belagerungszustand. An die
Bewohner Wien's! Von Seiner Majestät dem
Kaiser beauftragt und mit allen Vollmachten
ausgerüstet, um den [!] in Wien dermalen
herrschenden gesetzlosen Zustand ohne Zeitverlust
ein Ziel zu setzen ...
[Wien]Oktober 1848.Gedruckt bei M.Lell.
broadside. 38x22cm.
Lyser (Wiener-Ereignisse) p.78.
At head: Zum Andenken soll Jeder dies Blatt
aufbewahren.

(See next card)

Austria. Armee.   ... Wien im Belagerungszustand

*pGB8
V6755R
10.20.48

... 1848.   (Card 2)

Dated & signed: Lundenburg den 20. Oktober
1848. Fürst zu Windisch-Grätz, Feldmarschall.
Other editions have title: An die Bewohner
Wiens!

Austria. Reichstag, 1848-1849.

*pGB8
V6755R
10.20.48

Völker Oesterreichs! Durch Euer Vertrauen
zu dem friedlichen Werke der Constituirung
unserer Freiheit berufen, ist der Reichstag
durch die Gewalt der Ereignisse plötzlich mit
in den Kampf der Zeit gestellt ...
[Wien]Aus der k.k.Hof= und Staatsdruckerei.
[1848]
broadside. 45x28.5cm.
Dated: Wien am 20. October 1848.

Austria. Sovereigns, etc., 1835-1848

*pGB8
V6755R
10.20.48

(Ferdinand I)
Wir Ferdinand der Erste, constitutioneller
Kaiser von Oesterreich ... sanctioniren den
folgenden, von Unserem verantwortlichen
Ministerium Uns vorgelegten Reichstagsbeschluss
und verordnen, wie folgt: Erstens. Jn
Berücksichtigung der unabweisbaren Nothwendigkeit,
dem Staatshaushalte die erforderlichen Mittel
zu verschaffen ...
[Wien]Aus der k.k.Hof= und Staatsdruckerei.
[1848]

(See next card)

Austria. Sovereigns, etc., 1835-1848

*pGB8
V6755R
10.20.48

(Ferdinand I)   Wir Ferdinand der Erste
... [1848]   (Card 2)

folder([2]p.) 45x29cm.
Caption title; imprint on p.[2].
"Gegeben in Unserer königlichen Hauptstadt
Ollmütz am zwanzigsten October im eintausend acht
Hundert acht und vierzigsten ... Jahre."

Austria, Lower. Laws, statutes, etc., 1835-1848

*pGB8
V6755R
10.20.48

(Ferdinand I)
... Circulare der k. k. Landesregierung im
Erzherzogthume Oesterreich unter der Enns. Jn
Betreff mehrer zur Erleichterung des Verkehres
getroffener Anordnungen.
[Wien]Aus der k.k.Hof= und Staatsdruckerei.
[1848]

folder([3]p.) 38x23cm.
Caption title; imprint on p.[3].
At head: № 47506.
Dated: Wien am   20. October 1848.

Endlich, Johann Quirin.

*pGB8
V6755R
10.20.48

Zur Warnung und Belehrung für die Landbewohner.
Gedruckt bei Heinrich Liebergesell in Wr.
Neustadt.[1848]

broadside. 39x46.5cm.
Dated: Am 20. October 1848.

Vienna. Gemeinderat.

*pGB8
V6755R
10.20.48

Kundmachung. Der Gemeinderath der Stadt Wien
hat in seiner Plenarsitzung vom 19. October
die Absendung einer Deputation an Se.
kaiserlliche [!] Hoheit dem Herrn Erzherzog
Johann beschlossen, welche bereits am 20. d. M.
abgegangen ist und nachstehende Adresse zu
überreichen hat: ...
[Wien]Aus der k.k.Hof= und Staatsdruckerei.
[1848]
broadside. 45x29cm.
Dated: Wien am 20. October 1848.

Vienna. Gemeinderat.

*pGB8
V6755R
10.20.48

Mitbürger! Die vom Gemeinderathe der Stadt
Wien an Se. Majestät abgesandte Deputation ist
gestern Abends um 8 Uhr ohne in einer Audienz
empfangen worden zu seyn, mit folgendem
schriftlich mitgebrachten Bescheide zurückgekehrt.
Die Adresse des löblichen Gemeinderathes der
Stadt Wien ist Jhrer Majestät vorgelegt worden
...
[Wien]Aus der k.k.Hof= und Staatsdruckerei.
[1848]

(See next card)

Vienna. Gemeinderat.   Mitbürger! ... [1848]

*pGB8
V6755R
10.20.48

(Card 2)

broadside. 45x28.5cm.
Lyser (Wiener-Ereignisse) p.79.
The court reply is dated "Ollmütz den 20.
October 1848".

Vienna. Mobilgarde.
*pGB8
V6755R
10.20.48

An die Nationalgarde in Wien. Reactionäre
Unternehmungen des letzten Ministeriums haben
in der Hauptstadt der Monarchie einen
Freiheitskampf hervorgerufen ...
[Wien]Aus der k.k.Hof= und Staatsdruckerei.
[1848]

broadside. 45x58cm.
Dated & signed: Haupt=Quartier Belvedere am 20.
October 1848. General Bem.

Vienna. Mobilgarde.
*pGB8
V6755R
10.20.48

... Tapfere Wiener! Würdige Nachfolger Eurer
Vorfahren, die in zwei schweren Belagerungen
Wien gegen andrängende Barbarenheere
vertheidigten, Ihr steht auch jetzt gerüstet da,
und kämpft todesmuthig gegen einen mächtigen
Feind ...
[Wien,1848]

broadside. 42.5x53cm.
Dated & signed: Wien, im October 1848. Im
Namen des mobilen Universitäts-Corps.
Habrofsky, Corps= Commandant.

Vienna. Nationalgarde.
*pGB8
V6755R
10.20.48

... An Se. Durchlaucht den k. k. Herrn
Feldmarschall=Lieutenant Fürsten Alfred v.
Windischgrätz, Befehlshaber der am linken
Donauufer sich concentrirenden Truppen.
[Wien]Aus der k.k.Hof= und Staatsdruckerei.
[1848]

broadside. 45x29cm.
Lyser (Wiener-Ereignisse) p.79.
At head: Vom Nationalgarde-Ober-Commando.
Dated & signed: Wien den 20. October 1848.
Messenhauser, pro-visorischer Ober=
Commandant.

Vienna. Nationalgarde.
*pGB8
V6755R
10.20.48

Bekanntmachung. Allen jenen Garden und
Mitgliedern mobiler Corps, welche nicht auf den
vor dem Feinde befindlichen Wachposten stehen,
ist es strengstens untersagt, mit geladenem
Gewehre, in oder ausser Dienst, zu erscheinen
...
[Wien]Aus der k.k.Hof= und Staatsdruckerei.
[1848]

broadside. 45x29cm.
Dated & signed: Wien am 20. October 1848.
Messenhauser, provisorischer Ober=
Commandant.

Vienna. Nationalgarde.
*pGB8
V6755R
10.20.48

Kundmachung. Den sämmtlichen Bezirks-Chefs
und Befehlshabern selbstständiger Abtheilungen
wird hiemit aufgetragen, täglich um 1 Uhr
Mittags eine Ordonnanz zur Abholung des
Tagsbefehles in das Hauptquartier im
Schwarzenbergischen Garten zu senden ...
[Wien]Aus der k.k.Hof= und Staatsdruckerei.
[1848]

broadside. 45x29cm.
Dated & signed: Wien am 20. October 1848.
Messenhauser, provisorischer Ober=
Commandant.

Vienna. Nationalgarde.
*pGB8
V6755R
10.20.48

Kundmachung. Gleichzeitig mit der Deputation
des Gemeinderathes zur Ueberreichung einer
Adresse an Seine Majestät hat auch die Nationalgarde der Stadt Wien sammt den zur Hilfe der
Hauptstadt herbeigeeilten Wehrmannschaften der
Städte Brünn, Linz und Gratz eine Deputation zu
demselben Zwecke abgeschickt ...
[Wien]Aus der k.k.Hof= und Staats=Druckerei.
[1848]

(See next card)

Vienna. Nationalgarde.   Kundmachung ... [1848]
*pGB8   (Card 2)
V6755R
10.20.48

broadside. 45x29cm.
Lyser (Wiener-Ereignisse) p.77.
Includes the text of the address.

Vienna. Nationalgarde.
*pGB8
V6755R
10.20.48

Kundmachung. Nur durch einiges Zusammenwirken
ist im Dienste eine Pünktlichkeit zu erzielen
...
[Wien]Aus der k.k.Hof= und Staats=Druckerei.
[1848]

broadside. 45x28.5cm.
Dated & signed: Wien am 20. October 1848.
Vom Nationalgarde-Ober-Commando. Messenhauser,
provisorischer Ober=Commandant.
Ordering the unification of the Bürger-
Artillerie and the Nationalgarde.

Vienna. Universität. Medizinische Fakultät.
*pGB8
V6755R
10.20.48

Die medicinische Fakultät an die Bevölkerung
Wiens! Die medicinische Fakultät hat zu Folge
der Aufforderung des Gemeinderathes die
ärztliche Obsorge für Verwundete in allen
Theilen der Stadt übernommen ...
[Wien]Aus der k.k.Hof= und Staatsdruckerei.
[1848]

broadside. 44.5x29cm.
Dated: Wien am 20. October 1848.

Austria, Lower. Mercantil- und Wechselgericht.
*pGB8
V6755R
10.21.48

Kundmachung. Von dem k. k. N. Oest. Mercantil=
und Wechselgerichte wird hiemit bekannt gemacht,
dass über Ansuchen der k. k. priv. Grosshändler
und des bürgerlichen Handelsstandes in Wien,
das k. k. Justizministerium mit Decret ddo.
Wien am 20. October 1848, Z.4235, 4243, 4250 zu
erklären befunden habe ...
[Wien]Aus der k.k.Hof= und Staats=Druckerei.
[1848]

broadside. 45x28cm.
Lyser (Wiener-Ereignisse) p.81.
Dated: Wien am 21. October 1848.

Germany. Reichskommission nach Oesterreich, 1848.
*pGB8   Den 21. 1. M. Abends ist von den Reichs=
V6755R   Commissären nachstehende Zuschrift an das
10.21.48 Reichstags=Präsidium eingelangt: An ein hohes
         Präsidium der Reichs-Versammlung zu Wien.
         [Wien]Aus der k.k.Hof= und Staatsdruckerei.
         [1848]

              broadside. 44.5x28.5cm.
              Lyser (Wiener-Ereignisse) p.81.
              The address is dated & signed: Krems den 21.
         October 1848 ... die Reichs=Commissäre, C. Welker
         ... Mosle ...

Vienna. Universität. Ausschuss der Studierenden.
*pGB8   Bewohner Wiens! Eure Hochherzigkeit hat in
V6755R   dieser bedrängten Zeit schon so viele
10.21.48 ausserordentliche Opfer gebracht ...
         [Wien]Gedruckt bei U.Klopf sen.und Alex.
         Eurich.[1848]

              broadside. 25.5x39.5cm.
              Dated & signed: Wien, am 21. October 1848. Der
         Ausschuss der Studenten.

Vienna. Nationalgarde.
*pGB8   An die in den Bezirken eingetheilten zur
V6755R   Nationalgarde nicht gehörigen Wehrmänner.
10.21.48 [Wien]Aus der k.k.Hof= und Staatsdruckerei.
         [1848]

              broadside. 45x28.5cm.
              Lyser (Wiener-Ereignisse) p.83.
              Dated & signed: Hauptquartier Schwarzenberg=
         Palais am 21. October 1848. Messenhauser, prov.
         Ober=Commandant.

Austria. Reichstag, 1848-1849.
*pGB8   Beschluss des hohen Reichstages. Der hohe
V6755R   Reichstag hat unter dem 22. October 1848
10.22.48 folgenden Beschluss gefasst, und den
         Gemeinderath der Stadt Wien beauftragt,
         denselben zu veröffentlichen: ...
         [Wien]Aus der k.k.Hof= und Staatsdruckerei.
         [1848]
              broadside. 45x28.5cm.
              Lyser (Wiener-Ereignisse) p.93.
              Calling Windischgrätz's declaration of a state
         of siege and martial law illegal.

Vienna. Nationalgarde.
*pGB8   Kundmachung. Auf Anlangung der medicinischen
V6755R   Facultät wird behufs der Sicherung und leichteren
10.21.48 Erkennbarkeit der im Dienste der Nationalgarde
         und der mobilen Corps zu verwendenden Aerzte
         angeordnet: ...
         [Wien]Aus der k.k.Hof= und Staatsdruckerei.
         [1848]

              broadside. 45x28.5cm.
              Lyser (Wiener-Ereignisse) p.82.
              Dated & signed: Wien am 21. October 1848.
         Vom Verwaltungs-   rathe der Nationalgarde.

Austria. Reichstag, 1848-1849.
*pGB8   Reichstagsbeschluss vom 22. October 1848
V6755R   Nachmittags.
10.22.48 [Wien]Aus der k.k.Hof= und Staatsdruckerei.
         [1848]

              broadside. 45x57cm.
              Lyser (Wiener-Ereignisse) p.93.
              Calling Windischgrätz's declaration of a
         state of siege and martial law illegal.

Vienna. Nationalgarde.
*pGB8   Kundmachung. Die vielerlei Denunciationen,
V6755R   welche über das Vorhandensein von Waffen, von
10.21.48 Vorhandensein unterirdischer Gänge in
         ausgezeichneten Gebäuden, oder aber von dem
         Aufenthalte von Spionen, volksgefährlichen
         Personen, an andern Orten eingelaufen sind ...
         [Wien]Aus der k.k.Hof= und Staats=Druckerei.
         [1848]

              broadside. 44.5x28.5cm.
                             (See next card)

Austria. Reichstag, 1848-1849.
*pGB8   Reichstags=Beschluss vom 22. October 1848
V6755R   Nachmittags.
10.22.48 [Wien]Oberer'sche Buchdruckerei.[1848]

              broadside. 40.5x49cm.
              Lyser (Wiener-Ereignisse) p.93.
              Calling Windischgrätz's declaration of a state
         of siege and martial law illegal.

Vienna. Nationalgarde.   Kundmachung ... [1848]
*pGB8   (Card 2)
V6755R
10.21.48   Lyser (Wiener-Ereignisse) p.82.
              Dated & signed: Hauptquartier Schwarzenberg.
         Palais am 21. October 1848. Messenhauser,
         provisorischer Ober=Commandant.

[Donner, Eduard]
         Ein Nasenstüber. Der Granaten=Furst Bombowitz.
*pGB8   Bum! bum! bum!
V6755R   [Wien]Gedruckt bei Franz Edlen v.Schmid.[1848]
10.22.48
              [2]p. 1 illus. 39.5x25.5cm.
              Caption title; imprint on p.[2]; dated &
         signed: Wien im Oktober 1848. Eduard Donner.
         Directed against Windischgrätz.

Vienna. Gemeinderat.
*pGB8   Antwort des Gemeinderathes der Stadt Wien an
V6755R   Seine Durchlaucht Herrn Fürsten Windisch=Grätz,
10.22.48   Feldmarschall.
     [Wien]Aus der k.k.Hof= und Staatsdruckerei.
[1848]

     broadside. 45x28.5cm.
     Lyser (Wiener-Ereignisse) p.93.
     Dated: Wien am 22. October 1848.

Austria. Armee.   Proklamation ... [1848]
*pGB8   (Card 2)
V6755R   Small folio broadside.
10.23.48   Dated & signed: Hauptquartier Hetzendorf am
     23. Oktober 1848. Fürst zu Windisch-Grätz, k.
     k. Feldmarschall.
     Calling for the surrender of Vienna.
     Imperfect: cropped at foot, removing signature
(and imprint?).

Vienna. Nationalgarde.
*pGB8   Kundmachung. Mitbürger! Ein Plakat, gezeichnet
V6755R   "Fürst zu Windischgrätz, Feldmarschall" ist
10.22.48   heute an den Strasseneecken auf kurze Zeit
     gesehen worden ...
     [Wien]Aus der k.k.Hof= und Staats=Druckerei.
[1848]

     broadside. 45x57cm.
     Lyser (Wiener-Ereignisse) p.94.
     Dated & signed: Haupt=Quartier Schwarzenberg=
Palais am 22. October 1848. Messenhauser, prov.
Ober=Commandant.

Austria. Armee.
*pGB8   ... Proklamation. Jm Verfolg des von mir in
V6755R   meiner ersten Proklamation vom 20. d. M.
10.23.48   verkündeten Belagerungszustandes und
     Standrechtes für die Stadt Wien, die Vorstädte
     und nächste Umgebung habe ich befunden, als
     ferner Bedingungen zu stellen: ...
     [Wien,1848]

     broadside. 38x24cm.
     Lyser (Wiener-Ereignisse) p.95.
     At head: Nro.13373.   (See next card)

Austria. Armee.
*pGB8   Proclamation. Jm Verfolge des von mir in
V6755R   meiner ersten Proclamation vom 20. d. M.
10.23.48   verkündeten Belagerungszustandes und
     Standrechtes für die Stadt Wien, die Vorstädte
     und nächste Umgebung habe ich befunden, als
     fernere Bedingungen zu stellen: ...
     [Wien]Aus der k.k.Hof= und Staats=Druckerei.
[1848]

     broadside. 43.5x55cm.   (See next card)

Austria. Armee.   ... Proklamation ... [1848]
*pGB8   (Card 2)
V6755R   Quarto sheet broadside.
10.23.48   Dated & signed: Hauptquartier Hetzendorf am
     23. Oktober 1848. Fürst zu Windisch=Grätz,
     Feldmarschall.
     Calling for the surrender of Vienna.

Austria. Armee.   Proclamation ... [1848]
*pGB8   (Card 2)
V6755R   Lyser (Wiener-Ereignisse) p.95.
10.23.48   Large folio broadside.
     Dated & signed: Hauptquartier Hetzendorf am
     23. October 1848. Fürst zu Windisch-Grätz,
     k. k. Feldmarschall.
     Calling for the surrender of Vienna.

Teufel, Franz, fl.1848.
*pGB8   Liebe Landleute! Theuere Brüder! Wir erfahren
V6755R   von mehreren Seiten, dass bei Euch zu Hause
10.23.48   über die Zustände der Residenzstadt Wien,
     Gerüchte verbreitet werden, welche nicht nur
     diese, sondern auch uns Abgeordnete in ein
     falsches Licht stellen ...
     [Wien]Gedruckt bei Carl Ueberreuter,
     Alservorstadt Nr.146.[1848]

     broadside. 44x52.5cm.
     Dated & signed: Wien, am 23. Oktober 1848.
Franz Teufel,   Reichstagsabgeordneter.

Austria. Armee.
*pGB8   Proklamation. Jm Verfolg des von mir in
V6755R   meiner ersten Proklamation vom 20. d. M.
10.23.48   verkündeten Belagerungszustandes und
     Standrechtes für die Stadt Wien, die Vorstädte
     und nächste Umgebung habe ich befunden, als
     fernere Bedingungen zu stellen: ...
     [Wien,1848]

     broadside. 30x35cm.
     Lyser (Wiener-Ereignisse) p.95.
                   (See next card)

Vienna. Gemeinderat.
*pGB8   Mitbürger! Nachdem Se. k. k. Hoheit Herr
V6755R   Erzherzog Johann durch die Reichskommissäre
10.23.48   Welker und Moslé, Namens der deutschen
     Centralgewalt, so wie der h. österreichische
     Reichstag, die friedliche Lösung der Wiener=
     Angelegenheiten eingeleitet haben ...
     [Wien]Gedruckt bei Leop.Grund.[1848]
     broadside. 42x26cm.
     Lyser (Wiener-Ereignisse) p.96.
     Signed & dated: Vom Gemeinderathe der Stadt
Wien am 23.   Oktober 1848.

*pGB8
V6755R
10.23.48

Vienna. Mobilgarde.
An das mobile Universitäts=Corps. Brüder!
Die Stunde der Entscheidung naht. Schon hat der
hohe Reichstag selbst in einer energischen
Proklamation die Revolution anerkannt ...
[Wien]Gedruckt bei Ulrich Klopf sen.und A.
Eurich.[1848]

broadside. 41x51cm.
Dated & signed: Wien den 23. October 1848.
Habrofsky, Corps=Commandant.

*pGB8
V6755R
10.24.48

Ein erngtes Wort an Seine Majestät den Kaiser
nach Ollmütz gesendet von einem Wiener Bürger.
[Wien]Okt.1848.Gedruckt bei M.Lell.

broadside. 40x50cm.
Signed: S....r.
Dated in contemporary ms.: 24. Oktober 848.

*pGB8
V6755R
10.23.48

Vienna. Nationalgarde.
Bekanntmachung. Ausserordentliche Zeitumstände
erfordern ausserordentliche Massregeln. Je
wichtiger der Moment, je grösser die Gefahr ...
[Wien]Aus der k.k.Hof= und Staatsdruckerei.
[1848]

broadside. 45x57cm.
Dated & signed: Wien am 23. October 1848.
Messenhauser, provisorischer Ober=Commandant.

*pGB8
V6755R
10.24.48

Vienna. Nationalgarde.
Erklärung. Es verbreitet sich das Gerücht,
dass die sowohl als Deputirte an Se. Majestät
den Kaiser nach Ollmütz abgeschickten
Vertrauungsmänner der Nationalgarde, als auch
die Adresssteller an den hohen constituirenden
Reichstag verrätherischer Absichten gegen die
Interessen der Bevölkerung beschuldiget, und
persönlich bedrohlt werden ...
[Wien]Aus der k.k.Hof= und Staatsdruckerei.
[1848]

(See next card)

*pGB8
V6755R
10.23.48

Vienna. Nationalgarde.
Wegen Plünderung. Mitbürger!--In einem
feierlichen Augenblicke, wo allen gesetzlichen
Gewalten durch Militär=Herrschaft Gefahr droht,
ist es doppelt nothwendig, die Gesetze innerhalb
der eigenen Mauern zu achten ...
[Wien]Aus der k.k.Hof= und Staatsdruckerei.
[1848]

broadside. 44.5x29cm.
Lyser (Wiener-Ereignisse) p.95.
Dated & signed: Wien am 23. October 1848.
Messenhauser, provisorischer Ober=
Commandant.

*pGB8
V6755R
10.24.48

Vienna. Nationalgarde.   Erklärung ... [1848]
(Card 2)

broadside. 44.5x57cm.
Dated & signed: Hauptquartier Schwarzenberg=
Palais am 24. October 1848. Messenhauser m. p.
...
Broadside in 2 columns; the 2d column contains
the address, signed by 14 division commanders
of the Nationalgarde, beginning: An den hohen
constituirenden Reichstag! Es haben sich bei der
Nationalgarde   Wiens Zweifel erhoben
...

*GB8
V6755R
10.23.48

Vienna. Universität. Ausschuss der Studierenden.
Landsleute, Brüder! Seit mehreren Tagen sind
wir von der Verbindung mit Euch, von der
Verbindung mit der ganzen Welt abgeschnitten ...
[Wien,1848]

broadside. 21x13cm.
Dated & signed: Wien, im Oktober 1848. Der
Ausschuss der Studenten.

*pGB8
V6755R
10.24.48

Vienna. Nationalgarde.
Kundmachung. Durch den Parlamentär Herrn
Hauptmann und Ober=Commandanten=Stellvertreter
Thurn sind dem Unterzeichneten eine Anzahl
Exemplare der nachvolgenden Proclamation des
Feldmarschalls Fürsten zu Windischgrätz mit
dem Auftrage zugekommen, selbe ungesäumt zur
öffentlichen Kenntniss zu bringen ...
[Wien]Aus der k.k.Hof= und Staats=Druckerei.
[1848]

(See next card)

*pGB8
V6755R
10.24.48

Austria. Reichstag, 1848-1849.
Da Feldmarschall Fürst Windischgrätz im
offenen Widerspruche mit dem kaiserlichen Worte
vom 19. October, und in offener Nichtachtung
des Reichstags=Beschlusses vom 22. October in
einer neuen Proklamation ddo. Hetzendorf 23.
October 1848, Massregeln über Wien verhängt ...
[Wien,1848]

broadside. 45x57cm.
Dated: Wien den 24. October 1848.

*pGB8
V6755R
10.24.48

Vienna. Nationalgarde.   Kundmachung ... [1848]
(Card 2)

broadside. 45x57cm.
Dated & signed: Wien am 24. October 1848.
Messenhauser, provisorischer Ober=Commandant.
Includes Windisch-Grätz's "Proklamation" of
23 October.

*pGB8
V6755R
10.24.48

Vienna. Universität. Ausschuss der Studierenden.
Dringender Aufruf! Von den 48 Stunden, die Windischgrätz der Stadt Wien zur Bedenkzeit gab, ob sie der Freiheit oder dem Korporalstocke gehorchen wollen, sind bereits 12 Stunden verflossen ...
[Wien,1848]

broadside. 42x53cm.
Dated & signed: Wien, im October 1848. Der Ausschuss der Studenten.

---

*pGB8
V6755R
10.24.48

Vienna. Universität. Ausschuss der Studierenden.
Tapferes Volk von Wien! Endlich naht er, der ersehnte Augenblick der Entscheidung, der dem drückenden peinlichen Zustande der letzten vierzehn Tage ein Ende machen, der unseren schweren Kampf zu einem herrlichen siegreichen Ausgange führen wird ...
[Wien,1848]

broadside. 42x53cm.
Dated: Wien, den 24. Octob. 1848.

---

*pGB8
V6755R
10.24.48

Vienna. Universität. Medizinische Fakultät.
Die medicinische Facultät an die Bevölkerung Wiens. Durch den Edelmuth der Bevölkerung Wiens ist die Facultät in den Stand gesetzt worden, die sämmtlichen, unter ihrer Leitung stehenden Nothspitäler für den ersten Bedarf mit den nothwendigsten Verbandstücken zu versehen ...
[Wien]Aus der k.k.Hof- und Staatsdruckerei.
[1848]

broadside. 45x57cm.
Dated: Wien den 24. October 1848.

---

*pGB8
V6755R
10.24.48

Vienna. Zivilgericht.
Kundmachung. Der Gemeinderath der Stadt Wien hat in seiner Plenar-Sitzung am 23. Oktober 1848 den Beschluss gefasst, dass die Auszieh- und Aufkündigungs-Zeit neuerlich auf vierzehn Tage verlängert ...
[Wien,1848]

broadside. 42x26.5cm.
Signed & dated: Vom Civilgerichte der Stadt Wien am 24. Oktober 1848.

---

*pGB8
V6755R
10.25.48

Austria. Armee.
An die Bewohner von Wien. Es ist mir der Antrag gestellt worden, eine friedliche Vermittlung mit der Stadt einzugehen und mit meinen Truppen nach Wien einzurücken, um die von mir vorgeschriebenen Bedingungen selbst in Ausführung zu bringen ...
[Wien,1848]

broadside. 35x21.5cm.
Dated & signed: Hauptquartier Hetzendorf am 25. Oktober 1848. Fürst zu Windisch-Grätz, Feldmarschall.

---

*pGB8
V6755R
10.25.48

Austria. Armee.
... An die Bewohner von Wien. Es ist mir der Antrag gestellt worden, eine friedliche Vermittlung mit der Stadt einzugehen und mit meinen Truppen nach Wien einzurücken, um die von mir vorgeschriebenen Bedingungen selbst in Ausführung zu bringen ...
[Wien,1848]

broadside. 38x24cm.
At head: Nr. 13373.
Dated & signed: Hauptquartier Hetzendorf am 25. Oktober 1848. Fürst zu Windisch-Grätz, Feldmarschall.

---

*pGB8
V6755R
10.25.48

Austria. Armee.
An die Bewohner Wiens. Es ist mir der Antrag gestellt worden, eine friedliche Vermittlung mit der Stadt einzugehen, und mit meinen Truppen nach Wien einzurücken, um die von mir vorgeschriebenen Bedingungen selbst in Ausführung zu bringen ...
Gedruckt bei H.Liebergesell in Wr.Neustadt.
[1848]

broadside. 39x23.5cm.
Dated & signed: Hauptquartier Hetzendorf am 25. Oktober 1848. Fürst zu Windisch-Grätz, Feldmarschall.

---

*pGB8
V6755R
10.25.48

Austria. Reichstag, 1848-1849.
Eure Majestät! Der konstituirende Reichstag hat Euerer Majestät niemahls sprechendere Beweise von seiner unerschütterlichen Treue für die Freiheit, für das Wohl des Gesammtvaterlandes und für den konstitutionellen Thron zu geben vermocht, als er sie in der aufopfernden Thätigkeit der letzten Tage darlegte ...
[Wien]Aus der k.k.Hof- und Staatsdruckerei.
[1848]

broadside. 43.5x55.5cm.
Dated: Wien den 25. October 1848.

---

*pGB8
V6755R
10.25.48

Austria. Reichstag, 1848-1849.
Reichstags-Beschluss. Da Feldmarschall Fürst Windischgrätz im offenen Widerspruche mit dem kaiserlichen Worte vom 19. October, und in offener Nichtachtung des Reichstags-Beschlusses vom 22. October in einer neuen Proclamation, de dato Hetzendorf 23. October 1848, Massregeln über Wien verhängt ...
[Wien]Aus der k.k.Hof- und Staats-Druckerei.
[1848]

broadside. 45x56cm.

(See next card)

---

*pGB8
V6755R
10.25.48

Austria. Reichstag, 1848-1849.   Reichstags-Beschluss ... [1848]   (Card 2)

Dated "Wien am 24. October 1848"; also includes "Proclamation. Mitbürger! Das Vorstehende ist die Stimme des hohen Reichstages ..." dated & signed: Wien am 25. October 1848. Messenhauser, provisorischer Ober-Commandant.

*GB8
V6755R
10.25.48

Der Reichstag. Es ist bekannt, dass die volle Zahl der Reichstagsmitglieder 384 beträgt. Das Tagesblatt "Gradaus" vom 24. Oktober gesteht selbst, dass dermalen nur 196 davon an den Reichstagssitzungen theil nehmen ...
[Wien,1848]

broadside. 17.5x23cm.
Dated & signed: Wien den 25. Oktober 1848. F. K.

*pGB8
V6755R
10.26.48

Vienna. Gemeinderat.
Der Gemeinderath hat folgende Zuschrift erhalten, welche er zur Kenntniss seiner Mitbürger bringt: An den Gemeinderath der Stadt Wien! Hauptquartier Hetzendorf, am 26. October 1848. Jm Nachhange zum Puncte 3 meiner Proclamation vom 23. October ...
[Wien]Aus der k.k.Hof- und Staatsdruckerei. [1848]

broadside. 44.5x27.5cm.
The proclamation is signed: Alfred Windisch-Grätz m. p.,   Feldmarschall.

*pGB8
V6755R
10.25.48

Vienna. Gemeinderat.
Vom Gemeinderathe der Stadt Wien wurde in der Sitzung vom 24. October d. J. nachfolgendes Memorandum an den Herrn Feldmarschall Fürsten v. Windischgrätz beschlossen, und dasselbe am 25. d. M. durch zwei Mitglieder des Gemeinderathes in das Hauptquartier des Fürsten überbracht.
[Wien]Aus der k.k.Hof- und Staats=Druckerei. [1848]

broadside. 45x57cm.
Dated: Wien am 25. October 1848.

*pGB8
V6755R
10.26.48

Vienna. Gemeinderat.
Vom Gemeinderathe der Stadt Wien. Nachdem dem Gemeinderathe die Eröffnung gemacht wurde, der Fürst Windischgrätz beabsichtige in Bezug auf seine Proclamation, dem Gemeinderathe Erläuterungen zu geben ...
[Wien]Aus der k.k.Hof- und Staatsdruckerei. [1848]

broadside. 44.5x27.5cm.
Dated: Wien am 26. October 1848.
Includes Windisch-Grätz's proclamation of 25 October,beginning: An die Bewohner von Wien. Es ist mir der   Antrag gestellt worden ...

*pGB8
V6755R
10.25.48

Vienna. Nationalgarde.
Kundmachung. Die Stelle in meiner Proclamation vom 25. October: "Die Stadt Wien wird von heute Abend 9 Uhr als im Belagerungszustand befindlich, erklärt" hat die Besorgniss der Civil= Behörden erregt ...
[Wien]Aus der k.k.Hof- und Staatsdruckerei. [1848]

broadside. 45x29cm.
Dated & signed: Wien am 25. October 1848.
Messenhauser, provisorischer Ober=Commandant.

*pGB8
V6755R
10.26.48

Vienna. Nationalgarde.
Aufruf! Es hat in der akademischen Legion eine Abtheilung entschlossener Männer unter dem Titel "Todtenkopflegion" bestanden. Diese Schaar ist aufgelöst worden ...
[Wien]Aus der k.k.Hof- und Staatsdruckerei. [1848]

broadside. 44x28cm.
Dated & signed: Wien den 26. October 1848.
Messenhauser, prov. Ober=Commandant.

*pGB8
V6755R
10.25.48

Vienna. Nationalgarde.
Nachtrag zu dem Frühbefehle am 25. October 1848. Die Herren Bezirks=Commandanten sämmtlicher Vorstädte haben nach Erhalt dieses sogleich Alarm schlagen zu lassen ...
[Wien]Aus der k.k.Hof- und Staatsdruckerei. [1848]

broadside. 45x57cm.
Dated & signed: Wien den 25. October 1848.
Messenhauser, provisorischer Ober=Commandant.

*pGB8
V6755R
10.26.48

Vienna. Nationalgarde.
Befehl an alle Commandanten. Fürst Windischgrätz hat der Deputation des Gemeinderathes erklärt, er müsse bei seinen Bedingungen beharren, er verlange unbedingte Unterwerfung, und am Abende werde er die Feind- seligkeiten eröffnen ...
[Wien]Aus der k.k.Hof- und Staatsdruckerei. [1848]

broadside. 44.5x55.5cm.
Dated & signed: Wien am 26. October 1848. 5 Uhr Abends.   Messenhauser, provisorischer   Ober=Commandant.

*pGB8
V6755R
10.26.48

Austria. Reichstag, 1848-1849.
Kundmachung. Dem unterfertigten Reichstags= Ausschusse ist die betrübende Nachricht zugekommen, dass ein am gestrigen Tage aus dem militärischen Lager in die Stadt gelangter "Parlamentär" von einzelnen Personen unwirdig behandelt worden sei ...
[Wien]Aus der k.k.Hof- und Staats=Druckerei. [1848]

broadside. 44x28cm.
Dated: Wien den 26. October 1848.

*GB8
V6755R
10.26.48

Vienna. Nationalgarde.
Befehl an alle Commandanten. Fürst Windischgrätz hat der Deputation des Gemeinderathes erklärt, er müsse bei seinen Bedingungen beharren und am Abende werde er die Feindseligkeiten eröffnen ...
[Wien]Aus der k.k.Hof- und Staatsdruckerei. [1848]

[2]p. 20.5x12.5cm.
Dated & signed: Wien am 26. October 1848. 5 Uhr Abends.   Messenhauser, prov. Ober=Commandant.

Vienna. Nationalgarde.
*pGB8 Kundmachung. Das Ober=Commando hat mir laut
V6755R Proclamation vom 25. d. M., die Organisirung
10.26.48 einer Sicherheitsbehörde übertragen ...
[Wien]Aus der k.k.Hof= und Staatsdruckerei.
[1848]
broadside. 44x28.5cm.
Dated & signed: Wien den 26. October 1848.
Fenneberg, Hauptmann, Chef der Feldadjutantur
und Sicherheits=Behörde.

Vienna. Nationalgarde.
*pGB8 Kundmachung. Es kommen Fälle vor, dass
V6755R Commandanten oder einzelne Garden im Uebermass
10.26.48 des Eifers Gemeinderäthe zur Leistung der
Wehrpflicht anhalten ...
[Wien]Aus der k.k.Hof= und Staatsdruckerei.
[1848]
broadside. 44x27.5cm.
Dated & signed: Wien am 26. October 1848.
Messenhauser, prov. Ober-Commandant.

Vienna. Nationalgarde.
*pGB8 Kundmachung. Mit dem heutigen Tage um 12 Uhr
V6755R läuft die von dem Herrn Feldmarschall
10.26.48 Fürsten Windischgrätz der Stadt gestellte
Frist ab ...
[Wien]Aus der k.k.Hof= und Staatsdruckerei.
[1848]
broadside. 44x55cm.
Dated & signed: Wien den 26. October 1848.
Messenhauser, provisorischer Ober=Commandant.

Vienna..Nationalgarde.
*pGB8 Vom Generalstabe. Die Mannschaft des
V6755R Transport=Sammelhauses ist vom Herrn Militär=
10.26.48 Platz=Commandanten Generalen v. Matauschek
angewiesen, sich bei dem bevorstehenden Kampfe
neutral und ganz passiv unter Androhung des
Standrechtes in dem Transporthause zu verhalten
...
[Wien]Aus der k.k.Hof= und Staatsdruckerei.
[1848]
broadside. 44x27cm.
Dated & signed: Wien am 26. October 1848.
Haug, Chef des Generalstabs.

Vienna. Universität. Ausschuss der Studierenden.
*pGB8 Dringende Aufforderung an die Bewohner Wiens.
V6755R Der wichtigste, entscheidende Moment in unserem
10.26.48 begeisterten Freiheitskampfe, der Barrikaden-
kampf, steht uns bevor ...
[Wien]Aus der k.k.Hof= und Staats=Druckerei.
[1848]
broadside. 45x28.5cm.
Dated & signed: Wien am 26. October 1848. Vom
Studenten-Comité.

Austria. Post-Kurs-Bureau.
*pGB8 Kundmachung. Die eingetretenen Verhältnisse
V6755R haben schon gestern die Absendung der Posten von
10.27.48 hier nicht gestattet ...
[Wien]Aus der k.k.Hof= und Staatsdruckerei.
[1848]
broadside. 44x28cm.
Dated & signed: Wien am 27. October 1848. K. k.
oberste Hofpost-Verwaltung.

Austria, Lower.
*pGB8 ... Circulare vom k. k. N. Oe. Kreisamte
V6755R V.U.W.W. Womit die Statuten des Vereines "die
10.27.48 deutsche Flagge" bekannt gemacht werden.
[Wien,1848]
folder([3]p.) 36.5x23cm.
Caption title; at head: Nr.152 2/18741.1551.
Dated: Wien am 27. Oktober 1848.
"Allgemeine Statuten des Vereines: Die
deutsche Flagge": p.[2-3].

Vienna. Gemeinderat.
*pGB8 Kundmachung. Von Seite des Gemeinderathes der
V6755R Stadt Wien wird hiemit bekannt gemacht, dass
10.27.48 von demselben im Einverständnisse mit der
medicinischen Fakultät den inspizirenden
Aerzten der Nothspitäler für Verwundete ... in
Bezug des Transportes und der Pflege der
Verwundeten unbedingte Vollmacht ertheilt worden
...
[Wien]Aus der k.k.Hof= und Staatsdruckerei.
[1848]
broadside. 44x28cm.
Dated: Wien am 27. October 1848.

Vienna. Gemeinderat.
*pGB8 Vom Gemeinderathe der Stadt Wien. Der
V6755R Feldmarschall Fürst Windischgrätz hat in einer
10.27.48 an den Gemeinderath der Stadt Wien gerichteten
Zuschrift alle Aerarial- und Privat-Gebäude und
alles Eigenthum unter den Schutz des
Gemeinderathes gestellt ...
[Wien]Aus der k.k.Hof= und Staatsdruckerei.
[1848]
broadside. 44x27.5cm.
Dated: Wien am 27. October 1848.

Vienna. Gemeinderat.
*pGB8 Vom Gemeinderathe der Stadt Wien. Der
V6755R Gemeinderath hat sich veranlasst gefunden, heute
10.27.48 Nacht in der gegenwärtigen bedrängten Lage der
Stadt Mitglieder des Nationalgarde=Ober=
Commandos, der mobilen Garde, des
Verwaltungsrathes, der akademischen Legion, des
Studenten=Ausschusses und des Gemeinderathes in
gleicher Anzahl zu einer Commission zusammen zu
berufen ...
[Wien]Aus der k.k.Hof= und Staatsdruckerei.
[1848]
broadside. 44.5x28cm.
Dated: Wien den 27. October 1848.

Vienna. Nationalgarde.
*pGB8
V6755R
10.27.48
Aufforderung. Alle Sachverständigen, welche im Stande sind, Schiesspulver zu erzeugen, wollen sich so bald als möglich, bei dem Verwaltungsrathe, Stadt, Stallburg, melden ...
[Wien]Aus der k.k.Hof= und Staatsdruckerei. [1848]

broadside. 45x27.5cm.
Dated & signed: Wien am 27. October 1848. Vom Verwaltungsrathe der Nationalgarde.

Vienna. Nationalgarde.
*pGB8
V6755R
10.28.48
Kundmachung. Ich mache wiederholt darauf aufmerksam, dass alle wehrpflichtigen Personen auch ausser Dienst, in Waffen zu erscheinen haben ...
[Wien]Aus der k.k.Hof= und Staats=Druckerei. [1848]

broadside. 44.5x27.5cm.
Dated & signed: Wien den 28. October 1848. Der Chef der Sicherheits=Behörde Fenneberg.

Vienna. Nationalgarde.
*pGB8
V6755R
10.27.48
Kundmachung. Von 8 Uhr Abends an ist der 1. Stock sämmtlicher bewohnten Häuser in der inneren Stadt, bei Vermeidung strenger Ahndung, zu beleuchten ...
[Wien]Aus der k.k.Hof= und Staats=Druckerei. [1848]

broadside. 44x28cm.
Dated & signed: Wien den 27. October 1848. Fenneberg, Chef der Sicherheits=Behörde.

Vienna. Nationalgarde.
*pGB8
V6755R
10.28.48
Kundmachung. Im Falle wieder eintretenden Kampfes sind bei Vermeidung augenblicklicher standrechtlicher Behandlung der Dawiderhandelnden alle Thore und Fenster sogleich zu öffnen ...
[Wien]Aus der k.k.Hof= und Staatsdruckerei. [1848]

broadside. 44x27.5cm.
Dated & signed: Wien am 28. October 1848. Der Chef der Sicherheitsbehörde: Fenneberg.

Vienna. Nationalgarde.
*pGB8
V6755R
10.27.48
Tagsbefehl. Der Feldmarschall hat vom gestrigen Abend an keinen Angriff, wie es nach seiner Erklärung zu vermuthen war, eintreten lassen ...
[Wien]Aus der k.k.Hof= und Staatsdruckerei. [1848]

broadside. 43.5x55.5cm.
Dated & signed: Wien den 27. October 1848. Messenhauser, prov. Ober=Commandant.
Large folio broadside.

Vienna. Nationalgarde.
*pGB8
V6755R
10.28.48
Tagsbefehl. Cameraden! Mitbürger! -- Der heutige Tag wird entscheidend seyn. -- Es ist in der Nacht eine Depesche des Banus an den Herrn Feldmarschall=Lieutenant Ramberg, Befehlshaber der Truppen im Prater, aufgefangen worden ...
[Wien]Aus der k.k.Hof= und Staatsdruckerei. [1848]

broadside. 44x55.5cm.
Dated & signed: Wien am 28. October 1848. Messenhauser, prov. Ober=Commandant.
Large folio broadside.

Vienna. Nationalgarde.
*GB8
V6755R
10.27.48
Tagsbefehl. Der Feldmarschall hat vom gestrigen Abend an, keinen Angriff, wie es nach seiner Erklärung zu vermuthen war, eintreten lassen ...
[Wien]Aus der k.k.Hof= und Staatsdruckerei. [1848]

broadside. 20.5x12.5cm.
Dated & signed: Wien den 27. October 1848. Messenhauser, provisorischer Ober=Commandant.
Small octavo broadside.

Vienna. Nationalgarde.
*GB8
V6755R
10.28.48
Tagsbefehl. Cameraden! Mitbürger! -- Der heutige Tag wird entscheidend seyn. -- Es ist in der Nacht eine Depesche des Banus an den Herrn Feldmarschall=Lieutenant Ramberg, Befehlshaber der Truppen im Prater, aufgefangen worden ...
[Wien]Aus der k.k.Hof= und Staatsdruckerei. [1848]

broadside. 20.5x12.5cm.
Dated & signed: Wien den 28. October 1848. Messenhauser, provisorischer Ober=Commandant.
Small octavo broadside.

Vienna. Nationalgarde.
*pGB8
V6755R
10.28.48
Kundmachung. Die Besitzer von Greisslereinen, Spezereihandlungen und sonstigen Victualien= Verschleissen haben ihre Gewölbe, in so lange stets offen zu halten, als kein ernstlicher Angriff erfolgt ...
[Wien]Aus der k.k.Hof= und Staats=Druckerei. [1848]

broadside. 44x27.5cm.
Dated & signed: Wien am 28. October 1848. Der Chef der Sicherheits=Behörde, Fenneberg.

Vienna. Gemeinderat.
*pGB8
V6755R
10.29.48
Alle jene Arbeiter, welche bewaffneten Corps oder der Mobil=Garde eingereiht wurden und bestimmte Beztige bisher von der Commune empfangen haben ...
[Wien]Aus der k.k.Hof= und Staatsdruckerei. [1848]

broadside. 44x28cm.
Dated & signed: Wien am 29. October 1848. Vom Gemeinderathe der Stadt Wien.

Vienna. Gemeinderat.
*pGB8   An die Bevölkerung von Wien! Der provisorische
V6755R   Ober=Commandant ist gestern Samstag am 28.
10.29.48 October d. J., um 7 Uhr Abends in der
Plenarsitzung des Gemeinderathes erschienen ...
[Wien]Aus der k.k.Hof= und Staatsdruckerei.
[1848]
   broadside. 44x28cm.
   Dated & signed: Wien den 29. October 1848. Vom
Gemeinderathe der Stadt Wien.

Vienna. Gemeinderat.
*pGB8   Mitbürger! Nachdem der Herr Ober=Commandant
V6755R   so eben dem Gemeinderathe die Nachricht
10.29.48 überbracht hat, dass die stabile und mobile
Nationalgarde, so wie die academische Legion sich
entschlossen habe, die Waffen niederzulegen ...
[Wien]Aus der k.k.Hof= und Staatsdruckerei.
[1848]
   broadside. 44x27.5cm.
   Dated & signed: Wien am 29. October 1848.
Vom Gemeinderathe der Stadt Wien.

Vienna. Nationalgarde.
*pGB8   Dringender Aufruf. Es haben allsogleich von
V6755R   allen Compagnien der Nationalgarde, der
10.29.48 akademischen Legion und der Mobilen
Vertrauensmänner bis längstens 4 Uhr
Nachmittags im Bureau des Ober=Commandos mit
unumschränkter Vollmacht sich einzufinden ...
[Wien]Aus der k.k.Hof= und Staatsdruckerei.
[1848]
   broadside. 44x27.5cm.
   Dated & signed: Wien am 29. October 1848.
Messenhauser, provisorischer
Obercommandant.

Vienna. Nationalgarde.
*pGB8   Kundmachung. Die von der Sicherheits=Behörde
V6755R   unter dem 28. October 1848 erlassene Kundmachung,
10.29.48 dass bei Vermeidung augenblicklicher
standrechtlicher Behandlung der Dawiderhandelnden
alle Thore und Fenster im Falle wieder
eintretenden Kampfes, sogleich zu öffnen sind
...
[Wien]Aus der k.k.Hof= und Staatsdruckerei.
[1848]
   broadside. 44.5x28cm.
   Dated & signed: Wien den 29. October 1848.
Messenhauser, provisorischer Ober=
Commandant.

Vienna. Nationalgarde.
*pGB8   Mitbürger! Ich habe die Vertrauensmänner der
V6755R   Compagnien versammelt gehabt, ich habe mit
10.29.48 ihnen gesprochen, ob ein Verzweiflungskampf
stattfinden solle ...
[Wien]Aus der k.k.Hof= und Staatsdruckerei.
[1848]
   broadside. 44x55.5cm.
   Dated & signed: Wien am 29. October 1848.
Messenhauser, prov. Ober=Commandant.

Vienna. Nationalgarde.
*pGB8   Proclamation. Mitbürger! Der erste Kampf um
V6755R   unsere constitutionelle Ehre hat gestern Statt
10.29.48 gefunden. Wir stehen an der Gränze, um den
zweiten zu beginnen ...
[Wien]Aus der k.k.Hof= und Staatsdruckerei.
[1848]
   broadside. 44x56cm.
   Dated & signed: Wien am 29. October 1848.
Messenhauser, provisorischer Ober=Commandant.

Austria. Reichstag, 1848-1849.
*pGB8   Zur Nachricht. Zu der am gestrigen Tage
V6755R   abgehaltenen Berathung von Vertrauensmännern der
10.30.48 sämmtlichen Nationalgarde, über die fernere
Vertheidigung oder Uebergabe der Stadt ...
[Wien]Aus der k.k.Hof= und Staatsdruckerei.
[1848]
   broadside. 44x28cm.
   Dated & signed: Wien den 30. October 1848. Vom
Reichstags-Ausschusse.

Telegrafische Depeche angekommen am 30.
*pGB8   Oktober früh halb 10 Uhr. Fürst Windischgrätz
V6755R   an Oberst Horvath in Wiener=Neustadt. Wien hat
10.30.48 sich unbedingt unterworfen, heute belegen meine
Truppen die Stadt.
   Gedruckt bei H.Liebergesell in Wr.Neustadt.
[1848]
   broadside. 23.5x39cm.

Vienna. Gemeinderat.
*pGB8   Alle jene Arbeiter, welche bewaffneten Corps
V6755R   oder der Mobil=Garde eingereiht wurden und
10.30.48 bestimmte Bezüge bisher von der Commune
empfangen haben ...
[Wien]Aus der k.k.Hof= und Staatsdruckerei.
[1848]
   broadside. 44x28cm.
   Dated & signed: Wien am 30. October 1848. Vom
Gemeinderathe der Stadt Wien.

Vienna. Gemeinderat.
*pGB8   Kundmachung. Von Seite des Gemeinderathes der
V6755R   Stadt Wien wird hiermit bestätigt, dass Herr
10.30.48 Obercommandant Messenhauser so eben in der
Plenar=Versammlung des Gemeinderathes die
Erklärung abgegeben habe ...
[Wien]Aus der k.k.Hof= und Staatsdruckerei.
[1848]
   broadside. 43.5x28cm.
   Dated: Wien am 30. October 1848.
   Declaring Messenhauser's willingness to continue to serve as Commandant of the Nationalgarde until peace has been restored.

Vienna. Nationalgarde.
*pGB8   Kundmachung. Der heutige Tag ist wieder in
V6755R   Aufregung vollbracht worden.--Man hat das
10.30.48 anrückende Heer der Ungarn fechtend gesehen ...
          [Wien]Aus der k.k.Hof= und Staatsdruckerei.
          [1848]
          broadside. 44x28cm.
          Dated & signed: Wien am 30. October 1848, 8 Uhr
          Abends. Messenhauser, provisorischer Ober=
          Commandant.

Vienna. Nationalgarde.
*GB8   Vom St. Stephansthurme. Unterhalb dem
V6755R   Neugebäude steht ein Truppenkörper, wegen dem
10.30.48 Nebel lässt sich nichts Näheres bestimmen ...
          [Wien]Aus der k.k.Hof= und Staatsdruckerei.
          [1848]
          broadside. 14x21.5cm.
          Dated & signed: 2 Uhr Nachmittag. Messenhauser,
          prov. Ober=Commandant.
          In this edition, the last line of text begins:
          mer näher ...
          Describing troop actions on the 30th of
          October.

Vienna. Nationalgarde.
*pGB8   Mitbürger! Die gemischte Deputation, welche
V6755R   sich in das Hauptquartier Sr. Durchlaucht des
10.30.48 Herrn Feldmarschalls Fürsten zu Windischgrätz
          begab, ist zurückgekehrt, und hat über den
          Ausgang ihrer Mission Folgendes berichtet: ...
          [Wien]Aus der k.k.Hof= und Staatsdruckerei.
          [1848]
          broadside. 43.5x55cm.
          Dated & signed: Wien am 30. October 1848.
          Messenhauser, provisorischer Ober=Commandant.

Vienna. Nationalgarde.
*GB8   Vom St. Stephansthurme. Unterhalb dem
V6755R   Neugebäude steht ein Truppenkörper, wegen dem
10.30.48 Nebel lässt sich nichts Näheres bestimmen ...
          [Wien]Aus der k.k.Hof= und Staatsdruckerei.
          [1848]
          broadside. 14x22cm.
          Dated & signed: 2 Uhr Nachmittag. Messenhauser,
          provia. Ober=Commandant.
          In this edition, the last line of text begins:
          bar immer näher ...
          Describing troop actions on the 30th
          of October.

Vienna. Nationalgarde.
*GB8   Vom St. Stephansthurme. Die Schlacht scheint
V6755R   sich gegen Oberlaa und Inzersdorf zu ziehen.
10.30.48 Der Nebel verhindert eine klare Ansicht ...
          [Wien]Aus der k.k.Hof= und Staatsdruckerei.
          [1848]
          broadside. 13x21.5cm.
          Dated & signed: Wien am 30. October 1848.
          12 3/4 Uhr Mittags. Messenhauser, prov. Ober=
          Commandant.

Austria. Armee.
*pGB8   Mitbürger! Der Gemeinderath der Stadt Wien hat
V6755R   von jenem Zeitpuncte an, als der hohe
10.31.48 Reichstags=Ausschuss demselben aufgetragen hatte,
          in Vereinigung mit dem Nationalgarde=
          Obercommando die Stadt in Vertheidigungs=Zustand
          zu setzen, alle strategischen Massregeln dem
          Obercommando überlassen ...
          [Wien]Aus der k.k.Hof= und Staatsdruckerei.
          [1848]
          broadside. 44x56cm.
                              (See next card)

Vienna. Nationalgarde.
*GB8   Vom St. Stephansthurme. Man sieht deutlich ein
V6755R   Gefecht hinter Kaiser=Ebersdorf, ohne die
10.30.48 kämpfenden Truppen oder den Gang des Treffens
          ausnehmen zu können ...
          [Wien]Aus der k.k.Hof= und Staatsdruckerei.
          [1848]
          broadside. 13.5x20.5cm.
          Dated & signed: Wien am 30 October 1848.
          Vormittag 11 Uhr. Messenhauser, prov. Ober=
          Commandant.
          In this edition, the 3d line of text
          begins: den Gang ...

Austria. Armee.   Mitbürger ... [1848]
*pGB8   (Card 2)
V6755R
10.31.48   Dated & signed: Hauptquartier Hetzendorf, am
          30. October 1848, um 3 Uhr Nachmittags. Jm
          Namen und Vollmacht Sr. Durchlaucht des Herrn
          Feldmarschalls Alfred Fürsten zu Windischgrätz.
          Cordon m. p.
          Followed by a brief proclamation of the
          Gemeinderat, dated 31 October 1848, beginning:
          Nachdem der Herr Obercommandant erklärt hat,
          dass von Seite der ungarischen Armee keine
                              (See next card)

Vienna. Nationalgarde.
*GB8   Vom St. Stephansthurme. Man sieht deutlich ein
V6755R   Gefecht hinter Kaiser=Ebersdorf, ohne die
10.30.48 kämpfenden Truppen, oder den Gang des Treffens
          ausnehmen zu können ...
          [Wien]Aus der k.k.Hof= und Staatsdruckerei.
          [1848]
          broadside. 13.5x21cm.
          Dated & signed: Wien am 30. October 1848. 11
          Uhr Vormittag. Messenhauser, prov. Ober=
          Commandant.
          In this edition, the 3d line of text
          begins: Gang des ...

Austria. Armee.   Mitbürger ... [1848]
*pGB8   (Card 3)
V6755R
10.31.48 Hilfe mehr zu erwarten sei ...
          Large folio broadside.
          Specifying conditions for the surrender of
          Vienna.

Austria. Armee.
*pGB8
V6755R
10.31.48
Mitbürger! Der Gemeinderath der Stadt Wien hat von jenem Zeitpuncte an, als der hohe Reichstags=Ausschuss demselben aufgetragen hatte, in Vereinigung mit dem Nationalgarde=Obercommando die Stadt in Vertheidigungs=Zustand zu setzen, alle strategischen Massregeln dem Obercommando überlassen ...
[Wien,1848]

broadside. 43.5x27.5cm.
Dated & signed: Hauptquartier Hetzendorf, am
(See next card)

Austria. Armee. Mitbürger ... [1848]
*pGB8
V6755R
10.31.48
(Card 2)
30. October 1848, um 3 Uhr Nachmittags. Jm Namen und Vollmacht Sr. Durchlaucht des Herrn Feldmarschalls Alfred Fürsten zu Windischgrätz: Cordon m. p.
Followed by a brief proclamation of the Gemeinderat, dated 31 October 1848, beginning: Nachdem der Herr Obercommandant erklärt hat, dass von Seite der ungarischen Armee keine Hülfe mehr zu erwarten sei ...
Small folio broadside.
Specifying con-( )ditions for the surrender of Vienna.

Vienna. Bürgergarde.
*pGB8
V6755R
10.31.48
An die mobilen Corps! Die Herren Commandanten der mobilen Corps haben bis heute Nachmittags fünf Uhr dem Gemeinderathe die Standesausweise ihrer Truppenkörper, behufs ihrer weiteren Verpflegung einzureichen ...
[Wien]Aus der k.k.Hof= und Staatsdruckerei.
[1848]

broadside. 44x56cm.
Dated & signed: Wien am 31. October 1848.
Fenneberg, provisorischer Mit=Ober=Commandant
der Wiener ( ) Volkswehr.

Vienna. Nationalgarde.
*pGB8
V6755R
10.31.48
An die Nationalgarden der Hauptstadt Wien. Jm Nachhange zur Proclamation vom 30. October 8 Uhr Abends sehe ich mich verpflichtet, bekannt zu geben, welche Ursachen mich bestimmten, zu der mit Sr. Durchlaucht dem Feldmarschall Herrn Fürsten Windischgrätz einzurathen ...
[Wien]Aus der k.k.Hof= und Staatsdruckerei.
[1848]

(See next card)

Vienna. Nationalgarde. An die Nationalgarden
*pGB8
V6755R
10.31.48
... [1848]
(Card 2)
broadside. 44.5x28.5cm.
Dated & signed: Wien am 31. October 1848.
Ernst Haug, Chef des Generalstabes der Wiener Nationalgarde.

Vienna. Nationalgarde.
*pGB8
V6755R
10.31.48
Kundmachung. Das unterzeichnete Ober=Commando der Wiener Nationalgarde protestirt hiemit feierlichst gegen jede Zumuthung, als seien die am 31. October Nachmittags von Seite einzelner mobiler Corps gegen die kaiserlichen Truppen begonnenen Feindseligkeiten auf seinen Befehl geschehen ...
[Wien]Aus der k.k.Hof= und Staatsdruckerei.
[1848]

(See next card)

Vienna. Nationalgarde. Kundmachung ... [1848]
*pGB8
V6755R
10.31.48
(Card 2)
broadside. 45x28cm.
Dated & signed: Wien am 31. October 1848.
Messenhauser, provisorischer Ober=Commandant.
Fenneberg, Stellvertreter.

Vienna. Nationalgarde.
*pGB8
V6755R
10.31.48
Kundmachung. Um den verschiedenen Parteien, welche in dem kritischen Augenblicke des Verhängnisses der belagerten Stadt über die so hochwichtige Frage, ob ein Verzweiflungskampf gegen eine factische Uebermacht geschlagen werden solle oder nicht, Rechnung zu tragen ...
[Wien]Aus der k.k.Hof= und Staatsdruckerei.
[1848]

broadside. 44x28cm.
Dated & signed: Wien am 31. October 1848.
Messenhauser, provisorischer Ober=Commandant.

Vienna. Nationalgarde.
*pGB8
V6755R
10.31.48
Mitbürger! Es ist notorisch festgesetzt, dass unsere ungarischen Brüder der Waffen=Uebermacht unterlegen sind ...
[Wien]Aus der k.k.Hof= und Staatsdruckerei.
[1848]

broadside. 43.5x27.5cm.
Dated "Wien am 31. October 1848" & signed jointly by Messenhauser & Fenneberg for the Nationalgarde & by Stifft & Pranter for the Gemeinderat.
Calling for a ( ) laying down of arms.

Vienna. Nationalgarde.
*pGB8
V6755R
10.31.48
Nachricht. Die nachstehende Proclamation ist dem Nationalgarde-Ober=Commando von Seiten des Herrn Feldmarschalls Fürsten zu Windischgrätz durch einen Parlamentär in mehreren Exemplaren zugesendet worden ...
[Wien]Aus der k.k.Hof= und Staatsdruckerei.
[1848]

broadside. 45x55cm.
Dated & signed: Wien am 31. October 1848.
Messenhauser, prov. Ober=Commandant.
(See next card)

*pGB8
V6755R
10.31.48

Vienna. Nationalgarde.   Nachricht ... [1848]
(Card 2)
Windischgrätz's proclamation begins: Kund-machung. Ein Corps der ungarischen Insurgenten hat es gewagt, österreichischen Boden zu betreten ...

---

*pGB8
V6755R
10.32.48

Die bürgerliche Ehe und die Vortheile derselben beider Geschlechter.
[Wien]Gedruckt bei Franz Edlen von Schmid. [1848]
[2]p. 40x25cm.
Caption title; imprint on p.[2]; dated & signed: Wien im October 1848. Z.

---

*pGB8
V6755R
10.32.48

[Adler, ——]
Die Errettung des Feldmarschalls Radetzky aus Banditenhänden durch den hochherzigen Wiener Freiwilligen Ignatz Halfer. (Eine wahre Begebenheit.)
[Wien]Gedruckt bei Franz Edlen von Schmid. [1848]
[2]p. 40x25cm.
Caption title; imprint on p.[2]; dated & signed: Wien, im Oktober 1848. Adler.
Quoting a letter from Halfer.

---

*pGB8
V6755R
10.32.48

Kossuth, Lajos, 1802-1894.
Kossuths Abdankung uud [!] wie er den Plänen der Kamarilla auf die Spur kommt. Von ihm selbst niedergeschrieben.
[Wien]Okt.1848.Gedruckt bei M.Lell.
broadside. 50x40cm.

---

*pGB8
V6755R
10.32.48

An das Militär! Unsere Brüder in der Armee: Freunde, Brüder, Soldaten! Mit tiefer, unbeschreiblicher Wehmuth erblicke ich Euch mit Misstrauen und Verachtung auf Eure Brüder im Volke herabsehen ...
[Wien]Oktober 1848.Gedruckt bei M.Lell, Leopoldstadt,Weintraubengasse Nr.505.
broadside. 44x57cm.

---

*GB8
V6755R
10.32.48

Ein schwarzer Minister in Teufelsgestalt. Seit den Märztagen ist in Wien der Teufel los ...
[Wien]Okt.1848.Gedruckt bei M.Lell.
[2]p. 1 illus. 28.5x22cm.
Caption title; imprint on p.[2].

---

*pGB8
V6755R
10.32.48

[André, Rudolf, fl.1848]
Vorschlag zur Unterstützung Wiener bedürftiger Gewerbsmänner.
[Wien]Druck von Ulrich Klopf sen.und Alex. Eurich.[1848]
[2]p. 42x26.5cm.
Caption title; imprint on p.[2]; signed: Rudolf André, Jurist, Jägerzeile Nro. 27.
Suggesting the creation of a special paper currency.

---

*pGB8
V6755R
10.32.48

... Der Sturz des treulosen Kossuth! Die neue Einverleibung Ungarns mit Oesterreich. Heldenmuth der Deutschen auf den Barrikaden von Weisskirchen.
[Wien]Zu haben im Verlagsgewölbe:Stadt, Parisergasse Nr.411.Gedruckt bei U.Klopf sen. und Alexander Eurich,Wollzeile Nr.782.[1848]
[2]p. 39.5x25.5cm.
Caption title; imprint on p.[2]; signed at end: S.--T.
Austrian arms & "Oesterreich hat gesiegt!" in small type at head of title.

---

*pGB8
V6755R
10.32.48

Braun, Philipp, b.1805.
Kameraden. Ich war stolz an Eurer Spitze gestanden zu seyn, bei Euch gestanden in einer Zeit, wo es galt zu wachen, zu sorgen! ...
[Wien]Aus der k.k.Hof= und Staats=Druckerei. [1848]
broadside. 44.5x29cm.
Signed: Braun, Bezirks=Chef des 8. Bezirkes Mariahilf.

---

*pGB8
V6755R
10.32.48

Vienna. Nationalgarde.
Die Anweisung zur Fassung von Brot, Wein, Limito=Tabak, Licht, Holz, Hafer, Heu und Stroh erfolgt bei der Approvisionirungs= Commission im Magistratsgebäude ...
[Wien]Aus der k.k.Hof= und Staats=Druckerei. [1848]
broadside. 44.5x57cm.
Signed: Von der Central=Kanzlei des National-garde=Ober=Commando's.
This broadside is accompanied by 4 printed voucher forms for the issue of tobacco and of bread and wine.

Vienna. Nationalgarde.
*GB8
V6755R
10.32.48
Es werden Garden mehrseitig aufgefordert, ihre Sympathien für die akademische Legion insbesonders durch Einschreibungen kundzugeben. Der XI. Bezirk sympathisirt mit allen integrirenden Theilen der National=Garde ...
Wien,im October 1848,gedruckt bei Carl Ueberreuter,Alservorstadt Nr.146.

broadside. 29.5x23.5cm.

---

*pGB8
V6755R
11.1.48
Absichtliche Entstellungen und Verdrehungen ... [1848]   (Card 2)
Dated: Aus dem Hauptquartier Hetzendorf den 1. November 1848.
This edition is printed in 2 columns.
Recapitulating the events of 23-31 October.

Vienna. Universität. Ausschuss der Studierenden.
*pGB8
V6755R
10.32.48
Bürger, Landsleute! Die Zeit ist eine gefährliche! Wir warnen das Volk, und fordern es feierlich auf, vorsichtig zu seyn. Wir bitten, dass man keinen geheimen Schriften glaube, die man heute unter das Volk vertheilt oder vertheilen möchte ...
[Wien]Aus der k.k.Hof= und Staatsdruckerei. [1848]

broadside. 44.5x28.5cm.
Signed: Der   Ausschuss der Studenten.

---

*pGB8
V6755R
11.1.48
Absichtliche Entstellungen und Verdrehungen aller Thatsachen sind gegenwärtig so sehr an der Tagesordnung, dass es den Freunden der Wahrheit willkommen seyn muss, nachstehend eine getreue Darstellung der Fürgänge bei der Einnahme der Stadt Wien durch die k. k. Truppen zu erhalten ...
[Wien]Gedruckt bei U.Klopf sen.und Alex.Eurich. [1848]

broadside. 34.5x26cm.   (See next card)

---

*pGB8
V6755R
11.1.48
Absichtliche Entstellungen und Verdrehungen aller Thatsachen sind gegenwärtig so sehr an der Tagesordnung, dass es den Freunden der Wahrheit willkommen seyn muss, nachstehend eine getreue Darstellung der Fürgänge bei der Einnahme der Stadt Wien durch die k. k. Truppen zu erhalten ...
[Wien]Aus der k.k.Hof- und Staatsdruckerei. [1848]

broadside. 49.5x40.5cm.
Dated: Aus dem Hauptquartier Hetzendorf den   (See next card)

---

*pGB8
V6755R
11.1.48
Absichtliche Entstellungen ... [1848]   (Card 2)
Dated: Aus dem Hauptquartier Hetzendorf den 1. November 1848.
Recapitulating the events of 23-31 October.

---

*pGB8
V6755R
11.1.48
Absichtliche Entstellungen und Verdrehungen ... [1848]   (Card 2)
1. November 1848.
This edition is printed in a single column.
Recapitulating the events of 23-31 October.

Austria. Armee.
*pGB8
V6755R
11.1.48
An die Bewohner von Nieder= und Ober= Oesterreich. Der verlängerte Widerstand, den die in offener Empörung begriffene Stadt Wien meinen Truppen entgegen gesetzt hat ...
[Wien]Aus der k.k.Hof= und Staats=Druckerei. [1848]

broadside. 43.5x55.5cm.
Dated & signed: Hetzendorf am 1. November 1848. Fürst zu Windisch-Grätz, k. k. Feldmarschall.
Setting Vienna in a state of siege.

---

*pGB8
V6755R
11.1.48
Absichtliche Entstellungen und Verdrehungen aller Thatsachen sind gegenwärtig so sehr an der Tagesordnung, dass es den Freunden der Wahrheit willkommen seyn muss, nachstehend eine getreue Darstellung der Fürgänge bei der Einnahme der Stadt Wien durch die k. k. Truppen zu erhalten ...
[Wien]Aus der k.k.Hof= und Staatsdruckerei. [1848]

broadside. 43.5x55.5cm.
(See next card)

Austria. Armee.
*pGB8
V6755R
11.1.48
Proclamation. Jndem ich die unter meinem Befehle stehenden k. k. Truppen in die Hauptstadt Wien einrücken lasse ...
[Olmutz]Olmitzer k.k.pr.Kreisbuchdruckerei. [1848]

broadside. 44x57cm.
Dated & signed: Hauptquartier Hetzendorf am 1. November 1848. Fürst zu Windisch-Grätz, k. k. Feldmarschall.

Austria. Armee.
*pGB8   Proclamation. Jndem ich die unter meinem
V6755R   Befehle stehenden k. k. Truppen in die
11.1.48   Hauptstadt Wien einrücken lasse ...
     [Wien]Aus der k.k.Hof= und Staats=Druckerei.
     [1848]

       broadside. 44x56cm.
       Dated & signed: Hauptquartier Hetzendorf am 1.
   November 1848. Fürst zu Windisch-Grätz, k. k.
   Feldmarschall.

Vienna. Gemeinderat.   Kundmachung ... [1848]
*pGB8   (Card 2)
V6755R
11.2.48   broadside. 41x50cm.
     Signed & dated: Von dem Gemeinderathe der
   Stadt Wien, am 2. November 1848.

Austria. Armee.
*pGB8   Proclamation. Jndem ich die unter meinem
V6755R   Befehle stehenden k. k. Truppen in die
11.1.48   Hauptstadt Wien einrücken lasse ...
     [Wien]Gedruckt bei U.Klopf sen.und Alex.
   Eurich.[1848]

       broadside. 34.5x26.5cm.
       Dated & signed: Hauptquartier Hetzendorf am 1.
   November 1848. Fürst zu Windisch=Grätz, k. k.
   Feldmarschall.

Vienna. Gemeinderat.
*pGB8   Kundmachung. Vom k. k. Militär=Stadtcommando
V6755R   wurde in Folge der Zerstörung des Gasometers
11.2.48   und der hiernach eingestellten öffentlichen
   Beleuchtung der Stadt und Vorstädte angeordnet
   ...
     [Wien]Aus der k.k.Hof= und Staats=Druckerei.
     [1848]

       broadside. 44x27cm.

       Dated & signed: Wien am 2. November 1848.
   Vom Gemeinderathe der Stadt Wien.

       Telegrafische Depeche angelangt am 1.
*pGB8   November 1848 früh halb 9 Uhr. Fürst
V6755R   Windischgrätz an Oberst Horvath in Wiener=
11.1.48   Neustadt. Die ungarische Jnsurgenten=Armee
   hat sich hinter die Leytha zurückgezogen ...
     Gedruckt bei H.Liebergesell in Wr.Neustadt.
     [1848]

       broadside. 24x38.5cm.

Austria. Armee. Stadt-Commandantur, Vienna, 1848.
*pGB8   Proclamation. Die von Seiner Durchlaucht dem
V6755R   k. k. Herrn Feldmarschall Fürsten zu
11.3.48   Windischgrätz für die Dauer des
   Belagerungszustandes unter meiner obersten
   Leitung niedergesetzte Central=Commission hat
   am 2. d. M. ihre Functionen begonnen ...
     [Wien]Aus der k.k.Hof= und Staatsdruckerei.
     [1848]

       broadside. 44x55cm.

                  (See next card)

Vienna. Gemeinderat.
*pGB8   Kundmachung. Diejenigen, welche vom
V6755R   Nationalgarde=Ober=Commando zu
11.1.48   Dienstverrichtungen Pferde erhalten haben ...
     [Wien]Aus der k.k.Hof= und Staatsdruckerei.
     [1848]

       broadside. 43.5x28cm.
       Dated & signed: Wien am 1. November 1848.
   Von der Permanenz des Gemeinderathes der Stadt
   Wien.

Austria. Armee. Stadt=Commandantur, Vienna, 1848.
*pGB8   Proclamation ... [1848] (Card 2)
V6755R
11.3.48   Dated & signed: Wien am 3. November 1848.
   Von dem Vorstande der Central-Commission der
   k.k. Stadt-Commandantur. Freiherr von Cordon,
   k. k. General=Major.

Vienna. Gemeinderat.
*pGB8   Kundmachung. Es sind in der letzten Zeit
V6755R   verschiedene Militär=Effekten als: Mäntel,
11.2.48   Beinkleider, Kotzen, Betten u. s. w., so wie
   auch werthvolle Trophäen und geschichtliche
   Armatursstücke theils von dem Nationalgarde=
   Oberkommando requirirt, theils von dem
   Proletariate aus den Kasernen und ärarischen
   Depots genommen und fortgetragen worden ...
     [Wien]Gedruckt bei Leop.Grund,Hundsthurm Nr.1.
     [1848]

            (See next card)

Austria. Armee. Stadt=Commandantur, Vienna, 1848.
*pGB8   Proclamation. Jm Nachhange zu dem Proclam Sr.
V6755R   Durchlaucht des Herrn Feldmarschalls Fürsten zu
11.3.48   Windisch-Grätz vom 1. d. M., und auf hochdessen
   Befehl wird von Seite des Stadt-Commando
   Folgendes kund.gemacht.
     [Wien]Aus der k.k.Hof= und Staatsdruckerei.
     [1848]

       broadside. 44x56cm.
       Dated: Wien am 3. November 1848.
       Calling for the return of historic pieces of
   arms and armor   plundered from the
   armory on 7   October.

*pGB8
V6755R
11.3.48

Vienna. Gemeinderat.
Kundmachung. Das hohe k. k. Militär=Commando
hat, um die Versehung der Hauptstadt mit den
nöthigen Lebensmitteln so schnell als möglich
zu bewerkstelligen, nachfolgende Bestimmungen
getroffen: ...
[Wien]Aus der k.k.Hof= und Staatsdruckerei.
[1848]

broadside. 44x27.5cm.
Dated & signed: Wien, am 3. November 1848.
Vom Gemeinderathe der Stadt Wien.

---

*pGB8
V6755R
11.4.48

Vienna. Gemeinderat.
Kundmachung. Auf hohen Befehl bringt der
Gemeinderath der Stadt Wien folgende von der
Central=Commission der k. k. Stadt=Commandantur
angeordnete Massregel zur allgemeinen
Kenntniss: ...
[Wien]Aus der k.k.Hof= und Staats=Druckerei.
[1848]

broadside. 44x27.5cm.
Dated & signed: Wien am 4. November 1848.

---

*pGB8
V6755R
11.3.48

Vienna. Gemeinderat.
Kundmachung. Der Gemeinderath der
Residenzstadt Wien beeilt sich im Auftrage des
löbl. k. k. Militär=Ober=Commando's Folgendes
zur öffentlichen Kenntniss und genauer Beachtung
zu bringen ...
[Wien]Aus der k.k.Hof= und Staats=Druckerei.
[1848]

broadside. 43.5x55.5cm.
Dated: Wien den 3. November 1848.
Regulations for   traffic with the suburbs.

---

*pGB8
V6755R
11.5.48

Sankt Pölten, Austria. Kreisamt.
... Kundmachung. Um die Versehung der Haupt=
und Residenzstadt Wien mit den nöthigen
Lebensmitteln so schnell als möglich zu
bewerkstelligen, wurden laut Zuschrift des
Gemeinderathes der Stadt Wien ddo. 3., erhalten
am 5. d. M. Zahl 540 von dem k. k. Militär=
Stadt=Kommandanten Freiherrn von Cordon nach-
stehende Bestimmungen getroffen: ...
[Sankt Pölten,1848]

(See next card)

---

*pGB8
V6755R
11.3.48

Vienna. Gemeinderat.
Kundmachung. Jm Laufe der letzten Ereignisse
sollen beträchtliche Pulvervor-äthe theils in die
Stadt gebracht, theils daselbst auch erzeugt
worden seyn ...
[Wien]Aus der k.k.Hof= und Staats=Druckerei.
[1848]

broadside. 44.5x27.5cm.
Dated & signed: Wien am 3. November 1848.
Vom Gemeinderathe der Stadt Wien.

---

*pGB8
V6755R
11.5.48

Sankt Pölten, Austria. Kreisamt.   ...
Kundmachung ... [1848]   (Card 2)
broadside. 38x24cm.
Dated & signed: Kreisamt St. Pölten am 5.
November 1848. Weinberger, Kreihauptmann [!].
At head: Nro. 13502.

---

*pGB8
V6755R
11.4.48

Austria. Armee. Stadt-Commandantur, Vienna, 1848.
Kundmachung. Um den Verkehr zwischen der Stadt
und den Vorstädten zu erleichtern, habe ich zu
bestimmen gefunden ...
[Wien]Aus der k.k.Hof= und Staats=Druckerei.
[1848]

broadside. 44x27.5cm.
Dated & signed: Wien am 4. November 1848. Von
der Central=Commission der Stadt-Commandantur.

---

*pGB8
V6755R
11.6.48

Austria. Kriegsministerium.
Kundmachung. Seine Majestät der Kaiser haben
Sich mit allerhöchstem Handschreiben vom 3.
dieses veranlasst befunden ... den Herrn
Feldmarschall=Lieutenant Freiherrn von Welden
mit dem Titel eines Gouverneurs zu bestimmen ...
[Wien]Aus der k.k.Hof= und Staats=Druckerei.
[1848]

broadside. 44x27.5cm.
Dated & signed: Wien am 6. November 1848.
Vom Ministerium des Kriegswesens.

---

*pGB8
V6755R
11.4.48

Austria. Armee. Stadt-Commandantur, Vienna, 1848.
... Kundmachung. Um den Verkehr zwischen der
Stadt und den Vorstädten zu erleichtern, habe
ich zu bestimmen gefunden ...
[Wien,1848]

broadside. 37.5x24cm.
At head: Nro. 13785.
Dated & signed: Wien am 4. November 1848.
Von der Central-Commission der Stadt-Commandantur.

---

*pGB8
V6755R
11.6.48

Austria. Sovereigns, etc., 1835-1848
(Ferdinand I)
Wir Ferdinand der Erste, von Gottes Gnaden
Kaiser von Oesterreich ... Es hat dem
allmächtigen Gott gefallen, den Zeitpunct,
welcher eine namhafte Erweiterung der
constitutionellen Freiheit Unserer zur
königlichen ungarischen Krone gehörigen Länder
bezeichnet, in die Epoche Unserer Regierung zu
verlegen ...
[Olmutz,1848]

(See next card)

*pGB8
76755R
11.6.48

Austria. Sovereigns, etc., 1835-1848
(Ferdinand I)   Wir Ferdinand der Erste
... [1848]   (Card 2)
[2]p. 38x25.5cm.
Caption title; imperial arms at head.
"Gegeben in Olmütz am 6. November des Jahres
1848, Unserer Regierung im vierzehnten."

---

*pGB8
V6755R
11.7.48

Austria. Sovereigns, etc., 1835-1848
(Ferdinand I)
An die Landbewohner der Länder Meiner
ungarischen Krone. Die frechen Umtriebe Ludwig
Kossuth's und seiner Genossen, welche in Eurem
unglücklichen Vaterlande die Macht an sich
gerissen haben ...
[Olmütz,1848]

broadside. 38x51cm.
Dated & signed: Olmütz am 7. November 1848.
Ferdinand.

---

*pGB8
V6755R
11.6.48

Vienna. Gemeinderat.
Kundmachung. Die bedrängten Umstände, die
jeden Wehrpflichtigen zwangen, die Waffen zu
ergreifen, und sich dadurch dem Betriebe seines
Gewerbes zu entziehen, haben aufgehört ...
[Wien]Aus der k.k.Hof= und Staats=Druckerei.
[1848]

broadside. 44x28cm.
Dated & signed: Wien am 6. November 1848. Vom
Gemeinderathe der Stadt Wien.

---

*pGB8
V6755R
11.7.48

Vienna. Gemeinderat.
Kundmachung. Mit Genehmigung der hohen k. k.
Militär-Central=Commission hat der Gemeinderath
nach Anhörung der hiesigen Fiaker zur Fahrt
zu dem Bahnhof in Floridsdorf und zurück,
folgende Fahrtaxe festgestellt: ...
[Wien]Aus der k.k.Hof= und Staatsdruckerei.
[1848]

broadside. 44x28cm.
Dated: Wien den 7. November 1848.

---

*pGB8
V6755R
11.6.48

Vienna. Gemeinderat.
Vom Gemeinderathe der Stadt Wien. Um den
vielen bedrängten, durch die gegenwärtigen
Verhältnisse in Nothstand versetzten Mitbürgern
nach Möglichkeit eine Unterstützung angedeihen
zu lassen ...
[Wien]Aus der k.k.Hof= und Staatsdruckerei.
[1848]

broadside. 44.5x28cm.
Dated: Wien am 6. November 1848.

---

*pGB8
V6755R
11.7.48

Vienna. Magistrat.
Kundmachung. Gemäss [Paragraph].5 der Proclamation vom 23. October d. J. und des [Para-
graphen].6 der Proclamation vom 1. d. M. haben
die sich in Wien ohne legale Nachweisung der
Ursache ihrer Anwesenheit aufhaltenden Ausländer, so wie auch alle in gleicher Lage befindlichen, nach Wien nicht zuständigen Jn-
länder Wien sogleich zu verlassen ...
[Wien]Aus der k.k.Hof= und Staatsdruckerei.
[1848]

(See next card)

---

*pGB8
V6755R
11.7.48

Austria. Armee. Stadt-Commandantur, Vienna, 1848.
... Kundmachung. Um den Verkehr zwischen der
Stadt und den Vorstädten mit den ausser den
Linien liegenden Ortschaften zu erleichtern ...
[Wien,1848]

broadside. 38x24cm.
At head: Nro. 13785.
Dated & signed: Wien am 7. November 1848.
Von dem Vorstande der k. k. Central=Commission
der Stadt=Commandantur. Freiherr von Cordon, k.
k. General=Major.
Another edition   has imprint.

---

*pGB8
V6755R
11.7.48

Vienna. Magistrat.   Kundmachung ... [1848]
                            (Card 2)
[2]p. 40.5x25cm.
Caption title; imprint at foot of p.[1].
Dated & signed: Wien am 7. November 1848. Von
der Stadthauptmannschaft.
Calling for householders to provide a list
(form printed on p.[2]) of all occupants.

---

*pGB8
V6755R
11.7.48

Austria. Armee. Stadt-Commandantur, Vienna, 1848.
Kundmachung. Um den Verkehr zwischen der
Stadt und den Vorstädten mit den ausser den
Linien liegenden Ortschaften zu erleichtern ...
[Wien]Aus der k.k.Hof= und Staatsdruckerei.
[1848]

broadside. 43.5x28cm.
Dated & signed: Wien am 7. November 1848. Von
dem Vorstande der k. k. Central=Commission der
Stadt=Commandantur. Freiherr von Cordon, k. k.
General=Major.
Another edition   is without imprint.

---

*pGB8
V6755R
11.8.48

Austria. Armee. Stadt-Commandantur, Vienna, 1848.
Kundmachung. Das Ausrufen und der Verkauf von
Zeitungs=Blättern und Flugschriften auf den
öffentlichen Strassen und Plätzen wird im
Allgemeinen auf das Strengste untersagt ...
[Wien]Aus der k.k.Hof= und Staats=Druckerei.
[1848]

broadside. 44x27.5cm.
Dated & signed: Wien am 8. November 1848. Von
dem Vorstande der k. k. Central=Commission der
Stadt=Commandantur. Freiherr von Cordon, k. k.
General=Major.

Austria. Justizministerium.
... Kundmachung. Von dem k. k. Ministerium der Justiz wird über Einschreiten der Direction der privilegirten österreichischen Nationalbank zur Beseitigung erhobener Zweifel über den Sinn des zweiten Absatzes der Justiz=Ministerial-Verordnung vom 5. November 1848 erklärt ...
[Wien]Aus der k.k.Hof= und Staatsdruckerei.
[1848]

*pGB8
V6755R
11.8.48

broadside. 38x23cm.
Dated: Wien am 8. November 1848.

Sankt Pölten, Austria. Kreisamt.
... Von dem k. k. n. ö. Kreisamte B.O.W.W. Jn Folge der letzten Ereignisse zu Wien ist zu besorgen, dass die von dort flüchtige Parthei und deren Anhang sich auf das flache Land vertheilen, und daselbst versuchen werde ...
[Sankt Pölten,1848]

*pGB8
V6755R
11.8.48

broadside. 37.5x23.5cm.
At head: Nro. 13642.
Dated & signed: Kreisamt St. Pölten am 8. November 1848. Weinberger, Kreishauptmann.

Vienna. Gemeinderat.
An die wohlthätigen Bewohner Wiens! Jnmitten der ungeheuren Unglücksfälle, von denen die Hauptstadt betroffen worden, nimmt die bedrängte Lage Derjenigen zunächst unser innigstes Mitgefühl in Anspruch, welche durch die beklagenswerthen Kämpfe der letzten Wochen, durch Feuer und Plünderung um ihre Habe gebracht, theilweise ihrer Ernährer beraubt und obdachlos dem Elende Preis gegeben sind ...
[Wien]Aus der k.k.Hof= und Staatsdruckerei.
[1848]

*pGB8
V6755R
11.8.48

(See next card)

Vienna. Gemeinderat.   An die wohlthätigen
... [1848]   (Card 2)

*pGB8
V6755R
11.8.48

broadside. 44x28cm.
Dated & signed: Wien am 8. November 1848. Vom Gemeinderathe der Stadt Wien.

Vienna. Gemeinderat.
Kundmachung. Der Gemeinderath der Stadt Wien sieht sich veranlasst, hiemit folgende von dem Herrn Stadt=Commandanten und General=Major Freiherrn von Cordon an ihn gelangte Zuschrift zu veröffentlichen: "Es ist zu meiner Kenntniss gekommen, dass die Nationalgarden und sonstigen bewaffneten Corps sich noch immer als constituirt ansehen ...
[Wien]Aus der k.k.Hof= und Staatsdruckerei.
[1848]

*pGB8
V6755R
11.9.48

broadside.   44x28cm.
Dated: Wien den   9. November 1848.

Austria. Sovereigns, etc., 1835-1848
     (Ferdinand I)
     Wir Ferdinand der Erste, constitutioneller Kaiser von Oesterreich ... Wir haben mit Unserem Patente vom 22. October 1848 alle zum con-stituirenden Reichstage erwählten Volksvertreter aufgefordert, sich bis zum 15. November 1848 in der Stadt Kremsier zuverlässig einzufinden
...
[Wien]Aus der k.k.Hof= und Staats=Druckerei.
[1848]

*pGB8
V6755R
11.10.48

(See next card)

Austria. Sovereigns, etc., 1835-1848
     (Ferdinand I)   Wir Ferdinand der Erste
     ... [1848]   (Card 2)

*pGB8
V6755R
11.10.48

folder([2]p.) 44.5x29cm.
Caption title; imprint on p.[2].
Dated: Ollmütz den 10. November 1848.

Vienna. Gemeinderat.
Der Gemeinderath an die Landbewohner Oesterreichs! Durch die letzten Euch wohl bekannten Ereignisse ist ein grosser Theil der Bevölkerung Wiens in namenloses Elend gestürzt worden ...
[Wien]Aus der k.k.Hof= und Staatsdruckerei.
[1848]

*pGB8
V6755R
11.10.48

broadside. 44x27.5cm.
Dated: Wien am 10. November 1848.

Austria. Armee.
An den Herrn Feldmarschall=Lieutenant Moga und sämmtliche in Ungarn befindliche k. k. Generäle, Stabs= und Ober=Officiere.
[Wien,1848]

*pGB8
V6755R
11.12.48

broadside. 43x53.5cm.
Dated & signed: Hauptquartier Schönbrunn den 12. November 1848. Alfred Fürst zu Windischgrätz, Feldmarschall.

Large folio broadside, without imprint.

Austria. Armee.
An den Herrn Feldmarschall-Lieutenant Moga und sämmtliche in Ungarn befindliche k. k. Generäle, Stabs- und Oberofficiere.
[Wien]Aus der k.k.Hof= und Staatsdruckerei.
[1848]

*pGB8
V6755R
11.12.48

broadside. 44.5x28.5cm.
Dated & signed: Hauptquartier Schönbrunn den 12. November 1848. Alfred Fürst zu Windischgrätz, Feldmarschall.
Small folio broadside, with imprint.

Austria. Armee. Stadt-Commandantur, Vienna, 1848.
Kundmachung. Auf Befehl Sr. Excellenz des
Herrn Gouverneurs, Feldmarschall-Lieutenants
Freiherrn v. Welden, wird von heute an die
Passage zwischen der Stadt und den Vorstädten
wieder hergestellt ...
[Wien]Aus der k.k.Hof- und Staatsdruckerei.
[1848]

*pGB8
V6755R
11.12.48

broadside. 44.5x29cm.
Dated & signed: Wien am 12. November 1848.
Vom [!] dem Vorstande der Central-Commission der
k.k. Stádt-Com-   mandantur. Freiherr von
Cordon, k. k.   General-Major.

Austria. Armee.
Proclamation des Fürsten Alfred zu
Windischgrätz ... an die Bewohner jeder
Zunge und jedes Standes des Königreichs
Ungarn und des Grossfürstenthums Siebenbürgen.
[Wien,1848]

*pGB8
V6755R
11.13.48

broadside. 43x27cm.
Dated: Hauptquartier Schönbrunn den 13.
November 1848.
Another edition has a Hungarian translation
printed in a second column.

Austria. Armee. Stadt-Commandantur, Vienna, 1848.
Kundmachung. Da man wahrgenommen hat, dass
an öffentlichen Orten, besonders in Wirths- und
Kaffeehäusern von Fremden und Einheimischen
Reden geführt werden, welche zum Aufstande und
zum Aufruhr aufzureizen geeignet sind ...
[Wien]Aus der k.k.Hof- und Staats-Druckerei.
[1848]

*pGB8
V6755R
11.12.48

broadside. 44.5x28.5cm.
Dated & signed: Wien am 12. November 1848. Von
dem Vorstande der k. k. Central-Commission der
Stadt-Commandantur.   Freiherr von Cordon,
k. k. General-   Major.

Austria. Armee. Stadt-Commandantur, Vienna, 1848.
Kundmachung. Es ist sehr unangenehm
wahrgenommen worden, dass die in der Proclamation
Seiner Durchlaucht des Herrn Feldmarschalls
Fürsten zu Windisch-Grätz vom 1. November 1848
... angeordnete allgemeine Entwaffnung nicht mit
jenem Eifer und mit jener Bereitwilligkeit
durchgeführt werde, welche man zu erwarten
berechtigt war ...
[Wien]Aus der k.k.Hof- und Staatsdruckerei.
[1848]

*pGB8
V6755R
11.13.48

(See next card)

Austria, Lower. Laws, statutes, etc., 1835-1848
(Ferdinand I)
... Circulare der k. k. Landesregierung im
Erzherzogthume Oesterreich unter der Enns.
Betreffend die Blechdicke der Dampfkessel bei
Locomotiven.
[Wien]Aus der k.k.Hof- und Staatsdruckerei.
[1848]

*pGB8
V6755R
11.12.48

broadside. 38x23cm.
At head: № 49737.
Dated: Wien am 12. November 1848.

Austria. Armee. Stadt-Commandantur, Vienna, 1848.
Kundmachung ... [1848]   (Card 2)

*pGB8
V6755R
11.13.48

broadside. 44.5x27cm.
Dated & signed: Wien am 13. November 1848.
Vom Vorstande der k. k. Central-Commission
der Stadt-Commandantur. Frank, k. k. General-
Major.

Vienna. Gouverneur, 1848 (Welden)
An die rechtlichen und verständigen
Bewohner Wiens. Alle Folgen einer fürchterlichen
Anarchie sind in der schrecklichsten Gestalt an
Euch vorüber gezogen, und haben Zerstörung bis
in das Familienglück eines Jeden verbreitet
...
[Wien]Aus der k.k.Hof- und Staats-Druckerei.
[1848]

*pGB8
V6755R
11.12.48

broadside. 44.5x57cm.
Dated & signed: Wien am 12. November 1848.
Der k. k.   Gouverneur der
Hauptstadt Wien.   Welden, Feldmarschall-
Lieutenant.

Austria, Lower. Laws, statutes, etc., 1835-1848
(Ferdinand I)
... Circulare der k. k. Landesregierung im
Erzherzogthume Oesterreich unter der Enns.
Die Bestimmungen der Vorsichtsmassregeln
betreffend, welche die Zucker- und Mandoletti-
Bäcker und ähnliche Geschäftsleute bei ihrem
Geschäftsbetriebe in sanitätspolizeilicher
Hinsicht zu beobachten haben.
[Wien]Aus der k.k.Hof- und Staats-Druckerei.
[1848]

*pGB8
V6755R
11.15.48

(See next card)

Austria. Armee.
Proclamation des Fürsten Alfred zu
Windischgrätz ... an die Bewohner jeder Zunge
und jedes Standes des Königreichs Ungarn und
des Grossfürstenthums Siebenbürgen.
[Wien,1848]

*pGB8
V6755R
11.13.48

broadside. 38x51cm.
Dated: Hauptquartier Schönbrunn den 13.
November 1848.
This edition has a Hungarian translation
printed in a second column.

Austria, Lower. Laws, statutes, etc., 1835-1848
(Ferdinand I)   ... Circulare ... [1848]
(Card 2)

*pGB8
V6755R
11.15.48

[2]p. 38x23cm.
Caption title (at head: № 46898); imprint
on p.[2].
Dated: Wien am 15. November 1848.

*GB8
V6755R
11.15.48

Warum wurde Wien belagert? und Was haben die
Wiener jetzt zu thun?
[Wien,1848]
folder([4]p.) 26.5x21cm.
Signed at end: Sch—d—r.
On the October revolution.

---

*pGB8
V6755R
11.17.48

Vienna. Gemeinderat.
Kundmachung. Es ist in jeder Hinsicht dringend
nothwendig, dass in unsere schwer geprüfte Stadt
Ruhe, Ordnung und Sicherheit im vollsten Masse
zurückkehren ...
[Wien]Aus der k.k.Hof= und Staatsdruckerei.
[1848]
broadside. 44.5x28.5cm.
Dated & signed: Wien am 17. November 1848.
Der Gemeinderath der Stadt Wien.

---

*pGB8
V6755R
11.16.48

Vienna. Gemeinderat.
Kundmachung. Der Gemeinderath der Stadt Wien
hat durch Beschluss vom 6. d. M. in Anbetracht
der traurigen Verhältnisse zu Folge deren die
Möglichkeit mangelte, einen hinreichenden
Unterhalt bei Gewerben oder bei öffentlichen
Arbeiten zu finden ...
[Wien]Aus der k.k.Hof= und Staatsdruckerei.
[1848]
broadside. 44.5x28.5cm.
Dated: Wien den 16. November 1848.

---

*pGB8
V6755R
11.17.48

Vienna. Gemeinderat.
Wiederholte Warnung! Der Gemeinderath der
Stadt Wien hat die betrübende Erfahrung gemacht,
dass seine warnende Kundmachung vom 16.
d. M., bezüglich der Ablieferung der Waffen, den
beabsichtigten Erfolg nicht gehabt habe ...
[Wien]Aus der k.k.Hof= und Staatsdruckerei.
[1848]
broadside. 44.5x57cm.
Dated: Wien am 17. November 1848.
Large folio broadside.

---

*pGB8
V6755R
11.16.48

Vienna. Gemeinderat.
Mitbürger! Die Kundmachung des k. k. Herrn
General=Majors von Frank, Vorstandes der k. k.
Central=Commission der Stadt=Commandantur vom
15. d. M., durch welche die letzte Frist zur
Ablieferung der sämmtlichen Feuer=, Hieb= und
Stich=Waffen auf heute 10 Uhr Morgens
festgesetzt worden ist, spricht sich deutlich
dahin aus ...
[Wien]Aus der k.k.Hof= und Staatsdruckerei.
[1848]
                              (See next card)

---

*pGB8
V6755R
11.17.48

Vienna. Gemeinderat.
Wiederholte Warnung! Der Gemeinderath der
Stadt Wien hat die betrübende Erfahrung gemacht,
dass seine warnende Kundmachung vom 16. d. M.,
bezüglich der Ablieferung der Waffen, den
beabsichtigten.Erfolg nicht gehabt habe ...
[Wien]Aus der k.k.Hof= und Staatsdruckerei.
[1848]
broadside. 44.5x28.5cm.
Dated: Wien am 17. November 1848.
Small folio broadside.

---

*pGB8
V6755R
11.16.48

Vienna. Gemeinderat.   Mitbürger ... [1848]
                              (Card 2)
broadside. 44.5x28cm.
Dated & signed: Wien am 16. November 1848. Vom
Gemeinderathe der Stadt Wien.

---

*pGB8
V6755R
11.18.48

Austria, Lower.
Kundmachung. Da Seine Durchlaucht der Herr
k. k. Feldmarschall Fürst zu Windischgrätz über
Antrag Seiner Excellenz des Herrn Gouverneurs,
Feldmarschall-Lieutenants Freiherrn von Welden,
für die in Italien liegenden Truppenkörper unter
der Classe der für den activen Wehrstand
tauglichen Individuen der Bevölkerung eine
Werbung angeordnet haben ...
[Wien]Aus der k.k.Hof= und Staatsdruckerei.
[1848]
                              (See next card)

---

*pGB8
V6755R
11.17.48

Austria, Lower. Laws, statutes, etc., 1835-1848
          (Ferdinand I)
... Circulare der k. k. Landesregierung im
Erzherzogthume Oesterreich unter der Enns.
Betreffend die Einreihung des Schwefeläthers
und des Chloroforms in den Zoll=Tarif vom Jahre
1838.
[Wien]Aus der k.k.Hof= und Staatsdruckerei.
[1848]
broadside. 38x23cm.
At head: № 50510.
Dated: Wien am   17. November 1848.

---

*pGB8
V6755R
11.18.48

Austria, Lower.   Kundmachung ... [1848]
                              (Card 2)
broadside. 45x57cm.
Dated & signed: Wien am 18. November 1848.
Von der k. k. Nied. Oe. Landesregierung.

*pGB8
V6755R
11.18.48

Austria, Lower. Provinzial-Commission für die
Liquidirung der Jurisdictions-Kosten.
... Kundmachung. Ueber die Liquidirung der
Kosten für die Fortführung der Gerichtsbarkeit
und politischen Amtsverwaltung durch die
Communal= und Patrimonial=Behörden bis zur
Bestellung landesfürstlicher Behörden.
[Wien]Aus der k.k.Hof= und Staats=Druckerei.
[1848]
[5]p. 38x23cm.
Caption title (at head: № 1. L. C.); imprint
(See next card)

---

*pGB8
V6755R
11.18.48

Austria, Lower. Provinzial-Commission für die
Liquidirung der Jurisdictions-Kosten.
... Kundmachung ... [1848]   (Card 2)
on p.[2].
Signed & dated: Von der k. k. Nieder=Oester.
Provinzial=Commission für die Liquidirung der
Jurisdictions=Kosten. Wien am 18. November 1848.

---

*pGB8
V6755R
11.19.48

Austria. Armee. Stadt-Commandantur, Vienna, 1848.
Kundmachung. Jn dem fünften Absatze der
Proclamation Sr. Durchlaucht des Herrn
Feldmarschalls Fürsten zu Windischgrätz vom 1.
November 1848 wurde die Affigirung von Placaten
ohne hiezu eingeholter Bewilligung der k. k.
Militär=Behörde unter sonstiger Stellung des
dawider Handelnden vor das Militärgericht
verboten ...
[Wien]Aus der k.k.Hof= und Staatsdruckerei.
[1848]
(See next card)

---

*pGB8
V6755R
11.19.48

Austria. Armee. Stadt-Commandantur, Vienna, 1848.
Kundmachung ... [1848]   (Card 2)
broadside. 44.5x28.5cm.
Dated & signed: Wien am 19. November 1848. Von
dem Vorstande der Central-Commission der k.k.
Stadt-Commandantur. Frank, k. k. General=Major.

---

*pGB8
V6755R
11.19.48

Vienna. Gemeinderat.
Kundmachung. Der Gemeinderath der Stadt Wien
hat in Anbetracht der vielen Missbräuche, die
sich bei der Vertheilung der Brotzetteln eingeschlichen haben, den Beschluss gefasst, dass
die Ausgabe derselben mit Ende November
gänzlich eingestellt werde ...
[Wien]Aus der k.k.Hof= und Staatsdruckerei.
[1848]
broadside. 44.5x28cm.
Dated: Wien am 19. November 1848.

---

*pGB8
V6755R
11.19.48

Vienna. Gemeinderat.
Kundmachung. Mit auffallender Schnelligkeit
wird das Gerücht verbreitet, dass binnen sechs
Wochen keine Lebensmittel nach Wien geführt
werden sollen, wesshalb sich Jedermann für diesen
Zeitraum verproviantiren möge ...
[Wien,1848]
broadside. 37x22cm.
Dated & signed: Wien am 19. November 1848. Von
der Permanenz des Gemeinderathes.

---

*pGB8
V6755R
11.20.48

Austria. Armee.
Zum Armee=Befehl. Der Herr Feldmarschall Graf
Radetzky hat im eigenen und im Namen der unter
seinen Befehlen stehenden Armee an mich und die
unter meinem Kommando hier versammelten Truppen=
Worte der erhabensten Theilnahme an den
Ereignissen des 28., 30., 31. Oktober und 1.
November d. J. gerichtet ...
[Wien,1848]
broadside. 34x22cm.
Dated & signed: Hauptquartier Schönbrunn am
20. November 1848.   Fürst zu Windisch=Grätz,
k. k. Feld-   marschall.

---

*pGB8
V6755R
11.20.48

Austria. Armee. Zentral-Untersuchungs-Commission.
Kundmachung. Gemäss standrechtlichen
Urtheiles vom 18. d. M. ist Eduard Pallucci, in
Wien geboren, 35 Jahre alt, katholisch, ledig,
Doctor der Arzenei=Wissenschaft ... zum Tode
durch den Strang verurtheilt,--ferner ist Ludwig
Brzyiemski, aus Basel in der Schweiz gebürtig,
28 Jahre alt ... zur achtjährigen Schanzarbeit
in schweren Eisen condamnirt worden ...
[Wien]Aus der k.k.Hof= und Staatsdruckerei.
[1848]
(See next card)

---

*pGB8
V6755R
11.20.48

Austria. Armee. Zentral-Untersuchungs-Commission.
Kundmachung ... [1848]   (Card 2)
broadside. 45x29cm.
Dated & signed: Wien am 20. November 1848.
Von der k. k. Central-Untersuchungs-Commission.

---

*pGB8
V6755R
11.20.48

Austria. Justizministerium.
... Kundmachung. Durch die gegenwärtige
Hemmung des Verkehres mit Ungarn und die
hiedurch für die hiesigen Wechselschuldner
herbeigeführte Schwierigkeit, sich ihre in
Ungarn anzusprechenden Zahlungsmittel in der
gehörigen Zeit zu verschaffen ...
[Wien]Aus der k.k.Hof= und Staatsdruckerei.
[1848]
broadside. 44.5x28.5cm.
(See next card)

*pGB8
V6755R
11.20.48

Austria. Justizministerium. ... Kundmachung
... [1848]   (Card 2)
   At head: Nr. 4675/J.M. 1848.
   Dated & signed: Wien am 20. November 1848.
   Vom k. k. Ministerium der Justiz.

---

*pGB8
V6755R
11.22.48

Sankt Pölten, Austria. Kreisamt.
   ... Circulare. Wegen einer Sammlung für die
Verunglückten in Wien.
[Sankt Pölten,1848]
   broadside. 38x24cm.
   At head: Nro. 14460. 209.
   Dated & signed: Kreisamt St. Pölten den 22.
november 1848. Weinberger, Kreishauptmann.

---

*pGB8
V6755R
11.21.48

Austria. Armee. Zentral-Untersuchungs-Commission.
   Kundmachung. Johann Ritter von Vogtberg, zu
Wien geboren, 20 Jahre alt, katholisch, ledig,
Studirender; ferner Eduard Elgner, aus Ollmütz
in Mähren gebürtig, 25 Jahre alt, katholisch,
ledig, Schulgehilfe in der ersten Normal=
Classe am Neubau; endlich Ferdinand Schmalhofer,
zu Sechshaus bei Wien geboren, 20 Jahre alt,
katholisch, ledig, Kattundrucker=Geselle von
Profession ...
   [Wien]Aus der k.k.Hof= und Staats=Druckerei.
[1848]   (See next card)

---

*pGB8
V6755R
11.22.48

Vienna. Magistrat.
   Aufforderung. Von den durch die Ereignisse
der letzten Zeit abhanden gekommenen Effecten
sind nach sicheren Andeutungen viele in Privat=
Hände gekommen und werden, weil der Eigenthümer
nicht bekannt ist, zurückbehalten ...
   [Wien]Aus der k.k.Hof= und Staatsdruckerei.
[1848]
   broadside. 44.5x28cm.
   Dated & signed: Wien am 22. November 1848.
Von der Stadthauptmannschaft.

---

*pGB8
V6755R
11.21.48

Austria. Armee. Zentral-Untersuchungs-Commission.
   Kundmachung ... [1848]   (Card 2)
   broadside. 44.5x28cm.
   Dated & signed: Wien am 21. November 1848.
Von der k. k. Central-Untersuchungs-Commission.
Hipssich, k. k. General=Major.
   Changing the original death sentence of the 3
men to four years at hard labor.

---

*pGB8
V6755R
11.22.48

Vienna. Magistrat.
   Euer Wohlgeboren! Mehrere österreichische
Abgeordnete bei der constituirenden deutschen
Nationalversammlung zu Frankfurt am Main haben
sich aus Anlass der am 27. Oktober d. J. von
der letzteren gefassten, in den [Paragraphen].2
und 3 der künftigen deutschen Reichsverfassung
aufgeführten Beschlüsse, worin sie für die
Jntegrität des österreichischen Gesammtstaates
die grösste Gefahr erkennen, bewogen gefunden
...
   [Wien,1848]   (See next card)

---

*pGB8
V6755R
11.22.48

Austria. Armee. Stadt-Commandantur, Vienna, 1848.
   Kundmachung. Vom 24. des laufenden Monates
angefangen wird bei allen Linien die freie
Passage von 5 Uhr Morgens bis 8 Uhr Abends von
aussen nach innen, und umgekehrt den Fussgehern
und den Fahrenden ohne Vorweisung eines
Passirscheines gestattet ...
   [Wien]Aus der k.k.Hof= und Staatsdruckerei.
[1848]
   broadside. 44.5x28.5cm.
   Dated & signed: Wien am 22. November 1848.
Von der Central-Commission der k.k. Stadt-
Commandantur.   Frank, k. k. General=Major.

---

*pGB8
V6755R
11.22.48

Vienna. Magistrat.   Euer ... [1848]
                 (Card 2)
   folder([3]p.) 40x25cm.
   Caption title; signed & dated: Vom Magistrate
der k. k. Hauptstadt Wien am 22. November 1848.
   Includes (p.[2-3]) an address from the
Austrian delegates at Frankfurt, dated 1 November
1848.
   Printed address at foot of p.[1]: Sr. Wohlgeboren Herrn   als Wahlmann im Hauptwahlbezirke: Landstrasse.

---

*pGB8
V6755R
11.22.48

Austria, Lower. Laws, statutes, etc., 1835-1848
   (Ferdinand I)
   ... Circulare der k. k. Landesregierung im
Erzherzogthume Oesterreich unter der Enns.
Betreffend die Berichtigung eines in dem
allerhöchsten Patente vom 20. October 1848
wegen Ausschreibung der Steuern für das erste
Semester 1849 unterlaufenen Druckfehlers.
   [Wien]Aus der k.k.Hof= und Staats=Druckerei.
[1848]
   broadside. 38x23.5cm.
   At head: NO   52391.
   Dated: Wien am   22. November 1848.

---

*pGB8
V6755R
11.23.48

Austria. Armee. Zentral-Untersuchungs-Commission.
   Kundmachung. Joseph Aigner, aus Wien
gebürtig, 30 Jahre alt, katholisch, verheiratet,
Porträtmaler und Commandant der bestandenen
akademischen Legion, ist in Uibereinstimmung
mit dem erhobenen Thatbestande geständig und
überwiesen ...
   [Wien]Aus der k.k.Hof= und Staatsdruckerei.
[1848]
   broadside. 44.5x28.5cm.
                (See next card)

*pGB8
V6755R
11.23.48

Austria. Armee. Zentral-Untersuchungs-Commission.
Kundmachung ... [1848]   (Card 2)
Dated & signed: Wien am 23. November 1848.
Von der k. k. Militär-Central-Untersuchnngs[!]-
Commission.
Revoking Aigner's death sentence and setting
him free.

---

*pGB8
V6755R
11.26.48

Austria, Lower. Laws, statutes, etc., 1835-1848
(Ferdinand I)   ... Circulare ... [1848]
(Card 2)
broadside. 38.5x23cm.
At head: Nr.164. 3015/P.
Dated: Wien am 26. November 1848.

---

*pGB8
V6755R
11.24.48

Vienna. Gemeinderat.
Kundmachung. Der Gemeinderath der Stadt
Wien bringt hiemit den bei den sogenannten
Nothstandsbauten beschäftigten Arbeitern zur
Kenntniss, dass nicht nur die Vollendung der
begonnenen, sondern auch die Ausführung neuer
öffentlicher Bauten ...
[Wien]Aus der k.k.Hof= und Staatsdruckerei.
[1848]
broadside. 44.5x28.5cm.
Dated: Wien am 24. November 1848.

---

*pGB8
V6755R
11.27.48

Schwarzenberg, Felix, fürst zu, 1800-1852.
Cuvîntarea Prezidentului de ministeriu.
Rostită în sesiea Dietei împărăției în Kremzir
la 27. noemvrie 1848.
[Wien,1848]
[2]p. 44.5x28cm.
Title as above transliterated from Rumanian
characters.

---

*pGB8
V6755R
11.24.48

Vienna. Gouverneur, 1848 (Welden)
Bekanntmachung des k. k. Stadt=Gouvernements.
Die mir als Gouverneur der Stadt Wien von
Seiner Durchlaucht dem Herrn Feldmarschall
Fürsten zu Windischgrätz zugekommene
nachstehende Proclamation ...
[Wien]Aus der k.k.Hof= und Staatsdruckerei.
[1848]
broadside. 45x57cm.
Dated & signed: Wien am 24 November 1848.
Welden, k. k. Feldmarschall=Lieutenant und
(See next card)

---

*pGB8
V6755R
11.27.48

Schwarzenberg, Felix, fürst zu, 1800-1852.
Discorso del Ministro presidente tenuto a
Kremsier nella seduta della costituente li 27
novembre 1848.
[Wien,1848]
[2]p. 44.5x28.5cm.
Caption title.

---

*pGB8
V6755R
11.24.48

Vienna. Gouverneur, 1848 (Welden)
Bekanntmachung ... [1848]
(Card 2)
Gouverneur.
·Windischgrätz's proclamation is dated:
Hauptquartier Schönbrunn am 23. November
1848.

---

*pGB8
V6755R
11.27.48

Schwarzenberg, Felix, fürst zu, 1800-1852.
Govor ministarskoga presidenta u sjednici
državnoga sabora u Kromjerižu 27 novembra 1848.
[Wien,1848]
broadside. 44.5x28.5cm.

---

*pGB8
V6755R
11.26.48

Austria, Lower. Laws, statutes, etc., 1835-1848
(Ferdinand I)
... Circulare der k. k. Nieder-Oester.
Landesregierung. Jn Folge Erlasses des k. k.
Finanz=Ministeriums vom 24. November 1. J.,
Z.7024-F.M., wird die Ausfuhr von Monturstüchern,
Fussbekleidungen, Waffen und Munition in das
im Aufstande begriffene Königreich Ungarn bis
auf Weiteres verboten ...
[Wien]Aus der k.k.Hof= und Staatsdruckerei.
[1848]
(See next card)

---

*pGB8
V6755R
11.27.48

Schwarzenberg, Felix, fürst zu, 1800-1852.
Przemowa prezydenta ministrów miana na
posiedzeniu sejmu walnego w Kromiezyrzu dnia
27. listopada 1848.
[Wien,1848]
broadside. 44.5x28.5cm.

*pGB8
V6755R
11.27.48

Schwarzenberg, Felix, fürst zu, 1800-1852.
... Vortrag des Minister-Präsidenten.
Gehalten in der Reichstagssitzung zu Kremsier
den 27. November 1848.
[Wien]Aus der k.k.Hof= und Staatsdruckerei.
[1848]
[2]p. 40.5x25cm.
Caption title (at head: Nro.15644./225.);
imprint on p.[2].

*pGB8
V6755R
11.30.48

Vienna. Voters, 1st district.
An den Abgeordneten des 1. Wahlbezirkes der
Haupt= und Residenzstadt Wien zur deutschen
National-Versammlung Dr. Eugen von Mühlfeld.
[Wien,1848]
folder([2]p.) 42x26cm.
Caption title; dated & signed on p.[2]: Wien,
am 30. November 1848. Die Wahlmannschaft des
ersten Wahlbezirkes der Stadt Wien.

*pGB8
V6755R
11.30.48

Vienna. Voters, 1st district.
Eure Majestät! Als im letzverflossenen
Frühjahre in ganz Deutschland der Ruf nach einer
Neugestaltung seiner Bundesverhältnisse laut
wurde, fand derselbe auch in den zur Krone
Eurer Majestät gehörigen Ländern deutscher Zunge
den lebhaftesten Wiederhall ...
[Wien,1848]
folder([3]p.) 42x26cm.
Caption title; dated & signed on p.[3]: Wien,
am 30. November 1848. Die Wahlmänner des ersten
Wahl-Bezirkes der Stadt Wien.

*pGB8
V6755R
12.1.48

Austria. Armee. Zentral-Untersuchungs-Commission.
Kundmachung. Carl David, Civil-Schlossergeselle
aus Zwettl, V. O. M. B., in Niederösterreich
gebürtig, 28 Jahre alt, katholisch, ledig, ist
durch sein mit dem erhobenen Thatbestande
übereinstimmendes Geständniss überwiesen ...
[Wien]Aus der k.k.Hof- und Staats=Druckerei.
[1848]
broadside. 45x28.5cm.
Dated & signed: Wien am 1. December 1848. Von
der k. k. Militär-Central-Untersuchungs-Commission.

*pGB8
V6755R
12.1.48

Austria. Armee. Zentral-Untersuchungs-Commission.
Kundmachung. Mateo Padovani, aus Triest
gebürtig, 33 Jahre alt, israelitischer Religion,
verheirathet, kinderlos, vormals Agent einer
Triester Versicherungs=Gesellschaft, ist durch
übereinstimmende mehrere eidliche
Zeugenaussagen überwiesen ...
[Wien]Aus der k.k.Hof= und Staats=Druckerei.
[1848]
broadside. 44x28.5cm.
Dated & signed: Wien am 1. December 1848. Von
der k. k. Militär-Central-Untersuchungs-
Commission.

*pGB8
V6755R
12.1.48

Austria. Armee. Zentral-Untersuchungs-Commission.
Kundmachung. Wenzel Pova, aus Zeban in
Oesterreich gebürtig, 24 Jahre alt, katholisch,
ledig, Concepts=Practikant des hiesigen Criminal-
gerichtes ist durch sein mit dem hergestellten
Thatbestande übereinstimmendes Geständniss
überwiesen ...
[Wien]Aus der k.k.Hof= und Staats=Druckerei.
[1848]
broadside. 45x28cm.
Dated & signed: Wien am 1. December 1848. Von
der k. k. Militär- Central-Untersuchungs-
Commission.

*pGB8
V6755R
12.2.48

Austria. Armee. Stadt-Commandantur, Vienna, 1848.
... An die k. k. Armee. Seine Majestät der
Kaiser Ferdinand I., haben Kraft des
angeschlossenen Manifestes die Krone Seines
Reiches niedergelegt ...
[Wien]Aus der k.k.Hof= und Staatsdruckerei.
[1848]
broadside. 44.5x29cm.
At head: Nr.6134./M.K.
Dated & signed: Kremsier den 2. December 1848.
Cordon m. p., General=Major.

*pGB8
V6755R
12.2.48

Austria. Armee. Stadt-Commandantur, Vienna, 1848.
... An die k. k. Armee. Seine Majestät der
Kaiser Franz Joseph I. hat den Thron Seiner
Väter bestiegen ...
[Wien]Aus der k.k.Hof= und Staats=Druckerei.
[1848]
broadside. 45x28.5cm.
At head: Nr.6134./M.K.
Dated & signed: Kremsier am 2. December 1848.
Cordon m. p., General=Major.

*pGB8
V6755R
12.2.48

Austria. Sovereigns, etc., 1835-1848
(Ferdinand I)
Mi Első Ferdinánd, Isten kedvező kegyelméből
Ausztriai császár ... Visszatekintve
uralkodásunk tizenhárom évvel meghaladott
folyamatára, megnyugtató Reánk nézve azon tiszta
öntudat ...
[Olmutz,1848]
[2]p. 38x25.5cm.
Caption title; dated at end: Kelt királyi
fővárosunkban Ollmitzban, December hó 2-kán
az úr 1848-dik ...
Announcing his abdication.

*pGB8
V6755R
12.2.48

Austria. Sovereigns, etc., 1835-1848
(Ferdinand I)
Mi Ferdinand Prvi, po Božijoj milosti cesar
austrijanski ... Kada smo Mi, poslije smrti
Našega gospodina octa, pokojnoga Franja Prvoga,
uzišli na prestolje po zakonitomu nasljedovanju
...
[Wien,1848]
[2]p. 44.5x29cm.
Caption title.
(See next card)

*pGB8
V6755R
12.2.48

Austria. Sovereigns, etc., 1835-1848
   (Ferdinand I) Mi Ferdinand Prvi ...
[1848]   (Card 2)

"Dano u Našemu kraljevskomu poglavitomu gradu
Olomucu drugoga prosinca 1848sme, a Našega
carovanja 14ste godine."
Ferdinand's proclamation of abdication (2
December 1848) in favor of Franz Joseph.

---

*pGB8
V6755R
12.2.48

Austria. Sovereigns, etc., 1835-1848
   (Ferdinand I) Noi Ferdinand ... [1848]
           (Card 2)

[2]p. 44.5x28cm.
Caption title.
"Dat în regeasca Noastra capitala Olomuţ, la
doua decemvrie în anul una mie opt sute
patruzeci şi opt ..."
Transliterated from Rumanian characters.
Announcing his abdication.

---

*pGB8
V6755R
12.2.48

Austria. Sovereigns, etc., 1835-1848
   (Ferdinand I)
My Ferdinand Pervyi, Bozhieiu milostiiu
tsesar Avstrii ... Vstupivashi na tron po
otshestvii z sego sveta Nashogo gospodina
ottsa, s. p. tsesaria Frantsa Pershogo v
ustavnom nasledstve, pronikneni sviatostiiu i
strogostiiu Nashykh oboviazkov blagalismo pered
vsem Bga o ego pomoch ...
   [Wien,1848]

broadside. 45x28cm.
           (See next card)

---

*pGB8
V6755R
12.2.48

Austria. Sovereigns, etc., 1835-1848
   (Ferdinand I)
Noi Ferdinando Primo, per la grazia di Dio
imperatore d'Austria ... Allorquando dopo la
morte del Nostro genitore l'imperatore Francesco
I, salimmo per diritto di successione sul trono;
penetrati della santità e gravità dei Nostri
doveri implorammo prima di tutto l'ajuto divino
...
   [Wien,1848]
           (See next card)

---

*pGB8
V6755R
12.2.48

Austria. Sovereigns, etc., 1835-1848
   (Ferdinand I) My Ferdinand Pervyi
   ... [1848]   (Card 2)

"Dano v nashom korolevskom golovnom meste
Golomutsu dnia vtorogo grudnia roku tysiach
osmsotnogo chetirdesiat' i osmogo ..."
Transliterated from Russian characters.
Announcing his abdication.

---

*pGB8
V6755R
12.2.48

Austria. Sovereigns, etc., 1835-1848
   (Ferdinand I) Noi Ferdinando Primo ...
[1848]   (Card 2)

[2]p. 44.5x28.5cm.
Caption title; dated at end: Dato nella Nostra
regia città capitale di Olmitz li 2 decembre
dell'anno 1848...
Announcing his abdication.

---

*pGB8
V6755R
12.2.48

Austria. Sovereigns, etc., 1835-1848
   (Ferdinand I)
My Ferdynand pierwszy, z Bożej łaski cesarz
Austryjacki ... Wstąpiwszy na tron w prawném
następstwie po zejściu naszego ojca, s. p.
Franciszka pierwszego ...
   [Wien,1848]
broadside. 44.5x28.5cm.
"Dano w Naszem królewskiem głównem mieście,
Ołomuńcu, dnia 2go grudnia, tysiąc ośmset
czterdziestego ósmego a Naszego panowania
czternastego   roku."
Announcing his abdication.

---

*pGB8
V6755R
12.2.48

Austria. Sovereigns, etc., 1835-1848
   (Ferdinand I)
Wir Ferdinand der Erste, von Gottes Gnaden
Kaiser von Oesterreich ... Als Wir nach dem
Hintritte Unseres Herrn Vaters, weiland Kaiser
Franz des Ersten, in gesetzlicher Erbfolge, den
Thron bestiegen, flehten Wir, durchdrungen von
der Heiligkeit und dem Ernste Unserer
Pflichten, vor Allem Gott um Seinen Beistand an
...
   [Wien]Aus der k.k.Hof= und Staats=Druckerei.
[1848]
           (See next card)

---

*pGB8
V6755R
12.2.48

Austria. Sovereigns, etc., 1835-1848
   (Ferdinand I)
Noi Ferdinand întaiu, din mila lui Dumnezeu
împarat de Austria ... Când dupa mutarea din
vieaţa a dumisale parintelui Nostru,
împaratului Franţisku întaiu de ferice pomenire,
Noi în legiuita urmare klironomiceasca Ne
suiram pe tron, patrunşi de sfinţeniea şi de
înalta importanţa a datorinţelor Noastre, Noi
mai înainete de toate rugaram pe Dumnezeu pentru
al Sau ajutoriu ...
   [Wien,1848]
           (See next card)

---

*pGB8
V6755R
12.2.48

Austria. Sovereigns, etc., 1835-1848
   (Ferdinand I) Wir Ferdinand der Erste ...
[1848]   (Card 2)

[2]p. 45x28.5cm.
Caption title; imprint on p.[2]; dated at end:
Gegeben in Unserer königlichen Hauptstadt Olmitz,
den zweiten December im ein tausend acht hundert
und acht und vierzigsten, Unserer Reiche dem
vierzehnten Jahre.
Announcing his abdication.

Austria. Sovereigns, etc., 1835-1848
(Ferdinand I)
*pGB8 V6755R 12.2.48

Wir Ferdinand der Erste, von Gottes Gnaden Kaiser von Oesterreich ... Zurückblickend auf den über dreizehn Jahre dauernden Verlauf Unserer Regierung ...
[Olmütz,1848]

[2]p. 43x27cm.

Caption title; dated at end: Gegeben in Unserer königlichen Hauptstadt Olmütz, am zweiten December im Jahre des Heils ein tausend acht hundert und acht und vierzig ... Announcing his abdication.

Austria. Sovereigns, etc., 1848-1916
(Franz Josef I)   Noi Francesco Giuseppe Primo ... [1848]   (Card 2)
*pGB8 V6755R 12.2.48

[2]p. 44.5x27.5cm.
Caption title; dated at end: Dato nella Nostra regia città capitale di Olmütz il 2 dicembre dell'anno di grazia 1848.

Austria. Sovereigns, etc., 1848-1916
(Franz Josef I)
*pGB8 V6755R 12.2.48

Mi Első Ferencz-Jósef, Isten kedvező kegyelméből Ausztriai császár ... Miután fenséges nagybátyánk, ö felsége I. Ferdinánd császár ...
[Olmutz,1848]

[2]p. 38x25.5cm.

Caption title; dated at end: Kelt királyi fővárosunkban Ollmützban, December hó 2-kán az úr 1848-dik esztendejében.
Announcing his accession to the throne.

Austria. Sovereigns, etc., 1848-1916
(Franz Josef I)
*pGB8 V6755R 12.2.48

Noi Franţiscu Josif Întăiu, din mila lui Dumnezeu Împărat de Austria ... Prin abdicaţiea de tron a Înălţatului Nostru unkiu, Împăratalui şi regelui Ferdinand Întăiu ... Noi vestim prin aceasta foarte solenel tuturor popoarelor monarhiei suirea Noastră pe tron supt numele Franţisku Josif Întăilea ...
[Wien,1848]

(See next card)

Austria. Sovereigns, etc., 1848-1916
(Franz Josef I)
*pGB8 V6755R 12.2.48

My Frants Iosif Pervyi, Bozhieiu milostiiu tsesar' Avstrii ... Otrecheniem sia tronu Nashogo vysotnogo stryia tsesaria i korolia Ferdinanda Pervogo ... vozveshchaem sim nainarochneishe vsem narodom monarkhii Nashe vstuplen'e na tron pod imenem Frantsa Iosifa Pervogo ...
[Wien,1848]

broadside. 44.5x28cm.   (See next card)

Austria. Sovereigns, etc., 1848-1916
(Franz Josef I)   Noi Franţiscu Josif Întăiu ... [1848]   (Card 2)
*pGB8 V6755R 12.2.48

[2]p. 44.5x28cm.
Caption title.
"Aşa sau dat în regeaska capitala Noastra Olomuţ, la doă decemvrie în anul mântuirei una mie optsute patruzeci şi opt."
Transliterated from Rumanian characters.
Announcing his accession to the throne.

Austria. Sovereigns, etc., 1848-1916
(Franz Josef I)   My Frants Iosif Pervyi ... [1848]   (Card 2)
*pGB8 V6755R 12.2.48

"Dano v nashom korolevskom golovnom meste Golomutsu dnia vtorogo grudnia roku spaseniia tysiach' osmsotnogo chetirdesiat' i osmogo."
Transliterated from Russian characters.
Announcing his accession to the throne.

Austria. Sovereigns, etc., 1848-1916
(Franz Josef I)
*pGB8 V6755R 12.2.48

Wir Franz Joseph der Erste, von Gottes Gnaden Kaiser von Oesterreich ... Durch die Thronentsagung Unseres erhabenen Oheims, Kaisers und Königs Ferdinand des Ersten ... verkündigen Wir hiemit feierlichst allen Völkern der Monarchie Unsere Thronbesteigung unter dem Namen Franz Joseph des Ersten ...
[Wien]Aus der k.k.Hof- und Staats-Druckerei. [1848]

(See next card)

Austria. Sovereigns, etc., 1848-1916
(Franz Josef I)
*pGB8 V6755R 12.2.48

Noi Francesco Giuseppe Primo, per la grazia di Dio imperatore d'Austria ... Chiamati dalla sanzione prammatica, dietro l'abdicazione del Nostro augusto zio l'imperatore e re Ferdinando ... annunciamo solennemente colle presenti a tutti i popoli della monarchia la Nostra assunzione al trono col nome di Francesco Giuseppe Primo ...
[Wien,1848]

(See next card)

Austria. Sovereigns, etc., 1848-1916
(Franz Josef I)   Wir Franz Joseph der Erste ... [1848]   (Card 2)
*pGB8 V6755R 12.2.48

broadside. 44.5x57cm.
"So gegeben in Unserer königlichen Hauptstadt Ollmütz, den zweiten December im Jahre des Heils eintausend achthundert und acht und vierzig."

*pGB8
V6755R
12.2.48

Austria. Sovereigns, etc., 1848-1916
(Franz Josef I)
Wir Franz Joseph der Erste, von Gottes Gnaden
Kaiser von Oesterreich ... Durch die
Thronentsagung Unseres erhabenen Oheims,
Kaisers und Königs Ferdinand des Ersten ...
verkündigen Wir hiemit feierlichst allen
Völkern der Monarchie Unsere Thronbesteigung
unter dem Namen Franz Joseph des Ersten ...
    [Wien]Aus der k.k.Hof= und Staats=Druckerei.
[1848]

(See next card)

---

*pGB8
V6755R
12.5.48

Austria. Sovereigns, etc., 1848-1916
(Franz Josef I)
Wir Franz Joseph der Erste, von Gottes Gnaden
Kaiser von Oesterreich ... Haben in dem
Anbetrachte, dass die bisher in den militärisch=
conscribirten Provinzen bestehenden
Recrutirungs=Vorschriften dem Grundsatze der
Gleichstellung aller Staatsbürger vor dem
Gesetze nicht entsprechen ...
    [Wien]Aus der k.k.Hof= und Staats=Druckerei.
[1848]

(See next card)

---

*pGB8
V6755R
12.2.48

Austria. Sovereigns, etc., 1848-1916
(Franz Josef I) Wir Franz Joseph der
Erste ... [1848]   (Card 2)

[2]p. 44.5x28cm.
Caption title; imprint on p.[2].
"So gegeben in Unserer königlichen Hauptstadt
Olmütz, den zweiten December im Jahre des
Heils eintausend achthundert und acht und
vierzig."

---

*pGB8
V6755R
12.5.48

Austria. Sovereigns, etc., 1848-1916
(Franz Josef I) Wir Franz Joseph der
Erste ... [1848]   (Card 2)

folder([4]p.) 44.5x29cm.
Caption title; imprint on p.[4]; dated at end:
Gegeben in Unserer königlichen Hauptstadt Olmütz
am 5. December 1848.

---

*pGB8
V6755R
12.2.48

Vienna. Voters, 4th district.
Euere kaiserlich-königliche apostolische
Majestät! Die verhängnissvolle Richtung, welche
die constituirende deutsche National-
Versammlung zu Frankfurt durch die vorläufige
Beschliessung des 2. und 3. Paragraphen der
künftigen deutschen Reichs-Verfassung genommen
hat ...
    [Wien]Druck von Ullrich.[1848]
    [2]p. 39.5x25cm.
    Caption title; imprint on p.[2]; dated &
signed: Wien am 2. Dezember 1848. Die
Wahlmänner des   Haupt=Wahlbezirkes Wieden
für den Frank=   furtertag.

---

*pGB8
V6755R
12.5.48

Vienna. Magistrat.
Kundmachung. Zufolge Erlasses der hohen k. k.
Militär=Stadt=Commandantur wurde die Bewilligung
ertheilt, dass die Gast= und Kaffehhäuser in
den Vorstädten gleich jenen in der inneren
Stadt während des Belagerungszustandes bis 11
Uhr Nachts geöffnet bleiben dürfen ...
    [Wien]Aus der k.k.Hof= und Staatsdruckerei.
[1848]

    broadside. 45x29cm.
    Dated & signed: Wien am 5. December 1848.
Von der Stadt-   hauptmannschaft.

---

*pGB8
V6755R
12.3.48

Austria. Armee.
Kundmachung. Die freiwillige Werbung für
die in Jtalien liegenden Truppenkörper wird ...
in der Caserne der Alservorstadt und in dem
Gemeindehause am Schottenfelde fortgesetzt
werden ...
    [Wien]Aus der k.k.Hof= und Staatsdruckerei.
[1848]

    broadside. 44.5x56.5cm.
    Dated: Wien am 3. December 1848.

---

*pGB8
V6755R
12.6.48

Vienna. Magistrat.
Kundmachung. Durch die Wahrnehmung, dass die
Schank= Gast=, und Kaffehhaus=Localitäten,
welche nach der gegenwärtig bestehenden Vorschrift in der inneren Stadt und in den Vorstädten um 11 Uhr Nachts geschlossen werden
sollen, an manchen Orten noch über diese fest-
gesetzte Zeit offen gehalten werden ...
    [Wien]Aus der k.k.Hof= und Staatsdruckerei.
[1848]
    broadside. 44.5x28.5cm.
    Dated & signed: Wien am 6. December 1848.
Von der Stadt-   hauptmannschaft.

---

*pGB8
V6755R
12.3.48

Austria, Lower.
Circulare. Die allgemeinen Klagen über Wald-
und Jagdfrevel, verübt von Seite des Landvolkes,
an denen in einigen Orten sogar die Nationalgarden Theil genommen haben sollen ...
    [Wien]Aus der k.k.Hof= und Staatsdruckerei.
[1848]
    [2]p. 36x21cm.
    Caption title; imprint on p.[2]; dated &
signed: Wien am 3. December 1848. Von dem k. k.
Nieder-Oester. Landespräsidium. Lamberg.

---

*pGB8
V6755R
12.7.48

Austria. Armee. Stadt-Commandantur, Vienna, 1848.
Kundmachung. Da man neuerdings wahrgenommen
hat, dass an öffentlichen Orten, besonders in
Wirths= und Kaffehhäusern von Fremden und
Einheimischen Reden geführt werden, welche zum
Aufstande und zum Aufruhr aufzureizen geeignet
sind ...
    [Wien]Aus der k.k.Hof= und Staatsdruckerei.
[1848]

    broadside. 44.5x28.5cm.
    Dated & signed: Wien am 7. December 1848. Von
dem Vorstande der   k. k. Central-Commission
der Stadt-Com-   mandantur. Frank, k. k.
General-Major.

*pGB8
V6755R
12.7.48

Austria. Armee. Zentral-Untersuchungs-Commission.
Kundmachung. Johann Horvath, aus Csodno,
Oedenburger Comitates in Ungarn geburtig, 44
Jahre alt, katholisch, ledig, Schmidgeselle von
Profession und ausgedienter Capitulant des Inf.
Reg. E. H. Ernst ist bei erhobenem Thatbestande
theils geständig, theils durch Zeugenaussagen
rechtlich überwiesen ...
[Wien]Aus der k.k.Hof= und Staatsdruckerei.
[1848]

(See next card)

---

*pGB8
V6755R
12.9.48

Austria. Armee. Zentral-Untersuchungs-Commission.
Kundmachung ... [1848]   (Card 2)
broadside. 44.5x28.5cm.
Dated & signed: Wien den 9. December 1848. Von
der k. k. Militär-Central-Untersuchungs-
Commission.

---

*pGB8
V6755R
12.7.48

Austria. Armee. Zentral-Untersuchungs-Commission.
Kundmachung ... [1848]   (Card 2)
broadside. 45x28.5cm.
Dated & signed: Wien den 7. December 1848. Von
der k. k. Militär-Central-Untersuchungs-
Commission.

---

*pGB8
V6755R
12.9.48

Austria. Armee. Zentral-Untersuchungs-Commission.
Kundmachung. Johann Urban, von Wien geburtig,
37 Jahre alt, katholisch, verheirathet, vormals
als Geschäftsführer in einer Bandfabrik
bedienstet gewesen, und im Juli dieses Jahres zu
berittenen Abtheilung der Sicherheitswache
eingereiht ...
[Wien]Aus der k.k.Hof= und Staatsdruckerei.
[1848]
broadside. 45x28.5cm.
Dated & signed: Wien den 9. December 1848. Von
der k. k. Militär- Central-Untersuchungs-
Commission.

---

*pGB8
V6755R
12.8.48

Austria. Armee. Stadt-Commandantur, Vienna, 1848.
Kundmachung. Es hat sich, wie man vernimmt,
unter der Bevölkerung Wiens ziemlich allgemein
die Meinung verbreitet, dass in Folge der
Proclamation Sr. Durchlaucht des k. k. Herrn
Feldmarschalls.Fürsten zu Windischgrätz, vom 23.
v. M. ... das standrechtliche Verfahren für
alle Fälle überhaupt aufgehoben worden sei ...
[Wien](Aus der k.k.Hof= und Staatsdruckerei.)
[1848]
broadside. 45x26.5cm.
Dated & signed: Wien am 8. December 1848.
Von der k. k. Central-Commission der k.
k. Stadt-Com-   mandantur.

---

*GB8
V6755R
12.10.48

Frei-christliche Gemeinde, Vienna.
Memorandum der frei-christlichen Gemeinde in
Wien an den hohen Reichstag!
[Wien]Gedruckt bei J.N.Fridrich.[1848]
8p. 26x17cm.
Caption title; imprint on p.8; dated on p.4:
Wien den 10. Dezember 1848.
"Verfassung der frei-christlichen Gemeinde in
Wien": p.[5]-8.

---

*pGB8
V6755R
12.8.48

Austria. Armee. Stadt-Commandantur, Vienna, 1848.
Proclamation. Ungeachtet der Termin zur
Ablieferung der Waffen mehrmals verlängert
worden ist, und der Gemeinderath der
Residenzstadt Wien hierwegen an die Bevölkerung
wiederholte und wohlmeinende Warnungen ergehen
liess ...
[Wien](Aus der k.k.Hof= und Staatsdruckerei.)
[1848]
broadside. 45x28.5cm.
Dated & signed: Wien am 8. December 1848. Von
der Central=Commission der k. k. Stadt=Com-
mandantur.

---

*pGB8
V6755R
12.12.48

Austria. Armee. Zentral-Untersuchungs-Commission.
Kundmachung. Anton Heizerath, von Wien
geburtig, 55 Jahre alt, katholisch, verheirathet,
vormals herrschaftlicher Amtsschreiber, letzterer
Zeit Bau=Aufseher bei den hiesigen Erdarbeiten,
hat zu Folge seines mit dem hergestellten
Thatbestande übereinstimmenden eigenen
Geständnisses und mehrerer eidlicher Zeugenaussagen ...
[Wien]Aus der k.k.Hof= und Staatsdruckerei.
[1848]

(See next card)

---

*pGB8
V6755R
12.9.48

Austria. Armee. Zentral-Untersuchungs-Commission.
Kundmachung. Alexander Skarbek von Leszczynski,
aus Wien geburtig, 46 Jahre alt, katholisch,
ledig, Privatier, ehemals k. k. Lieutenant,
letztere Monate Chef des Nationalgarde=Bezirkes
Nr. 1, hat laut erhobenen Thatbestandes und
seines mit demselben übereinstimmenden
Geständnisses nicht nur den Pflichten eines
redlichen Staatsbürgers überhaupt zuwider ...
[Wien]Aus der k.k.Hof= und Staatsdruckerei.
[1848]

(See next card)

---

*pGB8
V6755R
12.12.48

Austria. Armee. Zentral-Untersuchungs-Commission.
Kundmachung ... [1848]   (Card 2)
broadside. 45:28.5cm.
Dated & signed: Wien den 12. December 1848.
Von der k. k. Militär-Central-Untersuchungs-
Commission.

*pGB8
V6755R
12.12.48

[Milde, Vinzenz Eduard, abp. of Vienna, 1777-1853]
Hohe Reichsversammlung! Der öffentlich bekannt gemachte Entwurf der Grundrechte der österreichischen Constitution muss die Aufmerksamkeit jedes Staatsbürgers auf sich ziehen, und die unterfertigten Bischöfe des Erzherzogthums Oesterreich ob und unter der Enns sind nicht nur durch die pflichtmässige Theilnahme an dem Wohle des Staates ...
[Wien]Gedruckt bei Leopold Grund.[1848]
(See next card)

*pGB8
V6755R
12.12.48

[Milde, Vinzenz Eduard, abp. of Vienna, 1777-1853]   Hohe Reichsversammlung ...
[1848]   (Card 2)
[6]p. 35x22.5cm.
Caption title; imprint on p.[6]; dated & signed at end: Wien, den 12. Dezember 1848. Vincenz Eduard, Fürsterzbischof von Wien. Gregor, Bischof von Linz. Anton Buchmayr, Bischof von St. Pölten.

*pGB8
V6755R
12.13.48

Austria. Armee.
Proclamation des Fürsten Alfred zu Windischgrätz ... Bewohner Ungarns und Siebenbürgens! Aus meiner Proklamation vom 13. November 1. J. konntet Jhr vernehmen, zu welchem Zwecke ich Euer Land betrete ...
[Wien,1848]
broadside. 38x51cm.
Dated: Hauptquartier Schönbrunn am 13. December 1848.
German version in left column; Hungarian version in right column begins: Herczeg Windischgrätz Alfred ... Proclamatioja. Magyar és Erdély lakosaihoz! ...

*pGB8
V6755R
12.13.48

Austria. Armee. Zentral-Untersuchungs-Commission.
Kundmachung. Franz Xaver Sinsler, aus Friedek in k. k. Schlesien gebürtig, 38 Jahre alt, katholisch, verheirathet, Mechaniker, ist theils durch Geständniss, theils durch Zusammentreffen der Umstände überwiesen ...
[Wien]Aus der k.k.Hof= und Staatsdruckerei.
[1848]
broadside. 44.5x29cm.
Dated & signed: Wien den 13. December 1848.
Von der k. k. Militär-Central-Untersuchungs- Commission.

*pGB8
V6755R
12.13.48

Austria, Lower. Laws, statutes, etc., 1848-1916
(Franz Josef I)
... Circulare der k. k. Landesregierung im Erzherzogthume Oesterreich unter der Enns. Betreffend das provisorische Gesetz für die Errichtung von Handelskammern.
[Wien]Aus der k.k.Hof= und Staatsdruckerei.
[1848]
folder([4]p.) 38x23cm.
Caption title (at head: № 55466); imprint on p.[4].
Dated: Wien am   13. December 1848.

*pGB8
V6755R
12.14.48

Austria. Armee.
Proklamation des Fürsten Alfred zu Windischgrätz ... an das Landvolk in Ungarn und Siebenbürgen. Mit dem allerhöchsten Manifeste vom 7. November 1. J. ist Euch bereits die Versicherung ertheilt worden dass die durch die Gesetze vom Monate April 1. J. gewährten Befreiungen von der Robot und vom Zehent unangetastet bleiben ...
[Wien]Aus der k.k.Hof= und Staatsdruckerei.
[1848]
broadside.   44.5x28.5cm.
Dated: Haupt-   quartier Schönbrunn am
14. December 1848.

*pGB8
V6755R
12.14.48

Austria. Armee. Zentral-Untersuchungs-Commission.
Kundmachung. Wenzel Blaszek, aus Podiebrad in Böhmen gebürtig, 27 Jahre alt, katholisch, ledig, Schneidergeselle, ist durch Zusammentreffen der Umstände überwiesen, am 27. v. M. in einem hiesigen Branntweinhause politische Reden gefährlichen Jnhaltes gegen die gesetzliche Ordnung geführt zu haben ...
[Wien]Aus der k.k.Hof= und Staatsdruckerei.
[1848]
broadside. 44.5x28.5cm.
(See next card)

*pGB8
V6755R
12.14.48

Austria. Armee. Zentral-Untersuchungs-Commission.
Kundmachung ... [1848] (Card 2)
Dated & signed: Wien am 14. December 1848. Von der k. k. Militär-Central-Untersuchungs-Commission.

*pGB8
V6755R
12.15.48

Austria. Armee. Zentral-Untersuchungs-Commission.
Kundmachung. Carl Pfanl, aus Sechshaus bei Wien gebürtig, 23 Jahre alt, katholisch, ledig, Fleischhauergeselle, ist durch die mit dem erhobenen Thatbestande vollkommen übereinstimmende eidliche Aussage mehrerer Zeugen überwiesen ...
[Wien]Aus der k.k.Hof= und Staatsdruckerei.
[1848]
broadside. 44.5x28.5cm.
Dated & signed: Wien am 15. December 1848.
Von der·k. k.   Militär-Central-Untersuchungs- Commission.

*pGB8
V6755R
12.16.48

Austria. Armee. Zentral-Untersuchungs-Commission.
Kundmachung. Franz Fizia, aus Czernisko in Schlesien gebürtig, 54 Jahre alt, katholisch, verheirathet, vormals Wachszieher, seit längerer Zeit ganz ohne Beschäftigung, ist bei ordentlich erhobenem Thatbestande, theils durch mehrere beeidete Zeugenaussagen, theils auch durch sein eigenes Geständniss überwiesen ...
[Wien]Aus der k.k.Hof= und Staatsdruckerei.
[1848]
(See next card)

*pGB8
V6755R
12.16.48

Austria. Armee. Zentral-Untersuchungs-Commission.
Kundmachung ... [1848]   (Card 2)
  broadside. 44.5x28.5cm.
  Dated & signed: Wien am 16. December 1848.
Von der k. k. Militär-Central-Untersuchungs-
Commission.

---

*pGB8
V6755R
12.26.48

Austria. Armee.   Proklamation ... [1848]
(Card 2)
  Dated & signed: Hauptquartier Nikolo am 26.
Dezember 1848. Alfred Fürst zu Windischgrätz,
k. k. Feldmarschall.
  A double impression on 2 sides of a folio
sheet 38x51cm., intended to be cut apart.

---

*pGB8
V6755R
12.17.48

Vienna. Magistrat.
  Kundmachung. Das hohe Ministerium für Handel
und Gewerbe hat den Magistrat, im Wege der hohen
Landesstelle, mit Erlass vom 10. d. M. Z.660,
beauftragt, in kürzester Zeit die nöthigen
Einleitungen zur Vornahme des Wahlaktes für
die zu errichtende Handelskammer der Haupt= und
Residenzstadt Wien, welche vorläufig den Bezirk
von ganz Nieder=Oesterreich vetreten soll, zu
treffen ...
  [Wien]Gedruckt bei Leop.Grund,Hundsthurm Nr.1.
[1848]   (See next card)

---

*pGB8
V6755R
12.27.48

Vienna. Gouverneur, 1848 (Welden)
  Kundmachung. Da in jüngster Zeit das Bestehen
eines Klubbs böswilliger Buben wiederholt
angezeigt worden ist, welcher sich mit der absurden
Jdee herumtreibt, selbe in den Kneipen der
Vorstädte bespricht, durch Kennzeichen von
Federn an den Hüten sich kund gibt, und ganz
vorzüglich Pläne entwirft, in Masse die
Verschanzungen auf den Basteien nächtlich zu
erstürmen ...
  [Wien]Aus der k.k.Hof= und Staats=Druckerei.
[1848]   (See next card)

---

*pGB8
V6755R
12.17.48

Vienna. Magistrat.   Kundmachung ... [1848]
(Card 2)
  broadside. 53x68cm.
  Signed & dated: Von dem Magistrate der
Stadt Wien am 17. Dezember 1848.

---

*pGB8
V6755R
12.27.48

Vienna. Gouverneur, 1848 (Welden)   Kundmachung
... [1848]   (Card 2)
  broadside. 44.5x56.5cm.
  Dated & signed: Wien am 27. December 1848.
Der Civil- und Militär-Gouverneur: Welden,
Feldmarschall=Lieutenant.

---

*pGB8
V6755R
12.19.48

Austria. Armee. Zentral-Untersuchungs-Commission.
  Kundmachung. Michael Schwind, aus Heiligenfeld,
Würzburgerkreises in Baiern gebürtig, 29 Jahre
alt, katholisch, ledig, Tischlergeselle, ist
geständig und überwiesen ...
  [Wien]Aus der k.k.Hof= und Staatsdruckerei.
[1848]
  broadside. 44.5x28.5cm.
  Dated & signed: Wien am 19. December 1848. Von
der k. k. Militär-Central-Untersuchungs-
Commission.

---

*pGB8
V6755R
12.28.48

Austria. Armee. Zentral-Untersuchungs-Commission.
  Kundmachung. Johann Grünzweig, aus
Rudolphstadt in Böhmen gebürtig, 39 Jahre
alt, katholisch, ledig, von Profession Weber,
dann Johann Furchtmayer, aus Wien gebürtig, 54
Jahre alt, katholisch, ledig, Taglöhner, und
Ignaz Szileczky, aus Teschen in Schlesien
gebürtig, 51 Jahre alt, katholisch, verheirathet,
Posamentirer=Geselle, sind durch ihr eigenes mit
dem erhobenen Thatbestande übereinstimmendes
Geständniss überwiesen ...
                    (See next card)

---

*pGB8
V6755R
12.26.48

Austria. Armee.
  Proklamation. Soeben wird mir ein Aufruf vom
19. d. M. überbracht, in welchem der Rebellen=
Commissär Alexander Lukács sich erfrecht, das
Volk gegen die Armee ihres Königs aufzuwiegeln,
indem er es auffordert, sich in Masse zu
bewaffnen, und ihr allen möglichen Abbruch zu
thun ...
  [Wien,1848]
  broadside. 38x25.5cm.
                    (See next card)

---

*pGB8
V6755R
12.28.48

Austria. Armee. Zentral-Untersuchungs-Commission.
  Kundmachung ... [1848]   (Card 2)
  [Wien]Aus der k.k.Hof= und Staats=Druckerei.
[1848]
  broadside. 44.5x28.5cm.
  Dated & signed: Wien den 28. December 1848.
Von der k. k. Militär-Central-Untersuchungs-Com-
mission.

Austria, Lower.
*pGB8 ... Kundmachung. Um das politische Recht der
V6755R freien Presse den Staatsbürgern unverklimmert zu
12.28.48 erhalten, und nicht durch fortgesetzten
Missbrauch beim besseren Theile des Publikums
um Ansehen und Theilnahme zu bringen ...
[Wien]Aus der k.k.Hof= und Staats=Druckerei.
[1848]

broadside. 41x25cm.
At head: Nr. 57773.
Dated & signed: Wien am 28. December 1848.
Vom k. k. n. öst. (Regierungs-Präsidium.
Lamberg.

Austria, Lower. Laws, statutes, etc., 1848-1916
*pGB8 (Franz Josef I)
V6755R ... Circulare der k. k. Landesregierung im
12.30.48 Erzherzogthume Oesterreich unter der Enns. Die
über die Beiziehung von politischen,
cameralistischen und montanistischen
Repräsentanten zu Urtheilsschöpfungen in
Rechtssachen geltenden Vorschriften werden
ausser Wirksamkeit gesetzt.
[Wien]Aus der k.k.Hof= und Staatsdruckerei.
[1848]

(See next card)

Austria. Armee.
*pGB8 An die Völker Ungarns. Nicht genug, dass der
V6755R Rebell Kossuth und seine Helfershelfer Ungarn
12.29.48 mit einer zahllosen Menge von Papiergeld
überschwemmt; nicht genug, dass er es wagt,
unsern geheiligten König und Herrn und die ganze
allerhöchste Dynastie in seinen schändlichen und
lügenhaften Plakaten zu schmähen und zu
entweihen ...
[Wien,1848]

broadside. 51x38cm.
Dated & signed: (Hauptquartier Raab, am 29.
December 1848. (Alfred Fürst zu
Windischgrätz, k. k. Feldmarschall.

Austria, Lower. Laws, statutes, etc., 1848-1916
*pGB8 (Franz Josef I) ... Circulare ... [1848]
V6755R (Card 2)
12.30.48 broadside. 40.5x25cm.
At head: № 57911. Nr. 13.
Dated: Wien am 30. December 1848.

Austria. Armee.
*pGB8 Magyarország népeihez. Nem elég, hogy Kossuth
V6755R Lajos pártütö és czinkosa Magyarországot roppant
12.29.48 számu papirospénzzel elárasztották ...
[Wien,1848]
broadside. 38x51.5cm.
Dated & signed: Kelt Györi tábori
főhadiszállásomon, karácson hó 29-kén 1848.
Herczeg Windischgrätz Alfred, császári királyi
tábornagy.
Also published in a German version beginning:
An die Völker (Ungarns ...

Adresse, wodurch die Unterzeichner auf
*pGB8 Ehrenworte erklären, die Errungenschaften der
V6755R Märztage gegenüber republikanischen,
12.32.48 communistischen oder reactionären Umtrieben mit
Wort und That zu vertheidigen ...
[Wien,1848]

broadside. 36x22cm.

Vienna. Magistrat.
*pGB8 Kundmachung. Jn Folge Auftrages der k. k.
V6755R Militär=Stadt=Commandantur vom 24. d. M. werden
12.29.48 alle Besucher von Gast= und Kaffehhäusern alles
Ernstes erinnert, sich längstens um 11 Uhr
Nachts aus den gedachten öffentlichen Orten
zu entfernen ...
[Wien]Aus der k.k.Hof= und Staats=Druckerei.
[1848]

broadside. 44.5x28.5cm.
Dated & signed: Wien am 29. December 1848.
Von der Stadt- (hauptmannschaft.

Allgemeines politisches Bürger-ABC.
*GB8 Pesth,1848.
V6755R
12.32.48 folder([4]p.) 22x15cm.
Caption title; imprint on p.[4].

Austria. Armee. Zentral-Untersuchungs-Commission.
*pGB8 Kundmachung. Bartholomäus Hofstädter, aus
V6755R Neusingen, Herrschaft Drosendorf in
12.30.48 Niederösterreich gebürtig, 28 Jahre alt,
katholisch, ledig, Kutscher, ist durch sein mit
dem erhobenen Thatbestande übereinstimmendes
Geständniss überwiesen ...
[Wien]Aus der k.k.Hof= und Staats=Druckerei.
[1848]

broadside. 44.5x28cm.
Dated & signed: Wien am 30. December 1848. Von
der k. k. Militär (Central-Untersuchungs-
Commission.

[Anthur, Ls.]
*pGB8 Juden Tritsch-Tratsch. oder: Warum [!] steckt
V6755R der Herschel seine Nase überall hinein?!!
12.32.48 [Wien]Gedruckt bei M.Lell.[1848]

[2]p. 38x23cm.
Caption title; imprint on p.[2]; signed: Ls.
Anthur.

[Armbruster, Heinrich]
*GB8   Offene Erwiderung des offenen Briefes an
V6755R Baron Sina.
12.32.48 [Wien,1848]

— folder([4]p.) 27x21cm.
Signed at end: Heinrich Armbruster, Anton
Bordan, Carl Bauernfreund, von der akad. Legion.
The anonymous "Ein offener Brief an Baron
Sina" accused him of not contributing to public
causes.

[Arthur, pseud.]
*GB8   Lachpulver zur Erheiterung. Die Frauen
V6755R Empörung oder Entwurf zur Einführung einer
12.32.48 Ehestand's Constitution ...
[Wien]Gedruckt bei Josef Ludwig,Josefstadt
Florianigasse Nr.52.[1848]

8p. 27x22cm.
Signed at end: Arthur.

Augustus, pseud.
*pGB8   Der katholische Geistliche in dem Wiener=
V6755R Gebärhause und die Predigten in den
12.32.48 gesperrten Zimmern des Spitals.
[Wien]Gedruckt bei M.Lell.[1848]

broadside. 38x23cm.

Ausführliche, wahrheitsgetreue Schilderung
*GB8   der gesetzwidrigen Hinrichtung des unglücklichen
V6755R Johann Calas zu Toulouse in Frankreich.
12.32.48 [Wien]Zu haben in Gumpendorf,untere Annagasse
Nr.507,2.Stock,Thür Nr.9.[1848]

folder([4]p.) 26x21cm.

Austria. Reichstag, 1848-1849.
*pGB8   ... Antrag des Abgeordneten ...
V6755R [Wien,1848]
12.32.48
11 broadsides. 38.5x23.5cm.
Each broadside has the deputy's number at head.
Present are motions from Deputies Gredler (1),
Sierakowski (2), Selinger (1), L. von Löhner (6),
& Kudlich (1).

Das Blutgericht über die Blutegel! Meine
*pGB8   Antwort den hochgeschätzten Herren, die mich
V6755R allenthalben suchen, sich mir anschliessen und
12.32.48 mit mir wirken wollen.
[Wien]Druck von U.Klopf sen.und A.Eurich,
Wollzeile 782.[1848]

broadside. 53x42.5cm.
Signed: N. N.

Die Börsianer und die Studenten.
*GB8   Wien,1848.Gedruckt in der Josephstadt,
V6755R Langegasse Nr.58.
12.32.48
folder([4]p.) 24x19cm.
Signed at end: M. F.

Brauner, Anton.
*GB8   Die Doppelart des Erdenlebens. (Von Anton
V6755R Brauner, ausübendem Arzte in Wien.)
12.32.48 [Wien,1848?]

[2]p. 24x15cm.
Caption title.
In verse; not in Helfert (Wiener Parnass).

Die braven und schlechten Männer ...
*GB8   [Wien,1848]
V6755R
12.32.48 folder([4]p.) 25x20.5cm.
Imprint on p.[4]: Gedruckt bei M. Lell,
Leopoldstadt, Weintraubengasse Nr. 505.
At end: Zweiter Theil folgt.
No more published?

[Carlo, pseud.]
*GB8   Dreizehn Teufeleien aus den Papieren der
V6755R dreizehn Mädchen in Uniform.
12.32.48 [Wien,1848]

folder([4]p.) 27x21.5cm.
Signed at end: Carlo.

Dallinger, Joseph, fl.1848.
An meine guten Brüder Arbeiter!
*pGB8
V6755R   [Wien]Aus der k.k.Hof= und Staatsdruckerei.
12.32.48 [1848]

broadside. 44.5x29cm.
Signed: Joseph Dallinger, Praterarbeiter.

Falk, Adolph.
Der Papst geht in Wien als Frauenzimmer
*pGB8
V6755R   verkleidet herum, und Napoleon ist nicht auf
12.32.48 der Insel Helena gestorben.
[Wien]Gedruckt bei A.Dorfmeister.[1848]

broadside. 39.5x24.5cm.
A satire on baseless rumors.

[Dörflinger, J   ]
Feldzug der falschen Studenten zur Bestürmung
*GB8
V6755R   des Klosters Heiligenkreuz im Wald.
12.32.48 [Wien]Gedruckt bei Josef Ludwig Josefstadt
Florianigasse Nr.52.[1848]

folder([4]p.) 26.5x21cm.
Signed at end: J. Dörflinger.

Die Freiheit in Krähwinkel. Nach J. Nestroy.
[Wien]Gedruckt bei M.Lell.[1848]
*pGB8
V6755R   broadside. 38x23cm.
12.32.48 In verse, but printed as prose.

... Entwurf eines Finanzsystems, welches
*pGB8   jedem Staatsbankerott für immer vorbeugt,
V6755R   sämmtliche Staatsbürger zufrieden stellt,
12.32.48 Agricultur, Gewerbe, Industrie, Handel, Kunst
und Wissenschaften begünstigt, allgemeinen Wohl-
stand verbreitet, durch eben bedingte
Hervorrufung des vielseitigen Verdienstes und
Arbeitsmöglichkeit das Proletariat aufhebt, auf
den moralischen Zustand der Nation verbessernd
einwirken wird und muss, und endlich den Wucher
auch ohne Gesetzesanwendung fast unmöglich macht.
(See next card)

[Frieser, J   ]
Keine Coelebat. (Keine Ehelosigkeit.)
*GB8
V6755R   [Wien]Druck von U.Klopf sen.und A.Eurich,
12.32.48 Wollzeile 782.[1848]

folder(4p.) 21.5x13.5cm.
Caption title; imprint on p.4; signed at end:
J. Frieser.

... Entwurf ... [1848] (Card 2)
[Wien]Gedruckt bei Leop.Sommer (vorm.Strauss).
*pGB8   [1848]
V6755R
12.32.48 folder(4p.) 44x29.5cm.
Caption title (at head: Beilage zur allgem.
österr. Zeitung); imprint on p.4; signed at end:
Th. N. [&] C. H.
"Ursprünglich für Ungarn bestimmt, aber gleich
anwendbar für Oesterreich und andere Staaten."

Die Geheimnisse des Bischofkellers als
Fortsetzung des Rundschreibens: Dornbacher
*GB8   Pfarrhof, Schottenkeller, Klosterneuburgerkeller
V6755R   &c.
12.32.48 [Wien]Verlag von A.Wenedikt,Lobkowitzplatz Nr.
1100.Druck von Franz Edl.von Schmid.[1848]

[2]p. 22.5x14cm.
Caption title; imprint on p.[2].
Protesting monastic ownership of inns and
taverns.

Errichtung eines Bordell=Hauses in Wien.
[Wien]Druck der M.Lell'schen Offizin.[1848]
*pGB8
V6755R   [2]p. 38x23.5cm.
12.32.48 Caption title; imprint on p.[2]; signed
at end: Ein praktischer Vokativus.

Gesellschaft der Volksfreunde, Vienna.
Ein die "Gesellschaft der Volksfreunde"
*pGB8   entehrendes Plakat zwingt dieselbe zu
V6755R   folgender Kundmachung: Die darin der
12.32.48 Gesellschaft unterlegten verbrecherischen
Thatsachen und Absichten werden als Lüge und
Verläumdung erklärt ...
[Wien,1848]

broadside. 27x43cm.

*pGB8
V6755R
12.32.48

Gesellschaft der Volksfreunde, Vienna.
Mitbürger. Man sucht Euch einen Verein, der den Namen Volksfreunde in den Tagen der Gefahr mit seinem Blute und Leben zu erkaufen bereit war, als geheime Gesellschaft zu verdächtigen ...
[Wien,1848]

broadside. 44x29cm.

---

*pGB8
V6755R
12.32.48

Hechler, Friedrich.
Die Revolution zu Madagaskar, und das fürchterliche Erdbeben daselbst.
[Wien]Druck von M.Lell.[1848]

broadside. 38x23cm.
Signed: Friedrich Hechler, Berichterstatter.
J. K. Verfasser.

---

*pGB8
V6755R
12.32.48

Gründe zur Beschwerde der Saal= und Gastwirthe, Musiker und Volkssänger, gegen das Bestehen des Elisiums und Odeons.
[Wien]Gedruckt bei Ulrich Klopf sen.und Alex. Eurich.[1848]

broadside. 42.5x26.5cm.

---

*pGB8
V6755R
12.32.48

Hehne, Anton.
Offene Klage gegen den Polizeikommissär Max in Hitzing.
[Wien,1848]

broadside. 39x24.5cm.

---

*pGB8
V6755R
12.32.48

Gschöpf, Rudolf, fl.1848.
Aufruf. Freie Völker Oesterreichs! Die Versorgung unserer lieben Angehörigen, deren Sicherstellung vor Noth und Elend nach unserem Tode, gehört unstreitig zu unseren ersten Pflichten ...
[Wien,1848]

broadside. 89x58cm.
On pensions.

---

*GB8
V6755R
12.32.48

Heimliche Sachen im Findelhause und im Gebärhause von den groben Krankenwärterinnen dann die spitzbübischen Bedienten. Von R. H.
[Wien]Gedruckt bei Josef Ludwig,Josefstadt Florianigasse Nr.52.[1848]

folder([4]p.) 26x21cm.

---

*GB8
V6755R
12.32.48

Hammerschmidt, J   B
Die erste Beschäftigungs=Anstalt des Wiener Kreuzer-Vereins zur Unterstützung arbeit-suchender Personen. Von Dr. Hammerschmidt.
[Wien,1848]

folder([4]p.) 25x20cm.
Caption title.

---

*pGB8
V6755R
12.32.48

Der Herr und der Knecht.
Wien,gedruckt bei Leop.Sommer (vorm.Strauss).
[1848]

broadside. illus. 37.5x28.5cm.
In verse; not in Helfert (Wiener Parnass).

---

*pGB8
V6755R
12.32.48

Haslinger, Carl, 1816-1868.
Die 3 [i.e. drei] März-Tage 1848. Character-istisches Tongemälde. Componirt und für das Piano-forte eingerichtet von Carl Haslinger. 49tes Werk ...
Wien,bei Tobias Haslinger's Witwe und Sohn,k. k.Hof- u.priv.Kunst- u.Musikalienhändler.Leipzig, bei B.Hermann.[1848] ...

11p. 32.5x25cm.
Engraved throughout; plate no.: 10,885.

---

*pGB8
V6755R
12.32.48

Kanocha, Ludmilla, b.1812.
Offener Brief an Sr. Hochgeboren den k. k. wirklichen Kämmerer und Major in der Armee Herrn Dominik Grafen von Wrbna und Freudenthal.
[Wien,1848]

broadside. 38.5x24cm.

[Komorny, Joseph]
*pGB8
V6755R
12.32.48
Damen=Vernunft wie die Männer von ihren
Frauen angeschmiert werden.
[Wien]Zu haben in der Stadt,Sterngasse Nr.452
im Hofmagazin.[1848]

   [2]p. 36.5x22.5cm.
   Caption title; imprint on p.[2]; signed at
end: Komorni.

Meisl, Karl, 1775-1853.
*GB8
V6755R
12.32.48
Weheklagen über das bestehende Gesetz, dass
den Grundherrschaften die Verleihung von
Gewerben übertragen ist. Für alle Gewerbsuchende
und mit ähnlichen Gesuchen Zurückgewiesene. Von
Karl Meisl.
Wien,1848.Gedruckt und zu haben bei U.Klopf
sen.und Alex.Eurich.

   folder(4p.) 20x12.5cm.
   Caption title; imprint on p.4.

[Komorny, Joseph]
*pGB8
V6755R
12.32.48
Medicin, wie man die bösen Weiber kuriren kann.
[Wien]Zu haben in der Stadt,Sterngasse Nr.452
im Hofmagazin.Gedruckt bei Leop.Sommer.[1848]

   [2]p. 41.5x26cm.
   Caption title; imprint on p.[2]; signed at
end: Komorn.

Die nationellen Bewegungen.
*GB8
V6755R
12.32.48
[Wien,1848]

   folder([3]p.) 23x14.5cm.
   Caption title.

Konrad, Johann.
*pGB8
V6755R
12.32.48
   Meine Freunde und Mitbrüder! Seit dem Jahre
1847, wo ich durch ehrendes Zutrauen zum
Mittelsvorsteher erwählt worden bin, habe ich
ohngeachtet vieler Anfeindungen stets meiner
Pflicht nach gelebt ...
   [Wien]Gedruckt bei U.Klopf sen.und Alex.
Eurich,Wollzeile Nr.782.[1848]

   broadside. 39.5x24.5cm.

Oeffentlicher Dank. Die Arbeiter des
*pGB8
V6755R
12.32.48
Brigittenauer Dammbaues, deren Anzahl sich
bereits auf 4000 beläuft, haben ihre Herzen
vereint, und drücken ihren innigsten Dank aus ...
   [Wien,1848]

   broadside. 45x28cm.
   Signed: Von dem Nachsteher der 52. Parthie im
Namen Aller.

Lagout, ———.
*pGB8
V6755R
12.32.48
   Der endlich entdeckte Mörder des
geviertheilten Frauenzimmers oder: die alberne
Behauptung Sedlnitzki habe die That verübt.
Juden und Liguorianer im ungerechten Verdacht,
indem ein Barbier=Geselle der wahre Thäter.
   [Wien]Gedruckt bei Joseph Ludwig.[1848]

   broadside. 38.5x24cm.

Ein offener Brief an Baron Sina.
*pGB8
V6755R
12.32.48
[Wien]Druck von Ulrich Klopf sen.und Alex.
Eurich.[1848]

   broadside. 40x23.5cm.
   Signed: R.

Leben und Thaten des allgemein bekannten
*pGB8
V6755R
12.32.48
Wiener=Fiakers Freyherrn von Vogelhuber und
seiner Gemalin Therese. (Genannt Vogelhurber
Res'l.)
   [Wien]Gedruckt bei Josef Ludwig.[1848]

   [2]p. 43x27cm.
   Caption title; imprint on p.[2]; signed at
end: Schon wieder ein Vocativus.

Ein offener Brief an Rothschild.
*pGB8
V6755R
12.32.48
[Wien]Druck von U.Klopf sen.,und Alex.Eurich,
Wollzeile 782.[1848]

   broadside. 40.5x25cm.
   Signed: R.

*GB8
V6755R
12.32.48

[Pizzighelli, Gaetano]
    Vorschlag zur Creirung eines Wiener Bürger=
Magistrats.
    [Wien,1848]
    folder([4]p.) 22x13cm.
    Caption title; signed at end: Gaetano
Pizzighelli; bürgl. Seidenhändler.

---

*GB8
V6755R
12.32.48

Schmerz, Friedrich.
    Das Serail in St. Helena. Ein ernstes Wort an
Pfarrer, ihre Köchinnen und Wirthschafterinnen.
Von Friedrich Schmerz.
    Wien,1848.Gedruckt in der Josephstadt,
Langegasse Nr.48.
    folder([4]p.) 26x21cm.
    Protest against the idleness of the clergy.

---

*pGB8
V6755R
12.32.48

Reburg, J
    Muster-Tabelle. Wie man aus der k. k. Zahlen=
Lotterie für Wien und Linz früher als in einem
Jahre 400 Percent gewinnen muss, nach dem
Jahre 1847 berechnet. Fond 50 fl.C.M.
    [Wien,1848]
    broadside. 30x46cm.

---

*GB8
V6755R
12.32.48

Die schreckliche Mordthat, die in Zombor
geschehen ist.
    Wien,1848.Gedruckt bei Joh.N.Fridrich.
    folder([4]p.) 23.5x19cm.
    Woodcut illus. on t.-p.
    Signed at end: G. B.

---

*pGB8
V6755R
12.32.48

Revolution in Petersburg.
    [Wien]Druck von M.Lell's Offizin.[1848]
    broadside. 40.5x24cm.
    Signed: C. F.

---

*GB8
V6755R
12.32.48

Sentner, Johann.
    Ich finde mich veranlasst, meinen Herrn
Mitmeistern meine Rechtfertigung öffentlich
kund zu geben.
    [Wien,1848]
    broadside. 30x24cm.

---

*pGB8
V6755R
12.32.48

Revolution in Russland.
    [Wien]Gedruckt und zu haben bei Joh.N.
Friderich.[1848]
    broadside. 38.5x48.5cm.
    Signed: L. S.

---

*pGB8
V6755R
12.32.48

    [Sheet containing 26 small lithographs showing
important events of the revolution of 1848 in
Vienna, beginning with the signing of the
students' demands in the Aula on 12 March and
ending with the taking of the city by the army
on 31 October.]
    Zu haben bei Fr.Wiener in Wien.[1848]
    plate. 44.5x58cm.
    Mounted on linen.

---

*GB8
V6755R
12.32.48

    Rundschreiben an die Weinschanken
Klosterneuburger=Keller, Schotten=Keller,
Dornbacher Pfarrhof &c.
    [Wien]Verlag von A.Wenedikt,Lobkowitzplatz Nr.
1100.Druck von Franz Edl.von Schmid.[1848]
    [2]p. 23x14.5cm.
    Caption title; imprint on p.[2].

---

*GB8
V6755R
12.32.48

Steiner, Friedrich, fl.1848.
    Chronik scandaleuse der Geistlichen, von
Friedrich Steiner.
    [Wien,1848]
    folder([4]p.) 21x13cm.
    Imprint on p.[4]: Eigenthumsrecht und Verlag,
Gumpendorf Gärtnergasse Nr.545, im zweiten
Stock.

[Swiedack, Karl, 1815-1888]
Ich fürchte mich nicht, meine Herren!
[Wien,1848]

*pGB8
V6755R
12.32.48

broadside. 38x46.5cm.
Signed: Elmar [pseud.].
Large folio edition.
Defending the production of his farce "Wie die
Reaktionäre dumm sind!"

Vienna. Nationalgarde.
Euere Excellenz' Die unterzeichneten
Nationalgarden, durchdrungen von der Ueberzeugung,
dass besondere, von den Officieren und Chargen
der Nationalgarde auch ausser Dienst zu tragende
Ehrenabzeichen nur vielfache Gelegenheiten zu
kastenartigen Absonderungen des Officiers-Corps
geben ...
[Wien,1848]

*pGB8
V6755R
12.32.48

broadside. 39.5x24.5cm.
A petition to change the rules regarding
uniforms; no names have been signed.

[Swiedack, Karl, 1815-1888]
Ich fürchte mich nicht, meine Herren!
[Wien,1848]

*GB8
V6755R
12.32.48

broadside. 21.5x18cm.
Signed: Elmar [pseud.].
Small quarto edition.
Defending the production of his farce "Wie die
Reaktionäre dumm sind!"

Vienna. 2. Berzirk (Leopoldstadt) Lese- & Rede-
Verein.
Entwurf der Statuten des Lese- & Rede-Vereins
in der Leopoldstadt.
[Wien,1848]

*GB8
V6755R
12.32.48

[2]p. 30.5x23.5cm.
Caption title.

Die unglücklichen Beamten. Mehrseitig hat sich
bei der Nationalgarde eine ungünstige Stimmung
gegen den Beamtenstand bemerkbar gemacht ...
[Wien]Gedruckt bei L.Sommer (vorm.Strauss).
[1848]

*pGB8
V6755R
12.32.48

broadside. 52x41.5cm.
Signed: M. M.

Vollständiger Leitfaden und auf langjährige
Erfahrung gegründete Anleitung, in der Lotterie
mit wahren Nutzen zu spielen, eigentlich dieses
Institut systematisch auszubeuten. Mit
sorgfältig ausgewählten Nummern zu Einsätzen auf
Wien, Linz, Prag, Brünn und Graz für Terno und
Ambo=Solo berechnet.
[Wien]Gedruckt bei M.Lell,Leopoldstadt,
Weintraubengasse,Nr.505.[1848]

*GB8
V6755R
12.32.48

folder([4]p.) 24.5x19cm.
Caption title; imprint on p.[4].

Verzeichniss jener Herren Einwohner Wiens,
welche zum Ausschuss vorgeschlagen werden ...
[Wien,1848]

*GB8
V6755R
12.32.48

broadside. 29x12cm.

Die Wiener Spiessbürger. Unter den Bürgern
Wiens, dieser Zierde der Stadt und schönen
Hoffnung des Vaterlandes, welchen die ganze
Welt die verdiente Lobeserhebung nicht versagt,
befindet sich ein kleines Häuflein, die den
Nahmen Wiener Bürger nicht verdienen und welche
man daher gerne "Spiessbürger" bezeichnet.
[Wien]Gedruckt bei J.N.Fridrich,Josefstadt
Nr.58.[1848]

*pGB8
V6755R
12.32.48

broadside. 42.5x52.5cm.

Vienna. Nationalgarde.
Commissionsbericht über die Frage, wie es
sich mit jenen Garden verhält, welche aus den
Kompagnien austreten und mit Armatur und
Monturstücken betheilt wurden.
[Wien,1848]

*pGB8
V6755R
12.32.48

folder([3]p.) 38x24cm.
Reproduced from ms. copy.

Index

This is an author and subject index of proper
names, pseudonyms, and initials only. Not included are proper names under corporate entries
in which the individual was acting in an official capacity, i.e., Windischgrätz signing an
official order for which the main entry is
Austria. Armee. Neither is the name of the
Emperor Ferdinand I included, since to have
done so would have resulted in a useless string
of hundreds of page numbers.

Since entries could not be numbered individually
in the method of card reproduction here employed,
index reference has had to be limited to page
number only, with the result that the user may
have to scan 10 different cards in order to lo-
cate the entry he is looking for. We hope this
will not prove too great an inconvenience.